HUNTER'S FIERY RAID THROUGH VIRGINIA VALLEYS

C-1900 "Idlewood"-New Castle: Built in 1852 by Alexander J. Minnick. Minnick joined the 28th Va. Infantry and was killed at the Battle of Seven Pines. In 1864 David Hunter occupied this home as he retreated into West Virginia. The home was bought by the Lee family in 1877. Photo courtesy of current owner, Robert O. Lee.

HUNTER'S FIERY RAID
THROUGH
VIRGINIA VALLEYS

by
Gary C. Walker

PELICAN PUBLISHING COMPANY
GRETNA 2008

To my mother, Mary Cassell Walker

First published by A & W Enterprise, 1989
Published by arrangement with the author by
        Pelican Publishing Company, Inc., 2008

First printing, 1989
First Pelican edition, 2008

ISBN-13: 978-1-58980-575-0

Printed in the United States of America

Published by Pelican Publishing Company, Inc.
1000 Burmaster Street, Gretna, Louisiana 70053

Chapters

Quick Reference to Major Characters:

Northern

1-Averell, Gen William-Cavalry Commander under Hunter
2-Blazer, Capt. Richard-Scout
3-Campbell, Col. Jacob-Commander 54th Pa. Infantry
4-Carlin, Capt. John-Artillery Commander
5-Crook, Gen. George-Commander of Infantry Division under Hunter
6-Duffie, Brig. Gen. Alford-Cavalry Commander under Hunter
7-Dupont, Capt. Henry-Artillery Commander under Hunter
8-Ellicott, Capt. George-Chief of Scouts
9-Ely, Col. John-Commander 18th Connecticut
10-Ewing, Capt. Chatham Artillery Commander
11-Glassie, Capt. Daniel-Artillery Commander
12-Grant, Gen. U. S.-Commander-in-Chief all Union Forces
13-Halleck, Adj. Gen. Henry-Part of Union High Command in D. C.
14-Hayes, Col. Rutherford-Commander 23rd Ohio Inf>
15-Hinkle, Thornton-Newspaper Reporter
16-Hunter, Maj. Gen. David-Commander of Union Force
17-Lincoln, Abraham-President United States
18-Martindale, Capt. Franklin-Commander Company 1st N. Y. Cavalry
19-Meigs, Lt. John-Chief Engineer
20-Moor, Col. Augustus-Commander 1st Brigade under Sullivan
21-Oley, Col. J. H.-Commander 2nd.Brigade Artillery
22-Powell, Col. William-Commander 1st & 2nd W. Va. Cavalry
23-Quinn, Maj. Timothy-1st N. Y. (Lincoln) Cavalry
24-Schoomaker, Co. James-Cavalry Brigade Commander
25-Sheridan, Gen. Philip-Cavalry Commander
26-Sigel, Gen. Franz-Hunter's Predecessor
27-Snow, Capt. Alonzo-Artillery Commander
28-Stahel, Maj. Gen. Julius-Cavalry Commander at Piedmont
29-Stanton, Edwin-Sec. of War
30-Starr, Col. William-Security Chief & Head of Prisoner Interrogation

31-Stearns, Maj. Joseph-1st N. Y. (Lincoln) Cavalry
32-Sullivan, Gen. Jeremiah-Infantry Division Commander under Hunter
33-Taylor, Col. R. F.-1st Brigade Commander under Duffie
34-Thoburn, Col. Joseph-2nd Brigade Commander under Sullivan
35-Town, Capt. Franklin-Commander Signal Corps
36-Von Kleiser, Capt. Alfred-Artillery Commander
37-Wells, Col. George-1st Brigade Commander under Sullivan
38-White, Col. Carr-2nd Brigade Commander under Crook
39-Wynkoop, Col. John-2nd Brigade Commander under Duffie

Southern

1-Beall, Maj. Henry-Scout
2-Berkeley, Lt. Carter-Artillery Commander
3-Blue, Lt. Monroe-Commander in Home Guard
4-Bragg, Gen. Braxton-Adviser to Pres. Davis
5- Breckinridge, Gen. John-Army Division Commander
6-Browne, Col. William-2nd in Command at Battle of Piedmont
7-Cochran, Lt. Col. James-Commander-14th Va. Cavalry
8-Creigh, Mr. David-Civilian
9-Davis, Jefferson-President Confederate States of America
10-Davis, Cap. Thomas-Commander Md. Battalion
11-Douthat, Capt. H. C.-Artillery Commander
12-Doyle, Capt. Robert-Commander in Home Guard
13-Early, Maj. Gen. Jubal-Senior Commander of Forces opposed to Hunter
14-Elzey, Maj. Gen. Arnold-nominal Cavalry Commander
15-Gilmor, Harry-Commander Md. Partisan Rangers
16-Gordon, Gen. John-Brigade Commander under Early
17-Hampton, Gen. Wade-Cavalry Commander
18-Harper, Col. Kenton-Commander in Home Guard
19-Hayes, Gen. Harry-helped with fortifying Lynchburg
20-Hill, Gen. D. H.-Commander under Early
21-Imboden, Gen. John-Commander-Shenandoah Military District
22-Jackson, Gen. "Stonewall" (Des.)-Past Commander Shenandoah District
23-Jackson, Gen. "Mudwall"-Cousin of "Stonewall"
24-Jones, Col. Beuhring-Commander Niter & Miner Corps
25-Jones, Gen. "Grumble"-Commander at the Battle of Piedmont
26-Lee, Col. Edwin-Commander town of Staunton
27-Lee, Gen. Fitzhugh-Cavalry Commander
28-Lee, Gen. Robert-Commander Southern Forces
29-Longstreet, Gen. James-wounded-recuperating Commander
30-Marquis, Capt. J. C.-Commander Boy's Artillery
31-McCausland, Gen. John-Commander of some mounted forces

32-McDonald, Col. Angus (Ret.)-personally hated by Hunter
33-McDonald, Harry-son of above
34-McNeil, Capt. John-Commander Partisan Ranges
35-Morgan, Gen. John-stationed in Southwest Virginia
36-Mosby, Col. John-Commander Partisan Rangers
37-Nicholls, Gen. Francis-Commander City of Lynchburg
38-Opie, Capt. John-Scout
39-Ramseur, Gen. Stephen-Division Commander under Early
40-Ransom, Gen. Robert-nominal Commander of all Early's Cavalry
41-Rodes, Gen. Robert-Division Commander under Early
42-Saunders, Maj. R. C.-Scout
43-Seddon, James-Sec. of War
44-Shaver, Cornelius-Home Owner
45-Smith, Gen. Frances-Commander VMI Corps
46-Vaughn, Gen. John-Cavalry & Mounted Infantry Commander
47-Wharton, Gen. Gabriel-Brigade Commander under D. H. Hill
48-White, Capt. Matthew-Regular Army assigned to Home Guard

A special thanks to those people who shared their time and information so generously for this book: John Jenkins, S.A. Bell, Kelly Chapman, Roderick Cline, J.W. Sites, Jerry McCray, Charles Hunter, III, Marquis G. Witt, William O. White, Mark E. Neely, Jr., Ph.D, Pat Trout, Brocky A. Nicely, George Whiting, Worichard Lavinder, Carol Tuckwiller, Keith Gibson, David Brown, John McIlhenny, Allen Allison, Scott Hutchison, Bob Fleet, Lorlys Elton Molter, Rev. Harold Skelton, John Jeffries, M. Robert Rogers, Doyle & Esther Howdyshell, Jack Fulton, Rowena Myers, Thomas W. Dixon, Jr., Jerry Markham, Randolph Kean, Kenneth Crouch, Peter Viemeister, Hiram Opie, Richard M. & Thomas B. Hamrich, Deedie Hagey, Mayor William McGraw, Toler Ransone, Sue Gilbert, Katherine Parr Claytor, June B. Goode, Thomas Ledford, Edwin L. Warehime, Gwyn Rowland Caouette, Larry Pickett, Mrs. Jessie Richards, Ralph Greenway, Minor Keffer, Kenneth Wolfe, R.T. Craig, Lloyd H. Jones, Roy Hayth, John & Pam Scott, Dorothy Whitesell, Arraga McNeil Young, Allan & Keith Wingfield, Lance M. Hale, Lila Huffman, Larry Huffman, Maj. Marshall Vass Hale, USAF (retired).

This book would not have been possible without the aid of numerous librarians. A special thanks to the employees of the National Park Service, the Virginia Park Service, the Bedford City/County Museum, and the Chesapeake and Ohio Historical Society.

Thank you beautiful wife for your love, your support, and for the countless hours you spent in helping to prepare this manuscript.

A very special thanks to: Stan Cohen — Pictorial History Publishing Company, Charleston, W. Va., and to Jim Comstock, (Richwood, W. Va) Editor and Publisher of *Porte Crayon Sampler* by David Hunter Strother, for allowing me the use of so many photos from their works.

HUNTER'S FIERY RAID THROUGH VIRGINIA VALLEYS

Artist unknown to author

Fortifying The Lines At New Hope, At Night, And In Rain

Chapter I

Weapons & Strategy

A very brief and general look at some of the strategies and the weapons is presented to help the reader more fully understand and appreciate the war in which many of our ancestors participated.

The Union's grand strategy for defeating the Confederacy called for cutting the South into two parts by taking the Mississippi River, by blockading the South to prevent shipments of supplies from overseas, and by taking Richmond, the capital of the Confederacy. By May 1864, the first two objectives had been accomplished. Hunter's raid was designed to accomplish the third objective: taking Richmond.

Because the army of the United States had a larger population to recruit from and because it had a larger manufacturing base for support, it was more standardized than was its Southern counterpart.

The army was divided into different classifications, and each had different field strategies and weapons. The main divisions were the infantry, the cavalry, the artillery, the signal corps, and the engineers.

The infantryman at the first of the war would most likely carry a .58 caliber Enfield or Springfield Rifle, which weighed fourteen pounds. Its "effective range, that is, the range at which massed infantry fire would hit often enough to be adequately damaging"[1] was approximately 200 to 300 yards. A sharp-shooter could drop a man at a half mile. The gun was muzzle-loading and was fired once before reloading.

By 1864, the Union had introduced the Spencer Repeating Rifle. It used a cartridge with a self-contained detonater. The bullets were fed into the chamber via a lever mechanism. The rifle could be fired seven times before reloading. The Southerners would say, "You can load it on Sunday and shoot it all week."

Because the Confederacy could not mass produce cartridges, even captured Spencers saw little action with the Southern Army. Confederate infantry was armed with a variety of weapons. There might be .58 caliber Enfields, smoothbore converted flintlocks, squirrel guns, and shot guns within the same unit. Men on both sides believed that, "A good infantry can always sustain itself against the charges of the cavalry."[2]

The cavalry carried a shorter rifle than the infantry. The breech-loading Sharps, a .54 caliber, could be fired once before reloading. An advertisement said that the Sharps was "...Just what a skirmish line needed for effective work."[3] By 1864, many Union units were equipped with a carbine (smaller) version of the Spencer Repeating Rifle. The duties of the cavalry included scouting, picketing roads and gaps to shield the slower moving infantry, quick raiding against weakly defended targets, and striking the enemy's infantry when there was disorder in the ranks or when a field gun was weakly protected. The cavalry could move up to fifty miles a day on a forced march.

The cavalry sword was used for close range fighting. There were very few engagements fought during the war in this manner. It appears that most Southern cavalrymen preferred a pistol to a sword.

Artillery, generally considered "the queen of the battlefield," was the most important weapon on the field. By 1864, there were a wide variety of field cannons and ordnance that could be used with each gun. The twelve-pound Napoleon smoothbore cannon was the most popular at the start of the war. It could fire a round ball that weighed approximately twelve pounds 1,600 yards.

The Three-Inch Ordnance Rifle came into general use after the war started. It could fire a cylindrical projectile with a cone-shaped nose weighing nine and a half pounds 1,800 yards. Many artillerists believed the rifled three-inch gun was much more accurate than the smoothbore Napoleon.

One of the largest field guns was the twenty- pound Parrott Rifle. It could send a projectile weighing twenty pounds 2,000 yards. The twenty-four pound James Rifled Gun could send its projectile almost 1,800 yards.

Whether the gun fired a round ball or a cylindrical projectile, the artillerist had a variety of ordnance that he could fire at the enemy. Solid shot was used against fortifications, buildings, and sometimes against infantry and cavalry formations. Some shells, filled with small round balls, were designed to explode in the air by means of a timed fuse. When the shells exploded, shell fragments and round balls might riddle enemy formations.

At ranges of less than 350 yards, the artillerist could load the cannon with grapeshot or canister. The solid grapeshot was larger than the round ball used in the exploding shell; some grapeshot measured an inch and a half in diameter. Loading the cannon with grapeshot turned it into a "big shotgun." Canister fire could tear large holes in infantry or cavalry formations. Soldiers feared cannons loaded with grapeshot more than any other type of projectile.

The Signal Corps sent messages by using flags during the day and by using lights and rockets at night.

The engineers were used mostly to build bridges and to clear blocked roads.

The Confederate Army augmented its force with the use of the Home Guard, which was under the control of the departmental commander. The commander would call the civilian men into service when there was danger in their area. The Home Guard was composed of men who were too old or too young or in too poor health to be in the regular army. Soldiers on furlough were expected to join the Home Guard if the local unit was activated. Because Home Guard members provided their own weapons, the weapons varied in type and quality. Home Guard units, basically composed of poorly trained civilians, were usually considered the poorest troops in the field.

Both armies grumbled about their food. By late war, many Confederates were poorly fed but most Union soldiers were adequately fed. Both sides cursed the heavy, hard bread called hardtack. Soldiers sometimes referred to it as crackers. Men sometimes complained that they almost broke their teeth trying to bite it. Often it was soaked in water or crushed with a rifle butt before it could be eaten.

The meat field ration was heavily salted pork or beef. The meat was usually soaked in water to remove some of the salt. As the ability of the Confederacy to feed the army decreased, the quality of the meat fell rapidly. By the end of the war, it was no longer called salt pork or beef but "salt horse."

Hardtack, meat, corn meal, an extra pair of socks, and coffee or sugar were carried in a haversack or knapsack slung across the shoulder. The standard forty rounds of ammunition were carried in a cartridge box strapped to a belt.

Modern route numbers are given in the book to help the reader locate the route of march. Because many roads have been rerouted since the war, modern route numbers are to be used as general, not specific, guides.

This account uses the language and ideas of those who fought and lived during this campaign, and reflects the attitudes of the time. No attempt has been made to impose a 20th Century morality standard on those who lived in the 1860's.

Chapter II

Setting the Stage

The Valley of Virginia is roughly bordered by the Blue Ridge Mountains on the east and by the Allegheny Mountains on the west. The Valley extends from the Maryland border south toward Lynchburg and then west to the Tennessee border. The large Valley can be subdivided into six smaller valleys, each drained by a main river. The three valleys of most importance to this work are the Shenandoah, the Fincastle or James River, and the Roanoke.

The Shenandoah River flows north (thus downgrade) toward the Potomac River that borders Maryland. The Shenandoah drains as far south as Botetourt County. The Cowpasture and the Jackson Rivers form the James River flowing through Lynchburg, east, and northeast out of the Valley. The Roanoke River empties into the Staunton River flowing generally southeast out of the Valley. Bedford and Roanoke counties are drained by this river system.

At the beginning of the war, there was a James and a Kanawha River Canal Company. The James River and its tributaries were navigable from Richmond through Lynchburg, from Lynchburg past Lexington to the north, and from Buchanan to the south. A system of locks and canals allowed boats carrying men and materials to flow across the state. Although the canal was slower than the train, it was still an important link in the Virginia transportation system.

The boys of 1861 were either the dead or grim men of 1864. The game of war was now a deadly occupation. The boys had learned their profession on the fields of Manassas, Fredericksburg, Sharpsburg, Chancellorsville, Gettysburg, and Cold Harbor. The dream of 1861 of a graceful, beautiful, independent Confederacy living in peace now was the mud, blood, and pain of 1864.

Federal forces had increased in strength, skill, and equipment, but Southern forces had decreased as there were very few replacements for soldiers. There was little equipment or food for the Rebel army. Federal forces were determined to increase the miseries of their opponents, and the Valley of Virginia gave them an excellent opportunity to do that.

Some of the war products from the Valley of Virginia would include men, iron, saltpeter, salt, lead, food, wool, shoes, and some manufactured items. Not only did the Valley produce war products, but its geography offered the Union an invasion route into the heart of Virginia. Since the first of the war, the Federal forces had been attempting to move into the Valley. Every attempt had been turned back.

Gen. John D. Imboden had been placed in charge of the Shenandoah Valley District (usually referred to as the Valley District) in July 1863. Forces had moved into and out of the Valley District to counter Union pressure.

The whisky-drinking but victorious general from the west, Ulysses S. Grant, had been moved east and given command of all Union field armies. Grant, perhaps more than any other general, knew and used a total war concept. Grant, knowing the war-making ability of both sides, ultimately relied on the civilian economy. He realized that the Union was superior in manpower and equipment. Even a Southern private could see that the Confederacy was having great difficulty providing and supplying an army.

Grant used his superiorities against the South's weaknesses. No longer would there be a single grand offensive"...On to Richmond." Grant used the telegraph to coordinate a general offensive across a whole region. His offensives would force each out-numbered, out-gunned Confederate army to stand and fight. No longer could Confederate reinforcements be shifted across a region to counter a single thrust because a thrust would be made against every sector.

Before Grant took command, civilians and their property were not considered official military targets. Grant now "...ordered his generals to burn and destroy all sources of Confederate supplies in their path of operations...(he was going after) the South's stomach."[3] Civilian resources were now legitimate military targets.

Grant realized that destroying civilian production would further cripple the Confederate Army. His army commanders were encouraged not to take much food or fodder when invading Dixie but to allow soldiers and animals to eat Confederate food. It appears that sources of production for food and manufactured products were now military targets. Homes, schools, and personal property were not.

Another area of radical change was the treatment of the slavery issue. Slavery was not a major contributory cause of the war, but the United States government began to use the issue as a weapon against the Confederacy for a variety of reasons.

The issue was used very effectively in international politics. By labeling the Confederacy as a slave-holding nation, the Union was successful in blunting Confederate efforts in winning diplomatic recognition from France and Great Britain. When President Lincoln issued the Emancipation Proclamation in January 1863, the masses of Europe believed that the Union stood for freedom, but the issue cut both ways.

Although the Proclamation would hurt the Confederate diplomatic efforts overseas, it might also hurt the Union at home. It was feared that a policy to free all slaves would seriously undermine Union support in the slave-holding states of Delaware, Maryland, Kentucky, and Missouri (all within the Union sphere of control); as a result, these states were quietly exempted from the act.

There was a strong and growing peace movement in the North. The movement had caused much violence and destruction in protest against the conscription act. Young men went to Canada or the Far West to avoid being drafted to fight a war they did not believe in. The peace movement, willing to allow the Southern states to remain out of the Union, was exerting strong pressure on the Lincoln Administration to sue for peace and bring the troops home.

To lessen the draft grievance of the peace movement, the Lincoln Administration changed the conscription rules shortly after issuing the Emancipation Proclamation. From January 1863 to the end of the war, state quotas would be filled by volunteers. If there were not enough volunteers, then *all* Negro males of draft age would go into service before the first white boy was drafted.

Starting in 1863 when Union armies invaded the South, male slaves were encouraged to leave their masters; many left willingly, but others were marched off at the point of a gun. Today's slave was tomorrow's black Union soldier. Some slaves exchanged involuntary servitude to a master, for involuntary servitude in the Union Army (where they might be killed). The Negro soldier was paid less than his white counterpart. Few black soldiers ever rose above the rank of private. Almost all colored units were commanded by white officers.

Because Southerners resented the fact that former slaves were now engaging them in combat (an act of treason from the Southern point of view), captured black soldiers were not treated as prisoners of war. Many were returned to slavery or executed.

The Union Army did not treat black soldiers as equals to whites. When the Confederacy did not treat them as equals either, the Lincoln Administration placed captured Southerners at hard labor as retaliation. This retaliation policy led to widespread privation and torture of Southern prisoners.

Men who looked the same and shared a common language were now divided by more than ideology or lines on a map; there was deep hatred between them.

In May of 1864, Grant decided to take the Rebel capital. On paper, Union forces were so strong that victory was assured. Grant would attack at points across the state. The South could not shift forces to counter any attack without losing the capital. Out-numbered Rebel forces would have to fight. Union victory would come in some sector.

The attack plan was simple: Grant would move directly upon Richmond. This move would force Lee to stand and fight. Grant's numbers might overwhelm Lee, and the capital would fall. Gen. Franz Sigel would attack the Valley. If he was successful, he would capture Lynchburg. Without a transportation link between Richmond and the critical supplies from Southwest Virginia, Lee could not hold the capital. Gen. George Crook would attack from the Union Department of West Virginia toward the long railroad bridge at Central Depot (Radford). If Crook was successful, the supplies from Southwest Virginia would stop. Gen. William Wood Averell with the Cavalry Division of West Virginia would strike directly against the vital saltworks (at Saltville) and the lead mines (in Wythe County). If Averell was successful, those vital war materials would not reach Lee, and the capital would fall.

General Lee was aware of the build-up of Union forces. Grant was right: the South had few troops that could be shifted to meet the increased Union pressure. The Confederacy was able to bring Gen. John Hunt Morgan and his command from the Knoxville area to the Saltville area without Union detection. Morgan was one of the South's most vicious cavalry soldiers. Unionists often referred to Morgan as "the devil himself" and called his soldiers "Morgan's terrible men." The very mention of Morgan's name sent fear through Union ranks.

With Morgan on his way to Southwest Virginia, Lee ordered Gen. John C. Breckinridge, Commander of the Department of Southwest Virginia, to move the bulk of his command to the Shenandoah Valley to counter Sigel.

Breckinridge and part of his command were near Lexington when Grant, the "Great Hammerer", opened on Lee and his Army of Northern Virginia. In a series of battles later known as the Wilderness Campaign, Grant attempted to out-flank or out-fight Lee and take Richmond. Lee showed great generalship as he out-maneuvered and out-fought Grant's massive army.

In the Valley near the small town of New Market, the German-born Franz Sigel and his superior army were turned back by Breckinridge and his rag-tag little army of regular and irregular forces. The Corps of Cadets from the Virginia Military Institute took part in the charge that broke Sigel's line. (Sometime after the battle, Breckinridge and his force would be transferred to the Richmond area. Breckinridge, the former Vice-President of the United States, was still the Commander of the Department of Southwest Virginia when he moved to Richmond).

When Breckinridge left Southwest Virginia, Col. John McCausland was instructed to continue gathering soldiers from the department and sending them toward Lexington to reinforce Breckinridge. McCausland was a twenty-seven-year-old graduate of V.M.I. He had graduated first in his class and was the only cadet to this point in time to have graduated without a single demerit.

Gen. John McCausland C.S.A.
Courtesy: Dr. Alexander McCausland.

When McCausland became aware that Union General Crook was advancing toward the New River Bridge, he stopped loading the trains going to Breckinridge. McCausland marched troops north out of Dublin toward Crook's advance.

George Crook, one of the North's most able generals, had graduated tenth from the bottom of his West Point class of 1852.

Col. Rutherford B. Hayes, U. S.

Lt. William McKinley, U. S.

Crook's Infantry had been pushing a small Confederate cavalry unit under Gen. Albert Jenkins. Jenkins linked-up with McCausland's Infantry and Artillery force a few miles north of Dublin near the summit of Cloyds Mountain. Jenkins ordered McCausland to make adjustments in the battle line. McCausland protested the adjustments, but Jenkins was the general, and Colonel McCausland moved his line.

The largest battle to occur in the Department of Southwest Virginia occurred on May 9, 1864. When the smoke cleared, Crook owned the battlefield. He started marching to Dublin, where the headquarters of the department were located.

In far Southwest Virginia, Averell had learned that Morgan had moved to the defense of the saltworks. Averell was no scholar (he ranked in the bottom third of his West Point class of 1855), but he knew better than to tangle with the "Devil" Morgan. Averell decided to abandon his attack on the saltworks and to move toward Wytheville. At Wytheville, he could destroy the railroad between his unit and Morgan's, and then move against the lead mines.

Gen. William Averell, U.S.   *Gen. George Crook, U.S.*

Morgan, aware that Averell had decided to move against Wytheville, drove his cavalry relentlessly from Saltville to Wytheville. In the nick of time, Morgan formed a battle line in a valley leading to Wytheville. In the engagement at Crockett's Cove, Averell was defeated and sent scurrying toward Crook's Infantry for protection from Morgan's "terrible men."

Grant, Sigel, Crook, and Averell had all met Southern resistance; only Crook was successful. According to Grant's plan, one victory was all it would take to capture the capital.

Crook's one victory should be enough. The plan called for Crook to advance on Lynchburg, destroying the railroad as he went. General Lee would be deprived of the supplies from Southwest Virginia, and the capital would fall.

It was near 2:00 p.m. when Crook realized that he had beaten the Confederates. He fainted because of both excitement and exhaustion.

Rebel General Jenkins lay wounded with hundreds of his dead and wounded men.

By sundown, Crook's victorious optimism had changed to defeated pessimism. Crook believed that Grant's grand plan had fallen apart and that he must retreat to save his army.

Crook's pessimism was based on two factors: (1.) John Hunt Morgan was not in Tennessee, where he should be, and (2.) a captured Confederate telegraph message from Richmond, stating that Lee had handed Grant a severe defeat and that Grant was scurrying north. True, Lee had beaten Grant, but Grant was only shifting forces to continue the attack on Lee. Neither the sender of the telegram nor Crook, the Yankee general who received it, was aware of that fact.

Crook believed that Lee had defeated Grant and that now Lee could shift troops into Southwest Virginia. The only course open to Crook was to retreat north. Before leaving the area, both the turnpike and the railroad bridges over New River near Central Depot were burned. The loss of these bridges was a major blow to the transport of military and commercial traffic.

Averell joined Crook as the Yankees withdrew north. The Union cavalry and the infantry were demoralized and were retreating toward Union, (West) Virginia. Colonel McCausland received his commission as brigadier general as he chased the Yanks.

Despite the one victory, Grant's grand strategy had failed. The capital of the Confederacy still stood defiantly. Many men on both sides lost their lives in Grant's offensive. Southern hospitals were full to overflowing from Richmond to Southwest Virginia. One of the generals that Lee depended upon the most, James Longstreet, was severely wounded near Richmond. He was later transferred to a Lynchburg hospital. Union men and material could be replaced; Southern losses could not be. Even though Grant's plan had failed; he still had gained a victory of sorts.

Gen. James Longstreet, C.S.A.

"...The memory of General David Hunter will live and be handed down through the generations to come — it may be, in the long future, only by legend and tradition — in connection with deeds that illustrate how far the passions, fanaticism, and hate engendered by Civil War can drag a man down...."

General J.D. Imboden

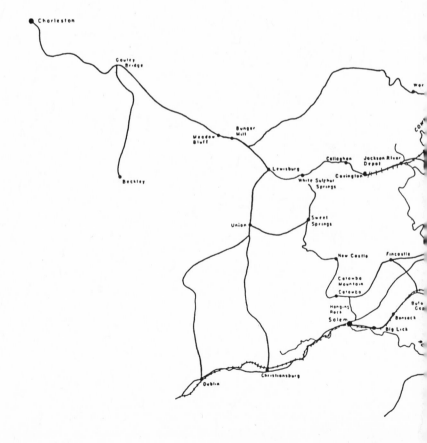

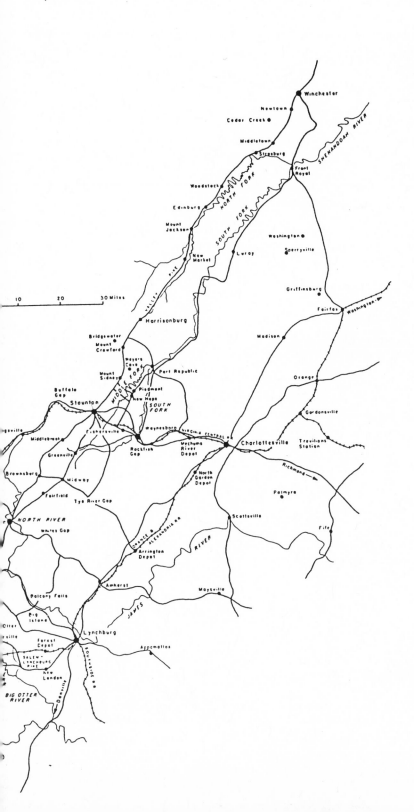

Chapter III

Thursday, May 19 — Monday, May 23

By May 19, Crook and Averell had moved from Union, (West) Virginia, to Meadow Bluff, (West) Virginia. Brig. Gen. John McCausland, commissioned May 18, 1864, who had been pursuing, fighting, and generally annoying Averell since the raid into Southwest Virginia, May 5-14, moved his headquarters to Union.

Crook's and Averell's men and horses were worn out. The generals had been trying to secure supplies: they were low on food, ammunition, clothing and shoes. For eleven days they had been waiting. The problem wasn't that the Union had no supplies to send; it was that those annoying Southern guerrillas had been cutting rail and canal supply lines and capturing wagon trains. On May 19, John S. Mosby, the Gray Ghost, had captured another wagon train near Strasburg. The Marylanders, John H. McNeill and Harry Gilmor, were harassing the defenses also. These guerrillas, usually fewer than forty men in a band and sometimes only three or four, snaked in and out of the mountain passes, striking isolated Union units or trains and vanishing in a gorge or over a mountain. Not only did they worry the Union like an unpredictable swarm of bees, but they also sent information back to other Confederate field commanders. The shortages, which they helped to produce, led to half rations and discontent for Crook's and Averell's men.

At Meadow Bluff, the officers were catching up on their paper work. Crook could write of his victory at Cloyds Mountain, the taking of military headquarters for the Department of Southwest Virginia at Dublin, and the destruction of the all-important, four-hundred-feet-long railroad bridge at Central Depot. The break in the Virginia-Tennessee line would slow for months shipment of the vital war materials of lead and salt to Lee. Trains had to stop at one side of the bridge, remove the load; ferry across, and reload on another train. This, of course, slowed the movement of troops, mail, freight, and passengers. The South employed slave labor to rebuild the bridge as quickly as possible.

(Crook could write his report truthfully and with some pleasure). Averell, on the other hand, decided that it would be wise to write high command a fairy tale. Averell's part in the strike into Southwest Virginia was to destroy the saltworks at Saltville and the lead mines at Austinville near Wytheville. He hadn't come close to achieving either goal. He was defeated in virtually every skirmish and battle he fought. He personally received a head wound at a battle near Wytheville. Now Averell was busy changing battlefield losses into paper victories. If that weren't bad enough, McCausland with troops of Jenkins' Cavalry Brigade (Albert Jenkins was mortally wounded at Cloyds Mountain) and troops under Gen. William "Mudwall" Jackson, were still pushing Averell's tired troopers back. (William acquired his nickname "Mudwall" earlier in the war when he was on the staff of his famous cousin Thomas "Stonewall" Jackson).

Meadow Bluff became Brigade Headquarters for the Department of West Virginia. Command Headquarters were now located at Cedar Creek, Virginia. That part of the army wasn't doing much better after its part in the grand offensive of early May either. Gen. Franz Sigel was ordered south to cut transportation from the Valley to General Lee. On May 15, John C. Breckinridge, then the commander of the Department of Southwest Virginia, met Sigel at New Market. Although Sigel had more troops and supplies, Breckinridge dominated the field. Breckinridge's rag-tag army of regulars and irregulars, including cadets from the Virginia Military Institute, thoroughly routed Sigel. Sigel left his dead on the battlefield and his wounded in hospitals, hotels, and private homes from New Market to Woodstock. Stragglers of the demoralized army were still coming in at Cedar Creek, located near Winchester and Strasburg.

Sigel depended on the same supply line that was supposed to feed Crook. The Confederate guerrilla raids were hurting Sigel, too.

General Grant was enraged over Sigel's defeat. One of Grant's subordinates suggested that Sigel be removed. Grant decided that removal of Sigel was wise. Grant telegraphed Adj. Gen. Henry W. Halleck "...to appoint Hunter, *or anyone else,* to the command of West Virginia...."[4] "Anyone else" may have reflected Grant's frustration with Sigel or that Grant was open to suggestions if Halleck didn't want Hunter to take charge.

Of the approximately 580 generals dressed in Union blue, only a handful earned the undying animosity of the Southern people. (Benjamin Franklin Butler, who was known as "the Butcher of New Orleans"; William Tecumseh Sherman, who raped Georgia; Philip H. Sheridan, who also earned infamy in the Valley of Virginia; and David Hunter).

Hunter was the son of a Virginia Presbyterian preacher. Born in 1802, (in Washington D.C.), he was an old man of almost sixty-two when he was appointed to command the Department of West Virginia. His whole military career could be described as a fire storm. One writer called him "...the war's highest ranking pyromaniac."[5] Southern by birth, he grew up to hate the institution of slavery and all those connected with it. A collection of comments on Hunter could easily fill a volume, such was the controversy the man invoked.

After graduating from West Point, class of 1822, Hunter started his army career. Except for the six years he was involved in real estate, Hunter was a professional soldier. As he climbed through the ranks, he literally left two dead bodies behind. He was not a man to be crossed since he had "...won a reputation as a duelist."[5] When Hunter decided that a commanding officer was to be body number three, he went too far. He was courtmartialed and sentenced to be dismissed from the service. It was then that Hunter realized that political power could be very beneficial. President John Quincy Adams overruled the military trial: Hunter would not be dismissed.

In the war with Mexico, many of the future Civil War generals on both sides practiced their deadly profession and gained reputations. Though Hunter was in service, he saw no action. After the war, he was assigned to a post in the Northwest. There he married an Illinois girl, Maria Kinzie.

In 1860, Abraham Lincoln, an Illinois attorney, was elected President of the United States. With the election count came the storm clouds of war. Between election and inauguration, Hunter sent a stream of correspondence to the President-elect in Springfield, Illinois, concerning "insurrectionary rumors."[5] When the steam train rumbled out of Springfield bearing the new President and his entourage to Washington, Hunter was on board. This was Hunter's trip from obscurity.

The close association with the President didn't hurt Hunter's military career. When Hunter first wrote the letters to the President-elect, he was a major; on May 17, he was a brigadier general.

Hunter was there at the first great battle of the war, Manassas or Bull Run. He was wounded early in the battle and evacuated from the field long before the disgraceful defeat and rout the Union suffered. He had the prestige of great battle and the wound of heroism, but he had none of the dishonor of defeat.

After Hunter recovered from his wound, he was assigned under Maj. Gen. John Fremont in the Western Department. Fremont recognized Hunter as a rival, anxious to climb the military ladder. Their relationship was not good. Fremont was reassigned after he failed to defeat a much smaller Confederate force. Hunter was assigned as temporary departmental commander. That position suited Hunter just fine.

His happiness was short-lived. In November, when the department was broken up; he was assigned to a much smaller portion of his old department. His new department was Kansas; this was a demotion in fact. The Department of Kansas included Colorado, Nebraska, and Dakota. It was Indian territory and a backwash of the war. Hunter was not happy, and he let Adjutant General Halleck in Washington know. When that correspondence bore no fruit, he addressed his letters to the White House.

Apparently Lincoln paid no attention to Hunter's letters, and conditions worsened for the disgruntled general. He saw officers of less grade receiving commands of vast armies while most of what few troops he had were taken to reinforce General Grant.

On December 23, Hunter sent a Christmas message to President Lincoln. He wrote, I am "...very deeply mortified, humiliated, insulted, and disgraced...."[5]

President Lincoln was already upset by the constant dispatches from the War Department, and the letters from Hunter were filled with discontent. Hunter's Christmas letter was too much! The President fired off a stinging rebuke to Hunter. He said that he found it difficult to make a "civil reply to so ugly a letter...the flood of grumbling dispatches and letters...you are adopting the best possible way to ruin yourself...."[5] Hunter knew that the letter could have been signed "your former friend, the President."

Hunter knew more than one politician. On March 31, 1862, he was reassigned to the command of the Department of the South, directing Union operations in South Carolina, Georgia, and Florida with headquarters at Hilton Head, South Carolina.

Hunter had replaced Brig. Gen. Thomas Sherman. He inherited Sherman's troops and plans for the attack on Fort Pulaski which guarded the entrance to Savannah Harbor. It was Sherman's plan and men, but Hunter got the glory.

His glory was gone shortly after May 7, 1862. Hunter's hatred of slavery had clouded his judgement. He issued his own Emancipation Proclamation for slaves in his area of operation. He then followed his proclamation with a recruitment drive and formed the "first black regiment"[6] in the United States Army, the First South Carolina Volunteers. These were political decisions that enraged the South and the North. He soon heard from the leaders of both countries.

On May 19, President Lincoln decreed "...repeal of emancipation in the Department of the South."[5] The First South Carolina Volunteers "...were discharged without pay."[6] The abolitionists, and the liberal Republicans applauded Hunter, but the President was not ready to make such a radical change of policy.

On August 21, Hunter heard from the other President, Jefferson Davis. Davis stated: "Hunter and other slave recruiters (were) common criminals liable to summary execution...."[5] Hunter was branded a felon and a price set on his head. "...If captured, he (Hunter) shall not be regarded as a prisoner of war, but held in close confinement for execution as a felon."[7] The South went on to declare that white officers that led negroes, many of whom were former slaves, would be hanged.

Hunter retaliated with orders of his own. Southern prisoners of the "aristocratic caste"[5] were to be held as hostages and executed if the South hanged any Northern officers. Hunter again heard from his former friend, the President, who "suppressed"[5] the order.

Despite the storm Hunter generated, he was not washed from the Department of the South. Things in the department were "...static and listless,"[5] but Hunter's ambition was lively. In November, he went to Washington to look for more fertile ground. Instead of the glory, excitement, and possible advancement of a battlefield command, he was assigned to shuffling papers on a series of review boards.

Hunter realized that this assignment was a mistake. "The President, without comment...allowed (Hunter) to return to Hilton Head,"[5] where he didn't remain in command long. His troops failed in another attack on Charleston, and he was re-assigned to Washington.

Though Hunter wore a general's uniform, he was an errand boy for the War Department. He remained in this position for almost a year. He carried orders, filed reports, and made field inspections. His travels brought him in association with General Grant in the West, where he cultivated a friendship with this winning general and waited.

During this time, the political climate in Washington was changing. The liberal Republicans were becoming dominant in the Lincoln Administration. The outrages Hunter committed in 1862, freeing slaves and recruiting Negroes for the ranks, were now administration policy. No longer was Hunter viewed as an uncontrolled radical but as a military Moses — out front, leading the fight against evil Southern slave owners. His actions which brought a reprimand from President Lincoln were now to bring him the offer of a reward. He was "...offered command of all Union forces on the Pacific Coast."[5] He declined. War, glory, and advancement were not to be found on the West Coast.

He wrote Secretary of War, Edwin Stanton, "I am an old man, but...if they give me a command I intend to make it fly."

When Sigel was defeated at New Market, May 15, 1864, his new friend Grant telegraphed "...appoint Hunter."[4] Hunter got his chance to "fly."

The energetic old man was now Maj. Gen. David Hunter, Commander of the Department of West Virginia. When he left Washington, he had Grant's orders and his own plans as he traveled to Cedar Creek.

When he arrived, he later wrote, "I found his (Sigel's) command very much disorganized and demoralized...and the three generals with it...Sigel, Stahel, and Sullivan, not worth one cent."[8]

Hunter assumed command at 7:00 p.m.[8] and wasted no time in relieving one of the generals not "worth a cent," his predecessor, Sigel.

Hunter then fired off a stinging telegram to Washington. "Our cavalry is utterly demoralized from frequent defeats by inferior forces and retreats without fighting...needs a commander of grit, zeal, activity, and courage...inefficiency of General Stahel."[8] Hunter also states that Sullivan "...had a limited background."[6] Hunter wanted both Brig. Gen. Jeremiah C. Sullivan and Maj. Gen. Julius Stahel relieved of command. They also had friends in high places, and Hunter did not get his way.

Hunter did make some changes in command. He incurred the resentment of some senior officers when he promoted Capt. Henry Algernon Dupont to Chief-of-Artillery. They were embittered that this twenty-six-year-old, just out of West Point, with less experience than they, was now their commander. The fact that he graduated number one in his class made little difference to them.

A part of the First New York (Lincoln) Cavalry under Major Quinn was chosen by Hunter as his personal guard. He chose several officers from the unit to command positions: Major Harkins, Provost Marshal; Cap. William Alexander, Quartermaster; and Charles G. Halphine acting Adjutant General with duties of personal secretary.

For his Chief-of-Staff, Hunter chose his cousin, David Hunter Strother. Strother was understandably proud of this promotion. He boasted that "We can afford to lose such battles as New Market, to get rid of such a mistake as Maj. Gen. Sigel." He considered his cousin "...experienced, well trained...."[7]

Strother was related to General Hunter. Strother came from the Shenandoah Valley, and they shared the same namesake, Col. David Hunter. Strother, however, was not a militarist. A close examination of his life and writing shows a man at war, not only with the South, but within his own spirit. He was an artist: he looked for the beautiful, the civilized, and the cultured, however, war is not comprised of these qualities. He couldn't forget that he was a Virginian; he was not driven by hatred of slavery, as was his cousin General Hunter. Before the war, he did sketches for *Harper's Weekly* and signed his work "Porte Crayon" (pencil box). He did many sketches as he traveled the Valley and visited in the homes of friends and relatives. The knowledge he acquired while he was sketching the beautiful Shenandoah Valley would be used to help destroy the Valley and even some of the beautiful homes where he had been entertained. One experienced cavalryman described Hunter's Chief-of-Staff as a "...genial man."[9]

Col. David Hunter Strother.

What history says of a general is largely written by the deeds of the legions of non-commissioned officers and privates under that general. Time has largely erased the names and the faces of these soldiers, but their opinions of their new general were important.

When Hunter rode in with his dyed mustache, dark-brown wig, and generally dark complexion, some soldiers were apprehensive. One wrote, "We don't like his looks."[6] One cavalryman with the First New York saw Hunter and later wrote "...stern appearance, prompt manner...but he (the Virginian with roots in the Shenandoah Valley, General Hunter) spared no Rebels for relations' sake."[9]

Hunter knew that the opinions the army held of him were important. He knew the value that an example could have at this critical point in time on a change of command. The next move would let the troops know that Sigel was a man of the past and that Hunter was the man they now had to please. This move could provide a new direction for this demoralized army. Captain Auer provided that example.

Capt. Michael Auer of Company A, Fifteenth New York Cavalry, was on picket duty with thirty of his men when Confederate guerrillas attacked. Within minutes, forty-five Union horses and fifteen of Auer's men were captured. The Rebs simply disappeared through some mountain valley with their booty. Captain Auer must have trembled before Hunter, who had a "...violent temper...(and showed) indifference to human suffering...."[6] Hunter dressed him down accusing him of being "...disgracefully surprised, (and) ...dishonorably discharged (Auer)...."[8] Then he said to "...all officers...strictly responsible for the performance of their duties, *...no excuse* (for failure)...."[8]

Partisans or guerrilla fighters for the South.

Hunter was to be as stern as his looks.

Hunter understood what his superior, General Grant, expected of him. Grant's policy was to exert constant pressure at every possible point on the Confederacy, destroy military stores, to take what the army needed from Southern soil, and to eliminate every Southern soldier because the South virtually had no replacements. Hunter's raid was only one of a multi-pronged attack designed to stretch Southern manpower and resources to the breaking point and end the war. Gen. Nathaniel Banks moved up the Red River off the Mississippi. Gen. William T. Sherman kept Confederate Gen. Joseph E. Johnston on the defensive as he pushed toward Atlanta. Gen. Samuel Sturgis pushed south out of Memphis, and Grant would keep enormous pressure on General Lee as Lee defended the capital. Because of the vast advantage Grant had in manpower, it was assumed that Lee would not spare a single man to defend the Valley. With the advantage enjoyed in troop numbers, Northern victory should be easy, but Sigel had enjoyed the same advantages.

Grant said that Lee was "...supplied through Staunton..."[8] and that "it would be of great value to us to get possession of Lynchburg for a single day."[10] Following Grant's instructions, Hunter sent orders to the Brigade Headquarters at Meadow Bluff. Crook and Averell were to move on May 25 toward Staunton and link both armies of the Department of West Virginia. On May 21, Hunter sent orders to Meadow Bluff and a telegram to Washington: "I hope to meet them there (Staunton) and then move directly east, via Charlottesville and Gordonsville...."[8] Then he would join Grant and apply pressure on Richmond.

During the same period, Hunter received a communique from President Lincoln. Strother recorded that Hunter was "...requested by the President to retain the Dutch (Sigel was born in Germany) in some position...."[11] Hunter placed Sigel in command of the railroad reserves far to the rear. In preparation for a move south, Hunter ordered that all excess transport (wagons) filled with the excess baggage of the army, were to be sent north to Martinsburg. Hunter now in effect made Sigel the porter boy for his former army. It was Sigel's job to form this wagon train moving north as the fighting portion of his old army moved south.

The dispatches reached Brigade Headquarters at Meadow Bluff, informing them of the change in command and the orders to move toward Staunton. Rutherford B. Hayes, Commander of the Twenty-Third Ohio Infantry Regiment, who wished history to remember him as "one of the good colonels,"[12] wrote that he had never met Hunter, but "...had for some reason formed an unfavorable opinion of the general."[13]

Near Meadow Bluff Averell's men were still being pushed back. On May 21, Averell reported that some of the men that were cut-off south of a ford on the Greenbrier River had made it back to camp. These men reported that there were 200-300 Southern troops on the north side of the Greenbrier and that they had "...heard drums this morning on the road toward White Sulphur (Springs)."[8] Averell reported that the South had driven his pickets back. Troops of Lt. Col. James Cochran, Company 1, Fourteenth Virginia Cavalry, under Col. William H. French's command were the troops pushing Averell's pickets. These troops reported back to McCausland that they believed a "big"[8] wagon train of supplies was moving toward Meadow Bluff.

On May 23, Gen. William E. Jones telegraphed the War Department in Richmond that he was assuming command of the Department of Southwest Virginia. This understaffed department was in a state of disorganization because of the moves against it and the Valley District earlier in the month. The last confirmed leader of the department was General Breckinridge. He moved with the bulk of the troops from Southwest Virginia to New Market to meet Sigel. Then General Lee decided that Breckinridge could best serve the Confederacy nearer Richmond, and Jones took it upon himself to assume command of the department. Although there was no official directive issued by Lee, the War Department acquisced to Jones's telegram and he was approved as head of the department.

In the Valley District, the Commander, Gen. John David Imboden, was also denuded of troops as Lee pulled troops to defend the capital. Imboden had about 1,000 men mostly members of the Fifteenth and Twenty-Third Virginia Cavalries scattered throughout the Valley. They protected strategic mountain passes and manned signal stations. Imboden had been criticized for not consolidating his strength, but having dispersed his troops through the Valley. The lack of food and fodder made it more difficult to supply massed troops; limited supplies could be obtained more readily in the countryside. Imboden had only one battery of light artillery in his command, Capt. John H. McClanahan's "Flying Artillery" (flying in theory meant that it could operate independently of the main forces for a limited period of time).

Imboden was not happy because of the potential threat of the Yankees massed at Cedar Creek and at Meadow Bluff. So far, the Federals had shown no inclinations to attack since their retreat from Southwest Virginia or their rout at New Market, but the threat was still there. Either wing of the Department of West Virginia could field an army that would dwarf his army and Home Guard combined. A telegram was sent to Breckinridge at Richmond, asking him to return Imboden's pride and joy, the Sixty-Second Virginia Mounted Infantry. Imboden wrote: "...that regiment is small now, and will be of little value to you but inestimable to me as a nucleus to form reserves (Home Guards) upon."[8] The regiment may have been "small," but Breckinridge was using it. Until Lee saw fit to transfer the regiment, Breckinridge was determined to keep it.

Imboden seemed to be at his best while organizing and recruiting. On May 20, he made a re-organization designed to increase the size of his Home Guard. Control of the Home Guard was turned over to Col. Edwin G. Lee, headquartered at Staunton. Colonel Lee inherited a force of approximately 1,100 old men, young boys, convalescents, and clerks, a force of questionable military value. Few had training, fewer had battlefield experience, and all were poorly armed and equipped. Lee assumed command with a determination to increase the size of his force. He sent out an appeal that echoed throughout the Valley. "It is deemed unnecessary to make an appeal to

Virginians to step forward without coercion; and lend their aid to the noble armies that are now winning; at such costly sacrifice; our independence; our bleeding country points to her wounds in an appeal stronger than words."[6]

Chapter IV

Tuesday, May 24 — Saturday, May 28

On May 24, McCausland, who had been commanding the Confederate cavalry since shortly after Cloyds Mountain, was headquartered at Union, W. Virginia. Here he received the official orders, making him commander in name as well as in fact. The Southern forces from Southwest Virginia were beginning to reorganize their command structure after the Union incursion of early May and the subsequent shift of troops from and to the department.

At Cedar Creek, the wagon train carrying the extra baggage had headed north on May 23. Since that time, rumors were that the army was going to move south. It had been only eight days since the rout at New Market. The new general had been in command only two days. It seemed too soon to move, but the wagon train had gone with the excess baggage. There was no doubt that Hunter intended to move south soon.

On the morning of May 24, Hunter called a conference of his officers. David Hunter Strother's appointment, was officially announced to no one's surprise. Hunter then informed his officers that they would move south on May 26. Also on that date, Crook and Averell would be "...advancing from Meadow Bluff with 16,000 men as directed"[11] (toward Staunton). Hunter seemed to be misinformed as to the drastic shortages that existed in Meadow Bluff, where the men had no shoes and only half rations, because he had stated that the men were "...in fine condition."[11] Crook and Averell were in no condition to march.

Hunter then issued orders for his own troops. He ordered that they would march on May 26. Each infantryman was to carry one hundred rounds of ammunition, four pounds of hard bread, ten rations of coffee, sugar, and salt. Each was to pack enough for four days, but the soldiers must make it last for eight days. Hunter permitted one pair of shoes and one pair of extra socks but "...nothing more."[14]

Soldiers marching to battle were usually required to carry forty rounds of ammunition, but Hunter was demanding each man lug one hundred rounds, over six pounds of weight. This led the men to refer to themselves as "...Hunter's ammunition train."[9]

Supplies for four days had to last eight days, but Hunter was to see to it that his marching army would not go hungry. It was to be "...supplied from the country; cattle, sheep, hogs, and if necessary horses and mules must be taken (from the civilian population) and slaughtered."[9] Hunter would allow "...(no)

pillaging...no waste...no straggling."[9] Officers were responsible for "...enforce-
ment of discipline...no excuses."[9]

Hunter went on to state that General Grant "...expects much from the
Army of the Shenandoah, and he must not be disappointed."[9] Sigel's army was
the Army of the Shenandoah before Hunter took command of it and the troops
at Meadow Bluff.

Hunter used the stick when he told the officers that Grant "must not be
disappointed...no excuses." He used the carrot to get his men to perform when
he said I "...will never cease to urge the prompt promotion of all officers,
non-commissioned officers, and enlisted men who earn recognition by their
gallantry and good conduct."[9] Victory was assured since even God was
fighting with General Hunter because he expects "...ever kind Providence for
the result."[9] The message was clear: Hunter, Grant, and God expected good
results; they would reward the faithful and accept no excuses for failure.
Hunter also informed them that he had heard from Grant via Washington.
Grant reported that Breckinridge was with Lee. There would be little the
South could do to oppose them.

Hunter then turned the group's attention to a matter that must be taken care
of today. Strother records: "An order is issued, threatening destruction of
property and reprisals for the attacks of guerrillas and bushwhackers. In case a
train or a man is fired on by *anyone* behind our lines, houses of secessionists
and their property are to be burned *without mercy*...."[11] In fact, a wagon train
was fired on at Newtown. Some of the Union soldiers were wounded, and
perhaps some were captured. As a result, "the houses of three secessionists
were burned...."[11]

On May 25, preparations continued for the march south. In the afternoon,
Hunter reviewed his troops and set the marching order for the next day.

Also on the 25th, a delegation of four men from Newtown came to call on
Hunter. He refused to see them and referred the matter to his Chief-of-Staff
Strother, who rode out to meet them. The delegation came to complain about
the three houses Major Timothy Quinn and the First New York (Lincoln)
Cavalry had burned. It informed Strother that one of the houses burned was
owned by "...a rich secessionist residing in Lexington."[11] The person most hurt
by the burning was the person renting the house. His furnishings were
destroyed even though he was "...esteemed loyal...(and had even) taken the
oath."[11] The house of "the parson,"[11] where shots were fired at the wagon train,
was burned. The delegation described the Rev. John Wolff as a "...sentimental
secessionist...a worthy, upright man."[11] Strother didn't tell the delegation that
he needed no testimony about John Wolff, a former classmate and friend. Now
Strother's army had stolen and destroyed Wolff's possessions and burned his
dwelling to the ground. The gravity of what occurred must have weighed
heavily upon his mind. The third house burned could have been considered a
military target according to the group. It was "Mr. Harman('s), a bushwhacker,
and the house was used as a rendezvous for guerrillas."[11]

Chief-of-Staff Strother, apparently gave no reply. He simply handed the
men a copy of Hunter's order for burning "...and told them that vengeance

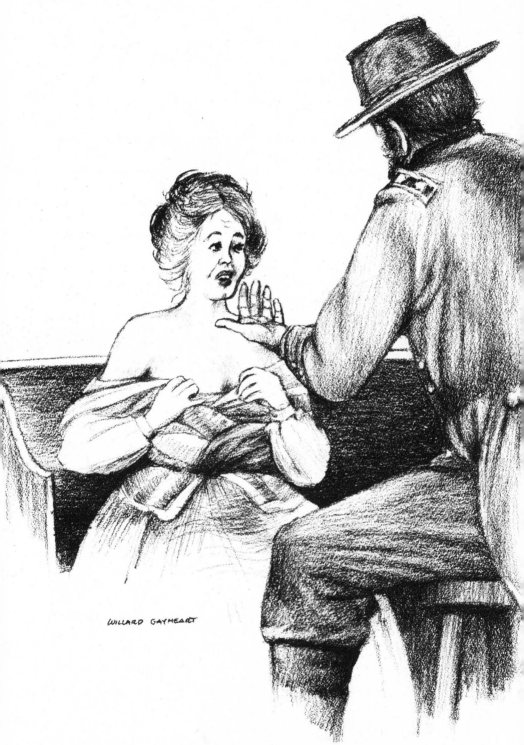

Union officer interrogates young southern woman. (Drawing by Willard Gayheart, Box 605, Galax, Va. 24333)

would surely fall upon the country if these robberies and murders continued and that the only way to protect themselves and their innocent neighbors was to indicate to us the quilty persons."[11]

The fear of reprisal was great, and the delegates began to blame others from outside of their community for the attacks on Union supply wagons. They said that a Captain Glen and his "...young men from Maryland"[11] were involved. They also sighted a Captain Sheerer of Winchester. The only local resident implicated was the "...house of a Mrs. Wilson in Newtown as being a rendezvous for guerrillas...."[11] As members of the delegation left, they promised to "...give all the information in their power"[11] to the Federals.

Strother informed General Hunter of the accusations against Mrs. Wilson, who was a widow. Hunter immediately issued orders for the burning of the house and for the arrest of Mrs. Wilson whom he wished to deport farther South.

When the Union forces arrived to burn Mrs. Wilson's house, they learned that the house was not hers, for she only rented it. They told her that their orders were to burn the house, and burn they must. Everything she owned must be taken out of the house. (The Yanks had learned from their previous burning). Mrs. Wilson "...thinking that the house was to be burnt, she and her daughters assisted in the removal with great alacrity, thanking the officer for his consideration. Her astonishment and grief was great when the heap of furniture instead of the house was set fire to and consumed. The woman herself was then arrested and trudged six miles to Starr's guard tent. Rough are the wages of war."[11]

At Lt. Col. William Starr's guard tent, Strother observed a young woman under arrest. When she was informed that she would be held prisoner at least another day or two "...she broke into loud lamentations, wringing her hands and tearing her hair. She had left a baby at home six weeks old, and it would perish with hunger."[11] (There was no nursing mother to feed the baby). Starr, at least, partially disrobed the young woman and "...felt her breasts, which were entirely flat and showed no signs of milking...."[11] Starr told her that she would not be released because she "...would be of little use to the baby...."[11] That insult to injury was too much for the young Southerner who "abused Starr"[11] (cursed him).

Re-creation: Union Cavalry returning without any Southern prisoners.

Strother concurred with Starr that the young woman was lying when he got a chance to observe the female prisoner before he left Starr's compound somewhat later. She was under a tree "...smoking a short clay pipe and chatting in a friendly manner with the guard."[11]

While Northern forces were preparing to attack a second time within the same month against General Lee's vital supply lines that ran from Southwest Virginia through the Valley, the strain of constant battle was showing on General Lee. Lee's battered army was only a little more than one third the number of Grant's well-supplied and equipped invasion force. Lee contested Grant's approach on the capital at every opportunity in a series of battles called the Wilderness Campaign. Lee's almost constant attention had to be focused on Grant. Lee's communication to the War Department on May 25 showed that he was mentally drained. Lee wrote, "Since I withdrew General Breckinridge from the Valley there is *no* general commander...a *good* commander should be at once sent to that brigade...is Morgan there? W.E. Jones, I believe, belongs to (Department of) East Tennessee...I shall return General Breckinridge as soon as I can."[8]

The Morgan Lee referred to was cavalry General John H. Morgan. Morgan was born in Huntsville, Alabama but adopted the blue grass state of Kentucky as his home. Among the South's most savage fighters, Morgan at this time was assigned to the Department of Southwest Virginia and East Tennessee. He and his "terrible men"[15] had been shifted to Southwest Virginia to oppose Averell's and Crook's forces. W.E. Jones, already in Southwest Virginia, had assumed command of the Department. Neither man was in the Shenandoah Valley; nor had either been ordered to move east at this point in time. It appears that either General Lee had forgotten that Gen. John Imboden was in command of the Valley District or that he held a low opinion of Imboden. It was a slap in Imboden's face when Lee stated "There is *no* general...(he needed) a *good* commander...."[8]

Gen. John H. Morgan, C.S.A.

Only now did Secretary of War I.A. Seddon inform Lee that in the
"...absence of General Breckinridge"[8] that W.E. Jones had been appointed
commander of the Department of Southwest Virginia and East Tennessee.

Before the sun set on May 25, Grant cabled Maj. Gen. H.W. Halleck,
adjutant, in Washington: "If Hunter can possibly get to Charlottesville and
Lynchburg, he should do so, living on the country. The railroad and canal
should be destroyed beyond possibility of repair for weeks. Completing this,
he could find his way back to his original base, or form about Gordonsville and
join this army."[16]

On May 26, Grant gave the order to General Philip Sheridan's Cavalry to
prepare to move toward Charlottesville and a link-up with Hunter.

On the morning of the 26th, Hunter was ready to make his command "fly."
To insure communications to the rear, he would set up a series of signal stations
on mountain tops. The first of these stations was placed on Round Top near
Cedar Creek.

Re-creation: Federal Signal Station.

As Hunter stepped off to the south in the early morning, he was sure that
the armies of Crook and Averell were also leaving Meadow Bluff for a
rendezvous at Staunton.

Hunter notified Washington that he was on the move. He said he would
"...depend entirely on the country (for food) and hope to form a junction with
Crook at Staunton, and then move *immediately* to Lynchburg."[17] It appears
that Hunter had already decided not to follow Grant's instructions to take
Charlottesville first, cutting the railroad to prevent the South from sending
troops from Richmond to attack him. Only after cutting the railroad was he to
move on Lynchburg. Perhaps Hunter was certain that Lee could not spare a
single soldier for the defense of the Valley and that a side trip to Charlottesville
was a waste of time. Perhaps Hunter did not wish to move eastwardly to
link-up with Grant. Hunter was an independent man with a big ego.

In the Valley, he would be a big man operating his army freely. With Grant,
he would be a subordinate. Once again slavery ("...on this issue he focused all
his toxic anger"[7]) may have clouded his judgement. He felt that it was his
mission to reap vengeance on Virginia because of the "suppressing (of) John
Brown."[7]

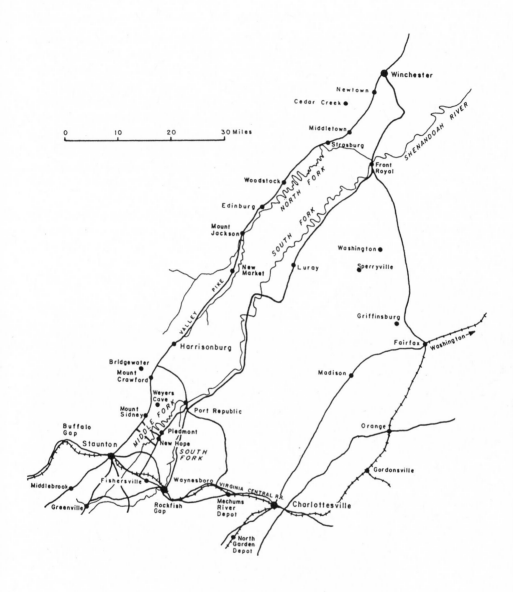

Hunter wisely deployed some of his cavalrymen to the front and the rear of the column. They would give early warning of any Confederate attacks. The balance of the cavalry was to march on a parallel road to the right of the main column. By using more than one road, he would be able to move more rapidly. The Signal Corps could be used if either column was attacked. Rockets fired from one column would indicate possible distress and the need for assistance.

Hunter started his massive army of approximately 8,000 officers and men with a complement of 21 guns and a supply train in motion. The advance cavalry was followed by the Hundred Sixteenth Ohio Volunteer Infantry. Most members of the Hundred Sixteenth would have been happy to have traded the honor of being first to some other regiment. Even with a cavalry screen, they knew that if a surprise action occurred, they would be the first under fire. The biggest advantage of being in front was that they knew all other units would eat their dust that day. Previous rain had taken this advantage away. They started their march at 8:30 a.m. over a muddy road. After wading Cedar Creek, they marched for four miles and through Strasburg and up Fishers Hill. Already it was getting hot.

If the soldiers looked back toward Strasburg, they could see the smoke from the Boyden house. Col. George D. Wells had burned it because it was "...a rendezvous for bushwhackers."[11] He knew that the recent deaths of five Federals near Fishers Hill could be traced to the activities from that house.

The Union soldiers had barely gotten their feet wet in Cedar Creek before Confederate scouts were rushing south toward Imboden with the news. They also reported accurately that Hunter had brought a "...pontoon (for bridging streams) train along."[8]

There was no significant Southern force to attempt to harass the Union on its march; the Southerners stayed a safe distance ahead and watched. En route the Federals detained two "refugees"[11] who turned out to be dissatisfied "conscripts."[11] They may have been drafted, but they weren't going to serve in the Confederate Army. They told the Federals they were going to Pennsylvania.

*Re-creation: Union soldiers block a road preventing a
Southern lady from returning home.*

A Mrs. Henry and her children who were traveling north met the Union Army coming south. She asked permission to pass through the advancing army. She also wanted a special guard so that she and her children would not be molested. She just knew that she would be accomodated because Hunter was a "Virginian" and a "gentleman."[9] Although he was a Virginian by heritage, she received no special guard.

An army is a rumor mill with feet. On May 24, Hunter issued orders for burning of private property as a reprisal for any firing on Federal troops. By the 26th, the order was interpreted and broadened by the rumor mill. Now "...the town nearest the scene of such attack would be burned,"[9] or "...the commanding general will cause to be burned every Rebel house within five miles of the place (of the attack)."[7]

The army marched approximately eleven miles and camped two and one half miles north of Woodstock on Pughes Run. Near the campsite was the Cheney home. As a Northern officer approached the house, Mrs. Cheney came out and asked if General Sigel was with him. He replied "No, he has been removed from command and sent North." She said, "...she thanked God fervently and said again she had never prayed for vengeance against anyone that my prayer had not been granted."[11] Her prayer had been granted again and Sigel was gone. Mrs. Cheney was glad to see Sigel gone, but some of his former troops did not care for his stern replacement. Sigel was "...a good officer...kind to the men...from a soldiers view, we need more like him...."[18]

Hunter ordered some of his scouts to go to Woodstock and to burn some houses that may have been used by Southern guerrillas. The people of Woodstock were less than cordial. They either refused to answer the enemy's inquiries or they gave conflicting answers. Because the Yanks couldn't find the houses Hunter ordered burned, they returned to camp without the stench of smoke on their uniforms. Hunter's own order called for burning in reprisal for guerrilla activity against his forces, but there had been no reported shooting upon them. In addition to reprisal burning, Hunter believed that it was a good policy to burn something everyday as general punishment for being a slave-holding state and for being on the wrong side in this war. "Hunter wreaked his vengeance on pro-Confederate civilians with an enthusiasm that sometimes disturbed his own men."[7] Along with his violent temper, which he often turned on his men, his stern appearance, and continual burning, caused his men to refer to him as "Black Dave."[7]

Grant's orders of May 25 reached Hunter on May 26 after passing through Washington. The communique now read: "...he (Grant) wishes you to push on, if possible, to Charlottesville, and Lynchburg, and destroy railroad and canal beyond possibility of repair for weeks; then either return to your *original base* or join Grant, via Gordonsville."[17] Hunter now felt relieved of the command to move eastwardly to Grant, but he must take Charlottesville before Lynchburg.

Hunter moved on May 26; Crook and Averell stayed. The men Hunter described as being in "fine condition" were on half rations and waiting for adequate supplies. Hunter, of course, believed his orders to march had been obeyed.

No military reason could be found for not marching on May 27. After starting a march which Hunter knew would alert the Southern forces that he was coming, he now took a break. He knew that this break would allow more time for the Rebs to prepare for him.

Hunter apparently didn't even consider issuing marching orders for May 27. He summoned Chief-of-Staff Strother to his quarters early in the morning. He ordered Strother to go to Woodstock to find out who had tried "...to confuse our scouts yesterday as he (Hunter) wished to burn a few houses."[11] It was clearly implied that if the guilty parties could be found, reprisals would be taken against them.

It was an unhurried day for Strother and the army. Strother stopped by General Sullivan's quarters, and the two rode to Mrs. Cheney's house. She entertained the Union officers with a piano concert. As the two men left the house, Strother (tongue in cheek) told Sullivan that he had better treat Mrs. Cheney very nicely or she may call wrath down on his head "...as her prayers seemed to be efficacious."[11]

At Woodstock, Strother found that "the whole town was squalling with women, children, chickens, and geese...feathers were flying like a cloud... excitement (because of the unwelcome visitors)."[11]

Strother sauntered his horse and rode to the Chipley house in an unobtrusive manner. Mr. Chipley was elderly, a "...fiery secessionist and took occasion to express his high scorn of Yankees and especially of *renegade Virginians.*"[11] Obviously Mr. Chipley knew that Hunter, a Virginian, now commanded the army, but he probably didn't realize that Hunter's Chief-of-Staff Strother, was also a Virginian. Strother apparently displayed no outward emotion, but to be referred to as a renegade and traitor had to have some effect on the artist, Chief-of-Staff.

While he was taking verbal barrages from Chipley, Strother noticed Chipley's two daughters, "the girls were dressed in flaming red and were evidently parading to attract attention...."[11] Strother's quick wit went to work and as the irritated Reb paused to catch his breath, Strother let go with a barrage of his own: "I told (him) the girls, both would marry Yankees, the first good-looking fellow who asked them...they (the girls) were not nearly so much horrified as I expected, although they got up some scornful airs."[11] Strother knew that he would get no useful information from this old Reb. Chipley was not likely to point an accusing finger at any of his neighbors, so that the Federals could burn their houses. Once again Chief-of-Staff, Strother, sauntered his mount unobtrusively down the street.

Soon Strother saw Chief Engineer John R. Meigs, and a fellow soldier, talking at the window with two Southern belles. Strother walked his horse close enough to overhear the conversation, but he didn't become directly involved. The girls "...got the better of the officers in the way of wit. They (the girls) twitted them politely about New Market (the Union defeat)."[11] The girls then attacked Hunter's burning order from a very sound and logical point of view and characterized it as "...uncivilized and unmilitary...."[11] They went on to state that "...attacking of trains and cutting off of escorts were legitimate acts of war,"[11] with the clear inference that reprisals upon civilians for such attacks were not legitimate acts of war.

Without a trigger being pulled or a shot being fired, Hunter suffered a casualty on his staff at Woodstock that day.

Strother could stand the mental assaults no longer. The emotional barrage of Mr. Chipley's calling him a traitor to his birth and heritage and an oppressor of his friends, relatives, and countrymen, coupled with the logical assault of the two nameless belles, was too much for this artist in a military uniform to bear. "...I rode off,"[11] he said.

In his diary, he makes a statement that seems incongruent with the rest of the text. "I also determined to have no more social intercourse with *the* people of *the* country as it interferes with my military duties too much and brought me continually in view of outrage and distresses which awaken my sympathies but which I could not prevent."[11]

In analyzing this statement: Strother could have written *my* country and *my* people. These weren't enemy people he was warring against but his own flesh and blood, neighbors, childhood friends, people who opened their homes and hearts to him, who cared for him. Strother already knew the logical, moral, and emotional issues, but he had suppressed them. Today they were "awakened," and he could hide his "sympathies" from himself no longer. The artist, the seeker of beauty and good, could no longer stand to "view the outrage and distresses" that he himself was helping to cause. The artist, creator, and the warrior, destroyer, were engaged in a battle for possession of this tormented man in blue. To preserve his sanity, this sensitive man carved a middle ground in an attempt to reject both the creator and the destroyer. He told himself that his actions made no difference, "...I could not prevent." He was "determined to have no more social intercourse with the (his) people...."

As Hunter's Chief-of-Staff, Strother should be implementing his bosses' policies with enthusiasm, but now he was only going to do "my military duties." Perhaps neither Hunter nor Strother fully realized the trauma that was occurring in this "Virginia Yankee('s)"[11] soul. From Maj. Gen. David Hunter's point of view, his Chief-of-Staff at his best was a mere observer of the repression policy; at his worst he was an advocate for those whom Hunter wished to punish. David Hunter Strother was a casualty of this house divided against itself. He resented the military institutions that forced him to war against his own.

Strother stopped his search for names of Rebels for reprisal burnings. "More than once Hunter put the torch to houses owned by his Virginia relatives!"[7] Hunter would find his Chief-of-Staff of little assistance in his reprisal campaign; he would perform only his duties.

Before he got back to headquarters, his new neutral ground decision was challenged again. He received a letter delivered by a cavalryman, from the Rev. John Wolff of Newtown. The former schoolmate of Strother, whose home had been burned to the ground, wanted to meet and talk with his old friend. "I did not see him...I could not have helped him...,"[11] wrote Strother.

While Strother had been hunting for Rebels, the infantry had been resting, but a portion of the cavalry had been active. Hunter, who had the name of a bushwhacker, sent Capt. George M. Ellicott to punish him. Other cavalrymen were foraging. Other units were sent out as scouts. Some of these units became turncoats. They shed Union blue and put on Confederate gray. "It was easier for a scout thus to get information...."[9] William Beach said that some of his company of the First New York Cavalry became "experts."[9] Men like Savacoch, Warren, the Goublemans, Forkey, and Valentine "...ran great risk without seeming to mind...dangerous...his life was forfeited if he should be taken."[9] The Southern people distained these Yankees in Rebel clothing and referred to them as "Jessie Scouts."[19] "Jessie"[20] was Mrs. Jessie Fremont, wife of Union General Fremont. She suggested the ideal for the deception. Captured Rebs lost their clothes, papers, passes, and names to a Yankee of the same apparent build. Confederate Captain John N. Opie got to know some of these turncoat Yankees. He found some to be "...bold, dashing, reckless, good fellows."[20] One group of Yankees of the First New York wasn't fast enough, and a group of Confederates charged them and cut Valentine off. To avoid capture, he jumped from his horse and hid in the woods. One gray-coated Yank felt fortunate to walk back to camp.

When Strother returned with no names, Hunter was less than happy. When Captain Ellicott came back and reported my "...heart failed (me),"[11] (he simply couldn't burn the home of a woman and three children) the badnatured "...General reprimanded him."[11] Ellicott retorted that "...the house was such a mean affair...it was not worth burning. The General laughed and excused him...."[11]

While the Yankee cavalrymen were riding through the countryside, the Rebel scouts had gotten word back to Imboden. Imboden informed Lee at Richmond that the army was now headed by Hunter and that Hunter was on the move south from Cedar Creek. Imboden sent word to the towns and farms, ordering his Home Guard to be ready for action.

It had been a rather quiet day at Regimental Headquarters at Meadow Bluff. There was scouting done by both sides, but it was mostly a day to rest and wait for supplies. Some reinforcements were coming in to Crook from the Kanawha Valley near present day Charleston. The Fifth Regiment (W) Virginia Volunteer Infantry arrived. It was well "...supplied with clothing, shoes, etc...."[21] This was a stark contrast to Crook's veterans. The men had not been informed of Hunter's order to march, but the rumor mill was active. "Some said they were going to Staunton; others thought Lynchburg."[21]

As the daylight hours of May 27 were rapidly coming to a close, Strother was approached by the owner of the house where General Hunter's staff was located. Although he had known Strother before the war, he was not overjoyed at this reunion. Strother referred to him as "our host (and) Old Painter."[11] The reluctant host approached Strother with a request. Some Union man had made off with his horse and he wanted it back. He described the horse as being "...over twenty years old, blind, spavined, split-hoofed, and threatened with the bolts and could not possibly be of any use to us and might communicate disease to our stock."[11] (This begs the question that if he was lucky enough to have the horse stolen, why would he want it back?) Strother told him that if he could find the wretched animal, he could order its return in the name of the Chief-of-Staff.

The "host" knew which "damned Yankee" had his horse. Strother spotted "old Painter" leading "...a respectable, sleek, well-made animal...."[11] The reluctant host knew that he had hood-winked Strother. "...He greeted me (Strother) with the first smile I had seen on his face since we arrived...."[11]

Some troops continued coming into camp from Cedar Creek late into the evening hours. The Fifth New York Heavy Artillery had lost its guns in a command reorganization but had retained its name. The heaviest gun it carried was a musket. The men were in the infantry now. When they trudged into camp that night they were hailed by cheers from their "old friends"[18] the Eighteenth Connecticut. The colonels of each outfit shook hands while they were still mounted.

The sun rose on May 28, but the Federal Army did not march. On May 26, Hunter set the army in motion, a move he knew would alert the Rebels, and made a short march. He was a deliberate, calculating man. He had planned and executed orders since he received word that he would be assuming command. Only in the area of slavery did he seem to lose his perspective. Why did the army rest the second day? Again, no military reason not to march was found. Could it be that the army did not march for Hunter's own personal political reasons? If Crook, a diligent officer, had moved his army from Meadow Bluff as he was ordered to do on May 26, he would now be at or approaching Staunton, the most important target in that area. It would be logical to assume that the Confederacy would shift any forces it could to defend that town and thereby relieve any pressure on Hunter's troops. Crook would either defeat the Rebel force or seriously weaken it, thus making it easy for Hunter. (Hunter could still share in any glory; it was his department and his plan).

If, however, Crook was routed and the mission had to be abandoned, who would receive the blame? Would it be Hunter, who could manufacture a reason for not pressing onward to Staunton or Crook, who would have been defeated in battle? Only questions are found: perhaps Hunter kept the answers locked inside his head.

On the morning of May 28, Hunter received word that confirmed that there were no substantial troops for many miles to his front. One of Col. Augustus Moor's cavalrymen had returned from Mt. Jackson approximately fifteen miles ahead. He was probably a Jessie Scout. He personally observed that there were no enemy troops that far, but he had gotten additional information from someone. Did a local citizen, or perhaps a Confederate scout talk with a Yankee dressed in gray? The scout reported that Southern forces had "...fallen back six miles beyond New Market and...(were) pressing transportation and supplies for a move."[11] Hunter believed that Crook was nearing Staunton, and that the "move" would probably be made on Crook.

Hunter consulted with Chief-of-Staff Strother and told him, that Halleck had ordered an attack on Charlottesville before moving on Lynchburg, cutting the railroad. Hunter sent Stahel's Cavalry out to forage with orders stating "...no wanton plundering...."[6] Col. John Meigs was a Chief Engineer who wanted action, not rest. Apparently without Hunter's approval, he went out on a scouting party.

While Hunter's army rested, scouted, and foraged, a sixteen-wagon Union supply train was approaching Newtown en route to the army. Despite its guard of eighty-three cavalrymen of the Fifteenth and Twenty-First New York, it would not make it. Harry Gilmor's men sprang suddenly upon them. In a brief, savage fight, Gilmor drove the escort off, killing, wounding, and capturing Federals in the process. The band of guerrillas loaded all supplies they could carry on their horses, burned the wagons and remaining supplies and vanished through some mountain pass.

Moor's scout was correct. Southern forces were falling back. From his headquarters at Staunton, Imboden was collecting his men and making plans to stop Hunter at the North River. It was the largest natural barrier between Hunter and Staunton. Imboden was not overly concerned with Crook who he had still not moved from Meadow Bluff.

Before the sun set, on May 28, Meigs returned from scouting and reported to Hunter. He had "...burned the house of a man who had assisted in killing and capturing stragglers during Sigel's retreat (from New Market)."[11] The news of the fire must have warmed Black Dave's heart. Meigs also repeated a rumor to Hunter. Apparently even some women had "...armed themselves... (and) assisted in the capture"[11] (of Sigel's fleeing troops). To Hunter, this was only additional justification for his reprisals against this pro-Southern, pro-slaveholding population. One historian says that the march was "...marred by Hunter's savagery toward pro-South civilians...."[7] Hunter could state that his army struggled not only against the Confederate Army but also against every man, woman, and child.

At last, Hunter decided to move the army and issued marching orders for May 29.

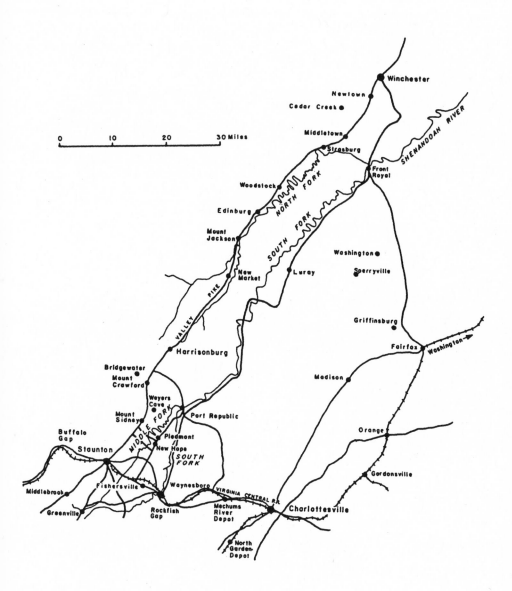

Chapter V

Sunday, May 29 — Saturday, June 4

At Meadow Bluff, (West) Virginia, Crook had received some fresh well-equipped troops and some supplies which were unevenly distributed. Some units received much; some received little. Crook was not satisfied with the supplies he had received, but he decided that he could no longer delay executing General Hunter's order to march. Staff members shuttled between Crook's Infantry headquarters and Averell's Cavalry headquarters. Crook informed Averell that the infantry would start the march toward Staunton the next day. Averell would delay his departure because the cavalry could advance more rapidly and overtake the foot soldiers.

Col. Rutherford B. Hayes, later President of the United States, lamented the inactivity of his command caused "...chiefly by rains and delays in obtaining supplies."[22] On this date he completed his staff which was composed of "...Lieutenant Hastings, Adjutant General, Lieutenant William McKinley (later President), Quartermaster, Lieutenant Delay, Thirty-Sixth, Commisary, and Lieutenant Wool, Thirty-Sixth Aide-all nice gentlemen."[22]

Near Woodstock, the Union Army started coming to life at four o'clock in the morning. The troops had eaten breakfast and were ready to march by dawn. They hoped that "...the plan of an extensive and damaging campaign... might now be successfully carried out."[16]

As the army entered Woodstock (First New York Cavalry in advance), Hunter ordered that the column halt and the jail be searched. He was looking for any Union soldiers or sympathizers that might be held there. Strother observed that Hunter "...was evidently seeking an apology to burn something...."[11] Hunter didn't find any prisoners, but he wasn't satisfied. He proposed burning the Hollingsworth Hotel. Chief-of-Staff Strother's sympathies were not with Hunter's plans of reprisal and punishment. He sprang to the defense of these people with whom he was determined to have no "social intercourse." He said the burning of the hotel would be unjust because Union wounded had recovered there after the defeat at New Market. Strother's lack of support caused Hunter to change his plan; Woodstock would not feel the heat of Hunter's wrath.

One soldier recalled that he saw very few people in Woodstock that early morning. Rumors circulated through the army that "They (the civilian population) still inform us that they hate the Yankees. Hope we will all be captured and be sent to Richmond."[18] It was early morning and already, "Hot, cloudy, muggy weather."[18] It wasn't the condition a foot soldier would prefer.

The army had advanced in good order only a few miles south out of Woodstock when it was halted again. This delay was caused by its own men's action. When the Federals were retreating north after the disaster of New Market on May 15, they burned the bridge over Narrow Passage Creek to prevent the Confederates from overtaking them. Now the Union Army would stop to rebuild a Southern bridge to allow the wagon train to cross. Chief Engineer Meigs put his expertise to work and soon had the bridge rebuilt.

BURNT RAILROAD BRIDGE, NARROW PASSAGE CREEK.

By David Hunter Strother.

The advance continued unopposed. As the troops moved "...through Edinburg we found a great quantity of salt, which we took."[14] Eight thousand blue-clad enemy may intimidate the Confederate Army, may cause her Edinburg neighbors to run or hide inside, but when one of the soldiers stole onions from a woman's garden, they had gone too far: "...a woman came out and drove him out with rocks."[14] The town may be theirs, but the onions were hers. The thieving Yank got rocks but no onions.

The march from Edinburg to Mt. Jackson was almost uneventful until a shutter ran through the entire army. The Rebs were making a stand. "...We can plainly hear the boom of the guns. The advance (cavalry) are having a hot time...,"[18] wrote one soldier. The First New York Cavalry thought that there was a good prospect for a fight. The infantry was quickly placed in line of battle (probably two ranks shoulder to shoulder) to absorb the shock of a Confederate assault. The artillery was rushed forward and dispersed along the line.

The preparations were in vain. The Southern troops on Rubes Hill outside of Mt. Jackson were too weak to attack, and they knew their weakness. They were just attempting to slow the Union advance. They limbered up their cannons and made tracks south toward New Market.

Rubes Hill would not be the scene of battle, but it became accommodations for the night for General Hunter and his staff. He took Mr. Rube's home for his headquarters. The day's march was ended, and the general opened some champagne (no doubt confiscated from some Southerner — perhaps Mr. Rube) which he shared with his Chief-of-Staff. In *The Rockingham Register*, dated May 27, was an article stating that the telegraph between Staunton and Richmond had been out of service for five days. Hunter was gleeful, but he was mistaken. He attributed the disruption in communications to Phil Sheridan's Cavalry from Grant. He believed that Sheridan held part of the Virginia Central Railroad, which would block General Lee from shipping troops from the East. Sheridan was making his way toward Hunter. Crook and Averell must be in or near Staunton, fighting the Rebs, who were in the Valley. Sheridan blocked troops to the east and was heading toward Hunter. Hunter marched about twenty miles that day with almost no resistance. Champagne was just the drink called for at the close of the day.

George E. Pond wrote *The Shenandoah Valley in 1864*. He wasn't as closely associated with General Hunter as was his Chief-of-Staff Strother. He painted a much different picture of Black Dave. At Mr. Rube's house, he said Hunter dressed down General Julius Stahel for "...the numerous and grave complaints against soldiers of his command for unauthorized pillaging...should cease." He pictured the kind General Hunter as saying "Many of the residents... Very kind to our wounded, and it is neither just nor politic to allow wanton outrage and injuries to be inflicted...." All this information came from the general, who that morning wanted to burn the Hollingsworth Hotel, where many Union wounded had been treated and who was now drinking stolen champagne.

At Staunton, General Imboden had spent most of the day calling out and collecting his "reserve", the Home Guard. He recalled that in his entire Valley District "...I had less than one thousand Confederate soldiers...."[23] Although Crook and Averell hadn't moved from Meadow Bluff, Imboden was convinced that they would move and that they would then combine with Hunter. "...I communicated it to General Lee and the Confederate Secretary of War, announcing my utter inability to cope with them...,"[23] wrote Imboden.

The frustrated Gen. John Daniel Imboden was forty-one-years -old. Staunton was not only his headquarters; it was his birthplace and residence. As a young man, Imboden had attended Washington College (now Washington and Lee) in Lexington where he studied law. He practiced in Staunton. When war clouds started gathering, he was elected to the Constitutional Convention and voted for secession. He became a captain with the Staunton Artillery. Imboden was a good lawyer, a whiz at logical thinking and an organizer. Soon he was out recruiting his own outfit, the First Virginia Partisan Rangers. He and the Rangers fought under Gen. Thomas "Stonewall" Jackson for the protection of his beloved Valley. By January, 1863, Imboden was a brigadier general, and the First Virginia Partisans were now the Sixty-Second Virginia Mounted Infantry.

Imboden and the Sixty-Second distinguished themselves on a raid into Northwestern Virginia, "...where he severed the B and O Railroad and captured several thousand cattle and horses."[24] He was also credited in saving General Lee's wagon train after the retreat from Gettysburg.

Imboden understood the need to shift troops from the Valley to General Lee after the Union defeat at New Market. It was difficult to watch his command shrink to fewer than one thousand men, especially when he was convinced that the Federals would be back soon to his vital Valley. When "his baby," the Sixty-Second was given to a Kentucky general, John C. Breckinridge, from the Department of Southwest Virginia and sent to Richmond, it was a personal loss. The Sixty-Second was not only the nucleus on which he could form his reserves; it was Imboden's greatest accomplishment. He resented that it was under the care and command of a stranger.

Imboden was forming his regular troops and his Home Guard even though he believed a contest with the vastly superior enemy was a foregone conclusion. These men weren't the gay boys of 1861, full of excitement and hope; these were survivors of a hundred pitched battles with a full knowledge of relentless war. One soldier wrote in his diary: "I believe it is growing hopeless, for the prospect of peace was still so far off, even though we had lost so much and struggled so hard."[25]

Brig. Gen. John D. Imboden, C.S.A.

On Monday, May 30, General U.S. Grant and his numerically superior army were constantly trying to run around or over General Lee's battle seasoned troops in order to capture Richmond. Lee was not only the commander of the Army of Northern Virginia but also Commander-in-Chief of all armies of the Confederacy. He had to approve troop movements within the department. He realized that even if he stopped Grant and held Richmond, it would be an empty victory if the Federals held the Valley, cutting off the vital supplies of salt, lead, and food to the capital. If he defeated Grant and lost the Valley, he would still lose the capital. He had no troops to spare. He decided that the already undermanned Department of Southwest Virginia would have to be virtually drained of manpower to protect against imminent danger in the Valley.

On this date, Lee informed Imboden that he could spare no soldiers but that he would direct General Jones "...to come...with every available men he could raise; and that I (Imboden) might retard Hunter's advance as much as possible...,"[23] wrote Imboden later.

Lee telegraphed Jones at Glade Spring near Abingdon: *"Get all the available forces you can* and move at once to Imboden's assistance to defend Valley;...call out the reserves to help your lines with what forces you leave behind."[8] The defense of the vital lead, salt, and railroad of Southwest Virginia now rested on old men and young boys of the Home Guard.

William Edmondson Jones was probably at his home near the Glade Spring Railroad Depot. Jones, born nearby on May 9, 1824, had just celebrated his fortieth birthday and the assumed command of the Department of Southwest Virginia. He had attended nearby Emory and Henry College and later graduated from West Point, class of '48. After graduation when he was traveling with his new bride to a post in Texas, she was swept away in a strong current and drowned. Jones was despondent because of this cruel fate life had sent upon him. It left him filled with "...unspeakable sorrow."[26] During this period, he acquired the nickname, which would follow him to the grave: "Grumble" Jones. He left service and became a hermit farmer until the South's need of his talent was greater than his need for withdrawal from activity. During this period he patented an improved military saddle. Although his nickname remained, his men were devoted to him, and he became a brigadier general in September 1863. He "...rendered excellent service,"[24] but had too many clashes with his superior, the man who wore a plume in his hat, J.E.B. Stuart. Jones was transferred to the Department of Southwest Virginia. He was serving there when General Breckinridge was called first to the Valley to fight Sigel and later to Richmond. Jones had appointed himself commander; now he was ordered to follow his predecessor to the Valley. One source said that Jones "...had the look of an old testament prophet...terrifying his enemies in battle...."[7]

Jones's forces were few and scattered. McCausland at far off Union, (West) Virginia, opposing Crook and Averell was technically under Jones's command. Jones had troops at Saltville and sprinkled along the railroad east to Central Depot (Radford). There were some fixed artillery positions. The field artillery

English Patent and Seal for W.E. Jones's "Adjustable" saddle.
Courtesy: Southern Comfort Antiques, Bristol, Va.

Brig. Gen. William E. "Grumble"
Jones, C.S.A.

consisted mostly of Bryan's and Ringgold's Batteries, and the Botetourt Artillery. Bryan's Battery was probably north of New River at Central Depot. Jones decided to leave the Ringgold and Botetourt Artillery there and ordered Bryan's six guns east. Because of the lack of rail transport, the horses were sent via the macadamized road, (Rock Road or Valley Pike, present day Rt. 11). The horses and their teamsters must be pushed to their physical limit to try and arrive at Staunton for the guns.

Jones took his order from Lee seriously. Lee's message was: send "all the available forces you can." On May 30, Jones moved every soldier he could find from each stop along the tracks as he too headed east.

At Meadow Bluff, Crook started part of the infantry in motion toward Staunton. The Reb scouts sent word to McCausland at Union. Some of the Union troops complained that they started the march "...almost as destitute as when we came (from Cloyds Mountain)...."[27]

Hayes with the infantry noted that he spent the day watching the Fifth and Thirteenth W. VA. drill. He heard rumors about the contest between Grant and Lee. "Grant's prospects (of defeating Lee or taking the capital) are fair."[22]

At Mount Jackson, Hunter's army rose early and moved freely toward New Market and the dark memories of two weeks ago. On the march, Hunter received some good news and some bad news. From the railhead and telegraph back at Beverly, (West) Virginia came an intelligence report. It was believed that the Valley was wide open. The South had only two battalions of the Eighteenth Virginia Cavalry, Mosby's guerrillas, the unreliable Home Guard, and four guns to oppose Hunter's departmental strength of over 18,000 men. The bad news came from Newtown. Apparently it was late on May 28 when Harry Gilmor's band ambushed the Union supply train. Due to Confederate guerrilla activity, the message did not reach Hunter until May 30. He was infuriated. The town had only tasted his wrath when he ordered three homes burned; now it would feel his full punishment: the town would be burned to the ground. Hunter sent a courier to the First New York Cavalry, ordering it to return to headquarters.

It was an easy march of just over seven miles from Mt. Jackson to New Market, and there was plenty of daylight left as the troops approached the scene of their earlier defeat.

Strother rode on the battlefield and retraced the positions of the Union troops during the battle. He noted that the dead horses had been skinned for the desperately needed leather, and that the shoes and nails had been removed. The South could not put good shoes on man or beast. It had rained much since the battle. Strother noted: "Our dead soldiers had been hastily buried and parts of their bodies were exposed."[11] About sixty bodies were reburied.

In a church yard, Strother found the fresh graves of forty-one Rebs. Thirty-three had names or unit identifications above them. Eight families would never know what happened to their loved ones missing in action. Among the dead were four from the corps at the Virginia Military Institute.

A scout reported to Strother that the army had been attacked and that the enemy had captured two men. Not long after, however, the two men returned, but they didn't return empty-handed. They had captured their would-be guards. The six prisoners were from the Home Guard — all over age 45 and armed with "old flintlock hunting pieces."[11] One had orders in his pocket from a Confederate officer to capture Union horses. When Hunter heard this order he wanted to "hang him."[11] Once again Hunter found his Chief-of-Staff resisting orders and arguing that the "...poor devils...should be paroled."[11] Hunter relented and when the prisoners took an oath not to bear arms against the Union forces again, they were set free.

It was the responsibility of the cavalry to forage for the infantry. The cavalry got the biggest and the best; the infantry shared what was left. Many young soldiers' appetites were far from satisfied. After the short march, there was still plenty of light. The homes and the fields had food. Lower ranking officers and many enlisted men decided to do some foraging on their own. If it was all right for the cavalry to steal, why not them, too?

When Hunter learned about the wanton pillaging by his infantrymen, he sent the cavalry to round them up, arrest them, and herd them back to headquarters. There he gave them "...severe reprimand...."[18] The non-commissioned officers were reduced in rank, the privates made to walk a beat four hours with "...a heavy fence rail over the shoulder... It did seem very strange to us that we could not forage in the enemy's country...a gloomy time for us."[18] The infantry would not be allowed to forage at will.

It wasn't that General Hunter had a change of his black heart and wanted to show sympathy to the civilian population. A well organized, large army would not allow the small Confederate guerrilla groups much of a target for attacks. Some disorganized bands of scavengers would be easy targets. Even though the possibility of a large-scale attack on his army was remote, Hunter did not want to chance that all his intelligence reports were wrong, thus giving the south a victory.

On Tuesday, May 31, Jones was at Central Depot. He had spent May 30 collecting troops from Bristol, Saltville and Abingdon, and moving them east via the railroad. He called out even the miners from the saltpeter works. Mining of saltpeter is essential to the production of gunpowder. Production would stop because the mines were under the control of the Nitrate Bureau. The 130 miners were called the Nitrate Mining Corps. On the morning of May 31, Jones was south of New River at Central Depot, supervising the transfer of his troops across New River. The Southern forces had burned both the railroad bridge and the Ingles Ferry Bridge as they retreated after losing the battle of Cloyds Mountain on May 9. This, of course, caused a major bottleneck and slowed troop transport to a crawl. Jones telegraphed that he would be in Lynchburg by June 1.

Bryan's Battery, already across the river, was heading toward Lynchburg and Staunton. Jones was bringing the Thirty-Sixth, Forty-Fifth, and Sixtieth Virginia Volunteer Regiments, and Beckley's Forty-Fifth Volunteer Battalion.

Jones left the Ringgold Battery north of New River to protect the bridge even though it was under reconstruction.

The last of Crook's army left Meadow Bluff by May 31. Most of the army moved toward Staunton, but a few troops moved north. For some of the volunteers, their time of enlistment was finished, and as the army moved south, they moved north to the sound of "...slow sad music."[22] Colonel Hayes noted that this was "A bad time to go to the rear,"[22] as it reduced the strength of Crook's army as it invaded. Before the day was over, the rear guard of Crook's army was at Bungers Mill about ten and one half miles from Meadow Bluff and about five miles from Lewisburg.

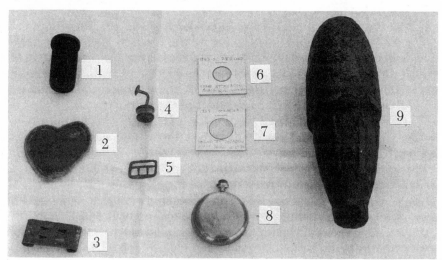

Some things lost by soldiers at Meadow Bluff.

1 - *U.S. Percussion fuse 20-pound Parrott*
2 - *Heart shaped Martingale from cavalry horse harness*
3 - *Belt keeper (rifle)*
4 - *Tompkins (stopper for gun barrel)*
5 - *Suspender (belt) buckle*

6 - *$2.50 gold piece, 1843*
7 - *Seated Liberty 1857 quarter*
8 - *Gold pocket watch*
9 - *12-pound shenkle shell*
Courtesy: Pat Trout collection

Confederate scouts had watched Crook's advance element leave; now these scouts raced to Union, W. Virginia with the news that Crook's entire infantry division had left Meadow Bluff. McCausland knew that he had to leave Union to get in front of Crook, who was heading toward Staunton. By late afternoon, McCausland started his cavalry toward Covington along a road at the base of the mountain.

It was probably late afternoon when the scouts of W.L. "Mudwall" Jackson reported Crook's movement to McCausland. McCausland said he knew that the "...objective point was Lynchburg...."[28] Crook and Sigel had failed to take and hold the railroad in early May, thus cutting off General Lee's supply line and forcing the South to abandon the capital. McCausland was correct: Lynchburg was the railroad hub, which the North could use to strangle Richmond. Mudwall's small brigade was to harass and delay the advance of Crook's army. McCausland knew that his small army of approximately 1,000 cavalry and 300 infantry were no match for Crook's massive infantry, but he would try to delay Crook. McCausland gave orders to his men to get ready to move at once. They must march rapidly from Union via Sweet Springs in order to be in front of Crook at Covington. If Crook reached Covington before they did, there would be no opposition between him and Staunton.

It is unlikely that McCausland knew that Jones was in the process of leaving the Department of Southwest Virginia and heading for the Valley when he sent couriers to both his department and, to Imboden at Staunton. McCausland was alerting them that Crook was on the move toward Staunton and that he would try to delay Crook's forces.

Apparently at New Market Hunter had decided that if his policy of punishment was to be carried out, it was best not to ask his Chief-of-Staff to help. It appears that he did not inform Strother that he was recalling the cavalry to headquarters on May 30. It is unlikely that Strother knew of Hunter's orders to Major Timothy Quinn. Quinn was to select 200 men from the First New York and burn Newtown to the ground, "...sparing only churches, and the dwelling of a Dr. Owens, who had been kind to the (wounded) Federals."[6] Early that morning the 200 men were placed under Maj. Joseph K. Stearns. As the cavalrymen headed north away from the enemy, speculations and rumors flew through the command.

It is not known for certain which day during this time frame that Harry Gilmor made his proclamation. Hunter's order for burning had been repeated to him. Gilmor considered reprisal against civilians as uncivilized warfare: He knew it struck directly at his guerrillas. A guerrilla movement needs the support of the civilian population. Without the safe hiding places, food, and information from the Southern population, his effectiveness would be greatly diminished. If Hunter's order of burning frightened the people to the point that his guerrillas received no aid, it would be a major defeat for him and the South. Therefore, Gilmor decided to raise the ante in this uncivilized warfare. In retaliation for reprisal burnings, Gilmor threatened to execute Union prisoners. There is no proof that either Hunter or the officers of the First New York had knowledge of Gilmor's proclamation when the 200 headed toward Newtown.

The cavalry is the eyes of the army. It protects the front from surprise attacks and sends information to the command officers with the infantry. The cavalry had been recalled; therefore Hunter wouldn't move.

Hunter and all but one of his General Staff were West Point graduates. They knew that time was as much a commodity of war as men, gunpowder, and food. He called another halt to the movement of the army. This was another day lost since he started the invasion. Hunter's own punishment policy became more important to him than the objective of the mission, which was the destruction of Lynchburg. It seemed a reasonable gamble because all the intelligence was good. He believed that Sheridan was destroying the Virginia-Central as he moved to join his main force. Hunter believed that Crook and Averell were now at or near Staunton and that there was only an impotently small band of Rebs between him and Harrisonburg with no major forces beyond that point.

It appears that there was no disclosure at the morning staff conference about the 200 cavalrymen heading north. Hunter stated that the army was waiting for Crook: "We are not to move until we hear from Crook."[11]

Orders were issued for foraging. Apparently Hunter saw his privates walk a beat with a fence rail on their shoulders and he had an idea. Not only would his army punish the pro-Southern population by stealing their vegetables and meat, but now it would interfere with future production. An army of 8,500 men in camp, consumes tremendous amounts of wood. "An order came today...forbidding us to burn anything but rails: strange order,"[14] said one soldier. Col. John Ely was ordered to drill and to inspect several companies of his Eighteenth Connecticut. Before the conference broke-up, Hunter, "...rebuked Provost Marshal Starr for permitting Rebels to come *within* our lines.[11] Starr was miffed that Hunter had singled him out.

After dinner (mid-day) one source recorded "...it was intensely hot and everybody (around headquarters) slept."[11] The foraging was paying off. Captain Kellogg with the One Hundred Twenty-Third Ohio stole a large amount of flour, wheat, and salt, which had been shipped to the country for civilian needs.

Headquarters were still in the Rube house. There was a "mountain bred"[11] woman who had two very married, very pregnant daughters with her. Both daughters delivered on the night of May 30. Quick-witted Strother put the births together with Starr's rebuke for a practical joke.

Strother said "...I approached him (Starr) with an alarmed look. 'Colonel,' I said, 'two Rebel citizens came into camp last night without papers and are now about headquarters kicking up a row.'" Starr knew that he was in deep trouble with his ill-tempered general. He "...called hastily to the guard to arrest them."[11] Then Starr turned to Strother for more information. He wanted to know who had seen them and where these Rebels were. Strother told Starr to see Dr. R.S. Hayes; then Starr realized that a practical joke had been played on him.

It was not a totally uneventful ride for the regiment of 200 under Major Stearns. At a rest stop, probably near Strasburg, a shot rang out, and a man from Company L was wounded. The troops grabbed a Reb nearby and "...it almost came to the point of hanging him...the arrested man protested his innocence, but faced his threatened fate bravely...."[9] When it was discovered that the troop was probably shot accidentally by a fellow Yank, the Rebel citizen was released.

After Colonel Ely had completed drilling his men at New Market, he secretly disobeyed his general as "...on the quiet (he), restored to their former rank the non-commissioned officers reduced by General Hunter for foraging."[18]

It was near nightfall when Stearns's regiment established camp on the Stickel farm not far from Newtown. The men knew something of Gilmor's attack on the wagon train for the camp was rife with rumor. One source says, "It began to be suspected that the purpose of this expedition was to burn the town...murmuring of disapproval. Burning houses of citizens was not the business of soldiers."[9]

It appears that Imboden turned over command of Staunton to Maj. Beverly Randolph with orders to recruit every man he could find and send him forward to Mt. Crawford on the North River. Imboden moved toward Harrisonburg.

At Staunton, Randolph issued an order to the citizenry "...every man who can fire a gun...required at Mt. Crawford...Fight for their homes...If it becomes necessary to make them fight, I will declare martial law...every man shoulder his musket...forced into ranks. If (a draftee is) killed, the loss is trifling."[6] Randolph personally searched for any able-bodied citizens; postal workers, tax collectors, clerks, telegraphers, anybody.

From Harrisonburg, Imboden sent out scouts to get and give information. One scout observed "What deserts these spaces between the lines of armies are...not a human being anywhere visible. The inhabitants do not show themselves...awful silence."[29]

Imboden not only wanted the scouts to provide him with information; he also wanted them to send information to Hunter "...to inform the people that we were...in expectation of large reinforcements then on their way to my support. I knew that any such statement would be repeated to the enemy, and cause him to advance with great caution."[23]

This Valley was Imboden's. He was born in the Valley and grew up here. He knew every road, mountain, hill, valley, and stream. A lawyer by training, he knew that his small force would stand no chance in an open field fight with Hunter's hordes. He had decided to make a stand on the south side of North River at Mt. Crawford. There was only one bridge to defend, and the natural barrier of the river would help make up for his lack of troops. He went to Harrisonburg to slow Hunter. He would fall back and join his reserves at Mt. Crawford and try to stop Hunter. Imboden informed high command that a "trust worthy scout" had reported that Hunter had "nine thousand infantry, two thousand-five hundred cavalry, and thirty-one guns."[30]

Imboden's Home Guard moved forward. Imboden had recruited many of the men personally. He was an excellent organizer and recruiter. In a seven-day period in April 1864, he recruited four companies of between forty-five and fifty men each and an artillery battery. He could report to Lee that he had between 1,200 and 1,500 Home Guard troops in Augusta, Rockingham, Page, and Rockbridge Counties.

On Tuesday afternoon, May 31, McCausland's men had left Union, (West) Virginia. They forced marched until 2:00 a.m. and went into camp approximately three miles from Sweet Springs. Tired men and horses would rest until dawn before moving eastwardly toward Callaghans, a few miles northwest of Covington.

Averell was still encamped at Bungers Mill, waiting for "...horses, shoes, clothing, etc."[8] from Charleston.

Crook's column snaked from Meadow Bluff through Lewisburg and White Sulphur Springs, over the Greenbrier River and headed toward Covington. Those troops in the rear characterized the move as an "...easy march"[22] with much foraging. The troops in front had a different view as each curve or stream could provide another Rebel ambush. Southern forces were much too weak to stop Crook; but they were determined to slow him. One forward soldier said that there was "Considerable skirmishing...along the entire route; the Rebel cavalry probing quite annoying, but in many instances suffering for their temerity by deaths and captures."[31] No mention was made of Northern casualties. It is assumed that they were very light but greater than Confederate losses.

When the Union soldiers entered Lewisburg, they were hailed by Erasmus. Erasmus was a slave and houseboy to a family in town; he wanted freedom. "Wishing to curry favor with the Federal officers to prevent being returned to his master...,"[32] he told them a story about David Creigh and the body of a Yankee buried on the Creigh property. The story had been repeated to him from a hired laborer for the Creighs. The Federals sent men to investigate. The men discovered the remains of a soldier killed in November '63. Confronted with the evidence, Mr. Creigh did not deny killing the Yank, but he told the officers that he had good reason. They may not have believed him, but they had no authority to act on their own. Either way David Creigh was wasting his breath. They arrested him, his wife, and daughters and forced them to return to headquarters at Bungers Mill. It was after ten o'clock that night that the group left Lewisburg. They even "compelled"[32] Mrs. Creigh and her daughters to ride horseback, not in a carriage (certainly not the custom of refined ladies).

At the Confederate Military Department of Southwest Virginia, General Jones spent the entire day moving as many of his soldiers forward to Staunton as possible. Some moved over the macadamized road on foot or on horse. Jones was on the train which had to go to Lynchburg via the Virginia-Tennessee line and then to Staunton via the Virginia-Central.

At New Market, it was a hot, lazy day for Hunter's army. Even the common soldier was getting bored "...waiting for orders to advance."[18] The foraging was good, and the army ate the fat of the land. Soldiers washed themselves and their clothes in the beautiful Shenandoah River. This wasn't war; it was a social event. Hunter, a West Pointer, the man who would make his command "fly", sat idle. He was giving the Confederacy the best gift he could: time.

Hunter believed that his column of cavalry should be nearing Newtown. He was correct. Early that morning Major Stearns confirmed the rumor that had been circulating in his command: Newtown would be burned! When they heard the order the men were silent, and some left camp observing that it was "...more like a funeral procession than a marching army."[9] It was only a short ride to the center of town, where the column halted. "The old people and children were standing in the doorways with an expression of mute helplessness on their faces,"[9] noted one soldier. These veterans, who had faced death unflinchingly as they charged Confederate positions, had no stomach for their task. As the column halted, there came low and anguished murmurings in the ranks "...to obey no orders to burn."[9]

The officers, too, struggled with their conscience. They vacillated about carrying out the orders. Horseback conferences among the officers were carried out in the main street of Newtown. The officers spoke with some of the citizens. The people claimed that they had nothing to do with Gilmor's raid; in fact, "...Union wounded in the attack...had been carefully nursed in (their) homes."[9] Stearns concluded the people "...were in no wise guilty."[11] "...The officers...consulted...and decided to disobey the order of General Hunter...the officers agreed to stand by Major Stearns if he should incur the wrath of General Hunter...It seemed best to have the people take the oath of allegiance to the Union and spare the town."[9] Apparently the men never dismounted, and the column returned south, stopping at Bushong's near Woodstock for the night. Because of the fear that Gilmor's men might spring suddenly upon them in the dark, many men slept with their guns.

As the sun descended at New Market, Hunter, who said that they would not move until they heard from Crook, issued marching orders for the next day.

By sundown, Imboden with his cavalry had established his headquarters in Harrisonburg. One citizen recorded in his diary that they were "...still looking for the Yankees" (to come).[33] Imboden put an advance picket post at Lacy Springs near Midway between New Market and Harrisonburg.

By late afternoon, the head of Crook's column was approaching Callaghans, a few miles from Covington. McCausland pushing his troops eastwardly had reached the main road. Crook was advancing toward Covington. The small force of "Mudwall" Jackson that Crook had been pressing all day, linked with McCausland at Callaghans. There was a brief skirmish at that time with no casualties recorded. The combined forces of McCausland and Jackson fell back on Covington. Crook apparently camped at or near Callaghans for the night.

Thursday, June 2:

On Thursday, June 2, Averell spent the day at Bungers Mill near Meadow Bluff, waiting for supplies. He knew that Crook's Infantry was moving deeper into enemy territory and that the "eyes" of the cavalry would soon be needed.

The decision was made to march on June 3, even if no supplies were received by that time.

The head of Crook's army was at Callaghans near Covington and its tail was not through White Sulphur Springs. As the head of the army moved out, it prepared for another day of brisk skirmishing with McCausland and Jackson. Troops back from the head of the column and danger were on a very destructive picnic. One Union soldier wrote: "The scarcity of rations was made an excuse for the most outrageous acts of robbery and plundering. Men would shamelessly enter a house and rob a poor woman of her last pound of flour and corn meal, while she was all the time begging them to leave enough to save the lives of her already half-starved children. The men would not hear a word...And if a house was foolishly forsaken, it would be ransacked from top to bottom; and sometimes when nothing had been found, the men in blue would destroy furniture...."[21] The Yanks called it foraging, the South called it stealing. Yankees took food stuff, clothing, and livestock at will from Southern farms to the main Union Army. "Every morning...thousands of pounds of beef could be seen left on the grounds, because the men had no time to cook it and no salt (to preserve it) if they had had the time."[21] The lack of cooking utensils forced many to eat under-cooked or raw vegetables and meat. This improperly cooked food made "many...too ill to march...."[21] Because the army was deep in enemy territory, these men couldn't be sent back to Meadow Bluff or left. They crowded the wagon train and slowed the march.

LIVING ON THE COUNTRY.

By David Hunter Strother.

The head of the army pushed the annoying Southern cavalry back on Covington. Grading for the tracks of the Virginia-Central had been made to Covington but no track had been layed. The war had stopped the construction. There was a skirmish at Covington, but Crook's overwhelming numbers forced the Confederates to fall back. Crook's men destroyed track and bridges.

While Crook was marching and fighting, Averell at Bungers Mill convened a formal courtmartial. The verdict was known before the proceedings began. Today there would be legal questions as to whether a military court could try a civilian, but David Creigh had no right of appeal. "...Mr. Creigh, a *Citizen* of Lewisburg, was tried by a *military commission* and found guilty of murdering a Union soldier in November."[34]

The soldiers did not listen to the poor mother who begged them not to steal the last bite of food from her starving children. Apparently the Courtmartial Board paid David Creigh's story little attention. He told the board members that on November 6, '63, the Confederates were defeated at Droop Mountain. On November 7, Southern soldiers retreated through Lewisburg, pursued by troops under Averell. When Creigh started to enter his home someone informed him that a Yankee was in his house "ransacking."[32] The Federal had gone upstairs and entered the bedroom of one of the daughters. Apparently the daughter was in bed "ill with fever"[32] and her mother was in attendance. The Yank broke into the room and was going through the trunks, looking for something worth stealing, while abusing Mrs. Creigh and her daughter with "...insulting language."[32]

David drew his pistol, ran upstairs and ordered the foul-mouthed, thieving Yankee to stop. The soldier did not listen to David and attempted to break into Miss Lewis's trunk. Miss Lewis was "...a young lady employed as governess...."[32] Unable to open the trunk, the Yankee demanded that David give him the keys. David refused the demand and again ordered the Yank out of his home. The Yank made no effort to leave, and David attempted to inforce his demand but instead of "bang" his gun just "snapped." The percussion cap detonated, but the charge and bullet were still in the gun. The Yank fired his weapon toward David, but the bullet hit the wall. David went after the Federal's gun. The two fought down the stairs to the front hall where the Yank's pistol discharged again. This time the bullet struck and severely wounded the Yank. Although the Yank was wounded he retained the weapon which "...he fired at Mr. Creigh (while) staggering on the porch."[32] The bullet missed David and went into the upper part of the door. The Yank fell on the porch; it is not known if he had lost consciousness. The family slave "Aunt Sallie" now appeared with an axe in her hand. She gave it to David. "Aunt Sallie" feared that the Yank might get up and renew the fight with David. She began "...begging that Mr. Creigh strike him with the axe."[32] David "...forthwith dispatched"[32] the Yankee. David Creigh concluded his testimony by "...declaring that he considered himself justified in what he had done and that he would do the same to any looter, whether Federal or Confederate...."[32]

In November '63 the Union controlled the town. It was not a good time to report the death of their own regardless of circumstances. With secrecy and without a preacher, the Union intruder was laid to rest on the Creigh's property. The Creighs wished that the story would end there, but a hired laborer of the Creighs, who probably helped bury the body, repeated the story to Erasmus, the slave houseboy of a neighbor.

The words of Creigh had no effect on the Union court. There was a body of a Yankee, and Creigh would pay with his own life. His wife and daughters were released. Hugs and kisses interspersed with love and goodbys exchanged. David Creigh beheld his family one last time through tear-blurred eyes.

It is not known if any legal questions bothered Averell or if he wanted the Department Commander, Hunter, to approve the verdict, for whatever reason Averell delayed in carrying out the death sentence on Creigh. David would be held prisoner until Hunter had time to review the matter and pass judgement.

Most of June 2, General W.E. Jones spent aboard a train heading for Lynchburg. Part of his forces with the Department of Southwest Virginia still had not started toward Lynchburg via the railroad or directly toward Staunton via the Rock Road. John Milton Hoge, with Co. F, Eighth Virginia Cavalry camped near Newbern, recalled "...we were awakened by the shrill notes of the bugle;"[35] at 3:00 a.m. and started riding toward Christiansburg en route to Staunton.

By nightfall Jones had arrived in Lynchburg with Bryan's Battery and approximately 3,000 men. He sent a message to Imboden that he would be in Staunton within twenty-four hours.

It was the early morning of June 2 when Stearns's First New York Cavalry started out from near Woodstock for what was expected to be a less than cordial reception from its commanding general. Hunter had reduced many officers in rank and had made privates walk a beat with heavy fence rails on their shoulders for stealing a little food. What would he do for the cavalry willfully disobeying an order to burn an entire town?

It was known that "McNeill (John) with a hundred men had been hanging on around the rear of Hunter. It would be a fine thing if this detachment could capture some of these fellows. Hunter might accept them as an atonement for not burning Newtown."[9] With much hope, probably the best company of troopers was sent forward after the elusive Confederate guerrillas. "But the captain was lacking in the skill and sharpness necessary to catch those lively Rebels...None of McNeill's men were caught that day."[9] The tired Yanks went into camp approximately six miles north of New Market. They dreaded the next day when they would rejoin the main army and face the wrath of Hunter.

Stearns believed that Hunter and the army were at New Market, but Hunter had started the army forward toward Harrisonburg early. The army took the main road, the Valley Pike, and two secondary roads out of New Market. All three roads then converged at Harrisonburg. By using the three roads, Hunter could advance his army much more rapidly, and the Signal Corps could keep the three wings in contact with one another as well as back to the rear at Cedar Creek.

Chief-of-Staff Strother was delayed from starting the march. Apparently the Union's foraging efforts were taking place both outside and within the Union camp. A Yankee thief with lots of brass made off with Strother's transportation: "My fine bay horse disappeared..."[11] mourned Strother.

Although he didn't have the strength to stop Hunter, Imboden contested every foot of ground as his men fell back. One Federal wrote: "Our advance are again having a hot time, judging by the booming of the guns."[18] Imboden said that the first real skirmish occurred at Lacy Springs. Strother records that the army was "stopped (at) Big Springs by a Rebel picket."[11] While the Union reconnoitered the Rebel position and brought more troops forward, the Signal Corps brought news of an attack on the rear of the army. "This produced some excitement and tremor...."[11] The attack was only a raid by Confederate guerrillas who were out foraging, but it showed the nervousness of high command and their lack of faith in their army. Maybe the misinformation Imboden had planted was bearing fruit. Rumor had it that Imboden had 3,000 men with him and that Colonel Bradley Johnson's Maryland men were on the way to join him.

The Rebs were pushed from the road, and the command continued its march to Harrisonburg where "...the air was full of flying reports."[36] Rumors flew, but no concrete news was received until a cavalryman came in the afternoon to report Hunter at Lacy Springs. With this news, a small group of Rebs rode approximately one half mile out of town toward the Yanks and stopped at a Mr. Liggett's place. Soon the head of the Union column was sighted "...Pour(ing) over the (Gambill's) hill in solid columns."[36] The group returned to town where it intended to stay until the Yanks were close at hand. Because the Federal column was still a little distance out of town, one member of the Confederate party dismounted to adjust the girthing strap on his saddle. At this moment, the idle group of Rebs saw another group of Southerners ride at a fast clip toward them. It was assumed that these Rebs were coming into town on a different road, "...when we observed them elevate their pistols and fire,"[36] (they were Jessie Scouts). The Yanks in Confederate gray, passed the group "...firing wildly and shouting...."[36] The Rebs fired back "...as all went down the street like a roaring tide...."[36] A cannon ball struck the Masonic Building as the group exited town with Rebs in the front and Yanks in the rear. The pursuit abruptly ended when both sides saw a skirmish line Imboden had established south of the town. The Yanks turned tail back to town; the Rebs rode forward to safety.

A resident observed that it was about 2:00 p.m. when the Union cavalry entered the town "...on a charge of great excitement."[33] The town was secured quickly, and some of the citizens came out and greeted the blue-clad cavalrymen.

The Rebs maintained their thin skirmish line outside town. It was manned by some Rockingham Reserves — Home Guards, a small group of cavalrymen, and the few Rebs that had just fled town "...barely more than a battalion" (approximately 150 men).[36] Soon Union cavalry challenged the far right of the line. "...Our cavalry became hotly engaged with theirs."[26] In the brief encounter, Union forces pushed the Rebs back, and the Rebs counter attacked, forcing the Union line back. The South fired a cannon toward the Union line from a position approximately one mile farther south. "A staff of officers (CSA) with glasses is seen observing from the old Methodist Church hill...,"[36] reported one soldier. The line cannot be held. "Our men retired sullenly toward Mount Crawford...."[36] Harrisonburg now belonged to Hunter's army.

Rebel scouts raced back toward Mount Crawford with the news. Other couriers were sent to Staunton. From Mount Crawford Imboden sent General Lee another dispatch, "...that with his (Imboden's) 3,000 men and ten guns he would fight to the last at North River...."[6] Imboden again appealed to Lee for aid.

Hunter's Cavalry had ridden and fought, while the infantry marched and marched. One infantryman complained that it was "hard marching over these rough, stony roads. Very tired tonight."[18] Apparently the cavalry camped in Harrisonburg that night where it destroyed *The Rockingham Register*. The advance of the infantry only made it to the hills overlooking the town. Hunter headquartered outside town in "...a fine brick house..."[11] belonging to Mr. Grey. That night Hunter heard the booming of distant guns and believed Crook must be close at hand. Citizens informed him that the reports he heard came from gun boats on the James River near Richmond. The guns ("one to two hundred pounders")[11] noise could be heard almost 100 miles away. The artist, David Hunter Strother, sought refuge from the military in the library of Mr. Grey. Here he found *Swallow Barn* by John P. Kennedy, and "Harper's Magazine" with the "Porte Crayon" series. Both contained Strother's illustrations. It was obvious to Strother that this Grey family had "taste."[11] The rain fell as the pickets observed and the command slept.

Friday, June 3

By June 3, Crook changed the direction of his army. He had moved southeast through Lewisburg to White Sulphur Springs to Covington. Now he turned northeast following the Virginia-Central Railroad toward Panther Gap and Buffalo Gap, heading toward Staunton.

McCausland was there, too, at Crook's front "...never losing an opportunity to harass and annoy him (Crook)."[29] The advance of Crook's army skirmished with McCausland and pushed on toward Staunton, destroying the railroad as it went. The troops at the front were in combat, but those to the rear considered the 3rd "a good day's march...."[22]

Early in the morning and still without supplies, General Averell advanced the cavalry section of Crook's command from Bungers Mill. He had approximately 2,000 troopers; 1,200 of which were dismissed (many of these had no shoes).[37] He had the condemned prisoner, David Creigh with him.

As Crook's Cavalry was riding to join him, Hunter's two hundred men of the First New York under Major Stearns were riding to rejoin him. When they left with orders to burn Newtown, the army was at New Market. They arose early, and started the six-mile ride to New Market and the confrontation with their ill-tempered general. They would rejoin the army without burning a single house in Newtown. When the troopers arrived in New Market, they learned the army had moved toward Harrisonburg. After a rest, they continued toward Harrisonburg.

At Harrisonburg, the Signal Corps had established another station on a hill out of town. As sunshine chased the darkness away, communications could be sent and received all the way back to Beverly, (W) Virginia. Men with flags and

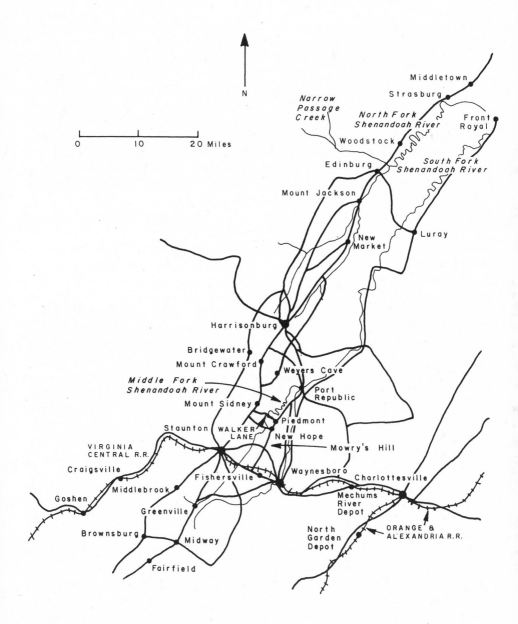

N

0   10   20 Miles

Middletown
Strasburg
Narrow Passage Creek
North Fork Shenandoah River
Front Royal
Woodstock
Edinburg
South Fork Shenandoah River
Mount Jackson
New Market
Luray
Harrisonburg
Bridgewater
Mount Crawford
Weyers Cave
Middle Fork Shenandoah River
Port Republic
Mount Sidney
Staunton
Piedmont
WALKER LANE
New Hope
Mowry's Hill
VIRGINIA CENTRAL R.R.
Craigsville
Fishersville
Waynesboro
Charlottesville
Goshen
Middlebrook
Mechums River Depot
Greenville
ORANGE & ALEXANDRIA R.R.
Brownsburg
Midway
North Garden Depot
Fairfield

field glasses "spoke" over many miles.

It was still early morning when the infantry moved from the hills into the town of Harrisonburg. The Yankee invaders were impressed with the town. One stated: "...(Harrisonburg) is the county seat of Rockingham County, and is a very pretty place. The Courthouse is a very pretty (rather old) brick building, situated about the center of the town, with a fine yard around it. Just outside the yard is a large spring about twelve feet in diameter, round and walled up several feet, with marble steps going down to the water. The whole is covered with a circular roof supported on pillars, which makes it look very nice. The streets immediately around the Courthouse are of respectable width...There are a great many fine residences in and near town."[14] Some of these "fine residences" had opened their doors to wounded Yankees after New Market, an act of Christian decency.

The charity and the beauty of the town were no protection against the ravenous hordes descending on it. "...It seems hard but it is necessary as the army must feed,"[11] commented one soldier. It was "hard" for the citizens also. The "fine residences" were searched for food "...flour, meat, etc., taking *all* they found."[14] The lawless soldiers stole not only food for their stomachs but continued their plundering. "...The men were busy as ants, bringing sacks full of shelled corn...The horses...were not unaware of what was going on. They (the horses were) watchful and appreciative."[9] After the men stuffed their stomachs with food, they stuffed their haversacks with stolen loot. One group of Yanks got muslin valued at $245.[14] Another group of blue-bellies stole twenty-five horses from the farmers of the area. They justified their theft by stating that it was "better" that the horses "...help us than help the enemy."[9] The Federals also destroyed three printing offices, including the office of the "Rockingham Register." It is little wonder that the citizens greeted the invading, destructive army with "...great consternation and disgust."[11]

Chief-of-Staff Strother observed the pillaging and recorded: "This is not necessary and should not be permitted...."[11] If the Chief-of-Staff had no power to control the men, who did?

The Eighteenth Connecticut Regiment was thrilled that Charlie Avery was alive. He was wounded at the Battle of New Market, and his fate was not known until he returned to camp. The unit said they had "re-captured"[18] him from the hospital where Union soldiers have been well-treated. Avery, still suffering from his chest wound, was returned to the hospital.

During the day, information came into the camp from Jessie Scouts and regular cavalry units. It appeared that Imboden was preparing to make a stand at Mount Crawford on North River (renamed after the war Murray River). The main road from Harrisonburg to Staunton had to pass over the North River at Mount Crawford approximately seven miles ahead. All reports indicated that the South was moving artillery forward and entrenching its infantry overlooking the river the Union must pass over. Although Imboden's force reported to be 2,500 was no match in manpower or equipment for Hunter, the river may prove too costly to cross.

Strother, the only non-West Pointer on staff, devised the next military move. He proposed to Hunter that the army be divided. Part of the cavalry would be sent forward to demonstrate against Imboden's defenses at Mount Crawford as if waiting for the infantry to launch a full-scale attack. This attack would hold Imboden in place. Part of the cavalry would be sent through Port Republic and then to Waynesboro to sever the Virginia-Central Railroad. This would prevent the Confederacy from moving rolling stock out of Staunton or troops in. The infantry would then proceed to Port Republic and cross the river. Once over, there would be no major river between the army and Staunton where Imboden could stand. Hunter approved the plan, which was to be executed in the morning.

It was probably after mid-day when Major Stearns and his group of two hundred approached the army. Because Stearns didn't burn Newtown, he was worried that "possibly he and all his officers would be dismissed from service."[9] He decided to approach his harsh general in a harsh way. He "...saluted and reported, 'General Hunter, I am the officer that was ordered to burn Newtown and didn't do it!'"[9] Hunter may have been caught off balance by Stearns's insubordination and belligerent manner and didn't have Stearns imprisoned, but Hunter did become "...angry and ordered him to make a written report."[11] Hunter may have been "...somewhat pleased to find one who could be almost as gruff as himself...."[9]

As Stearns left Hunter; Strother commended him for not burning the town. Then Strother took up Stearns's cause and the cause of the Southern population of Newtown, as he tried to convince Hunter that Stearns was right in his willful disobedience of a direct order. Hunter might have been wondering on which side the sympathies of his Chief-of-Staff lay. Hunter allowed the matter to drop.

While the Federals spent the day sacking Harrisonburg, the Confederates spent the day preparing for battle. Imboden's Cavalry, McNeill's Rangers, and citizens fleeing south kept Imboden informed on the lack of movement and wanton destruction of the enemy.

Mount Crawford offered the best defensive position between Harrisonburg and Staunton, and Imboden was determined to use it and his small forces the best he could. There was skirmishing near Harrisonburg with Hunter's Cavalry. Imboden admitted that he had "...a few men killed and wounded."[23] Imboden left one unit north of the North River as an observer unit and pulled the rest of his men south of the river.

The reserve (Home Guard) units sent from Staunton were there at Mount Crawford. Imboden augmented his manpower with slave labor and started preparing defensive works along the river "...by throwing up some works on the hill tops overlooking the bridge and felling trees in the fords for several miles above and below (Mount Crawford)."[23] Imboden anchored his line on the right at Rockland Mills and the left at Bridgewater.

Imboden began placing his troops in positions to take maximum advantage of the terrain and of their firepower. He had approximately 1,200 cavalrymen (part Home Guard) that he brought south with him from Harrisonburg. At Mount Crawford, he joined with an unknown number of Home Guard units sent from Staunton. There was a total of 1,000 to 1,500 men in Home Guard units in four counties. Not all the units were there, and not every man was with his unit. Marquis' Boys' Battery was there. Imboden used it as his centerpiece to guard the bridge, which with the main road going over it, was expected to receive the main thrust of the Union attack. Most field artillery batteries consisted of six-to-nine-pound cannons. This was a Home Guard unit supplied with equipment that other regular army units did not want. These young boys, sixteen to eighteen years old, were equipped with enormous field guns. They had a twenty-four-pound Howitzer and a twenty-pound Parrott rifle.

It was late afternoon when the first of General Jones's men from Southwest Virginia began to arrive in Staunton. They disembarked rapidly and began to make their way toward Mount Crawford seventeen miles away. They knew that the emergency was upon them and that time was accentual. Jones's men were not organized above the company level. Each company rushed toward Imboden with its men.

One of the first groups to debark from the train was commanded by Colonel Beuhring H. Jones. It was the Niter and Miner Corps from the saltpeter works in Southwest Virginia. One company was under Capt. Will Clark and one was under Capt. F.P. Clark. They were equipped with old "smoothbore rifles"[6] and had no bayonet or cartridge belt. The quartermaster at Staunton helped equip them and sent them forward to Imboden. Imboden was happy to receive the new manpower and the news they bore. Bryan's Battery was at Staunton, but it would be delayed because of the lack of horses and harnesses. The horses with their harnesses on were being driven over the mcadamized road from Southwest Virginia and had not arrived yet. The quartermaster was helping provide the battery with horses, and improvising harnesses. He had "...singletrees attached to the splinter bars of the guns and caissons."[30] Singletrees were used to attach horses and harnesses to wagons, guns, or caissons. Small logs were used. Because of the lack of tools and time, it is likely that rods of iron were heated red hot in a fire and used to burn a hole through the center of one of the logs. Once the hole was large enough to permit the second log to pass through, a lynch pin or bolt was inserted in a hole which was burned also at the end of the first log, thus holding the two together. The two logs now formed a "T" and harness and reins were mounted to the "T" and then to the horses.

It can be assumed that the supply depot at Staunton was well stocked and well run because of its effectiveness in equipping soldiers on their way to the front and in improvising ways to transport guns.

There was much confusion in Staunton. There were soldiers milling about asking for information, food, and supplies. Some of those soldiers wearing gray were "blue-bellies" (Jessie Scouts). They didn't stand out in anyway, and no one realized that they were collecting valuable information for the enemy, General Hunter.

Not only did Imboden receive word about Bryan's Battery, but also about General Jones's expected arrival that night in Staunton. Imboden also learned that Gen. John Crawford Vaughn's Brigade of Tennesseans was on its way.

After sunset, both sides were treated to a show. Hunter was sure that the faithful Crook must be close at hand by this time. He ordered the Signal Corps to try to contact Crook. A soldier wrote; "Sat up very late last night watching the Signal Corps using rockets and roman candles. A wonderful sight."[18] The rockets were launched from the top of a house in Harrisonburg. The soldiers on both sides enjoyed the fireworks. Crook the man for whom the display was made did not see it.

As the Yanks prepared for sleep, there were "heavy rain storms...(and) our shelter tents are poor protection...,"[18] one soldier reported. Southern soldiers at and across North River had little or no protection from the rain. Some of the top commanders did not even think of sleeping this night. Capt. Frank B. Berkeley was a constant aid to Imboden thoughout the night. Imboden recorded that he received about 2,000 men sent by General Jones from Staunton during the night. "To my dismay, I found they were not generally organized in bodies larger than battalions, and in companies and fragments of companies hastily collected from Southwest Virginia, between Lynchburg and Tennessee, and in large part indifferently armed. Indeed, many of the men were convalescents taken from the hospitals, and furloughed dismounted cavalrymen who had gone home for a remount, and were taken possession of by General Jones wherever he could find them...."[23] General Imboden, the great organizer, used his aides to make a list of each unit or individual that came up the main road from Staunton. The unit was bedded down as comfortably and quickly as possible on the rain-soaked ground in the dark of night. The list was then rushed to Imboden. (The list included not only the names and the number of soldiers, but also a description of arms and equipment). Harry Gilmor came from Staunton with about fifty men. There were thirty Marylanders, who had just come from service with the heavy coastal artillery at Charleston, South Carolina. They were sent to McClanahans's Battery. Imboden records, "I spent the entire night of the 3rd in obtaining a list of all these small bodies of men, (plus the troops he knew to be underway to Mount Crawford) out of which by daybreak on the fourth I had composed, on paper, two brigades and assigned officers to their command."[23]

Saturday, June 4

It was near dawn, Saturday June 4, when the two tired, blurry-eyed Southern generals met at Mount Crawford. Imboden and his aides had been up the entire night collecting information and trying to bring this hodge-podge of soldiers into some sort of organized fighting unit at least on paper. Jones had been in constant motion with little sleep since he received orders to leave Southwest Virginia on May 31. The night of June 3 he spent sending his troops from Staunton toward Mount Crawford, where he joined them near dawn.

There was no time to rest on this morning and no time to reminisce about the other time they met for battle. Imboden briefed Jones on the situations. Since Hunter was in Harrisonburg, Staunton was the logical target. The main road from Harrisonburg to Staunton crossed the bridge at Mount Crawford. This was the last river barrier between Hunter and Staunton, and it was here that Imboden had chosen to make a stand. Because of time and Imboden's knowledge of the terrain, Jones accepted Imboden's decision to fight here at the river.

Imboden then presented Jones with his suggested organization of the present army at Mount Crawford. According to the plan, Jones's forces were to form the nucleus, and Imboden's men were to form around them.

The generals reviewed Imboden's organization chart. The First Brigade was under Col. Beuhring H. Jones, Commander of the Sixtieth Virginia Regiment. Colonel Jones would command the Sixtieth and the Thirty-Sixth Virginia Regiments of the infantry plus one regiment of Home Guards mostly convalescents from the hospital at Lynchburg. The Second Brigade was placed under Col. W.H. Browne of the Forty-Fifth Virginia Infantry. He was to command the Forty-Fifth Regiment, the Forty-Fifth Battalion Beckley's Battalion, and two regiments of approximately 700 men under Lt. Col. Robertson of Imboden's Home Guards (reserve). There were three batteries of artillery: McClanahan, Marquis' Boys', and Bryan's Battery from Southwest Virginia. The thirty Marylanders from the fortifications at Charleston, South Carolina were assigned as teamsters to Bryan's Battery.[38] General Jones accepted Imboden's organizational plan.

Imboden then informed Jones that Hunter had "...eleven thousand superbly appointed troops of all arms... (and thirty-one guns)."[23] Imboden's plans of battle, organization, and report were accepted and commands of all troops in the Valley District were transferred from Imboden to Jones.

Imboden's headquarters, Mrs. Robert Gattan's house, were now Jones's headquarters, but neither man remained long. The army and the battle would be at North River.

According to one source, Jones "...refused to wear insignia or other trappings of office...(but his men knew him and) were fiercely loyal to him."[23] Jones was "...a fighter.."[23] who hated parades and ceremonies. For a commanding general, he had a squeaking voice.

Troops were still struggling in from Staunton during the morning. Captain Jones's company of Niter Miners (130 men) came in about ten o'clock. The men were placed under the command of Maj. Richard Brewer.

Before noon, General Jones was happy to receive word that Vaughn's Tennessee Brigade of mixed cavalry and mounted infantry (500-800 men)[39] had arrived. General Vaughn received his commission somewhat sooner than Imboden; therefore, Imboden, who was number one, was now third in command. The Tennesseans, too, were placed on the hills above North River. Jones had approximately 4,500 men and three artillery batteries south of North River. Imboden had placed Peck's and Opie's Home Guard companies north of the river. They were there as an early warning that Hunter was approaching.

Imboden records that "...a spirit of defiant optimism gripped the little army"[6] as it awaited battle.

It was approximately 10:00 a.m. when the first contact was made. According to Strother's plan, the cavalry unit was to demonstrate against the

Southern lines as if waiting for the infantry to move forward and launch a full-scale attack. Chief Engineer Meigs, had an itch for action. Apparently without orders from Hunter, he joined the cavalry at Mount Crawford.

The enemy observed that Jones had "...the mount strongly fortified, a commanding position."[18] Imboden wanted Hunter to test the defense he had prepared. "I am holding out every enducement I can to Hunter...If he does, and we can get him on 'a run' we can ruin him, (but) he is playing devilish cautions, however, and may not take the bait."[16]

While the Rebs were waiting on the hills above North River, the Union infantry began its advance. The infantry was surprised when it was ordered off the main road to Staunton shortly after leaving Harrisonburg.

The Yanks weren't the only ones surprised that morning. Capt. John H. McNeill was watching from a hill as the Union Army left Harrisonburg. Although McNeill's Partisan Rangers operated from the Valley District, they were not under the District Commander and could range freely. After harassing Hunter's rear, they had moved toward Hunter's front. "He (McNeill) would not permit a single man to show his head above the crest, though at a great distance from the enemy."[29] "After gazing at the scene, with sundry ejaculations, he exclaims, 'Where do they go to? They do not appear on sketches of the Valley Pike visible farther south, yet they keep agoin' (sic) out of the edge of the town.'"[29] One of the soldiers crouching below the crest line suggested that he look toward Port Republic. "Ah! There go the rasicals (sic) horse, foot and dragoon...."[29] A courier was sent via Bridgewater to warn Imboden.

The Yanks marched toward Port Republic and the old battlegrounds of Cross Keys. During the battle action, the bridge over the South Fork of the Shenandoah River was burned. The advance of the Union infantry was halted at the unbridged river at one o'clock. A small band of Rebs withdrew rapidly as the enemy approached. The Federals knew that it was only a matter of time before the Confederate generals knew the army was going to Port Republic, not to Mount Crawford.

Hunter ordered the pontoons to be brought forward and assembled. Orders were issued, but no pontoon bridge was built. "There seemed to be no one of the engineers who understood how to put up the canvas pontoons."[11] It was then that Hunter angrily discovered that Chief Engineer Meigs was with the cavalry demonstrating at Mount Crawford. Hunter's "superbly appointed troops" sat.

The Signal Corps kept the divided and strung-out Union Army in contact with its different columns and officers. No doubt Hunter ordered it to send a flag message to get Meigs to the river at Port Republic.

It was about twelve noon when Imboden suspected something was going wrong. The infantry from Harrisonburg should be there to do battle, but there was no blue-clad infantry in sight. Imboden sent his brother Col. George W. Imboden, commander of the Eighteenth Virginia Cavalry, over North River to ascertain what was happening.

Back at Port Republic, the bridging "...was awkwardly done and so slow that it was evident that we would lose all the benefit of our early march."[11] The army lost three precious, critical hours at the stream. Some soldiers with the One Hundred Twenty-Third Ohio forded the river and burned "...a large woolen factory just across the river..."[40] just for fun and to relieve the boredom. Some officers sat "...under an apple tree"[11] and read a captured Rebel newspaper. Strother found the paper "...ludicrous and yet painful to read...."[11] There was a letter from a Sanitary Commission Agent thanking people for their contributions to help the army. The letter drove home "...the dreadful poverty of the country..."[11] to Strother. The letter thanked one person for "...a bundle of rags, (another for) three eggs, (another for) four chickens, (another for) three red peppers and two onions."[11] The list went on and on. The destitute people were supporting their destitute army as best they could. While Strother was reading this, he could count thirteen captured wagons, full to overflowing, with supplies waiting for the bridge to go over the river.

While the officers relaxed and read at the head of the column, Confederate McNeill was busy at the Union's rear. One of his men said, "Hurrah for John McNeill, a prompt and gallant fighter... pushing right into Harrisonburg... (Northern) stragglers scattering here and there as they recognized the dreaded gray coats... Out (of town) up the Valley Pike he swept, eagle-eyed, fierce, daring everything. Harrisonburgers stared with wide-eyed wonder...(and) hope...to see that Hunter was 'surrounded.'"[29]

About five miles south of town, McNeill did strike the rear guard of Hunter's army. While battling troops to his front, McNeill was set upon by Yanks on his flank. His command was under much pressure, and there was confusion in the ranks but they were "...speedily brought to order and led out by that cool, brave man in language more forcible than graceful."[29] McNeill withdrew.

McNeill knew that he had harassed Hunter and that was all he could do. He returned to Harrisonburg before moving his command toward Imboden at Mount Crawford.

"...A cavalry trumpeter..."[11] decided not to wait for the pontoon bridge. He attempted to swim his horse through "the high, swift-running, dirty water...."[11] "Half a dozen men stripped and went in to save him...."[18] "The Shenandoah River was his grave...."[18] The cavalry would make no dash on Waynesboro.

While the Union Army sat waiting to cross the river, a scout from the Eighteenth raced to Jones at Mount Crawford. The enemy was not coming; it had turned toward Port Republic. Sometime thereafter, John McNeill's command rode to Imboden and reported the same. McNeill did not want his Partisan Rangers under anyone elses command so he rode off toward Staunton. Imboden knew immediately that they had been out-flanked. "This flank movement *disappointed* and somewhat *disconcerted* General Jones." Jones consulted with Imboden. There were three courses open to them. (1.) Remain in position. This would stop nothing and would not save Staunton; (2.) move over North River to Harrisonburg and strike Hunter at Port Republic. This plan held the possibility of two negative consequences: (A) Hunter could turn his large army on them in open field combat with a vast numerical advantage. Or: (B) Hunter could cross the Shenandoah and leave the Rebs standing on the bank, out of position to save Staunton. The only feasible option: (3.) Jones saw was to attempt to move the army off of North River and interpose it at some point between Hunter and Staunton.

Because Jones didn't know the country, he turned to Imboden for advice. Where was the best place between Port Republic and Staunton to do battle? Imboden did not "...hesitate...(this was) my native county, Augusta. I know every road, and almost every farm over which Hunter would pass. Mowry Hill,"[23] was Imboden's reply.

View of Mowry House (hill) near

Mowry Hill is located about eight miles northeast of Staunton. It is "...an eminence overlooking the beautiful little vale of Long Meadow Run (Creek)."[23] The big problem was that Mowry Hill was closer to Hunter's army than it was to Jones's. Jones and his part of the army were tired and had had no sleep the night before. But if they were to be at Mowry Hill and set-up defenses, they could not wait. This "...imposed on him (Jones) the necessity of a night march over roads he had never seen to get in position between Port Republic and Staunton."[23] The two generals agreed that it was likely that the slow moving Hunter would camp that night at or near Port Republic and not make a dash on Staunton. With this in mind, Jones reorganized the army. Imboden knew the land. He would take the cavalry and move that night to a point near Hunter at Port Republic. He would attempt to delay Hunter in the morning, giving Jones with the slow moving infantry and artillery time to reach Mowry Hill and set-up a defensive line. It was estimated that if Hunter did camp at Port Republic and if Imboden slowed him, Jones's men could be ready at Mowry Hill by noon on the fifth. Because Vaughn was senior to Imboden, he remained with Jones "...so as not to supersede Imboden in the

command of the cavalry."[30] Both generals started their respective parts of the
army in motion.

The delay at Port Republic cost the Federals their "benefit" in the diversion
and flanking movement. It was well into the afternoon when the army readied
to cross the pontoon bridge, "...a frail thing for an army to cross on."[18] Hunter
himself was worried about the contraption.

One of the troops recalled that Hunter "...sat on his horse very close to the
frail bridge, anxiously watching us (his troops) cross, and shouting, 'Men,
break step' (to)...divide the weight while we were on the bridge... a duty that
the General would not trust to anyone else."[18] The army did pass over safely,
but the cavalry forded at another point.

As Imboden guessed, Hunter decided to camp at Port Republic. Captured
Confederate supplies were distributed unequally to the troops. The Eighteenth
Connecticut ate well; the One Hundred Sixteenth Ohio "...were now out of
rations, except coffee, sugar, and salt."[14]

One soldier recalls "A number of packages of coffee came to our company
(Company C), which gave to us a great surprise as they were put up in our
hometown by Selden & Willard, Norwich, Conn. ...It has often been reported
that there are people in the North getting rich by running supplies through the
blockade. These people are anxious to prolong the war when they should
remember that every battle kills soldiers, and by the help they give to the
foes."[41]

As the Yanks slept, the weary Confederate Army was on the move. Hunter
decided that it was raining too much to make a night march with his rested
troops, but Jones knew that if he didn't push his exhausted little army that
night, he couldn't save Staunton.

The plans called for Imboden with his cavalry to lead the way south from
Mount Crawford over the Valley Pike Road to above Mount Sidney and then
east to a road that intercepts East Road above the village of Piedmont. The
cavalry was to turn north at East Road and move to Hunter's advance near
Port Republic. Jones ordered Imboden to delay Hunter with strict orders not
to commit the cavalry to a general engagement. Jones would need every
cavalryman and infantryman that he had if there was any hope of defeating
Hunter.

Because Opie's and Peck's Home Guard Cavalries were across the river,
they would join up with Jones's Infantry, not Imboden's Cavalry on the march.

The infantry and the artillery under Jones was to continue straight down
Cross Road and turn south at the intersection at East Road (south of Piedmont)
and go approximately three miles and establish a line of battle on Mowry Hill.
If all went according to plan, Imboden would slow Hunter's advance from
Port Republic and combine with Jones at Mowry Hill to do battle with Hunter
at high noon.

It is not certain if Jones and Imboden were together when Jones received a
telegram from General Lee. If the two were not together, their parts of the
army could not have been far apart because Imboden (the former Valley
District Commander) knew that the telegram had arrived. Lee had tele-

graphed Jones that no troops would be sent from Richmond to help him. He must fight Hunter and very soon before Hunter made junction with Crook. The combined army would be too awesome to attack. Jones must strike Hunter now and defeat him before turning on Crook. Jones read the telegraph and put it in his pocket without advising anyone, including Imboden of its contents. Until the war, Jones had withdrawn from the world; he kept his own council. Imboden must have felt a little miffed. He was, and would be probably in the future, the commander of the department. Although Jones, a highly temporary commander (by virtue of his commission as brigadier general pre-dating Imboden's), was using Imboden's facilities and personnel, he did not even bother to inform him as to the communication with the most important general of them all. Imboden wondered about the telegram but had no authority to demand that Jones reveal its message to him.

That night Jones requested that a telegraph operator be sent to him, near Mount Sidney. The operator found Jones "...seated at the foot of a giant white oak tree, *apparently intent on some map of the country, and alone.*"[29] He thought that Jones was showing the effect of his lack of rest. The operator asked the general which of the three available operators he would prefer to open a station at Meechum's River Depot. The weary general had a weary army and an overwhelming opponent to worry about; he didn't give a damn which one went. Jones replied, "If one of you don't go immediately, I'll put you all in irons."[29] One of them went.

Jones, the hermit farmer, was accustomed to working and being alone. According to one report, Jones was "...surprise(d) ...disappointed...disconcerted..."[7] by Hunter's flanking movement toward Port Republic. Jones studied the map. If his forces were at Mowry Hill three miles south of the crossroad at Piedmont, what was there to prevent Hunter from side-stepping him again? Hunter could easily turn west over the same road that Jones had come to Piedmont on and be back on the main road (Valley Pike) to Staunton. All of Jones's plans and marching would be in vain. Hunter would take Staunton with no resistance. He would there link-up with Crook and become awesome, almost invincible to attack from Jones's small command. Of course, the telegram in his pocket from Lee reminded Jones that he must — regardless of circumstances — strike Hunter before he combined with Crook. This time, there would be no road open to Hunter for a detour. Jones would plant his army and feet at the crossroads and at Piedmont.

That night an error occurred. It is possible that the sleepless Rebel general simply forgot or chose not to inform Imboden and the cavalry of his change of plan for the expected battle the next day. It is more likely that a messenger was sent to Imboden that night. Because it was not known for certain where Imboden would be stopping, the messenger and message may have gotten lost in the dark. Or Jones may have decided to inform Vaughn, his second in command and according to the plan, the projected leader of the cavalry at tomorrow's expected battle, and choose not to inform Imboden. It is not known why Imboden was not informed; it is known that he knew nothing of Jones's change of plans.

Apparently Opie's and Peck's Home Guard Cavalries, and the Eighteenth Virginia Cavalry, under Imboden's brother George, were still north of North River when the plan for the night march was agreed upon and the troops started moving. Imboden sent word to them to move south of the river and toward Port Republic. It was not until scouts from the Eighteenth arrived that Imboden learned that the Union Army had used a pontoon bridge to cross the river.

On this day, miles to the west, Crook continued toward Staunton. Crook left Covington and skirmished again with those pesky Rebs on Bratton's farm. Crook entered Jacksons River Station, (near Clifton Forge) which was the western terminus of the Virginia-Central Railroad. Here the destruction of the rails began. McCausland and Jackson fell back to Panther Gap where "...we took a strong position in the western entrance of the Gap behind natural stone breastworks, extending from the road through the pass to the top of the mountain, and awaited the onset of the enemy."[19] Apparently McCausland was anxious for Crook to attack; he knew that he would slow Crook's progress and inflict considerable casualties before Crook's numbers would force him to withdraw. Crook reconnoitered McCausland's position. One of the Rebs reported: "General Crook was too good a general to attack us...."[19] Crook found an old road to the left of the Southern line and tried to use it to out-flank McCausland and seal off McCausland's escape route. Crook sent Second Brigade, composed of the Twelfth & Ninety-First Ohio, and the Ninth & Fourteenth (W) Virginia Regiments, to do the job. McCausland detected Crook's movement and recognized the danger. There was a "...fight...not of long duration, (and) the Rebels giving way suddenly in great confusion."[31] McCausland was forced to give up a very strong position without much of a fight. Crook continued advancing; McCausland continued retreating. McCausland's men felled trees to slow Crook.

Colonel Hayes and the Twenty-Third Ohio were back from the advance of Crook's army. They were at Warm Springs but still saw some action. Partisan Rangers, "...said to be McNeill's and Marshall's Cavalry"[22] attacked the Twenty-Third. The Rebels apparently inflicted no casualties and did little damage before being driven off, but the action kept the guards on their toes.

Farther to the north, Averell was pushing his cavalry toward Staunton. This was a switch in normal tactics. The cavalry usually screened the infantry troop movements. Because Crook left first for Staunton and followed a more southernly route along the railroad, he was drawing the attention of the Rebels while Averell moved undetected over a more northernly route.

The forces that General Jones had ordered to Staunton from his department were still trickling in. John Hoge was a trooper with Company F, Eighth Virginia Cavalry, but he was walking to battle. On June 4, he left Salem, and marched to nine miles west of Buchanan and camped near a paper mill. It rained that night.

Also later that night from Southwest Virginia, the horses, harnesses, and teamsters from Bryan's Battery arrived from Staunton. Now there were extra teams to transport guns.

Chapter VI

On Sunday, June 5, General Jubal Early (Old Jube), near Richmond, received notice of his appointment as Lieutenant General.

Hoge and the Eighth Virginia marched to Natural Bridge during the day.

Crook pushed his force to Goshen. In the process, he lost "...two or three slightly wounded...(but) captured four or five Rebels and wounded three others badly."[22] McCausland retreated toward Buffalo Gap.

The Virginia Central Railroad was suffering much damage from Crook's troops with "...the rails being pried from their fastenings thrown over precipices into ravines, beyond all possibility of recovery...(also) rails were piled up several tiers high and fires were built about their middle."[31] When the rails got hot enough, they were bent.

The Confederates were pushed back with little loss; the destruction of the railroad was going well but not all of the day's news was good. The Yanks knew that McCausland and Jackson had consolidated forces trying to stop their huge army, but now there were rumors that the "Devil"[42] himself, John Hunt Morgan, was on his way to oppose them. Morgan and his savage fighters from Kentucky were perhaps the most hated and feared troops in the South. Although their numbers were not great, their courage and combat skills were. None of Crook's troops wished to tangle with Morgan's men. The rumor caused concern throughout the army, but it proved to be false.

Destroying Southern railroad.

Hunter VS Jones: Collision Day

"No resident of Staunton then living and over the age of infancy will ever forget Sunday, June 5, 1864."[43] At the small village of Piedmont, the Shavers retired as usual on Saturday night. Piedmont was a sleepy farming community of no particular note. Little did the residents of the community realize that fate had selected their small community for the scene of a major battle. The Shavers were suddenly awakened in the pre-dawn hours by part of Imboden's Cavalrymen. When the Shavers peeked out, they saw that "...the yard fence was hitched full of horses and soldiers were lying on the porch and in the yard."[44] The soldiers told them that the Yankees were coming; and they were there to try and stop them.

Near dawn, Confederate infantry under Jones reached the crossroads (intersection of East Road [which runs from Port Republic to Staunton] and Cross Road [which runs from East Road to Valley Pike Road]) and following orders began to dig trenches and rifle pits. Somewhat later in the morning, Jones arrived and observed the terrain and his men digging.

Jones rode forward over East Road toward Port Republic. He rode only a few hundred yards up the road, before he found ground more to his liking. Middle River made a loop toward East Road. By anchoring his left flank on the river, he had only approximately 400 yards to defend to the road. About 400 yards across an open crop field, there were a small stream and a wood which would restrict Hunter's movements on the right. The crest of the hill he chose offered a mild elevation over the next hill over which East Road runs to Port Republic. It didn't have everything that Jones wanted, but it was superior to the original line he had chosen looking at a map in the dark. Jones sent orders to his troops to stop digging at the crossroads and move north and resume digging. The order was met with little enthusiasm, but the men moved forward.

At Port Republic, Hunter woke his Chief-of-Staff. At an early morning conference, they agreed, "We felt certain that this would be a day of battle...."[11] Accordingly, the cavalry was sent out at 4:00 a.m., on a rainy morning, to ascertain the enemy's position and strength.

At approximately 5:00 a.m., the infantry was set in motion "...without having made even a cup of coffee for breakfast, but with a promise that we should get something to eat soon."[14] Hunter seemed to sense the presence of Confederates, because he sent infantry skirmishers to the left and to the right of the road before he even observed the enemy.

Hunter believed that this would be a day of battle. There was no time for breakfast, but there was time to inflict punishment on this pro-Southern population. Near Port Republic, "By order of General Hunter, a large woolen mill was burned...."[18] A soldier said, "I noticed a number of women were crying as the mill burned. (But he excused the punitive burning by stating) that the mill had been used to make cloth for the South."[18] Who else could it be for? The soldier stated, "Death and destruction follows in the path of war,"[18] but wanton destruction was not normal procedure in this war.

By 6:00 a.m. the army had advanced approximately four miles from Port Republic when scouts with the First New York Cavalry returned "...reporting the enemy (was in) force."[9] Hunter ordered his cavalry forward. The infantry was ordered to form battle lines and advance.

The advance of the Union cavalry had struck Capt. Frank M. Imboden's (another brother of General Imboden) Company (approximately 20[6] to 40[30] men) of the Eighteenth Virginia Cavalry. General Imboden called it "...one of my best Companies."[23] Frank Imboden was at or near the crossroads south above the Alexander Givens farm near Mount Meridian.

General Imboden and the remainder of the Eighteenth were farther south, eating breakfast on the farm of Col. Samuel D. Crawford, called "Bonnie Doon," located one mile south of Mount Meridian and four miles north of New Hope.

The Union cavalry (part of First Brigade — First New York Cavalry under Col. William B. Tibbets) apparently caught Frank's Company by surprise and pushed the "panic stricken"[6] Company along the road. General Imboden and his men had just finished breakfast and were mounting their horses when they heard the shooting. Imboden ordered his troopers forward, uncertain as to how many troops he might engage. Jones had ordered Imboden "...to avoid any risky engagement."[23] Technically, Imboden violated orders by sending his men on an uncertain foray.

Some in Frank's Company were apparently wounded or captured. Soon Colonel Tibbetts' Yanks were taking firm control of the skirmish.

The Yanks knew that there were Confederates in the area, perhaps in force. Colonel Tibbets ordered skirmishers to be thrown out front as early warning sentinels for the main body of the cavalry. The troopers were deployed in a skirmish line with Company A on the left and Company C on the right. They were to advance in unison forward, and remove some fence rails to allow the others to pass through. When the Union troopers left the woods, they were "...surprised to see immediately in front of them a broad, rounded hill filled with the enemy."[9] Imboden had arrived with the main force. Instead of dismounting and deploying, the broken skirmish line continued forward. When it came to within range of Imboden's troopers' guns, the line received a "murderous fire."[9] Despite the fact that the men were at a "disadvantage...they held their ground and...returned the enemy's fire."[9] Lieutenant Vermilya was shot from his horse and not one leader was there to order them to charge, or deploy, or retreat. There was no support on the right flank because Company C was delayed removing the fence. The decision to retreat was made for them by "A Confederate officer with uplifted sabre (who) led a charge down the slope of the hill with such vigor that these companies were forced back into the woods."[9]

During the charge as the two cavalry lines met, Lieutenant Savacools' horse bolted into the Confederate line. Because of the rain, Savacools was wearing "...a light-colored rubber coat."[9] In the confusion of the thunderous attack, Savacools blended in with the Rebel cavalrymen. He simply turned his mount about and charged toward his unit with the enemy. When the Reb advance slowed at the tree line, he continued galloping forward and rejoined his unit unscratched.

In less than five minutes, the First New York had taken twenty casualties including Sergeant Buss and George Mason of Company M. Lt. Clark Stanton was shot in the thigh. Many horses were killed also. Private Thomas Gorman was captured; while retreating he attempted to jump the fence; neither he nor his horse made it over. His buddies could see two Rebel soldiers free Gorman from under his horse and take him prisoner. Major Quinn led a group of his men forward and overtook Gorman and the two Rebs. As they were being surrounded, Gorman announced to his captors, "Now you are my prisoners."[9]

Major J.K. Stearns was "skillful"[6] to be able to retreat the First New York in good order.

Imboden's attack continued to push the men in blue to the rear. Lieutenant Vermilya who "...was universally respected as an honest, faithful soldier,"[6] was shot. Doctor Douglas and others rushed to his aid but "...in a few minutes (he) was dead."[6] The First New York had lost another trooper.

Imboden's attack had hit the Federals with such force that they fell back toward the river to a point one mile north of Mount Meridian. As the First New York fell back toward its army, it picked up additional reinforcements. The men were joined by:

The Twenty-First New York Cavalry (Griswold's Light Cavalry, Maj. Charles G. Ottis commanding).

First New York (Veteran) Cavalry.

First Maryland Cavalry, (regiment of the Potomac Home Guard).

Fourteenth Pennsylvania Cavalry.

Fifteenth New York Cavalry, (Lieutenant Colonel Augustus I. Root commanding).

Twenty-Second Pennsylvania Cavalry, (Col. Jacob Higgens commanding).

Twentieth Pennsylvania Cavalry, (Lt. Col. Gabrich Middleton commanding).

Some units from the Second Cavalry Brigade (John E. Wynkoop commanding). Members of the Signal Corps deployed to the front and flanks to keep the general's staff informed of the action.

Re-creation:

Union cavalry.

Confederate cavalry.

With this increased strength, the Union horsemen were able to halt the Southern advance. Battle lines were drawn as Imboden endeavored to resist the increasing Federal pressure. Despite orders to the contrary, Imboden had his cavalry involved in a general engagement. Instead of retreating and delaying the enemy, Imboden chose to fight. He sent a courier toward Mowry's Hill to hunt up Opie's and Peck's Cavalry units and send them forward.

Imboden had stalled the Union advance for an hour, but the forces to his front were too much. Imboden's men were forced to withdraw to their original position on the high ground of the hill.

It appears that the companies of the First New York Cavalry that didn't get to support their unit on the field because of the fence were at the head of the Union's mass attack on Imboden's hill position. It was a "determined"[6] and furious charge. Imboden's line could not hold and it broke in "confusion."[6] One Union soldier vividly recalled seeing "...riderless horses running wild over the dead and wounded and among the living."[6]

Capt. Frank Imboden's Company had been mauled early. It was now cut off from retreat. Captain Imboden and eighty-two[6] of his men were captured in a "...hand-to-hand contest."[45] (After capture, Frank was personally interrogated by Chief-of-Staff Strother and held prisoner). General Imboden was almost captured. He apparently leaped from his horse and ran for his life to keep from being taken.

Imboden had violated his orders and became totally engaged in a "...running fight that...threatened to destroy the whole regiment."[30] Now his troopers were retreating without organization. As Southern troops retreated, Opie's and Peck's men advanced. Opie stated, "We were passed by hundreds of men on horseback, who seemed to be utterly demoralized, fleeing from the enemy."[20]

The two companies of Home Guard cavalry continued to advance until they found Imboden and a few of his men "without formation."[20] Opie had every fourth man hold the horses, and the three dismounted men formed a line behind a rail fence. It was the first fight for many of these Home Guard men. Opie, worried about the courage of his men, shouted an order to his troops: "Now men, if it is necessary to run, I will start first, but, if any man runs before I do, I will shoot him."[20]

Opie's order worked for him. They held the line, turning back several Union attacks. The Yanks attacked across the open field. The Twenty-Third Virginia Cavalry under Col. Robert White and the Maryland Battalion of Cavalry under Major Sturges joined the fray. The Marylanders and the Twenty-Third "...made a charge that checked the enemy,"[30] and saved Imboden's Cavalry from possible destruction.

Although the Home Guard and Imboden's few men were holding the line, they had to retreat when they received word that the Yanks were rounding their right flank. The South fell back through Mount Meridian. The skirmishing grew more violent and confusing.

The Yanks moved a battery of artillery to near Bonnie Doon. Capt.

Chatham T. Ewing fired several ineffective shots toward the Southern line. Imboden observed the Union infantry moving forward. He knew that if he were to hold the line to give Jones the time he needed at Mowry's Hill, he needed artillery support. He sent a courier back to Jones requesting a battery and 500 infantry troops.

It was now mid-morning. In the morning skirmishing, the North had lost approximately seventy-five men killed, wounded, and captured. The South had lost well over eighty captured and many more wounded and missing.

The sound of furious cavalry skirmishing could be plainly heard in the Village of Piedmont. The villagers knew that the battle action was heading their way. Soldiers moved into position and others dug breastworks as all prepared for battle. Lt. Carter Berkeley's Battery, a section of McClanahan's artillery comprised of six guns, waiting near Piedmont had not been ordered to any location, but he knew that orders would soon come. He had the horses in harness and men waiting. When Jones approved Imboden's request for artillery, Berkeley was ready to go. One observer recalled that when Berkeley's outfit raced through Piedmont "...the artillerymen were shouting and singing, while ladies stood on porches and waved, cheering them on."[6]

To General Imboden's "...astonishment these reinforcements arrived within a half hour."[6] This was the first clue Imboden had that the battle plan had been changed. It was physically impossible to get artillery from Mowry's Hill to his location south of Mount Meridian in one half hour, but Berkeley's Battery was here. The confused general situated the artillery on a "rock bluff"[20] and had his men form a line to protect the guns.

Unlike his Union counterpart, Berkeley put his two guns to effective work. One of Berkeley's first shots put one of Ewing's guns out of action. Another source indicates that "Two 3-inch rifles of horse battery "B" West Virginia Artillery...had been crippled by the loss of horses in the fight with Imboden...."[30] Southern guns also found their mark on the First New York Cavalry; at least one horse was killed and Major Quinn barely escaped one of the rounds. A member of the Eighteenth Connecticut recalled Berkeley's guns being fired on them from a "...distance of about two miles, getting range on our colors (flag)."[18] The fire was so intense that it forced the Eighteenth to leave the road and open field and seek protection in the woods. The men continued to advance despite the incoming Rebel fire. They could not fire back because their cavalry was between them and the enemy.

Berkeley's Battery continued to pour lead on the Northern cavalrymen for about one half hour. Some infantry (the two companies of Niter Miners) began to arrive.

A mill was set afire at Mount Meridian, "...Hunter adhering to his policy of destroying at least one structure in each community...."[6]

During this time, the confused General Imboden rode to the rear to confer with Jones. He found Jones above Piedmont, not at Mowry's Hill, where he was supposed to be. The river afforded a good anchor for the South's left flank, but the hill-line Jones had chosen offered the South very little advantage, and Imboden told Jones so.

Many years later, Imboden recalled the conversation.

Imboden: "We have no advantage of ground, and he outnumbers us nearly three to one and will beat us."

Jones: "I don't want any advantage of ground, for I can whip Hunter anywhere."

Imboden: "General, I will not say you cannot whip him here, but I will say, with the knowledge I have of his strength, that if you do, it will be at the expense of a fearful loss of life on our side, and believing we have no right to sacrifice the lives of our men where it is possible to avoid it as it is now, if you will even yet fall back to Mowry's Hill, I enter my solemn protest against fighting here today."

Jones: "Sir! I believe I am in command here today."

Imboden: "You are, Sir, and I now ask your orders and will carry them out as best I can; but if I live, I will see that the responsibility for this day's work is fixed where I think it belongs."[30]

Imboden's remarks had no effect. Jones would permit no discussion; they would fight and fight here. Imboden once more "...made a solemn and angry protest."[6] Again it had no effect on Jones. Jones acted and spoke with extreme confidence. He knew that his army would defeat Hunter; he belittled the fighting abilities of his opponent. He was "...entirely confident that if he could engage Hunter anywhere that day he could beat him...."[23] Jones may not have believed his remarks as much as he wanted those under him to believe. He knew the odds were stacked against him. He didn't want his men to look at the situation logically. If they did, they would develop a defeated attitude. Imboden listened to Jones and decided "...his over-confidence (had) led him into (a grave) error...."[23]

While Imboden protested and Jones ignored, Capt. Henry A. Dupont moved a total of ten guns on line against Berkeley's two. Dupont brought John Carlin's (W.Va.) Battery, Alonzo Snow's (Md.) Battery, Alfred Von Kleiser's (N.Y.) Battery, Battery "B" Fifth U.S. (Dupont's own battery), to join Ewing's (W.Va.) Battery. Dupont directed a holocaust of fire against the Southern line. Opie recalled that "We lay in the rear of the battery, under heavy fire, for about an hour...."[20]

With the increased intensity of the artillery reports, both generals knew that the battle was heating up. They decided to ride forward and direct the troops. Jones told his staff before leaving to stay where it was: "Gentlemen, I don't want any of you killed and don't want to be killed myself."[6]

As the two generals approached the line of battle the cavalry had set up, the men "...cheered the commanders...."[6] Jones and Imboden rode forward for a first hand assessment. Shells from some of Dupont's guns began to fall when the generals left the tree line. It didn't take the two generals long to conclude that they couldn't hold the line against the North's cavalry, backed by infantry, and supported by Dupont's overwhelming batteries. The generals raced back to the relative safety of the woods.

Jones gave orders for the withdrawal. The artillery and cavalry were to draw off line first, and the two companies of Niter Miners were then to fall back toward Piedmont. Jones told his men to make each shot count: "Aim low, boys, and hit 'em below the belt."[6] Some of the Niter Corps didn't complete its retreat. A determined Northern cavalry charge on its left resulted in some of the corps being taken prisoner.

Men clad in blue and men clad in gray (perhaps tattered or in homespun) were on a collision course. With weapons of iron, courage of steel, and resolute determination, they would meet in combat. Each man had full knowledge that this sunrise might be his last this side of eternity. Today would determine if Hunter would be defeated and be sent scurrying north like his predecessor Sigel; or if the South would be defeated and the all important Valley with its rail link to Richmond be opened to Northern domination. Men of flesh and blood had been classified from private to general, and assigned to squads, companies, battalions, regiments, brigades, and divisions. These are the units that fate brought to the obscure village of Piedmont on June 5, 1864.

FORCES OF THE UNITED STATES OF AMERICA
Major-General David Hunter, Commanding
Colonel David Hunter Strother, Chief-of-Staff

Infantry
Sullivan's Division, Brigadier-General J.C. Sullivan
   First Brigade, Colonel Augustus Moor
   Eighteenth Connecticut, Colonel W.G. Ely
   Second Maryland Eastern Shore, Colonel Robert S. Rodgers
   Twenty-Eight Ohio, Lieutenant-Colonel, Gottfried Becker
   Hundred and Sixteenth Ohio, Colonel James Washburn
   Hundred and Twenty-Third Ohio, Major Horace Kellog
Second Brigade, Colonel Joseph Thoburn
   Thirty-Fourth Massachusetts, Colonel George D. Wells
   Fifty-Fourth Pennsylvania, Colonel Jacob M. Campbell
   First West Virginia, Lieutenant-Colonel Jacob
   Twelfth West Virginia, Colonel William B. Curtis
   Fifth New York Heavy Artillery, (four companies serving as infantry) Lieu-
      tenant Colonel Edward Murray.

Unassigned
   Second Maryland Infantry Regiment — Potomac Home Brigade, Lieuten-
      ant-Colonel G. Ellis Porter

Cavalry
Cavalry Division — Major Julius Stahel
   First Cavalry Brigade, Colonel William B. Tibbets
   First New York (Veteran) Cavalry, Colonel Robert Taylor
   First Maryland (Cole's) Cavalry — Potomac Home Brigade, (Detachment)
      Major J. Townsend Daniel
   Fourteenth Pennsylvania Cavalry, (Detachment) Captain Ashbell F. Duncan
      (and Lieutenant William Blakely)

Second Cavalry Brigade, Colonel John E. Wynkoop
Fifteenth New York Cavalry, (Small Detachment) Lieutenant-Colonel
    Augustus I. Root
Twenty-First New York Cavalry, (Small Detachment) Lieutenant-Colonel
    Gabriel Middleton
Twenty-First Pennsylvania, (Small Detachment) Colonel Jacob Higgins
Artillery
    Artillery Brigade — Captain Henry Algernon Dupont
    Light Battery "B", Fifth U.S. Artillery — six, 3-inch guns rifled, Captain
        Henry A. Dupont
Snow's Light Battery "B", Maryland Artillery, sixty-three rifles
    Carlin's Light Battery "D", First West Virginia Light Artillery, six, 3-inch
        rifles, Captain John Carlin
    Thirteenth Independent New York (Veteran) Light Artillery, four Napolean
        guns — Captain Alfred Von Kleiser (Von Kleiser's Battery)
    Battery "G", First West Virginia Light Artillery, three-inch rifles, Captain
        Chatham T. Ewing
    Thirty-First Independent New York (Veteran) Light Artillery, Captain
        Gustav Von Blucher
Signal Corps
    Captain Franklin E. Town
Engineers
    Lieutenant John R. Meigs

FORCES OF THE CONFEDERATE STATES OF AMERICA
Brigadier-General William Edmondon "Grumble" Jones, Commanding
Infantry
    First Brigade, Colonel Beuhring H. Jones
    Thirty-Sixth Virginia Regiment, Major William E. Fife
        (fewer than 500 men)
    Sixtieth Virginia Regiment, Colonel Beuhring H. Jones
        (approximately 600 men)
    Second Brigade, Colonel William H. Browne
    Forty-Fifth Virginia Regiment, Colonel William H. Browne
        (approximately 500-600 men)
    Forty-Fifth Virginia Battalion, Lieutenant Colonel H. M. Beckley
        (Beckley's Battalion — approximately 175 men)
Cavalry
    Vaughn's Brigade (approximately 600 to 800 men)
    Brigadier-General John Crawford Vaughn (second in command to Jones)
    Imboden's Brigade, Brigadier-General John D. Imboden (third in command
        to Jones)

Eighteenth Virginia Cavalry, Colonel George W. Imboden
    (Brother of John — Now a Union prisoner)
Twenty-Third Virginia Cavalry, Colonel Robert White
Artillery
    Bryan's Battery, Light Artillery, Captain Thomas A. Bryan
    six guns (4 long-range) (one account states that Bryan had a 12-pound
    Howitzer and a bronze, 3-inch rifle, slightly drooped by rapid fire at New
    River Bridge)
    Marquis' (Boys') Battery, Captain J.C. Marquis (two guns recorded at
    battle, 20-pound Parrott and a 24-pound Howitzer — "Lads under
    eighteen"
    McClanahan's Battery, Maryland Artillery, Captain John H. McClanahan
    (six guns) (supplemented by thirty Maryland cannoneers)
    Berkeley's Section, Lieutenant Carter Berkeley (two guns)
    Fultz's Section, H.H. Fultz (two guns)
    Flying Artillery Section, Captain John H. McClanahan
Unassigned
HOME GUARDS (RESERVES), PARTISAN RANGERS, AND IRREGU-
LAR TROOPS
Harper's Regiment Reserves, Colonel Kenton Harper
    Company A, Captain Hardy
    Company B, Captain Robert L. Doyle
    Company C, Captain J.M. Templeton
    Company D, Captain Henry H. Peck
    Company E, Captain John Newton Opie
    Company F, Rippetoe
    Company G, Hilbert
    Company I, Bacon
    Company K, Lieutenant Monroe Blue
    (four companies cavalry reserves)
    One-Captain J.F. Hottle
    Two-Captain Robert W. Stevensib
    Three-Captain James C. Cochran
    Four-Captain John Nunan
Harman's Brigade of Reserves, Colonel William H. Harman
Robertson's Regiment of Reserves, Lieutenant Colonel Robertson
Niter and Mining Corps Battalion, Captain James F. Jones (less casualties,
    missing and captured at this time in battle)
McNeill's Partisan Rangers, Captain John H. McNeill
Gilmor's Maryland Battalion, Major Harry Gilmor
Davis's Maryland Battalion, Captain Thomas Sturgis Davis

Estimates of troop strength and quality vary widely. Estimates vary in part
because of the lack of records and the fact that many units in both armies had
been depleted because of casualties taken in May in the Valley (New Market)
and in Southwest Virginia (Cloyd's Mountain). Vaughn estimates Southern

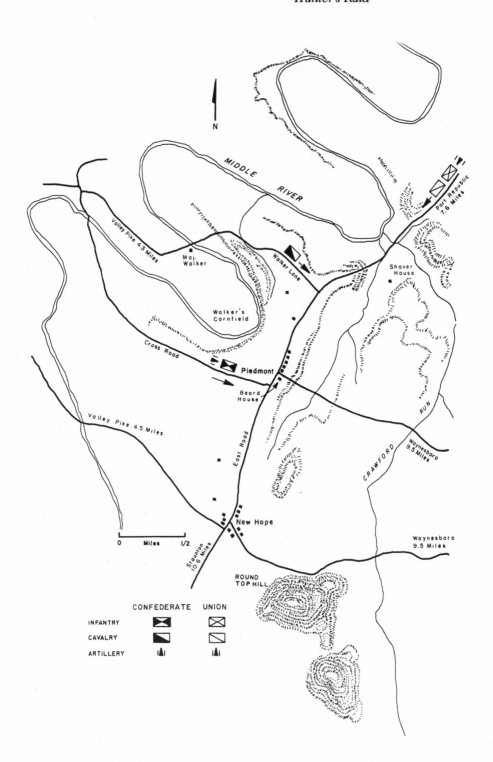

forces at 3,600 infantry and 2,000 cavalry, for a total of 5,600 men. Imboden estimates 2,400 infantry and 1,800 cavalry, for a total of 4,200 men. Hunter put the number between 6,000 to 7,000 (probably much too high, but it looked good on his record). Most sources estimate that the Confederacy fielded approximately 1,000 men who had no combat experience and little training. The South had approximately fourteen pieces of artillery on the field.

Union estimates are little better. One source estimates 9,078 infantrymen and artillerists, and 2,910 cavalrymen, for a total of 11,988 men. Imboden estimates 9,000 infantry and 2,500 cavalry, for a total of 11,500 exclusive of the artillerists. The North had between 22 and 31 guns. It can be stated factually that the North was superior in number of men and guns, in quality of equipment and supplies, and in trained combat soldiers.[46]

As with other battles, such as Antetium or Gettysburg, the obscure village of Piedmont with little economic and no military value, through a twist of fate, was to be the scene of a desperate battle. Piedmont is located on East Road which leads directly to Staunton approximately thirteen miles away. Jones originally intended to fight at Piedmont at the intersection of Cross Road and East Road, but since better terrain approximately one mile north on East Road offered a somewhat better advantage, Jones relocated his line. Because Hunter had simply side-stepped a battle at Mount Crawford, Jones was obsessed with preventing a recurrence.

Jones was also pressed by time. He had to fight Hunter before Hunter could link-up with Crook, and Lee's order in his pocket was a reminder of the importance high command attached to this situation.

The terrain, the quality and quantity of soldiers, and Jones's obsession that Hunter not be allowed to round his flank, dictated Jones's placement of troops on the battlefield. Jones decided to anchor his left flank on Middle River at a point where the convex of the river was nearest east Road. Hunter could not easily round this flank. There was a slightly wooded ridge line that runs from the river to East Road. Jones chose this as his main battle line and threw skirmishers forward across a slight dip to the next ridge line which was only a few feet lower in elevation than the main ridge line. Jones placed his veteran Southwest Virginia units from left to right: Second Brigade; Forty-Fifth Regiment, then Forty-Fifth Battalion. First Brigade, Thirty-Sixth Regiment, then the Sixtieth Virginia was placed along the ridge line. "...Soldiers of these units had earned reputations as fierce fighters and fairly well disciplined soldiers."[6] The soldiers made rail pen breastworks. They took the fence on one side of the road (Walker Lane) and piled it on the other side and made a kind of breastwork...."[44] At approximately fifty yards behind these breastworks to support his left flank, Jones placed the six guns of McClanahan's Battery. Near East Road, Jones placed the Marquis' Boys' Battery with their huge guns, the twenty-pound Parrott and the twenty-four pound Howitzer (Dupont indicated there were four guns). Jones was counting on these large guns to counter Hunter's superiority in number of guns. The right side of the line which was closer to the Union's anticipated advance was expected to receive the main thrust of the attack.

Because it was important to Jones that Hunter should not round the flank, Jones told his cavalry "...to remain there (in place) and protect the right flank. The order was considered as leaving them (Imboden and Vaughn) no discretion: They were not to move without orders."[30]

Imboden was to the east of East Road and south of Cross Road with his flank near Crawford Run. (He even had a contingency occupy Round Top Hill, which is below New Hope, the highest point in the area, and far detached from Jones's main line. This picket was to observe and to make sure that Hunter didn't attempt to skirt the flank). Along the wooded lane (Cross Road) leading back to East Road, Vaughn placed his command. Both Vaughn's and Imboden's cavalries were dismounted. Four long-range guns of Bryan's Battery were placed along this line. Two short-range guns ("A 12-pound Howitzer and a bronze 3-inch rifle slightly drooped by rapid fire at New River Bridge"[30] [after Cloyd's Mountain]) of Bryan's Battery were placed near the junction of Cross Road and East Road.

From Cross Road north to the Sixtieth Virginia's flank on East Road there was a gap perhaps as much as 400 yards wide with no troops.

Because of the importance this gap would have in the battle, there has been much debate as to its cause and who was at fault. Some imply that Jones in his battle plan simply overlooked this area. That tantamounts to accusing Jones of gross incompetence. Jones's previous war record would tend to indicate that he was not a leader who would overlook such a glaring error.

Some want to blame both Vaughn and Imboden. One rumor was stated that the two generals paid a visit to David Beard's distillery near the intersection of Cross Road and East Road. According to the rumor, the generals had a few too many drinks and returned to the field and failed to direct their units properly during the entire battle.

This theory has many holes in it. First there is no definite proof that David Beard's distillery was in operation. The first records found indicate that whisky was produced there five years after the end of the war. Even if the records are incomplete and if there was a still, it is not likely that two men who rose to the rank of Brigadier General would have so little self-control as to give way to temptation and get drunk immediately before a battle. Also it is to be remembered that Imboden with the cavalry was retreating before Hunter's troops. There was simply no time for the two generals to sit around reminiscing about old times and drinking.

Then why the gap? No absolute answer could be found. A glance at command structure listing shows the Home Guard, Partisan Rangers, and irregular troops as being "unassigned." One historian noted, "The exact position of the irregulars is immaterial."[30] Since all other units had a specifically assigned area, it is possible that the Home Guard was to fill the gap. The same historian noted that, "They (Home Guards) were held in reserve...."[30] It is very unlikely that Jones would select the least reliable troops as his reserve. At the Battle of Cloyd's Mountain the Home Guards broke and ran. Jones knew that if he were to get any service from them, they must be placed on the front line. It appears likely, but not provable beyond a shadow of a doubt, that the Home

Guard was to cover the area that became the gap. Either Jones's orders were not issued, or they were not executed. Perhaps Vaughn, second-in-command, was given the duty of placing the Home Guard in Imboden's absence. Most of the Home Guard remained near the intersection of East Road and Cross Road.

Based on the terrain, the troops, and the time element one historian concluded, "...the position on the whole was sound...."[6]

The Battle of Piedmont started in earnest about 10:00 a.m. The last of the Confederate cavalry and Home Guard units that were attempting to delay Hunter fell back to the Southern line. Skirmishers were placed along the ridge line in advance of the Rebel breastworks. As Opie's men fell back, they were not ordered to join either Imboden or the Home Guard; they were assigned to the far left of the line. Opie, observing the terrain, stated "...General Jones had selected a most miserable position...."[20] There was no height advantage or artillery advantage. Imboden agreed that there was "...no advantage of ground...."[6]

At the Shaver house, teenager Milton Shaver, had seen the Confederate cavalry that had rested about the property before daylight and then moved toward Mount Meridian. He saw Southern forces then move past the house heading toward Piedmont. When he saw "...Yankees coming back of Crawford's orchard...,"[44] he knew that it was time to hide the horses. By the time he and Dan Scroghem got the horses in the woods "...minie balls commenced flying pretty lively."[44]

The Union cavalry continued to advance until it came within range of Southern artillery. When six shells[44] were fired at it, the cavalry knew that it was time to wait for the infantry and artillery; to continue forward would be disaster. Some of the officers were "lounging"[9] closer than they thought to Confederate guns. A shell passed over their heads and exploded only a short distance to their rear. "It seemed best to move the regiment to the left to a less exposed position."[9]

"Forward was the word to horse, foot, and artillery."[11] The cavalry rested out of Confederate gun range, and the infantry began to move forward. As the infantry was being formed for battle, Hunter reviewed some of his units. He decided the Eighteenth Connecticut needed a pep talk. The Eighteenth had "disgraced itself"[11] and had been "...reprimanded repeatedly for invalorous conduct at New Market."[6] Now the men of the Eighteenth would "...have a chance of retrieving their reputation";[11] a chance to "wipe out the stain of disgraceful retreat at New Market."[6] "They didn't seem much elated with the prospect and scarcely got up a decent cheer in the response;"[11] "...with the resentful mutter that the Eighteenth was being blamed for Sigel's ineptitude...."[6] They formed with their first brigade.

First Brigade under Colonel Moor moved to the Confederate left flank near the river. He placed his troops as follows from (Confederate left to right): Eighteenth Connecticut Volunteers (under Colonel Ely), then the Fifth New York Heavy Artillery (no cannons), Moor's old regiment the One Hundred Twenty-Third Ohio, with the Second Maryland Eastern Shore in reserve. Colonel Thoburn's Second Brigade formed on First Brigade's left, perhaps to

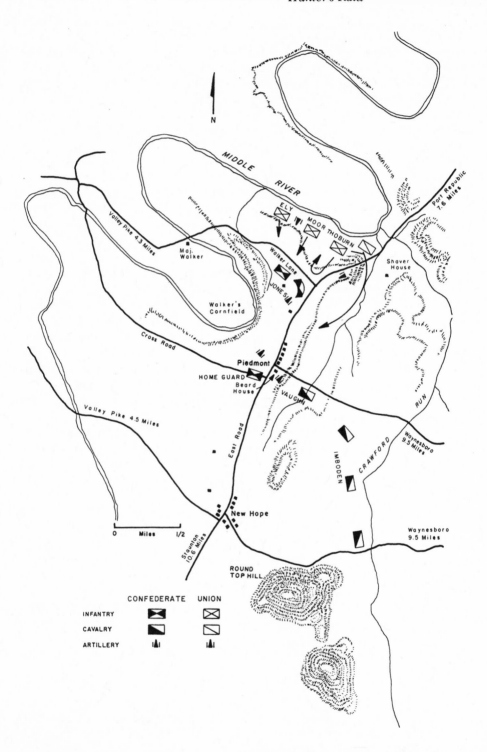

the right of East Road. The cavalry was placed out of danger in a hollow behind First Brigade. It would be used if rapid movement against an inferior target was required.

Southern gunners could no longer strike the Yanks' cavalry, but the deploying infantry was within range. Colonel Strother records: "Already the shells and shot began to whistle around our ears."[11] Hunter ordered the artillery forward. Dupont posted most of his strength in an orchard against the Confederate left. He placed only two of his Napoleons on the Confederate right wing across East Road.

Dupont's overwhelming numbers took effect on Southern guns. When the smoke of Southern guns revealed their position, Dupont ordered his guns to return the fire en masse. Dupont used "mounted orderlies"[47] to coordinate his cannon fire. Having over twenty guns return fire against one Southern battery was overwhelming. This fire forced the South to pull much of her artillery farther from the line of battle. The Confederate artillery was at a disadvantage.

Union guns continued to pound, troops deployed until about 11:30 a.m. when "...the enemy's artillery seemed to be silenced...and...retiring at all points."[11] Hunter and his staff had been behind Dupont's guns watching the enemy from a distance. Now Hunter moved his staff forward for a closer look. It apparently advanced toward the Confederate right wing across East Road.

On the Confederate far right was a cloverfield running 500 to 800 yards. ("The clover was in head about knee high."[44]) Vaughn's and Imboden's cavalries were placed along the woods just below Cross Roads which borders the cloverfield. The cloverfield extended up the hill toward East Road on the left (Confederate line).

Hunter's staff saw the cloverfield which extended up the hill toward East Road, where it observed "...the twenty-pounder battery (Boys' Battery)."[11] Along the wooded ridge line the staff saw the rail breastworks the South had constructed. The breastworks "...rested on a steep and impractical bluff 60 feet high and washed at its base by the Shenandoah"[11] (Middle Fork). Many Southern commanders lacked confidence in their position, but the Northerners had a different view. They admitted that "The enemy's position was strong and well chosen."[11] Hunter described Jones's position as "advantageously posted."[8] The Rebs were "...well protected behind rail and log breastworks."[14]

When Hunter and his staff rode out on "...open, rising ground...the whole of the enemy's heretofore silent guns opened on (them)."[11] The cannon fire did not scare the general who "retired...after a satisfactory view."[11] One shell from Berkeley's gun came close enough to Hunter "...stirring the general and his staff to seek cover...."[6] Southern guns tried to find their range on him as he entered the woods. Dupont took command of two guns and silenced the Confederate batteries.

As Hunter was retreating on the right, Moor started attacking on the Confederate left. The Confederates had skirmishers on a ridge top between the Yankees and their main breastworks below Walker Lane. Walker Lane intersects East Road and runs west to the ford at Major Walker's on Middle River. Southern cavalry had passed over this road in the pre-dawn darkness.

Moor ordered his men "...to crawl up (the hill) on our hands and knees"[18] so as not to present the Rebs on the hill with a target. If the Dixie boys stood to get a shot at the attackers, other Union infantry were set to cut them down. Even though the Confederates couldn't fire, they knew that the Yanks were coming. "Reaching the brow, we were ordered to rise; at the same time the enemy poured a deadly volley into our ranks. A number fell; the stock of my gun was shot off,"[18] recorded a soldier with the Eighteenth Connecticut.

Jones's battle plan didn't call for holding the hill. Under increasing pressure, the Confederate soldiers on the skirmish line began to fall back toward their breastworks. "We poured a sharp fire into their ranks,"[18] recorded one Federal. The Rebs in retreat encouraged the attackers to pursue them, and the Yanks attacked. "The advance was gallantly made, and the roar of musketry continuous."[11] The Northern soldiers pursued until they found themselves in the open field with the main Confederate defensive work at their front. "...Here the soldiers fought desperately and at some disadvantage, being entirely in the open field."[7] The Eighteenth Connecticut, whom Hunter lectured, sent Company C to protect its right. The "...company suffered heavy losses from withering fire."[6] Colonel Washburn's (of the One Hundred Sixteenth Ohio) horse was shot from under him. The Northern attack was checked. Colonel Ely of the Eighteenth Connecticut sent a request to Dupont for artillery support. The Yanks were taking heavy casualties as Dupont moved two guns to within fifty yards of the Confederate line and began to pepper the breastworks with solid shot. The artillery "...did excellent service in knocking the rail pens to splinters amid great slaughter."[7] "...Though probably serviceable enough against an infantry attack, (rail pens) proved to be of no value whatever so far as artillery fire was concerned."[47]

The Union could not maintain its position. It began to fall back "...with considerable loss."[20] Hunter and his staff had seen the "gallant" attack, "But in a few moments we had the mortification to see the lines break and retire in confusion...."[11] Colonel Ely added, "Our colors were riddled by three cannon shot and thirteen bullets, and all of our color guard but one was killed or wounded."[7] Within minutes Moor's Brigade had taken over 150[7] casualties. The South had beaten the right of First Brigade, "...Moor's soldiers fled frantically into the woods."[6]

Seeing the enemy in flight made the adrenalin flow through the defenders' veins. "The long, lean, and lank Confederate, hair in strings, and tobacco saliva creeping out of both sides of his mouth, was always the equal of the most pampered of the Federal soldiers...He was a dangerous man...."[48] The rout "...seemed to encourage the enemy...with earsplitting yells, made a determined assault upon our whole line."[7] Browne commanded that section of Jones's line. It does not appear that he gave orders to attack but the men themselves "...advancing from their works with yells of triumph, mingled with the derisive cries of 'New Market, New Market',"[11] came over their breastworks.

The Confederate counterattack put Southern soldiers in the open between their breastworks and the hill that had just been taken by the enemy. The North rushed troops to the hill and brought artillery support forward. With more

Union soldiers on the hill and with Dupont's guns, the Southern attack halted and Confederates quickly returned to the relative safety of their breastworks.

During this time, Jones moved from the right of his extended wing toward the action on his left. Soon after the Northern attack halted and the Southern counterthrust ceased, he took command in the sector.

Hunter and his staff watched the action. As the Union line stabilized, they knew that they had struck the main Confederate force. There seemed to be no thought of sidestepping this fight. The enemy's position was only slightly better than their own; with the tremendous advantage they enjoyed in manpower and number of guns, this seemed like a good place to fight. As Hunter knew that this wouldn't be a quick action, he and his staff drew off to a house near the center of the Union line. They headed toward the Shaver house.

The Shavers and their Piedmont neighbors had been making preparations for their unwanted guests. Shaver's son Milton, and Dan Serogham had taken the horses to the woods. At the house, the Shavers, like their neighbors, were hiding valuables, food, and locking doors. At the David Beard place, Belmont in Piedmont, the family was frantically hiding hams and food stuff in the attic and putting other valuables under lock and key. No one noticed that little Gleaves Crockette Beard, age four, had wandered off. When he was missed, panic broke out in the family. Hiding assets from the enemy was forgotten as all members of the family searched for the boy. Attic, hallways, cellar, and yard were searched as the boy's name was screamed above the sound of battle. No boy or reply was evidenced. Finally a family member located the youngster calmly sitting on the fence, "...watching the smoke from the battle."[49]

News was sent to Staunton. Imboden's "...intricate signal system told them shortly after midday...battle was in progress at Piedmont."[6] Some citizens climbed the hills and looked toward Piedmont. They could see the smoke of battle and hear the cannons roar.

As he approached the Shaver house, Hunter ordered his staff to tie their horses behind the house in order not to attract Confederate attention and fire. Upon entering the house, the staff found two terrified women, Shaver's wife Catherine and daughter Mary, "...crying bitterly."[11] Yankee atrocities were already under way, even though the battle was in progress. There were "...some skulkers plundering..."[11] but these skulkers wore Union blue uniforms. "The soldiers were kicked and driven out and the women reassured."[11] Hunter then asked the women where the owner of the property was. He was going to inform the man that the house would be his headquarters during the battle and that the owner was to cause him no inconvenience. The women said that Cornelius Shaver was "...in the cellar with the little children."[11] This appeared to Hunter and his staff to be a complete reversal of roles. The women attempted to defend the house while the head male hid with the children. Hunter "...had him brought out and reviled him for his cowardice."[11] Cornelius was making every effort to uphold his faith and position in his church by avoiding violence. It would make him appear a coward. When Hunter paused in his rebuking, Shaver tried to justify himself as a man of peace, "He said he was a Dunkard preacher...."[11] Furthermore, Shaver added that Hunter shouldn't speak to him that way because he, too, was a "...Union man."[11] After his profession of loyalty to the Union, Hunter seemed to be moved and more open to Shaver. Cornelius, who had bought the farm only ten years before, had worked hard to improve the land. He had planted an orchard several years ago, and only now was he expecting some return from his investment of money and labor. With Hunter's more receptive attitude, Shaver "...begged we would not let our horses bark his apple trees."[11] Hunter and the Union Army had not come to his home for a Sunday picnic. There "...bloody battle was going on with death around and the fate of an army uncertain...."[11] Hunter and his staff were "disgusted"[11] by this apparent coward's request. Staff-Major Daniel H. Harkins "...cursed the fellow and ordered him into the cellar again with his whimpering boys...."[11]Hunter didn't have time to worry about a few fruit trees, this was war; besides he had burned finer homes than this.

Hunter believed the best chance for success lay with another attack on the Confederate left. Neither the open cloverfield nor Jones's left wing with those monster guns seemed to afford much opportunity for victory. Orders were sent to renew the attack.

Union forces which had been beaten back with "heavy loss"[41] in their first attempt on the Confederate breastwork were re-formed and reinforced. The command "Attack" was given, and men in Union blue sprang from the hill crest heading down to the open field between the two hills. Southern cannons and rifles tore into the Union ranks with devastating effect. The soldier whose rifle stock had been shattered by Confederate fire in the first attack now found a bullet hole in his "...tin coffee cup, hanging on my haversack...."[41] There had been two very close calls within minutes. The attack was short lived. The Yankees fell back "...with even greater loss than before."[19]

Field commanders quickly realized that another immediate attack on the South's defensive line would be a waste of fine infantry. They called for increased artillery support. Dupont moved more guns on line and began to pound Confederate positions. One soldier with the One Hundred Sixteenth Ohio recalled that a twelve-pounder (from Von Kleiser's Battery Thirteenth Independent New York Light) was brought on line in their sector. It "...did terrible execution, with solid shot thrown into the enemy's rail breastworks... The demoralization which every shot created in their ranks would be plainly seen; crowds of the enemy fleeing from the spot where a shot struck the rails (then) our infantry would open fire upon them the moment they showed themselves, the guns of the battery also saluting them at the same time with grape and canister."[14]

The two Napoleons of Von Kleiser's Battery between the Eighteenth Connecticut and the Fifth New York about 300 to 500 yards from the Confederate line, did devastating work when they "...blasted holes in the defense, scattering the rails, and driving the Southerners out like bees swarming from a hive."[6]

To counter the Union artillery, Jones sent orders to his artillery to open on the Union artillery on the left. Jones ordered Bryan's and the Boys' Battery to

Re-creation: Union artillery pounding Confederate positions.

Confederates return Union fire from their rail breastworks.

fire on Von Kleiser. Bryan did fire but, "...the ammunition, especially of the Howitzer, was found to be in every way bad...."[30] If that weren't bad enough, the time fuses were malfunctioning. The heat of the gun barrel was enough to detonate some shells in Southern guns. This was dangerous to the gunners and also rained shrapnel down on part of the Sixtieth Virginia "...probably wounding or killing men in the right wing of the Sixtieth Regiment."[30]

The Eighteenth Connecticut had been severely mauled in both attacks on the Confederate left. Jones thought that he saw an opportunity to break through the weakened regiment's line and capture the twelve-pounder that was causing so much trouble. It was only three hundred yards from their line. He launched an attack toward the gun, but the Eighteenth wasn't as cut-up as he supposed. The South was taking casualties as she pressed the attack.

The battle had been raging since dawn, and it was well past noon. In Staunton, the booming of the artillery had been heard for several hours. There were wild tales and speculations circulating. One could hear claims of total

Southern victory or shameful rout. No one had accurate information, but the lack of information didn't stop the effectiveness of the supply depot. Wagons were loaded with supplies and horses fed, watered, and harnessed. They would be ready to move on short notice.

Back at Piedmont, some Southern guns were trying to counter Dupont's increasing artillery fire; and Jones just received word that some Southern men were becoming casualties of their own guns (the Sixtieth Virginia). It was then observed that a "...20-pound Parrot, was sending projectiles turning end-over-end like a stick cast by the hand, would have enfiled the right wing of the regiment..."[30] attacking the twelve-pound Union gun behind the Eighteenth Connecticut.

(End-over-end indicates the boys were firing cylindrical type shells — not round balls. The wind resistance was causing the shells to fall short into the attacking Southerners. The attack faltered and died. The short falling shells only added to their troubles and casualties).

Jones probably concluded (incorrectly) that the casualties in the Sixtieth Virginia on the far right and the short fall of shells on the Southerners attacking on the left were both caused by Capt. J.C. Marquis' Boys' Battery. He transferred command in that section of the line back to Colonel Browne and raced back to the far right. Dupont and his gunners focused their attention on the Confederate right. Bryan's Battery and the Boys' Battery became "...the target of the concentrated fire of 22 cannons, some of them at a very short distance and all of them near enough for very accurate practice with good guns and ammunition."[30] Von Kleiser worked on Bryan while Carlin and Snow worked on Marquis.

Jones arrived during the intense fire. He ordered Bryan's guns moved to the rear. They relocated either down East Road to the wood line and then moved west off the road to a house at the edge of the woods with an open field to their rear: or they may have moved directly through the woods if passage were allowed. Either way their location was bad because the woods allowed little forward view. They located to the west side of a house to shield themselves from Von Kleiser's Napoleons.

General "Grumble" Jones was not known for his sensitivity and cordiality. In this time of crisis all compassion was gone. One can only imagine the verbal barrages Jones must have flung at Captain Marquis and his boys as he told them to get completely off of the battlefield. Most historians agree that Marquis' Battery was "...manned by boys under eighteen without previous experience and consequently ineffective as a unit."[50] Jones probably expressed opinions in stronger terms. Feeling that Marquis' Battery was of no help, but in fact a lethal menace to his other troops, he sent it toward its former commander and organizer, Imboden. So great was the impetus of Jones's squeaky voice and their haste, the soldiers of the battery left piles of shot and shell on the battlefield. They moved down East Road toward Imboden's position and halted with other Home Guard Units and remained near the crossroad "inactive."[6]

Marquis and his boys were humiliated. They knew that Jones was counting on them to anchor the right wing of his line, and counter the Union artillery. They had failed and were disgraced by being sent from the field. They were judged unfit to be on the same field with Southern "men." The transition from boyhood to manhood is difficult at best. Their manhood had been tried and found wanting. (In civilian life, it would be as if they were hired for labor by a neighbor, and he had found them so unqualified as to have driven them from the field and back to their father [Imboden being the father figure]. All of their neighbors [fellow soldiers] knew of their disgrace. Now they were standing idle in an open road for all to see and point at while others fought. It even felt as if the Yankees across that long cloverfield were pointing at them and laughing).

It can be imagined that the boys milled around aimlessly, with heads bowed in disgrace. They scarcely looked toward the battle in which they were not wanted or at one another. If they spoke at all, it was "What did we do wrong?" Some may have tears running down their faces. This only confirmed to the men present that they were still babies and worthy of no place with real men. They lowered their heads even farther to cover their shame. Most, if not all, of those young boys lived and died with that painful memory.

But the pain, shame, disgrace and memory were in no way their fault. "Someone had committed a crime: this beautiful new 20-pound Parrott had been thoroughly tested by Captain Chapman of Chapman's Battery, and it was found to be worse than useless, — a fact obviously unknown to Imboden."[30]

The gun, captured from the Federals, was just too new and too pretty to discard. Somehow the gun had been sent to a Home Guard unit where it may never have been used in combat. It is strange how fate sometimes uses the apparently trifle to undo the mighty. The unanswerable question: what if the gun had worked properly, would the boys be heroes, not the rejected? The boys were not disgraced babies but wrongfully condemned, brave young men.

Dupont's guns were doing their job on Confederate artillery. The Rebs were "...compelled to abandon their position and fall back rather precipitately."[7] One account states that all of the Rebel cannons along Jones's front had been pulled back by 11:30 a.m.[7]

General Hunter had been observing Confederate movements from the Shaver's front porch. When he saw the huge guns of the Boys' Battery being withdrawn, he examined the Confederate right wing again. Without those guns, could he now attack here? There was a small creek somewhat below the Shaver house. By following the creek up the ravine, it may be possible to move troops undetected to the base of the hill below the Confederate right where the Sixtieth Virginia held the line. Hunter ordered the Thirty-Fourth Massachusetts and the Fifty-Fourth Pennsylvania detached from Second Brigade, "Leaving skirmishers in place to mask their intentions...."[7] They were to march to the rear and out of sight of the Confederate line, in a wide swinging move to pass the Shaver house and follow the ravine. With any luck, the South would not detect their movements either off line or up the ravine. Hunter was unaware that Vaughn and Imboden were at the tree line along Cross Road and would have a clear view of the movement up the ravine.

To occupy the Confederates' attention, Hunter ordered another assault on the South's left flank. It is very difficult to fix the time of the attack because accounts either indicate no time or give widely separate times for each attack. It is probable that Moor's First Brigade surged forth against rail breastworks for a third time between 1:30 and 2:00 p.m.

The Rebels had been taking a considerable pounding from Dupont's guns. Not only had the South been compelled to move the artillery support back, thus lessening the effectiveness, but also the Confederate infantrymen had been taking a beating. Solid shot into rail pens turned chunks of wood and splinters into shrapnel. When they were forced to expose themselves, Northern rifles and cannons filled with grapeshot, would tear at the Reb line. Confederate breastworks were being destroyed, casualties taken, and no effective counterfire was being made by Southern artillery.

The South was weakening, but most of the men lying wounded or dead between the lines wore blue uniforms. The soldiers of the First Brigade saw their fellow comrades there, and had no desire to join them. It was a weakened, disheartened First Brigade that was ordered to attack again. Though it had failed twice, now it must try again.

Hunter, too, was discouraged at high losses and no apparent progress, saying, "The Confederate line had reached like a prodded snake to every Federal initiative, lashing out and fighting the attackers to a stand still."[7]

One officer added, "...although the defenses were under constant effective artillery fire the Confederates continued to surge out of the gaps and drive the Federals back."[50]

Jones, who seemed to be everywhere during the battle, apparently arrived as the Union was falling back again. The South once more attempted to take Von Kleiser's Napoleons. There was "...a severe hand-to-hand encounter,"[50] but the South was unsuccessful again. The weakened North had lost many more men and gained nothing. The attack "...was repelled without further efforts to win the battle."[30]

A soldier with the Eighteenth Connecticut recalled: "The enemy's fire was too hot for us, and we were losing many good fellows...The colors went to the ground, the corporal of the color guard, who was carrying them, being shot down. I jumped and picked up the flag, waving it and holding it up."[41]

Jones, upon viewing the results of the third repulse, told his Adjutant General, Captain Walter K. Martin that Hunter was "...desperately beaten...."[45] He only wished there was some way to get word to McNeill's Partisan Cavalry so that McNeill could attack the fleeing Hunter. Jones was sure of victory. He apparently knew nothing of the removal off line of the Thirty-Fourth Massachusetts and the Fifty-Fourth Pennsylvania. The first part of Hunter's plan was working.

Southern morale was boosted. Colonel Beuhring H. Jones, with the Sixtieth Virginia approached General Jones. He requested that one gun be sent to him saying "...he would guarantee to knock out a Federal artillery section at every shot."[6] This pompous offer was too good to turn down. Jones sent orders that one of the inactive guns with Imboden be brought forward. In the confusion of battle, it never occurred.

After the assault there was virtually no infantry contact. The infantry exchanged some shots at a distance, while the artillery continued to pound Confederate positions. There may have been as much as a two or three-hour interval of relatively low activity.

Confederate guns were not as effective, but they did continue firing. Apparently a wild shot still found a mark in the cavalry. Maj. Gen. Julius Stahel was wounded in the arm. A member of Hunter's staff rode off to check on him. A shell fragment had struck the general's arm, and it was much too painful to allow him to ride a horse, but General Stahel refused to transfer command. This cavalry general would direct his troops from the ground.

Besides the bad news that the head of the cavalry division was wounded, the Union staff members received word that their wagon train was on the wrong road. It was heading straight for Staunton and possible capture. Hunter dispatched a courier to the wagon train.

Jones and most of his staff believed that the North would start retreating after the disastrous third attack, but Northern cannon fire still pounded his position and the enemy showed no signs of withdrawal. Jones knew that ammunition was running low in Browne's Second Brigade on the left. The brigade had been attacked three times already. It had taken casualties, and the South could not provide effective counterfire. How many more assaults could it repulse?

Jones decided to withdraw to the original position he had picked on the map the night before. He knew that a partially dug trench line was at Cross Road and East Road. A move back would also allow him to utilize the cavalry under Vaughn and Imboden.

Jones rode back through the woods and located Bryan's Battery near the old house. Bryan's Battery had been firing at a long distance at the enemy, and all but the short-range canister ammunition was exhausted. Jones directed the battery (two guns) to a place "...midway between the East Road and the extreme left of the woods, (but Jones was not happy with this position so he)...conducted them to the extreme left at the north edge of the field or south edge of the woods."[30] They were 300 yards behind Browne's Second Brigade. Jones then told the gunners his plan and their duty: "I am going to withdraw the infantry from these woods to the edge of those (pointing to the woods lying southward of Cross Road) where they will be in line with the dismounted cavalry. You are to remain here, reserve your fire till the movement is made, and enfilade the enemy with canister if they press closely after. Hold your position with confidence: you will be amply protected by infantry."[30]

Jones's plan apparently called for Browne to move off line along the tree line to avoid enemy observation to East Road and then move south to Cross Road and redeploy. Browne was to supply infantry support for Bryan's guns. Browne's men did start moving off line but did not provide Bryan with the promised protection.

While Jones was starting the redeployment, the Thirty-Fourth Massa-

chusetts and the Fifty-Fourth Pennsylvania (now reinforced with a detachment of First New York Cavalry all under Colonel Thoburn) had reached the
creek below the Shaver house. They advanced up the ravine along the creek.
The area was partially wooded. Numbering approximately 800[6] men they
moved "...double quick or rather ran in seemingly disorganized masses when
passing through some cleared places..."[30] to try and avoid detection.

The efforts to move unseen were in vain. Once sighted, the gun crews of
two cannons supporting the right wing behind the Sixtieth turned their
attention and guns on the Yank column. "The first gun (was named)
'Maggie'..."[30] and she spoke to the Federals. After the first few shells came
whistling their way, Union commanders gave orders for the column to hit the
ground in the woods. Because of the contour of the hill and the shielding of the
woods, Confederate gunners could no longer see their target, but kept firing in
the area where the blue-coats were last seen.

Vaughn and Imboden and their men knew that the Yankee column was
there "...the farthest advance men being within musket range of Imboden
from whom they (Southern cavalrymen) were concealed by timber."[6] The
veteran cavalrymen saw the opportunity, and shouted, and begged to be
allowed to attack, but Imboden and Vaughn "...resisted their men's pleas to
dash to the aid of their embattled comrades."[6] The generals had no orders to
do so from the strict Jones. Captain Opie recorded later, "Had Vaughn and
Imboden... attacked half wheel, Hunter (column in the ravines) would have
been surrounded by fire and water...."[20] (Half wheel: using Vaughn's command as the hub, Imboden's line would rotate like a spoke of a wheel toward
the column in the ravine, bringing the cavalry as an organized unit to bear upon
the column). Those Confederate soldiers were veterans of many battles. They
knew a critical point with an easy prey was there. Some individuals and small
groups wanted to leave their line and attack even though there were no orders.
Vaughn and Imboden prevented the attack. Imboden states, "But Vaughn's
orders, like mine, as he informed me that night, were peremptory to take the
position assigned him and hold it till further *orders*."[30] Vaughn and Imboden
had more than twice as many men as the Yank column, "...but these two
geniuses stood by, silent spectators...."[20]

While the Union column in the ravine occupied the attention of Vaughn,
Imboden, and the artillery, Jones was apparently approaching East Road at
the advance of Browne's men from the Second Brigade. Some accounts
erroneously state that Jones knew at this point of the gap between the rear of
the Sixtieth Virginia and Vaughn's line almost a quarter of a mile away. Jones's
words and actions in the next time frame prove that he had no knowledge of
the gap. This provides further evidence that Jones believed the gap was
guarded, and probably guarded by the Home Guard.

Once again fixing a specific time is difficult, but it was probably after 3:00
p.m. Jones, approaching East Road, saw that his cannons were firing in the
wrong direction. They were turned on the Union column in the ravine.
Uncertain as to what was occurring, and where the troops he was leading
might be needed, Jones halted the column and rode quickly toward the

battery.

At the battery, he was told of the Union column. Apparently he and Capt. Thomas Bryan, of the gun crew, moved east of East Road to the edge of the hill which afforded a better view into the ravine. Because of the woods and the fact that the Federals were on the ground, Jones could not get an accurate measure of Union strength. There were approximately 800 Union soldiers, who couldn't be completely concealed. Jones knew that this was far more than a scouting party. With this knowledge, Jones turned to the gunners and said, "Those people are doing us no harm: Fire at that battery in the orchard."[30] The orchard was occupied by Union Second Brigade (weakened by the withdrawal of the Thirty-Fourth Massachusetts and the Fifty-Fourth Pennsylvania). If Jones was aware of the gap and knew that the artillery was keeping the Union from advancing, he would never have turned those guns. Jones and Bryan left their spot of observation, but Jones was to return there one last time, later.

Jones returned with Bryan to the artillery. He felt the artillery could be more effective at a different position. A considerable amount of time was lost in redirecting the guns. The spot Jones first chose would have exposed the guns to almost certain capture. Jones countermanded his order and kept them well inside Confederate lines. The guns then began bombarding Union Second Brigade. It was paramount to Jones that his right wing hold the line so that the men from the left could reach the road and fall back.

Jones, like his cavalry leaders, Vaughn and Imboden, recognized that the Union column was far extended from a protective line. Jones wrote a dispatch to Vaughn and Imboden to attack the column at once. (This gives additional credence to Imboden's assertion that he was to hold his ground unless ordered otherwise). Jones gave the dispatch to a courier named Reuben T. Tanner and sent him racing toward Cross Road.

Once again, if Jones had known of the gap, he would have certainly sent men from Browne's Second Brigade to that point on the line. As it was, men of Second Brigade were milling about. When Jones halted the column to assess the situation, he halted the flow of Second Brigade to East Road and then south. As Browne pulled more and more men from the breastworks and sent them behind First Brigade, they became bunched. Some men moved into the woods; others, into the open between the woods and the rear of First Brigade.

Hunter and his staff, of course, had been observing the Confederate line, and incorrectly interpreted the Rebels' movement. Hunter was sure that Jones had outfoxed him. Jones with a smaller army and less artillery fire was going to win the battle. There was increased artillery fire against Second Brigade. "The troops could be seen moving from behind the more distant works...It became evident that the enemy was massing his whole power in front of Sullivan (Second Brigade) for a decisive attack."[11] It was obvious to Hunter that Jones knew that troops had been pulled away from Second Brigade (the Thirty-Fourth Massachusetts and Fifty-Fourth Pennsylvania which were in the ravine). The First and Twelfth West Virginia and a thin skirmish line from the two removed regiments were all that held the Federal center.

Hunter could visualize hundreds of screaming Confederates charging off their hill and into the weakened Second Brigade. The center could be taken. First Brigade had been mauled in fighting all day, and now it would be cut off on the right by Jones and the left by the river. Panic gripped high command. Hunter ordered the wagon train turned to retreat. The Hundred Twenty-Third Ohio was the guard for the train.

Before conceding defeat and retreating, Hunter decided to make one more attempt. He knew that the Confederate left was now weakened because the troops had been moved to the right opposing his center. Perhaps by moving against the weakened left, and attacking the Confederate right from the ravine, Hunter could snatch victory from the jaws of defeat. If he struck Jones before Jones could attack him, there might be a chance. Time was of the essence, "The critical point of the day had arrived...."[11] A courier was sent toward First Brigade and Colonel Starr from Hunter's staff was sent toward Colonel Thoburn in the ravine.

Because the troops in the ravine were closer to Shaver's house than to First Brigade, they attacked first. "At length Thoburn's columns appeared moving in gallant array across the open field. He crossed the meadow and was rising on the opposite slope before the enemy seemed to notice his movement. Even then only a few shots from the distant battery struck his lines. The shells struck and burst, and the line closed up without confusion or appearance of trepidation....This gallant infantry moved in line and column to its destination, ...the enemy's flank."[11]

The detachment of First New York Cavalry joined the attack from the ravine. "To get under good headway Major Quinn led the regiment off somewhat to the left (away from the Confederate line), then wheeled to the right and bore across a cloverfield toward the woods. To the Confederates in the woods, that long line of horsemen with drawn sabres bearing down upon them, must have been a formidable sight."[9]

Vaughn and Imboden, of course, saw the Federals attacking from the ravine. Imboden said, "...a rapid charge on the left flank of the flanking brigade of the enemy would have at least checked it and given Jones time to charge front to the right and repel it."[50] Even in the face of danger, Vaughn and Imboden adhered strictly to orders and remained in position.

As the attackers struck the rear of the Confederate wing, they gave a great shout. By this time, the First Brigade had received orders on the Confederate left. When the men of First Brigade heard the shout from the hill, they took it up and came pouring over toward the Rebel breastworks for a fourth time. Although Hunter knew the South had pulled men off line, it appears that the Yanks nearest the line didn't know most of their opposition had been withdrawn. Bravely and grimly, they renewed their attacks.

The Confederates attempted to block the attack on their right wing, but there were virtually no defenders on the line. Both Bryan and McClanahan turned their guns toward the ravine, "...but so sudden was the onslaught that only a few shells fell among the Federals."[6] Officers of the Sixtieth Virginia tried to move units completely about to their side and rear in time to meet the attackers. "The attempt to adjust the Sixtieth to this situation led to confusion in that regiment...."[30], reported one officer.

Jones apparently rode toward the commotion. Only now did he discover the unprotected gap. Where were the Home Guardsmen? Jones must have seen them near the intersection of East Road and Cross Road. Jones sped toward them in hopes of bringing them on line before the Northern attack hit. The Home Guardsmen were civilians, not veterans. Unlike the cavalry veterans who begged and cursed to do battle, these men were not anxious to fight. Unlike regular army, they didn't jump when a general spoke; nor did they obey without questioning his orders. Many in the Home Guard reacted as civilians to Jones; many failed to move toward the fighting. Men were being killed there, and they would not rush blindly toward possible death. The men who did follow Jones did so as individuals, not as units; thus only weakened units moved, and precious time was lost.

As the armies collided "...the earth shook with the roar of guns and musketry...."[11] One Union infantryman said that on the Confederate left, "This time we scaled their works...."[14] The Yanks were into Confederate lines. What few defenders were left were shot, bayoneted, made prisoner, or fled. The Federals took possession of the breastworks and then chased the fleeing Rebels.

Back on the Confederates' right wing, the Thirty-Fourth Massachusetts was the first to engage the Rebels, striking the rear of the Sixtieth. Some units of the Sixtieth were ready and met the first two companies of the Thirty-Fourth on the hill to the right of East Road. The Sixtieth poured volley after volley into the two companies and "...within minutes killed nearly sixty of them."[50] A Lieutenant with them said, "In less than five minutes, we lost our major, adjutant, senior captain, and fifty-five men killed or wounded."[7] The company colors fell, but were picked up and advanced. Those two companies of the Thirty-Fourth Massachusetts were in trouble. Three companies of the Fifty-Fourth Pennsylvania and the cavalry were sent to their aid.

The cavalry was of little help because "...between the cloverfield and the woods was a high rail fence...it would be necessary to dismount and take down the fence..."[9] causing it to be delayed. Some Rebs fired at the cavalry from the woods, but "...their firing was wild and high."[9] Corporal Oliver's horse was shot. Captain Jones's horse was also shot and fell on him, pinning his leg. "To get free he had to pull his foot out of his boot and leave the boot there, and he came...with one foot bootless,"[9] noted one soldier.

The plight of the Thirty-Fourth Massachusetts made some Yankees less than courageous about continuing the attack. One cavalryman with the First New York saw the fence that couldn't be jumped and the Rebels firing at them. He decided not to remain a sitting duck and rode away from the battle. Another fleeing infantryman was collared by an officer who demanded to know why he was running the wrong way. The officer said, "You are not wounded." To which the soldier replied, "No, but I am fearfully demoralized!"[9] Another cavalryman was struck in the back, so "he broke from the ranks..."[9] and went looking for a doctor. The doctor examined the trooper and could find no wound. Maybe a bullet had not hit him, but he didn't have to continue the charge.

As the three companies of the Fifty-Fourth Pennsylvania approached the Thirty-Fourth Massachusetts and the fighting, they "...flung themselves on the ground and fired a volley, then charged across East Road into the flank and rear of the Sixtieth Virginia."[6] In the next half hour "...furious and desperate fighting took place."[50] Desperate men in blue, gray, butternut, and tatters went at one another "...with rifles, bayonets, clubs, even bare hands."[6]

While this action was occurring on the right wing, on the left the remnant of the former defenders of the breastworks were streaming south toward Cross Road. The retreat was on. They didn't gather around the two guns of Bryan's section which Jones had directed to the field. Jones had promised adequate infantry protection, but he hadn't provided it. Shortly after the Confederate infantry fled by, "...a strong Federal line of skirmishers appeared on the sky line of the hill in front...."[30] This time a detachment (Fourteenth Pennsylvania under Col. James M. Schoomaker, a crack regiment) of Stahel's Cavalry (dismounted) carrying "Spencer repeating rifles..."[7] joined the infantry attack. To halt the Yanks, the Southern gunners fired one shot of canister (grapeshot) at the blue-bellies. Canister was the only type of ordnance they had left, but "...that one shot betrayed the location of the guns...."[30] Because these guns had been silenced since Jones brought them on the field, Dupont at first was not aware of their presence. Northern guns began to pound the position, but the South could not reply because all it had was short-range ammunition. Somewhat of a stalemate developed on the left. The Northern guns pounded, but Southern guns could not reply, and Northern soldiers could not advance because of Southern guns with canister. Although the situation was grim, it was not completely humorless. One Rebel gunnery sergeant jumped suddenly to one side. Other Rebs laughed because it appeared to them that he had almost jumped into the path of an incoming shell. He replied to their laughter, claiming that he had seen the shell heading straight for him and had jumped out of the way.[30]

Near the intersection of East and Cross Roads, Lt. Carter Berkeley recorded: "General Jones...ordered me to follow him with my section (artillery)...(together) with Harper's and Harman's (Home Guard) Regiments. He proposed to stop the stampede, which was getting serious. How vain the attempt to rush untried soldiers through a stampeding line of battle to check and drive back a victorious line advancing. Old veterans could hardly have stood it. We were soon surrounded by our own flying men, and in sight of the Yankees. (Fewer and fewer Home Guard members continued forward with Jones). Our men began to give way. Jones became desperate, rushed impetuously to the front, followed by many of Harper's men...."[30]

This is a graphic illustration by a member of the Home Guard, showing why Jones would never have used such units as his reserve. Harper's Regiment "...burst into the 34th Massachusetts, killing several men,"[6] but the 34th "...poured a deadly volley into them, killing Jones and many others."[30]

Another account is the following: "There came a burst of firing (from the 34th), and Jones, shouting encouragement, rode toward it, then fell from his horse, shot through the head."[6] Jones fell near the spot where he and Captain Bryan had observed the troops in the ravine and proclaimed, "These people are doing us no harm...." Jones's earthly life of pain and loneliness had ended. An admirer stated that the brave and gallant "Jones was instantly killed...A braver soldier never lived...."[23]

The most contagious war disease, battlefield panic, was now becoming epidemic in Southern ranks. Walter K. Martin, Jones's adjutant general, galloped away from Jones's body, shouting, "General Jones is killed! We have no leader now!"[20]

The Union Army now attacked the "...panic-stricken men."[20] The Southern line "dissolved,"[6] as the "...men broke in panic."[50]

The Yanks on the Confederate left who couldn't advance because of Bryan's two guns loaded with canister, now fell on the panic-stricken right wing. One Confederate reported that the Yankees "...pierced the line at this point, and striking the right flank of our left wing, doubled the line back on itself, resulting in the wildest confusion and great loss to us."[23] Union soldiers "...thrust through the Confederate defenses."[6] "They were again driven back with slaughter...decimated by withering fire kept up by these cold-blooded Federals...."[45] Some Southerners didn't run in panic but continued "...loading and firing as they fell back...."[45]

It was clear to all observers that the Federals were winning. Union non-combatants cheered their side on. "Stretcher men, ambulance drivers, wounded men, butchers, bummers, and all took up the shout...Negroes, teamsters, and camp followers re-echoed the joyful shout...hearty cheers rose with the smoke and sounded like victory."[11]

The Union troops on the field, encouraged, continued pressing the Rebels. The First New York Cavalry followed the infantry as it attacked. This is what a cavalryman saw: "Behind the rail and earth entrenchments was a long line of dead men lying two, three and four deep. In places this line had been set on fire, and bodies were partly consumed. All through the woods the dead and wounded were lying."[9] "Union and Rebel dead (were) being found side by side all over the field."[9]

The disaster only intensified. To add to the South's trouble, second in command to Jones, Colonel Browne was wounded in the thigh and could no longer command.

The Southern infantry was now truly leaderless. The regular Confederate infantry soldiers saw their lines dissolving and recognized that they were being surrounded. Sergeant Fountain Shackleford of Co F, Thirty-Sixth Virginia saw the lines crumbling. He shouted to Lt. Patrick Duffy, "Pat, are you going to leave us here to be captured, while the rest of the command is seeking safety by retreating." With the situation hopeless, "Duffy...ordered each man to take care of himself."[51] Part of the Thirty-Sixth fled the field. For others the only option was surrender or death.

One soldier recalled: "I saw streams of greybacks and butternuts passing from the woods at a double-quick guarded by cavalrymen with drawn sabres. The cheers redoubled as the squads of captives continued to stream across the

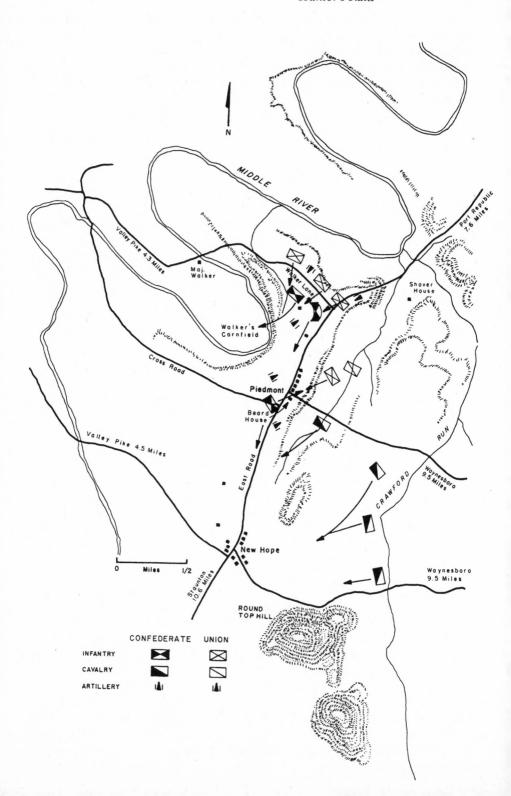

open ground to our rear...."[11] At points there were too many surrendering Rebels for the Yanks to handle. The Confederates were disarmed and told to go to the rear and find someone to surrender to.

Other individuals saw a chance to escape through the gap between First Brigade and the Union thrust that started in the ravine. They ran toward Bryan's guns. Men with the Fifty-Fourth Pennsylvania saw these running Rebs. They gave chase, firing as they went. Many Rebs fled for safety south to Cross Road; others went over the high river bank, and "...some plunged over the cliff into the Middle River...."[50] Hunter said he was "...crushing his (Jones's) whole line and driving a portion of his forces over the steep bank into the river...."[8]

Bryan's gunners did not know that Jones was dead, but they saw the rout and concluded "...the day was lost."[30] Disobeying their last order, they limbered up the guns and "...started at a gallop..."[30] southwestwardly to Cross Road. The Southern infantrymen threw down guns and equipment, some jumping off the "...cliff into Middle River and then racing across the cornfield in the river loop."[6] The Fifty-Fourth Pennsylvania took a great many prisoners on the bluff and fired at the Rebs running through the cornfield. "One man told me there was corn in the bottom (of Dr. B.F. Walker's farm) nearly waist high, and the bullets cut the corn like hail and one bullet hit his canteen."[44] These Rebs continued running toward Staunton. Some units near the center marched "...in an orderly and undisturbed manner and joined Vaughn's Regiment."[6]

The Home Guard was having no better luck trying to form and hold a line against the Union onslaught. Jones was dead, and it had no leader. Lt. Monroe Blue, Company K, a West Pointer, recognized the rout. In order to slow the Yankees and let other Home Guard units escape, he tried to establish a skirmish line. He was shot through the neck and died instantly. Another Home Guard company commander Capt. Robert Doyle was "...shot through the head, the ball entering the cheek and coming out at the base of the skull. He was perfectly conscious after receiving this wound...(and) was set against a tree by his men...."[45]

A few Home Guard units continued to fight. One member stated: "The more experienced soldiers said (that) the raw troops did not know when they were whipped and kept on fighting when they should retreat."[43] The well-trained, well-equipped Federals were too much, the Home Guard took casualties and joined the rout. Wounded Captain Doyle was bayoneted to death under the tree.

East Road was jammed with fleeing soldiers, with horses, wagons, and cannons. The residents no longer cheered their boys on, but most took refuge in the cellars.

Dupont's guns had done well all day. They continued to sling lead at the routed Rebels. Some houses in Piedmont were damaged by Yankee fire.

As the gunners searched for targets away from the former lines, (their own soldiers were now in Confederate lines) one gunner spotted a prime target on Cross Road — the Boys' Battery. Union cannon quickly found the range. The beautiful but worthless twenty-pound Parrott "...was put out of action by a solid shot which bent the axle, making it impossible to move...."[30] The barrel of the gun weighed 1,983 pounds and the carriage 1,000 pounds.[30] The Union would reclaim its gun.

Reuben Tanner, Jones's courier to Vaughn and Imboden could not locate either general due to the confusion. Vaughn and Imboden remained, "silent spectators," to the holocaust. Vaughn and Imboden felt compelled by Jones's orders not to attack and refused their men's anguished cries to aid their brothers in uniform. News of Jones's death, like the battlefield panic, spread fast. After learning of Jones's death, Vaughn and Imboden "...at last felt at liberty to act."[30]

Vaughn was now nominally the head of the army, but because of his lack of knowledge of the terrain he deferred most command decisions to Imboden. Because Imboden was, in fact, the commander and because "...their troops (cavalry) had not been engaged in the battle..."[20] Imboden came under severe criticism after the battle and especially after the war.

There was a period after the war when certain Southern generals claimed that they could have singlehandedly won the war if a certain Southern general had acted gallantly. There was much criticism and much distortion of the facts. One writer said that Imboden and Vaughn simply "...rode off without making any attempt to renew the struggle or check the enemy."[20] That statement tantamounts to accusing Imboden of incompetency, cowardliness, and murder.

Imboden saw the fine Northern infantry mauling and routing the Home Guard. East Road was clogged with "...Confederate wagons and horses ...entangled in a muddled traffic snarl. Shouts of drivers, blasts of bugles, and the rumble of wagon wheels could be heard afar."[6] Imboden was also aware that Northern gunners could train their guns on his sector because of the barrage unleashed on the Boys' Battery. If Imboden were to offer aid to the routed Home Guard, he could not use East Road to move forward. The only way to the collapsing front was through the knee-high clover which would provide no protection from Union cannons for his cavalry. His units would have been cut up and disorganized, thus useless in blocking the Northern infantry advance. Even if he could have moved his mounted cavalry completely unmolested between the Home Guard and the Yankee infantry, the cavalry would have only been a bone to be chewed by the Federals. Firing from a moving horse is an "ify" proposition at best. The infantry firing with somewhat longer barreled, more accurate rifles from the stationary ground would have cut the Southern cavalry to shreds.

Most of the Southern artillery had by now been drawn off the field. Some of the horses that were wounded in battle were replaced by those from Southwest Virginia. Thus Imboden would have no artillery protection. He suggested to Vaughn that they move south to Mowry's Hill and fight again. If the infantry and the artillery with full powder wagons couldn't stop Hunter, how would the cavalry with little artillery support do it? Vaughn decided that they must retreat, and Imboden made the decision to move toward Waynesboro. Not wishing to expose the cavalry to enemy fire, Imboden didn't move eastwardly over Cross Road; instead he gave orders for both cavalry outfits to move south across country to the road heading east toward Waynesboro below New Hope community. The cavalry did not fire a single shot during the main battle. It was now past 5:00 p.m. and the rout was well in progress.

Other than the disabled twenty-pounder, the only two (recorded) guns left on the field were the two of Bryan's section. Jones had posted them on the far left to cover his redeployment. They had started off the field at a gallop when they saw the army collapsing. Their flight was not a smooth one. After a team horse was wounded, an officer dismounted, and his mount was used to pull the gun, but "before the guns had gone twenty paces, a singletree was shattered."[30] It is unclear if enemy fire caused it to break or if one of the rapidly fashioned singletrees made at Staunton had given way. The gunners rigged the trace lines directly to the splinterbar and the gun was brought off the field. The guns were brought to Cross Road and headed west toward Staunton. The guns had only started to Staunton when a cavalry major halted the artillery section. The guns were unlimbered and faced toward the battlefield, pointing up Cross Road. The artillery was situated on a bluff to provide coverage for the fleeing remnants of the army. No clear target could be seen in the distance, and the unit was unaware that a Federal infantry unit was very close to its position. The Yanks started climbing the bluff and were not more than twenty feet[30] away when they were discovered. No record was found of an exchange of rifle fire at this point, and the Confederate cannons quickly limbered up and continued toward Staunton. As the unit crossed Middle River and started upgrade, it encountered a wagon load of wounded Confederate officers standing in the road. One of the team's horses had been wounded and the wagon halted. A sergeant with the artillery outfit dismounted and hitched his personal horse to the wagon. Then running about one half mile with his saddle on his back, he overtook his unit. The artillery continued unmolested to the macadamized road, Valley Pike, toward Staunton.

The last unit to draw off the field was the Niter and Miner Corps, which followed Imboden's Cavalry.

During the time between the attack that broke the Confederate line and the rout, it became apparent that Stahel's arm wound was too grave to allow him to command further. Hunter placed Col. Andrew T. McReynolds in command of the cavalry. With the Southern collapse, Hunter realized that fast moving cavalry might bag the rest of the fleeing Southern infantry. (Hunter never knew that Vaughn and Imboden were at the battlesite). McReynolds set the cavalry in motion toward Cross Road. Southern soldiers were cut off from retreat. One soldier said, "The cavalry followed in swift pursuit, gathering in prisoners and capturing guns...."[9] The cavalry attack may have been one composed of as few as two hundred men.[50] Imboden referred to it as a "demonstration."[23] Despite its size, it was doing effective work on the fleeing infantry. "...Rout and panic became universal, save among the artillery...(all the way to New Hope) was choked with broken infantry, reserves, cavalry, wagon, etc."[45] The Northern cavalry charge carried through Piedmont and down the road toward New Hope.

Lt. Carter Berkeley of McClanahan's Battery became aware of the Federal cavalry's onslaught. He had the fence along East Road broken down. He and Lt. H.H. Fultz placed their six guns in the wheatfield on the west side of East Road about three hundred yards south of the woods between Piedmont and New Hope. Imboden, too, was aware of the cavalry charge and Berkeley's defensive measure. He moved his brigade and about seventy-five to eighty of Vaughn's Tennesseans toward the guns to protect them.

Soon the Yankee cavalry came out of the woods southeast of the Dunkard Church. It was interested in bagging even more Southern prisoners. There were cannons but few if any of Imboden's men were there to form a line. As the Union troopers emerged from the woods, they formed a skirmish line to the right and the left.

The Southern guns were charged with canister. The Union horsemen galloped forward. Many fleeing Southern soldiers were trapped between the attacking cavalry and Berkeley's guns. Berkeley realized that fellow Southerners in the middle would be torn apart by grapeshot intended for the Yanks. Those men would be sacrificed to halt the Union charge.

"Fire!" shouted Berkeley, but nothing happened. Rebel gunners could not bring themselves to fire on their own men. Berkeley "sprang from his horse and fired the cannon himself, the discharge of grape and canister which annihilated an entire squadron of cavalry."[20] The other Southern cannons cut loose: "...the guns plowed wide gaps in their ranks, hurling horses and riders to the ground."[45] The Northern cavalry was attacking the hapless Rebels between the lines "...sabring men right and left."[45] The Southern cannon fire was too much. Records show that "there ensued a tangle of bodies, falling horses, horseless riders fleeing, the cavalry seeking refuge...."[6] After "suffering heavy losses (it) fell back...."[50] The cavalry retreated toward the woods. Apparently Imboden's and Vaughn's cavalries had not arrived upon the scene in much strength. The Northern cavalry commander saw an opportunity. Instead of concentrating on the few Rebs left between the lines, the cavalry would attack directly upon the guns.

The Federal cavalry re-formed. Some of Imboden's men were moving near the guns.

"Charge!" The Union moved forward a second time. This time dismounted Confederate cavalrymen fired from the right and "...brought down such numbers of the horsemen that the regiment retreated...(Berkeley's) well directed guns continued to scatter death in the Federal ranks...."[45] The Yanks "...receive (d) another severe raking...."[50] The Northern cavalry retreated through the woods toward safety at Piedmont.

The Union cavalry had been "...devastated. Mighty limbs were torn from trees...clover and wheat...trampled."[6] Imboden asked Berkeley how long he thought he could maintain his position. He replied, "...permanently."[6] Berkeley wanted to continue the fight, but he received orders to retreat. Berkeley did retreat, apparently taking some Union prisoners with him.

Col. Sturgis Davis ordered Opie's company to the church to form a line to cover the retreat. Davis ordered Opie "...to hold, at all hazard, and against all comers."[20] Davis tried to halt the panic-stricken fleeing Confederates still coming from Piedmont. Though he "...begged, swore at, and threatened them..."[20] few joined the defensive line.

The cavalry and artillery drew off unmolested. Opie's punie defensive line was an empty threat, a threat that was not challenged further. In fact, Chief-of-Staff Strother urged Hunter to pursue with vigor, but said, "The worthlessness of our cavalry was probably what induced the general to content himself with the affair as it stood."[11] Dupont also added, "...its pursuit of the enemy was very feeble...."[47] Obviously, neither man had accurate information of the encounter between Berkeley's guns and the Union cavalry. They knew nothing of the great gallantry their cavalry had shown and the high casualty rate. Even if Hunter had realized the lack of resistance the South could offer, he had no organized body of troops to move forward. He recorded, "...If the pursuit had been more vigorous it would have been far worse for us."[23] The hacking of sabres and report of rifle decreased, as the length of late evening shadows increased. The day and the battle belong to history.

The sound of battle was gone, but other sounds filled the evening air. There was the rush of feet as Confederate soldiers ran for their lives in all directions in an attempt to avoid death or capture. There was the gallop of horses' feet as Union cavalrymen gathered in prisoners. Cavalrymen "...brandishing drawn sabres..."[6] marched prisoners to Hunter's battlefield headquarters, the Shaver house. According to one witness, "The Yankees took them down in our field and built a rail pen around about an acre and put them in it."[44] There were approximately nine hundred[6] captured Rebs. Wynkoop's Cavalry was assigned to guard the prisoners. The cavalrymen "shouted taunts"[6] at the defeated Rebs. They also inspected the prisoners to see if any could be identified as members of Moseby's or McNeill's Rangers. They considered the rangers outlaws, not soldiers. Any they caught might be shot. The Shavers had been awakened the night before by Confederate cavalrymen; tonight Federal cavalrymen would camp about their place and watch the prisoners.

CONFEDERATE PRISONERS.

By David Hunter Strother.

A Confederate prisoner demanded a personal meeting with Union General Hunter. Presently, he and a companion were brought into the commander's presence. The prisoner introduced himself as Capt. Boyd Faulkner of Martinsburg, (W) Virginia. He claimed kinship with Hunter. When he learned that Col. David Hunter Strother, Hunter's Chief-of-Staff was also present; he remarked, "What, Colonel Strother, are you here, too?"[11] Faulkner soon learned that kinship and heritage meant little to Hunter, who "...was curt and hardly civil,"[11] and soon ordered his Rebel kin back to imprisonment.

Hunter had received reports that the Rebel General Jones, was dead. He sent Strother to check them out. Hunter then ordered a cavalry detachment be sent toward Staunton to provide intelligence on Confederate troop strength and intentions. Next, he ordered the army to camp on the battlefield and then moved his headquarters to a small cottage in the village of Piedmont. He also ordered the Signal Corps to get the news back to Beverly and the telegraph line. Then the whole Union Army would know of his glorious victory.

During the day at Staunton, there had been many rumors and much speculation on the course of the battle. It was near dark when a Rebel scout arrived with definite word that the battle was lost and Staunton would fall. Col. Edwin G. Lee, Commander of Staunton, ordered the remaining quarter-master supplies be loaded on the wagon train, carrying salt, leather, ammunition, and other military supplies. Lee had office papers, bank valuables, records, stores and other non-military goods loaded on the railroad cars. The railroad train was then sent via Charlottesville towards Lynchburg.

Near dark, Opie's Home Guard near New Hope drew off toward Waynesboro.

The evening air reverberated the anguished cries of the wounded and the dying. Amid the pain, Union soldiers dined. Many didn't even have a cup of coffee for breakfast. "We were under fire from 7 a.m. to 5 p.m. Sorrow came to us over our loss (killed and wounded), but we must have something to eat in order to keep up,"[18] wrote one soldier.

Most soldiers could rest, but Union doctors, assistants, stretcher bearers, and grave diggers would be busy throughout the night. Apparently the Middle River Church of the Brethern was used as a Union hospital, but it was soon filled to capacity and field tents were used. Most Confederate wounded were treated last and housed in field tents. Rank still had its privilege even for the defeated, wounded enemy. Col. William Browne, Jones's second in command was moved to Hunter's old headquarters, the Shaver house, for treatment. He had been shot in the upper thigh and apparently bled profusely. Unlike other Confederate wounded who were bedded on the ground, Browne had a soft feather bed. A hook may have been placed in the ceiling so that a rope hoist could be used to elevate the leg and decrease the bleeding.

Many Northern soldiers "...wandered over the field seeking trophies... some stopped to dress wounds of fallen Confederates."[6]

As a Union soldier was returning from Middle River where he had gone to fill his canteen he came upon a wounded Rebel. He reported: I "Bathed his wound on his foot with the water from my own canteen. He thanked me kindly as he lay on the ground, patiently waiting for his turn to be cared for."[18]

Not all were that lucky. One Union soldier reported on the suffering: "A wounded man lying by the side of a tree wished to change his position so that he could partly sit up...A Union soldier helping him observed that the wounded man's leg did not turn as the man himself turned. The leg, broken at the thigh, was limp and helpless...death came over him...One was lying on his back with a bullet hole in his forehead. 'That poor fellow never knew what hurt him,' said one standing by him. The supposedly dead man opened his eyes and looked at the speaker as if he had heard the remark and was conscious of his condition, but could not speak. The woods were full of such sights."[9]

Dupont saw the effect his artillery had "...by the terrible mangled condition of a great number of the Confederate dead..."[47] but he was happy to learn that his artillery fire had hurt few civilians.

EFFECT OF BATTERIES.
By David Hunter Strother.

One Union lad gathered blankets to take to the hospital to cover his company's wounded. He said, "It was a sickening sight to me. No more desire to visit a field hospital after a battle."[18] That night the Yankees camped with the "dead and wounded around us."[18]

The Confederates established a hospital at the Methodist Church in New Hope. The floor was blood-stained for over a hundred years.

The sound of shovels continued throughout the night. Notations of soldiers' graves were made so that relatives could possibly remove the corpses for reburial. Confederate Maj. W.C. Sanders had his place reserved. He "...was shot though the chest and consigned to a burial party."[6] He was discovered to be alive moments before his scheduled interment.

Sanders stated he "...was shot through just above the heart with a minie ball...was laid out...in a Mr. Crawford's yard and left there...Mr. Crawford poured nearly half a pint of whiskey in (Sanders), which produced a reaction and revived him."[52]

Teenager, Milton Shaver, summed it up: "I can't forget the suffering soldiers."[44]

Hunter was not the only one who had heard reports that Rebel General Jones was dead. The "grapevine" had informed a common soldier and curiosity seekers found Jones before Strother did. The soldier stated: "We saw his body in the woods a short distance behind the works with a bullet hole through his forehead."[14] Another stated: "He had the appearance of having been an intellectual and cultured gentleman."[9] Yet another stated: "In a short time, every button was cut off the coat for souvenirs and the clothing was searched for official documents."[6]

Some papers were taken by a cavalryman to Hunter.

Strother recorded, "I found a crowd around a body coarsely clothed in a dirty grey suit without any military trappings or insignia about it. He had on a pair of fine military boots well worn and fine woolen underclothes perfectly clean and new. His hands were small and white, and his features, high white forehead, brown beard, and long hair indicated the gentleman and man of the upper class. I concluded that this was truly the body of the General."[11]

While Strother was still near the body, "four Rebel prisoners came with a stretcher to carry the body to burial under the orders of the Provost Marshal."[11] Each of the Confederate prisoners identified the body as being that of General Jones. A further search of the pockets yielded a letter to Jones from Imboden and a memorandum showing Confederate troop strength to be 7,000 men and 16 guns. This was proof enough for Strother, who took the papers with him to report to Hunter.

Looting had begun before the battle occurred at the Shaver house. Now that the battle was over, looting had intensified. All the homes in the area were searched for food and valuables. Many of the residents saved goods by hiding them. Many years after the battle, Mr. Reegan re-visited the battlefield where he was a Pennsylvania soldier of age sixteen years.

At David Beard's house, he recounted this story: He was part of the group that "plundered"[49] the house. The Yanks burst in and ransacked the home. They missed the hams that were hidden in the ceiling over their heads. It was discovered that the cellar was locked and no one could find a key. In their haste and with their wanton disregard of personal property, they decided to chop a hole in the hall floor to gain entrance to the cellar. As soon as the hole was large enough, an impatient young officer without the aid of a candle or lantern, decided to drop himself through the hole. Boy, was he ever going to soak those people for their goods, but he was the one who got soaked. Splash! He fell into a vat of soft soap. He fumed, sputtered, and spit in his fit of anger, while no doubt, his comrades laughed.

After they were looted, the homes of the Beards, the Shavers and both

Walkers (Dr. B.F. and Maj. James), and the McCue home across Middle River were used as hospitals. Other field hospitals were opened both north and south of the battlefield.

General Hunter and his staff "...had a good supper and a triumphant evening,"[11] for the Federals had "...a clear cut victory...,"[6] in the Valley. "Verily they had wiped out the disgrace of New Market."[11] "The Eighteenth Connecticut exulted at its first triumph...,"[6] although about one third of the unit was killed or wounded.

Many men recalled their personal victories of the day. General Sullivan received "...a very complimentary letter..." from Hunter, himself. Sullivan had three horses shot from under him "...and won laurels for gallantry... The bands played and the men sang and shouted,"[11] and the good news kept coming.

A Union wagon train following Hunter did not turn toward Piedmont but continued unprotected toward certain capture at Staunton. That night Hunter received word that his couriers had reached the supply train and turned it away from danger. There was more good news: The cavalry force which Hunter had sent toward Staunton returned. Lt. Edward Muhleman reported that he had "...been nearly at Staunton..."[11] and found no Confederate defense works or organized troops. The town was wide open to invasion. Hunter reorganized the army for the march on Staunton in the morning. It is no wonder that Strother could write, "The army was intoxicated with joy."[11]

While the Union Army celebrated victory, the Confederate Army started picking up the pieces. Vaughn and Imboden were retreating toward Waynesboro. Most of the artillery, including the Boys' Battery, were on the same road. Units, remnants of units, and individuals followed the cavalry or made their way toward Staunton, either directly south over East Road via Mowry's Hill or Cross Road to Valley Pike, and then south to Staunton. Many soldiers simply ran in any direction leading from the battlefield. They rested in houses, barns, or fields as darkness and fatigue overtook them.

In Staunton the word spread like wild fire: "General Jones is killed and our army is routed!"[43] The citizens knew that Staunton was Hunter's next target. Many people left town immediately.

The Southern Army "...came pell-mell into Staunton..."[43] and so did information and rumors. The two guns of Bryan's section made it to Staunton. A cavalryman came via Mowry's Hill and said "...he had seen the rest (of the artillery) captured by Federal cavalry."[30] Since most of the men folk of Staunton were at Piedmont, their relatives hung on every word, whether fact or fiction. Capt. Robert L. Doyle, Harvey Bear, and John W. Meredith were reported killed; many others were reported killed, wounded, or captured. There was anguish in the hearts of the people of Staunton that night.

The telegraph clicked, and the South became aware of defeat. In Richmond, officers and high government officials were awakened and conferences held. General Lee was informed. Some people in Lynchburg had been following the events with no particular alarm until now. The Yankees had been attempting to invade the Valley since the first of the war and had always been turned back. Now there was a real possibility that Lynchburg itself might be attacked.

Some reports said that Vaughn got a courier through to the quartermaster at Staunton, ordering the wagon train be sent to him at Waynesboro. It is more likely that town commander, Col. Edwin Lee, acted on his own authority. If the order came from Vaughn, then the most logical and quickest route would be directly east to Waynesboro. Lee didn't know Vaughn's position or intentions; the wagon train headed south over the Greenville Road. The safety of the wagon train was Lee's primary motive. The train made it to Smith's Tavern "...long after dark."[43] It would rest there until morning. The tired men and horses with the two guns of Bryan's section elected to try and link-up with Vaughn and Imboden. They moved directly east toward Waynesboro, not stopping until after midnight.

After the wagon train left, Colonel Lee distributed some food stuffs from the supply depot. As there was no room for it on the wagons and there was no reason to let it remain for the Yankees, he gave it away to the townspeople.

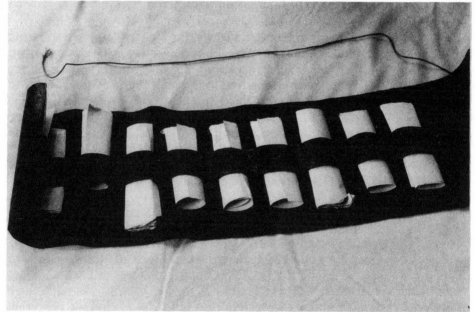

Gen. William E. "Grumble" Jones's leather field records file — probably used at Battle of Piedmont. Courtesy: Southern Comfort Antiques Collection, Bristol, Va.

View of Shaver house — Piedmont.

Shaver's smokehouse — holes remain where Union soldiers used bayonets in vain attempts to force door open.

Shaver house — bedroom and maybe bed where Col. William H. Browne died — Piedmont.

Prayer book and comb of Col. William H. Browne — Piedmont.

"Belmont" home of David Beard — Piedmont.

From battlefield at Piedmont.

Projectiles and fuses from Piedmont battlefield.
Courtesy of Doyle & Ester (Beard) Howdyshell.

It can easily be seen that the Union "...had dealt the Confederate Army a smashing blow...."[7] There are numerous statistics but no authoritative count known.

Union Losses (Aggregate)

Source:
Conquest of a Valley — Brice   Vaughn estimates 1,500 killed, wounded, and captured.
                                       Hunter estimates 500 killed.
                                       Brice estimates 150 killed, 650 wounded, 75 missing.

History of Augusta County
Virginia — Peyton   "Loss" 250 (assumed killed)

"The Shenandoah in Flames"
Time Life Books — Lewis   420 killed

The Shenandoah Valley in
1864 — Pond   420 killed

A History of the Lynchburg
Campaign — Humphreys   500 killed

Civil War Times Illustrated
"The Battle of Piedmont" — Kimball   500 killed "...but that is likely conservative."

Untitled manuscript — Shaver   800 plus (killed and wounded).

From "...official reports and semi-official documents...

Unit	Killed	Wounded
Eighteenth Connecticut	19	103
Twenty-Eight Ohio	33	105

Thirty-Fourth Massachusetts	13	97
Fifty-Fourth Pennsylvania	2	29
One Hundred Sixteen Ohio Volunteer Infantry	54	127
Fifth New York Artillery (Infantry)	6	28
First New York (Veteran) Cavalry	12	9

Add forty 'slightly wounded' to the Fifty-Fourth Pennsylvania."[6]

Northern cavalry losses after the initial battle at Piedmont, may not be included in the figures.

General Julius Stahel was among the wounded.

A detailed and accurate account of the One Hundred Sixteenth Ohio Volunteer Infantry shows the Northern casualties might have far exceeded the foregoing source estimates.

Forty-one men were killed outright and thirteen died of their wounds shortly afterwards, and an additional 127 were wounded. "Every color bearer and every one of the color guard were wounded, some of them seriously."[14]

Killed — Company A	Nathaniel D. Hayden
	Addey Brock
	Jacob Zimmerly
	Elijah Bennett
	Newton Meeks
Killed — Company B	Sylvester C. Shumway
Killed — Company C	Fred F. Neptune
	John Latchaw
	George W. Gannon
	Henry Pfeifer
	Isaac Barrett
	Robert E. Chambers
	James B. Mobberly
	Corp. Adam Rodecker
Killed — Company D	John Detwiler
	Robert H. H. Dryer
	Elias B. Brock
	Joseph Seimons
	Samuel Alford
	Henry B. Hixenbaugh
	Richard Mahoney
	Washington Bryan
	Scott Dixon
	Corp. Robert Armstrong
Killed — Company E	Moses McCulloch
	Frances Swarts
Killed — Company F	Morris Krouse
	Garrison Miracle
	George W. Johnson

	James F. Hughes
	Richard Phillips
	Joshua Mercer
	William Sutton
	Corp. William King
Killed — Company H	Stephen C. McCoy
	James Harrison
	Solomon Rich
Killed — Company I	Frederick Warren
	Corp. Richard B. Miller
Killed — Company K	Edward Henshaw
	Nelson B. Clements
Wounded — Company A	Jacob C. Keyler
	James Kimpton
	David Barcus
	Cyrus Spriggs
	Samuel Tidd
	Robert McCammon
	Robert Smith
	John Smythe
	John A. Harmon
	Albert Gates
	James C. Hall
	Serg. Mann Smith
	Corp. Fred R. Rose
	Corp. William Brock
	Serg. Daniel C. Hunt
	Corp. Benjamin F. Dye
Wounded — Company B	Marion Coleman
	George W. Keyes
	John Baker
	John Anderson
	Wells Grubb
	Davis Watson
	John Doland
	Serg. Uriah Hoyt
	Serg. William H. Bush
Wounded — Company C	George Kistner
	Thomas South
	William Metz
	Elwood Chambers
	John Buchwald
	John J. Montgomery
	James A. Presbaw

Edward Yockey
Philip Schoupe
Albert Vickers
Franklin Barnes
Miles H. Davis
Riley Thornburg
Emmon H. Beardmore
Serg. Matthew W. Maris
Serg. John S. Heald
Serg. John L. Beach
Color Serg. David K. Barrett
Corp. John G. Barrett

Wounded — Company D William T. Flowers
Charles W. Blowers
Josiah Norris
James C. Headly
Henry B. Hixenbaugh
James A. Sinclair
John H. Windland
John W. Hall
Jacob Hall
Eldridge Moffitt
Daniel Bennett
Henry Mowder
Hugh Thompson
Samuel Forsyth
Jessee M. Stine
Joshua Nixon
Peter Hickman
Alfred Gray
Peter Schultz
Thomas Rowley
David Conger
Lt. Richard T. Chaney
Serg. James K. Drum

Wounded — Company E Ephraim Henthorn
Madison G. Miller
Harrison Cochran
Charles Palmer
William Fisher
Joseph A. Hall
Corp. James Skiles
Corp. Lewis Barcus
Corp. John J. Atkinson

Wounded — Company F   William Sutton
                       James Carson
                       Elijah Bunting
                       Samuel Stephens
                       Jacob Dillon
                       Joseph Rake
                       Wesley McGee
                       Thomas Patterson
                       Emanuel Okey
                       James Piggott
                       Lempenious Efaw
                       Serg. Stephen A. Brown
                       Corp. Robert Martin

Wounded — Company G   Alexander McFarland
                       John Rawlings

Wounded — Company H   Nathaniel Butler
                       David Bock
                       Dighton M. Bates
                       William T. Cain
                       John A. Groven
                       John Wesley James
                       John W. Knockley
                       John H. Keyser
                       Eki T. Kirkbride
                       John Larrick
                       John W. Mott
                       William McBride

                       Andrew Powell
                       Simon Sechrist
                       Thomas Spear
                       Reason Baker
                       James Dudley
                       Capt. W. B. Teters
                       Serg. Joseph Purkey
                       Serg. Benjamin C. Drake
                       Color Serg. Reese Williams
                       Serg. William A. Arnold
                       Corp. Benjamin B. Tilton
                       Corp. Jacob Gregg
                       Corp. Joseph C. Wilson

Wounded — Company I   Joseph Morrison
                       Jesse Annon
                       Bradley P. Barrows
                       Luther Cayton
                       Samuel P. Fleak

Ephriam W. Frost
Consider Frost
James H. Gilehrist
Jonathan C. S. Gilbert
Nathan Hatch
Mark W. McAtlee
Samuel McCulloch
Elijah Patton
Rufus B. Stanley
George W. Tasker
Serg. John C. Chick
Corp. Edwin G. Fuller
Corp. Fayette Paugh
Wounded — Company K   Samuel Spencer
John Kulow
Thomas Witham
George Lyon
Andrew C. Cagg
Lt. Gottlieb Sheifley

(Dupont reported his personal Battery "B" Fifth U.S. Artillery fired 801 times during the battle).

Confederate (Aggregate)

Source:
"Shenandoah in Flames"
Time Life Books — Lewis   Approximately 600 killed and wounded; over 1,000 prisoners.

*The Shenandoah Valley in
1864* — Pond   Prisoners 1,000 plus (includes 60 officers) additional 400 sick and wounded taken prisoner on June 6, 1864, three guns, many small arms.

*The Lynchburg
Campaign* — Humphrey   Approximately 1,500 killed, wounded, captured.

Civil War Times Illustrated
"The Battle of Piedmont" — Kimball   Approximately 1,500 killed, wounded, captured; more than 1,000 small arms, no artillery.

Conquest of a Valley — Brice	Hunter reported 600 killed and wounded, 1,000 captured, and 1,000 more captured "...from straggling and desertion." Vaughn estimates 1,000 captured; 60 wounded on field; 1,000 small arms; no artillery. Brice estimates 1,500 killed, wounded and captured.
The First New York (Lincoln) Cavalry — Beach	1,500 captured; 3 cannons, 3,000 small arms.
The Annals of the War "Fire, Sword, and the Halter" — Imboden	1,500 killed, wounded, captured.
The Campaign of 1864 in the Valley of Virginia and the Expedition to Lynchburg — Dupont	600 killed and wounded; 1,000 captured including 60 officers.
Untitled — Shaver	800 men (assumed) killed and wounded "...many men taken prisoner."

Some Unit Figures:

Thirty-Sixth Virginia Infantry Regiment — 29 dead, 36 wounded, 112 captured.

(Company F took over 30% casualties). "Piedmont had claimed more lives from the regiment than any battle had before or any would subsequently."[51]

Niter and Miners Corps Battalion — 18 wounded, 9 killed.[6]

Forty-Fifth Virginia Infantry Regiment — 450 killed, wounded, captured.[30]

Harper's Reserves (Home Guard) — 52 killed and wounded.[6]

Individuals Killed:

Brigadier General William Edmondon "Grumble" Jones
Lt. Col. Robert L. Doyle
Maj. Richard Brewer
Harvey Bear — Home Guard, Augusta County

From the Thirty-Sixth Virginia Infantry Regiment —

Lieutenants	Thomas Jarrell — Jacob Wickham — George S. Rector — Squire Thompson.

From Harper's Reserve —

Company A	Captain Hardy
Company B	Capt. Robert L. Doyle (Augusta County), Jonathan Meredith
Company C	Capt. J.M. Templeton (Rockbridge County)
Company E	McKaney

Company H   Joseph Granitto

Company I   First Serg. W.W. Moore

Company K   Lt. Monroe Blue

Some wounded

Col. William H. Browne, (mortal) Forty-Fifth Virginia Infantry Regiment, second in command to Jones — "...shot in the thigh. They brought him to our house that evening."[44] "...I (Dupont Federal Artillery) knew (Browne) personally very well...I went to see him. (Not think) seriously injured... (asked Browne if have money for recovery period) 'not one cent'...(Dupont gave Browne) all the money I then had in the world...(a) $10 bill."[47]

Maj. W. C. Sanders — Forty-Fifth Virginia Infantry Regiment — "...shot through the chest and left for dead...next day resuscitated by Mr. Crawford..."[30] also captured.

Harper's Reserves (Home Guard)

Company A	Steinbuck — D.H. Snyder — Lieutenant Wright
Company B	G.F. Myerley — William Cason — Sergeant Helms
Company C	
	James Welch — A.L. Hanger — James Michell — Corp. A. H. Lackey
Company D	William J. Rush
Company E	McCormick
Company F	A. Staulus — J. Brown — Captain Rippetoe
Company G	Lt. J. A. Syms — Charles Ridgway — William L. Kyser
Company H	James Locker — W. Kerford — W. Reswick — Harmon J. Lohr — Robert Birtreit (mortal)
Company I	Taylor Coffman — Joseph Baldwin — Charles Schendle — Thomas Walls — Jonathan Smith
Company K	Sergeant Binford
No Company	John Phillip Strider age 17 — student — Washington College "...wounded severely."[6]
Boys' Battery	Joseph Shoemake — leg wound

Some captured

Col. Beuhring H. Jones — Sixtieth Virginia

Lt. Col. A.M. Davis — Forty-Fifth Virginia

Capt. William L. Clark

Lt. Robert L. Howard

Capt. Andrew J. Buford — Thirty-Sixth Virginia Infantry

Capt. Christopher Roles — Thirty-Sixth Virginia Infantry

Harper's Reserves
Company K

Sergeant Taylor — Serg. T.W. Wilson — Jonathan Roebuck — Jonathan Condor — Thomas Bunworth — Thomas Kelley — James Hackett — Hy. Kress — R.W. Goodman — William Kenney

Chapter VII

Monday, June 6 — Friday, June 10

Gen. Jeremiah C. Sullivan — U.S.

On Monday, June 6, Hunter prepared his army to march. The wounded Stahel had to be removed from command. Because Sullivan's Infantry had performed well the day before, Hunter awarded him command of both the infantry and the cavalry.

Many of the cavalrymen and the officers considered themselves to be more elite than the infantry. They rode while the infantry walked.

Hunter was not impressed by his cavalry's actions after the battle. As a form of punishment, he ordered two companies (over 100 men) to perform menial tasks. They were to bury the dead, care for the wounded, and collect small arms from the battlefield. Hunter wanted nothing left that could aid the Confederates. It appears that the soldiers might have collected at least some of the pile of artillery ordnance that was left by the Boys' Battery, even though it was too large for any of the Union's guns. Part of the One Hundred Twenty-Third Ohio was ordered to join the cavalry as it scavengered the field.

As these men worked, the rest of the army prepared to march toward

Staunton. To replenish his ammunition, each man was issued 50 rounds, 40 for his cartridge box, and 10 to carry in his pockets. This large an issue started some "...wondering what was in store for us."[18]

The soldiers gathered up "...some one thousand two hundred stands"[53] (of small arms). Another source indicated "...they burnt 1,500 guns on two piles."[44] A pile of rails was covered by a pile of rifles, and consecutive tiers were formed. Captain Chamberlin and Lieutenant Husted stood near cautioning the men to place the rifles pointed all in one direction and then to stay out of that direction (because some might still be loaded). Sergeant Baroff didn't follow instructions and was in the direction of fire when another rail was tossed onto the pile. Bang! One more Yankee was wounded at Piedmont: "...the ball passing nearly through his right leg...shattering the bone very badly and rendering amputation imperatively necessary."[53]

After the arms were burned, more units joined their comrades on the march. There was still time for some looting. One Yankee decided a goose dinner would be nice, but the "fighting gander"[11] alluded easy grasp. The soldier decided to let the goose dinner come to him. He baited a hook with bread and threw his line toward the goose. The goose took the bait, and the soldier took the goose by simply tying the string around his leg and walking off "...the goose following and flapping his wings in a vain struggle to escape."[11] The old woman that owned the goose heard the commotion and opened the door to see a soldier rapidly leaving with the flapping goose following. She yelled, "Oh, don't run, sir. He won't hurt you...He is not dangerous at all."[11] The soldier made no reply but kept walking with his dinner in tow.

When the Union left Piedmont, so did some area slaves. It can be assumed that the number of slaves was low and that there were few males of draft age. The Union Army had been actively seeking slaves. Because the war was less popular in the North, there was a growing peace movement; as a result, there were fewer volunteers for army ranks. Shortly after the Emancipation Proclamation (1-1-63), the Lincoln Administration changed the draft rules. Now troop quotas were filled first by volunteers and then by *all* Negroes of draft age; only after the last black was inducted was the first white boy drafted. Today's black slave was tomorrow's black Union soldier. Potential draftees usually joined freely, but sometimes they joined at gunpoint.

Most slaves were not enthusiastic about donning a blue uniform and possibly being killed in battle; nor were they thrilled with the idea that they might be captured on the battlefield. Many former slaves were executed as traitors to the South if they were taken prisoners by the Confederate Army.

The Confederate cavalry had retreated from Piedmont (Vaughn in advance and Imboden covering the rear) to Fishersville. Stragglers followed as the cavalry continued moving toward Waynesboro. Vaughn sent a messenger to telegraph Richmond, requesting reinforcements. He sent Secretary Of War James A. Seddon some details of the defeat. He said that the "...artillery and wagon trains (are) safe...enemy is pursuing...Staunton can not be held."[6] He also sent a messenger toward Staunton to inform Col. Edwin Lee of the defeat. Vaughn sent Lieutenant Colonel O'Ferrall with an empty wagon, three soldiers, and a note to General Hunter. Vaughn's note requested the return of General Jones's body. O'Ferrall would also attempt to assess Union strength and intentions. He proceeded toward Staunton and then north toward Piedmont. He had crossed Mowry's Hill, heading north early in the morning.

Imboden had been miffed that he had not been informed about the telegraph from Lee to Jones before the battle. At approximately 1:30, he was to receive a copy. After seeing the duplicate telegram, Vaughn and Imboden concluded that they could expect no reinforcements from Lee. Vaughn no doubt deferred the next move to Imboden. Where could his small army, estimated to be near 3,000[6] men including Jones's remnant and the Home Guard, make a stand? Imboden suggested Rockfish Gap, and the army continued retreating from Fishersville toward Waynesboro.

Vaughn's courier to Staunton bore a message Colonel Lee didn't need to read. He knew that the Federals were coming and "Our scouts were on the hills..."[43] awaiting the invaders. Few people could sleep the night before "...with knowledge that on the morrow they would be under the heel of a foe widely known for his savage marauding."[6]

In the predawn hours, the telegraph operator whom Jones had sent the night before his death to Meechum's River Depot had only now arrived in Staunton. He went to the railroad and asked his friend and depot agent, William A. Burke, for a hand car. Told that there was none, the operator proceeded toward Fishersville. He apparently had not been informed of the defeat at Piedmont.

It is assumed that the railroad train full of bank records, money, and other nonmilitary goods had been sent to Lynchburg via Charlottesville.

The wagon train which Lee had sent south toward Greenville had started toward Tye River Gap at daylight.

Colonel Lee telegraphed General Lee saying that he needed "...prompt reinforcements...I fear Staunton will go."[6]

The Eighth Virginia Cavalry (partially dismounted), which Jones had ordered from Southwest Virginia on June 2, made its way to Staunton in the early morning. One soldier said, "We met a great many refugees from Staunton."[35] The unit continued into town. Colonel Lee and the quartermaster were rendering service to the last. The Eighth Virginia Cavalry received forty rounds of ammunition each and was sent toward Waynesboro. It is possible that a cavalryman from the Eighth was tired of walking. Warned that the Union was approaching, he said that he would stay "until he could capture a horse."[35]

Sometime well before noon, a Yankee cavalry patrol reached Staunton, but "...received no loyal greeting. Only a few colored people seemed glad to see the old flag."[9]

It may have been the First New York Cavalry that lost a horse and a man to the Rebel who was tired of walking. "Almost in the presence of a large body of Federal cavalry, he singled out a man in advance, and presenting his gun ordered him to dismount."[9] The tired Reb took the horse and cavalryman and joined his unit heading for Waynesboro.

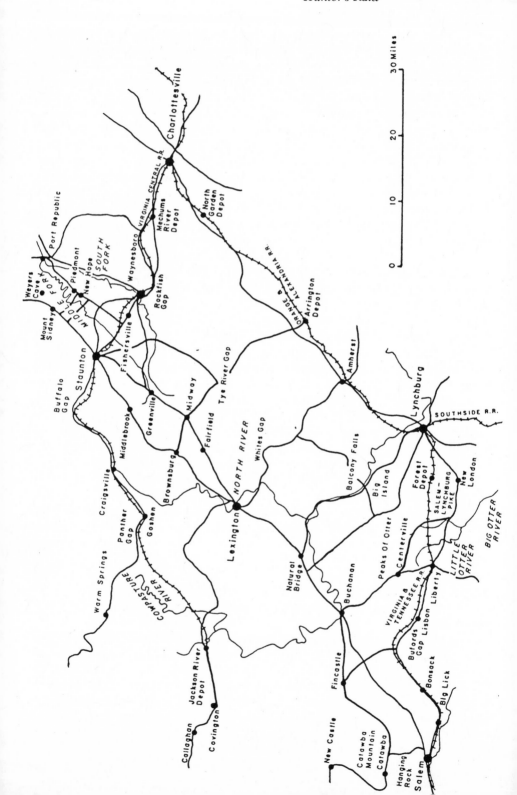

After being "...fired on by several men (the Confederate scouts) from the hills adjoining,"[9] and losing a horse, the cavalry unit withdrew toward the main army.

"After being under way for about two hours, suddenly, great cheering was heard...reports came to us by scouts that our cavalry was in possession of Staunton, where we expected to meet with stubborn resistance,"[18] one soldier recalled. The infantrymen with cartridge boxes and pockets full were glad that there was no fight expected that day.

Hunter now knew that there was no Confederate Army at Staunton. His chief-of-staff suggested that they forget Staunton and turn up the Waynesboro road after the Reb Army. Hunter refused the request. He wanted to link with Crook and Averell at Staunton, besides burning was to be done there.

One Northern soldier wrote: "There was much to be seen by (us) inquisitive Yankees."[18] Another wrote: "The people...were either much frightened or very glad to see us...waved their handkerchiefs...brought buckets of water or milk to quench our thirsts."[11]

One of the sights an inquisitive Yankee might have seen was an empty wagon and four Rebs under a flag of truce which had just left. O'Ferrall and his men were about six miles north of Mowry's Hill when they were intercepted by Maj. Charles G. Otis, Union cavalry. Otis took Vaughn's note to Hunter. Hunter was made aware of their presence and their request. Hunter was not a civilized warrior, magnanimous in victory. He considered the dead general a war prize. "Brig. Gen. William E. Jones, commanding forces, was killed on the field *and his body fell into our hands,*" wrote Hunter. Hunter sent word they would not receive Jones's corpse from his hand. O'Ferrall requested again, and the cavalry rode back to find Hunter.

At this time an old man, George W. Mowry, rode up. He said that all the Yankee prisoners should be "hanged."[6] When he was told that yesterday's battle was a Union victory and that the enemy was on its way, he "...blanched with terror and rode hastily away."[6]

In approximately one and a half hours, Otis returned with a note signed by Hunter: "All the Reb dead have been decently buried and the wounded are being well cared for. The bearer of this communication must return to his lines forthwith."[6] O'Ferrall departed for Rockfish. Jones was buried "on the spot where he was killed...and where he said 'those people are doing us no harm.'"

Back at Staunton, many residents were fleeing south, but a messenger was by now racing northwest. He was carrying word about Piedmont to General McCausland.

Crook, who had pushed McCausland through Panther Gap, advanced toward Goshen Station. Crook moved slowly, not only because McCausland was constantly harassing his advance units but also because he wanted to allow his army time to feed and destroy. A newspaper account says: "The fat of the land was appropriated by foraging parties...each morning...rich country, some of the best of Virginia and abounding in corn, wheat, bacon and apple brandy (which the Yankees stole)...the men did not leave the sweets of the beehive...."[21] Despite the amount and the quality of food they were able to steal, some infantry units were still hungry because of an inequitable distribution system in the army itself. Some units feasted; some units went hungry.

Crook was determined to take his part of the Virginia-Central Railroad out of service and keep it out. He planned to "burn culverts and tires as far as possible...easier to destroy than to build up, as our Rebel friends are learning to their cost."[22]

Crook kept stealing and destroying as he pushed McCausland back toward Buffalo Gap. McCausland kept the pressure on Crook's advance; "on many days not a half dozen miles progress..."[48] was made by Crook.

Averell continued closing in on Staunton also.

At or near Buffalo Gap in the afternoon, McCausland received the courier from Staunton. He learned that Jones was dead and that Staunton might fall any hour. McCausland quickly realized that his little column could be trapped between Crook and Hunter. He broke off contact with Crook's advance. Apparently Mudwall Jackson was in front as McCausland and his men ran from the path of the two overpowering armies. They moved south, avoiding the main road to Staunton. He would circle Staunton and station his troops south of the town. One cavalryman wrote: "We barely made good our escape...had a dead race to get to Middlebrook."[54] They camped on the farm of Archibald Sproul three miles south of Middlebrook at the foot of the mountains on the Staunton-Lexington Pike.

The citizens of Staunton knew that the enemy might be in town at any moment. They continued to leave. Colonel Lee also left heading toward Imboden at Waynesboro. The citizens in Lexington, Lynchburg, and other towns and villages were becoming aware of the disaster at Piedmont and the possibility that their town might be invaded also.

In Richmond, high level conferences, both civilian and military, were being held. Each piece of information was being examined in an effort to assess the situation and find a response. Secretary of War Seddon put the question succinctly to General Braxton Bragg. "Can anything be done to avert the advancing army?"[6] Bragg's response was that the only troops that could possibly be used were General Lee's.

General Lee's immediate opponent to his front was General Grant. Grant had him far outnumbered and outgunned. It might prove impossible to keep Grant at bay with his present troop strength, but something must be done about the Valley. As Lee's information did not present him with a clear picture of the situation, he decided to provide a limited response until he had a better grasp of the magnitude of the situation.

Lee had refused both Imboden's and Jones's requests for additional troops; now there could be no refusal regardless of the conditions at his front. Breckinridge had produced one miracle a couple of weeks before at New Market in the Valley: could he do it again? General Lee told President Davis, "He (Breckinridge) can do a great deal personally in rallying troops and people...."[55] The President concurred and sent orders.

The orders did not have to travel far. Breckinridge was in the city where he was recuperating. Breckinridges's horse was killed at the line, and it had fallen on him, pinning him to the ground. His leg was not broken, but it was very badly bruised. Breckinridge felt more pain at the loss of his horse than from his leg. He looked at his quivering horse: "My horse! My noble horse; poor old Sorrell, he had carried me so gallantly through so many battles and through such dangers that I even fancied he bore a charmed life and would survive the war; but he is gone."[55] Breckinridge turned over command to Gen. Gabriel C. Wharton and was transported to Richmond to rest. Upon receipt of General Lee's order, he sent word to Wharton to make the command ready to move immediately and left his bed of rest.

Part of the troops General Breckinridge had used in the Valley were also used in Richmond. Although these troops were instrumental in Breckinridge's victory, they were not Confederate troops. Stonewall's old school, Virginia Military Institute, had furnished its corps for duty to the South, but it was under the control of the state of Virginia, not the Confederate States of America. Breckinridge sent a request to the governor for the corps of boys. The request was honored, and the corps prepared to move.

The news that was spreading alarm and worry throughout Virginia and the Confederacy was having quite the opposite effect on the North.

President Lincoln was at the National Union Convention (Republican) in Baltimore (a city with much pro-Southern sympathies) to receive the party's nomination a second time for the presidency. When news of Hunter's victory was announced, rolls of applause and shouting broke over the convention. Secretary of War Stanton, probably acting at Lincoln's request sent a congratulatory telegram to Hunter.

The news that brought alarm and worry to one side of the lines in Richmond was like music to Grant's tone-deaf ears. Grant looked beyond Hunter's victory to total victory. The Valley was open. Lynchburg could be taken. The supplies to Richmond could be cut. The Rebel capital would fall. The war would be over.

Grant fired off a telegram to Hunter. He was to proceed to Lynchburg via Charlottesville, severing railroad access to Richmond. Grant knew the importance of Lynchburg. He wrote Hunter "...the complete destruction of this road (railroad) and of the canal on the James River is of great importance to us...it would be of great value to us to get possession of Lynchburg for a single day."[56]

Grant had been holding Sheridan in readiness for a move to help Hunter. It appeared that Hunter and Sheridan could link at Charlottesville. Orders were issued to move the cavalry west. With any luck, Lee would not discover that they were gone until it was too late.

Despite Southern troop movements, it was already too late for Staunton. One trooper wrote: "Staunton was an important town in a pleasant valley...."[9] Staunton was indeed important. It was the seat of Augusta County with a population of over 4,000 people. The best road in the area, Valley Pike, a macadamized road, ran north and south through the Valley. The Virginia Central Railroad provided rapid transport east and west. There were five stage coach lines serving the area. There were shops, a large hospital, a lunatic asylum, hotels, a shoe factory, a woolen factory, and a wagon factory. The military had a depot, a commissary, an arsenal, storehouses, a workshop, and, of course, troop campsites about the town. The town was modern: it even used gas to illuminate the streets and the houses.

A soldier with the Hundred Twenty-Third Ohio Volunteer Infantry records that his unit "...arriving there about 4 p.m. ...being the first Union infantry that had ever been there. We met with no resistance whatever...."[53]

Here an incident occurred that reveals how family life had been shattered by the war. Fathers, brothers, cousins, and boy friends were away fighting; and the girls on the home front were lonely. The day before, virtually every man that could hold a gun was at Piedmont. Many were killed, wounded, captured, or missing. Their fate was unknown. Four o'clock p.m., June 6, 1864, is an hour of eternal shame for Staunton. The invading enemy hordes, killers of family and friends were greeted by "...a dozen or more girls in their Sunday dresses (who) ...presented us with bouquets."[11] One Union officer noted the warmth and the sincerity of the girls. Some relationships went beyond innocent flirtation. One cavalryman noted "...some pleasant acquaintances were made that were kept up long after the war...."[9]

Chief-of-Staff Strother organized the victory parade. Two bands with large United States flags followed the general's staff through the streets of town, playing "Hail Columbia" and "Yankee Doodle." Few in the occupied town greeted the conquerors. Most houses were closed and shuttered. "A few skinny, sallow (under-nourished) women peeped from between the half-closed window blinds...."[11] Strother, torn between his loyalty to the Union and his heritage, was disappointed that so few citizens greeted the army. David Hunter made his headquarters at the Virginia Hotel.

David Hunter Strother established headquarters in the American Hotel run by the former Confederate States of America Colonel John Nadenboushe. (Wounds forced him to retire). Hunter ordered the Signal Corps to set up observation posts on the hills to keep an eye open for any Rebels. Hunter also ordered Capt. Franklin E. Town, head of corps, to attempt to contact Crook and Averell. Captain Town sent 200 cavalrymen toward Buffalo Gap. Citizens, seeing the cavalry column leave town, guessed that they were reinforcements for Averell.

American hotel — Staunton.

After dining with the general, Strother went to his room and slept: however he was unable to make peace with the war going on inside himself through sleep.

His sleep was of short duration. Hunter, who had a "...penchant for pillaging and burning..."[57] sent the man on his staff (Strother) that resisted his policy to deal with the local citizen delegation.

Strother met with the mayor, town council, leading citizens, and heads of the insane asylum and of schools for women. Their spokesman was former United States Congressman Alexander Stuart. Stuart first complimented Strother on his "literary fame"[11] and then got to the matter at hand: the safety of the town and its citizens.

Strother told them that Confederate military stores and manufacturing facilities would be destroyed "...but that private property and noncombatants would be respected. The schools and charitable institutions would be carefully protected."[11] Because Strother's mind didn't believe what his lips were saying, he gave himself an out. "I warned them that disorders might take place such as were to be expected among an ill-disciplined soldiery (his troops)...."[11] He promised to try and keep order although he had given up on the idea back at Woodstock. His words seemed to calm the committee as it was dismissed.

HOSPITAL FOR THE INSANE.
By David Hunter Strother.

Virginia female institute — Staunton.

Even as the committee left, some plundering was occurring.

Strother was present when Col. William Starr reported to Hunter on his actions at the jail. All the inmates were freed to prey on the population. There were "...thieves, spies, forgers, deserters, Irishmen (not citizens of either country), Union men, Yankee soldiers, Confederate officers, murderers, and rioters...(As) iron works were knocked off,...there was a general rejoicing...."[11] A Confederate officer who was accused of shooting a fellow soldier refused to be liberated by the Yankees and remained in the jail. Starr first threatened to place the former jailer in his own irons and then ordered him to get his family and belongings out of the jail as he intended to burn it. Hunter told Starr not to burn but to save it for the prisoners from Piedmont.

The hospital contained about 400 sick and wounded Confederates. They were first "captured" and then "paroled." The Yanks didn't need 400 invalids to care for. "Paroled" meant that each man who was capable was to make his mark or sign his name. By doing so, he agreed not to fight again for the Confederacy. If he broke his word and was captured, he would be subject to execution.

While the Union Army was taking possession of Staunton, the tired remnant of the Confederate Army was evacuating Waynesboro. It fell back on Rockfish Gap, where the railroad passed through a long tunnel, heading toward Charlottesville. It was here that Imboden believed that the best defense of the line and Charlottesville could be made.

Moving just ahead of the army was the uninformed telegraph operator. Jones had told him to open a station at Meechum's River Depot. He kept his one-horse — one-wagon train moving. Totally ignorant of Piedmont, he observed "the little darkies in their white cotton shirts dancing on the back porch to a sort of crooning rhyme, and tune of their own heard never before nor since...(He also noticed) the fair women who looked out upon me as we passed, saluting kindly."[36]

Colonel Lee's wagon train made it to Tye River Gap on the Blue Ridge and camped for the night. Many refugees and their livestock from Staunton passed.

At dark in Staunton, Union army units camped about the town. The Twenty-Second Pennsylvania and the Thirty-Fourth Massachusetts camped on the grounds of the lunatic asylum. The Eighteenth Connecticut camped west of town.

Since Strother apparently didn't enjoy doing his boss's bidding and instilling false hope in the citizenry, he left his hotel and "...wandered about... (and) stumbled upon (General) Sullivan's quarters."[11] He apparently didn't inform Hunter about his whereabouts. Here away from "Black Dave" he slept.

The Eighth Virginia Cavalry, which came from Southwest Virginia, didn't make it to the battle at Piedmont; it had left Staunton hours before the Union had arrived. The members of the cavalry rested some that day; at dark they started a night march toward Waynesboro, the last known location of their army.

Sometime during the night, rockets were seen in the western sky. The

Signal Corps was trying to locate Crook and Averell. Many soldiers in Staunton believed that the rockets were from the western wing of their army and that they would surely link tomorrow. Incredibly there was no mention made that Crook's forces observed the fireworks.

By 11:30 p.m., troops under Breckinridge were marching off the line and toward Richmond. The two brigades were under Gen. Gabriel C. Wharton and Gen. John Echols. Not only was Breckinridge suffering, but General Echols was too ill to command; he placed the brigade under Col. George S. Patton. The men would march through the night to Richmond.

June 7 (Tuesday)
Shortly after dawn on Tuesday, June 7, Sheridan and approximately 8,000 Northern troopers pulled off the line near the Pamunkey River. They would leave the Richmond area, heading west toward Charlottesville.

Other troopers were leaving Richmond and going west also. Breckinridge and his two brigades (approximately 2,100 men) boarded a train in Richmond at approximately 8:00 a.m.

Back at Lexington, Colonel John T. Preston was making preparations for possible Yankee visitors. He knew Hunter was in Staunton and heard reports that Averell was near "...with not a Confederate soldier between the enemy and Lexington...."[58] Colonel Preston obviously did not have information on McCausland's move to the south of Staunton. Preston began precautionary packing of records and valuables.

Some time during the night of June 6, the uninformed telegraph operator finally reached Meechum's River Depot between Rockfish Gap and Charlottesville. He and his aides spent the night in a box car at the siding. In the morning, he strung line and tapped into the telegraph line. He attempted to contact Staunton. A telegraph operator with Vaughn intercepted the message. Back at Meechum's, there was shock when they received the news: "Staunton is no more — its depot burned — Jones routed and killed — Vaughn in command — I am at Rockfish Gap."[36] The shocked operator recalled that Richmond sent hourly requests for information concerning Hunter.

At Rockfish Gap where the train tunnel penetrates the Blue Ridge Mountains, Dixie boys were digging in. They were expecting an attack from Hunter; it was just a question of when. Vaughn had concluded that he couldn't resist a determined attack by Hunter's mighty army. He wouldn't be able to prevent the Yanks from taking Charlottesville and marching on Lynchburg. He could inflict casualties on Hunter, but he could not stop him. Mounted cavalry patrols were sent out to report on Hunter and to harass his army when possible. Vaughn used Imboden's locals where possible on these patrols. They knew the terrain. Vaughn requested that John Opie attempt to go to his hometown of Staunton and bring back intelligence. Opie and seven men moved cross-country, avoiding the roads and traveling toward the north of Staunton.

As the patrols left, stragglers from Piedmont were still moving toward Rockfish Gap. The Eighth Virginia Cavalry, traveling all night, made Waynesboro near daylight. It would rest there during the day.

The wagon train Colonel Lee had sent from Staunton left Tye River Gap and continued moving slowly through the mountains.

At Middlebrook, McCausland's little force may have been growing in numbers as soldiers and Home Guard members who fought at Piedmont continued to straggle from occupied Staunton. He was still estimated to have fewer than 1,500 men. The soldiers knew that Hunter would destroy as much of the upper valley as possible. Members of McCausland's units, who were from the local area, approached the general and requested that they be allowed to go to their homes and drive livestock to the hills and hide valuables. McCausland refused permission saying "...he intended to fight...."[19]

Just like high command at Richmond, McCausland wanted to know what Hunter was up to. He sent James McChesney of Rockbridge County along with three members of Company C, Fourteenth Virginia Cavalry: William I. Kunkle, J.R. McCutcheon, and George Fishburne (also locals from Augusta County) to scout Hunter. They were sent over North Mountain at Pond Gap. The four had just passed over the mountain's crest and were halfway down to the Virginia Central Railroad when McCutcheon and Fishburne dismounted to adjust their saddle blankets. The other two stayed mounted and spotted a group of mounted men moving up the mountain toward them. Not knowing which side they were on, the two mounted men pulled their pistols and rode toward the group. When they were about fifty yards apart, both sides stopped. Seeing their gray uniforms, pistols were returned to holsters, and the two groups advanced. This scouting mission may be easier than expected thought McChesney. Surely these Rebs would know of Hunter's location and movements.

The two met with the other group of approximately twenty men. Greetings were exchanged. Something seemed wrong. Unlike the two men, the group of twenty still had their pistols in hand. McChesney inquired if the other Rebs had spotted any Yanks. A simple "no" was the reply.

By this time, the two men were abreast of the advance of the twenty mounted Rebels. The Rebel captain asked where they had come from. McChesney was uneasy and gave a general reply. The Confederate captain then demanded to know specifically where from. McChesney recorded "...they wore grey coats or jackets and slouch hats like our men, they all wore blue pants, their horses were branded (U.S.), and their saddles, bridles, and all of their equipments were such as the Yankee cavalry used. I knew at once that I was in the midst of the Jessie Scouts...."[19]

McChesney guessed that his next stop would be Yankee prison or the grave. He decided to buy time to think by continuing his conversation with the Union captain in Confederate clothing. He reasoned that as long as the captain believed he would get information, he would continue interrogating him. McChesney worried that Kunkle would discover their predicament and bolt, leaving him alone with these deceiving Yankees.

Hoping Kunkle would follow suit, he began to back his horse up and announced in a loud voice (so Kunkle could hear) words to the effect that if the twenty men had seen no Yankees in that direction, there was no need to advance farther. He rapidly turned his horse and spurred the animal.

The surprised Yankee captain yelled "Halt!", too late, because McChesney had dashed through the woods. Some Southern clad troopers shot. Kunkle attempted to follow suit, but a Union bullet found its mark. Kunkle was wounded and captured.

Some of the deceiving Yankees chased McChesney but halted when they saw Fishburne and McCutcheon — perhaps fearing an ambush.

Kunkle later wrote about his capture. He said he didn't have "...the remotest idea that they were Yankees until you (McChesney) wheeled...."[19] Kunkle indicated fifteen to twenty shots were fired at McChesney, one at only ten feet. McChesney was lucky; Kunkle was not. One Yankee bullet grazed his head, stunning him but not so much that he didn't attempt to continue his escape. He passed two Yanks also firing at him; and now there was only one left until he could run for freedom. This one didn't miss. The bullet "...shattering my left arm and another passing through my right at the elbow. With both arms helpless, I could not guide my horse...."[19] The Yank moved close in on the disabled man and his unguided horse. "...Taking deliberate aim..."[19] he missed, but the discharge frightened Kunkle's horse which bolted up a path on a steep bank. The Yank chased and caught the horse by the bridle. He then leveled his pistol on Kunkle "...I quietly succumbed...,"[19] recalled Kunkle.

The deceiving captain rode up to Kunkle and "...in a savage tone said: Now, old fellow, we have you safe; and if you don't tell where your general is and the number of forces, I'll damn soon put you up the spout!"[19] Kunkle replied: "Captain, I am a Confederate soldier...I intend to be true to my country. I have...(guarded) some of your men, and I have never spoken an unkind word to one of them; and if you were a gentleman and a brave man, you would not do it either."[19] The captain rode off, after instructing two of his men to escort Kunkle to General Crook.

His two escorts were worried about an ambush for, "they thought a blood-thirsty Reb lurked behind every bush."[19] They were in a big rush to get down the mountain. "They beat the horse (Kunkle) was riding with two long poles to hurry him...everytime they struck the horse he would lunge forward (besides being very lame) and caused me excruciating pain, (Kunkle was bleeding profusely) and I could feel the shattered bones of my left arm grating together. I begged them to desist,...but all to no purpose...I shut my teeth hard together and bore the pain with the stoicism that would have done honor to an American Indian. I allowed no cry or groan to escape me, but I registered a silent vow to even up things if I ever got the chance."[19]

Kunkle was interrogated by Crook and his staff. He gave his name, brigade, regiment, and his colonel's name and nothing on troop strength or movements. The interrogation completed, a surgeon inspected his arms and said that they would have to be amputated. Kunkle was from Augusta County, and as luck would have it, the surgeon took Kunkle to his uncle's house and began dressing his wounds. His wounds were not as serious as were thought, and his arms did not have to be amputated. As the surgeon covered the wounds, Kunkle's aunt dashed in with word that other Yanks were looting the place. The doctor left Kunkle and drove the skulkers out, saying, "Brave men go to the front, where there is fighting to do. Cowards and thieves stay (in) ...the rear and plunder... (returning to Kunkle's side, he added) such men are a disgrace to any army."[19] The surgeon told his medical director that Kunkle could not be moved.

Kunkle concluded, "I shall never forget that man as long as I live. Had he been a brother, he could not have been kinder to me. Who do you suppose he was? He was a son of Dr. Warrick, who practiced medicine in Middlebrook, Virginia, years before the war and moved to Ohio."[19] Except for the move, he would probably be wearing Confederate gray.

McChesney sent McCausland word of the Jessie Scouts by Fishburne. Then McCutcheon and McChesney returned to the top of the mountain by another route, hid their horses, and observed the valley below. The same Jessie Scouts, who had just left, were seen at the advance of a Union column. McChesney and McCutcheon estimated nearly 6,000 blue-bellies passed. The army passed over and camped at Dunlap's near Summerdean.

McCutcheon's home was near Shermariah Church about one mile from Dunlap's. After the army passed by, the two Rebs went to visit McCutcheon's family, then returned toward their regiment. It was about 4:00 p.m. when they found out it had moved to near Brownsburg, farther south toward Lexington. Indeed, McCausland had moved his whole army south. His unit was camped on a relative's farm, Adam McChesney's. After they reported to General McCausland, McChesney was given a pass to visit his home three miles from Brownsburg.

West of Staunton, Crook was moving toward junction with Hunter. The main Yankee Army moved from two miles west of Craigville. The Yankees didn't know that McCausland had withdrawn south of Staunton. Because they believed McCausland's army was ready to do battle at Buffalo Gap, they took a detour at Pond Gap and crossed the Central Virginia Railroad. McChesney observed the movement to Summerdean. The foraging was good, and news that "Hunter flogged the Rebels badly and took Staunton..."[22] came. They moved approximately eighteen miles this day and were only about ten miles from Staunton.

Staunton was the epicenter of action on this day.

Many of the Northern soldiers were too weary from their march of the day before to appreciate the beauty of the Staunton area. One homesick soldier wrote that the hills "reminds us somewhat of our hometown..."[41] in Connecticut. As at Harrisonburg, beauty was not to save Staunton from the "...unleashed...orgy of destruction."[7] The looters and destroyers rose with the sun.

Hunter did nothing to control his soldiers' plundering, thus encouraging them. He did, however, put the cavalry in motion. The majority of horse soldiers moved east toward Waynesboro. Hunter wanted to assess Reb troop strength, movement, and intentions. Part of the First New York Cavalry was sent to Piedmont. It was to escort the wounded to Staunton.

Hunter's next move shows his contempt for anything Confederate. Since he knew that his wounded would be coming, he sent orders to have the large General Hospital cleared of the Confederate rabble. The Southern sick and the wounded were literally thrown into the streets to fend for themselves. Hunter's men would need the bed space.

In the streets, there were "a mixed mob of Federal soldiers, Negroes, Secessionists, Mulatto women, children, Jews, and camp followers and the riff raff of the town were engaged in plundering the stores and depots. (The mobs stole) blankets, clothes, a thousand saddles, shoes, tobacco, etc...."[11]

Besides the mobs stealing and burning, units of the army operating under Hunter's orders destroyed also. The railroad depot was burned, tracks were ripped up, telegraph lines were torn down, and bridges and culverts were destroyed. Despite Colonel Lee's efforts "...large quantities of commisary and ordnance stores,"[8] were taken, what couldn't be used by the troops were destroyed. The Yankees stole twenty barrels of flour, ten barrels of meal, 600 sacks of precious salt, hogsheads of sugar, five bales of cloth, eight bales of yarn, 1,000 wooden buckets, fifty wagons, saddles, spurs, horseshoes, spikes, shovels, plus a twelve-pound Napolean and three defective Howitzers. Estimated value was 400,000 dollars.[6]

Destroyed Southern railroad depot.

Public workshops and storehouses were ransacked: The Staunton Steam Mill (flour mill) — destroyed. Trotter's Shop and Stages — destroyed. Crawford & Young's Woolen Factory — destroyed. Two livery stables — destroyed. Garber's Mill — destroyed. The shoe factory — destroyed. Tobacco warehouse — looted — destroyed. A steam distillery — destroyed. A foundry — destroyed. A "Tax — in-Kind" storehouse — destroyed. The offices of the "Staunton Spectator" were broken into. Printing type was thrown in the streets, and the office burned. Most of the equipment had been removed from "The Vindicator," but Federals did destroy a printing press.

Office furniture and about 1,000 small arms were piled in the street and burned.

The Thirty-Fourth Massachusetts tried to destroy a railroad culvert near the insane asylum with Reb gunpowder. There was a lot of noise and smoke but little damage. Hunter ordered the destruction stopped. He was not interested in saving Confederate property: he needed the gunpowder.

The orgy continued at the Virginia Hotel. Acting under the order of the Provost Marshal, soldiers rolled barrels of apple brandy to the street and broke them open. One observer noted, "The precious stream was running over the curbstones in cascades and rushing down the gutters with floating chips, paper, horse dung, and dead rats. This luscious mixture was greedily drunk by dozens of soldiers and vagabonds on their hands and knees and their mouths in the gutter...."[11] Others filled canteens for later consumption.

Alexander Stuart came to Hunter's headquarters and asked that the carriage (wagon) factory not be burned. He was afraid flames would spread to his property. He suggested letting the mob loose on the building. Strother agreed to let the mob have it, but Hunter had it burned anyway.

Alexander Stuart House — Staunton.

The owner of the American Hotel also asked that a warehouse next door not be set afire. It, too, was gutted by looters, not by fire.

Through the smoke came an Irishman to shake Strother's hand and to thank him for releasing him from jail. After the handshake, Strother discovered the man's hand was infected with a contagious skin disease. Strother drove him away saying, "...you damn scoundrel!"[11] Strother disinfected his hands with apple brandy.

Some Yankee soldiers did try to save houses next to the factories and warehouses that they were instructed to burn. Their help was much needed because other Yankees had destroyed the equipment of the Volunteer Fire Department.

Hunter knew that he was in Imboden's hometown. He sent out inquiries as to the location of Imboden's home. After considerable searching, a scout located the property. Much to Hunter's disappointment, Imboden had sold it only months before. When he found out that the new owner was pro-Union, he just couldn't burn it.

To add insult to injury, some of the Jessie Scouts that had entered Staunton while it was under Confederate control went to visit some of those residents they had talked to while wearing Rebel uniforms.

There were some Union sympathizers among both the white and the black population. It is not certain from whom Hunter received information about a wagon train, perhaps two trains, loaded with military supplies that had left by the Greenville Road. It is known that "Negroes" told him they had seen Averell's force at Buffalo Gap. If they did see a Union force near there, it was Crook's Infantry, not Averell's Cavalry. Hunter apparently did not know that Crook and Averell were on different routes to Staunton, but he knew that they should be close. If they were advancing together, and that would be his logical assumption, then Averell's Cavalry would be in front of Crook's Infantry. He believed the Negroes' report.

He believed the report but did not have current intelligence on the whereabouts of McCausland's small force. His latest report placed McCausland in front of the Union advance along the railroad. Hunter saw an opportunity to destroy McCausland. He would catch him between himself and the Union advance via the railroad. But there was a problem: he had sent most of the fast-moving cavalry toward Piedmont or Waynesboro. He couldn't strike as fast with infantry, but infantry was about all he had. The possibility of crushing McCausland was worth the effort. Hunter issued orders to move west. Much of the destruction of the town was being carried out by organized units. These were relatively easy to locate and direct, but many individual soldiers were among the looters and out of communication with their units. Many did not know that their army was force marching until they saw units, leaving town; some never knew the march was on.

If McCausland was to be caught, time was precious. Hastily formed units began to leave town about 12 noon. Misinformation and rumors flew through the ranks and through the civilian population. All that the soldiers knew for sure was that they were making a forced march away from the Piedmont battlefield. Were they running? Some soldiers were "...dejected and alarmed."[6] Most law-abiding citizens were happy to see them go. Rumors spread that another Union supply wagon train had been captured and that Hunter had decided to high-tail it north.

By 1:00 p.m., most of the Union Army was on the road. It moved west with what cavalry it had in advance, followed by the artillery, which was flanked on both sides by infantry brigades.

As soon as the last Federal unit left town, Confederate scouts from the hills were in town. The Yankees referred to them as "adventurous guerrillas."[11] Several of the looting Yanks were now Southern prisoners.

Union cavalry scouts had gone almost to Buffalo Gap and had found no Confederate or Union troops. Perhaps the scouts were with the Signal Corps and had sent up sky rockets the night before. One soldier noted: "What was singular and vexatious, they (the scouts) brought us no news of the enemy or of Crook."[11] Hunter used part of the cavalry to halt his columns in place while he gathered information and planned his next move.

To show how disorganized the army was, different units recorded their mileage marched, when they received the command to halt. Most units reported that they had force marched five or six miles, but one unit recorded only two miles. Hunter reached Swoope.

Other scouts were sent out. Presently they returned with news that there were Confederate troops operating south of Staunton. Hunter correctly deducted that McCausland had pulled his command south before Hunter's arrival. Hunter located McCausland's old camp near Buffalo Gap. Apparently while the units were still halted, two scouts reported that Crook was at Goshen, destroying the railroad. He could be in Staunton tomorrow. Hunter ordered the bridge or culvert at Swoope destroyed and turned his army east toward Staunton again.

One disheartened resident of Staunton noted it was about 4:00 p.m., and, "...the town was perfectly alive with Blue Coats again."[43]

Shortly after returning to town, Hunter held a conference with his Chief-of-Staff, and asked him to give his views on the future campaign. Strother had been contemplating that question since early morning. He originally favored following Grant's directive and moving on Charlottesville and later on Lynchburg. He knew that the remnant of the Confederate Army was between them and Charlottesville, but they had soundly beaten the army once. Couldn't they do it twice? That was his reasoning, but other officers had approached him expressing their desire to avoid the Rebs and move directly south via Lexington and attack Lynchburg. These officers had asked Strother to use his influence on Hunter. By evening, Strother had come around to their plan. He then advised his general, in effect, to disregard Grant's order and to move on Lexington and Buchanan, cross the Peaks of Otter, strike Liberty (Bedford), and drive on to Lynchburg (the prize). One member said, "In fact, we would have our grip on the vitals of the Confederacy...."[11] Hunter listened but gave Strother no indication of his next move.

It is uncertain when Hunter received the telegram Secretary of War, Edwin

Stanton, had sent him. The secretary thanked him for the great victory. He personally praised Hunter when he said the army was "...led on by courage and guided by the experienced skill of its commander...."[17] Hunter could imagine that he saw a smiling president. The telegram came over the signature of the Secretary of War; but it may as well have been signed, "Your regained friend, Abe Lincoln."

Another Union column was moving on Staunton, this one from the east. It was the cavalry Hunter had sent to recover his wounded from Piedmont. The mission had been accomplished but not without incident, for "mounted Confederates, singly or in small squads, were riding about, ready to pick up anyone so unfortunate as to wander a little way from his command."[9]

One incident occurred when two thieving Yanks left the column to visit a Confederate corn crib. While they were inside, a Confederate soldier emptied two revolvers into the building, firing with deadly intent. None of the bullets penetrated Union skin, and by the time the thieves were able to return the fire, the Reb had galloped off.

Not only did the column protect Union wounded that could be transported, it also brought some residents of the Staunton area home. They were among the prisoners captured at Piedmont. The column arrived after nightfall.

Around nightfall, John Opie's small party of Rebs took shelter at a farm off the main road. The party had not made it to Piedmont yet.

The residents of Staunton held a different view of the destructive Northern invaders from that which the invaders held for themselves. "We are soldiers doing hard service for our country in cruel war...."[18] Hunter concluded, "...the troops have behaved admirably."[8]

Wednesday, June 8

General Breckinridge's Infantry Brigades had been moving from Richmond. They had been delayed because the train had derailed twice. This derailment showed the poor conditions of Southern railroads. They moved toward Charlottesville.

Sometime between midnight and dawn, Averell's Cavalry joined Hunter at Staunton. One infantryman noted that we now have "...quite a formidable little army."[53]

Also moving towards Charlottesville was Sheridan's Union Cavalry. Sometime in the early morning hours, it damaged much of the railroad track. The track damage report told General Lee two things: one, that the Union cavalry had been pulled off line, and two, that it emphasized to him the importance Grant placed in the Valley operation. Lee gave orders to his nephew, Gen. Fitzhugh Lee, to intercept the Yankee cavalry.

About daylight, John Opie and his men started out toward Staunton to gather information for Vaughn. They left the isolated farm to observe the main roads toward town.

Vaughn and Imboden had by now established headquarters in the railroad tunnel at Rockfish Gap. The tunnel area was fortified. Vaughn decided to send some forces to Waynesboro. They would act as an early warning for the troops at the Gap. They could also slow Hunter's expected advance.

After Vaughn had received Colonel Lee's report on Staunton, he sent scouts to locate the wagon train full of military supplies.

The partially mounted Eighth Virginia Cavalry had been making its way from Southwest Virginia. On June 7, it camped at Waynesboro; on June 8, the cavalrymen had just left camp heading toward Rockfish when they were intercepted. They joined Vaughn's other units west of Waynesboro, waiting for Hunter's advance.

They didn't have to wait long, however, the cavalry Hunter had sent out the day before approached Waynesboro from the north, not from the west as expected. This caused Southern cavalry to be "maneuvered around..."[35] to meet the Yanks. The Union cavalry had taken possession of the northern end of town when the Confederate cavalry came on line. There were no figures on troop strength found, but the Union cavalry apparently felt that it could defeat the Rebs. The cavalry attacked. The Yankees were "...surprised at the severity of their repulse."[6] A Rebel cavalryman simply recorded we "...had a skirmish, the enemy fell back...."[35] There is no record that the South counter-attacked the surprised Yanks. Although many men were assumed killed, wounded, and captured, only William Mulligan of Company C, First New York Cavalry, is recorded as killed on the field of honor.

Back at the battlefield at Piedmont in the Shaver house, Col. William Browne, Jones's second-in-command, was in a soft feather bed. Milton Shaver recorded: "Wednesday morning he died."[44] Browne was "...buried side by side (to General Jones) in a grass lot in the hamlet of Piedmont."[45] Union signal men flashed the news back to Staunton. Captain Dupont didn't think that Browne's wounds were too severe. He said that he felt "very great regret..."[47] when he received news of Browne's death.

In Staunton, Strother's records show that he was awakened at dawn by a disturbance among the Confederate prisoners. As this irritated him, he started thinking of a way to dispose of the problem.

Also near dawn, troops were preparing for another day, working on the railroad — destroying it. They knew that Confederate scouts and guerrillas were near and that they might strike isolated groups or individuals at any time. Despite the danger, ties were piled up and set afire. Rails were placed upon them and heated until they bent, making them useless to the already deteriorating Southern railroad system. It was not easy, and "there is much kicking over the hard work."[18]

A resident of Brownsburg, Henry Jones, kept a diary for many years. He was a religious man and more concerned with heavenly events than earthly ones. He simply noted that on this date that McCausland's Brigade was there.

Strother knew that the enlistment time for Ewing's Battery and for the Twenty-Eighth Ohio Infantry was growing short. They would be going home. Why not pack his sleep disturbing, captured Rebels off with the home bound column? He rushed to General Hunter, who was still in bed, with his idea, which Hunter approved. Col. Augustus Moor, of the Twenty-Eighth was to supervise the move. Sometime that day Colonel Moor began preparing the eight commissioned officers and 350 men of the Twenty-Eighth for the march.

Hunter also ordered the Thirty-Fourth Massachusetts Cavalry to make a house-to-house search, looking for guns or Rebel stores.

Opie's group had been moving since dawn. By late morning, it had circled Staunton and was to the west of town. Opie and his men tied their horses in a dense patch of woods off the main road. They crept forward and found concealed positions to observe the main road. Apparently they were not there long when they sighted a single Union rider. The men whispered to Opie their desire to capture or shoot him. Opie guessed that this one man might be the advance of either Crook's army or Averell's army and refused permission.

Presently a squadron of Union cavalry appeared with livestock in tow. Now Opie was perplexed. Was this an army's advance, or was it one of Hunter's foraging parties? Opie observed: "In a short while, a long column of infantry appeared, and with it several batteries of artillery."[20] It was indeed Crook, and he would be linking with Hunter in Staunton. Opie had the intelligence Vaughn had asked for. He instructed the men to retire quietly to their horses; they must get the news back to Rockfish Gap.

It was about 12 noon when the first of Crook's units began arriving in Staunton. Crook considered it "...an enjoyable march, varied by a few skirmishers...."[59] Colonel Hayes with the Twenty-Third Ohio wrote his wife: "We have enjoyed this campaign very much." Hayes enjoyed moving toward Staunton but had a deep foreboding about meeting his new boss. "...Hayes, who had never met Hunter, had for some reason formed an unfavorable opinion of the general...."[60]

Crook's and Hunter's armies had destroyed almost fifty miles of the Virginia Central Railroad when they combined at Staunton.

Once again exact figures are hard to arrive at. Averell brought approximately 4,400 cavalrymen with him. Most estimated Crook's strength at 10,000 men. Crook had 2 batteries, (12 guns). One source places the aggregate number of troops at 17,000,[59] another at 25,000.[61] Most sources suggest a figure of 18,000. Most sources agree that there were 30 pieces of field artillery. The bottom line is that Hunter now commanded far more men and fire power than the South had in the entire Valley of Virginia or on its way, and Southern troop strength was dispersed.

The most authoritative figures come from the Union Chief-of-Staff. He stated there were 20,000 (5,000 were cavalrymen) and 36 cannons.[11]

Hunter was very happy finally to have his entire command united. He sat about the task of organizing the two armies into one army, and planning strategy for its use.

Hunter was happy that Crook and Averell were in Staunton, but at least one resident was not. He said "...the locusts of Egypt could not have been more numerous, our yard and kitchen were overrun...streets were filled from end to end."[43]

The Thirty-Fourth Massachusett's search for arms and Reb stores had degenerated into just another excuse to loot. Food, clothing, and livestock were stolen at will. Only the "...homes of Negroes and Union sympathizers"[6] escaped looting. They soldiers found some arms in one resident's outhouse and arrested him. Arms were found just outside of town and "...A.K. Trout, Mayor of Staunton, has been arrested and charged with ordering their concealment."[11] George W. Fuller was arrested as a spy because he had letters from Southern soldiers and was attempting to deliver them in town. B.F. Points was arrested "...for showing pleasure at the hasty departure of the Federals the previous day."[6]

Word of the harsh treatment and lack of food of the Southern prisoners Hunter had placed in the Staunton jail, spread. Ladies of the town braved smoke, arrest, and looters to bring what food they could to their incarcerated heroes.

Meanwhile during the day, Breckinridge's troops had been moving toward the Valley. He did not have a current picture of events about the area in which he was to command. It is known that the train derailed and delayed twice on the journey. One writer said that Breckinridge took a "circuitous route."[55] It appears that his force moved from Richmond to Gordonsville and then to Charlottesville. At Charlottesville, most of his command debarked. His command then started marching toward Rockfish Gap. These moves indicate that Breckinridge believed, as did Grant, that the best way to attack Lynchburg was via Charlottesville. Breckinridge had decided to fight the battle for Lynchburg at Rockfish Gap. While his troops marched west, Breckinridge moved south to Lynchburg. He intended to pick up an artillery battery and any available troops. At Lynchburg, he learned that Staunton was now an occupied town. A telegram from Vaughn stated that Crook and Averell had combined forces. It is not known if Breckinridge received word about the cavalry skirmish at Waynesboro earlier in the day. If he did, then he might have believed the cavalry attack was only the prelude to a full-scale attack by Hunter toward Charlottesville.

At Lynchburg, Breckinridge sent a telegram to Richmond, requesting that the "Devil" himself and his "terrible men,"[42] be sent to him from Southwest Virginia. Breckinridge wanted John H. Morgan's savage cavalrymen, but they would not be coming. Morgan had left the department on an unauthorized raid into his beloved Kentucky. He notified high command in Richmond of his departure after he left. Breckinridge did not know that he could not count on Morgan's support. It is uncertain, but likely, that Breckinridge spent the night at Lynchburg.

Back in Richmond, the governor okayed Breckinridges's request for use of the Corps of Cadets from V.M.I. The corps was now placed under the control of the Confederate States of America, specifically Breckinridge. By the time the corps was ready to entrain, word was received of Sheridan's destruction of the Virginia Central Railroad. Alternate but slower transport was obtained. The majority of the corps moved from Richmond via the Richmond-Danville line toward Burkes Station (Burkeville) and then toward Lynchburg. A few of the boys moved from Petersburg via the Southside Railroad. A wounded soldier from the Staunton area records that he was with "...Captain Semmes and 8 to 10 cadets..."[62] and their artillery and horses. The soldier, Edward A.

Moore from the Stonewall Brigade, was wounded at Cold Harbor. He was still too badly hurt to fight, but he was able to travel. To help relieve crowding at the hospital, he was sent home to recuperate.

While troops were moving toward the Valley from Richmond, Opie and his cavalry scouts were circling Staunton, heading toward Rockfish Gap with the news that Crook's and Hunter's forces were now combined. As they circled town, they intersected the Staunton-Lexington Pike. There was evidence that a large cavalry unit had passed. This cavalry was undoubtedly McCausland's, which was falling back on Middlebrook. Opie, unaware of McCausland's position, believed that they were Federal tracks he had seen. Proceeding toward Lexington, they saw three Federal cavalrymen. Before the Union soldiers were aware of what was happening, they were prisoners of the Confederates. Opie now had a bold idea: he would turn the tables on the deceiving Yanks. With the three uniformed yanks in the center, his men would pose as Jessie Scouts. He gave orders to his men not to act nervous or to shoot, unless in self-defense. To make sure the prisoners helped in the charade, Opie gave orders "...to shoot the prisoners if they raised an outcry...."[20] Now the cocky Opie and his men were able to "...proceed leisurely down the road."[20]

They moved without encounter to the Staunton-Waynesboro Pike. As they moved toward Waynesboro, they came upon forty to fifty Yankees at a mill, still mounted, eating and drinking. Now, Opie's brazen disguise would be tested. While some distance away, Opie ordered his men to draw their pistols and continue their steady pace. Eight Rebs with three prisoners were going to attack fifty of the enemy. The ruse worked. The men disguised as Jessie Scouts rode into the midst of the Yankee position. Before the Federals knew it, these counterfeit Jessie Scouts had taken eight of them prisoner. The rest of the startled group galloped down the road and then formed a skirmish line to attack the non-Jessie Scouts.

Opie also formed a line. He placed his command facing the Union skirmish line; then he lined up the Federal prisoners. To make sure the prisoners did not try to run, Opie was behind them with drawn pistols. The Yanks knew that they could attack and overwhelm the Rebs that beat them at their own game of deception, but any bullet that missed a Reb in front was likely to strike their own man behind. The price of victory was too high. The brazen Rebs were allowed to ride off without firing a shot.

Opie wrote from memory after the war. He does not record that he camped that night as he had done going toward Staunton. Opie wrote: "That evening, I reached Waynesboro with my prisoners and reported to General Breckinridge (not Vaughn or Imboden) that Crook and Averell had joined Hunter at Staunton."[20] Imboden, too, recalled that Breckinridge was at Rockfish Gap on June 8. Imboden added that Breckinridge "...Immediately began the defense of Lynchburg, shifting troops to that city."[23] At this point in time, Breckinridge operated on the assumption that Hunter would move first to Charlottesville and then Lynchburg. He concentrated his troops at Rockfish Gap. Breckinridge's biographer indicates that Breckinridge was not at Rockfish Gap until June 9. No information was found to reconcile the accounts.

During the day at Lexington, citizens and institute personnel had been making arrangements for the possible unwelcome visit of Hunter's army. At the Virginia Military Institute, a seriously wounded cadet was moved and hidden.

Quartermaster stores, a large amount of ammunition, four 6-pound cannons, and two 3-inch rifles were removed from V.M.I. and packed on six canal boats. If Hunter approached, these boats would be sent to Lynchburg. Some of the archives were removed from the college grounds, but there was neither time nor manpower to remove the books from the library.

Some time after nightfall, a scout from Vaughn reached the wagon train that had been sent south from Staunton. Vaughn's courier told the men to move toward Waynesboro at sunup.

Apparently the Superintendent of the Institute had communicated with McCausland. Hunter's forces were considered overwhelming. The Superintendent believed that the fall of Lexington was a foregone conclusion if Hunter chose to move by this route. He urged that no defense of the town be made, saying that it would "...only expose the town and the institute to retaliatory measures...."[58] (A ludicrous position: Staunton had offered no resistance).

At Staunton, the two armies had combined, but there was much confusion in the ranks. No one, including Hunter, was certain whose army units were where. He spent a great deal of the afternoon trying to organize and meet with his commanders. If he could align them, they in turn could align their troops.

As the streets were full of troops, civilians, bums, and Negroes, Hunter, who hated slavery, took no notice of Ned, a slave. There was nothing unusual about ignoring a slave, however, Ned had a "...tendency...to sleep, (that) was wonderful. He would sit down on a rock and be sound sleeping in one and two-tenths seconds by the watch...his hat...was full of nap just by being worn by that somnolent wooly head!"[21] Hunter would probably be enraged if he knew what was unusual about Ned. His owner was not a secessionist Reb but a member of the Fifth Regiment (West) Virginia Volunteer Infantry. Ned "...was the Quartermaster's Nigger."[21]

In Staunton, one group of soldiers looked on the Southern population with no apparent emotion. One observer noted: "Many of the women look sad and do much weeping over the destruction...We feel that the South brought on the war and the state of Virginia is paying dear for her part. The loss of our good boys brings us many sad hours...Who will be the next one to give his life for our country?"[18]

As Hunter was attempting to organize his army so that he could use it, there was much discussion in command circles as to the direction it should take. All commanders seemed to agree that the immediate goal should be Lynchburg, but they couldn't agree which way they should move. Col. Rutherford Hayes with the Twenty-Third Ohio said that they should have "...reflected on Grant's language. The supreme commander had made it plain that he desired Hunter to grasp the Charlottesville-Gordonsville line before proceeding farther south...."[60]

General Averell held the opinion of other ranking officers. He called on Chief-of-Staff Strother that night and laid out a plan similar to the one Strother had proposed to Hunter the day before. Averell wanted to present his plan to Hunter the next day and wished for Strother's support. The only drawback either officer saw was the lack of ammunition.

In the camps, the common soldiers did not struggle with long-term goals: the problem of feeding and moving an army, the worry over battlefield strategy, or the effects events in Richmond might have on the campaign. They were simply "...wondering what the morrow has in store for us."[18]

Thursday, June 9

From the highest commanders to the colonels involved, there was agreement that Lynchburg was the next major target of the campaign. Grant, Lee, and now Departmental Commander Breckinridge agreed that the advance should move toward the railroad at Charlottesville and then south to Lynchburg. At Staunton, debate was taking place in the high command as to the route to follow.

Breckinridge would not get Morgan from Southwest Virginia, but he would get the Botetourt Artillery (six guns). To show the importance Confederate high command placed on the need to stop Hunter, the next to the last artillery unit in the department would be sent to the Valley. The all-important New River Bridge would be virtually wide open. With Morgan gone, the defense of the whole department rested almost entirely on the shoulders of the old and the young — the Home Guard. Captain Fielding C. Douthat of the Botetourt Artillery received his orders to move on June 9. Because of time, the artillery horses were left behind and the guns moved toward Lynchburg on flat cars attached to a mail train.

Whether it was June 8 or 9, Breckinridge did arrive at Rockfish Gap. The train was packed inside, and some soldiers rode on the tops of cars. The saviour of the Valley was back, and command of the department was transferred. Breckinridge (a politician before the war) delivered "...a powerful oration which seemed greatly to revive their courage."[30]

Breckinridge believed in offensive war, not defensive. His first intentions were to organize his forces and then proceed toward Hunter and do battle. However, after receiving reliable reports that Crook and Hunter had combined forces and that now there were more than 18,000 men to oppose him, he changed his mind.

The combined forces of Vaughan, Imboden, and Breckinridge numbered approximately 5,023 infantry, and 4,000 mounted troops.[55] Breckinridge divided the infantry and placed it under Vaughn (second-in-command) and Wharton (third-in-command); the cavalry was placed under Imboden (fourth-in-command). Apparently Breckinridge held a low opinion of Imboden and his ability to handle the cavalry. He described it as "...wild cavalry — of the inefficiency of which there was constant complaint and almost daily exhibition."[55]

Breckinridge ordered scouts sent out to report on Hunter. He then sent additional forces to Waynesboro, including at least one artillery unit. Because of Breckinridge's injuries from the fall from his horse, he turned most of the details over to his subordinates and rested as much as possible.

John Opie, who had just returned with solid information that Crook and Hunter had combined, was sent out again. When he returned to the campsite of his brazen seven comrades of the day before, he could not locate them. They had been shifted to another position. Because of the urgency of his orders, he decided not to continue looking for them but rode off alone to scout the Union Army. He decided to watch Staunton, not from the east but from the south. Bravely he rode alone into enemy-controlled country.

Near daylight, most of the wagon train from Staunton began moving toward Vaughn. This train had crossed the Blue Ridge and had camped near Arrington Station on the Orange & Alexandria Railroad. Because some of the horses were worn out, part of the wagons, men, and horses, stayed behind while the majority of the supply train headed toward Vaughn.

In Staunton, the destruction started again and early. "It certainly looks bad for this town,"[18] concluded one observer. Amid the continuing destruction, some troops from Crook's command were allowed to rest. Others from Meadow Bluff received much needed shoes, stolen from the factory at Staunton. Ammunition was issued.

The Union soldiers had not forgotten their wounded comrades from Piedmont. Hunter had literally put Confederate wounded in the streets so that his wounded could have the hospital. When Yankees broke into the tobacco warehouses, they brought some of the stolen goods to the wounded.

Most of the Confederate wounded had been taken into the hotels that the Yanks did not occupy.

Having stolen, eaten, or destroyed most of the food in Staunton, troops now went into the countryside foraging both horses and cattle. Because there were also pesky Rebs around to capture or kill an individual or any small group that wandered too far from the main body, men remained in groups, armed and alert.

Some infantry soldiers stole some meal and flour. It was better to have it in their bellies than to chance having to divide it with others or having it stolen upon their return. They pulled the farmers' rail fences down for firewood. They tore canteens apart and used a stick for a handle: thus a frying pan. They made small pancakes which they called "toe jam."

A foraging party of the First New York was attacked by about thirty Confederate guerrillas, but the Yanks put the Rebs to flight.

South of town it was the Yanks who ran. McCausland advanced from Brownsburg up the Valley Pike Road. After a constant retreat since Meadow Bluff, McCausland was glad to advance. According to one soldier, "Nothing daunted we turned our backward march into a forward one, shewed (sic) our ragamuffins on the mountains...."[54] ("Ragamuffins" refers to the sad condition of clothing, horses, equipment, and men). The Union picket was attacked in force and driven in, back to one mile from Staunton. Here the Federals were reinforced, and the advance was halted. It was a minor operation but a morale builder. There was no mention of casualties, but both sides probably received some. A few casualties most days were simply a fact of life for these soldiers.

Since early morning, members of Hunter's high command evaluated the latest intelligence reports, conferred, and tried to reach a consensus on the next move of the army. All agreed that Lynchburg should be taken. One officer wrote, "We hoped thereby to drive Lee out of Richmond by seizing and threatening his southern and western communications and sources of supply."[11] According to another officer, all agreed, "...we could easily beat all the force that the enemy had in the Valley and in (South) West Virginia combined...."[11] It was also believed that Lee couldn't shift any significant force to help in the Valley, because of the pressure Grant was keeping on him. Even if Lee were to attempt to send troops, Sheridan's Cavalry would cut them off by destroying the railroad. Lynchburg and the Valley were theirs for the taking. The only question was which way to proceed: via Charlottesville and the railroad or overland via Lexington. Crook was less optimistic than the others. He knew that a thousand incidents could change or occur to change the military situation. What he saw was an open Lynchburg *NOW*. He wanted to move *NOW*. He wanted to "...move upon it (Lynchburg) immediately and rapidly."[11] When he was reminded that there wasn't enough gunpowder for sustained combat over a long period, "Crook said he had plenty and if permitted would march on Lynchburg with his division alone...."[11] Crook realized that time was just as much a commodity of war as gunpowder, shoes, and food. Lynchburg was open then, but it might have been more difficult to take later.

New intelligence came in for the officers to ponder. A Negro, who came to Staunton from Waynesboro, reported that Imboden's men were demoralized. The cavalry attack the day before had caused many men to desert. They were frightened by the prospect of tangleing with the Union Army again. Also the Negro reported that McCausland and Jackson had moved their men to join Imboden. He also reported rumors that additional troops were being brought from Richmond. The Negro's report was given more credence because of other reports that General Breckinridge was coming from Richmond.

Hunter was aware of the new reports and of the discussion among his officers. He was also working on a command structure for his army. The organizational chart he made at Staunton remained basically the same for the rest of the campaign.

ORGANIZATION OF FEDERAL FORCES AT LYNCHBURG
Department of West Virginia
Maj. Gen. David Hunter, Commanding

1st DIVISION: Brig. Gen. J. C. Sullivan
1st Brigade: Col. G. D. Wells
34th Mass.
116th Ohio
123rd Ohio
5th N.Y.H.A. (Cos. A, B, C, D)

2nd Brigade: Col. J. Thoburn
4th West Va.
18th Conn.
1st West Va.
12th West Va.

Unassigned:
2nd Md. Eastern Shore
2nd Md. Potomac Home Brigade

2nd DIVISION: Brig. Gen. George Crook
1st Brigade: Col. R. B. Hayes
23rd Ohio
36th Ohio
5th West Va.
13th West Va.

2nd Brigade: Col. C. B. White
12th Ohio
91st Ohio
9th West Va.
14th West Va.

3rd Brigade: Col. J. M. Campbell
54th Penna.
3rd & 4th Penna. Reserves (Bttn.)
11th West Va. (6 Companies)
15th West Va.

ARTILLERY: 1st Ky. Lt. Arty.
                1st Ohio Lt. Arty.

FEDERAL CAVALRY
1st DIVISION: Brig. Gen. A. N. Duffié
1st Brigade: Col. R. F. Taylor
15th N.Y.
1st N.Y. (Veteran)
21st N.Y.
1st Md. P.H.B.

2nd Brigade: Col. J. E. Wynkoop
20th Penna.
22nd Penna.
1st N.Y. (Lincoln)

ARTILLERY: 1st West Va. Lt. Arty., B

2nd DIVISION: Brig. Gen. W. W. Averell
1st Brigade: Col. J. N. Schoonmaker
8th Ohio
14th Penna.

2nd Brigade: Col. J. H. Oley
34th Ohio Mt. Inf.
3rd West Va.
5th West Va.
7th West Va.

3rd Brigade: Col. W. H. Powell
1st West Va.
2nd West Va.

ARTILLERY: Capt. H. A. DuPont
B, Md. Lt. Arty.
30th N.Y. Lt. Arty.
D, 1st West Va.
B, 5th U.S.

It is not known what time of day Hunter started making decisions. To Crook's request to go it alone, Hunter replied "No." The army would remain in one unit, fully under his control. The "No" to Crook's request to move with all possible speed was given because, Hunter thought, a good deal of delay was unavoidable. Hunter, like most of his officers, didn't see a need to rush. The South could do little or nothing to stop them from taking Lynchburg; besides, he was having the time of his life burning, destroying, and punishing this part of a slave-holding state.

Hunter had been giving the direction of the march a considerable amount of thought. The latest rumors placed Breckinridge heading toward the Valley. He had taken a vastly inferior army and routed Hunter's predecessor. Could he do it again?

Although Grant's orders seemed clear as to the army's course of march, Hunter began to interpret them as giving him "...some latitude...."[11] He decided that Grant's orders weren't chiseled in stone. After all, "strategy is the science of contingencies; a military campaign is an evolution of the unexpected."[56]

It was Gen. William W. Averell's turn to "...suggest a plan of operation...(to) capture Lynchburg...in five days."[59] Averell's plan called for moving upon Lynchburg overland via Lexington. Hunter might not have had to meet the man that sent his predecessor scurrying.

Gen. A.N. Duffié was to take some of the cavalry and move through a gap in the Blue Ridge, strike out Amherst Courthouse, cut the Southside Railroad and Canal, and then move toward Lynchburg.

Hunter "...approved and adopted..."[56] the plan: the army would move tomorrow.

By now Colonel Hayes of the Twenty-Third Ohio had had time to assess his new boss. He held an unfavorable opinion of Hunter even before they met. Now he concluded that "Hunter was an easy man to dislike...had a violent, almost a crusading desire to eradicate slavery...prejudiced and intolerant and likely to fly in sudden fits of anger and denunciation."[56] He also considered Hunter a stubborn man.

Dupont, Hunter's Chief-of-Artillery, admired Hunter's physical strength and endurance for his age but also expressed distrust of his judgement when dealing with civilians.

Hunter gave orders to help insure the success of the plan he had adopted. To help reduce the army's burden, the prisoners, the convalescents, and those with expired enlistments would start north the next morning.

To occupy the Confederacy's attentions and to mask Union intentions, Hunter ordered another cavalry raid on the Rebs at Waynesboro. This raid would hold Southern units in place as they would think that the real attack was headed their way. Hayes saw a political motive: "Hunter's push was probably intended as a token to show he had attempted to follow orders...."[60]

Some in Hunter's army had already advanced on Lexington, two of Hunter's spies (Jessie Scouts) arrived "...claiming to be from the far South, and ostensibly enjoying a furlough."[36] They took a room at the Lexington Hotel. A

local son came back to town about the time the strangers took boarding at the
hotel. The local was Capt. Matthew (Matt) X. White, with Company H,
Fourteenth Virginia Cavalry. He was home on leave. The men met. Matt did
not know they were Yankee spies. Matt and "...his supposed friends...(were)
enjoying together a glass of whiskey...."[36]

It was 11:00 in the morning when the V.M.I. cadets reached Lynchburg by
train. Here they learned that Hunter had occupied Staunton and might march
on their Institute at Lexington. Only McCausland was in Hunter's path.
Quickly the cadets were transferred to canal boats going toward Lexington.

The train bearing the artillery and horses for the corps also reached
Lynchburg. The cadets started overland toward their school. The wounded
soldier from the Stonewall Brigade was given a ride on an artillery horse.
Because of the severity of his wound, he soon had to dismount and move
slowly toward Staunton on foot.

Troops, sometimes, are not eager to march, dig trenches, or fight, but they
are quick to obey the order to go home. Apparently it was the idea of Colonel
McReynolds who was with the First New York Cavalry to have a formal dress
parade to bid farewell to the lucky troops going back to "America."[60] The
band played "Home, Sweet Home" as the color guard stepped off with the
flags. The flags were to be presented to the Governor at Columbus, Ohio.
Apparently, Col. Augustus Moor was the highest ranking officer to leave with
the 800 men whose terms of duty were expiring. Moor carried personal
dispatches from some of the officers. Most of these soldiers were from the
Twenty-Eighth Ohio or Ewing's Artillery Unit. There were approximately
1,000 Southern prisoners from Piedmont plus Negroes and refugees moving
north toward Martinsburg. The wounded Gen. Julius Stahel, and some of his
cavalrymen were to guard the wagon train. At Martinsburg, Stahel was to
escort a supply wagon train back to Hunter's army. One member, the chaplain,
of the One Hundred Twenty-Third Ohio was in the parade. Apparently the
preacher and his flock did not get along too well as "...his resignation (was)
being accepted at once...."[53]

In the 800, there were nine officers and 100 men from the Twenty-Third
Ohio. The future president, Rutherford B. Hayes, used the occasion for
transporting war booty and personal property. He sent his horse back with the
hope that someone in the family would sell it. He also sent "...a pistol captured
at Blacksburg from Lieutenant-Colonel Linkus, Thirty-Sixth Virginia, Rebel...
(and) (A) handbill showing (Colonel) Lee's appeal to the people of this
(Augusta) county."[11] Hayes recognized Col. Edwin Lee's abilities in writing.

Along with the happiness for the lucky ones going home, there was a note
of sorrow. "There was a general feeling of regret at the separation of the
Colonel (Moor) from his command."[9] The dress parade was on June 9, the
column would leave on June 10.

As some Yanks were preparing to leave Staunton, others were approaching
Waynesboro. One Confederate remarked: "We were in line of battle again,
had another skirmish, the enemy (Union cavalry) again fell back...."[35]

Back at Staunton, the unlucky troops began to prepare for the march the next day. There was much to be done. Because the march would be carried out over three separated roads, the Signal Corps would have a big job to do. It must keep the three Union columns in contact in order to prevent a sudden unexpected Confederate attack from crushing one of the columns. Men from the Signal Corps were assigned to the commander's staff of each marching column.

Although it had been a day of almost continuous conferences, organizational tasks, and parades for the officers, Colonel Hayes found some time to mingle with some of the native population. He found them to be "...friendly and polite; not the slightest bitterness or unkindness...."[22] Although he referred to all Southerners with the derogatory name "secesh," he appreciated Southern hospitality. He concluded if he ever had to be hospitalized "...this is the spot."[22]

Some time in the afternoon, Hunter became aware that a lady and nine children were waiting to see him. If that wasn't enough, there were others accompanying the brood. These people all wanted to speak with Hunter on behalf of Alexander T. Stuart, the arrested Mayor of their town. Hunter wanted nothing to do with an anguished wife and nine bawling children. He knew Mayor Stuart's fate was decided when he referred the matter to Strother to "...release"[11] him.

During the day, McCausland's forces had driven a Yankee picket back to within a mile or so from Staunton. With Northern reinforcements, the balance of power turned; and Confederate forces were pushed back. By nightfall, the Rebs had been pushed back six miles. Southern sentries were posted on Arbor Hill (the area also referred to as Palmer's Store).

Most soldiers of both sides slept, but many members of the First New York Cavalry were on alert all night. McCausland's attack of the day caused Federal forces to stay on guard during the night.

Alfred Duffie — U.S.

Friday, June 10

Duffié's Cavalry was the first to move from Staunton on Friday, June 10. Gen. Alfred Napoleon Alexander Duffié was born in Paris in May, 1835. He was an 1854 graduate of the Military College of St. Cyr. He was a veteran of the bloody Crimean War. With his French accent and military background, this soldier of fortune achieved the rank of Brigadier General in the United States Army in June, 1863. He was known as a very tough disciplinarian. Some of his units started as early as 3:00 a.m. He headed east over the Staunton-Waynesboro Road to Fishersville. There he cut south on the Waynesboro Pike toward Tye River Gap. He skirted the base of the Blue Ridge. At the mouth of Rockfish Gap, he used part of his cavalry to screen the main column so that Confederate forces could not attack the main body without detection. Near the base of the Gap, his men burned buildings and destroyed property of the Mountain Tenny Iron Furnace. As the South was not aware of his presence, he encountered little resistance.

During the day, he sent ten men to destroy the track on the Orange & Alexandria near Arrington Station.

Once again Confederate scout, John Opie, gives no information where he slept on the night of June 9. On the morning of June 10, he was at Col. James C. Cochran's farm, about five miles south of Staunton on Valley Pike, the main road from Staunton to Lexington. The occupants of the house knew he was on their land; it is possible that he had spent the night or dined there. South of the house on the road leading to Brownsburg on the west side of the road in a thick woods, John Opie staked out a spot to watch the road. In a short time, five riders dressed in gray were heading north. He saw the Jessie Scouts and was sure that they didn't see him. He was wrong. The five rode to the Cochran house and told a slave they were looking for a scout from their outfit that was supposed to be on this farm. The slave gave them Opie's location. Then the Jessie Scouts were sure that the Confederate scout in a Confederate uniform in the woods was indeed a Confederate.

Opie heard a noise in the woods and turned to see the five Jessie Scouts, pistols drawn, heading toward him. They wanted to drive him out of the woods and into the main road. Opie recalled, "Leaping into my saddle amidst a volley of balls, I had a race for life."[20] Opie refused to leave the woods, using trees to shield him and to attempt to escape through. Because he was riding through the woods, he could not return the fire because a limb might knock him from his horse as he turned. After a mile or so of chase, the Jessie Scouts gave up. The brazen Opie deducted that the only place they would not look for him was the spot where they had found him in the first place. Only a crazy man would return to the same spot. Opie went back and continued his vigil.

Opie wasn't the only Confederate scout in the area. In the early morning, McCausland had sent Lt. Sam Cochran (Commander) and Andrew Snider, James Long, and James E. McChesney from Brownsburg toward Staunton. The four rode to about one mile south of the tollgate below Staunton. At this point, they sighted a squadron of Yankee cavalry. The Yankees began to deploy as if getting ready to do battle with the four. Because the Northern cavalrymen couldn't be sure if they were Confederates or their own Jessie Scouts, they didn't fire. Before they came close enough to be identified as Rebs, the four turned unhurriedly about and withdrew slowly. After they were out of sight of the cavalry, the four moved more swiftly away from danger.

While scouting was going on and preparations were being made to move at Staunton, a train was approaching Lynchburg. The six guns of the Botetourt Artillery arrived with no horses or orders. They were to remain in Lynchburg until otherwise ordered.

In Staunton, last-minute stealing was going on. Colonel Starr caught a fellow, probably a fellow Yank, trying to steal his horse. He took him to Hunter. Hunter was subject to sudden fits of anger, but he didn't curse. According to one observer, "The General...abused him to the extent of his limited vocabulary, cuffed and kicked him around...."[11] Because he was a Yankee, he was not shot.

Hunter didn't believe that there was sufficient ammunition for the drive to capture Lynchburg, but time was important. He would move before he was re-supplied. He was not aware that the supply wagon train was approaching Staunton. It was probably the same one he had ordered Sullivan to bring forward after he had safely escorted the column to Martinsburg.

The farewell dress parade was June 9. This morning, probably near 8:00 a.m., the column began to leave Staunton. The prisoners (except one man), Negroes, and lucky troops, moved out.

It was approximately 11:00 a.m. when the Yanks began to stream out of Staunton, following three different roads. The Signal Corps was charged with the responsibility of keeping the column in communication.

Averell was to move his cavalry on the road to the west, Crook with infantry was on Valley Pike, and Sullivan (with Hunter) moved to the road on the east side with his infantry. One group of Federals did not leave Staunton. These Federals were the sick and the wounded too weak to be transported. The three hundred men, several doctors, and about forty attendants were left behind.

It was already hot when Averell rode out of town. The roads were dry. A lot of blue-bellies would eat dust that day. McCausland's troops were strung from Staunton to Brownsburg on the Valley Pike. Averell said they "...appeared sporadically to contest the way...."[60]

Crook encountered opposition from McCausland about one and a half miles south of town on the Valley Pike Road. The Yanks estimated McCausland's strength at 2,000 men and one battery. McCausland probably had fewer than 1,500 men. Because of the narrow roadway, neither side could bring many men to bear on its opponent. No doubt, Signal Corps scouts took the news to Hunter with Sullivan's column. Hunter did not realize that part of the Negro's report was wrong; McCausland had not gone to join Vaughn and Imboden.

McCausland knew that he couldn't stop the Union advance, but he was a shrewd general. He knew that time was important in military operations. Every minute he delayed the Union advance, it was a victory. Every casualty for the North weakened and slowed its progress. Very few with the Northern army and very few Southerners could see any use in the skirmishes McCausland fought, but he continued his skirmishing.

McCausland built barricades of fence rails across the road. His men would fire at the enemy from their protected position until the Union halted and deployed units to flank the barricade. Then they would fall back and repeat the process. The Union column would remain halted until the barricade was removed.

One Confederate soldier took Crook's advance personally. He believed that the Federals were striking back in anger because the South had pushed their picket force almost into Staunton the day before. "This so enraged them that...next morning Crook and Averell...marched out against us, swearing that they would drive McCausland to Hell, and really from the way he has put us through from there to this place seems like he would be able to keep his word,"[54] reported a Confederate soldier.

Another Confederate soldier saw it differently: "The Federal cavalry attempted to ride over us...we planted a few in the ground...put them in a condition to be returned to Mother Earth...."[63]

Very few casualties were taken on either side. The Fifth (West) Virginia Regiment reported that three men including officer Lieutenant A. Miller were killed, and three men were wounded. They had five Rebel bodies to confirm their count.

The four scouts McCausland had sent forward toward Staunton had encountered the enemy column also. As they, too, fell back to their position of the night before on Arbor Hill they "...found a strong barricade of fence rails...."[19] The four took cover behind the already deserted obstacle and waited for the enemy. One scout wrote: "I determined then and there to send my compliments to the enemy...."[19] The first shots from the barricade caused the Yanks to "retire...only to reappear in a few minutes...dismounted men deployed on each side...It was a grand sight, and we felt rather stuck-up that we...had caused such a display of force. (Soon) The rattle of bullets against our frail breastwork was terrific...We hastily retired...."[19]

The Rebel scout Opie also encountered the Union Army. He had returned to his original position on the west side of the Valley Pike Road. When Crook's men marched, Opie could not cross the road to take the information to Vaughn. He sat for three hours, watching Crook's men march by. Opie reported later: "I was so close to them, that I could hear their conversation."[20]

The Confederates fell back "slowly and stubbornly...."[19] McCausland found a good place for another ambush. On the Beard farm, the road made an oblique curve at the bottom of a high hill, crowned by woods. The horses were sent a little farther down the road toward Lexington. The men were placed along the wood line. The Fourteenth, Sixteenth, and Seventeenth Virginia Cavalries composed most of the line. It was about noon, and the Confederates didn't wait long for the cavalry that proceeded Crook's Infantry to arrive. The cavalry advanced four abreast. The sides of the Union men were exposed; thus it "...gave the whole firing line timber to work on."[63] One Confederate reported that the Federal cavalry was stunned when "...A roar went out from our lines...."[63] Many Yankees were blown from their saddles. It was "quite a spirited skirmish...."[19] The panicked cavalry retreated a short way up the road. To this point, it was a total Confederate victory (no losses). Then Capt. E.E. Bouldin's (also recorded Boulden) company of the Fourteenth on the right, chased after the Yanks in an attack McCausland did not order.

Within minutes, the Reb advance struck the Union infantry. "Several of the Charlotte Cavalry were wounded, (including) Norman B. Spraggins...,"[63] the South "losing several men, but inflicted greater loss upon the enemy."[19] There was no time for a body count. "The killed and wounded...we had to leave for their disposal, as we had to move on when the infantry came up,"[63] was one report. Two dead Rebels were buried at a fence corner. The Confederates fell back with the Fourteenth Virginia as rear guard.

One of the wounded was Norman Spraggins who couldn't stay with the column. He was left at the house of Capt. Tom Smiley. As the Confederates continued to retreat, James R. Crews also of Company B, Fourteenth Virginia Cavalry was wounded. He was left at Capt. James Strain's house near New Providence Church on the road to Brownsburg.

Apparently without authorization from McCausland, James McChesney left the retreat and rode to his family farm near Brownsburg. He would help save the livestock and valuables from Union plunderers.

Meanwhile, closer to Staunton, the brazen Opie was getting bored eavesdropping on Union soldiers' conversations. He saw a single mounted officer ride from Valley Pike up the long roadway to the Cochran house. Satirically Opie said, "I was very lonesome and determined to enjoy this man's company...."[20] Opie crept back through the woods and mounted his horse. From the woods, he observed that the Union officer had dismounted and was standing close to his horse. Out of the woods Opie dashed, pistol in hand. The Federal went for his pistol. Opie exclaimed, "Draw, and you are a dead man!"[20] The officer must have thought that Opie was a madman because the infantry was marching on Valley Pike only one hundred and fifty yards away. The infantry would be after him as soon as Opie pulled the trigger, but when he did pull the trigger, the officer knew he might meet his maker. The officer surrendered. Opie disarmed his prisoner. About this time, as a Union cavalry detachment thought that something funny must be going on at the house, it turned from Valley Pike. Opie ordered the officer to mount and stay in front of him in the woods or he would shoot him. The officer complied. They rode about a mile toward the west and lost the Union Cavalry. Opie chose a hill with a good view, and there he rested. He found out that this Yankee was Captain Johnson from Crook's personal staff, a fine intelligent catch who also wrote for the "Wheeling Intelligencer" a popular newspaper.

Opie concluded that it was too dangerous to move now. They would wait for nightfall.

In the same time frame that Opie took a prisoner and escaped, McChesney had gone to his family farm and returned. He caught up with his unit below Brownsburg. Here he was ordered to fight a delaying action as Crook

advanced. He was at Zack Johnstone's farm awaiting the enemy advance over
Valley Pike when the Yankee cavalry unexpectedly, from Walker Creek struck
McCausland's column closer to Lexington. McChesney's group was caught
between the Yanks that attacked McCausland to his rear and Crook's advance
over Valley Pike. McChesney's men struck out across country toward
Fairfield. They would attempt to circle the Yanks on the road and rejoin
McCausland.

The North kept advancing as the South kept retreating. "What availed
courage against such odds?"[54] The Union high command did not think much
of Southern efforts. The high command reported that McCausland "...was
easily driven..."[8] and that he "...did not seriously impede progress...."[59] "Not
withstanding the opposition the regiment marched twenty-three miles that
day."[21]

Union soldiers at the rear hardly took notice of the fighting. They took "all
cattle and horses that can be found."[18]

The Hundred Sixteenth Ohio was the last unit to leave Staunton. It had
marched seven miles at the dusty end of the column, when it was halted and
reversed. The men must march rapidly back to Staunton. A mounted unit
reported that a Union supply train was at Staunton and needed protection
before it could move forward. Back went the Hundred Sixteenth. There were
two hundred wagons to be guarded. The Hundred Sixteenth was less than
happy to have to march the same piece of road three times in one day.

Hunter was with Sullivan's Infantry that went toward Lexington via the
Greenville Road. The supply train was guarded by the Hundred Twenty-
Third Ohio. Sullivan encountered little or no resistance. Hunter's desire to burn
had not been quenched at Staunton. He had mills at Greenville and Fairfield
burned.

At Waynesboro, the Union cavalrymen kept Breckinridge's forces occupied. They "had a fight at the same position and the enemy fell back; the
artillery was used."[35] The Northern cavalry withdrew after "...losing several
men."[6] Breckinridge must have wondered when Hunter would attack in force.

As the last units left Staunton, the citizens began to take possession of their
once beautiful town. They couldn't believe the destruction that had been
visited on them. The hatred of the Yankees ran high, but some kept a balanced
perspective of their invaders. They said that some "...seemed to be gentlemen...having no heart for their business; others were mere plunderers and
robbed blacks and whites alike."[43] Most of the ladies of Staunton retained their
self-respect during the horrible ordeal; they were "...neither rude nor pleasant,
only coldly polite."[6] One slave owner said, "Our servants were such a comfort
to me. They could not have behaved better, and I really feel thankful to
them."[43] All were glad when the reign of terror was over.

Through the night and into the early morning hours, the cadets moved up
the James River Canal by boat. They debarked at the mouth of North River
and marched into Lexington arriving at 3:00 p.m. Their commander, Scott
Shipp, held the rank of colonel in the Virginia Militia.

As dark approached, the men of the Hundred Sixteenth Ohio and the wagon train they had been guarding made camp. They were still well back from the main body of Crook's army on Valley Pike Road. The soldiers discovered that there was food in the wagons. One soldier wrote "...for the first time in a week, had a good square meal."[14] There was a cargo more precious than food on board for the common soldier — letters from home. It had been a long march for the Hundred Sixteenth, but there were many happy soldiers lounging on the ground.

A courier with letters was sent toward Hunter at Midway. At Midway, Hunter was happy to hear about the train with "...necessary supplies and some ammunition...."[11] Hunter sent a courier back to the train, ordering it not to camp but move forward until it linked with Crook. Soldiers at Midway did not get a square meal, but they were very happy for the letters. One soldier remembered talking with an elderly resident who said, "It does me good to see the old flag. I have not seen it for more than three years."[41]

The heavenly minded Henry Jones simply noted in his diary that the Union camped in Brownsburg.

No reason was found why the following event occurred where and when it did. It was near sundown at Belleview about three miles west of Brownsburg on Hays Creek with Gen. William W. Averell in command. Hunter was not present, but he knew of the proceedings. One writer refers to it as "The story of Hunter's crime...."[63] All of the able bodied Southern prisoners had been sent toward Martinsburg except David Creigh of Lewisburg, (West) Virginia. An armed, drunken man who had entered Mr. Creigh's house was stealing and destroying his property and verbally abusing the women folk and threatening to assault them. When Creigh demanded that the unwelcome visitor leave, the intruder attempted to kill Creigh. In self-defense, Creigh killed the intruder who had trampled on almost every right that Creigh was granted by God, the United States and State Constitution. There is no evidence that the prosecution challenged any of these facts at his trial. Indeed, credence was given Mr. Creigh's testimony because according to several sources, he was "a most excellent Christian gentleman...,"[64] "one of the most prominent and devoted members of the Presbyterian Church of Lewisburg, a church Elder."[63] He was the father of eleven children, with a "reputation of the highest order (and of) the highest social position."[23] Apparently the prosecution didn't challenge Creigh's honor or honesty.

Not a court in the country should convict a man based on these facts, but in this court, the judges wore blue, and the dead intruder was wearing blue also. Guilty! The death sentence had not been carried out because the court wanted the head of the army to give his approval. On the evening of June 10, David Creigh was to meet his maker, or so Hunter thought.

Of all the places that Creigh could have been executed, fate had brought him to the farm of the Rev. James Morrison. Creigh, a devoted Christian, knew the Rev. Mr. Morrison well. When Creigh was informed that his sentence was to be carried out at the Morrison farm, he had but two requests. To allow Mr. Morrison to pray for him, and the other was that he be allowed to write one last letter home.

The Rev. Mr. Morrison remembered a knock at his door and seeing an elderly man from Uniontown, Pennsylvania. He was Rev. Mr. Osborn, an army chaplain. He informed Morrison of Creigh's last request. David Creigh was being held in a slave cabin on the farm. Morrison attempted to go to him to comfort him, but a Union guard prevented this visit. Morrison could speak to God but not to David Creigh.

What does a Christian man, ready to face his own death, write to his wife and family? What does an innocent man write to those he loves but will never see again on this earth? It must have been a hard letter to write and to read. Averell saw no reason to rush a dead man; he allowed Creigh this last night to write his last letter.

Back at his camp at Midway, Hunter did not know of the delay in the execution. He had apparently not told Strother of the incident. Strother knew that the wagon train had arrived with some ammunition, and he believed that this news is what made Hunter happy this evening. He noted, "The general is in high good humor."[11]

Hunter was in a good mood, but the Superintendent of V.M.I., F.H. Smith, was not. By 6:00 p.m. he had finished a conference with McCausland, who gave the position and estimated troop strength of Averell and Crook, but he was not aware of Sullivan. It was stated, "If pursued by either column, McCausland will not be able to hold Lexington."[58] V.M.I. would be occupied.

The residents of Lexington prepared for Hunter by hiding valuables, and food. They also sent livestock and slaves to the mountains. Many residents decided to flee south. Col. Angus McDonald was one to leave. He and his family had left the Winchester area, too, because of Union pressure. McDonald, a staunch Confederate, was old and partially crippled by rheumatism. His wife wrote "...he looked so little able to undertake even a short journey that it filled me with misgivings."[25] He could no longer serve his country actively. Since pressure from the Union Army and pro-Northern sympathizers had made life unbearable for the family, he had moved to Lexington. Now the war and General Hunter in particular had come to town. McDonald and his son, Harry, moved south over Valley Pike. McDonald gave his wife instructions, but she hardly heard them. "The future was nothing... portentous and dreadful, and I thought only of his going, and that he might not ever come back,"[25] she recorded.

One of the prominent citizens to also leave town was the former Governor of the Commonwealth of Virginia, John Letcher. He returned to his birthplace, Lexington, after his term expired in January 1864. He was governor when the war started, and "...his belief in eventual Confederate victory never wavered."[65] He knew if he stayed to face the ruthless Hunter, his freedom, and perhaps his life, would be forfeited.

Before he left town, he issued a proclamation to all Virginians never to surrender but continue to the struggle if only by guerrilla tactics.

The former governor was not a wealthy man, "war time inflation...had ruined him financially...."[65] He had to leave his greatest asset, his home, to his wife and the mercy of a merciless enemy.

On the evening of June 10, Matt again joined his friends at the hotel. The town was buzzing with rumors of Hunter's advance and Jessie Scouts. Matt told his new friends that he had been on patrol and "he had met an armed man dressed in citizens clothing." Matt decided that he was a Jessie Scout and shot him. The two new friends were very interested that he had shot a Jessie Scout. The dead man was a local farm laborer named John Thorn, who may have had Union sympathies, but no proof existed that he was a Jessie Scout. Matt was a man of war; this armed man in civilian clothes may have been a Jessie Scout so Matt shot him at the tollgate over North River at Lexington.

Later Matt excused himself from his new acquaintances, saying that he was returning to the family farm three miles west of town for the night.

The courier from Hunter arrived at the wagon train. The train and its infantry escort started forward. "It was a dreary, tiresome night march,"[14] said one infantryman.

The Signal Corps which was to keep communications open among the three columns had not done well today. Because the hills and the mountains had stopped direct communication, couriers had been used. Duffie's Cavalry force marched toward Tye River Gap, where it camped for the night. A Union cavalryman noted that it was much cooler that night at the base of the Blue Ridge than it had been in Staunton.

At Midway, a regiment of soldiers went to bed very tired, but sleep was not to be their companion. They were soon ordered to the line to protect an artillery battery. They must be ever vigilant lest a Rebel guerrilla attack succeed.

By sundown at Rockfish Gap, Breckinridge had heard reports that Hunter had moved troops south out of Staunton. He had no idea if this was a diversionary move or the real move. He had not received hard intelligence from any of his scouts.

If it were a diversionary attempt, he wanted to know. If it was the real move, perhaps his cavalry units could do some damage to Hunter's rear. About dark, he sent orders for Imboden to move toward Staunton in force. A cavalryman noted that his unit was now under Imboden and that they had marched all night.

With hard intelligence, Opie and a Union officer prisoner started toward Waynesboro at nightfall, but the road was occupied by Federals. He directed his prisoner into deep woods and they dismounted. Opie told his prisoner that he had been scouting five days and was exhausted. He said that he couldn't stay awake and watch him, but he really didn't want to shoot him either. Opie's bluff worked. The prisoner promised, "Oh, for God's sake don't kill me! I swear, upon the word of an officer and a gentleman, that I will not attempt to escape."[20] Opie said that he would accept the Yank's word, but if he as much as raised his head during the night, he would be shot. To keep the prisoner from getting his pistols during the night and reversing the tables on him, Opie slept on his guns.

Unlike Opie, James McChesney was able to rejoin his unit of McCausland's army, two miles below Brownsburg.

The wounded soldier from the Stonewall Brigade who had come to Lynchburg with the cadet artillery had been walking toward his hometown, Staunton. He heard from refugees that Hunter had moved south out of Staunton and that "the whole country seemed now to be overrun by the Federals."[62] He spent the night within an estimated ten miles from Staunton.

Two miles above Lexington at 7:00 p.m., Gen. Francis Smith from V.M.I. had a second conference with McCausland. McCausland at this time indicated that he could hold Lexington with support from the cadets and that he expected support from Breckinridge. Smith replied, "I was prepared to make any sacrifice necessary to this end. But that if a resistance in front of Lexington could only retard the advance...a few hours, involving thereby a useless sacrifice of life and endangering...the cadets...I was not willing to make such a sacrifice...."[66] McCausland restated his position that "...he deemed it important to retard the advance of the enemy...."[66] Neither side had changed its position, and McCausland was not sure of the corps's support.

Maj. Achilles James Tynes remembered that he was camped two miles below Lexington when he was awakened at 11:00 p.m. and told to go to a conference at the Institute. When he arrived, McCausland was conferring with General Smith again, but this time the direct commander of the corps, Col. Scott Shipp (Virginia Militia) was present. Tynes, not realizing what was occurring, found it difficult to stay awake. Tynes came alive when General Smith's "...fair daughter..."[54] began to serve them coffee (a luxury at this time in the war). The women's fashions dictated dress from neck to floor; there wasn't much for a man to see, but Tynes noted that she had a pretty face "...and oh such a pretty foot, too!"[54]

Apparently Colonel Shipp agreed with McCausland that retarding Hunter was worth the sacrifice. Colonel Shipp ordered the corps to help slow Hunter. To this end, the cadets' Howitzer was placed on a hillside overlooking the covered wooden bridge over North (now Maury) River, going east from Lexington. Capt. Henry A. Wise was ordered to blow "...out the piers, upon the approach of the enemy."[58]

A group of cadets was sent to load the bridge "...with bales of hay saturated with turpentine, leaving space just sufficient for the passage of McCausland's retreating forces."[58]

All waited for Hunter and the morrow.

Chapter VIII

Saturday, June 11 — Monday, June 13

On Saturday, June 11, the wagon train and its escort had been ordered to keep moving until they joined Crook's column. At 2:00 a.m. it was deemed impossible to push on until man and beast rested. It was a brief two hours, and they were back on the road again.

As the wagon train started at 4:00 a.m., most of Hunter's three columns began to rub the sleep from their eyes and prepare to march.

At 5:00 a.m. some units were lucky enough to draw rations. Most all units began marching south toward Lexington. The wagon train came upon the army just as the army started marching. Because of the tired condition of the horses and men, they were allowed to rest in the camp where their comrades had slept the night before.

Not all of Averell's command started forward at dawn. David Creigh had finished his letter the night before. This was to be the innocent mans last sunrise. "...He was brought out, put into a wagon, and conveyed up a little vale, about a quarter of a mile north of the house, and in full view of it, and was there hanged...."[23] "I have often seen the tree upon which this good man was hanged in the meadow of the Reverend James Morrison, and an uncontrollable desire seizes me to see his judge (Hunter) dangling at the end of a rope...,"[36] wrote one Confederate soldier.

His body was left hanging until the last Federal trooper rode off. Then Mrs. Morrison took the body down, wrapped it in a blanket, and buried it. The Reverend Mr. Morrison was too feeble to assist her.

David S. Creigh, May 1, 1809 - June 11, 1864

As the last Yanks left Brownsburg the religious Henry Jones recorded in his diary, "The people have suffered considerably but praise be to God our lives have been spared."[68]

South of Staunton, John Opie awoke. To his delight he had not been killed during the night by his Union prisoner; nor had the prisoner escaped. Opie woke the former member of Hunter's staff, who in turn greeted him "...cheery...."[20] There was no time for chit-chat. Imboden must be told that Hunter's army had left Staunton and was moving south. Opie commanded, "Let us mount and away."[20] Opie found his path toward Waynesboro open because all of Hunter's column had moved farther south toward Lexington.

In the early morning light, pickets exchanged shots near Trevilian Station

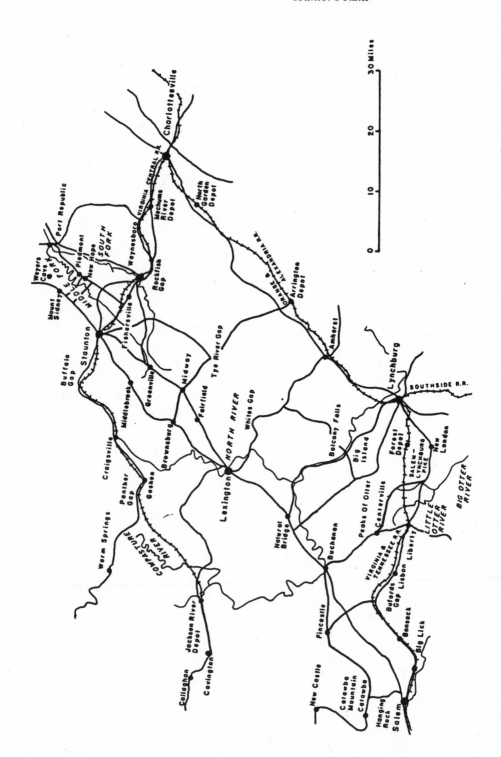

on the Virginia-Central Railroad. Advance units of Sheridan's Cavalry had struck advance units of the Confederate cavalry under Fitzhugh Lee and Wade Hampton. The fighting would intensify as each side brought more troopers forward.

Gen. John Cabel Breckinridge — C.S.A.

Back at Rockfish Gap, Breckinridge had been resupplied by the wagon train Colonel Lee had sent from Staunton. (A small part of the train was still camped near Arrington Station). Breckinridge was unsure of Hunter's location or intentions. He was anxious to secure information and wished to seize the offensive. He sent his cavalry towards Staunton. As reports of Union cavalry activity began to filter in, Breckinridge realized that his command could be in a very difficult situation very soon. The Union cavalry was obviously moving to link with Hunter. Hunter would try to link with the cavalry. With the Federal cavalry moving west and Hunter's army moving east, Breckinridge realized that his command could attack from both directions.

At daybreak, Duffié sent a courier from his camp at the bottom of the mountain below Tye River Gap toward Hunter at Midway. He told Hunter of his operations the day before. He lost one man killed and one man missing as he brushed with the Rebels near Rockfish. He also captured one Reb, who told him that Mudwall Jackson's Cavalry was moving to join the main Rebel army at Rockfish. The two small groups of men he had sent out toward the Orange & Alexandria Railroad on June 10 had failed to reach and destroy any track because of guerrilla forces in the area. He waited for some time in camp for a courier from Hunter. Receiving no courier, he posted a picket to hold the gap in the mountain and started moving toward the summit. "...The march was continued up a steep and stony road and along the bed of a swift mountain stream."[9] Luck was with Duffié. His men captured a Confederate courier. The dispatch he was carrying told of the wagon train from Staunton heading toward Rockfish. Duffié sent the First Maryland Potomac Home Brigade forward to try and overtake the wagons.

In Lynchburg, the Botetourt Artillery had received word to entrain and move over the Orange & Alexandria Railroad to Rockfish Gap and General Breckinridge.

Hunter's men moved slowly forward toward Lexington. They burned a mill, and were busy collecting in any livestock and vegetables that they could steal. When they heard Crook's Artillery firing upon McCausland's troops, they decided to quicken their pace. The Chief-of-Staff found time to talk with some Southern ladies. They indicated that the Union troops passing through had caused them less trouble than had their own Southern forces.

Although McCausland's gallant little band of men tried to slow Crook's column, it caused Crook no real worry. It was about 9:00 a.m. when the advance of Crook's forces began approaching Lexington, "great excitement prevailed in town...."[69]

At least two men in Confederate uniforms did not fall back toward Lexington. These men, Jessie Scouts, advanced toward the Yankees. They would help direct the Union army forward.

Re-creation: Jessie Scout

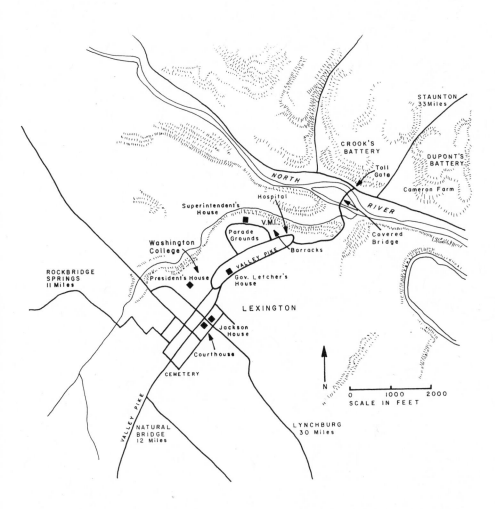

STAUNTON
33 Miles

CROOK'S
BATTERY

DUPONT'S
BATTERY

Toll
Gate

Cameron Farm

NORTH

RIVER

Superintendent's
House

Hospital

V.M.I.

Parade
Grounds

Covered
Bridge

Washington
College

Barracks

VALLEY PIKE

ROCKBRIDGE
SPRINGS
11 Miles

President's House

Gov. Letcher's
House

LEXINGTON

Jackson
House

Courthouse

CEMETERY

N

0   1000   2000
SCALE IN FEET

VALLEY PIKE

NATURAL
BRIDGE
12 Miles

LYNCHBURG
30 Miles

Near dawn advanced elements of McCausland's command began moving from his camp approximately two miles above Lexington to the town. Here he deployed his limited forces. They were troopers of the Fourteenth, under Col. James Cochran, the Sixteenth, under Maj. James Nounnan, the Seventeenth, under Lt. Col. W.C. Tavenner, and the Twenty-Second, under Col. Henry Bowen (?) Virginia Cavalries. He was augmented by some locals and the Corps of Cadets under Lt. Col. Scott Shipp and Gen. Francis Smith. McCausland, a proud graduate of V.M.I., had three pieces of light artillery in addition to the corps artillery. The total strength was approximately 1,400 men.

Most of McCausland's forces moved across the bridge before 8:00 a.m. McCausland had a rear guard to slow Crook's advance. To cover the bridge so that his rear guard could cross, McCausland posted men "...on the cliffs commanding approaches to the crossing."[28] McCausland moved to Institute Hill to have a better view and to direct his troops.

Observers recorded the following: "The sound of shooting approached the hills just north, and then a swarm of several hundred mounted men in gray poured up the road and over the bridge...."[70] "...Union skirmishers...dashed after them down to the hills."[7] "...at 9:00 a.m. three lines of their skirmishers occupied the hills...."[66] These skirmishers were the cavalry advance of Crook's column.

After the rear guard had passed over the bridge, McCausland gave the order, and the cadets, who had placed bales of hay on the bridge, lit them. The turpentine soaked hay caused "...a fine column of black smoke (to) roll heavenward."[71] "The blackened timbers were falling into the current as Federals came up."[72] Their task completed, the cadets moved up the hill to their barracks. They rejoined their respective companies that were by this time forming on the parade grounds.

At the first sound of battle Col. John T. Preston, from Washington College, started the six canal boats downstream. It appears that McCausland was not informed of the canal boats and their contents. If he had known of the cannons and the ammunition on board, chances are that he would have put them to use with his little army.

McCausland "...planted a section of artillery on Magazine Hill...."[66] The other two cannons were placed several hundred yards down the river from the bridge. After his rear guard had crossed, the artillery on the hill opened on the Union skirmishers. Sharpshooters also opened from the cliff. The artillery and the rifle fire caused most Union skirmishers to move back to the tops of the hills.

The Yanks referred to McCausland's gun as "a masked battery...which opened on the column...(and) killed and wounded several men."[73] The Union continued to bring men forward and to reconnoiter the Confederate defenses.

Crook placed his artillery (First Kentucky Battery) on Shaners Hill to the right of the road. One source said, "About 11 o'clock the enemy commenced a severe fire from six or eight pieces, the shells screaming, shrieking, bursting, and whizzing all over the crest of the hills...."[54]

Crook also directed Col. C.B. White to take the Second Brigade up river two miles. Apparently someone with Crook had detailed knowledge of the area (Jessie Scouts). The troops moved toward Leyburns Ford.

Apparently the only Rebel gun that had fired on the Yankees was the one on Magazine Hill. This was the gun that the Northern artillery concentrated on. The Union aim was high, and the shell passed above the Confederate artillery, but it hit the Institute. "The first shell that struck crashed in the hall of the society of cadets, sending down showers of brickbats and plaster when it exploded."[71] The cadets were on the parade ground, awaiting orders when the shell exploded. One cadet wrote that if the Union had aimed for the center of the building, it "...would have exploded in our midst."[71] The corps was ordered to move to the west end of the campus "...under the parapet..."[71] (wall about campus). The cadet artillery was still on the parade ground. It is assumed that it, too, now opened fire on the Yanks.

The artillery dual continued. One soldier with McCausland wrote home: "It was here (on Institute Hill) that you had like (sic) to have been a widow...(a) shell passed so near as to nearly take my hat off."[54] This was so close that McCausland's man decided to move back. He had just started his withdrawal "...when another (shell) came shrieking through the air, passing just before Jeff's (his horse) head, and plunged into the ground, some fifteen feet past me, seemingly boring itself two or three feet ere it exploded (timed fuse), when it did so throwing a large quantity of earth upon everything, made a grave nearly large enough to bury horse and man. Poor Jeff, he was completely paralyzed with fright...he only trembled and perspired in a foam. He shook so terribly that I could hardly keep my seat, and for three hours after, he was in a perfect quiver."[54] His rider, Maj. Achilles James Tynes, admits that he was as frightened as his horse.

Crook's Second Brigade marched upstream, shielded from Confederate eyes and fire by the hills. Crook's other men continued to move forward. They used the hills and the trees to protect themselves from Confederate fire.

Hunter with Sullivan and his column began arriving on the scene. A member of Hunter's staff wrote: "The skirmishing was sharp and so keenly did the balls whistle about us that we were obliged to dismount and hide our horses...."[11] Hunter surveyed the Confederate position. "I found the enemy's sharpshooters posted among the rocks and thickets of the...cliffs and in some storehouses at the bridge, and also occupying the buildings on the Virginia Military Institute...."[8] "The river was deep, being...a branch of the James River Canal. The opposite bank was a perpendicular cliff fifty or sixty feet in height and crowned by a thicket of cedars."[11]

Hunter's first thought was to put his pontoon bridge across North River. Covering fire was provided as the engineers moved toward the river. They attempted to put a "...pontoon bridge across the pool of water formed by canal and Jordon's Mill Dam."[28] The South had "...some sharpshooters along the shore, to harass our men, while constructing their pontoon bridge...."[53] Despite the covering fire, McCausland's men killed some of the engineers, and the rest fell back.

By 12:00 noon most of Hunter's infantry, cavalry, and artillery were near
North River. Hunter placed the artillery that had just arrived on a hill on the
Cameron farm (now referred to as Hunter's Hill). It was across the road from
Crook's artillery on Shaners Hill.

Re-creation: Union artillery and troops waiting for orders to attack Lexington.

Although there was some periodic firing of the artillery, there was no general cannonade. One Union soldier decided that Hunter didn't reduce the town by cannon because of his concern for potential loss of civilian life and property: "Hunter desiring to avoid opening fire on Lexington, as he might have done...."[17] Hunter had other thoughts which he recorded: "Their artillery was screened behind the buildings of town...the unsoldierly and inhuman attempt of General McCausland to defend an indefensible position against an overwhelming force by screening himself behind the private dwellings of women and children might have brought justifiable destruction upon the whole town, but as this was not rendered imperative by any military necessity, I preferred to spare private property and an unarmed population."[8] Hunter had shown no concern for private property or Southern human life before. Why now? Why didn't he use his power to "...crush...the place with my artillery."[8] It is believed that Hunter didn't use his guns to raze the town, primarily because of his lack of ammunition.

Hunter was probably irritated that this handful of Rebs and a river had stopped his grand army in its tracks, but he knew that the delay was only temporary: he would cross over. Hunter ordered Averell to take the cavalry upriver using the hills to conceal his movement. Averell was to ford the river and approach the town from the north. Now all that remained to do was to wait and keep McCausland occupied. With any luck, McCausland's escape route would be cut, and this pesky Rebel cavalryman would be history. Crook could have told his boss that this was wishful thinking. He had tried many times since Meadow Bluff to catch McCausland, but each time McCausland slipped through his fingers.

As Averell advanced upriver to ford at Rockbridge Baths "...active artillery fire was kept up for several hours...."[66] The Institute was an easy landmark above the tree lined hills; there was also an artillery battery there which received Union artillerists attention. Every member of Hunter's staff except his Chief-of-Staff was a West Point man. V.M.I. was the West Point of the South. Some officers must have thought: "What if the tables were turned and Southern guns were shelling West Point on the Hudson?"

One resident of Lexington said, "One can imagine the infinite satisfaction the Federal witnesses derived from this bombardment of the 'Hornets Nest' in Lexington. Hunter, Crook, Hayes, and McKinley were too well informed not to understand the infinite value to the Confederacy of Virginia's school of arms...."[58]

A cadet recorded, "...we were nearly in the line of fire of the shots directed at our battery. A number of shells struck the parade ground, some exploding there, and others ricocheting over our heads."[71]

A Union soldier recalled, "Our gunners put several shells through the Institute and one burst immediately in the cupola, one of the towers rather."[11] Some balls struck the heavy walls but failed to penetrate or do damage.

The veteran Union artillerists didn't consider it much of an affair after Piedmont. Capt. Daniel Glassie, with the First Kentucky Battery, said that he "...fired a few rounds...."[8] Dupont stated that his "...Regular Battery...opened with its six pieces on the stone barracks of the cadets, but after one round...ceased firing...."[47]

Later, a Southerner said that the Yanks "...dropped a few shells around the Institute and into the lower course of main street."[73] "Very noisy affair, but not dangerous."[22] It was "...an artillery's and sharpshooter's dual."[60]

The citizens, who had never experienced war, thought that the Yanks "...bombarded quite vigorously,"[25] "...setting fire to houses and doing a great deal of damage...."[25] Approximately forty houses[74] were damaged, "...frightening the inhabitants terribly."[25]

"The first shell that struck our part of the town passed through Mrs. Johnston's house...tearing a circular hole just the size of the ball...we heard the whizzing near us...one had passed through our garret wall and struck the rafter, exploding with a thundering noise. It knocked nearly all the plastering off and all the sash out of the windows, and made a great many large holes in the wall and floor...shells were flying thick and fast...I never before had an idea of the terror caused by the shelling of a town, never seemed to realize what it meant. I seemed to have spent a lifetime in one day...we went to the cellar..."[69] wrote a female resident of Lexington. Also "The residence of the Misses Baxter, Professor John I. Campbell, and others were struck, and two shells pierced the walls of the county jail...."[36]

One resident recorded that he "...barely escaped being struck by a leaden band of a shell."[25] Mrs. Cornellia McDonald records that her house was struck several times but "...I was past being frightened...."[25]

Many residents took shelter in their cellars. Others felt that no place in their house was safe so they fled in fear. Some came to the home of Colonel Preston "...our house was filled with women and children,"[58] recalled a member of the Preston family.

The wounded cadet who was removed from the Institute earlier was relocated to the president's home by fellow cadets. This wasn't the special occasion that Mrs. Margarett Jenkins Preston, wife of Col. John Preston and daughter of former Washington College (now Washington & Lee University) president, Dr. Jenkins, had been saving some of Jackson's personal stock of Blackberry wine for, but it was a welcome comfort to "...the frightened and almost fainting ladies."[58]

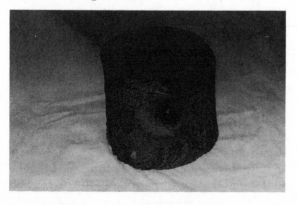

"War Log" — section of tree with cannon projectile embedded. Courtesy: Virginia Military Institute.

Presidents house Washington College (Washington and Lee University) — Lexington.

The Yankees on the hills simply laid down below the crest to avoid Southern bullets and shells. "The Fifth (West Virginia Regiment) was in the thick of the fight, but the Rebel shells went to their rear...."[21]

White's Second Brigade had been moving upstream toward Leyburns Ford, but Averell's Cavalry had made a much broader sweep of Lexington. Averell had crossed at Rockbridge Baths eight miles upstream and had circled to the west end of town. James McChesney recalled: "While on vidette duty on the Reid farm, in the rear of Washington College, I discovered a large body of cavalry descending a distant hill in the direction of the barrens...."[19] He quickly reported the news to McCausland, who knew that "...it was getting time to leave."[70] He knew the enemy "...was aiming to cut off our retreat."[19] McCausland "...did not call on the cadets,"[19] for battle duty. The cadets were infantry and would need more time to evacuate the town. By now Union infantry had been sighted at Leyburns Ford. McCausland sent word to General Smith to move his cadets.

General Smith's heart had never been in the fight for Lexington. He knew that the result was a foregone conclusion: he would be hastily retreating to attempt to save the young men of his beloved corps. He had been giving considerable thought as to the best route for retreat and the best use of the corps at that point. General Smith knew that many citizens of the area had moved with their livestock and transportable valuables south along the James River Canal. It was very likely that Hunter's Cavalry would pursue them. It was also possible that Hunter might attempt a large-scale cavalry thrust toward Lynchburg via the canal. The North River branch of the canal connected with the James, which flows through a gap in the Blue Ridge heading for Lynchburg. Near the gap, a family named Waugh ran a ferry.

It was about 1:00 p.m. when General Smith received the expected word from McCausland: he was ready. "I deemed it prudent to move at once to withdraw and gave orders to Lieutenant Colonel Ship (sic) to move...."[66] He told Shipp to move the corps by North River to the James and the cut in the mountain. "I determined to hold the pass at the Balcony Falls."[66]

Colonel Shipp moved his corps from the west wall of the Institute to Valley Pike. It is not certain where Col. Thomas H. Williamson was and why he didn't move with the corps. It is assumed that he had permission to stay behind. Apparently his wife was dead. He had daughters that he didn't wish left to the mercy of the Yankees.

There are contradictory statements about the cadets' artillery. One cadet reported: "As we were leaving, the artillery was limbering up...."[7] Another cadet reported: "...the five venerable pieces had to be abandoned to the enemy, for lack of teams to draw them off. They were left in the gun shed with their caissons and equipment."[58] A Union officer noted later: "In the court of the main building were several pieces of light artillery with a number of limbers and carriages."[11] More experienced officers should never have allowed such a prize to fall undamaged into the enemy's hands.

The corps did take "...4 brass pieces, 2 rifle guns 3-inch and ammunition...."[66] The Union officer was probably referring to "...the section of the Letcher Battery (probably Governor Letcher) given to the Institute"[66] which was left in private hands.

"No words would describe our feeling...it galled and mortified us that we had been compelled to abandon it (V.M.I.)...The place was endeared by a thousand memories...."[58] "With heavy hearts we passed through the town, bidding adieu to such of its residents as we had known in happier days,"[71] wrote some cadets.

The boys of the corps marched up Valley Pike and passed the graveyard where the remains of the school's most famous professor, Thomas J. Jackson "Stonewall" lie. They passed the graveyard and turned left on Fairground Lane. The march took them past the boatyard. They crossed the bridge over North River and continued south.

A Yank on the hill wrote: "We noticed our cavalry working around the Reb flank."[75] It was near 2:30 p.m., and McCausland knew that the corps was now out of town. Hunter believed that they could catch and swat this pesky Confederate bee, but McCausland knew that it was time to go. He assembled his troops on Valley Pike in front of Governor John Letcher's home.

Tynes remembered that he was in front of the Lexington Hotel, getting ready to leave town when the Federal artillery found its range. Tynes states: "...(they) let fly a *shell* among us...passed over our heads about five feet, passing up the stream about 100 yards...striking the bannister of a porch...."[54] Tynes was lucky. His life had been spared twice because of timed fuses. The first time the shell had gone deep into the ground before it exploded, thus muffling the blast; the second shell did not detonate because of a faulty fuse.

The Yanks saw an opportunity to capture at least one of McCausland's unprotected guns. One soldier recorded: "...it ceased firing, limbered up, and left the field at a gallop."[75] McCausland had some cavalry to protect the gun, which flew from Averell's grasp.

As McCausland moved down Valley Pike (Fancy Hill Road) toward Buchanan, the Union cavalry swept into town from the northwest and the infantry, from the east. A resident "...ran up a white flag...."[25] According to witnesses, "...several white flags were hoisted by some of the citizens, when the enemy in turn raised one and the firing ceased."[69] By 3:30 p.m., the Union controlled Lexington. The firing decreased.

Hunter had been observing his cavalry from the hill. He had McCausland almost in his grasp. Hunter saw Averell closing in, but McCausland, "Perceiving the movement in time,"[11] "...conducted a masterly retreat...."[19] Hunter and most of his staff were disheartened. One staff member stated: "The General was dissatisfied with the movement of Averell's, believing that if it had been promptly and boldly executed, he might have caught the enemy and have captured or dispersed the greater part of his force."[11] Another said, "...Hunter commenced losing confidence in..."[73] Averell. Crook was also on the hill: he probably just smiled.

"A strange quiet followed their (Southern troops) departure...."[70] One citizen noted that all Confederate forces had left town, "...leaving the terror-stricken people to their fears, (and she added satirically) to the tender mercies of the enemy."[25]

With the Rebels gone from their front, some Union infantrymen began to work their way gingerly over the remains of the burnt bridge. Once over the bridge, the troops made sure that the area was secure. Then the engineers also passed over. They tore planks from the buildings near the bridgehead and formed a makeshift foot path so that more infantry could pass.

Other engineers began assembling the pontoon bridge a little farther downstream. With no Rebel sharpshooters to oppose them, they soon had a bridge.

As the infantry entered the town from the east, Averell decided to chase the fleeing Rebels. His fast-moving cavalry could easily overtake the marching corps of cadets. A lady resident deliberately gave the Union cavalrymen wrong directions. Part of the cavalry charged down the wrong road in pursuit of the corps.

Averell's advance fought with McCausland's rear guard which it contested "...every foot of the way..."[19] as both cavalry units moved toward Buchanan. Unlike some generals who try to glorify themselves, McCausland simply noted: "The enemy drove my cavalry brigade from Lexington on the 11th. They now occupy the town." Although inevitable, it must have saddened McCausland to leave his school to the uncivilized warrior Hunter. McCausland was probably the only cadet ever to graduate without receiving one single demerit.

The corps force marched four miles and took a rest break. There was a large cheery tree there, and "...a kind old farmer turned (it) over to the cadets...it has never afforded more real enjoyment than it did to those hungry pedestrians on June 12, 1864,"[58] wrote one cadet. After the rest break, they continued toward Balcony Falls.

During the day, the Union supply wagon train from Staunton had been making its way from the Greenville area forward. It had left camp near 10:00 a.m. At noon it passed a house where several women were in the doorway. The women apparently hailed the wagon drivers and told them that they had "...walked several miles...to get one more look at the old Stars and Stripes."[14] The show of Union sympathy this deep in Confederate territory was music to the Union soldiers' hearts. The flags were unfurled and the women received "...three lusty cheers..."[14] for their show of patriotism. Then the soldiers and the women spontaneously joined in singing "The Union Forever." This show of support made the soldiers' advance less tiresome as they continued toward Lexington.

Since daylight John Opie and his prisoner had been moving toward Waynesboro with information for Breckinridge. During the ride Opie had been eyeing his captive's boots: "...the best pair of cavalry boots I had ever seen...,"[20] remembered Opie. Almost everything in the South was in short supply. Opie's boots were about worn out, and prospects for another pair were not good. As Opie figured that the Yank wouldn't be doing much riding or walking in a Confederate prison camp he wouldn't be needing that good pair of boots. Opie suggested to his prisoner that they exchange boots. The Yank's negotiating position was weak: Opie held all the guns. Opie had threatened last night to shoot him in cold blood. The prisoner believed that it was better for him if Opie had his hand on his new boots than on an old gun. "Certainly; really, with great pleasure,"[20] was the desperate Yank's reply. The Yank concealed his glee when he found that Opie's foot was much too big for his boot.

Opie made no mention of seeing any Rebel cavalry moving toward Staunton. At Waynesboro he found some regimental headquarters staff. He turned his prisoner over to Provost Marshal, Capt. John Avis. Avis had acquired some fame before the war: he was the man who had hanged John Brown.

After turning over his prisoner at Waynesboro, Opie moved to Rockfish Gap and reported to General Breckinridge. Now Breckinridge knew that Hunter was moving toward Lexington in force. He was not coming to Rockfish Gap to do battle. Breckinridge had also received information on the Union column under Duffié. Breckinridge probably assumed that the Union's mission was to cut the railroad north of Lynchburg and to return to the main body. If this was the case, it would be natural to assume that the Yanks would return by the same road they took going up the Blue Ridge. Breckinridge wanted his cavalry to be ready to receive the blue-clad horsemen. With this in mind, Breckinridge sent a courier toward Imboden with the cavalry. The cavalry was to reverse course and then swing south to the road leading to Tye River Gap.

Apparently the tired Opie rested near headquarters. He later related the story of a captured Jessie Scout. The man looked like a Confederate and said he belonged "...to a certain cavalry company, but could not give the name of his colonel or captain. The poor fellow was taken out...and shot as a spy."[20]

A cavalryman with Imboden recorded that the cavalry had moved out "slowly"[35] that morning. The advance had moved only twelve miles[55] all morning. It is no wonder that Breckinridge held a low opinion of Imboden. The column was halted when it received Breckinridge's courier. It does not appear that Imboden felt that time was of the essence in his pursuit of the Union column. One cavalryman said, we stopped "...grazed our horses and cooked some."[35] It was late afternoon before the cavalry started toward Tye River Gap and the Yanks.

During the morning the Union cavalry under Duffié had reached the summit of the mountain and enjoyed "...a magnificent view...."[9] The column moved slowly down the east side of the mountain because it "...was a fearful road."[9] The First Maryland Cavalry, under Maj. J. Townsend Daniel, preceded the main body in search of a wagon train.

The wagon train was only a small part of the supply-filled train which Colonel Lee had sent from Staunton before its fall. Those wagons that had stopped a few miles west of Arrington Station (the Orange & Alexandria Railroad in Nelson County) were the ones with exhausted horses. The wagons containing what were considered more critical supplies had been pulled by the better teams, leaving spent horses and less needed supplies. The exhausted horses were allowed to graze around a vacant house which the teamsters dubbed "Hubbard's Quarter."[43]

The teamsters had no idea that the Yankees were anywhere about. It was near noon when, according to one account, "...to their infinite astonishment a party of Federal cavalry burst upon them...firing pistols and demanding the surrender of the Rebels."[43] Duffié indicated that there was a fight "...driving back the guards..."[8] but no other account tells of resistance. The total captured (forty-one) indicates that there was no fighting. The surprise capture was almost complete. Only one man, a civilian teamster from Staunton, Anthony D. Wren, was not captured. He managed to hide in a wheatfield.

Eye witnesses agree that it was a "...small remnant...."[6] of the larger train. A Union cavalryman said that it was only "...a few wagons...."[9] One report indicates that there were seven[6] wagons. Duffié's report to Hunter indicates that he had captured a much greater prize, "...capturing a considerable number of wagons."[8]

The Union soldiers continued their practice of looting. They confessed that they took "...valuable papers and much jewelry..."[43] and "...other stores of some value."[9] Duffié indicated that it was "...of very great value....Hundreds of thousands in Confederate money and bonds...all the books and papers belonging to the several quartermasters....The damage could only be estimated by millions."[8] The cavalry got "a considerable number of horses...(and) some six or seven wagons, loaded with hams, flour, and other stores...."[8] There was too much loot for a fast-moving cavalry to carry. They had to "...destroy the remainder...."[8] Some wagons, books, papers, money, and bonds were burned.

Not surprisingly, a lot of money that was supposed to have been burned didn't get scorched. Duffié later showed a fellow officer "...a package containing several millions of Confederate money...."[11] They also burned the "Hubbard's Quarter."

Duffié said that he captured forty prisoners. There were seven officers among the group. Three of the seven were quartermasters.[8] Of the forty only three are named: Capt. R.H. Phillips, William D. Candler, and the feeble James H. Blackley.[43] To add to Blackley's troubles, he had hidden his gold watch in his boot. He would have to walk three days with this irritation.

The capture and the destruction took place in about one half hour. Duffié had his men mount and ride to Tye River. The Yanks found "...good foraging..."[9] in the area and went into camp on Tye River. It is unknown why Duffié sent only ten men and their sergeant[8] to do such a big job: cutting the Orange & Alexandria Railroad.

Farther down the Orange & Alexandria at Lynchburg, the Botetourt Artillery began moving north. The order to join Breckinridge at Rockfish Gap had come in the morning, but it was nearly two o'clock when the train pulled away from the station. The six guns rode on flatcars attached to an ammunition train.

Lynchburg was a city caught in a whirlwind of rumors. The whole population knew that the main objective of the invading Yankees was Lynchburg. They also knew that there were very few Confederates to stop them. Information and misinformation filled the air. Yankees were everywhere in tremendous strength and were preparing to march toward the city. There were "...great fears..."[76] for the safety of the trains. The leader of the artillery, Capt. H.C. Douthat, a veteran of many battles, knew not to put full credence in wild rumors. Without hesitation he entrained his company of approximately 100 men.

The train ride was uneventful until the train reached Amherst Station about fourteen miles from Lynchburg. Here the conductor was "...informed that the enemy was in our front, destroying the road."[76] The conductor's first thought was to back up to Lynchburg and safety. Captain Douthat, a native of the area, knew the strategic importance of the railroad to the defense of Lynchburg. The conductor was worried about the safety of his train but "...Douthat prevailed on the conductor to take his company on...."[76]

The train moved a few miles to the next station, New Glasgow. Here the men could see smoke rising in the sky six miles farther along the line. One account said that the eleven Yanks were burning "...Arrington Depot, containing a large quantity of boots, shoes, and other quartermaster stores...."[8] At New Glasgow Station, a scout informed the Confederates that there was "...a large raiding party..."[56] ahead.

Between New Glasgow and Arrington Depot, Tye River flows under a large wooden bridge. Douthat "...knew if the enemy got to that bridge the loss would be great."[76]

Douthat wanted to push on, but one of his men asked what can we fight with? They had six cannons and one hundred men, but "Without the aid of horses or loading ramps the guns...were of no value to defend the bridge."[77] Captain Douthat wasn't going to give up the all-important bridge without a fight. "Let's rock them,"[76] he said.

This was an ammunition train, and one of Douthat's men said that he had seen "...small arms on one of the cars. I saw them put on in the city before we left."[76] In a few minutes, the arms were located. "...Breaking open the ordance boxes, (Douthat) armed his men with muskets and forty rounds...."[76]

One account states that "...Douthat at once pushed forward with the train...."[76] It is highly unlikely that the train would leave New Glasgow Station. There was a "large" number of Federals ahead; the train could be seized and destroyed too easily. The train reversed engines and started backing to Lynchburg. Most probably, the men were moved "...double-quick three miles to that bridge..."[76] "...with the avowed purpose of defending it to the last extremity. Such a stance of heroism should not be left unrecorded."[76] About dark, the Confederates reached the bridge, which was still intact. Douthat placed his men in good defensive positions and then sent a three-man group forward as an early warning for the main group. A.H. Plecker was a member of that group. He remembers Douthat's instructions: Be "...sure of your game (know who you are shooting at in the dark), fire on them and fall back to the bridge."[76] The group climbed a hill overlooking the tracks about 500 yards in advance of the main group. The Confederates rested and waited.

The eleven Yanks were moving south from Arrington Station. They were "...tearing up the railroad for a distance of three or four miles."[8] The telegraph wires were also cut. It is not known if the Union cavalrymen had knowledge of the area. They were moving toward the big Tye River Bridge but may not have known that there was an important bridge just ahead of them.

As darkness was falling in the Valley of Virginia, the Confederates were at the bridge, and the Federals were working their way toward it, destroying the railroad as they went.

The morning fighting between a few cavalry pickets near Trevilian Station on the Virginia Central had intensified into a full-scale battle. Sheridan was trying to break through to assist Hunter and also to deliver orders from Grant. Hunter was to proceed to Charlottesville and then to Lynchburg and follow the railroad to Richmond to squeeze the life out of the Confederacy. Generals Fitzhugh Lee and Wade Hampton were fighting desperately to stop him.

General McCausland had lost another battle and more ground, but he had won a small victory also. He had slowed Hunter and had inflicted more casualties than he had received. His command was intact as he fell back toward Buchanan, and his troopers' morale was still high. He promised that they would fight "...back like Spartans of old, and fight them into the city of Richmond"[54] (never giving up).

Tynes wrote his wife saying "...remember you are a soldiers' wife...do not let...(the news of his close brushes with death, defeat, and retreat) disturb or make you sad."[54] They still had their love for each other and their country. He was anxious to continue fighting for both.

The corps made Balcony Falls by dark. There were rumors that the

Northern cavalry was pursuing. General Smith had selected Balcony Falls for the battle. It offered excellent defensive positions. The James River and canal snakes through a small opening in jagged mountains. It would be very difficult for the enemy to flank the corps because of the mountains. A few men could hold many at bay for a long period. Colonel Shipp placed his fighting young men in advantageous positions to receive attack. They were ordered to sleep "...on their arms..."[58] so that they would be ready for the enemy whatever time it arrived.

The corps made it to Balcony Falls, but the six canal barges did not. The water level was already low. At nine miles out of Lexington, there was a break in the canal. The heavily loaded barges were stuck. A decision was made: the barges would not be destroyed to keep them from falling into Union hands. Apparently it was decided not to offload some stores to lighten the boats so that they and some stores could be saved. An attempt to conceal the barges was made.

Angus McDonald and his son, Harry, had left Lexington before the Yanks arrived. They had used an ambulance for travel because of Mr. McDonald's inflammatory rheumatism. They had traveled about fifteen miles from town to the home of Mr. Thomas Wilson near Natural Bridge. They were seeking a place of refuge from the invaders. Soon after they arrived at Mr. Wilsons, word came that Union raiders were not only in Lexington but also in the countryside. It was decided that because the house might be located by the Federals, they must move to the mountains.

Mr. Wilson packed some valuables. He also took some of his male slaves and moved with the McDonalds to a mountain valley, apparently still on the Wilson farm where they camped.

Breckinridge's Infantry under Wharton and Vaughn remained near Rockfish Gap during the day. Breckinridge's cavalrymen under Imboden had first advanced toward Staunton; then they were ordered to halt. They reversed to pursue Duffie's Federals. Apparently after ascending the mountain, Imboden allowed his men and horses to rest. Now dark was approaching; "boots and saddles" was the order. There would be no rest tonight for Imboden's men as they followed Duffie's path over the Blue Ridge into Nelson County.

Back at Lexington, McCausland had fled town, and the Yanks were taking possession. Several witnesses observed: "...the wretches galloped into the town yelling and whooping like so many savages."[69] Most residents bolted their doors, "...nailed up all the windows..."[58] and pulled the shutters against the invaders; (the windows, shutters, and doors were) "...closed all the time they were here"[69] "...but (some residents) peeped..."[25] out to see what the Yanks were doing.

At one house at least one soldier was not considered a "wretch." Maj. Timothy Quinn with the First New York (Lincoln) Cavalry rode rapidly into town, seeking the Col. Angus W. McDonald house. Major Quinn rode to the front door. One resident said: "He was the same kindhearted Irishman who had so often befriended the citizens of Winchester...We had known him there...he offered to use his influence to prevent the house being searched (ransacked)."[25] Mrs. McDonald "...thanked him, but told him that if her neighbors were to suffer that indignity she did not wish to be exempted."[25] Major Quinn rode off, having fulfilled his duty as a gentleman.

Apparently Averell established a guard at both V.M.I. and Washington College to protect the school against Union looters. Col. J.M. Schoonmaker with the Fourteenth Pennsylvania Cavalry headed one of the guard units located at V.M.I. Later he recalled Hunter, "...taking me severely to task for not burning the Institute...."[58]

Mrs. Letcher, the wife of the former governor, was not happy to open her doors to the invaders, but she treated the two soldiers with respect after they coerced admission. Captain Towns, head of the Signal Corps, and Capt. James F. Berry (probably also with the Signal Corps) dined and slept at the house.

Hunter sent what cavalry was on North River along with the artillery to cross above town at Leyburns Ford. Then Hunter and his staff crossed over the bridge footpath the engineers had made. One officer noticed soldiers already "...peeping about for plunder."[11] "Many of the victorious troops began to plunder at once....It appears that their primary want was food."[70] At her house Mrs. Preston recalled that they "...pour(ed) into our yard and kitchen, half a dozen at a time....At first, they were content to receive bacon, two slices apiece...soon became insolent; demanded the smokehouse key...I protested against their pillage...(but they) proceeded to the smokehouse and threw it open...(she begged the soldiers to respect her as they would) their wives, mothers, and sisters....They heeded me no more than wild beasts...swore at me; and left me not one piece (of meat from the smokehouse). (They also stole)...newly churned butter."[58] They did not force their way into her house.

From a military point of view, Virginia Military Institute was "...the pride of old Virginia...."[18] Hunter and his staff went straightway to inspect their prize. The blue-uniformed soldiers of this Union army had under Hunter degenerated into blue-uniformed thieves. At the Institute they "...found the sack already far advanced, soldiers, Negroes, and riffraff disputing over the plunder."[11] One cadet recalled: many of the cadets' personal trunks had been removed to private homes, but some remained on the campus grounds. Some trunks were "...quite fat...I heard that one soldier got one hundred dollars in gold from one...."[11]

An army on the move had little excess storage space. Troops with supply trains might have found a little room in wagons for loot; cavalrymen might have found space in a saddlebag or over their horse's neck; foot soldiers carried only what they were willing to pay for with each stride. An officer was amused when he observed men working to remove booty that they in turn had to fight other soldiers for and which later had to be simply discarded. He recalled that grown, rational men with sweat running down their faces, were looking and fighting over "...beds, carpets, cut velvet chairs, mathematical glasses and instruments, stuffed birds, charts, books, papers, arms, cadet uniforms, and hats....Most ridiculous...."[11] Most of their work was in vain; the majority of the stolen property would be discarded when the next march began.

Hunter's family roots were in the Valley. He knew something of the area
and the people. However, it is not known why he selected the house of Maj.
William Gilham, a professor at the Institute, for first destruction. Major Gilham
had left with the cadets. One cadet recalled: "...rude officials..."[58] told the wife
to move what she could quickly to the lawn, because the house was to be
burned. She accepted the news in an "...eminently ladylike..."[11] fashion. She
"...was a soldier's wife and a soldier's daughter..."[11] and a soldier's sister.
Strother, the Southern-born artist trapped in a Union uniform, had much
difficulty watching the proceedings. Strother's blue uniform said that it was
okay to burn the house because it "...was a state building...."[11] The sensitive
artist said "...yet it was her only home...."[11] Also watching were Captain
Dupont, Capt. William McKinley, and Capt. Richard G. Prendergast. Mrs.
Gilham's next act, the ultimate expression of Southern hospitalty and the
Christian virtue of forgiving one's enemies, must have kindled the warfare
taking place in Strother's spirit. She offered Hunter and his staff, the same
people who were going to burn her home "...some good applejack,
apologizing she had nothing better..."[11] recorded one observer. Apparently
the pain inflicted on Strother by the gentle actions of this Southern lady was too
much to bear. He left before all the furniture was removed. Prendergast
recognized Mrs. Gilham as the sister of Union Colonel Haydon. Now several
of the officers became "...only too glad to assist her..."[47] in moving out
furniture. Even with the help of a few Union soldiers, most of her private
property was destroyed.

Strother's feet and mind retreated from the Gilham house. He soon met
with a fellow officer whose intentions were more to his liking. The young army
officer had spotted a house with "...a number of sweet-looking girls...."[11] The
young officer had been reconnoitering his target and contemplating strategy to
accomplish his mission. There were two major obstacles he had to overcome.
First there was a heavy guard posted with the girls, "...some matrons,"[11] and
there was the same problem faced by all men since the beginning of time:
"How do I break the ice?" The young man lamented to Strother that he wished
"...he had the boldness to go up and make their acquaintance."[11] Strother had
experience at this type of maneuver. He knew that an opening line was all
important. The situation gave him just the line he needed. The young man
recalled that Strother "walked up...with the pretense of inquiring whether
they had been disturbed by the soldiers...."[11] As Strother could have told the
young officer, many times when the male is looking over his target, the target is
also looking over the male. These sweet-looking girls were delighted that their
defense had been breached. A young man noted: "They seemed cheerful and
talkative."[11] Strother's campaign tactics were working well. He knew that his
strategy had succeeded when "We were invited to tea...."[11] Strother, fearing
personal involvement with his Southern people and knowing that his part of
the mission was over, withdrew. He left his young friend there, a willing
"...inmate of the house while we stayed in town."[11] The young army officer
may have never fully appreciated the masterful planning and bold executions
of his mentor because of the grace, the style, and the subtleties of the

complicated maneuvers.

While Strother was involved in complicated maneuvers, Hunter apparently ordered a second professor's home burned. Col. Thomas Williamson and his daughters were probably watching their neighbor, Mrs. Gilham, and the Yanks. When the order came to burn their house, they didn't invite the destroyers to tea. Colonel Williamson, not in uniform, probably slipped into the crowd. The daughters frantically ran from the house with armloads of anything they could carry. A neighbor recalled: "Colonel Williamson...had to keep quiet and say nothing when his daughters were driven from their house and all its contents burned, even the old black mahogany desk where hidden away was a yellow lock of his wife's hair, and her letters tied up with a blue ribbon...the greatest loss of all."[25]

When the flames started at the Williamson house, Mrs. Gilham was attempting to protect what she had saved. She had her "little boys"[25] with her, "...she sat in the midst, firm and ladylike."[11] Her presence kept the cowardly looters at bay.

The Williamsons had removed a considerable amount, but who could stand guard? If Colonel Williamson came forward, he would be arrested and there would still be no guard. If the girls attempted to stop the looters because of their youth, they would probably simply be ignored. The father feared that with the approach of darkness not only would his furniture be taken but that his daughters' virtue would be taken also. He must have communicated to the girls to take what they could carry and go to the neighbors' homes when he attempted to leave town.

Mrs. Gilham would remain with her furniture (on guard duty) during the night.

By now, Strother had left his young friend at the residence of Gen. R.E. Colston of the Institute. Hunter and his staff, the protectors of the Constitution and the Bill of Rights, violated both by quartering themselves in the residences of private citizens. They moved into the home of Gen. Francis Smith. Hunter, the great hater of slavery, was served by the family slave "Robinson."[11] Averell's headquarters were in the Presbyterian Church.

Superintendent's house — V.M.I., Lexington.

From his headquarters, the house of the Superintendent of the Virginia Military Institute, Hunter began to collect intelligence. He had captured a number of prisoners, but he seemed to trust the reports of the Negroes more than those of any other source. He wrote "...they are the only persons upon whose correct truth we can rely."[11] The white masters seemed to delude themselves: "They seem to believe firmly that their Negroes are so much attached to them that they will not leave them on any terms...(but) the Negroes take the first opportunity they find of running into our lines...."[11] Then the slave would often betray his master by revealing the master's hiding place and where the family assets had been stored. Slaves "...were continually running to us with information of all kinds...(but) we can not always rely upon their reports for (their) lack of judgement...."[11] Hunter continued, slaves were uneducated and not used to making abstract evaluations and "...they have...a tendency to tell us what they think will be agreeable to us rather than what they know."[11]

There was a fire on some mountain outside town, and the slaves told them that it came from the camp of some residents who had fled town before the Federals arrived. The weather had been hot and dry, and someone's camp fire had set the mountain on fire. Hunter's source of information is unclear, but he knew that the cadets had marched off toward Balcony Falls. Averell, of course, reported that McCausland had retreated toward Buchanan.

As many of the infantry troops had not made it into town by nightfall, they camped above North River. Pickets were placed outside of town as weary troops took shelter for the night. They slept on the Institute grounds and buildings, private homes, lawns, stables, anywhere they wished. According to one infantryman, part of the Fifth West Virginia camped "...in a cloverfield, where a professor of the military academy...was found hidden in the tall grass."[21] Almost certainly this was Col. Thomas H. Williamson, attempting to leave town.

As far as the common soldier was concerned, the day had been a noisy one but not a bloody one. There is no indication that the corps took even a single casualty. McCausland may have had a few men killed, but the only record on the subject indicates that he had "...a few prisoners...taken."[8] Colonel Hayes of the Twenty-Third wrote that in action from Staunton to Lexington, the Fifth (West) Virginia lost one lieutenant and one private killed; the Thirty-Sixth Ohio had three privates killed and ten to fifteen men wounded. Hayes's personal regiment, the Twenty-Third Ohio, took no casualties. Another report on the Thirty-Sixth Ohio indicates one officer was wounded, three privates were killed, and seven others were wounded. The First Ohio Battery had one man (Private George W. Tank) killed and four wounded.[70]

Hunter had another victory and another town. McCausland had been pushed back again. Lexington was a beautiful town on a peaceful river; the sounds of war had never been heard there before: what a difference a day makes! One resident cried, "...we had nothing between these ravagers and us, but God's protecting arm."[58]

Something occurred for which no military reason can be found. Averell's plan called for being at Lynchburg in five days. Hunter approved the plan. Averell's Cavalry and the infantry were to march into Lexington, over the Peaks of Otter, and on to Lynchburg. Duffié with the cavalry was to cut Lynchburg off from reinforcements that might be sent from Richmond. He was to cut the Orange & Alexandria north of Lynchburg, continue circling, cut the James River Canal, and circle south and cut the Southside Railroad. So far, Averell's plan was moving as it should.

There was no military reason why Hunter should have "...sent Duffié a peremptory order to come at once to Lexington!"[30] But he did so, apparently without consulting any of his staff. He sent a courier via White's Gap to find Duffié.

It appears that Hunter's obsession to punish and burn had overruled his military judgement. There seemed to Hunter to be no military reason to rush on Lynchburg. It would be just as weak later as it was then in his judgment. He had captured a great psychological prize, Lexington and, more specifically, the Institute. He was planning to do some serious burning, and he wasn't about to be rushed.

Apparently that was the reason for Duffié's recall order. Hunter didn't want Duffié isolated far from the main army.

It was 8:00 p.m. in Lynchburg when the train going to Rockfish Gap came backing into town. The only thing that was known for certain was that the railroad was blocked by a group of the enemy. Speculation and rumors sprang from this information faster than ears can hear and mouths repeat. Soon the city was afloat in hearsay. Was Lynchburg on the verge of being cut off from Richmond?

No doubt the brave Gen. Francis T. Nicholls, City Commander, was informed. The war had claimed Nicholls' left arm and left leg in two battles. Other men would have felt that they had given enough for their country after a loss of half of their appendages and gone home, but Nicholls stayed to serve. In other armies, in other wars, Nicholls would have been sent home, but the South was being bled white. She needed the service of any of her children. One Rebel described Nicholls' determination: "He still managed to mount a horse and do heroic service."[56]

At the Orange & Alexandria at Tye River Bridge, it was nearing midnight when three Confederate pickets Douthat had positioned about 500 yards north of the bridge "...heard the tramp of horses...."[76] "Halt" was shouted to the horsemen in the dark. They stopped but did not identify themselves. A Reb shouted, "...if you don't tell me (who you are) we will fire on you."[76] It was the eleven Yanks who "turned tail and went back at a rapid rate."[76] The Confederates fired in their direction in the dark but made no effort to follow them.

It happened quickly with very few troops involved. Only a few shots were fired in the dark. The bridge was not burned. There was only one casualty, a Confederate, "who accidentally lost his life at the bridge..."[76] perhaps in a fall. It could be assumed that this was an insignificant incident in a four-year war that consumed one half a million men, but it could have been paramount to the outcome of the war. Duffié "...committed a double blunder of the most serious consequences."[30] He had sent only eleven men to cut the Orange & Alexandria, partially isolating Lynchburg. One historian went so far as to hang the fate of Lynchburg at the bridge. According to his logic, if the bridge had "...been destroyed, Lynchburg must have fallen...."[56] He added that the "...prompt and bold action of Captain Douthat and the gallantry of his men on this occasion is worthy of all praise...."[56]

Sometime between midnight and dawn on Sunday, June 12, the eleven Yanks joined their comrades in camp at Tye River and reported to Duffié. They told him that they had destroyed three or four miles of track and had cut telegraph wires. As they moved along the tracks, they made "...contact with what seemed a heavy infantry picket" (the three Rebs). They assumed that there was "...a large infantry force on hand...(so) they retired...."[56] Duffié praised his men saying, "This work was very brilliantly executed...."[8]

Duffié's men were allowed some rest while "...keeping horses saddled."[9] Duffié was not sure of the disposition of enemy forces in the area, and he didn't want to be unprepared if attacked suddenly.

The courier that Hunter had sent with a recall order for Duffié moved through the night toward Tye River.

Since Hunter could not be sure that the lone man would make it to Duffié, he ordered Capt. George Ellicott, Chief of Scouts, to take twenty men and find and recall Duffié.

In the morning Douthat's men at Tye River Bridge buried their comrade who had been killed in an accident the previous night. They would spend most of the day marching the twenty-three miles back to Lynchburg. Breckinridge at Rockfish would not receive their artillery support.

At Lynchburg General Nicholls was unsure of the enemies strength and intentions. All he knew for sure was that there were Federals at Arrington Station. Nicholls mobilized his Home Guard unit, the Silver Grays. Their ages varied "...from fifteen-year old E.C. Hamner to eighty-one-year-old Mike O'Connel...."[78] Nicholls scoured the hospitals for any man who could stand and hold a gun.

The Home Guard and former hospital patients moved north of town to Amherst Heights. Here they dug in overlooking the Orange & Alexandria Railroad.

The telegraph had been cut between Lynchburg and Charlottesville, but it was open into Southwest Virginia. Nicholls received a message from Col. G.B. Crittenden reporting that Federals were sighted at Pound Gap near the Kentucky border. Crittenden said that he only had 250 Home Guard to try and stop them. Nicholls could empathize with him but could send him no troops.

Nicholls then telegraphed Richmond that he needed more troops.

In Richmond the high command was receiving not only telegrams from Nicholls but also reports from Trevilian Station. The few shots fired there by pickets had escaladed into a major battle. Grant had been quiet since Cold Harbor. Lee reached a decision and called for his profane general, Jubal Anderson Early "Old Jube."

Gen. Jubal Anderson Early C.S.A.

Early was born in Franklin County, Virginia, in 1816. He was a West Point graduate and was described as "...notorious as a woman hating bachelor with a coarse and unbridled tongue."[7] He could use "...profanity so shocking and a sarcasm so biting..."[7] as to leave men in laughter or tears. He did not readily accept advice but was "...formidable in battle."[7] He had an "ever present wad of chewing tobacco..."[7] in his mouth and did not care much about his personal appearance. He was probably the only general who could curse in General Lee's presence and get away with it. He had just been appointed Lieutenant General and had command of Lee's Second Corps, 8,000 men.[7] They were not the Second Corps 8,000 *strong*. By mid 1864, they were almost always hungry and ill clothed, and many were barefooted.

Lee informed his corps commander of the situation in the Valley and the importance of the supplies that funneled through Lynchburg. The Valley could not be lost if the Confederacy was to survive. Lee placed the fate of the Confederate States of America on Early's shoulders.

Sometime later in the day, Early returned to his camp headquarters near Gaines Mills. An officer near headquarters saw Early "...sending for Heads of Departments and Major Generals...Convinced all, that an important movement was on hand...,"[74] but he had no details.

Back at charred Staunton, news about Hunter's latest moves came filtering in. One person counted twelve dead horses between Staunton and Waynesboro. The railroad was reported destroyed as far east as Fishersville. A man who came in from Midway reported on Hunter's advance and McCausland's defense. He said that he had seen many Union graves (no mention of Confederate) and "...puddles of blood here and there."[43]

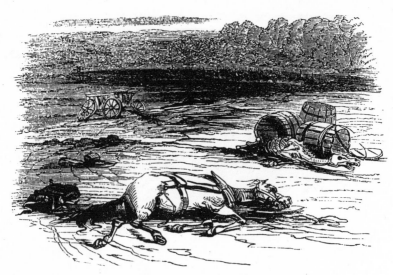

By David Hunter Strother.

At Rockfish Gap, a Home Guard colonel, Kenton Harper from Staunton informed Breckinridge that he had reports "...that the slaves in the town...have been greatly demoralized and are acting quite as badly as the enemy did while occupying the place."[8] He suggested sending a small force back to Staunton to restore order.

The McDonalds and Thomas Wilson were camped about fifteen miles from Lexington when a stray horse wandered in. The horse was being fed when its owner came searching for the animal. After the owner left with the horse, Mr. Wilson gave the McDonalds his opinion about the owner. Wilson said that the man was "...an avowed Union man, and not by any means an honest and reliable one.... Mr. Wilson expressed some uneasiness..."[25] that the man may reveal their location to the Federals.

The exact location of General Breckinridge and the infantry is in dispute. Several historians place him with the cavalry moving toward Tye River. It would be impossible for the infantry and artillery to be anywhere near the cavalry as it moved up very steep and stoney mountain roads. A member of the Confederate cavalry makes no mention whatever of Southern infantry in his report. Union intelligence reports from the Tye River area mention only Confederate cavalry and Imboden, nothing about Breckinridge and the infantry.

It seems likely that Breckinridge was at Rockfish Gap Tunnel. He was too sore from his horse's fall to ride a horse. At least one telegraph message was directed to him at Rockfish Gap. The infantry was probably spread from Rockfish through Waynesboro. Breckinridge was one who wished to seize the offensive, but where was an appropriate target for his infantry? He knew that Union cavalry had moved toward Tye River and he sent his cavalry after it. The infantry would stand no chance of catching the Union cavalry. Hunter's army was 18,000 strong; Breckinridge's Infantry would stand no chance in an open-field-pitched battle.

Breckinridge had received confirmed reports that Hunter was at Lexington. Breckinridge could assume that Hunter knew nothing of the Union cavalry now fighting at Trevilian Station. If Hunter had known of the cavalry, he would have advanced toward Charlottesville and a link-up. Breckinridge could breathe a little more easily, knowing that his small command would not be attacked from two sides.

If the Union cavalry did break through at Trevilian Station, it would probably move along the railroad toward Hunter. Breckinridge would be waiting at Rockfish Gap to meet the cavalrymen.

Breckinridge's Cavalry under Imboden had been moving all night. Sometime in the early morning hours, the men rested at the Nelson County Courthouse at Lovingston.

Imboden's target was Duffie, who had camped the night before on Tye River. Duffié had been expecting a courier from Hunter, but as he had received none, he moved toward Amherst Courthouse. According to Averell's plan he was to take the Orange & Alexandria out of service. According to one report Duffié was to "...destroy bridges and the track, and push a force across to the Virginia and Tennessee Railroad, east of Lynchburg, with the purpose of destroying the railroad bridge over the James River about eight miles from Lynchburg."[8] Duffié made an error in the name. The Virginia-Tennessee entered Lynchburg from the west. It was the Southside Railroad that ran east.

A cavalryman recalled that they "...marched for a few miles along the pleasant bank of the Tye...."[9] The command was about five miles from Amherst Courthouse at 10:00 when the courier from Hunter arrived. Hunter's order said to return "at once." Duffié had no options. The shortest way to Lexington was through Whites Gap. Duffié turned west "...and entered upon a road that skirted the eastern base of the mountain. It was one of the worst roads the regiment had ever traveled — rocks, ravines, steep pitches up and down, and sidling places where it was difficult to keep the wagons from tipping over....More than a hundred horses gave out,"[9] reported one soldier.

As the Union column started its tiresome ride toward Whites Gap, a Confederate from Breckinridge's command was getting ready to end his journey. Breckinridge had sent scouts to gather information about Hunter. One group was headed by Lt. Bushrod C. Washington, who had two men under him: a Private Creighton and Maj. Henry D. Beall. The three rode from Rockfish Gap to Midway, which is on the road that Sullivan used to advance on Lexington. One man recalled that it was hot, and that Sullivan's advance of the day before had turned the road to dust. The men were very thirsty. They stopped at a house and inquired if any Union units were in the area. The resident replied "no" but there was "...a detachment of Confederate cavalry... an hour's ride in advance of us."[25] This was a safe place for a rest and a drink.

Beall went over the fence to "...a spring of crystal water gushing from the side of a hill...."[35] He had just reached the spring when twenty Confederates were seen coming up the road. These were their comrades that the resident had spoken of, but there was no need for alarm. Lieutenant Washington, who was suspicious, shouted to Beall to come back over the fence, but Beall saw no reason to leave the cool spring in any rush.

Lieutenant Washington halted the advancing cavalrymen. The leader of the twenty asked who the three were. Lieutenant Washington answered, "We belong to Rosser's command."[80] The twenty drew pistols and started firing. They were Jessie Scouts from the First New York Cavalry under Capt. George M. Ellicott.

Now Beall felt a need to hurry over the fence. Washington and Creighton returned the Jessie Scouts' fire and tried to wait for Beall to cross the fence and mount. There were too many Yanks and too little time. The two rode off as Beall made it to the top of the fence. Beall pulled his pistol and fired at Captain Ellicott at the same instant Ellicott fired also. One was on the top of a shaking horse: the other, a shaking fence. Both men hit their targets. Beall said that his "...shot inflicted a slight flesh wound in the upper part of his (the Yank's) leg, went through the saddle skirt and entered his horse's flank."[80] The Yank's bullet "...went through the left sleeve of my (Beall's) coat, merely grazing my arm...."[80] In less than a heartbeat, another Yankee had "...his revolver almost in my face."[80] The contest was over, said Beall. "...I threw up both hands...."[80] It was then that Beall saw the man behind the revolver. He was a "...beardless private...perhaps the most insignificant looking Yankee in Hunter's army...."[80]

The Jessie Scouts did not pursue Beall's two companions. The captain's wounded horse was unsaddled and turned loose. Beall was now to ride his own horse behind Captain Ellicott. The one real Confederate and the twenty counterfeits rode toward Lexington. Ellicott's mission to find and recall Duffié was over. On the ride Ellicott showed Beall "...great kindness...."[80] As they talked, Beall stated that he knew the artist of "Porte Crayon...who was a friend of other days."[80] Ellicott knew that Beall was speaking of Col. David H. Strother, the Chief-of-Staff. Ellicott promised to tell Strother of Beall's presence when they got to Lexington.

As these Jessie Scouts were riding south toward Lexington, two other Jessie Scouts were riding west of Lexington. These two were the supposed friends of Capt. Matt White. He had told them that he had shot a fellow Jessie Scout. Later they would arrest White at a farm three miles west of Lexington and bring him back to the Lexington jail.

The Jessie Scouts, plus one, rode east toward Lexington. South of the town going toward Buchanan, McCausland's Cavalry was spread along the road. Many of the cavalrymen were resting and grazing their horses; others were felling trees to slow Hunter's expected advance.

Back at the village of Buchanan which rests on the banks of the James River, rumors were starting to circulate that the yanks might be coming. Mrs. James Boyd had heard the rumors before, but when some of McCausland's cavalrymen began to drift into town, she took the rumors seriously.

Tales of the furor of Hunter and the thievery of his men spread through the town. The residents began, "...storing their valuables of every description in trunks and boxes (which) the villagers conveyed...to a secluded spot in the mountain and concealed them in the clefts of the rocks and other places."[81] One woman concealed her valuables by prying up "...a board from the floor of the outhouse and hid them beneath it...."[81]

As rumors flew and the valuables disappeared from sight, citizens heard "Harrowing accounts...of the exhausted condition of McCausland's troops, and of the length of time during which they had been without food...."[81] The first troops were now entering town. One historian gives this account: "Citizens prepared the provision which could be spared from their scanty larders, and putting it into baskets, stationed themselves along the streets down which the troops passed and distributed it...."[81] Some of the men in Confederate uniforms were "blue-bellies." Some Jessie Scouts mingled with McCausland's troops, gathering intelligence on McCausland's strength, intentions, and morale. They also observed civilian morale and provisions. Some also gathered information on valuables that were being hidden from the invaders. The army's appetite far exceeded the supply. One family was giving each soldier one cup of soup intended for their noon meal. They would miss one meal to feed their men who had missed many.

As some of the soldiers moved up main street, "...one colored Mammy, weighing in the neighborhood of 300 pounds..."[81] went on the front porch to see the long lines of ragged soldiers. One soldier caught sight of the fat slave and exclaimed, "Look at that old Nigger, boy! That don't look much like starvation."[81] The group of soldiers burst into laughter. One of the household children saw what was happening and was worried that her Mammy's feelings would be hurt. She took the slave "...gently by the hand and would have drawn her away...(but the slave said) 'Lor' chillen, let 'em laugh if it'll do 'em any good. Let de po' creeters laugh: Mammy don't mind it.'"[81]

Since daylight, more Union troops had been moving from their campsites east of North River and into Lexington. Looting and plundering that began June 11 continued. One Southern soldier said that Hunter was "...more of a terror to women and children than to the Confederate battalions."[80] The people of Lexington "...the most hospitable and cultured people the sun ever shone on..."[36] were to drink from the bitter cup of the defeated. The Union Chief-of-Staff also noted: "There seemed to be a very few people of the lower class and loose Negroes in this place."[11]

Hunter came to Lexington "...with fire and sword...."[36] "...The outrages committed by Hunter, or his orders...(would) not insult the memory of the ancient barbarians of the North by calling them acts of vandalism."[10] Hunter's deeds (savage and cruel) were those of a malignant and cowardly fanatic, who was better qualified to make war upon helpless women and children than upon armed soldiers."[36] Many slaves were terrified.

The once well-dressed, well-organized, well-disciplined Union army had under Hunter degenerated to a mob composed mostly of thieves and plunderers. The soldiers "...took their tune from Hunter...."[58] "He let the troops loot...."[60] "Hunter gave the soldiers liberty to roam at will...."[21]

Mrs. Margarett Preston, the daughter of the former president of Washington College, recalled that her slaves woke her early saying that Yankees had forced their way into the house. She went down and begged them to leave: "I might as well have appealed to the bricks,"[58] for they had stolen "...every piece of meat..."[58] from the smokehouse. Now they were stealing her china. What could soldiers do with stolen china?

They didn't listen to her appeal to leave but instead demanded the key to the cellar. They told her that if they didn't get the key, they would burn the house. She still refused the thieves' demand.

Not every Federal had degenerated. One officer from Philadelphia stopped the plundering and forced the soldiers to leave the president's house. Mrs. Preston confided that she was a "...Northern woman, but...was (now) ashamed of my Northern lineage...."[58] After the Philadelphian left, she sent (probably a slave) to Hunter to ask for a guard.

Another resident remembered staying as quiet as possible indoors. Through closed shutters she saw the milk house robbed and the soldiers "...picking up everything they could use or destroy."[25] Her terrified little children wept "bitterly" saying "The Yankees are coming to our house and they will take all our breakfast, and will capture me...."[25]

As he had done at Staunton, Hunter sent squads of men to search houses for guns. They not only searched but robbed and destroyed as they went.

Not every door was bolted against the unwelcome visitors. The chaplain of the Eighteenth Connecticut found himself the guest of "Mayor" Adams. Mr. Adams asked the chaplain to breakfast, but he was shocked when he was served "...one plate of very small biscuit (sic) made of poor flour."[41] There was some rye coffee "Jeff Davis coffee" (the blockade had made real coffee a luxury). Mr. Adams said, "This is the best we have."[41] During their conversation, Adams said that his father had come from the North and that he believed that "Slavery was not at all profitable to the owners...."[41] The chaplain found Adams to be a polite gentleman but was concerned because there seemed so little for the citizens to eat.

A couple of soldiers with the Thirty-Sixth Ohio knocked on one resident's door and asked for water. The man who answered the door said, "I will give you a drink!"[7] He gave one man lead, not water, as he cut down one Union soldier with a shotgun blast. Nearby were other Union troops who turned their guns on the resident. By the time the Union gunfire ceased, the bullets had "...perforated his body...until his skin looked more like a pepperbox than a human being."[7]

Governor Letcher's home had been opened to the Yankees. Captains Towns and Berry had eaten supper and spent the night at the house. "Governor Letcher's wife had to take in two Federal officers and feed them with her family. After a chatty breakfast..."[82] Mrs. Letcher said that she had heard rumors that her house would be burned. Captain Towns said, "...It could not be possible..."[23] but he would go to Hunter to confirm it for her. Both officers then left.

General Hunter's headquarters were in the house of the superintendent of the Virginia Military Institute. All morning, officers had visited Hunter. They knew what was on "Black Dave's" mind. Crook stated, "I did all in my power to dissuade him...."[73] "This does not suit many of us,"[60] wrote Hayes. Hunter's desire to burn and destroy Lexington had overruled his military priorities. Capturing Lexington had "...aroused all of Hunter's crusading zeal."[60]

It seems clear that Hunter had already made his decision, but he put the question to his Chief-of-Staff, Strother. What did Strother think of burning the Institute? Strother had argued against every civilian target Hunter wanted to burn. Now Hunter could probably not believe the music his ears were hearing. Had his Chief-of-Staff finally seen the light? What he was hearing was better than an abolitionist preacher.

Yes, Strother was all for burning the Institute considering it a "...most dangerous establishment where treason was systematically taught...States Rights conspirators had with subtlety and forethought established and encouraged the school for the express purpose of educating the youth of the country...as would render them ready and efficient tools where with to overthrow the government....The same infamous and treasonable doctrines were taught at the University of Virginia...(Many officers from the Institute had) raised up against the government of the country....The professors and cadets had taken the field...as an organized corps. The building (was) used as a Rebel arsenal and recently as a fortress."

The man who wore a blue uniform was at war with himself. He who had denounced wanton destruction was now demanding destruction. Why an apparent change of heart? Strother was a sensitive artist who wished to draw only beauty. The war had forced him to put on a uniform and draw a sword and to look on mankind and destruction at its ugliest. To Strother the Virginia Military Institute, West Point, the United States Army, and the Confederate Army had all forced him into a uniform and a battle with himself which he could not win. If none of them existed, then he would be a happy artist, not a miserable soldier. Yes, burn it, burn it to the ground!

A gleeful Hunter issued the orders to burn the Institute and the professors' homes.

Captain Towns approached Hunter and told him that he and Captain Berry had spent the night in the home of the former governor, John Letcher, and that Mrs. Letcher was concerned that her house might be burned. Towns might have told the general that she had treated both house guests kindly. The home was private property, and Hunter said that he had no intentions of burning it. Towns left Hunter and started toward the Letcher house.

Slaves and citizens had been to Hunter's headquarters all morning, asking for protection from his men. They had all been sent away. The colonel of the Fifth West Virginia would not be turned away. He went to see Hunter "personally."[21] He informed Hunter of the "...outrages...and asked permission to employ some of his men to protect women and children from the robberies and abuse of soldiers. It was refused...."[21]

Hunter's orders to burn the Institute and now the refusal to control any of

Gov. John Letcher. Courtesy: Virginia Military Institute.

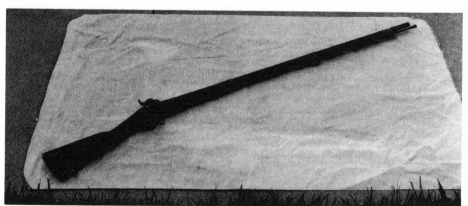

Virginia Military Institute cadet musket. Courtesy: George Whiting collection.

his men upset those officers present. They "...freely expressed their (disappointment) of these proceedings...."[21] The intolerant, short-tempered Hunter flew into a rage and "...bluntly reminded them that *he* was bossing that job."[21]

Before the flames started at the Virginia Military Institute, "...Home of the Cadets, our gallant little enemies of New Market...,"[83] the looters had their way. "A general upsetting of the college furniture and fixtures followed,"[21] recalled one soldier. "The barracks, mess-hall, officers' quarters, a library containing 10,000 volumes..."[36] were ransacked. "The books of the library were scattered over the floor...."[41] What had taken twenty-five years to accumulate was destroyed in one day. The distinguished collection of scientific books by Col. Claude Crozet was destroyed. "A priceless mineralogical collection"[58] donated by General Cocke was destroyed. The laboratory equipment of the engineering, chemistry, and agricultural departments were stolen or destroyed. Chief Engineer Meigs took mathematical instruments. Doctor Patton took "...a beautiful human skeleton."[11] Teaching aids once used by "Stonewall" Jackson were stolen. Paintings of three former Virginia governors, McDowell, Wise, and Letcher, were taken off of the walls. The desk, the files, and the private library of the superintendent were ransacked.

The cadet hospital was plundered. The shoe shop was wrecked, all leather being stolen.

There was much uncertainty as to the fate of the bell on the public clock. Many thought that it had been stolen; many believed that it was destroyed. Later reports stated that it had been stolen.

Soldiers scurried about with all types of loot. Trunks of the cadets were broken open. Watches, uniforms, hats, and some "tidy sums of money"[6] were found. Charts were pulled from the walls. Beautiful new carpets and curtains were taken from the Society Hall. "Negroes were seen scudding away in all directions bearing away the spoils...books, furniture, trunks full of clothes of the absent cadets..."[25] recorded one observor. Most looters' arms were full of "...the most useless and impractical articles."[11] Colonel Hayes said, "I got a pretty little cadet musket here which I will try to send to the boys."[22] Chief-of-Staff Strother could have had his choice of the spoils, but he took only "...a new gilt button marked V.M.I. and a pair of gilt epaulettes...."[11] Some officers brought out "...beautifully illustrated volumes of natural history...." One resident recalled that her household slave returned with "...a beautiful brocade curtain...."[6]

During this time frame, Captain Towns returned to the former governor's home. He told Mrs. Letcher "...that he was directed by General Hunter to assure her that the house would not be destroyed, and she might, therefore, rest easy...she dismissed her fears...."[23]

During the same time period a group of Federals discovered a printing press in the woods. The editor of the "Rockbridge Gazette" had removed the press and much material from the office in an attempt to save the paper. Now the press was discovered. He was arrested and the printed material with the press seized. Part of the printed material was the proclamation by ex-Governor Letcher. A Federal read the proclamation and decided to send a copy to General Hunter.

Most of the officers were against burning the Institute, and they told Hunter so. A rumor, perhaps colored by time, arose many years later. According to this rumor, "...A number of officers were placed in arrest for refusing to execute..."[58] Hunter's orders. Although there was much grumbling in the officers' corps, no first-hand reports were found to confirm the arrest of any officer.

Captain Dupont summed up the feeling well: "In my judgment, as well as in that of every other Union officer who expressed himself on the subject, the destruction of the cadet barracks was fully justified by the laws of war, but the burning of the buildings containing the library, the philosophical apparatus, the large and extensive mineralogical collection and other objects used solely for educational purposes...being contrary to the conventions of civilized warfare...."[47]

Various reports give differing times for the burning of the Institute. Two residents offer the most accurate accounts. One said that it was "...about ten o'clock, the Yankees set fire to the Institute, blew the walls down, and destroyed the mess hall...."[69] The other account states: "They set fire to the Institute about nine o'clock, the flames are now enveloping it; the towers have fallen; the arsenal is exploding as I write."[58]

Another account gives this description: "It was a grand and awful sight to see so many buildings burning at the same time."[41] By destroying the Military Institute, Strother had struck a blow against his internal war. For a brief moment, he felt some peace. The artist and the warrior held hands for a moment, and Strother found a scene worth sketching. He said, "The burning of the Institute made a grand picture, a vast volume of black smoke rolled above the flames and covered half the horizon."[11] Hayes saw something quite different in the flames and smoke: "...Hunter will be as odious as Butler or Pope to the Rebels...."[22]

The smoke was visible at Balcony Falls. The corps from the Institute was there, defending the mountain pass and expecting an attack at any time. It had signal posts on the mountain to warn the main body of the enemy's approach. One cadet recorded: "The day was bright and clear, and we saw the towers and turrets of the barracks, mess hall, and professors' houses in full blaze, sending up great masses of flame and smoke."[71] As the news spread to the main body, many young men climbed the heights to view the sight with much anger and sadness.

To Hunter, the fire and smoke of destruction represented one of the greatest achievements of his life: "He stood looking at the burning buildings, saying as he rubbed his hands and chuckled with delight, doesn't that burn beautifully?"[9] Strother remembered the incident: "The General seemed to enjoy this scene and turning to me expressed his great satisfaction *at having me with him.*"[11] Hunter meant not only in a physical sense but also with him on the policy decision to burn Southern property.

As Hunter was enjoying the fires of his punishment policy, an officer gave him a piece of paper discovered with the "Rockbridge Gazette". The

"...foolish and abusive paper..."[11] sent Hunter into a rage. He was reading a proclamation to the population calling for continued struggle, even guerrilla warfare, against the hated Northerners. "...It denounced (the Yankees) in most violent and fiery adjectives."[47] The proclamation was issued over the signature of the man whose house Hunter had vowed to protect, the former governor, John Letcher.

Captain Towns had left earlier to inform Mrs. Letcher that her house was safe, but Captain Berry was still with Hunter. Hunter knew that Berry had stayed at the Letcher house and he directed him to carry out the order. Hunter ordered Berry to go "...forthwith...(only) allowing his family ten minutes to get out of the house...(and) to burn the property."[11] The angry Hunter gave Berry no leeway: "The order was (to be) executed without delay."[11]

Captain Berry and some men "...rode up to the door...Berry dismounted, rang the door-bell, called for Mrs. Letcher, and informed her that General Hunter had ordered him to burn the house."[23] She replied: "There must be some mistake;"[23] and requested to see the order. He said that it was verbal. She asked if its execution could not be delayed until she could see Hunter. Berry replied: "The order is peremptory, and you have five minutes to leave the house."[23] Captain Towns had said that her property would be safe; now soldiers were here to burn it. Mrs. Letcher thought that Towns was "...guilty of (a) willful and deliberate falsehood...."[23]

Mrs. Letcher asked permission to remove family clothing. Request denied! Berry started to burn "The beautiful private residence...."[83] He poured "camphene, benzine, or some inflammable fluid"[25] on the furniture and the floor of the lower part of the house and then started upstairs. Mrs. Letcher knew that there was no time left. The house was gone, but she must save her family. She rushed upstairs "...and snatching her sleeping baby from the cradle, rushed from the house with it, leaving everything she had to the flames."[25] The cradle had been given to Mrs. Letcher by the people of Richmond. Elizabeth (Lizzie or Lizzy) Letcher followed her mother closely; she removed the cradle from the house to save it from the coming flames. Then Elizabeth ran upstairs and got some of her father's clothes and had them over her arm getting ready to descend the stair when "Captain Berry came near her with a lighted match and set fire to the clothes as they hung on her arm."[25] The house guest of the night before was returning none of the respect he had received. The daughter ran out and joined her mother in the street. Berry then piled clothing and bedding in the center of the room and set them on fire. Coming downstairs, he lit the flammable liquid.

A neighbor saw the fire at the Letchers' house. Most women would not leave their houses, but Mrs. McDonald pulled her sunbonnet on and rushed toward the house: "I was too used to their ways to be afraid of them..."[25] (the soldiers). By the time she arrived, she was "Breathless...(and) the house enveloped in flames."[25] She could do nothing to save any of the property and she knew no words that would comfort Mrs. Letcher who was "...sitting on a stone in the street with her baby on her lap, sleeping, and her other little children gathered around. She sat tearless and calm, but it was a pitiable group,

sitting there with their burning house for a background to the picture."[25] Even
the cradle did not survive. Some "...Yankees threw it back into the flames."[84]

The house next to Governor Letcher's belonged to his mother. Strother had
traveled in the area. He recalled in the good old days before the war, the house
was a boarding house. The Governor's mother was seventy-eight-years-old. It
is unclear if the Yankees deliberately set fire to her stable or if flames from the
governor's house spread to it, but it burned. There was real danger that the
house of the Governor's mother might catch fire also. Captain Towns was now
on the scene. "Our soldiers with some difficulty saved it."[11] One observer
noted, "Owing to the active exertions of Captain Towns, who made his men
carry water, the house was saved."[23] Mrs. Letcher saw Towns on the scene. She
probably went to her grave with resentment for this officer whom she
considered a lying Yankee.

"The destruction of Letcher's residence — in a sense Northern recognition
of his contribution to the Rebel war effort — left him more destitute than ever
but still confident that Lee could somehow salvage final victory,"[65] wrote one
citizen.

The smoke from the homes and the Institute mingled with the smoke from
the lower part of town, next to the river. Buildings along the stream had been
damaged the day before when boards were ripped from their sides to make a
walk over the burned bridge timbers. Today, recorded one resident, "Several
large mills, many warehouses, with all their contents, (and) the gas works..."[83]
were burned. For some reason the property of "...the Millers' and Toll
houses..."[83] were not burned. One resident seeing the fire and smoke,
remarked, it "...seemed as if the Evil One was let loose to work his will on that
day."[25]

Many soldiers had more than the stench of smoke on their clothing. They
had bad breath because the "...onions planted for the Confederate soldiers"[72]
were now in their Yankee bellies.

Other agricultural commodities suffered also. One soldier noted: "Within
sight of our encampment, are...fields of wheat, the yield from which...would
seem to be enough to supply the wants of Lee's entire army...except that our
horses and mules are turned upon them, to graze...."[83]

One house on the grounds of the Institute was not set afire. It was the home
of Superintendent General Francis Smith. Hunter used this house as his
headquarters. Most accounts agree that it was spared because "...of the illness
of a member of the Smith family."[47] "Mrs. Smith pled for her (house) to be
spared, on account of her daughter (Mrs. Morrison) who lies there desperately
ill (in child birth); that alone saved it,"[58] stated one account. The hard Hunter
may have been softened by reports that he had heard while using the house as
headquarters. The reports said that General Smith considered McCausland's
defense of the town "...futile, purposeless, and unnecessarily exposing the
town...."[8] Most sources agree that the labor pains of a family member saved
the house, but Chief-of-Staff, Strother believed that it was spared because it
was used as headquarters, and that "...the roof which has sheltered us and the
house where we have been entertained should be saved, whatever be its

character...."[11]

The fire at the Institute was burning itself out at 2:00 p.m., but the criticism leveled at Hunter for starting the fire has never burned out. Many residents, cadets, soldiers, officers, and historians have labeled it as a "war crime."[72] "General Hunter has been severely censured for burning the buildings...."[14] "It will always remain a deep reproach to General Hunter...."[14]

While looting and destruction were taking place at the Institute, Lexington's other college, Washington College, was being "...raided upon and despoiled...."[83] The library of 20,000[14] volumes was sacked. What wasn't carried off was destroyed. The soldiers didn't know that part of the books belonged to the Virginia Military Institute. They had been moved to Washington College for safe keeping. Very little was saved. Classroom equipment was stolen or destroyed.

To prevent further destruction "A trustee of Washington College....and"[11] "....one of the oldest alumni..."[72] (a Mr. Moore) approached Strother, who was at the Institute. He asked Strother for a guard to stop the plundering at his college. Strother's personal war was against the military, not education. He said, "I ordered it (the guard) immediately...."[11]

Strother then attempted to justify the burning of the Institute as a military objective. The alumnus listened but did not reply. In a high-handed manner, Strother said "...We were disposed to treat his college in a different manner from the Institute."[11] Strother expected a reply, stating that the alumnus understood and that he thereby gave passive approval to the destruction of the Institute. At the very least, Strother expected a "thank you for not destroying the school further." He received neither. The alumnus said, "I do not wish to discuss the matter, Sir."[11]

The shocked and hurt Strother fired a verbal barrage at the alumnus. With a sweep of his hand toward the burning building, Strother replied, "You perceive that we do not intend to discuss it either."[11]

The guard was sent, but by now Washington College had been "overhauled."[21] "The Federals used the lecture rooms of the college as stables for their horses..."[36] but the buildings were not burned. Like travelers of all ages, the many common soldiers left their marks on both colleges. Names, dates, and graffiti (some including derogatory messages to the Southern people) were scribbled, painted, and carved on walls.

One soldier noted "...Some things done here are not right...."[85] Another soldier said, "But for the vandalism in the (Washington) College, there can be no excuse."[14]

The looting that started when the first Yanks crossed the river was continuing. "Till now, this region had known nothing of the ravages of war,"[83] but they were learning. One observer noted: "The town people were so frightened that few dared to show themselves on the streets, and Yankees and exultant Negroes had their full satisfaction."[25] Hunter had ordered men to break into private homes and search for weapons. They, of course, stole what they wanted as they performed their official business. Other Union soldiers just stole.

Although the civilians suffered greatly, the conquerors, too, were strained by their victory. Only weeks ago, most of the Federal Army Hunter now commanded was composed of decent, hard-working men. Now in only a short time under Hunter, the thin veneer of civilization had come off many men. Men who respected women and private property and abhorred thieves now trampled on the principles they had lived by. After a few weeks, the poison of Hunter's hate had blinded the eyes of his own men to their crimes. Now a soldier could write home for all to read: "The houses of wealthy citizens were entered, and trunks and drawers searched for gold and silver or any valuables."[21]

Not only were the homes of the rich broken into but also "The houses of our poorest operatives, including seamstresses, laundresses, and laborers, were searched....Some persons were left (in) destitute and almost starving conditions. The kindness of friends...(who) had opened their homes to receive the trunks and effects of cadets, such houses were made the peculiar objects of vindictive spoilation,"[58] recorded one resident.

One lady recalled that Hunter's search squad came to her door and "...demanded arms."[58] They took the guns from her house and broke them upon the lawn. Since the search squad could be reasonably sure that the property owner could not retaliate, they "...broke into the cellar; carried off... lard..molasses, and whatever they could find."[58] One Yankee wrote about his fellow soldiers: they "...stole all they could take away."[21] One woman recalled that the squad "...pressed into the house and began to search my dressing room. What they took I don't know. They seized our breakfast and even snatched the toasted bread and egg that had been begged for the sick man's breakfast. My children were crying for something to eat: I had nothing to give them but crackers."[58]

At the house of the president of Washington College, some cadet trunks were discovered and broken into. Mrs. Preston decided that it was time to tell a Union officer about the wounded cadet she had been hiding. She took the Yankee to where the cadet was lying, "...pale and motionless, never opening his eyes."[58] The Yankee spoke "...so kindly that quiet tears began to steal down the poor wounded boy's face, for he is only seventeen,"[58] she stated. The wounded cadet would be neither captured nor moved.

Yankee thievery was not isolated to a few houses but was almost universal. Another lady records that a squad of men came to her house "...to search for provisions and arms."[25] The Yankees laughed because the family had only "a half barrel of flour and a little tea, *all the supplies we had*...."[25] When they searched the attic, they found that it was filled with chickens, hidden from the invaders. When the Federals saw the fowls in the house, "...their laughter was immense...."[25] Apparently the soldiers found nothing worth stealing at this house and left.

When the Yankees left her house, she peered out toward her neighbors' homes. Yankees were "...breaking in...and robbing them."[25]

"Ladies trunks...rifled...their dresses torn to pieces in mere wantonness: even the Negro girls had lost their finery."[86] One lady said that they even

"...carried off the coffee pot and everything they could lay their hands on... they emptied the corncrib."[58] A hungry blue-belly came to the house. He was no thief. He offered the lady of the house some silver for some bread. Other Union soldiers before him had cleaned out her pantry. Because he was polite, the lady gave him some of the crackers which she had to feed her children. In a conversation with the polite Federal, she discovered that he was born in Virginia. She told him "...that he was on the wrong side for a Virginian. He looked decidedly ashamed."[58]

After the Yankees had cleaned out one house, a soldier asked the lady of the house if she had anything else worth stealing. The soldier must have been shocked to hear a "yes." The she added, "but it is in the mountains."[58] It had been taken out of town before the Yankees had arrived.

Frightened women and children saw the smoke, the fire, and Yankees. Rumors circulated that the invaders "...would fire the entire town."[58] Other rumors were "...that General Smith, Colonel Williamson, and Colonel Gilham, with some of the cadets, have been taken prisoners!"[58] There were so many blue uniforms that they couldn't be counted. The rumor mill put the number at 40,000 in Lexington and at 8,000 in Staunton.

One lady from Lexington who had seen the destruction and whose house had been ransacked wrote, "I am in despair."[58] That would be natural and understandable, but her concern was not for her and her family's safety and the next meal. She was worried about her country. She continued, "Richmond must fall — how can it withstand such numbers?"[58]

One citizen said, "...The lamentation on the part of the white population is both loud and deep."[83] Colonel Hayes wrote, "Many of the townspeople had Union sympathies, but Hunter had alienated them beyond recall."[60]

Strother sent a guard to keep Washington College from being burned. Somewhat later he rode to the school to make an inspection. On the top of one of the main buildings was a statue of the namesake of the college. Residents affectionately call it "Old George." Because of its height, the detailed features can not be seen clearly from the ground. Some of the common soldiers might not have known the name of the campus where they were. They decided that the statue on the roof was that of the Rebel President, Jefferson Davis. As they were throwing rocks at the statue, Strother rode upon them. He commanded the throwing stopped and informed the soldiers that they were defacing the father of their country.

Lexington's Jackson

Tens of thousands of men had died in this war, but the pall of one of them covered the town of Lexington and permeated the air. Before the war, Thomas Jonathan Jackson had been an obscure professor. Only after he left Lexington did he achieve fame. At First Manassas, he lost his first two names. Thereafter his deeds and legends are recorded under the name "Stonewall" Jackson.

In two years, this Bible-carrying general had plotted strategy, pushed his men to the limit of their endurance, and defeated the superior foes of his Southern country time and time again.

Washington College (Washington and Lee University) building with "Old George" Washington on top —
Lexington.

"Old George" Washington.

An error in the dark at Chancellorsville led to Jackson's return to Lexington. Southern soldiers mistook the general's party for the enemy and let fly a volley in the night air. Doctors tried to save the great "Stonewall," but it was his time to "pass over the river." His remains were borne to Mrs. Jackson in Lexington up the same canal where the cadets from his Institute guarded Balcony Falls. The ground held the body, but nothing could erase the memory.

When the common soldier left Staunton, he knew where he was headed. "Lexington was the home of 'Stonewall' Jackson...Jackson's remains were buried..."[14] (at Lexington). One blue-clad soldier told a resident: "...We think as much of him (Jackson) as you Southern people do."[74]

After the town was secured, the plunder started. The most prized spoil a Yank could carry off was an item associated with General Jackson. It appears that some Union officer recognized this fact before the troops came over North River. Probably without Hunter's approval, a guard was placed around the Jackson house. Although most houses were entered and ransacked, no evidence exists that the Jackson house was desecrated. It was not left untouched because the soldiers were unaware of its location. Guided tours of the town were organized while the Northern army was in control. "The house of Jackson was pointed out, as well as other places of note, owing to their relations to the Rebellion."[41] Men who would steal food from crying children would have ransacked the house except for the fact that an armed guard was posted.

The gravesite was not guarded. Virtually every soldier, from the lowest to highest rank, made a pilgrimage to the grave. Even Jackson's mortal enemies came to honor him. Men who hated everything he fought for, came to honor him. Men who had fought against Jackson in the field, men who were wounded by Jackson's command, men who had lost friends, comrades, and relatives fighting Jackson came to honor him.

Accounts of the vandalism at the gravesite offer some confused and sometimes contradictory insights. The Chaplain with the Eighteenth Connecticut said, "When Hunter's army entered Lexington, the Rebel flag was found flying on a staff at the head of Jackson's grave."[41] It might have been Averell who said that he saw "the unique monument of a silk Confederate battle flag, made by certain secession sympathizing peeresses of England, which hung on a tall pine flagstaff near the grave...."[85]

In his history of the Second West Virginia Cavalry, J. J. Sutton indicated that it might have been a cadet that rescued the flag: "A young man, or rather a mere boy, went to the cemetry (sic) and removed a flag from the grave of Stonewall Jackson; and although efforts were made to capture the lad, he mounted a horse, and waving his flag at the pursuers, boldly and defiantly made his escape. It is needless to add that this chivalrous act elicited the admiration of all who saw it."[34]

One can assume that the boy took both flag and staff and waved them at his pursuers. Another account states that the Yankees took the flag down.

It was General Hunter's Adj. Gen. Charles G. Halpine, who was "...surprised that the flag which had flown above the grave had been removed, as a

matter of precaution, by McCausland's troops."[85] When private J.O.
Humphreys with the First Ohio Battery arrived, he saw that "Stonewall's grave
is unmarked except by a pine flagstaff, which serves to show where a great,
brave, and good enemy sleeps."[85]

Definite documentation that the hate-filled Hunter also paid homage at the
grave was not found. It is known that early in the day Hunter had been
denounced by every ranking Yankee officer, except one, for the burning of the
Institute. It is likely that Hunter felt that he was being ostracized and that he
was grateful that at least Strother was "with him." Strother records that he rode
to the grave. His text seems to indicate that he had a conversation with Hunter
as he rode from the grave back to town with the inference that Hunter, too,
paid honor to a great Southern general. Strother stated that there was a
flagpole but no flag at the grave. Sometime after Strother left the gravesite
"...the flagstaff and the head and (the) foot-board of his grave were fairly
whittled away and carried off for relics."[41] The "...staff was chopped up for
souvenirs."[7]

Another account said that the head was not marked with a board. One
viewer said: "One soldier scrawled in pencil on the general's marble headstone,
'A good man and a brave soldier but a traitor to God and his country.'"[7]
Another viewer said: "The chief pastime was making rings and other trinkets
from the black walnut boards captured from Stonewall Jackson's grave."[41]

It appears that the sword of Jackson "...that sword that had flashed so
victoriously over many a battlefield"[74] was also taken to the house of the
president of Washington College. Mrs. Preston had hidden it "...in a dark loft
above the portico."[58] When the president's house was searched for weapons,
the sword was not found. Later in the night of June 12, Mrs. Preston began
thinking of the sword more as a weapon than a symbol. At 1:00 a.m., she
quietly retrieved the sword. She took the excalibur (King Arthur's sword of the
South) to a neighbor that he might use it upon the Yankees. When he told Mrs.
Preston that he already had a sword, she returned to her house and hid "...it in
Anna Jackson's piano."[58]

Mrs. Preston decided that the piano was not a safe hiding place. Soldiers
were entering houses and stealing at will. The sword might be discovered.
Hunter had burned more than one house — it was possible that the president's
house was next. Mrs. Preston wrote: "With great trouble we carried it (the
sword) under our clothes...and finally concealed it in an outhouse...."[58] What a
low depository for such a high prize! It worked for Yankee fingers never
grappled the handle of Stonewall Jackson's sword.

While the destruction was occurring in Lexington, Hunter sent Averell on a
raid into the countryside. His major objective was to destroy iron furnaces in
the area. He destroyed the Buena Vista, the Jordan, and four other furnaces.
His men raided farmhouses and stole food and horses. One Southerner
reported seeing twelve barns burning. Many slaves ran to the woods from the
invaders, but others left with the invaders.

Some slaves told Hunter of six canal barges hidden nine miles from town.
Captain Richard Blazer and a company of scouts were sent to check out the

information.

Outside Lexington, the camp of the McDonalds and Mr. Wilson had been entered by "an avowed Union man" that morning. In the afternoon, the white men and slaves were resting or sleeping when "suddenly they heard the sound of horses feet, and a voice calling on them to surrender."[25] They saw only three Union troopers closing in on their camp. Harry McDonald had his gun lying next to him on the ground. He grabbed it and fired "...emptying one of the saddles."[25] The other two Yanks drew off. Because they were now sure that the Yanks knew their position, they decided they would cross North River under the cover of darkness.

Strother had had a conversation with Hunter, probably as the two returned from Jackson's grave to town. Strother, the artist and lover of beauty, suggested to Hunter that the bronze statue of President Washington at the Virginia Military Institute be taken "...as a trophy for West Virginia."[11] Since Hunter was no respecter of Southern property, public or private, he thought the suggestion was a great idea.

The statue, a bronze replica of Jean Antoine Houdon's Washington, was placed at the Institute by an act of the General Assembly. Because of concern that it might be damaged in shipment, Chief Engineer Meigs was given the task of removing the statue and making it ready for transport. When Meigs learned that Strother had ordered it to be sent to West Virginia as a war trophy, he confronted Strother. Meigs pointed out to Strother that this school was the West Point of the South and that any war trophy from this "West Point" should go to West Point on the Hudson. Meigs "insisted"[11] on this point. Strother agreed with Meigs, but the man with the final word, Hunter, either was not present or did not get involved with the discussion. Meigs did not perform his task faultlessly; the statue was damaged in the effort to take it from its pedestal.

When soldiers saw the statue being readied for transport, many wondered why it was being taken. One officer said, "...I felt indignant that this effigy (statue of President Washington) should be left to adorn a country whose inhabitants were striving to destroy a government which he founded."[11] Another officer added, "...Virginians should not be allowed to possess a relic of the first president."[60] Still another officer who saw the preparations wondered at what he considered a waste of manpower and time. Why take it? It could not "...give aid and comfort to the enemy, nor be of any service to our arms."[83] Another writer was more to the point: it was simply "stolen."[10]

There appears to be a discrepancy in the number and the type of artillery captured at Lexington. The usually accurate Strother said that there were "several pieces of light artillery (cadet artillery)...(and) twelve pieces of bronze cannon of the old French pattern."[11] The Military History of V.M.I. speaks of "....six French guns and the two bronze guns of the Letcher Battery...."[58] A soldier with the One Hundred Sixteenth Ohio counted, "Four pieces...which belonged to Lafayette...."[14] Chief-of-Artillery, Dupont, said that he was ordered to destroy "...the artillery trophies belonging to the Institute...the most important objects consisted of two ancient French bronze pieces...carriages were destroyed and guns left on the ground as utterly worthless for any military purpose."[47] Hunter's report only talks of destroying the five guns of the cadet battery. Another official report called Hunter a liar: "Hunter did not cause the five pieces of the cadet battery...to be destroyed...."[58]

Statue of George Washington stolen from V.M.I. — Lexington.

One of the cannons stolen from V.M.I. — Lexington.

It is known for certain that the two (24-pound) guns whose carriages were destroyed by Dupont were left. Whatever the number, the French cannons were crated. It would seem logical that the five serviceable guns of the corps would be kept and put to use.

After Strother had started the statue removal project, he rode by the burned houses of professors Williamson and Gilham. He saw Mrs. Gilham who had been sitting all night and all day with her furniture to keep Yankee scavengers from stealing it. Prendergast had helped to save Mrs. Gilham's furniture. Strother ordered him to bring two wagons to transport her belongings. Strother also noticed that the belongings from the Williamson residence were gone. He believed that they had been moved by the family, but with no protection they were more likely removed by Yankee thieves.

It appears that someone had told Hunter of the jailed Capt. Matt White. Hunter was probably told that White, by White's own admission had stated that he had killed a Jessie Scout in cold blood. Hunter probably issued orders to do the same to White.

One resident remembered: "At sunset we saw a man led by with a file of soldiers. The children came in and told me that it was Capt. Matt White that they were taking him out to shoot him. I thought they knew nothing about it and gave the matter no attention."[25] Matt White knew his fate. As he passed a friend, he called, "Goodby...I am gone up."[36] He was taken over North River to the tollgate. "He was told to walk in front of the two men (Jessie Scouts) who were his guards, and they evidently shot him when he was not aware of their intentions...he was shot in the back, the large ball going entirely through his body...his body was left where it fell...."[36] His friend said, "Poor Matt, friend of my youth and boyhood days, you deserved a better fate."[36] The body apparently rolled down the bank toward the river.

The two Jessie Scouts thought they had avenged the death of one of their own. They rode back to town. The Jessie Scouts knew where White's mother lived in Lexington. One source said they had stayed at her house on the night of June 11 and had eaten breakfast there. The mother knew her son was in jail. The two Jessie Scouts rode to "...the poor old mother..." and lied like dogs. They had executed her son less than an hour before. They now told Mom that her sonny boy was okay. "...He was temporarily detained, but would be immediately released."[36] The two deceiving Jessie Scouts had deceived another Southerner.

It was near twilight when Matt White met his fate; it was at this time that Jessie Scout Captain Ellicott and his prisoner, Maj. Henry Beall were approaching Lexington. Beall saw the town and the Institute. He recalled: "...a scene of desolation was presented to my eyes...(V.M.I.) was a smoldering ruin."[80]

Soon Beall was taken to the superintendent's house which was Hunter's headquarters. Captain Ellicott left Beall with the general and exited. Apparently Ellicott had taken a liking to Beall.

As soon as Ellicott was gone, Hunter started to interrogate Beall. He wanted to know where Breckinridge was, his strength, and intentions. Beall said that Hunter "...showed considerable irritation when I called his attention

Virginia Military Institute in ruins. Courtesy: *Virginia Military Institute archives.*

to the fact that I was a prisoner of war...that he could not reasonably expect me
to give him any information which could be used to the hurt of a cause in which
all my sympathies were heartily enlisted."[80] Beall's refusal to answer lit a short
fuse to Hunter's explosive temper.

Captain Ellicott knew that this confrontation might occur. He had gone to
see Strother. He told Strother that a pre-war friend and newspaper editor was
now being interrogated by Hunter.

Strother went to the room where Beall was being questioned. Beall records
that he was lucky that Strother appeared when he did: "...the General
was...getting ready to give me a sample of that roughness of manner and
speech for which he had an unenviable notoriety."[80]

Strother wanted to rescue his friend, but he didn't want to get on the bad
side of his general in the process. The verbal tactician, Strother, informed
General Hunter that he wished to see the prisoner when the general was
through with him. Hunter's fuse of patience was almost gone. "Take him now; I
do not wish to have any further conversation with him,"[80] growled Hunter.

Beall was taken to Strother's room, the dining room. Each had a glass of
whisky. Beall toasted the occasion by saying, "Here is to a speedy and
honorable peace."[80] Both agreed to the toast although it had a very different
meaning for each man. Strother had supper served to his prisoner. "Then
followed a long conversation on old times and about the colonel's relatives in

Charlestown and Jefferson County, all of whom were strong in upholding the Confederate cause, but of whom he spoke in the kindest manner, with perhaps an exception."[80] (Strother had no love for Angus McDonald).

Beall showed Strother some letters he was carrying from fellow soldiers to their homefolk. Strother banded the letters and endorsed them, "examined and permitted D.H. Strother, Colonel and Chief of Staff."[80] Beall could keep the letters.

Beall refused Hunter's demands for information but talked freely to his old friend Strother. He informed Strother that Imboden and the cavalry were at Waynesboro. He also gave Strother "...a great account of Lee's victory over Grant...."[11] Beall was very complimentary to Strother.

When Strother had finished collecting the information and reminiscing, he ordered the guard to take charge of the prisoner. Beall was taken "to the courthouse and dumped in with about 125 companions in misery...most of whom were wounded men or at home on sick leave."[80]

By late afternoon or early evening, Captain Blazer had located the canal boats "...with commissary stores, artillery ammunition, and six pieces of cannon...."[8] Blazer destroyed all but two of the boats. He had some of the men dismount and tie ropes from the boats to their horses. They then started walking back upstream toward Lexington. In the two boats were "...two six-pounders, one twelve-pounder and three mountain howitzers — nine thousand rounds of artillery ammunition, a ton and a half of powder, and commissary stores in great variety and abundance."[16]

By dark, Averell's troops were coming into town. Hunter had decided to allow them little rest. Through the Chief-of-Staff, Hunter directed them to be under saddle by two o'clock in the morning of June 13, heading for Buchanan. Hunter wanted Averell to surprise McCausland and capture the bridge over the James River at that place. Perhaps McCausland wouldn't get a chance to burn this bridge and slow Hunter's army again.

Apparently Hunter had not informed Averall that his timetable for taking Lynchburg had changed and that he had sent a recall order to Duffié. Averell sent men to Duffié.

Some of Averell's troopers had picked up additional horses from the countryside; they would be used to replace their own tired mounts. These troopers also brought in many slaves. The slaves "...were a husky lot and could run as fast as a horse."[41] Slave owners noted that most slaves ran to the mountains or stayed close to their masters' sides to avoid the Union invaders. "All the regular Negro servants of the Institute (V.M.I.) showed a marked fidelity."[58] The Union invaders saw a much different slave, the runaway. One soldier said, "The Negroes...are wild with joy, and throng our camps, giving information...."[83] Another soldier said, "They all held high carnival."[25] The more things change, the more they stay the same. Some slaves exchanged Southern masters for Northern ones, "Many of them engaged as officer's servants...."[83]

General Hunter decided that Duffié could not or would not be able to accomplish his work of destroying the Orange & Alexandria line. When

Averell returned, Hunter ordered him to detail 200 hand-picked men and send them to circle Lynchburg. Averell sent the Fourteenth Pennsylvania under Captain Duncan. Averell, "Fearing that (Duffié) might fail in the execution on the most important part of this work"[30] sent the men toward Whites Gap. They were to destroy rail transportation and gather information. Once they rounded Lynchburg, they were to move westwardly and join the army in the Liberty (Bedford) area.

At Lexington, the home of Jacob Fuller, taken over by the Yankees, soon became a gathering place for Negroes. There was even a band playing music. A resident was on her porch and observed "...a very fat and very black Negro woman...she was arrayed in a low-necked short-sleeved brown silk dress, with a large pink rose pinned on her breast, and several others fastened in her wooly hair. In her hand she held another red rose which she smelled vigorously, fanning herself slowly at the time."[25]

Neither the fat Negro nor the resident's personal slave, Susan, was aware of the resident's presence. The fat Negro called the house slave to the basement window and asked, "Are you going to the camp, Susan? I am. I went up there yesterday and a white gentleman treated me like a queen and invited me to come and spend the evening. You had better come."[25] The house slave must have found the thought of a white gentleman's company repugnant. An observer noted: "Susan, with an expression of contempt drew her head in without replying, and the lady continued her walk."[74]

By the evening, Hunter had received word that a 200-wagon-supply train was approaching from Martinsburg. It was decided that the statue, the cannons, and other loot would be sent back to Martinsburg by the same wagons when the army left Lexington. The one-hundred-day terms of some Ohio soldiers were about to expire. Col. David Putnam was put in charge of a regiment and a half of these men. They were to guard the train back to Martinsburg. No doubt, celebration broke out among the fortunate soldiers.

Hunter and his men could celebrate, but the residents certainly did not feel like celebrating. "How awful is war! Who would think that this is Sunday and our intended communion?"[35] said one resident.

Sometime during the day, a young Confederate officer named Marshall Greenlee had joined the McDonald party. The Greenlees ran a ferry near Natural Bridge. Earlier in the afternoon, Thomas Wilson and the McDonalds had shot one of the three Yankees that had charged their camp. They decided to relocate after sundown.

Their camp was located in a thicket bounded by a rail fence. On the other side of the fence was a cleared field with a few stumps. Capt. Franklin G. Martindale, Commander of Company A with the First New York Cavalry, noticed some Negroes in the woods. When a shot rang out from the thicket, "this intensified their (Union cavalry's) interest."[9] Upon further investigation, the Yankees saw several wagons and men defending them.

Martindale called on the men to surrender. The demand was answered by gunfire by the four white men.

The four men thought they were facing fifty men.[25] One Union source said there were twenty-two Federals;[9] another puts the number at twelve.[11]

There ensued some "...lively skirmishing...."[9] The small party of white men were armed to the teeth. They had twenty to thirty "...muskets, carbines, pistols, and double-barreled guns."[11] Most of the six slaves and Greenlee fled for their lives. Apparently Harry McDonald quit firing at the Yanks. He directed the remaining slaves and together they reloaded the guns. The remaining two men kept a strong fire toward the Union cavalry. They fired the guns "...as rapidly as they could be loaded."[11]

Several cavalrymen were wounded. Their return fire wounded the father, Angus McDonald, in the hand. Though outnumbered "...they fought desperately."[11] Apparently after the hand wound to his father, Harry joined in firing on the Yanks also. The three men kept the cavalry company "...at a distance till all their powder was spent...."[25]

When the firing stopped, the Federals came over the fence and surrounded them. The three white men had no ammunition, but they had courage. They did not surrender. Apparently the three were willing to fight with swords, knives, or bare hands. A Yankee sabre found its mark on Wilson's head, "...to all appearances his death wound. Not satisfied with that, he came near (the Yank), and stooping, fired his pistol into his temple, so near did he place it, that the ball glancing slightly, took his eye out, and his whole face was filled with powder,"[25] stated one observer. Angus saw what had happened to Thomas. He was an old and sick man of seventy; he did not fear for himself but for his young son of fourteen, Harry. Angus surrendered and young McDonald followed his lead. They "...were quickly overpowered."[62] A Yankee said that they surrendered after they were "...in no condition for a further fight."[9]

One account said that there were "several"[9] Yanks wounded. Another account said that there were two or three "...wounded and several of their horses were killed."[11]

Angus was a former military man. He knew that the Federals would search both men for weapons and steal anything else they found. Angus gave Harry eight dollars in silver, which he kept clinched in his hand.

The Federals did search and steal. They found no weapons but took Mr. McDonald's cap and the contents of both prisoners' pockets. Harry never opened his hand, and the Yanks didn't get the eight dollars.

With the one man apparently dead on the ground, and the other two secured, the Yanks ransacked the camp and wagons and broke open the trunks. Cavalrymen stuffed their pockets and saddlebags with all they wanted or could carry.

Angus McDonald had records with him from the "Institute,"[9] or they were "Provost Marshal or tax collector"[11] records. The records, bedding, and the remainder of the personal effects of the men were burned. At this time, Timothy Quinn rode up. He was the same Quinn who knew the McDonalds at Winchester and had offered Mrs. McDonald protection for their house at Lexington. He "...was as civil and merciful as he dared...."[25] He allowed Angus to ride in the ambulance. The Yanks left Thomas Wilson for dead on the ground.

The Yanks and their prisoners rode to a Union camp on North River, probably near Greenlees Ferry (also called Rupe Ferry). The prisoners were placed inside a house. A number of Federals also shared the house that night. There was one wounded Federal who Harry believed was the Yank whom he had shot earlier in the afternoon.

Harry McDonald was allowed to care for his decrepit father. He pulled grass and covered a board for his father to sleep on. He covered his father with the only blanket that was saved from the campsite. The guard and the prisoners would spend the night there.

During the day, McCausland's men had fallen back on Buchanan. They were camped in and about town. McCausland's scouts and civilians had kept him informed of the destruction taking place at Lexington. McCausland sent scouts to Breckinridge at Rockfish Gap.

The infantry rested another day at Rockfish Gap. Breckinridge's Cavalry under Imboden had been trying to locate Duffié. One Rebel cavalryman complained: "...marched around in Nelson (County) all day...."[35] Duffié was difficult to locate because he had changed direction. Early in the morning, he had moved his command toward the railroad and was only five miles from Amherst Courthouse. About ten o'clock, he received a courier from Hunter, ordering him to return "at once." It was probably late afternoon when part of Duffié's and Imboden's Cavalries met at Piney River. Very little information exists on the clash. One account said: "Imboden...was very roughly handled, losing prisoners, horses, and a considerable portion of his train."[88] No other source alludes to a wagon train. The writer may have confused the capture of a portion of Colonel Lee's wagon train near Arrington Station with the skirmish with Imboden. If the engagement had been furious enough to cause Imboden to abandon his supply train, more records would have probably survived. As it is, one Union soldier didn't even make a note in his daily dairy about the action. A Confederate with Imboden simply noted, "...had a skirmish."[35] It appears that the engagement was not great enough to cause Imboden to abandon his wagon train, nor was it great enough to block Duffié as he moved toward Lexington. Duffié used totals for both the eleventh and twelfth in his report. He probably inflated his figures. Duffié said that he had captured about eighty-three men, seventeen officers, and four hundred horses.[17]

After the skirmish, Imboden moved the cavalry back toward Breckinridge at Rockfish Gap. A courier was sent to Breckinridge to inform him of their activities and location. The Southern cavalry would rest during the night, but there was no rest for Duffie's men. One soldier recalled: "All day and all night the slow and toilsome march has kept up."[9] Hunter's order told Duffié to return at once. There would be little rest for man nor beast as Duffié tried to execute Hunter's order. "As the team horses gave out, some of the few wagons...could be taken no farther. These were burned...The night was intensely dark...There was only the light from the abandoned wagons that were burning at intervals along the steep road,"[9] recorded one soldier.

During the eleventh and the twelfth, Duffié had destroyed two iron furnaces.

Most of the day the Botetourt Artillery had been walking from Tye River Bridge to Lynchburg. Once back, it was given no rest. General Nicholls was unsure of the location, the strength, or the intentions of the Union cavalry. There was a possibility that Lynchburg would be attacked. He ordered the tired artillerymen to move their six guns to a redoubt (fortification) north of the river on Amherst Heights.

Nicholls sent scouts to attempt to locate the Union cavalry and to assess damage done to the track at Arrington Station.

What had begun at Trevilians Station with a few shots by pickets on the morning of June 11 and then had burst into full battle was ending near sundown on June 12. One source said that Sheridan had lost 85 men killed and 400 wounded. The Southern cavalry had suffered 59 killed, 258 wounded, and 295 missing.[89] Another source said that Sheridan had 8,000 troopers and 1,007 were killed and wounded and that Southern "...losses are uncertain but probably comparable."[90] Whatever the body count, it was a Confederate victory. Sheridan retreated toward Grant. He would not reinforce Hunter, and he would not deliver Grant's order to Hunter. In no uncertain terms, Grant had ordered Hunter to move first on Charlottesville and then on Lynchburg. Hunter received neither reinforcements nor orders.

On Monday, June 13, General Lee had issued orders to General Early to move his 8,000 soldiers to the Valley. The newly promoted Early was commanding troops that were weary of battle but high in morale. They "...had been for the last forty days constantly fighting...the Wilderness, Spotsylvania Courthouse, Gaines Mill, and Cold Harbor...no time or place for rest...bad condition for so arduous an undertaking."[56] Early knew both the importance of time and the condition of his men.

The soldiers near headquarters on the twelfth knew that some movement was planned because Early had summoned all the Department heads. At 2:00 a.m., the move was on. "No one but Early knew where they were going, but all felt that if Lee ordered the march it was right...."[56] The command left its camp one mile west of Gaines Mill. Because of the fighting between Sheridan and the Confederate cavalry, Early knew that the Virginia-Central tracks were blocked. This cavalry action would compel Early to force march his tired troops.

Some of the troops under Early were members of the famous Stonewall Brigade. This force march may have reminded them of service under General Jackson. The brigade had almost been wiped out at Spotsylvania Courthouse. The last general to command the brigade, James Alexander Walker, lay in a hospital with part of his left arm missing. The few men who remained for service after Spotsylvania were reassigned, and the Stonewall Brigade all but disappeared.

The men, covered by dust, would march twenty-five miles that day and camp at Auburn Mills on the South Anna River.

At the same hour that Early started his march, Averell's men climbed into their saddles at Lexington. Hunter said, "...I sent Averell forward to Buchanan with orders to drive McCausland out of the way and, if possible, secure the bridge over the James River at that place."[8] He had at least one section of artillery and a small supply train with him. He also had wagons loaded with the parts of a pontoon bridge in case he failed.

McCausland knew that the Yanks would be chasing him again. His troops slowed the Union cavalry "by cutting trees across the roads, burning bridges in front of them, and stationing cavalrymen, armed with Enfield Rifles, behind trees, rock, etc. He was able to check the advance of Averill's (sic) 5,000 cavalry...."[28] Many of McCausland's troopers were tough men from the hills in the western part of the state (including West Virginia). "Their courage was of the unflinching kind, natural hates of those who were despoiling their homes and woe to the Yankee who came within range of their unerring aim,"[28] wrote one commentator.

McCausland would place his men in a good defensive position and wait for Averell's Cavalry. Averell's Cavalry would stop and deploy for battle. After a few shots, McCausland would retreat and start the process over again. He couldn't stop Averell, but McCausland could slow him.

Despite the praise of McCausland and his tactics, it appears that Averell's advance at 2:00 a.m. caught McCausland unprepared. It is approximately twenty-four miles between Lexington and Buchanan. Averell had covered most of that distance by 8:00 a.m. Eight miles from Buchanan, Averell pushed his command to a "dog trot,"[34] trying to secure the bridge. At four miles from Buchanan, he sent a courier to Hunter saying that he was still "...driving McCausland."[11] Some of the Jessie Scouts that had been to Buchanan joined the army as it approached town.

Averell's push was almost successful. At 9:00 a.m., McCausland arrived at the covered bridge. He ordered that hay be brought and that the east end of the bridge be covered. McCausland was not a general to command from a safe distance. He was willing to accept the same risks that he had his men endure, gaining for him much respect from his troops.

Averell pressed him hard at the bridge; there was neither time nor manpower for McCausland to use. He and Captain St. Clair were the only ones between the capture of the bridge and Averell. McCausland lit the hay "...with my own hand..."[91] at the east end of the bridge. If he were to attempt to run across the bridge, it is likely that Union gunfire would cut him down. McCausland jumped from the bridge into the water. Captain St. Clair was on the east side of the bridge and the fire. He ran up the bank of the river, trying to escape the Union onslaught. The advance of Averell's Cavalry was on the east end of the bridge. One cavalryman saw that "...the oil flashed up and set fire to the hay in the bridge...."[91] The fire frightened the horses, and the advance stopped. The stalled cavalrymen saw St. Clair and gave chase. They didn't see McCausland in the water. McCausland spotted a canoe tied near the east of the bridge. He swam to the canoe and started paddling toward the west bank. He stayed under the burning bridge so that the Yanks could not see him. McCausland said that they "...did not discover me until I was going up the bank on the opposite side...."[91] The Union troopers probably shot at the wet Reb, not knowing it was General McCausland; however they did capture

Buchanan — note covered bridge over James River — painting by Beyer.

Remains of support columns of bridge burned at Buchanan.

Captain St. Clair.

McCausland stayed near the bridge until he saw it burning vigorously; then he fell back to join his men.

The small community on the east bank next to the end of the bridge was called Pattonsburg. The wind was blowing from Buchanan on the west bank. The wind carried sparks and set some houses on fire on the east side of the river. "Clouds of smoke rolled upward, and the despairing cries of those thus rendered homeless mingled with the roar of the flames,"[81] reported one observer.

By this time, Averell's Cavalry was arriving in force. A rumor sprang up among the troops that "the people...begged McCausland not to set fire to it (the bridge)..."[11] because it might spread to their homes, "...but McCausland, with his characteristic recklessness, persisted in needless destruction...."[34] McCausland "...disregarded their prayers...."[11] It is highly unlikely that any citizen protested the burning. McCausland barely had time to light a match; he had no time for a chat.

There were soon "...eleven private dwellings in the conflagration."[34] "...Many people (were)...homeless."[92] Yankee troopers carried water from the stream and put out the fire. The James River was at a very low level. One person remembers residents crossing the river coming into town, "...palefaced women with helpless children clinging to their skirts and bearing in their hands such valuables as their hasty exit permitted them to collect...."[34] They apparently crossed the river at the rapids several hundred yards below the burning bridge.

McCausland's forces moved up a small hill that had a commanding view of the river. Here on Oak Hill, he formed a battle line. Colonel R.H. Burks knocked on Mrs. Jane Boyd's door at the big house on Oak Hill. He advised her to leave the house immediately because it would be in the range of the Union fire.

Mrs. Boyd decided not to leave but gathered her house slaves and children and went to the cellar. Soon some of the people whose houses had been burned came to join her in the cellar. Others of the homeless people found refuge in cellars along main street.

A Negro mammy took one last look before entering the cellar toward the river from Oak Hill. She saw the blue column halted at the river and a stream of blue-clad soldiers covering the road as far back as the eye could see. She said, "Good lord, ain't thar no end to dem men!"[92]

In the cellar, her mistress recalled that it was "...a fearful time...(and) filled my heart with deep sorrow."[92]

Averell's troops controlled the north bank of the James. Averell could see some Confederate troops in town, and he knew that they would resist when his troops attempted to cross into town. Averell moved his artillery and men back from the river to the foot of Purgatory Mountain to increase their elevation and effectiveness.

Averell started a cannonade of the town. One resident said that it was only a single volley from each cannon, but it "...terrified inhabitants. Bomb shells

"Oak Hill" at Buchanan.

exploded in our very midst...."[81] Very little damage was done to the town. Another resident recalled that the "...facing of our back passage door was splintered by a shell, and a canister shot went through the end of the kitchen; a minie ball went through the front yard fence...."[92] One house was destroyed. "Aunt Eliza's house was struck by a shell and away it went."[92] Most of the frightened people in the cellars bemoaned their situation, but one resident said other Southern towns had been attacked by the brutal Hunter: "Why shouldn't we?"[81]

McCausland knew that his small force could not successfully oppose Averell's crossing. Averell kept shelling the town because he thought "...the damned Rebels..."[92] were hiding there. McCausland didn't want to give Averell an excuse to continue the cannonade. Most of McCausland's men withdrew from town toward the Peaks of Otter near Bedford.

When Averell observed McCausland's forces withdrawing, he halted the cannonade because he "...found out that he was wasting his ammunition upon helpless women and children...."[81] The contest for Buchanan was very brief. The cannonade ceased in less than forty minutes.

Jessie Scouts knew where the ford was. About one mile north of the bridge site was a ford (later Mr. Looney was to start a ferry here). The first Federals came over the ford. The residents saw "...a horseman, mounted upon a foaming steed (showing the effects of the hard ride), dashed down the main street hurraying and waving an unsheathed sabre about his head."[81]

The Federals were beginning to take control of the town. Because of the lack of uniforms, it was not easy for the conquerors to distinguish between civilians and soldiers. They caught one man attempting to leave town. The "...vandals killed Newton Painter as they came into town...Mr. Painter was trying to escape with his provisions...They ordered him to halt which he did, but the dastardly brute shot him through the heart,"[92] remembered one resident.

At the river "Several Batteaux loaded with ammunition stores were captured...."[34] This is another indication that McCausland had been forced back and through Buchanan more rapidly than he had anticipated. The engineers started constructing the pontoon bridge. Averell directed more troops to cross at the ford and secure the town. They chased some of McCausland's forces toward the Peaks, but returned to town shortly.

These troops who had served under Hunter, started to repeat a familiar pattern. While Averell was on the north side of the river, some troops began looting in town. At one home "...some of the soldiers...(were) very rough... (and) with many oaths..."[92] broke into one resident's cellar. They stole "...fine old wines..."[92] and drank them.

Union soldiers entered another cellar also looking for something to drink. They came out "...waving sealed bottles, exultantly above their heads. These happened to contain spoiled tomatoes (which someone had forgotten to throw out)...in their eagerness to get at the supposed liquor, they broke off the necks of the bottles and swallowed a considerable portion of their contents before discovering their mistake. If the drunk which followed...was bogus, (sic) the illness was genuine...."[81] Other Federals, "...clearing our garden fence at a bound, tore up the young vegetables by the roots...,"[81] recalled one housewife.

At one house, they stole a high hat and green cockades and "...amused (themselves) in putting them on."[92]

While some fellow soldiers were looting in town, the remainder of Averell's men rested on the bank of the river, waiting for the engineers to construct the bridge. To reduce the boredom, some soldiers began pulling mountain ivy and wrapping it around their bayonets and gun barrels. The new fashion became a rage in the army immediately, and a thousand men pulled vine and flowers and decorated their rifles.

Soon the bridge was constructed, and Averell and the mass of troops entered town "...like a moving mass of bloom."[81] Averell sent the artillery and wagons upstream to cross. When Staunton fell, the Union band played "Hail, Columbia." The residents of Buchanan now heard the same tune.

Averell moved down main street and established headquarters on the lawn of the Presbyterian rectory. Perhaps Averell was a devout follower; he had used the Presbyterian Church in Lexington as headquarters also.

The residents had heard of the brutality of Hunter's men. They saw the first troops starting to loot. They were afraid of what the whole army was going to do to their town and their property.

Averell and his force were Hunter's men, but Hunter was not there to command. Averell was determined that his men would conduct themselves as Union soldiers while they were under his command. Averell gave orders, and the looting began to decrease. The citizens were very shocked and pleased at this unexpected behavior. The fear and foreboding of Hunter turned to admiration for Averell. Their town would not be sacked by these Yankees. Reported one Confederate: "Deeds of vandalism...were not permitted...General (Averell) looking very elegant to our Confederate eyes in his well-made clothes and varnished boots...."[81] He posted Union guards to protect homes against Union men. Despite Averell's order, some looting continued. One resident said that the Yanks stole forty hams and forty bushels of corn[92] and other food from her house. They also entered her house: "Ned's Bible and little old music box...gone."[92]

Back at the ford, a man in a Confederate uniform had joined a Union wagon train. He was not a Jessie Scout but posed as one. Southerners were learning to beat the Yankees at their own game of deception. This brave Confederate was attempting to take advantage of the confusion to lead a wagon train west away from town so that it could be captured by McCausland's men. It appears that he had turned the wagon train the wrong way and was nearing the home of Col. John Anderson (C.S.A.) at Mount Joy when he was discovered. The Confederate in a Confederate uniform was arrested for not being a lying Jessie Scout.

A rider informed Averell at his headquarters about the situation. Averell rode to the wagon train to take personal command. The Confederate was deemed "a Rebel spy..., and by order of General Averell was shot."[34] Averell apparently ordered that the body neither be moved from the side of the road nor buried. This was his warning to other Rebels who might try to use deception in this war.

The Confederate was not the only soldier Averell had shot. "A Negro who was attached to his command attempted to rape a white woman and was seized and shot immediately."[11] "There was a Negro there who seemed to think when the Yankees came he could do as he pleased, and one night got into a lady's house and behaved badly. General Averell had him shot,"[92] wrote an observer.

Averell took a few prisoners in town, but they appeared to be citizens and not any of McCausland's men. The prisoners were held at a compound at Averell's headquarters.

One lady told Averell of her concern that her husband's office might be looted. Averell not only gave her permission to move books and materials but assigned some troops to aid her. While the troops, lady, and her slaves were moving the material, she conversed with a soldier who told her "...that the burning of V.M.I. was a shame."[92]

Averell sent a squad of men up the road (now Route 43) that goes over the Peaks of Otter toward Liberty (Bedford). The road had "...high cliffs on one side and a deep ravine and a precipice on the other."[92] A rumor was that a couple of Buchanan citizens named Goff and Burkholder might have directed McCausland's forces to a particular cliff overhang. There gunpowder was exploded, and the road was blocked by rocks and earth.

The squad returned and reported to Averell that infantry could pick their way around the side, but it would take three days to clear the road for artillery and wagons. This would force the Federals to advance up the Peaks by a steeper road farther west of Buchanan.

With the town secured, Averell sent a courier back to Hunter.

During this day, the corps continued to hold the pass at Balcony Falls. It received a courier from McCausland and tried to keep abreast of developments. The cadets also sent word to Lynchburg as to their position. Lynchburg was still afloat in rumors that Union cavalry would soon attack, but no cavalry came.

Sometime during the night of the twelfth, Breckinridge received Imboden's courier. Breckinridge then knew that the Union cavalry (under Duffie) was moving back toward Hunter at Lexington. Breckinridge had been receiving reports about the battle at Trevilians Station, he probably did not know that Sheridan had broken off contact with the Confederate cavalry. Breckinridge sent a courier to Imboden to move the cavalry toward Lynchburg. Breckinridge would remain at Rockfish Gap with the infantry. If Sheridan did break through, Breckinridge would attempt to stop him before he could link with Hunter, and Imboden would be in a position to intercept him before he reached Lynchburg.

Imboden also received a courier from Lynchburg. A Federal force of unknown size had damaged the tracks near Amherst Courthouse. These were the two hundred men Averell had sent to circle Lynchburg. They caused great panic among the civilian population. They also did slight damage to the James River Canal when they crossed it, still heading east.

It was early morning, and Imboden was apparently twenty-five miles from Lynchburg. The information that he had indicated that the Yanks were east of the James, but their direction and numbers were unknown. He crossed the James so that his command would also be east of the river. He then moved up the river toward the last reported sighting of the Union cavalry.

Averell's two hundred did not continue east, but started circling south around Lynchburg.

Despite Union cavalry activity, railroad workers had moved to Arrington Station and had begun repair work on the tracks.

Duffié had pushed his cavalry through the night. It had moved approximately twenty-four miles in the darkness over very rough roads. At approximately 4:00 a.m., the animals needed rest. Duffié allowed a three-hour break, and then weary men and beast started toward the top of the Blue Ridge and through Whites Gap. He kept the command moving until it struck the river at the base of the mountain. Here he allowed another rest break.

Outside of Lexington, a Confederate scout sent word to his commander that the two hundred men from Averell's command had given the Confederates the slip. "The cavalry which crossed the mountain has not been heard from,"[8] he said.

Near Natural Bridge, the two McDonalds and their captors awoke to find that the wounded Yank had died during the night. After he was buried along the river, the party started toward Lexington.

At Lexington, Hunter waited for the return of Duffié, word from Averell, and the supply train, which he believed would replenish his ammunition.

The infantry knew that it would not be moving that day. Most of the men rested; many washed the only clothes they had — their uniforms. Some bathed and swam.

For the first time since the march began, the artist, David Hunter Strother, made an appearance. Burning the Virginia Military Institute had been the first blow struck on this march that had satisfied both the Southern artist and the Northern warrior that struggled within Strother's spirit. He took his pad and sketched "...the ruins of the Institute."[11]

Hunter sent word to have the captured canal boats destroyed. The boats should be safe at Lynchburg at that time. One soldier noted, "There is a slack-water navigation of the James River at Lexington..."[14] combined with the canal and the boats captured.

The barges with their six cannons and ammunition were burned. "...A heavy cannonade from the bursting of shells which they contained reminded me of a well-contested battle,"[11] wrote one observer. Several locks on the canal were destroyed also.

While destruction was taking place in town, an irate Irishman named O'Brien was approaching town. He claimed that he was neither a United States citizen nor a Confederate one but a British subject. He was going to see Hunter and reclaim some horses (neither Yankee nor Rebel) that Averell had stolen from him the day before.

Hunter and his whole army were happy to see the wagon-supply-train roll in, but none were more overjoyed than the regiment and one half of the 100 volunteers that would be going home with the empty wagons. The volunteers would be replaced by the One Hundred Fifty-Second and the One Hundred Sixty-First Ohio Regiments that had escorted the train forward.

"Hunter was greatly disgusted when a fine supply arrived of everything except what he needed"[30] (ammunition). Some sources indicate that Grant had decided not to re-supply Hunter with ammunition because (1.) he had not followed orders to march via Charlottesville and (2.) he was fearful that Southern troops would capture the ammunition. These reasons seem to have no basis. Grant would not intentionally send to an army a supply train loaded with supplies but no gunpowder. An army that can't shoot is an army without use. Others argue that Hunter was only inventing excuses for not moving the army and for a critically low supply of ammunition for political reasons. Piedmont had reduced ammunition supplies to a low level. Hunter now realized that he had made a major error in ordering the barges loaded with ammunition destroyed.

The civilian population was aware that a supply train was in the town of Lexington. The Union Army had stolen all they had to eat. Many Southerners swallowed their pride and went to the Federals for food. Mothers, who would rather starve than ask a damn Yankee for help, stood and begged for their hungry children's sake. The Federals did fill some of the requests and stomachs.

Hunter did not want his superiors to believe that the only reason he stayed at Lexington was to set his fire of punishment. He now added to his excuse list, "I had also begun to feel anxious in regard to Duffié...."[8] Duffié was following orders until Hunter decided to tarry at Lexington and sent him recall orders. Duffié had started back at once and moved all night. Duffié, who was only following Hunter's orders to the best of his abilities, now became a scapegoat for delay. According to one report "The troops remained at Lexington because General Duffié...had not been heard from."[88] The hard-working Duffié was much maligned: "I learned upon his return that he had been mostly engaged in pilfering...this...prevented us from..."[73] leaving Lexington. One source said that the army was, "...waiting for Duffié and sinning away its day of salvation."[4]

It was afternoon when the tired "...sunburned and dusty..."[11] Duffié arrived at Lexington. He reported to Hunter that he had defeated Imboden "...in every attempt to harass or impede the movements of our troops...damage done to the railroad...captured 100 prisoners, about 500 horses, and destroyed large quantities of stores...."[8]

After talking to some of Duffié's subordinates and examining some prisoners, Strother concluded that Duffié's report was "exaggerated."[11] Strother did find two prisoners willing to talk. They told Strother "...that Fitzhugh Lee had defeated a body of cavalry sent by Grant...(and) that Ewell was advancing with a powerful column..."[11] toward the Valley, when in burst Duffié.

Strother was uncertain if the Rebs were telling the truth, but he never had a chance to find out. Duffié got into a quarrel with the men "...as to whether (Duffié) whipped them or not."[11] Strother concluded, "Two officers should never examine prisoners at the same time...."[11]

Strother was uncertain if the information he had gotten from the prisoners was reliable, but he relayed it to Hunter. Hunter said, "...I had assurance that there was no considerable force of the enemy in or near Lynchburg,"[8] but this information from Strother worried him.

Hunter sent word to Colonel D. Putnam and the regiment and a half of going-home volunteers that their trip had been cancelled. They and the train were to remain with the army. The order was received with much dismay and grumbling.

The courier from Averell had not arrived at Lexington by late afternoon. Hunter did not know for certain that the small but important town of Buchanan was now under Union control. Buchanan was the western terminus of the James River Canal. Much vital iron and food were moved down stream to Richmond. Hunter did not know that Averell had taken the town and that the important bridge over the James was burned.

Hunter sent a messenger to Averell informing him that the infantry would move from Lexington the next day and should be approaching Buchanan in late afternoon. Hunter told Averell that the last report he had received from Averell's Cavalry was in the very early morning. He knew that Averell was "driving" McCausland at that time. He told Averell, "You will ...hold the bridge, if possible, while we come up...from the reports...received, not anticipating that you will have much difficulty...."[8]

As darkness settled in on Buchanan, guards were posted at some homes. At one house the Yankee guard started making eyes at two young Southern belles. He "...had been persuading her and Lena Taylor's Becky to go away with him, and that Becky was going."[92] No information if the Yank was serious, if mom found out, or if Becky went too far.

Buchanan was a town awash with rumors: "We were distressed beyond description...heard they had killed pa, Captain Wills, and Captain Barton, Doctor Hamilton, and Doctor Mayo, but they certainly had killed pa."[92] Although this rumor was totally false, it was still disturbing.

Henry Beall had spent a quiet day in the Lexington jail, courtesy of General Hunter. "Two sweet young girls..."[80] whom Beall knew, brought him some food. When his Yankee guard saw that Beall had on an extra good pair of cavalry boots, he decided that a prisoner didn't need good footwear where he was going. Soon Beall was pacing about the jail in socks.

By this time, Quinn had brought his prisoners, the McDonalds, to town. Apparently they were placed in a stockade, not in the jail. Quinn struck up a conversation with Chief-of-Scouts Ellicott. Quinn told Ellicott that he had captured two old acquaintances from the Winchester area. Ellicott told Quinn that he too had captured a resident of that area — Henry Beall.

Quinn, whom Southerners described as kind, went to the jail to see Beall. When Quinn noticed that Beall had no footwear, he asked him what had happened. Beall told him that his Union guard told him to "shuck them."[80] Now his boots were walking around with Federal feet in them. Within minutes, Beall had his boots back: "I have always retained a grateful recollection of Colonel Quinn's kindness,"[80] recorded Beall later. That was the last time Beall saw Quinn during the war.

It was late afternoon when the irate Irishman O'Brien was approaching Lexington. He intended to see Hunter personally and demand that his horses be returned. By the time O'Brien approached North River, the Union Army had passed over the town. The pontoon bridge was disassembled and reloaded in the wagons. When O'Brien saw that there was no bridge but only a shaky footpath of boards remaining, he decided to look for another way across the river. One source says "...He went down through unfrequented woods to where he knew there was a canoe...."[36] Going down the hill, he discovered the remains of Captain Matt White.

Apparently the sight of the dead body changed the Irishman's mind and mission. He seemed to have decided quickly that these Federals play for keeps and that they could keep his horses. O'Brien went to the nearest house, the Camerons' and told the unmarried daughters of the body near the river. The two young girls and one old man decided that they could not move the body up the hill. O'Brien turned toward home. The girls remained with the body through the night to keep wild animals from eating and mauling it.

On the other side of the river, Matt's mother anxiously waited. She knew that her son would soon be released from jail as the two scouts had promised this morning.

Most of the female residents of Lexington had not dared to venture on the streets of their town that day. One lady recalled that the only outside contact she had today was a male member of her church who came to check on her safety. The church member told her that the Federals had caught and slaughtered all the livestock in and near town. They had stolen any horse that could carry a rider. There were rumors that the corps had been captured and that many slaves were running away. That night she said her "...heart and soul are weary."[74]

Hunter issued marching orders for the next day.

At Lynchburg sometime in the afternoon, General Nicholls received a courier sent from Imboden early in the morning. When the courier was sent, Duffié was still going toward the railroad and had not received his courier from Hunter.

The courier's report indicated that Duffié had 3,500 to 4,000 men heading toward the railroad at Amherst Courthouse. The 200 men Averell had sent from Lexington had been lost by Confederate scouts there, but Imboden's men discovered their movement. The 200 had grown to 2,000. Imboden wrote Nicholls: "You are in no danger of attack, except by cavalry, for a day or two."[8]

Nicholls had only a few Home Guards, convalescents, and soldiers to protect Lynchburg. He decided to shrink his perimeter and consolidate his forces. "I have to hug the town; want of force has compelled me to give up some strong positions,"[8] he wrote.

He wired Richmond of the immediate danger he faced: "I have prepared to the best of my ability...I will do my best against them, (but he didn't believe that he could hold the town) the condition of this place is well-known to you...I earnestly request reinforcements."[8]

Lee had sent Ewell's old corps, now under Early, toward the city. Lee hoped that Early would arrive before Hunter. He sent a North Carolinian, Maj. Gen. Robert Ransom, Jr., from Richmond to command all the cavalry in the Valley District. Ransom was allowed to select his own staff.

Chapter IX

Tuesday, June 14 — Thursday, June 16

On June 14, General Early had his army on the move from sun to sun. The army crossed the South Anna and marched to Gardiners Cross Roads. As the sun set, the tired army had moved much closer to Charlottesville, where it had expected railroad transport to Lynchburg. Some men were foot-sore, but most were "...in fine spirits."[79]

Gen. Daniel Harvey Hill — CSA.

The exact date and the mode of transportation that D.H. Hill used to leave the Richmond area is not known. Gen. Daniel Harvey Hill was a very important non-person on no official mission. Hill, a native of South Carolina, was almost forty-three years old. He had had war experience in Mexico and had taught military tactics; he was the Superintendent of the North Carolina Military Institute at the outbreak of the war. He had enlisted in Confederate service as a colonel and had risen to lieutenant general by 1863. At that time he was a man without official command or rank.

After Braxton Bragg's failure in the Chattanooga Campaign, Bragg blamed

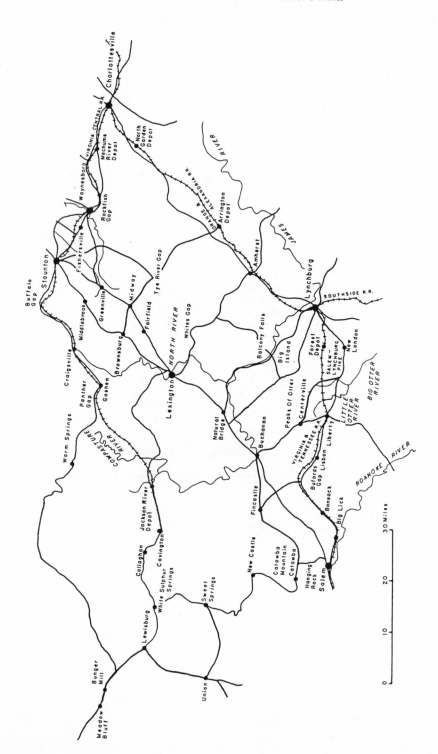

his failure on many of his subordinates. Bragg accused Breckinridge "...of being drunk and unfit for duty...."[94] Hill would let no criticism from Bragg go unanswered, but Bragg was one of President Davis's favorites. Bragg went to Richmond as the President's personal advisor, and Hill became unemployed. "His outspoken criticism of Braxton Bragg as a field commander caused not only his relief shortly thereafter but also the President's refusal to nominate Hill to the Confederate Senate at the grade to which he (the President) had earlier appointed him."[24]

Hill was too valuable a general to be retired. Soon he linked with General Beauregard in the Richmond area. Beauregard requested that Hill be confirmed as a volunteer on his staff. "The assignment was approved by Davis...not (as) active but informal service."[95]

Because it was informal service, Hill had more flexibility than most officers. Perhaps when Hill heard of the damage Hunter had done in Lexington, he was prompted to move from Richmond toward Lynchburg to do all in his power to defeat the destroyer Hunter. Hill had a personal attachment to Lexington: he had taught at the Washington College before the war.

He headed toward Lynchburg for county, school, and to aid General Breckinridge who had also felt the unjust wrath for Bragg's failure.

General Breckinridge spent the day at Rockfish Gap gathering intelligence. He knew Hunter's objective was Lynchburg. He was aware that Hunter was at Lexington and would not be moving on Lynchburg via Rockfish Gap. Breckinridge by then became aware that the Union cavalry had broken off the fight at Trevilians Station. He could not be absolutely sure that it would attempt to ride around the Confederate cavalry and move to link with Hunter. If it did, the most logical route would be via Rockfish Gap. If this route was followed, Breckinridge would be in a position to intercept the Federal cavalry. Since Breckinridge knew that his army would be needed at Lynchburg, he wanted to be there before Hunter but not at the expense of allowing Federal cavalry a free ride to join Hunter. Breckinridge had already sent his cavalry to reinforce Lynchburg. Breckinridge also spent the day, waiting for the railroad to be repaired to Lynchburg.

Sheridan's Federal Cavalry, soundly defeated at Trevilians Station, was moving toward Richmond.

Breckinridge's Cavalry under Imboden entered Lynchburg empty-handed this day. Imboden had made no contact with the Union force of unknown size that had damaged the railroad and the canal near Amherst. Imboden and Nicholls no doubt conferred. Nicholls apparently guessed incorrectly as to the direction the Union force was heading. Imboden's men got some rest, rations, arms, and ammunition and went back into Amherst County, looking for the Federal cavalry. It was probably believed that this group, like Duffié's, was going to rejoin Hunter, but that was not the plan. The 200 hand-picked men continued their sweep of Lynchburg. They probably struck the Southside Railroad in the afternoon or early evening. At Concord Station between Lynchburg and Appomattox, they captured and burned two trains and severed telegraph lines to Richmond.

The wounded Gen. James Longstreet had been moved from a Lynchburg hospital to recuperate at his friend's (Col. John D. Alexander) home near Campbell Courthouse. When the Yankees struck Concord Station they came near Longstreet's resting place. The Federals did not know that the great General was there, but some Confederates believed his capture was the object of the raid, "A Federal raiding party...from five hundred to one thousand in number, after burning the railroad at Concord...moved toward Campbell Courthouse for that purpose; the attempt failed when friends rescued him...."[108] Longstreet was later moved back to Lynchburg.

Soon Imboden had his cavalry in motion. It moved to Buffalo Spring and camped for the night. The men had received some rations but they were "...without feed for our weary horses."[35]

As the sun rose at Lexington, Hunter's army started to march toward Buchanan. The army used two roads (one was "...an old plank road...")[53] to speed the movement over the twenty-four mile journey. The Signal Corps would attempt to keep both columns in communication, but the rugged terrain prevented communicating.

As the army was starting to leave town, couriers from the two hundred troopers from Averell's command that were sent toward Lynchburg returned. They had done very little damage but had triggered false reports and panic. They returned with captured newspapers both from Richmond and Lynchburg. Hunter and his staff examined these papers with great interest. The Richmond paper confirmed that Grant's siege of Richmond was intensifying. This was good news for Hunter because he knew General Lee could send little force to oppose him, if any. Perhaps the rumors that a large Confederate force was moving from Richmond were only rumors.

"Sheridan is on a raid toward Charlottesville," the Lynchburg paper stated. This was more good news for Hunter. The Virginia Central Railroad was blocked. No reinforcements would be coming to Lynchburg from that direction. It was also likely that Sheridan would be bringing even more reinforcements to join the army soon. The Confederate position appeared to Hunter to grow weaker with each passing hour. There appeared to be no military person available to make a hasty dash on Lynchburg.

The soldiers were glad that their general was not pushing them hard because "the road is rough, crooked and rocky, with occasional deep holes, which cause us no little trouble, and considerable delay."[83]

Every soldier soon became aware that the army would pass within two miles of Natural Bridge. The soldiers wished to see this natural wonder of the world, but they were soldiers, not tourists.

A few adventurous officers and men disobeyed orders and went to see the Bridge. They knew that it was likely that they would never pass this way again in their lives, and this opportunity should not be missed. Of course, Lieutenant Meigs was among them. Chief-of-Staff Strother had sketched the Bridge many times, but he did not leave the army to go see it.

There was a saltpeter mine near the Bridge. Saltpeter was used in making gunpowder. The miners were not there when the few blue-clad soldiers arrived. There is no account that the Federals took time to destroy any of the miners' equipment. They enjoyed a forbidden look at the enemy's stone bridge.

NATURAL BRIDGE.

By David Hunter Strother.

The army was slowed not only by bad roads but also by some Confederate guerrillas, who "...invariably fired at our appearance."[83]

The first regiments began leaving Lexington at 6:00 a.m. One resident wrote: "...I was aroused early by the rumbling of the artillery racing out of town with all speed; before breakfast, the whole street as far as the eye could see up and down was jammed with their wagon trains, which seemed to be in the greatest possible hurry, and before twelve o'clock all were gone except a few horsemen who seemed to be left as scouts. We were in high spirits, you may know, and there never was so much rejoicing in town."[69] The One Hundred Sixteenth Ohio Infantry was the last to leave town.

One soldier with the wagon train lamented "...in our wagons, in place of hardtack and meat, the beautiful statue of Washington..."[83] rides. The prisoners, guarded by the One Hundred Twenty-Third Ohio Infantry, were marched off also. There was still much grumbling among the soldiers whose enlistment was near expiration, but "The General has concluded not to send back the grand wagon train, but will retain it until it becomes troublesome."[11] Some prisoners who were wounded, sick, or elderly were released at Lexington because they would slow the army. Finally, after almost three days James H. Blackley (captured near Arrington Station), could remove the watch from his boot. He was a free man.

The army continued the hot, dusty, and toilsome march throughout the day.

At Lexington, the few remaining Federals were captured by Confederate scouts that entered the town as the last Federal units left. One resident had mixed emotions about the Union's departure; she was Mrs. Matthew White, the mother of Capt. Matt White. She was told that her son was in jail but that he would be released soon. The Yankees were gone, but her son had not been returned to her.

The Camerons' daughters had sat with the body throughout the night. Some time after twelve after the Union had left, they sent word to Mrs. White. Only now did she become aware that her son had been gunned down and that the killers had calmly lied to her.

One resident wrote: "That afternoon...I saw a wagon pass on its way up the street, and in it a stiff, straight form covered with a sheet. It was poor Matt White on his way to his mother."[25] His body lay corpse that day, and arrangements were made for the funeral the next day.

Also, some time in the afternoon, two of Thomas Wilson's slaves came into town. They had run when the Yankees fired at the campsite of their master and of the McDonalds. They saw the Yankees wound and capture the McDonalds. Several residents heard the news. As the report circulated, it became distorted, and many believed that all three men had been killed. The rumors circulated, and everyone assumed that Mrs. Cornelia McDonald had been informed of the fate of her husband and son, but she had not received any news.

Above Buchanan near the Peaks of Otter, there was a clash between some of Averell's cavalrymen and some of McCausland's scouts. Private K.P. Kahea with Company B, Jeff Davis Legion was struck by a Union minie ball near the heart, severing the artery. Kahea bled profusely as the Yankees chased him almost three miles. He then rode five miles farther and was taken into a private home. Despite the hard riding, the bleeding ceased. He would remain several days in this home.

Averell's men were scouting and testing McCausland's defenses. They would make no major push toward Liberty (now Bedford) today.

At Buchanan, Averell was becoming a respected conqueror because he had not turned his troops loose to burn and steal as the residents had expected. Now a Southern lady could write: "Our colored servant had the *honor* of cooking for General Averell...."[81]

The kindness of the enemy general in a blue uniform was shown in his attitude toward children. A young one approached Averell and asked, "Are you going to have any more firing?" "No," he replied, smiling; "would you like us to have some more?"[81]

Most of Averell's forces remained in or near Buchanan. Averell did send some out to raid and destroy. Important iron works like the ones at Purgatory Mountain, Arcadia, and as far as the Fincastle area were destroyed. "In the vicinity of Buchanan several iron works were burned, one a branch of the Tredegar Works (at Richmond) which employs five hundred hands."[11]

There were no large-scale Confederate forces to guard the iron works but the Partisan Rangers that dogged every step of the Union Army, made some Yanks pay with their lives for the destruction. The Union troopers knew that destroying these furnaces today would prevent the Confederacy from making cannons and ordnance that could be used against them tomorrow.

Most if not all of the furnaces were run by the Tredegar Iron Works at Richmond. The agent in charge of the furnaces did try to find men to defend the works, but did not evacuate any of the portable assets of the works.

The Union troops easily overpowered the few men at the furnaces. What followed was a "disaster (and a) catastrophe" for the South. The "...South's chief supplier of gun metal, Grace Furnace, another producer of cannon iron, and Mount Torry Furnace...were left in smoldering ruins. Many of the slaves escaped and the raiders captured large numbers of draft animals and destroyed extensive stores of provisions."[87]

Remains of iron furnace at Purgatory Mountain.

Iron furnace at Arcadia.

Because the residents knew the Federal Army was coming, they had hidden possessions on their property and even had taken much wealth to the mountains to protect it from the invaders. The Jessie Scouts that were in town before the Confederates left took note of where the valuables were taken. Now that they controlled the town and made and enforced the rules, "...the wretches..."[92] simply went to the mountain and stole the hidden wealth.

In many cases slaves helped their owners hide valuables. In some cases the slaves were not as loyal as their owners believed. When the Federals came, the slaves took the opportunity to run to freedom. Some of the slaves directed Union soldiers to their former owner's wealth. "The Union soldiers went direct to the place where our valuables were concealed, and our family plate, our jewelry, and even portions of our clothing fell into their hands,"[92] said one resident. Some of the valuables that the slaves did not help hide remained safe.

The thievery was not confined to Yankees and Negroes only. Some neighbors stole from neighbors. The less wealthy had aided the wealthy in hiding valuables. Some people who were rich were then poor, and some who were poor were rich.

Hunter and his army had been moving toward Buchanan all day. The prisoners were guarded by the One Hundred Twenty-Third Ohio Infantry. Among the prisoners there was a reunion of sorts. Henry Beall met Angus McDonald and his son Harry. They exchanged stories of their captures and showed their wounds. Beall remembered that old man McDonald "...by his cheery words encouraged others who had become faint-hearted under the depressing surroundings."[80] There was very little food for the prisoners.

It was late afternoon when the advance units of Hunter's army reached the James River at Buchanan. Hunter was disappointed that Averell had failed to secure the bridge. He was not happy that Averell had ordered his men to put out the bridge fire that McCausland had started.

Hunter sent the cavalry, artillery, and wagon train upstream to ford. The captured canal boats were used to ferry troops. Engineers used boards to form a footpath over the burned bridge and its abutment. Even with the boats, footpath, and ford, it took a long time to move the massive army over the stream. Units were still crossing at 3:00 a.m. Some couldn't cross that night. At the ford Hunter lost "...several mules and wagons, in the darkness."[83] Because the wagon train was separated from the infantry; many blue-bellies remained empty after the long march.

Hunter could blame the toil, lost time, and equipment on Averell's failure to secure the bridge.

At least one good thing occurred at the crossing: The invaders "...were greeted with cheers of welcome, and the old flag was waved by a company of people on the veranda of a large house...this was the first demonstration of the kind since the departure from Winchester, and each regiment responded with hearty cheers as they passed, causing no little excitement in the staid-looking town...The crowd that had cheered were called, 'Northern people....'"[41]

Colonel Hayes's most pleasant moment came when he bathed in the James.

It appears that Hunter and his staff took quarters at the Haynes Hotel north of the James and did not ford or enter the town that day. One account indicates that Hunter "...camped on the magnificent estate of Col. John Anderson"[23] (Mount Joy). This encampment is not likely. It is probable that many Union officers and men were on the plantation at Mount Joy, west of town. There were Yankees camped everywhere. The town and its surroundings were crushed under a wave of men dressed in blue. They camped in wheatfields, barns, porches, homes, and anywhere they wished. The troops who were lucky enough to eat noticed, "Our hardtack was all gone, and flour getting scarce, but fresh beef and mutton still plenty."[53] (They were still able to steal and slaughter the Southern farmers' livestock).

Crook was somewhat aloof from Hunter and his staff. He forded the river and camped at Oak Hill. The lady of the house feared that the Yanks would burn her home. Mrs. Boyd had more to fear than most because "...my husband had been a member of the secession convention."[92]

After supper Averell called on Hunter at the Haynes Hotel. He reported to Hunter that "he drove McCausland, pressing him as rapidly as possible but was unable to save the bridge."[11] Hunter's reaction and words to Averell are not recorded, but he was not pleased.

Averell then told Hunter about the Confederate who had pretended to be a Jessie Scout and was attempting to lead a wagon train straight to McCausland. Hunter roared, "Let him be hung forthwith." "Well, no," Averell answered cooly. "I had him shot yesterday."[11]

Hunter set the order of march for the next day. Crook and Averell would take the lead, and Sullivan and Duffié, the rear.

The townspeople knew, Averell knew, and the men knew that Hunter was commanding in person. Averell's rules were gone; almost anything was acceptable. Here Hunter, continuing his "outrages,"[93] was hated and feared by the residents, but "...Averell's men were very civil and acted with as much as we could expect from enemies."[92] One lady said that Averell "...was very courteous and polite,"[92] in contrast with Hunter.

Hunter was angered that these conquered people would admire any general on his staff. Hunter's anger and contempt for Averell was growing.

J.W. Jones's Foundry and large storehouse north of the river were burned. The foundry was used to mold brass. A warehouse that was burned contained a large amount of sorghum. The Yankees "...danced around the fire, saying it was the biggest molasses stew they ever saw."[92]

Not only did the Federals steal food; in some cases they forced the slaves to cook it for them. Any spirits that could be stolen were consumed. Alcohol lowered their inhibitions even further, and they continued the reign of terror on the defenseless citizens.

The troops entered one house and stole everything. The owner of the house said, "The Yankees left me without one mouthful of anything to eat...(but they did leave) one tablespoon, that was generous, wasn't it?"[92]

That night they broke into a smokehouse. The mother of the house and her child were alarmed. Some of the Yankees became aware of the woman's presence. I "...leave out all the horrible oaths and brutal language of an infuriated drunken man,"[92] wrote the mother. Not only was she worried about the stealing, but she was terrified of what might be forced upon her person. When the Yankees made good their promises to pay her a personal visit, she knew that she must do something to protect herself and her child. The slaves tried to talk to the Northern intruders and to discourage them as they entered the house. This delay gave her enough time to run out another door with her child. She "...ran through that deep ditch, was wet up to my knees, ran to Captain Harvey's (house) did not know that my clothes were open"[92] (because of hastily dressing and the rigors of the run). In the Harvey house, she covered herself and protected her child.

The woods outside of town were not safe either. Yankees searched them for Rebels. They captured three local citizens: a Mr. Talbert, Walter Johnston, and Charles Farris.

One frightened lady said, "General Hunter had no feeling for the people, but the other two generals (Crook and Averell) were gentlemen."[92]

Some Yankees, too, were fearful of Hunter. They worried because they were "...going farther in the enemy's country, and away from our base of supplies."[18]

A cadet at Balcony Falls exhibited no fear of Hunter. It is uncertain if he used a youthful boast or graveside sarcasm when he said, "Fortunately for General Hunter he did not come our way!"[91] What was certain was that Hunter's move on Buchanan had left the corps without a mission. Neither Hunter nor his cavalry would move on Lynchburg via the James. The corps was in a useless position.

Back above Lexington at Brownsburg, the pious Henry Jones had heard of the destruction the Union Army had caused from Staunton to Lexington. He wrote in his diary: "They have done us much injury, oh! Lord, have mercy upon us and *them.*"[68] He knew that both the defeated and the conqueror would suffer for the wanton destruction.

On Wednesday, June 15, at 4:00 a.m., reveille sounded, and Hunter's army started to stir. Breakfast was cooked, units started to form, and units north of the James continued to cross into town.

Shortly after Strother awoke, Hunter came to his room at the hotel. Hunter told Strother: "We have captured that old vagabond, Col. Angus McDonald."[11] Strother's mind was flooded by bad memories: "...I remembered my father and bitter tears rolled down my cheeks...My blood boiled...."[11] Strother stated that McDonald "...was responsible for my father's treatment at Winchester."[11] One source indicates that once again the war had caught Strother between loyalty to the Union and loyalty to family. Because Strother wore Union blue, McDonald had accused Strother's father of disloyalty to the Confederacy. Strother's father had been subjected to shame and discrimination as a Union sympathizer. A Union officer wrote about McDonald: "He is...a cruel and hoary-headed Rebel Commissary, who had caused the death of Colonel Strother's father by arresting that gallant old patriot for his avowed Unionism, and casting him — an old man over seventy years of age...into a dark cellar-cell in the common jail of Martinsburg, until death put an end to his life and miseries together."[107]

In a strange turn of fate, Yankee Strother now had the opportunity to redress the wrong done to his loyal Confederate father by another Confederate. Hunter turned "...the prisoner over to me that I might work my pleasure with him...After three years the hour had at length come and this tyrannical old brute who had treated my aged father with such wanton indignity was himself a prisoner in my hands and I clothed with authority for life or death,"[11] recalled Strother.

McDonald had been captured while the army was at Lexington. McDonald sent word to Hunter that he wished to see him. Hunter declined to meet him; McDonald belonged to Strother.

Once again the struggle within Strother's spirit would allow him no pleasure in the war. The Union side of his spirit wanted revenge for McDonald's, "...insolent and inhuman manner toward my father...."[11] The Southern, sensitive artist said, "I did not care to use my position in the United States service to avenge a private quarrel or injury."[11] As in the past, Strother sought a middle ground where there was no war or peace but coexistence within his spirit, "...I was not a fit judge in McDonald's case."[11] Strother declared his neutrality.

Somewhat later Strother went downstairs from his hotel room and saw McDonald sitting on the porch. The Southern artist's spirit said, "That single look was vengeance enough for me. I could see remorse in his countenance when he recognized me and his aged appearance filled me with pity. If I had followed my impulses...I should have liberated him."[11]

McDonald saw Strother and greeted him with a civil, "Good morning."[11]
The soldier's spirit took over. "I made no reply but eyed him sternly."[11]
McDonald was getting ready to say something when Strother growled, "Do
you know me, Sir?"[11]

McDonald retained a civil, almost apologetic voice, "Yes, I know you and
you know me very well. And yet, Sir, you do not know me. No, you do not
know me."[11]

Strother recognized that further conversation would compel him from his
neutral position and start the fighting in his spirit that had caused him to weep
earlier. "I could not listen to more...."[11] He could enjoy no vengeance; neither
could he release McDonald. "Old and young or both parties accused him of so
many acts of petty and vindictive tyranny that while my own wrong was
forgotten, I considered that I had no right to interfere with the course of public
justice...,"[11] Strother said.

Strother ended his encounter by replying to McDonald, "I think I do know
you, Sir; and (I) then turned on my heel and went away."[11]

McDonald's son Harry later remembered that Strother "...looked insolently
at him, turned around without any greeting, and shut the door in his face."[80]

There was still grumbling among the 100-day militia whose terms were
ready to expire. There seemed no danger that would require their services to
the army. For a second time Hunter issued orders that they should go north
with the wagon train and prisoners. Hunter told General Sullivan to "make
arrangements,"[8] but no time was set for their departure. They would remain
with the army for this day at least.

Hunter also ordered that McMullen's First Independent Ohio Battery be
transferred from Crook's command directly to Chief-of-Artillery, Dupont.

Later Strother learned that McDonald had requested parole because of old
age and disease. The parole being denied, he asked to be transported in an
ambulance. Despite McDonald's age and health, Strother, "...determined to
leave him to his fate...he must walk."[11]

When McDonald was told to walk, he said that he could not and would not
"...they would have to shoot him first."[11] His guard responded that "...he was
sorry they had not shot him when they captured him...."[11] Another soldier said
McDonald became "...a marked character thereafter."[41]

A fellow prisoner recalled: "...Colonel McDonald footed it all day though
there was an abundance of conveyances in which he might have ridden had
the Federal train master so ordered."[80] Harry McDonald recalled that his
father rode "...not in his own ambulance, but in a wagon loaded with boxes of
nails...In the uncomfortable conveyance...."[25]

Harry drove the wagon "...(and) with one arm supported his father who
was obliged to lean on him, there being no support for his weak frame and
nothing to prevent him being josted off the seat at every lurch of the wagon."[25]

Because the direct road to the Peaks of Otter mountain pass had been
blocked by the explosion and subsequent rock slide, Hunter was forced to use
the narrow road west of town. The huge army had trouble and delay moving
along the one narrow road. Although units had formed, they couldn't move

because other troops and wagons had blocked the road. Many men used this opportunity to bathe in the cool James, knowing that it would be a toilsome, hot day for them.

As soldiers hurried up just to wait, a shot rang out in the town. "...A resident who had the temerity to shoot a Union soldier who attempted to enter his home,"[28] had fired the shot. The extent of the Yankee's wound was unknown. The homeowner paid with his life: Hunter ordered him hanged. Rumors spread among the population that it was Hunter's policy to kill "...one of the citizens as they do wherever they go."[92]

Hunter did single out at least one place to burn in each community. As the advance of the army started to turn left from Valley Pike Road and start up the narrow road to the Peaks, it passed Col. John T. Anderson's home "Mount Joy" on the right. Mount Joy "...crowned a high wooded hill, was very large, and furnished in a style to dispense that lavish hospitality which was the pride of so many of the old-time Virginians. It was the seat of luxury and refinement, and in all respects a place to make the owner contented with his lot in this world."[23]

Colonel Anderson, (John's son) who had been in the Confederate Congress earlier in the war, was in Richmond when the Union Army came to town. Both John Anderson and his wife were elderly. "He was in an office, and too old to fight...there was no military or public object on God's earth to be gained by ruining such a man."[23] Colonel John's younger brother was Gen. Joseph R. Anderson of the Tredegar Iron Works in Richmond. Many a Yankee had been sent to his maker because of weapons produced there. Because of the position of Joseph Anderson, Hunter ordered that Mount Joy was "...to be laid to ashes."[23] After issuing the order, Hunter continued with the army, going up the mountain.

The officer charged with carrying out Hunter's order had no stomach for war on innocent civilians. He burned the outbuildings and left.

When Hunter learned that his orders had not been executed, he summoned the officer in charge of the burning detail. The short-tempered, bad-natured general made it abundantly clear that Mount Joy was to be burned.

The officer and his men returned to Mount Joy and told Mrs. Anderson that she had one hour to carry out what she could, for the house would be burned. Mrs. Anderson and her slaves carried out china in skirts and aprons. Union soldiers entered the house and stole small items that were valuable. Most of the family's silver service was stolen. The goods removed from the house were not safe. Some Federal cavalryman "...slashed their clothing with his sabre and crushed the china."[23]

Mount Joy was burned. Much of the goods taken from the home were damaged or destroyed. The slaves were able to retrieve some of the stolen silver service from Union saddlebags.

As Mount Joy burned and as troops, wagons, and cannons were jammed along the narrow road leading from town and starting toward the Peaks of Otter that morning many miles away at Rockfish Gap, Breckinridge received a telegram from Early. The telegram was sent at 8:00 a.m. from Louisa Courthouse. Early informed Breckinridge that he expected to be at Mechanicsville in Louisa County by dark that night and to be at Charlottesville by the night of June 16. He reported that, "Sheridan's force has been driven back from this place...."[8]

Breckinridge now knew for sure that Sheridan was not coming to join Hunter. Breckinridge's army was serving no purpose where it was. Breckinridge sent the news to General Nicholls at Lynchburg and requested rail transportation to Lynchburg. Because Breckinridge was uncertain of the condition of the tracks and availability of transportation, he started most of the infantry marching toward Lynchburg. Breckinridge also sent a courier to the Corps of Cadets at Balcony Falls, ordering them to move toward Lynchburg.

At Lynchburg, Nicholls ordered trains to be sent to Breckinridge. It was late morning or early afternoon before they would leave town. Nicholls also realized that Sheridan was no longer a threat to Lynchburg. He sent a courier to Imboden's Cavalry to return to the city from Amherst County. Nicholls ordered the Home Guard, convalescents, and the Botetourt Artillery, which he had stationed on Amherst Heights, to move from the north approach to the city to defend against Hunter's advance from the west. He also sent a request to Richmond for more supplies for the armies moving toward his city. He was desperate for shoes for his men.

The old men and the convalescents were happy to leave their line, though none complained "...of the hardships of picket duty, scanty rations ill cooked, and mother earth for a sleeping couch and not one of them reported at sick call...."[91] They had been isolated from the rumor mill in the city. When they returned, they heard the "alarming rumors"[91] that Hunter was ready to pounce on the city with up to 40,000[91] troops. Soon the men were back on a line very near the city's west side.

While Nicholls was preparing for battle, the terrified residents at Lexington were emerging from their homes. They were cleaning up, trying to gather information on their loved ones separated by the enemy action, listening to rumors of army movements, looking for food, and trying to bring direction back to their lives. Part of the community was organized enough to attend the funeral of Capt. Matt White. "Everybody who knew the family was there."[25] Mrs. McDonald was there at the grave for "...the poor fellow...I turned and walked sadly away with some ladies...."[25] Something odd occurred to Mrs. McDonald. "...I met Mrs. Powell, my dearest and most intimate friend. She looked very pale, and turned to me as if she would speak, but passed on."[25] Mrs. Powell knew and assumed that Mrs. McDonald knew about the death of Mr. McDonald. The news came to Mrs. McDonald from an unexpected source. Late that evening "...one of the neighbor's little boys (Willie Crocken) came and climbed up on the porch till he reached my ear...he...whispered, 'Did you know that Colonel McDonald and Harry were killed and were lying in the woods fifteen miles from here?'"[25]

Mrs. McDonald hoped "...it was not true,"[25] and sent another son, Allen, to see if he could get any additional information. In his absence Willie's father came and said that he knew that they had been attacked but "...there was no certainty that they had been killed; that it was thought they were prisoners."[25]

Mrs. McDonald spent the day and night in agony, not knowing if her husband and son were dead or prisoners.

All morning Hunter's army had been slowly moving. Troops were still crossing the river into Buchanan. In the morning light they saw, "Several wrecked team wagons...still in the river...."[41] They saw, "Two darkies...sitting in a wagon, minus a horse, waiting for a power of locomotion to 'take them over Jordan...hard road to travel.'"[41]

'JORDAN IS A HARD ROAD TO TRAVEL."

By David Hunter Strother.

As troops passed out of town to the west, they saw the body of the Confederate who had played at the role of a Jessie Scout, attempting to lead a wagon train to capture. Averell had ordered him shot and left unburied as a warning to any other brazen Rebel. Death is a fact of life to a soldier. Many Federals cracked jokes as they passed the body. "It would shock anyone to repeat the trifling remarks made by the men as they passed him,"[14] recalled one soldier.

That pesky bee, McCausland, was always at the front, felling trees and ambushing the advance. Since Hunter had been unable to catch or disperse him in reality, he decided to beat him on paper, "...our advance feebly contested by some light parties of the enemy...easily cleared..."[8] wrote Hunter.

Averell's Cavalry and the advance infantry paint a much different picture of McCausland's work. "...We were greatly impeded by trees felled...rocks rolled in, and streams of water diverted from their course into the road."[14] "The pioneer corps are having a hard work to clear the road."[18]

McCausland's troops skirmished with Hunter's advance. No figures are given for Union casualties. Many units report passing a single Confederate body "...laid out by the roadside...."[41] "Here and there, upon the road, laid stretched the body of a guerrilla, shot by our advance while ambushed for their devilish game of bushwhacking."[83] One soldier observed that several bodies, "...looked frightful, with their long black beards and white faces, in death."[18] "...Twelve bushwhackers under the lead of a wealthy citizen of Buchanan, fired upon the advance, and were all killed and captured by some of the infantry. The captain was laid out by the roadside, so that his friends might find him, the other killed were left to rot in the bushes, as the captain should have been."[21]

Although Union casualties are believed to have greatly exceeded Southern, only one is mentioned. One soldier wrote, "I mourn over the body of a dead captain, one of our advance guard. They are digging his grave by the roadside...."[41]

The Union soldiers were greeted with two pleasant surprises on the mountain top. One was the picturesque view from what most believed to be the highest mountain (Peaks of Otter) in Virginia. Following are the reactions of some of the viewers: "As the troops came over the summit, they gasped at the sight of the entire side of the mountain covered with rhododendrons in full bloom."[60] "...The whole scene one never to be forgotten."[41] "Bubbling up from the mountain top...were springs of delicious water, which gave us much refreshment."[83] "...Drank from the cool water of this strange mountain spring,"[14] indicating Mother Nature's cooperation.

THE PEAKED MOUNTAIN FROM NEW MARKET.
By David Hunter Strother.

McCausland's men were falling back on Liberty (Bedford), already "...filled with conflicting rumors."[96] Panic set in as news arrived that Hunter was on his way. The often repeated scenes of hiding of livestock and valuables were being repeated. McCausland picked up at least one more soldier. An artilleryman with what had been the Stonewall Brigade was recuperating at his aunt's house in Bedford County. When he knew that Hunter was near, he determined to help stop the pillager. He said that before he left his aunt's house "...she gave me the pistol which her son Robert, Colonel of the Twenty-Eighth Virginia Regiment, was wearing when he fell in Pickett's charge at Gettysburg."[62]

A band of thirty men,[97] Home Guards and citizens apparently operating independently of McCausland, was moving from Liberty toward the Peaks. These thirty would try to stop Hunter's thousands.

Some troops who had been up since 4:00 a.m., were still waiting in Buchanan well past noon. The huge army snaked up the mountain on its tiresome march. The road was narrow, winding, and steep. One soldier remembered the gruesome march: "...Mountain is piled high upon mountain. Far above our heads, we catch occasional glimpses of the moving column, the heavy rumbling of the artillery carriages coming to our ears, like the low muttering of distant thunder; far below us, we see the wagon train, as it winds along its slow and heavy way. The road, in places, is very narrow, and its windings short and sharp; and several of our wagons went down the almost precipitous sides of the mountain...."[83] "Army wagons can be seen down among the trees."[18] Harry McDonald, driving his aged father stated, "Every hour there was danger of their being backed down and pushed off the edge of the road over the frightful precipice."[25]

The village of Buchanan breathed a collective sigh when the last of the army left. Hunter's army wasn't in town many hours, but the citizens had much cleaning to do. The main road from town to the Peaks was closed by the Rebel explosion. It took three days to clear it. One resident said, "Buchanan is a desolate looking place, just a mass of ruins...fit for the habitation of owls and bats."[92] Another resident commended her slaves: "...Servants were faithful, except two, who left with the army."[92]

At Rockfish Gap, the trains, packed both inside and out with soldiers, began to arrive from Lynchburg in the afternoon. The trains were delayed by a brief but hard hail storm that drove "...many of the soldiers under the cars."[36] During this interval, the telegraph operator from Staunton asked Breckinridge if he should return to his hometown and work, saying, "...that section was now in the rear...." General Breckinridge replied in the negative: "It is in the rear now, but it may very soon be in the front again."[36] This remark shows that Breckinridge felt he was not only physically able to fight Hunter but that he was also anxious to take him on. Breckinridge was interested not only in defending Lynchburg but also in the destruction of Hunter. He felt that after defeating Hunter that the Union Army might flee north via Staunton: Staunton would not be in the rear but in the front. The storm passed, and Breckinridge ordered the trains back to Charlottesville and toward Lynchburg. There was no room for Berkeley's Battery on the train so it started toward Lynchburg via the road.

It was near noon when "...the easy calm life at the "Big House" was shattered."[98] The "Big House" was the Saunders home on their tobacco plantation, located about twenty-five miles south of Liberty (now within the ground of Smith Mountain Lake State Park). The Saunders family owned many slaves, but "...the master was never cruel to his slaves...He never sold slaves and unless there was reasonable justification, would not allow his overseer to punish the Negro workers. The Saunders family enjoyed a pleasant, prosperous life."[98]

Almost certainly these were the advance of Averell's 200 hand-picked men. They had circled Lynchburg and were starting toward Liberty. According to one source "The Union troops strode up the steps of the Big House, forced the (white) occupants to open the dining room and cook meals while the Negro kitchen help looked on. After the Yankees had eaten, they would call in enough slaves to fill the dining room; then force the Saunders girls to wait on the Negroes. This action embarrassed the slaves..."[98] for they had "...deep affection...for 'their white folks.'"[98]

Soon the main column of Union cavalry arrived. It appears that the advanced unit in the house went out to greet and confer with their leader. "As more and more Northern soldiers came up the driveway to the mansion, the Saunders girls, warned of the enemy's approach, fled to the Negro cabin and hid. Never once did the slaves betray their mistresses' sanctuary to the blue-uniformed soldiers of Abe Lincoln, who arrived with shouts of freedom for the blacks."[98]

The Union soldiers stole and plundered before they continued toward Liberty. There is no record that indicates even a single slave asked to leave with them.

By late afternoon, the courier whom Breckinridge sent reached Balcony Falls. He was to order the corps to move to Lynchburg. When he arrived, the movement was under way. When General Smith had concluded that his corps would be of no benefit at the falls, he started moving toward Lynchburg before the courier arrived. The corps boarded canal boats and floated toward Lynchburg.

As the corps was floating, Hunter's army was still climbing the mountain. Soon after the first Federals reached the summit, they opened an observation or signal flag station. The summit allowed a view of any mass Rebel movements to the front. There was "...no sight of the enemy."[11] Neither was there a way for the army snaking up the mountain to communicate with flags. Of course, thrill-seeking Lieutenant Meigs was one of the first officers to arrive at the station. Some troops climbing the mountain mistook their signal post for a Confederate position. The station "...at first was supposed to be Rebel, but when it appeared to be Union, there was great excitement and joy in the Union line."[41]

The column halted at the hotel between the Peaks. Here the cavalry stole "...a hundred pieces of bacon."[11] A Yankee officer signing the hotel register

SOUTH PEAK OF OTTER, FROM THE HOTEL.

By David Hunter Strother.

wrote after his name, "He didn't pay his bill."[11]

After a rest, cool water, and a view of the scenery, the troops continued down the mountain. After the exhausting climb, the downgrade march was fun. Soldiers broke shoots of rhododendron off and put them in their gun barrels. Colonel Hayes's adjutant said that he saw a "...mass of color...a moving bank of flowers."[60]

The Second West Virginia Cavalry continued forward and occupied Fancy Farms, where it stole supplies and waited for the infantry to follow. It is uncertain when the first infantry units under Crook began to arrive. Hunter was with Crook. Several hours of daylight remained when Hunter arrived at Fancy Farms. Hunter ordered Averell to occupy Liberty. Averell again sent the Second West Virginia in advance.

As the cavalry left, Hunter decided to take quarters for the night at the large brick home on Fancy Farms.

The Fifth West Virginia Infantry must have been one of the first units to arrive at Fancy Farms because "...the men found plenty of flour and corn meal and went for it...The corn (in the fields) was in splendid condition and an abundance of it, and the mules and horses fared sumptuously...."[21]

After the cavalrymen left Fancy Farms, they saw that "...a body of about thirty Rebel cavalry were observing our movements, and their capture was attempted."[34] The Home Guard unit, having made contact, was doing an effective job. "...The little force of the enemy imagined that they had checked further advance."[34]

Powell saw an opportunity to bag the Home Guards. He dismounted the members of Company H of the Second West Virginia and sent them behind the hills to screen their movement. They were to circle to the rear of the

Manor house "Fancy Farm" at foot of the Peaks of Otter.

Confederate position while the brigade continued a steady fire on these irregular troops. The plan was going well until the man leading Company H "...was horrified to see a huge mountain rattlesnake."[34] He later swore the snake came "...eight feet high (off the ground) as it prepared to strike."[34] The report of his carbine rang through the hills as the monster snake fell dead.

When the Home Guard heard the shot coming from the sneaking Yankees, "...the Johnnies beat a hasty retreat."[34] A Southern writer said, "...the men defending their homes were forced back with the loss of three wounded."[97]

With the Home Guard now in full retreat, the cavalry continued its advance. Apparently, McCausland withdrew his forces from the town as the Union entered. McCausland positioned his artillery on a hill just east of town on the Lynchburg-Salem Pike, probably on Piedmont Hill near the hospital a quarter of a mile from town.

McCausland's men weren't the only ones to leave town. The roads were crowded with refugees. Among them was Micajal Davis, Jr. (Sheriff of Bedford County). Davis feared that he would be arrested for being a Confederate lawman. Davis "...entrusted everything to (Uncle Billy Haden — family slave) — everything on the place, silver, funds, and the papers of Bedford County."[99] Uncle Billy cared for the home, Chestnut Hill, and performed his duties for his master. Also, State Legislator, Edward Burks, did not leave his home "Woodford" but went into hiding inside.

McCausland's gunners were probably surprised when they saw Yankee troopers coming into town not from the north but from the south. These were the 200 hand-picked Federals that had circled Lynchburg. They didn't know

Piedmont — Liberty (Bedford).

Grapeshot — Recovered at Piedmont. Courtesy: Bedford City/County Museum.

where their army was. Several ladies had taken refuge in Burks at Woodford. The ladies saw the "...Northern soldiers come up Burks Hill...."[100] Southern cannons on Piedmont Hill let fly: "...We gave the Yankees much trouble with our four 6-pounders, with which we shelled them and made farther progress impossible for a time."[100] A local story states that the Yankees entered Woodford and rounded up the ladies. "The Northern soldiers then put the women in front of them, and the firing ceased."[36] Confederate soldier accounts mention no women.

The Yankees' orders were for them to rejoin the army near Liberty. They were there, but where was the army? They simply held their position and a stalemate developed.

It was 7:30 p.m.[99] when Averell's forces entered town from the north. "...In minutes after they arrived, the depot, the Hay house, and Turpin's house were in flames."[36] Some pillaging took place, but these were Averell's men back under his independent command. There was no wanton disregard for personal property.

The Yankees, held up at Woodford, now knew where their army was. A Southern soldier said it was, "About night (when the Federals) struck both our flanks, and we had to give back."[99]

At Woodford, the Yankees did not find Burks, but they did steal his "...underwear which they filled with flour, or sugar or other food, after knotting the arms and legs; then rode out with those grotesque articles on their saddles in front of them. Before departing...they piled all the other food they could not carry with them in the center of the kitchen floor and poured over the heap molasses and oil."[96]

While the Yankees stole and plundered, Mrs. Burks was standing with the family silver service suspended from her waist and under her long dress. These unwelcome guests could not stay because they had to report directly to Hunter. When the Yanks left, so did Mrs. Burks, who headed to a farm in the countryside, taking her children with her. No mention was made of Mr. Burks.

"Woodford" — Liberty (Bedford).

According to another report, Liberty may have fallen much earlier in the day. This report states that McCausland was already six miles east of town and that the depot was "burning" at 6:00 p.m.[96] The report also stated that McCausland had observed a big camp near the Peaks of Otter, which he "...supposed to be Hunter's forces."[96]

As Averell's forces were taking Liberty, the trains with Breckinridge's forces were entering Lynchburg. The anxious population was happy to see these "...very dilapidated veterans, true good men but worn with fatigue and hunger."[91] The hopes of the civilians were much boosted by their arrival.

One Home Guard soldier recalled that he thought that he had seen Breckinridge in the Senate of that foreign nation, the United States in 1859. Now he saw Breckinridge five years later, but "Now he looked twenty years older, his hair and moustache having turned iron gray, almost white, and he looked sick and worn."[91] The war was making men of young boys, and old men of young men. The strain of war was exacting a toll on the combatants.

Apparently Hill had made it to Lynchburg before Breckinridge arrived. Hill had already inspected the Hill City and was formulating a plan for the defensive implacements. There was no record found, indicating the exact time that Breckinridge became aware that Hill, too, was in the city.

Breckinridge and Nicholls conferred. Breckinridge learned that Imboden had been riding about the city but that "They had done...less than nothing... (Breckinridge was) fed up with Imboden's inefficiency...."[55] Breckinridge fired off a telegram to Richmond, requesting a replacement for Imboden. The wise general had foreseen the need of replacing Imboden earlier. General Lee had instructed Maj. Gen. Robert Ransom, Jr., to take command of all cavalry in the department upon his arrival. Ransom was a North Carolinian and West Point graduate. He joined the service as a colonel with the North Carolina Cavalry. He became a major general in May of 1863. Before being detached from the Richmond theater, he had defended Lee's vital supply link, the Weldon Railroad. Command of the city was transferred to Breckinridge, who sent a courier to Amherst County to find Imboden, but Imboden was to move his cavalry to join McCausland west of the city. Breckinridge also requested that scouts be sent to provide more accurate information on Hunter. This request was despite a newspaper report that said, "Day by day and almost hour by hour scouts would arrive and report the progress and precise locality of the foe."[101] Breckinridge wanted his own men's report.

As Breckinridge's troops moved through town, "...residents rushed to the street to cheer them."[78] "...A reassuring sight and never were a lot of bronzed and dirty looking veterans, many of them barefooted, more heartily welcomed...people...waved hats and handkerchiefs...."[55]

The populace's morale was greatly boosted, but one Home Guard soldier who saw them move into position west of the town concluded that still "...we had no adequate force to resist...in point of fact, we did not have men enough to make any resistance with any hope of success...though all had determined to do or die in the attempt to hold the town."[91] Despite the bolstered morale, citizens hid livestock and valuables.

On an injured general, a fatigued army, some cavalry, a Home Guard with few men, and convalescents from the hospitals rested the defense of Lynchburg. These men guarded the arteries that supplied Richmond. As long as Richmond stood, there was hope for the Confederacy. Lynchburg was the funnel for the supplies General Lee had to have to hold the capital. Troops alone could not keep Grant at bay. If Hunter could seize the canal and railroads, the life blood of the defense of the capital would cease. The Confederate States of America would be doomed. Not only would supplies and food from the Valley which were being sent to Richmond via Lynchburg be stopped, but also the salt and the lead from Southwest Virginia. Without lead there would be no bullets to defend the capital. Without salt to preserve the food, the South would be starved into submission. Life or death of the Confederacy centered on control of Lynchburg. With the easy transport and relative safety that it provided, Lynchburg became a major hospital town. Virtually every warehouse in the city was converted to use for the sick and the wounded. Many private homes were opened to Confederate casualties also.

Other troops would continue toward the city throughout the night.

Major R.C. Saunders was selected to scout Hunter. General Nicholls summoned Saunders, who had an intimate knowledge of the area to his office. Saunders was the Chief Quartermaster for the collection of taxes in kind for the state. He knew every farm and road in the Lynchburg area. Nicholls told Saunders, "I want you to start out in the morning, find out where he (Hunter) is, what force he has and when in your judgement he is likely to get here."[91]

Saunders asked for a squad of men to help him. Nicholls denied the request because there was not a man to spare. Saunders would ride alone.

Darkness was setting in on the Valley district. On the mountain north of Liberty, Hunter's men were camping. Some of the advance units started to establish camps well before the sun set. Because of the long snakey road, other units would march until past 9:00 p.m. before they would bed down. The cavalry was in possession of Liberty. The infantry camped from Fancy Farms near the foot of the mountain back to the top of the Peaks of Otter. Hunter issued a strange order to his tired troops: "...Keep very quiet and not make any fires."[18] One tired soldier complained, we "must go without our coffee for the night."[18] A prisoner was upset not only because "...they were not allowed to make coffee...(but all) they had (was) some fat meat and crackers...."[25]

Two prisoners did not stay with the others. Harry and Angus McDonald were "...dragged up close to Hunter's Headquarters. No one spoke to him (Angus), and no courtesy or kindness was extended him, and only the coarsest food furnished him."[25]

At least one soldier decided to disobey the order and have his coffee. He built a very small fire to heat his brew. He might not have even noticed the root of the pine tree near the fire at first. The pine was dead and apparently decayed from the center of the root and into the trunk of the tree. When flames from the small fire ate to the center of the root, the decayed center acted like a chimney. The pitch of rotting pine burns almost as fast as kerosene. The soldier's disobedience to Hunter's orders was signaled to all. The tree

"...quickly caught fire, the blaze shooting out at the top like a chimney."[18] The soldier threw dirt on the tree in a vain attempt to conceal his guilt, but because "the tree being away up the mountain, the blaze could be seen for miles...."[18] The embarrassed soldier might have received no punishment for his deed.

Although Hunter forbade fires for others, he allowed fires at his headquarters. A correspondent with *The Cincinnati Gazette*, Thornton M. Hinkle, wrote: "The Peaks of Otter tower above us, the stars and silvery moon shine, while all around us the campfires and signal lights add brilliance to the scene."[102]

Chief-of-Staff Strother was not looking at the beauty of the sky or of the big oaks at Fancy Farms. He was looking at "...a horse of extraordinary ugliness...."[11] The animal was a gift. Strother may have wondered at the donors true feelings as the horse stared back with "...one eye milky like a huge opal, a hanging nether lip, a barrel like a rhinoceros, and prominent hip bones and a long, thin neck. (Strother) Named him the Giraffe...."[11] The donor said that the horse was "...swift and powerful...he may be useful to me (Strother) as we are going into the jaws of the enemy, blind."[11]

When Strother said, "blind," he was talking about the confusing information at headquarters. The 200 hand-picked troops from the Fourteenth Pennsylvania Cavalry made it to the infantry after dark. They had to wait for Averell's men to secure Liberty before they proceeded. Captain Duncan told Hunter that he had lost between twelve and twenty men but that he had circled Lynchburg. They had cut the Orange & Alexandria Railroad near Amherst and had damaged the James River Canal nearby. Circulating south they had captured and burned two trains at Concord on the Southside Railroad. The latest intelligence indicated that Lynchburg was held only by a few Home Guards and cripples. Hunter had received the two newspapers, one from Lynchburg and one from Richmond which they had sent. The prize was open for the taking. Captain Duncan left headquarters.

Captain Duncan's information wasn't the only intelligence which Hunter had received that day. Because his command was spread out with Averell at Liberty and Sullivan and Duffié on the mountain somewhere, Hunter tried to evaluate the information without his staff.

Hunter could be happy that "...the challenge of the Blue Ridge had been met and overcome."[103] Averell at Liberty was only twenty-four miles away from the prize — Lynchburg. He was at Fancy Farms, having moved approximately sixteen miles that day. Some of the troops were as much as five miles closer to Buchanan than Hunter was.

Both positive and negative information had reached him that day: "Negro refugees from Lynchburg represented that people were leaving the city and that the city was guarded only by a few thousand armed invalids and militia."[96] Some captured prisoners "reported that Sheridan had been defeated near Louisa Courthouse, while others said he was already in Lynchburg."[17] One source said, "Nothing lay between the Union Army and the Confederate base save the worn and shattered forces of Generals John McCausland and John Imboden. Dogged as were these Rebels, they had been unable to do more than slow Hunter's columns and could hardly be expected to do that much longer."[103] Another report states "...that Breckinridge is at Balcony Falls with ten thousand men and that some detachment from Lee's army is at Lynchburg."[11] "Hunter said that...he could obtain no clue or reliable information of the enemy, that there were exaggerated rumors of disaster to both Grant and Sherman, that Sheridan had been defeated near Louisa Courthouse, and that he was already in Lynchburg. ...Also...that the enemy were in force at Lynchburg, and that Ewell's corps, 20,000 strong, had reinforced them."[88] Added to this disastrous report, Hunter had the recently captured newspapers that stated Richmond was under siege and that Sheridan was moving on Lynchburg.

Hunter could find no clear information on which he could base his next move. He decided in order "to develop the truth, I determined to advance on Lynchburg immediately."[8] He sent couriers to Sullivan and Duffie on the mountain to be ready to move early in the morning. Hunter was concerned that the wagon train and the prisoners would slow the army.

"The night (of Wednesday, June 15) passed quickly and revealed a splendid morning among the mountains,"[41] records one of Hunter's infantrymen. "...A rough stony road..."[18] "...did not give much encouragement to sore-footed and tired-out men."[41] The view was splendid. As the soldiers entered the foothills they found an abundance of crops. We "Passed through a large peanut field. The vines were fine but not much left of them after the army passed through..."[18] said an infantryman.

As the men in the infantry marched toward Liberty, they came to the small community of Centerville about three miles northwest of Liberty on the Peaks Road. At Centerville, B.E. Owen had his home and tobacco business. He grew, cured, stored, and processed tobacco. When he heard that the army was coming, he took his livestock to the mountain. Former slaves who had been granted freedom "...but who preferred to remain with their late master"[102] went with him. Mr. Owen, his former slaves, and livestock were safely hidden when Averell rode by on June 15.

When Hunter's infantrymen arrived, they broke open the storage barns and stole the tobacco. What they couldn't carry, they threw on a fire made from Mr. Owen's fence rails.

Next they broke into the house. "These men in the uniform of the United States Army used much profane and abusive language and one of them even went so far as to shake his fist in Mrs. (Virginia) Owen's face in a very threatening manner...the home was ransacked for valuables...,"[102] reported an observer. Mrs. Owen concealed her silverware under her long dress.

It is reported that "Hunter's ruthless destruction of property made him the most hated Union general of the war who operated on Virginia soil."[102]

Other tired and foot-sore men were also on the march early that morning. If these men had regulation uniforms, they were Confederate gray. Early had made it to the vicinity of Trevilians Station on June 15. With any luck, he would be at the railhead at Charlottesville by sunset. Time was of the essence. Early sent a telegram to Breckinridge: he wanted trains sent to Charlottesville

immediately. He told Breckinridge to order the trains of both the Virginia
Central and the Orange & Alexandria to be commandeered. To emphasize the
priority Early attached to his order to Breckinridge, he threatened both
Breckinridge and the railroad employees, saying *"I have authority to direct
your (Breckinridge's) movements,* and I will take the responsibility of what
you may find it necessary to do. I will hold *all* railroad agents and employees
responsible with their lives for hearty co-operation with us."[104] The heat of the
day was relentless, and so was Early as he drove his army forward. Early
turned his infantry into foot cavalry.

It was early in the morning when R.C. Saunders left Lynchburg on his
scouting mission. He traveled west by the Forest Road. Near St. Steven's
Church, he came upon a Home Guard unit also traveling west. He told the
sergeant with the Home Guard about his mission, and the sergeant gave him
permission to join his group. As the men continued west, they crossed the Big
Otter River at Walkes Mill. The road was already blocked by "...fleeing
citizens, their Negroes, horses, and other stock."[91] The fleeing citizens reported
that the Yanks were just to their rear. Saunders and his party decided to move
to the right to the Big Island Road and scout along Hunter's left.

In Lynchburg, "...nearly every able bodied man, (except a few skulkers
whom no appeal to patriotism could move...) was under arms or busy making
trenches...."[91] The ladies of Lynchburg had been doing more than their share
in the war effort. Now that the war was coming to their town, they doubled
their efforts to aid and feed the soldiers now filling the lines around the city.
Since the war started, these women had become "So worn...every cent they
owned was invested in Confederate bonds, most of them had sold their jewels
to buy proper food for the wounded soldiers who crowded the city; sick,
suffering boys of the far south...homesick and sad. Food was so scant they
could barely produce enough to stay the hunger of their own children and
servants...the best was saved to provide boxes to send to the camps, and to
furnish the hospitals. All their sheets and table-linen had been torn up for
bandages, all their time was given up to nursing the sick, and to sewing and
knitting for the fighting men...Life for those in Lynchburg had become a grim,
hand-to-hand struggle with death and despair...Every day brought news
which desolated some household, every hour some woman's heart was wrung
with anguish. Only their homes remained and their sorrow can be imagined as
they awaited Hunter's approach."[10] "...Our noble women the finest in the
land...(are) supplying food...lot of drinks...(and) praying for Early...to
come."[91] Even with the increase in troop strength, the ladies began to realize
their troops would be no match for Hunter's masses. They continued to serve
"with brave but despairing hearts...."[10]

At 8:00 a.m.,[66] their hearts must have lifted slightly. The Corps of Cadets
came floating into town from Balcony Falls. They had taken some artillery
with them from the Institute. "I have brought with the command 4 brass
pieces, 2 rifle guns 3-inch and ammunition...."[66] The days the corps lay at
Balcony Falls, and the long slow boat ride had given general of the cadets,
Francis H. Smith, time to reflect on the burning of his school. "In a time of war

it was not to be expected that the Virginia Military Institute should escape the effects of the devastation...It was a painful (experience?) to all associated with the Virginia Military Institute, to know...(that V.M.I. was) in the hands of the (spoiler?) and when the clouds of heaven reflected the conflagration lighted by the torch of the invader every eye was moistened that the home of the V.M.I. cadet was gone! But the Virginia Military Institute still proudly stands. The brick and mortar which gave a temporary shelter to her nurturing sons, while they were buckling on the armor for the conflict, constituted not the Military School of Virginia. Thank God, that still lives. The Governor — its Board of Visitors — its professors — its cadets — still remain in organized being, ready to work — and able to send forth, year by year, its alumni, to fill up all the ranks of those who have fallen in the deadly struggle...All are prepared to sacrifice...to promote the end of our Revolution...It cheers the heart of the patriot and especially of every friend of the V.M. Institute to witness the filial affection displayed by the cadets as they cluster around the proud standard (flag) committed to their charge by the Governor of Virginia...."[66]

Command of the city was under Breckinridge, but not all was running smoothly at headquarters. There were no orders or positions for the corps. One cadet recalled, "...we loafed around on the streets most of the day...I was setting on the curb-stone...on Main Street with several cadets, munching on cold potatoes and waiting..."[91] for orders.

Headquarters were not running smoothly; many reports state that the commanding general was in pain and not able to discharge command responsibilities. There is no report that he injured his leg again between Rockfish and Lynchburg, but he might have. "I saw General Breckinridge several times and considered him entirely unfit for active service suffering as he was...compelled in consequence to take to his bed...."[91] Breckinridge himself lay near collapse, bedridden...unable even to inspect or attend defensive lines,"[55] wrote one soldier in his report.

Breckinridge received and sent some telegrams. He received Early's telegram, requesting trains be sent to Charlottesville. Early also informed Breckinridge, "My first objective is to destroy Hunter, and (for) the next (objective) it is not prudent to trust to telegraph."[8] Some historians interpret this remark to mean that Early was already thinking of turning the tables and invading Union soil with a touch of vengeance.

Breckinridge informed Richmond that he was sure that Hunter had crossed the Blue Ridge and was descending on Liberty. He said "...trains have been sent him (Early) ...hope we shall be able to destroy Hunter."[8] Again he asked if a replacement had been selected for Imboden.

Sometime during the night hours or early morning, General Imboden sent approximately 400 cavalrymen and a section of artillery to reinforce McCausland. Sometime later that day, he arrived with the rest of his command "...and assumed command, being the senior brigadier outside of the city."[30]

Back on the mountain, it was becoming a routine: another pretty town, fleeing refugees, another triumphant entry, destruction, thievery, wanton

pillaging, and passing on. Now it was Liberty's turn unwillingly to become
part of the routine. "Down at the base of the mountains was the pleasant village
of Liberty. It seemed almost an ideal situation with its mountain background,
while before it lay the broad, rich plains...."[9] Strother recalled that Liberty
"...is much improved since I saw it last."[11] The triumphant entry: "We entered
Liberty, with bands playing 'Hail Columbia,' (and) 'Yankee Doodle.'"[16] It was
about noon when the town began to feel the conquerors' boots against its
throat. Hunter was not about to rush to Lynchburg to learn the truth when he
had important burning and pillaging to do.

Crook had destroyed railroad from near Covington to Staunton. Hunter
knew that he could do the job. At Liberty, Crook worked on "...their old
railroad target, the Virginia and Tennessee...."[60] Crook had burned the "long
bridge" over New River in Southwest Virginia in mid-May. As before, "Rails
were torn from the cross ties and great fires were built from the ties. The rails
were then placed on burning ties and heated and twisted out of shape."[102]
"...Utter destruction was made of...depots, track, etc., as usual in such cases."[14]
"A thorough job of wrecking consumed most of the sixteenth."[103] Another
source noted that Hunter had committed, "...another unnecessary delay."[59]
Seven miles of track would be destroyed before the day was over.

Destruction of Southern Railroad.

Destruction of Southern Railroad.

The Liberty Steam Mill was destroyed. Also destroyed was W.R. Terry's Steam Mill which he used in his foundry works. The production of castings, parts for agricultural machines, and such, halted abruptly.

Also "...public stores were destroyed,"[9] "Ad's Mill was visited and all the produce that was in it taken out...,"[100] and "they plundered the stores and destroyed everything in them, giving goods to Negroes and everybody."[100]

According to one Union source, the whole Liberty area was used as a Confederate hospital: "...Almost nothing but a hospital, the houses were nearly all filled with the wounded...there were four large hospital buildings...Every country house and barn was filled to repletion with wounded men."[14]

Liberty was indeed a major hospital area for General Lee. Before the end of the war, the Baptist Church, the Episcopal Church, Mr. Miller's home, Crenshaw's, Davis's, and Reese's warehouses, Henry Osborne's home (Piedmont), Toler's furniture warehouse, Clark's carriage shop, and Campbell's business were all used as hospitals. Piedmont was described as "...one of the principal ones in the South."[99] Reese's Hospital was a "wayside" hospital which means that it was a first stop and classification hospital. Here the diseased men and the wounded men were classified. After classification, they were transferred to a hospital which specialized in their classification for further treatment. Since there were no patients at Reese's when Hunter arrived, his forces burned it. The patients at the other hospitals "...we did not disturb."[109]

The heat from the fires only increased the misery of the army. Some men who could not tolerate the heat stopped burning and looting and sought shade.

While the organized destruction of commercial property was taking place, Hunter's thieves were stealing at almost every house. "...The Yankees have occupied our town and played the devil generally...our dining room, backyard and garden were filled by them, everybody was visited. They demanded something to eat and were given all we had,"[100] wrote one Southern victim. "Some of the more ignorant people, who had never seen a Yank before, were surprised to see us without horns and all the other traditional appendages of 'Old Nick,'"[14] said a Yankee soldier.

"Chestnut Hill," the home of Micajal Davis, Jr., which was located on the Peaks Road coming into town, was probably one of the first pillaged. One observer said, "The soldiers were so hungry that they ate the green things growing in the garden...."[99] The trusted slave with three names, Uncle Billy Haden, protected his mistress, Mrs. Ellen Davis, and the family cow. He also guarded the secret where the family assets were hidden. Master Micajal Davis had entrusted him with that responsibility; he did not fail his master.

Chestnut Hill — Liberty (Bedford).

Slaves quarters Chestnut Hill — Liberty (Bedford).

A.A. Bell and O.P. Bell lost heavily. Almost every family in or near Liberty had goods stolen. The Yanks robbed Mr. Rosebrugh of all his meat, corn, flour, and a male slave. "William Claytor had two Negroes carried off, or they went off."[100] Frederick Anspuagh said, "They didn't ransack or pillage our house at all, except the basement."[100]

Some Yanks with the Fifth New York Heavy Artillery (infantry) went into a large house and were stealing everything they didn't need and could hardly carry. Some of Crook's Ohio boys, Company A, Hundred Twenty-Third Ohio ran them out at the point of a bayonet.

Strother in gross understatement wrote: "Our troops, I fear, are plundering the town and misbehaving terribly as women and children are besieging the General's door for protection...."[11] For Strother, it was an understatement; for the women, it was an exercise in futility.

Many reports state that the home pillaging had a silver lining. The new fashion in women's clothing was tableware suspended from the waist and resting on petticoats.

With all of the destruction going on, the correspondent with *The Cincinnati Gazette* noted that it was very hot as he took lunch at the Bedford Hotel. The surgeon with the Eighteenth Connecticut noted blood coming from his lungs. He blamed it on the fatigue of climbing the Peaks of Otter and the high mountain air. Apparently while guards were distracted with the destruction, Harry McDonald found a bag of coffee in his wagon. He gave some of it to his ailing father. It seemed to make the old man feel better.

At Liberty, Hunter started his move east toward Lynchburg. Duffié's Cavalry was to take the Forest Road on the left toward the Hill City. He was to send reconnaissance in force to Balcony Falls. Hunter wanted to know if Breckinridge with 10,000 men was really there. The majority of Crook's command moved east, destroying the railroad as it went. Hunter sent most of his army over the Salem-Lynchburg Pike. Averell's Cavalry took the advance. Sullivan and the remainder of Crook's forces followed. All of Dupont's artillery except a two-gun section which was detached to Duffié followed. The wagon train, prisoners, contraband, and their guard brought up the rear. The wagon train was also divided.

As the army started the advance toward Lynchburg, the roads ahead were filled with fleeing refugees, Negroes, livestock, and wagons. There was a wounded soldier, Edward Moore, who had come back to the area to recuperate. When it became known that Hunter was near, he picked up a gun and hobbled on his crippled leg when he was not riding his horse. He was not attached to any unit. He was moving east out of Liberty on the Salem-Lynchburg Pike toward McCausland. About noon, he stopped at a house and asked for food. He was just getting seated at the table when "...there arose a great commotion outside, with cries of 'Yankee cavalry! Yankee cavalry!'"[62] There was not time to eat; in the rush, he forgot the pillow he used to cushion his leg. Outside he saw "...a stream of terrified school children crying as they ran by, and refugees flying for the woods."[62] He saddled and moved at a very fast pace. He recalled that a twelve-year-old boy riding bareback on a yearling colt "shot by me with the speed of a greyhound."[62]

No Union cavalry had actually been seen, but Ed continued to ride. He came upon Lindsay Reid, a mixed blood — freeman from Liberty. Reid wanted to fight the whole Union Army. "It is a shame to fear anything; let's stand and give them a fight!"[62] he shouted. If Lindsay fought, it would be without Ed. Edward rode to a farmhouse well off the main road. There the elderly and blind William Hurt and his two daughters cared for him.

As Hunter's army left Liberty, the wagons, almost empty of food, bounced and rattled. Grant's policy of living off the land not only hurt the Southern people but caused disunity and tardiness in the Union Army. Soldiers who must forage and steal do not march forward rapidly. The Eighteenth Connecticut had just left town when a member discovered a smokehouse that had not been pillaged by troops in their advance. The Eighteenth stopped as men stole meat, and were "...marching into the woods with hams elevated upon their bayonets."[41]

Sam Taylor with Company A, Eighteenth Connecticut Infantry, recalled that he had stopped at one house and stole three pints of meal. Meal was the only food the family had in the pantry.

Strother, riding on the Salem Pike, recalled that as he was passing one house a fellow officer hailed him, saying that there were two young ladies that wished to meet him. He dismounted and went to the door. "They had my book, *Virginia Illustrated*, and professed themselves admirers of my literature." While they were talking in the front, other Union soldiers broke into the back of the house and started stealing. "In the confusion which ensued, I mounted and *escaped*,"[11] he later wrote. Escaped from the ladies? No. He escaped from a situation in which he would be forced to leave the neutral ground in his spirit and choose between heritage and duty.

Some Yankee soldiers lost time but found a lot of strawberries. The stolen food was unequally divided. Some feasted, but many went hungry. An army can not march and fight with a little meal and strawberries. Also it lost much time.

The lack of food and water, combined with the dreadful heat, caused men to fall "...out in large numbers...large number on the sick list."[41]

The troops to the rear could indulge in foraging, but the troops in front had to be constantly ready for combat. McCausland's men fired often to slow their advance.

McCausland's little force continued to resist Hunter's forward motion. One soldier reported: "The advance are skirmishing, as we can plainly hear...Sharp skirmishing kept up all day, showing the enemy is contesting our advance on Lynchburg."[11] Averell continued pushing McCausland, "But with increasing difficulty, indicating that he had now been reinforced by Imboden."[17]

At Little Otter River, the Yankees were not surprised to find that McCausland had burned the bridge. McCausland's men fired on the Union advance. Soon more Union men arrived, forded the stream, and forced McCausland back. Hunter claimed that he "rebuilt"[8] the bridge, but an infantryman recalled that he crossed by a "narrow footbridge"[83] over the ruins.

The cavalry proceeded to the Big Otter River. Here again the bridge was burned, and McCausland gave the Union cavalry another hot welcome. Dupont recalled that his Light Battery B, Fifth United States Artillery under First-Sergeant Jeremiah Weaver, was "warmly engaged."[47] Again sufficient forces were brought on line, and McCausland was forced to fall back toward New London. Averell pursued McCausland, but the Union infantry was well back from Big Otter River.

As McCausland was falling back on New London, Imboden and his cavalry were moving toward New London.

The other wings of Hunter's army were encountering little resistance. Crook moved slowly along the railroad, destroying as he went. An officer with Hunter's staff indicated that the Union used gunpowder to destroy some Confederate bridgeworks. Duffié moved most of his command by the Forest Road toward Lynchburg. He detached a large force with orders to go to Balcony Falls to see if Breckinridge was there. Apparently the force moved by the Big Island Road. Saunders and his Home Guard party had left the Forest Road to scout Hunter from what they thought would be a safe road on Hunter's left. Saunders became aware that the Union cavalry was advancing up the Big Island Road also. The scouts left the road and moved into cover between the Big Island Road and the Forest Road. Then they became trapped between the two columns of Duffié's Cavalry. There was nothing to do but wait for the cavalry to pass and pray that they would not be discovered.

Back at the Hill City, one report states that Breckinridge decided to transfer command to his infantry subordinate, General Vaughn. The two generals were worried that fleeing citizens would cause disruption in transportation. Efforts were made to reassure the citizens that Hunter was advancing very slowly and that Early would arrive well before Hunter. This was little reassurance as many citizens fled east and south from the city.

Another report states that it was "...late in the afternoon..."[55] when Breckinridge asked Hill to assume command of the city. Hill was happy to be a general with a command again. Neither Breckinridge nor Hill informed Early or Richmond of the change of command. Their old commander and now joint enemy Braxton Bragg, was the President's personal adviser. He was sure to become aware of the change of command if the telegraph was used. Neither Hill nor Breckinridge needed Bragg's personal wrath at this critical point. Vaughn might have been miffed to learn that the unofficial general (with no rank or unit) had been chosen to command.

Hill was joined by Gen. Harry Thompson Hays, who was in Lynchburg recovering from wounds he had received at Spotsylvania Courthouse. He left his bed to join Hill. The two generals ordered redoubts and trenches constructed on the western approaches to the city. Citizens joined the soldiers in the digging on College Hill. General Hill constructed a short line close to the city because there were few soldiers and because he did not know when or if Early would arrive.

It was late afternoon when Crook's men crossed the Big Otter River as they destroyed the Virginia-Tennessee Railroad. Sullivan's Infantry and Hunter's staff on the Salem Pike reached Big Otter. There was no bridge left to allow the infantry easy passage. The tired, hot men were looking forward to the cool of the evening.

Imboden had moved to New London. Using a tributary of the Big Otter River as a defensive barrier, he placed his 2,000 men on the right of the Lynchburg-Salem Pike. As McCausland's men fell back, they were placed to the right of the road. They were backed with some artillery. Because of stragglers and incomplete reports an exact count of troops is impossible. It appears that Southern forces were approximately 3,000 men. Averell's cavalrymen were heading straight for them.

No detailed accounts were found of the fight at New London. It appears that Averell's advance men were shocked and sent reeling by the large force that they encountered. This unexpected counter-force caused Averell to halt his forward movement, reconnoiter the situation, and send a courier back to Hunter with Sullivan's Infantry.

Hunter received the courier from Averell, stating "...that the enemy had been reinforced and was becoming stubborn."[8] Hunter and Sullivan were in no position to send reinforcements because the bridge was burned. Hunter had the Signal Corps flash a message to Crook on the Virginia-Tennessee lines to see if he could aid Averell.

The tireless Crook divided his forces. He left some at the Big Otter River and moved with White's Second Brigade to the south toward New London.

Averell continued to bring men forward but made no attempt to strike hard at Imboden's and McCausland's line. The Southern cavalry was dismounted and hoped that Averell would attack before dawn.

It was about dark when Averell became aware that Crook's Infantry was moving in on the Confederates' right. He began to mass his troops on the Confederate line. When McCausland became aware of Averell's troop movements, he sent word that he expected an attack at any moment.

McCausland's courier reached Imboden about the same time that Imboden became aware of troop movement not only from his front, where he expected it, but also from his right side. When it was learned that the troops on his side were infantry, not cavalry, Imboden knew that it was a whole new ballgame. Imboden was fearful that Crook's heavy infantry assault would turn his flank and stop an orderly retreat to the rear. Because most of his troops were dismounted, he feared that the horses might be lost to a sudden Union thrust. Word was sent to McCausland to retire toward Lynchburg.

Apparently McCausland was the first to draw off line. Averell became aware of the Southern withdrawal. He sent a courier to Crook and his men forward to press McCausland's rear guard.

Crook knew that he must strike now or that the Rebs would move off. As the Twelfth and Ninety-First Ohio charged forward, they were "...warmly engaged."[31]

There was rear guard action as both McCausland and Imboden drew off. It appears that the rear guard of McCausland's forces suffered the greatest loss. "The Charlotte Cavalry, under Captain E.E. Bouldin, deserves special mention...."[106]

A Union soldier called it "...a slight cavalry brush...."[59] Twelve Confederates died in the slight brush; no Union figures were found. The Confederates said that they withdrew. The Yankees said that they drove the South two miles. The truth is probably somewhere between. At the next creek east of New London, Imboden formed another line. It was dark when the Union force reached the area. Crook decided to halt the attack.

Some soldiers believed that Hunter was on the field by that time. An observer wrote, "An enterprising commander might have exploited the success by going right into Lynchburg even in a night assault, which was what some of the regimental officers thought Hunter might do. The general elected, however, to call off the battle and to go into camp."[60] "General Hunter missed his opportunity for capturing Lynchburg (that night) when he forbade the regiments...to carry the Rebel works."[106] The best information places Hunter west of the Big Otter River, waiting for information from Averell and Crook. They did send a courier later that night.

By nightfall, General Early had moved to the Charlottesville area. Some men could see the University of Virginia from their camp. Early had moved his command approximately eighty miles in four days. Old Jackson couldn't have done any better. Early was glad that his men were at the open railroad to Lynchburg; he was very disappointed that there were no trains there for his troops. Despite his orders and threats, he expected no trains until the early

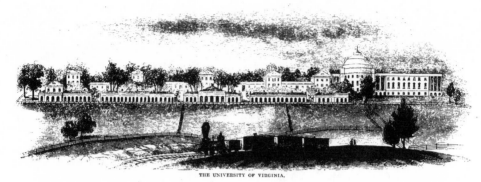

THE UNIVERSITY OF VIRGINIA.

By David Hunter Strother.

morning hours.

Early sent Breckinridge a telegram from Charlottesville: "If you can hold out till morning and the railroad does not fail, all will be well."[8]

The rapid movement was not without cost. A soldier recalled, "My feet were so sore that I had to crawl around the fire and cook on my hands and knees. I got no sleep the whole night."[107]

Although Breckinridge had turned the command over to Vaughn and then Hill, he tried to keep abreast of developments. It was night, and Breckinridge received word that Vaughn still had not placed his soldiers on line. Breckinridge became upset and sent Vaughn a stinging note. Vaughn was upset too!

A cadet recalled it was afternoon when they were finally ordered to their position "...in a graveyard...sitting upon graves and among tombstones...was anything but cheerful."[71]

Before the night was over, men were "stationed at all the passes by which ingress to the city was afforded; it was not doubted that the militia, the reserves, the convalescent soldiers, and the volunteers would be able to keep the enemy at bay until reinforcements could arrive."[101] "Nearly every man was determined to defend the town to the last extremity,"[106] wrote one loyal man.

Already the citizens were looking upon McCausland as their protector. "...The brave and indomitable General McCausland, to whom we owe a debt of lasting gratitude...materially retarded their progress from Staunton to this place,"[101] commented one citizen.

Hunter was slow this day also. Some units had only moved five or six miles; even the advance had moved only fifteen miles. The prize, Lynchburg, was still sixteen miles away from the infantry. The army was spread out with units still in Liberty. Sullivan's Infantry with Hunter was at the Big Otter River. Some units had crossed the stream by dark, but most of them were west of the river. Crook's Infantry was divided. Part was near the Big Otter River at the Virginia-Tennessee Railroad Bridge; part was in or near New London. Most of Averell's Cavalry was also in or near New London. Duffié was nearing Lynchburg by the Forest Road. He held up the column, waiting for the return of his reconnaisance in force, that had been sent to Balcony Falls.

Back at Liberty, terrified citizens wearily watched the unwelcome quests. Micajal Davis's slave, Uncle Billy Haden, became more than a slave. A member of the family said, "Uncle Billy absolutely saved the lives of the people in the house…slept at the door of my grandmother's room. He said to her, 'Miss Ellen, nobody shall come into your room except over my dead body. Don't you worry.'"[99] Uncle Billy was willing to sacrifice his life to protect his master's home and family at Chestnut Hill. There is no record that any more Union soldiers harassed the family. No one died.

Not all slaves in Liberty were as dedicated to their master as Uncle Billy. "You may imagine my feelings. The two Negro women that lived with us (Emily and Mary) and Joe (Mary's husband) left with the Yankees. I believe I wish every Negro had gone with them,"[100] said one resident of Liberty.

It appears that General Hunter took shelter in a house near the Big Otter River. By early evening, he knew that Averell had been engaged by a reinforced cavalry unit. He knew that Crook had been ordered to advance toward New London to help Averell, but he didn't know the outcome of the action. Some time in the early evening, Hunter "…obtained a report from a woman informant that Lynchburg was not heavily defended. The fortifications on the west side of town were nothing more than shallow rifle pits, and only sick and wounded soldiers were guarding Lynchburg."[78]

Apparently Hunter decided to regard Duffié's and the informant's reports and good, hard intelligence and to disregard the rumors of large numbers of troops alleged to be on their way to the Hill City.

Hunter had been holding the one-hundred-day volunteers who might be needed for battle. The latest reports indicated that it would be another cakewalk into Lynchburg. There was no need to retain them and the almost empty wagon train. It was a good time to send both the volunteers and the wagon train back north. Hunter knew that his troops were strung out back to Liberty. From Liberty north to the James, there was no known enemy force. The train should be free from attack at least that far. Hunter ordered that most of the little remaining food on the two-hundred-unit wagon train be divided among the troops. Some troops received two rations; others received none. Colonel Putnam and the one hundred volunteers were to escort the train. Hunter ordered them back through Liberty, over the Peaks, and toward New Castle because the bridge was out at Buchanan. They were to take the refugees, both white and Negro. All the prisoners except one were also to be taken. The statue of Washington and other articles stolen at the Virginia Military Institute were on the train.

When soldiers at the front received the unexpected rations from the wagon train, they built fires to cook their food. The light of the fires silhouetted their Union forms, and the constantly lurking Southern scouts opened fire upon the Yanks. "It was soon found necessary to extinguish the fires.…"[31] Hungry Union bellies growled; after a period of time, the fires were re-lit with the same results. There was another period of time, and again the fires were lit. The Rebs opened fire again. It was plain that by ignoring the Rebels, they weren't going to go away. The hungry blue-bellies decided to ignore the incoming fire, (and) "...persisted in their attempts at cooking, not withstanding bullets were flying thicker than hailstones."[31] There were no reports of the number killed or wounded or of the indigestion from the late night supper.

Hunter and his army saw no major problem between them and the taking of Lynchburg. A soldier stated, "With us, it is now on for Lynchburg, which we seem confident that we can capture."[18] Strother also contemplated their goal. If seized and held, the lifeblood of the Confederate capital at Richmond would be stopped. There would be no lead from Southwest Virginia. Guns without bullets are useless. The salt from Southwest Virginia would cease. Without salt to preserve the food, Richmond would be starved into submission. Strother was not as confident as that soldier. He said, "I felt a vague uneasiness as to the result of our move. Lee will certainly relieve Lynchburg if he can. If he can not, the Confederacy is gone up. If he does succeed in detaching a force, our situation is most hazardous."[11]

Saunders and the cavalry Home Guard unit had to wait until the Union Army was bedded down before they felt safe to move from their hiding place between the Forest and Big Island Roads. It was decided that the Home Guard would follow the Union cavalry force seen moving on the Big Island Road (heading for Balcony Falls) to see what they were up to. Saunders moved by the Forest Road toward Lynchburg at approximately midnight.

Chapter X

Friday, June 17 — Saturday, June 18

On Friday, June 17, R.C. Saunders had been moving toward Lynchburg over the Forest Road since near midnight. He reached the railroad depot at Forest at approximately 2:00 a.m. He woke the agent and told him that the Union would be there sometime early in the day. The agent and his assistant set about hiding railroad property. The exhausted Saunders, spread corn on the depot platform for his horse, took the horse's reins, and lay down. Soon he was fast asleep.

As Saunders was falling asleep at Forest Depot, Strother was being awakened by General Hunter six miles east of Liberty. Hunter showed Strother a dispatch Averell had sent about the fighting at New London. Uncertain as to the extent of Southern opposition, Hunter determined to move forward and assess the situation. He and his staff moved toward New London via the Lynchburg-Salem Pike. Strother was to get Sullivan and the infantry on the move.

Strother told the sergeant in charge of headquarter escorts to provide him with two orderlies. Strother was mounted and waiting for his escort when he became aware of a disturbance. One of the orderlies did not like being awakened, "...the fellow was mutinous and drew a pistol."[11] Strother recalled that he went in, "...sword in hand to quell..."[11] this orderly who refused to cooperate. After confrontation, discussion, and delay, Strother left with one orderly.

Strother was further delayed because he could not locate Sullivan. "...I never saw such damnable ignorance and carelessness. The greater part of the sentries did not know where the headquarters of their regiments were. This want of system in this respect is common to our army and is the cause of great delay...."[11] Providing food for the army by theft rather than from supply trains by necessity creates disunity; other problems were created by Hunter's encouraging his men to commit acts of wanton pillaging against civilians and the fact that the army no longer functioned as a single unit. Because of the disorderly orderly and the difficulty Strother had in locating Sullivan, Strother felt that he had lost two hours of time. Strother knew that Hunter was depending on him to bring the infantry forward. A two-hour delay in the infantry might prove to be critical. Strother was very anxious as he and Sullivan followed Hunter over the Pike.

There was also a delay near Charlottesville. Early wanted the trains to greet his men by sundown June 16, but it was well past midnight before the first trains arrived. At 2:00 a.m., Early started his army in motion. Men were "...grumbling, and stumbling around in the dark...."[103] Reports indicated that more trains were on their way. The line was not open. All had to wait; some troops had begun to board the train shortly after 2:00 a.m. They didn't know about the additional trains. To them it was just more foul-ups, hurry-up, and wait.

When the soldier with feet so sore he had to crawl around the campfire on his hands and knees to cook supper was alerted in the pre-dawn darkness about the march, it was too much to bear. The foot pain had prevented him from getting any restful sleep, and now another day of marching lay ahead. He hobbled to his regimental surgeon and "...showed him my feet and told him that it was impossible for me to march any farther."[107] The doctor told him that today he would ride. The soldier decided that he could make it to the train.

Shortly before sunrise, the other trains arrived. Early soon discovered that there was only enough transport for half of his command. It is assumed that Ramseur's and Gordon's Divisions were closer to the railroad and that Early ordered them to entrain. This decision did not set well with General Rodes.

Gen. John Brown Gordon — C.S.A.

Gen. Stephen Dodson Ramseur was a North Carolinian; Gen. John Brown Gordon, a Georgian; and Gen. Robert Emmett Rodes, a Virginian. Rodes, a V.M.I. graduate, was born and reared in Lynchburg. He and his men were told to wait while others commanded by out-of-staters went to the rescue of his hometown. General Rodes's wife, child, and father were in Lynchburg; if anyone was to fly to their rescue, it should be he. His intimate knowledge of the area might be invaluable. If any one of the three was to reap vengeance on Hunter for the destruction of V.M.I., it should be Rodes. He heatedly confronted Early.

Early was not a man to accept other's counsel readily or worry about subordinates' feelings when there was a job to be done. Early would not hear "...Rodes's demand to go first in defense of his native town...It is not surprising that there were hot words between Rodes and Early...."[10]

The air may have turned blue between the angry Rodes and the profane Early, but Early's order stood: Gordon and Ramseur would take the train. The artillery, wagon train, ambulances, part of Gordon's Division (one brigade under Brig. Gen. William Richard Terry, who was born at Liberty and educated at V.M.I.), and Rodes's Division were to march on the road running near the railroad toward Lynchburg. The angry Rodes probably rode off on his march before Gordon's and Ramseur's men boarded the train.

Early boarded the first train which was occupied by Ramseur's men. Near dawn the train puffed off toward Lynchburg, sixty miles away. Would the Second Corps be in time to oppose Hunter, or was the delay fatal to Lynchburg and the whole Southern Confederacy? Early had not been informed that Breckinridge had relieved himself of command. Early sent a telegram at 7:40 a.m., stating that he would be in Lynchburg by 12:00 noon or 1:00 p.m. Because of the poor maintenance of both rolling stock and rails, the train crept along at a snail's pace of less than twelve miles per hour.

Lynchburg was the focus of the entire campaign, but not all troops were moving toward that city. It was approximately 3:30 p.m. when the two-hundred wagon wagon train, started back toward Liberty. It was almost empty except for stolen war trophies. Many refugees, mostly contraband, left willingly. Most prisoners followed unwillingly. The train was guarded by the regiment and one half of the hundred day volunteers (Hundred Fifty-Second & Hundred Sixty-Second Ohio). The commander was Col. David Putnam, but the last recorded order was issued to the Quartermaster, Capt. William Alexander. "You will direct division quartermasters to burn all wagons that break down or cannot be transported; also, shoot all horses that give out on the road. Nothing must be allowed to impede the progress of your train."

Prisoner Beall recalled seeing old Mr. McDonald, "...ailing considerably. He was greatly exhausted by the long, hot march, and was suffering from his wound. But his spirit was as proud as ever."[80] It was then that Captain Berry (the same one who burned Governor Letcher's home) rode up. Getting ready to march, he took the prisoners, and then he turned to Angus McDonald and shouted, "You will go with us, you old scoundrel. General Hunter has not decided what he will do with you — whether he will shoot or hang you."[80]

"The poor boy (Harry) heard with bitter grief that they were to be separated, for he knew that only his care and kindness could keep his father from severe suffering."[25] "...Harry McDonald — as brave and noble a boy as ever lived —advanced a step and begged to be permitted to go with his father...Harry commenced shedding tears."[30] Colonel McDonald turned to his son in a firm but fatherly way and said, "Harry, my son, do not shed a tear, but, if necessary, shed your blood in defense of your country."[80] Then in a tone too low to be heard by the guard, he told Harry to try to escape. Harry recalled, "He told me never to let them see that I was afraid of them but to bear all they would inflict like a soldier."[25]

Then the defiant, courageous McDonald took command, ordering Captain Berry to separate him from the other prisoners. This was soon done, and Angus found himself in the area of Hunter's guards. He was ordered to march, "But here Colonel McDonald's superb courage again asserted itself, and he said not one foot would he march...."[80]

Captain Berry reacted to this defiance with anger. He "...ordered a rope to be brought with which he (McDonald) was to be dragged by the neck at the rear of one of the wagons."[25] Apparently Harry was marched off at this point. The last view he had of his father was one of an old man, broken in body, but with the heart of a courageous patriot with a rope tied about his neck.

Prisoner Beall was there after Harry was marched off. He observed Captain Berry's threat and rope; Colonel McDonald showed that he was not "afraid of them." Captain Berry decided to make another threat. He told McDonald to move, for if he didn't move, he would run him through with a bayonet. McDonald bet his life and called Berry's threat: "...whereupon the old Confederate hero threw open his vest, exposed his bosom and exclaimed, 'You may shoot and kill me, but you cannot make me march. Now do your worst.'"[80]

Defiance and hatred shot between the two men. Berry may have wanted to kill him on the spot, but McDonald was the general's prize. Berry knew that he was beaten and lowered his eyes. Then Berry ordered the worst wagon in the train to be brought and "the old scoundrel"[80] was to be thrown into it. The conquered had beaten the conqueror.

As dawn approached, Duffié was approaching the Forest Depot. Two Southern men aroused the sleeping Saunders, telling him the enemy's advance was only a few hundred yards away. Saunders engaged in no dialogue but quickly mounted and galloped away. In about one mile he slowed down and looked back to see smoke rising from what was the Forest Depot. He continued to ride to Lynchburg to report on the enemy's advance.

Four Yankees broke into Edward Sextus Hutter's home "Popular Forest" near the depot. They were starting to take Hutter's personal goods when a band of Confederates rode up. Soon three of the four were Southern prisoners. The one escaping Yankee yelled threats that he would return and burn the home as he ran.

As Duffié moved upon Forest Depot, Sullivan's Infantry with Strother had begun the march over the Lynchburg Pike. Strother was concerned that the two-hour delay might have a bad effect on the army. It appears that most of the infantrymen were two miles west of Big Otter River although some advanced units had made it to the stream the night before. Establishing an exact time is difficult. Most sources agree that the infantry was on the move by 5:00 a.m. and had only moved two miles when it came to a complete halt at Big Otter River. The time was probably near 7:00 a.m. Hunter and his staff were there. All were waiting for Meigs and his engineers, "Pontoon Corps or Pioneer Corps," to bridge the river. Strother then realized that the two-hour delay would have no effect on the army because the army would be delayed crossing the stream.

Strother rejoined Hunter and his staff. The reports Hunter had received from Averell caused him some concern. He had sent a courier to Crook, ordering him to abandon his destruction and march over the Virginia-Tennessee Railroad and to move to New London with his entire force. Thus the Union would advance on Lynchburg from two, not three routes.

Although Hunter was approximately fourteen miles from Lynchburg, he had very little information about the defense of the Hill City. The Jessie Scouts, who had served him well as the army proceeded down the Valley, continued to report that only a small force was at Lynchburg, but rumors circulated about large reinforcements coming from Richmond.

As the sun rose in the sky, so did Hunter's short temper. The bridge work was proceeding at a snail's pace. During this time, Capt. Thomas K. McCann approached Hunter with the news that Union armies had suffered defeat in both the east and the west. Hunter asked for the source of information. McCann said that a Rebel by the name of William Leftwich had been boasting of the Union defeats. The Leftwich home "Greenwoods" was nearby, and the army could not move because the replacement bridge had not been constructed; Hunter decided to visit the big mouth, Leftwich.

Strother recalled that Leftwich had "...a very pretty country residence...a sweet daughter about sixteen and a nice family."[11] Hunter was irritated with Leftwich's news and the gleeful manner in which it was delivered. Leftwich was arrested and his house burned as he, his family, and soldiers, watched. One soldier remarked, "General Hunter, for reasons best known to himself, has ordered the burning up of many fine old Virginia mansions with all the contents. Many fine appearing ladies weep while their homes are burning...one cannot help but feel sorry...."[18] The family wept, the soldiers felt pity, and most of Hunter's staff rode away. "...We did not wish to look upon the scene."[11] Only Hunter seemed to enjoy the sight.

Hunter returned to the river to wait. News filtered in about continued guerrilla activity. Hunter ordered one house where supposed guerrilla fire originated, burned. Again through Strother's intercession, the home was spared.

Lynchburg was the focus of the entire campaign from Meadow Bluff and Cedar Creek to here. Hunter "...expected to walk into Lynchburg and take it like a piece of cake."[110] Lynchburg was a massive warehouse of military goods. The two railroads and the canal made it ideal to funnel supplies through to Lee.

There were warehouses that contained small arms and ammunition. There were firms that repaired small arms, harnesses, and wagons. The Piedmont Foundry, later called the Phoenix, made or repaired artillery. It also produced ordnance for the cannons. Many uniforms were made in the factory. There was also food for his hungry army. Hunter knew that there were many hospitals in the town. He probably had no idea that he might capture Lee's number one general, Longstreet, in one of them.

Because of concern that Lynchburg would fall and that Longstreet might be captured, he was moved to a private residence, the Gordons. Mrs. Eliza Gordon sent word to a nurse, Susan Blackford, that Longstreet wanted to see her personally. Mrs. Blackford said the general "...is very feeble and nervous and suffers much from his wound. He sheds tears on the slightest provocation and apologizes for it. He says he does not see why a bullet going through a man's shoulder should make a baby of him."[115]

The biggest reason that Lynchburg was so important was that it was the conduit for the salt and the lead from Southwest Virginia. If supplies of either were cut for too long, Richmond would be starved into submission or there would be an army that couldn't shoot. Without Lynchburg, Lee could not hold Richmond; without Richmond, the Confederacy would collapse. Lynchburg was critical to the South and Hunter was eagerly standing on the front porch of the town. Hunter was going to eat Lynchburg like cake.

R.C. Saunders was in Lynchburg quite early in the morning. He reported to the city's former commander, Nicholls. Nicholls informed Saunders that the city had been reinforced by Breckinridge and that Early's army was expected any time. Saunders remarked that if Hunter was aware of the reinforcements that Hunter would not mount a full-scale attack on Lynchburg but would head on to Danville. General Nicholls made no comment on Saunders' remark but told him to report back later.

Nicholls did not tell Saunders that there was more than a little friction between the generals. Vaughn had not taken his rebuke from Breckinridge well. He had been arguing and opposing the plans and deployments of Hill and Hays. The ailing Breckinridge considered Vaughn another pain in the side.

Gen. John C. Vaughn — C.S.A.

Despite Vaughn's uncooperative attitude, Hill's line of defense was proceeding. Hill was a general who recognized the value of the terrain. Either Hill had intimate knowledge of Lynchburg or he used the services of someone who did. Local historian, Ed Warehime, pointed out that Hill's defense line used the hills, the valleys, and the creeks to the west of town as a natural defense. By using the terrain, Hill hoped to make up for the lack of troops.

Because of the lack in quantity and quality of forces, Hill's line must be short. It hugged the city closely. (For clarity, all battle positions will relate to the Confederate side. The line ran generally south to north; directions assume that the Confederate line stands facing west; thus the south is on the Confederate left, while the north is on the right). Somewhat south of town on the Rustburg (or Campbell Courthouse Road) was a fortification which commanded the road and offered a view of the Valley framed by Fishing Creek. Hill felt that this fort would help if the Union attempted to turn his left flank and march into the city. Following the line of site from the fort across Fishing Creek, up by Diamond Hill is the summit of Cralle Hill (College Hill). College Hill was near the outer limits of the city at this time. On the hill stood a tall building belonging to the military school, Lynchburg College (not directly related to the current college of that name). Hill threw up breastworks and cannon implacements on the hill. The hill provided a good view down to the Fishing Creek Valley. Thus the Valley would be commanded by high ground on both the left and the right. The line followed the brow of the hill to the right and extended almost straight to the Methodist Cemetery (now Old City Cemetery). There the line arched back along the ridge, moving eastwardly. The right side of the line was anchored on the hill overlooking Blackwater Creek. It is only a short distance between Blackwater Creek and the James River. The line covered every likely invasion route that Hunter could use as he approached the city from the west.

Hill placed the best available troops on College Hill: Breckinridge's Infantry. Next he placed some dismounted cavalrymen on the line. Between them and the City Cemetery, he placed the Home Guard, invalids, and stockade prisoners. From the point of the City Cemetery back to Blackwater Creek, he placed his second best troops, the young soldiers of the corps. They had their own artillery support. The Botetourt Artillery was moved from Amherst Heights across the James to the top of the hill above the city to a location on Church Street, back in the city from the defense line. The street ran parallel to the defense line from College Hill to the Cemetery. Hill held the battery in reserve, "...every man at his post."[76] Hill could move the battery to most any section of the line within minutes to stop a Union attack. Hill's line took advantage of the terrain. Only a narrow strip along the turnpike on Forest Road offered Hunter any high ground toward the city. Because the hills sloped so rapidly off on both sides, Hunter could advance only a limited number of men forward along the roads. The creeks, the valleys, the ravines, and the cutbacks would not permit mass formations to move in unison on the line. Hill had used the terrain and available manpower well, but the sure numbers of Hunter's army would probably be able to overrun the line in some place.

Could Hill withstand an attack until Early arrived?

Vaughn was causing command difficulty. At 9:00 a.m., Richmond directed a wire to Breckinridge, who they believed was commanding Lynchburg, telling him that General Ransom should be in Lynchburg to take command of all cavalry some time in the afternoon. He would be coming by the Southside Railroad. At least one command problem would be gone: Imboden would no longer be in command.

Some time in the early morning, Nicholls called Hill's attention to the report from Saunders. Union cavalry under Duffie was approaching the city by the Forest Road. It was advancing almost unopposed. Hill sent a messenger over the pike toward Imboden, requesting that he send some troops to the Forest Road.

At the Big Otter, Hunter waited. The building of the bridge was proceeding slowly. As it was already quite warm, some troops forded above the engineers "...and enjoyed themselves in looking on and talking with citizens of different color...."[41] Some Negroes inquired about leaving with the army. There was already a lack of food and uncertainty if the army would achieve its goal and return to friendly territory. The Negroes were not encouraged to join the column.

While Hunter with Sullivan's Infantry waited, Averell and Crook continued to push up the Pike. Imboden and McCausland "...resisted our advance at every step...."[8] East of New London, Confederate opposition increased. Averell sent a courier to Crook to send the infantry forward. There was a sharp skirmish between the cavalries of Averell and McCausland on Samuel Miller's farm. As Crook advanced, McCausland retreated. The Union Army was only eight miles from Lynchburg, both time and distance were running out. McCausland had slowed Averell, giving Lynchburg a few more minutes.

After McCausland retreated, the Union "...ransacked Miller's home, threatened his life and devoured a forty-five-year-old barrel of French Brandy."[78]

The sounds of skirmishing could be heard back at the river, but the bridge work continued very slowly. Meigs "...was bound to see that it was put up only after the most approved methods of regular army bridge building. But the plans were too elaborate and tedious, and everybody got out of patience...."[14]

Capt. John F. Welch was in charge of the Pioneer Corps from the One Hundred Sixteenth Ohio. He got fed up with waiting and vented his frustration on Meigs. He told Meigs that he could get a bridge over the stream in a hurry. Since Colonel Meigs did not want to hear any more from Welch, he said in effect, "Show me."

Welch accepted the challenge. He put the men of the One Hundred Sixteenth to work. Some felled trees; others carried them to the bank. He supervised the bridge laying. "...In less than an hour..." the red-faced Meigs watched "the artillery...crossing, on the gallop...."[14]

Hunter had lost between three and four hours of precious cool morning marching time. The time was now between 10:00-11:00 a.m. A report with some inconsistencies stated that Hunter and his staff rode up to "Liberty Hill," the farm of William Read near New London at "about ten o'clock."[111] Unlike most other receptions Hunter had received, the family and the slaves welcomed him. They invited him to breakfast, which they cooked with "...*no undue haste*...."[111]

While waiting for breakfast, Hunter and his staff were served Mint Juleps. While they were having drinks, the slaves came to report that the Yankee soldiers were stealing. Hunter responded to the Read family's kindness by posting a guard. No Yankees discovered the family silver which was put in gunny sacks and thrown into a pond near the house.

After breakfast, the general and his staff were taken into the parlor, where the ladies played the piano for them. This allegedly was followed by song and dance. McCausland had been trying to slow Hunter with bullets; the Reads had slowed him with a breakfast party.

If this incident did take place, it is stated that as Hunter rode off but while still in hearing range, William Read's sister began playing "Dixie" on the piano.

During this general time frame, the courier from Lynchburg reached Imboden with the request that the cavalry troops be sent to oppose the Union cavalry advancing over the Forest Road. McCausland's fatigued men and horses who had done the most to oppose Hunter's advance from Meadow Bluff, were sent cross-country to the Forest Road. McCausland left part of his command and took approximately 1,000 troops and two guns.[91]

Imboden decided to make another stand at the stone house of worship, the Quaker Church, about four miles from Lynchburg. The Quakers opposed the war. Ironically their church and cemetery with a stone wall would be a place of battle. As Imboden fell back, he did a good job of screening McCausland's movement. No Union report indicating that they were aware that McCausland was gone has been found.

Old Quaker meeting house — Lynchburg.

Some time after noon, Crook reported back to Hunter via a courier, that he knew the Reb troops with their artillery were digging in near a church. Hunter ordered Crook "...to remain and wait for the arrival of our other troops before making the attack."[73]

By 12:00 noon, the heat was oppressive. Marching, riding, and fighting combined with the heat to sap the strength from the troops. The only troops that were recovering their strength were the weary men of Early's command riding slowly to Lynchburg. It is uncertain which train in Early's convoy was on the bridge over the James River when the rear car jumped the tracks. "...Soldiers commenced halloing (sic) to the engineer, he stopped. Some of the men jumped off for fear the whole train would be pulled off the bridge. One or two were killed, and some fell on the bridge, and some (were) caught in the timbers and were badly hurt."[107] Without a shot being fired, Early's command had taken its first casualties in its effort to save Lynchburg. Soon, some mother, wife, or sister would weep bitter tears and try to understand how her loved one could have given his life in defense of the country while he was riding on a train.

To the families the loss was great. To Early's veterans of a hundred pitched battles, it was insignificant. Injury and death were a part of the routine. Nothing must prevent the movement upon Lynchburg. The derailed car was simply pushed off the bridge, and the journey was resumed.

The last communication Early had received from Lynchburg earlier that morning indicated that a weak force was opposing Hunter's hordes. Early must have wondered who would greet him at the station — friend or foe. If Hunter had made a quick dash and captured the city, one half of the Second Corps would be riding directly into grave peril.

The townspeople and those who defended them were "...praying for Early...to come."[91] "People eagerly gazed toward the north to see if they could see any signs of Early...."[106] "With every whine of an engine, or the noise of moving cars a report would be circulated that Early and his men had come."[91]

With a rumble, puffing smoke, and belching ashes, prayers were answered at 1:00 p.m. Early had arrived! "A thrill of joy went like an electric shock through the whole place as the train came over the bridge into the city, the cars packed with men and many hanging on the outside. When the soldiers disembarked, cheer after cheer rent the air. Early had come, and Lynchburg was safe once more."[106]

As Early started detraining his command, he received reports that the enemy was still several miles away. He was in time. His first order of business was to move his troops off the trains as soon as possible. The trains must be serviced and sent back to pick up Rodes and the rest of the infantry. The wagon train and the artillery would have to continue over the road. Early used soldiers familiar with the terrain and defense lines to direct his troops. Early gave orders to his troops to move to points in advance of the defense line and to camp.

Most of Early's men moved up Fifth Street to the breastworks on College Hill. Fifth Street, though steep, was not the upgrade presented by streets nearer the center of town. The march was made in double-quick time because their services at the front might be needed. Most soldiers had neither hats nor shoes, but the people cheered their ragged heroes on. A citizen described the soldiers as looking "...like long, lean grayhounds."[10] Sally Scruggs was a young girl standing on a wall at the top of the hill (Fifth and Church Streets). She had a wide-brimmed straw hat which she had proudly and gayly decorated. Upon viewing the hatless soldiers marching rapidly toward battle with heads exposed to the scorching afternoon sun, she made a decision: her pretty straw hat went sailing through the air to a red-haired soldier. He caught it and immediately covered his head. Without breaking stride, he raised his gun to the "present arms" position as a show of gratitude. His comrades had been watching the proceedings. Sally's selfless gift to one of them was a gift to all. Loud cheers rang out from the whole brigade.

Most troops moved to the west of the breastworks on College Hill. They rested along the Western Turnpike (Salem Pike). There a lucky few received the gratitude of some of the ladies of the city. From the meager food stocks, homemakers brought meals and liquid refreshments to the men who would protect their town.

Re-creation: Early's men moving out of Lynchburg.

As his troops marched off, Early was taken to see Breckinridge. He was
surprised to find Breckinridge in bed. Breckinridge expressed his joy that
Early had arrived in time. Early showed him his "...confidential instructions
for the impending campaign...."[55] General Lee, the master strategist, had
looked beyond the present peril posed by Hunter to Richmond's supply line,
to an opportunity. Lee envisioned Early dealing a decisive defeat to Hunter
and then attacking Washington City as a means of relieving pressure on
Richmond. Breckinridge saw the soundness of the plan and offered his
unconditional support to Early. Then he told Early that high command at
Richmond believed that he commanded the department, but because of his
debilitating injury, Hill was in fact in command. "A potentially sticky situation,
this, because Early had no great admiration for Hill, and Hill's position was
unofficial."[103]

After giving Early a little taste of salt, Breckinridge gave Early some sugar.
He told Early that Hill's number one aide in setting up the city's defense was his
old friend and former subordinate, Brig. Gen. Harry Hays, the Tennessean
who was wounded at Spotsylvania. Early was glad to have Hays on his staff,
and "Hill at least could be trusted...."[103]

Early said he would accept the situation and inform Richmond of the
change. Early's position with General Lee allowed him to go over Braxton
Bragg's head, a step Breckinridge could not make.

Then Breckinridge called Early's attention to another command problem.
Vaughn had not acted with the speed that Breckinridge wanted in deploying
the troops around town. After a formal rebuke, Vaughn had only grown more
uncooperative. "...Vaughn had turned obstinate and was impeding efforts by
refusing to comply with General Hill's orders."[6] Some soldiers said, "...they
lacked confidence in him."[30]

Early said that he would put Vaughn in his place. It is unclear if Vaughn was
temporarily relieved of command or told to confine his activity to make sure
that his brigade followed orders.

Early knew that his telegram would pass under Bragg's nose before it got to
General Lee's eyes. Early was a good salesman. He started his short telegram
with words of confidence and reassurance. Then he presented the problem
and concluded with a solution.

"Lynchburg June 17, 1864
General Bragg — Richmond

Arrived here at 1 p.m. with sufficient troops to make all safe. Hunter's
force is all east of the mountains and his main body is between here and
New London. He is reported advancing on this place. General Breckinridge is so disabled from injury to old wound as to be unable to ride, and
he thinks he will be so for several days, and at his request I ask that
General D.H. Hill, who is here, be assigned to temporary command of
Breckinridge's troops. It is of the utmost importance to have another
commander than the senior Brigadier (Vaughn).

Answer at once."[8]

General Lee was usually able to think one step ahead of his opponent and his subordinates. Lee managed his soldiers much like a loving father. To "answer at once" was no problem. Major Gen. Arnold Elzey would be arriving on the afternoon train with Ransom. Elzey lived under an assumed name. He was born Arnold Elzey Jones in Maryland on December 18, 1816. At West Point, he decided simply to drop the name Jones; in 1837, he graduated as Arnold Elzey. He rose to the rank of Major General near his forty-sixth birthday in 1862.

Gen. Arnold Elzey — C.S.A.

After the conference with Breckinridge, Early went out to inspect Hill's defense line. It is assumed that Hays accompanied Early and Hill. Early noted Hill's excellent use of the terrain. Because of the small amount of manpower, Hill's line hugged the city tightly. Early at once recognized that Hunter could shell Lynchburg at will without breaking Hill's line. More troops were available. Early gave orders that the troops on Hill's defense line would remain in place. They would form an inner-defense line. Early's troops would move farther from the city and form an outer-defense line. It is likely that the same personnel who assisted Hill and Hays was used to establish an outer-defense line.

Assessing Relative Strength

It is difficult to assess the strength of troops since figures vary widely or are incomplete. On the high side, a Confederate estimated that Hunter had between 30,000 and 50,000 men.[91] Hunter officially estimated Confederates to number between 10,000 to 15,000.[8]

Milton Humphreys' account appears to be the most detailed and complicated. He indicates that Hunter had 19,680 total troops of which 16,643[30] were available for duty. Chief-of-Staff Strother for the Union Army said that there were approximately 25,000 men when the armies combined at Staunton. Although there were some men moving in and out, the figure would remain near that estimate to Lynchburg.

Humphreys states that the Confederacy had 11,623 present plus the approximately 4,000 men under Early, which would give a figure of 15,623 men. Although the individual figures used to achieve that total can be disputed, the aggregate figure is probably correct. (Early had nearly 4,000 men plus artillery and wagon trains coming from Charlottesville on June 17, but they are not included in the above figure).

As Union forces approached Lynchburg, there were two 3-inch guns detached for service with Duffié's Cavalry and thirty-four guns with Dupont, who accompanied Sullivan. These thirty-four were classified as four Napoleans and thirty 3-inch guns. Ammunition for the guns was not abundant.

The South enjoyed a distinct advantage in artillery. At or approaching Lynchburg were these batteries: Bryant's Battery, six guns; Chapman's, four guns; Lowry's, four guns; Jackson's, six guns, Lurty's, four guns; McClanahan's, six guns; the Botetourt Artillery, six guns; Marquis' (Boys' Battery), four guns; Stamp's, three guns; the Cadet Artillery, six guns; and the Home Guards, possibly four guns. The total number of guns would be forty-six or fifty. They could be classified as follows: One 24-pound Howitzer, two 20-pound Parrotts, seven 12-pound Napoleans (Corps Artillery referred to as "four brass pieces" assumed 12-pound Napoleans), eight 12-pound Howitzers, three 10-pound Parrotts, sixteen 3-inch rifles, two 6-pound Smooth Bores, and fourteen 3-inch guns. The four guns possibly manned by locals were old "Smooth Bores."[30] McCausland and Imboden had parts of one battery split between them. Some artillery was still approaching the city. Most of the artillery was protected in redoubts (earthworks forts) or behind breastworks, giving it an additional advantage if attacked. The Confederates had more guns which were better positioned and defended, and storehouses in Lynchburg that could provide adequate ammunition and artillery to defend the city. This weighed heavily in the Confederates' favor.

Even with the Confederates' good defense line for Lynchburg, their morale was low. Morale is an important factor in battle. It cannot be quantified and it can change rapidly. The morale factor would appear to be heavily weighed in the Union's favor because they had just won a clear cut, smashing victory at Piedmont. Part of the Confederate troops were the same ones who had been defeated by Union forces. A great number of the Confederates were untrained, inexperienced Home Guards; they lacked confidence. A high number of the soldiers should be lying in hospital beds, not in the trenches. Many of Early's men were battle-weary. Some of the units under his command were nearly wiped out at Spotsylvania Courthouse (the famous Stonewall Brigade nearly passed out of existence here). All of Early's men were dog-tired from three days of long marches. The morale factor favored the Union.

ORGANIZATION OF FEDERAL FORCES AT LYNCHBURG
Department of West Virginia
Maj. Gen. David Hunter, Commanding

1st DIVISION: Brig. Gen. J. C. Sullivan
1st Brigade: Col. G. D. Wells
34th Mass.
116th Ohio
123rd Ohio
5th N.Y.H.A. (cos. A, B, C, D)

2nd Brigade: Col. J. Thoburn
4th West Va.
18th Conn.
1st West Va.
12th West Va.

Unassigned:
2nd Md. Eastern Shore
2nd Md. Potomac Home Brigade

2nd DIVISION: Brig. Gen. George Crook
1st Brigade: Col. R. B. Hayes
23rd Ohio
36th Ohio
5th West Va.
13th West Va.

2nd Brigade: Col. C. B. White
12th Ohio
91st Ohio
9th West Va.
14th West Va.

3rd Brigade: Col. J. M. Campbell
54th Penna.
3rd & 4th Penna. Reserves (Bttn.)
11th West Va. (6 Companies)
15th West Va.

ARTILLERY: 1st Ky. Lt. Arty.
1st Ohio Lt. Arty.

FEDERAL CAVALRY
1st DIVISION: Brig. Gen. A. N. Duffié
1st Brigade: Col. R. F. Taylor
15th N.Y.
1st N.Y. (Veteran)
21st N.Y.
1st Md. P.H.B.

2nd Brigade: Col. J. E. Wynkoop
20th Penna.

22nd Penna.
1st N.Y. (Lincoln)
ARTILLERY: 1st West Va. Lt. Arty., B
2nd DIVISION: Brig. Gen. W. W. Averell
   1st Brigade: Col. J. N. Schoonmaker
   8th Ohio
   14th Penna.
   2nd Brigade: Col. J. H. Oley
   34th Ohio Mt. Inf.
   3rd West Va.
   5th West Va.
   7th West Va.
   3rd Brigade: Col. W. H. Powell
   1st West Va.
   2nd West Va.
ARTILLERY: Capt. H. A. DuPont
   B, Md. Lt. Arty.
   30th N.Y. Lt. Arty.
   D, 1st West Va.
   B, 5th U.S.

ORGANIZATION OF CONFEDERATE FORCES AT LYNCHBURG
General Jubal A. Early
Department of South West Virginia
Maj. Gen. John C. Breckinridge,
(Temporarily under Command of Gen. D. H. Hill & Gen. Elzey)
Brig. Gen. G. C. Wharton's Brigade;
Col. Aug. Forsberg
   45th Va.
   50th Va.
   51st Va.
   30th Va. Bttn. S.S.
Col. Geo. S. Patton's Brigade
   22nd Va.
   23rd Va. Bttn.
   26th Va. Bttn.
Col. T. Smith's Brigade
   36th Va.
   45th Va. Bttn.
   60th Va.
Maj. Gen. S. D. Ramseur's Division:
Brig. Gen. R. D. Lilley
   13th Va.
   31st Va.

49th Va.
52nd Va.
58th Va.

Brig. Gen. R. D. Johnston
5th N.C.
12th N.C.
20th N.C.
23rd N.C.

Maj. Gen. John B. Gordon's Division (Partial):
Brig. Gen. Z. York
5th La.
6th La.
7th La.
8th La.
9th La.
1st La.
2nd La.
10th La.
14th La.
15th La.

Gen. Francis T. Nicholls
Convalescents & invalids
"Silver Grays" City Home Guard
V.M.I. Cadets

Brig. Gen. W. G. Lewis
6th N.C.
21st N.C.
54th N.C.
57th N.C.
1st N.C. Bttn.

Brig. Gen. C. A. Evans
13th Ga.
26th Ga.
31st Ga.
38th Ga.
60th Ga.
61st Ga.
12th Ga. Bttn.

RODE'S DIVISION arrived late on June 18th; The rest of Gordon's Division also.

CONFEDERATE CAVALRY FORCES: Gen. Robert Ransom

Gen. J. McCausland
   14th Va.
   16th Va.
   17th Va.

Col. W. L. Jackson
   1st Md.
   19th Va.
   20th Va.
   46th Va. Bttn.
   47th Va. Bttn.
   26th Va.
   37th Va. Bttn.

Gen. J. D. Imboden
   18th Va.
   23rd Va.
   62nd Va.
   25th Va.

Gen. J. C. Vaughn (Mounted Infantry)
   1st Tenn.
   43rd Tenn. Mt. Bttn.
   16th Tenn Bttn.
   16, 61, 62nd Tenn. Mt. Inf. (remnants)

Gen. W. E. Jones (under Gen. Vaughn)
   8th Va.
   21st Va.
   22nd Va.
   34th Va. Bttn.
   36th Va. Bttn.

ARTILLERY:
   Botetourt Arty.
      (6 Guns) Capt. H. C. Douthat
   Berkeley's Btty.
      (2 Guns of McClanahan's Arty.)
   W. S. Lurty's Btty.
      (2 Guns)

Maj. Floyd King's Battalion (Breckinridge)
   Chapman's Va. Btty.
   Bryan's Va. Btty.
   Lowry's Va. Btty.

Just like Hunter's army, the Confederates were also in a somewhat confused state. The rapid influx of so many units from so many locations and the many changes in command structure had caused confusion. It was difficult to determine who was in charge of which units and where those units were located. News and rumors about new units and Hunter's moves added to the confusion in the ranks. It is no wonder that Early chose to keep his troops separated from the units already in town. He would feel more comfortable fighting with his troops than trying to integrate the whole army. That is the reason he left the forces in place and advanced his soldiers only to establish a line farther from the city.

Hunter told Duffié "...to attack resolutely on the Forestville Road...."[8] At 1:30 p.m., Duffié struck McCausland about five miles out of Lynchburg. McCausland who had "...refined delaying tactics to an art,"[28] now brought Duffié's Cavalry to a complete halt. Duffié had no infantry support and little artillery. McCausland chose to stop Duffié where "the road was narrow, and the woods so dense as to forbid the use of cavalry."[8] Because the foliage was dense and because McCausland's men were firing from concealed positions, Duffié was unsure of the size of the force opposing him. McCausland had "...a section of artillery..."[8] with him, but the number and the type of cannons is not known for certain. Imboden stated that he had "...four rifles (3-inch guns?), and three small Howitzers (Mountain Howitzers?)" with him on June 16. Some of this artillery was sent with McCausland. It appears that Imboden was reinforced by additional artillery on June 17 (perhaps his Boys' Battery with twenty-pounders). Because Mountain Howitzers are smaller and easier to transport, it is likely that McCausland took these as he moved cross-country from Imboden earlier in the day. McCausland used them effectively. Duffié dismounted his cavalry and by pure numbers began to push McCausland back. The firing was intense, and the advance was very slow.

The time was probably after 1:30 p.m. when Early, Hill, Hays, and their staffs rode forward to establish another defense line so that Hunter could not shell the town at will. It is unlikely that Early was informed that the Union cavalry was sighted moving toward the city by the Forest Road. If he was informed, no mention was made, and Early's action indicated that he did not feel threatened by that column. Early believed that most cavalrymen were dandies who would rather find an isolated house and sit on the porch, sipping buttermilk while the infantry fought. He sometimes called them "Buttermilk Rangers."[112]

The generals and their staffs, probably including those locals who helped lay off the present defense line, rode forward. About two miles out of town, there was a tollgate. Part of the reason the tollgate was constructed at that location was to try and insure that everyone who used the road to Lynchburg paid a toll. The Lynchburg-Salem Pike follows the higher, relatively flat ridge crest toward town. At the tollgate the flat land falls very steeply on both the left and the right, leaving only a small area on either side of the road that deadbeats could use to go around the gate into Lynchburg free.

Early didn't want Hunter to go into Lynchburg free. About 1,500 feet east of the tollgate toward the city, Early established an outer-defense line. He was

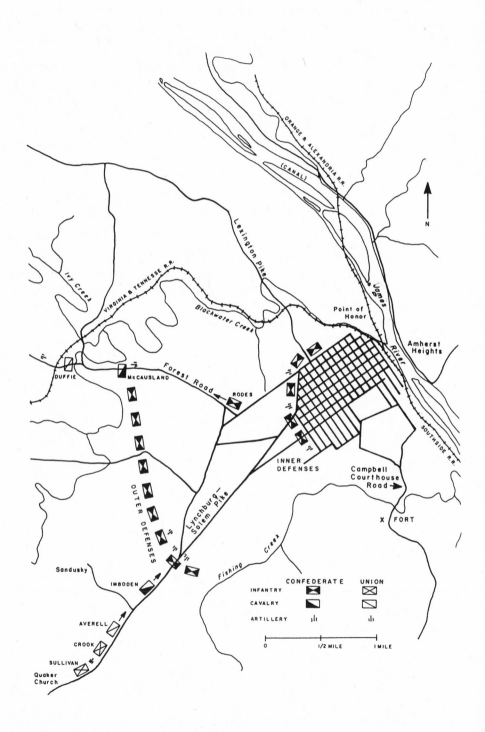

determined that if Hunter moved closer to Lynchburg, Hunter would pay a toll. Early used a redoubt constructed near the intersection of the Pike and a farm road entering from the right. (The present remains of the earthworks, "Fort Early," can be seen near the intersection of Fort Avenue and Memorial Avenue). From the fort, going both left and right, Early ordered trench works and breastworks constructed. The line to the left followed the crest to the Spring Hill Cemetery. There the line curved back along the hill toward town. The curve and the view it provided of Fishing Creek would make it difficult for Hunter either to turn or try to move about without being detected. The line to the left of the fort was approximately 1,000 yards long. The line to the right also generally followed the high ground. It extended approximately 3,350 yards (almost two miles) and covered other roads that could be used to approach the city. It dead ended on a hill which afforded a view of the Forest Road and Blackwater Creek.

The following events probably took place in the following order, but that cannot be proved beyond a shadow of a doubt. It appears that once Early approved the location of the line, he sent a courier to his troops camped near the inner-defensive line to move double-quick to the new line. He probably placed the responsibility for the actual construction on Hays and the staffs. It appears that because he wanted a better look at the enemy, Hill and he with their escorts rode west over the Pike.

Early's men had hurried to wait for the train and hurried to be told to rest in camp. They received another hurry order. Soon thousands of men with picks, shovels, and bare hands were moving dirt and rocks and were felling trees. These men knew that their lives could depend on a few inches of dirt. Time counted and protection counted, but neatness did not count. These men were experienced soldiers who said that they were at their "...old trade — fortifying."[107]

One resident, a Home Guard soldier, thought about Hunter's march from near Winchester to near the city; he knew the new line was being constructed and concluded, "...somebody would (be) hurt before the invaders got possession"[91] (of Lynchburg).

Possession of Lynchburg was the objective of the entire raid. Since shortly after noon, Averell and Crook had been watching Imboden at the Stone Church or Quaker Church about four miles from town. Hunter had sent word not to attack until the rest of the army came forward from New London. The church stood on a hill where Imboden had placed "...irregular rifle-pits and rail-fence barricades..."[109] to form a line. Imboden had three pieces of artillery with him on June 16, and he was reinforced by two more monster guns (20-pound Parrotts),[83] perhaps the Boys' Battery. There was probably some sniping as Averell's Cavalry attempted to slow Imboden's preparations.

It was about 2:00 p.m. when Sullivan's column began approaching the rear of Crook's army. The afternoon heat was intense. One soldier remembered seeing Hunter "...on his swaggering horse...(wearing) a straw hat...."[54] Hunter saw that the Rebels were "...strongly posted and entrenched...,"[8] and "...the enemy seemed determined to give battle in earnest."[34] Strother noted: "The chiefs looked troubled."[11] Not only were the "chiefs" troubled but also the "Indians" (common soldiers). "Many of the boys with pencils wrote their names, companies and regiments, and that of a parent or relative. By this means should the worst happen, they would not fill a nameless grave."[105] Despite the tension of the situation, there appeared to be no rush: "...everything went on as leisurely as (at) a legislature."[59]

Most sources agree that it was near 4:00 p.m. before the proceedings started in earnest. Crook and Averell had been in a position to attack since shortly after 12:00 noon. Hunter had ordered them not to start battle. During the afternoon, they watched Imboden's men preparing defenses. Now that Imboden's line would be much harder to take, Hunter ordered Averell and Crook to take on the task. Crook, the good soldier, made no recorded complaint at that time, but he was not happy that the delay would cause increased Union casualties.

As a general rule, cavalry should never attack an entrenched enemy that has artillery support. General Hunter committed another error this day. This time some cavalrymen would pay for the mistake with their lives.

"The ground made it very difficult to handle cavalry, being rough and broken by sharp ravines,"[34] noted one cavalryman. Averell placed his First Brigade under Col. J.N. Schoonmaker in the rear. Members remained mounted, forming a long skirmish line. Col. J.H. Oley's Second Brigade, formed on the right of the road. The men of Third Brigade (First and Second West Virginia) under Col. William Powell, were dismounted and placed to the left of the road. Dupont sent a section of artillery to support Averell.

Averell gave the order, and his cavalry advanced. There was some very light skirmishing as the cavalry division advanced. As the Third Brigade started up the hill there was "...a roar of muskets and carbines, and the crash of bigger guns. Powell's Cavalry was engaged...."[59] "...A rapid artillery fire was opened upon us, and their small-arms become unmasked,"[8] recorded a soldier.

Imboden records that he had three brigades; a Southerner estimates that there were 1,000[36] Confederates to oppose more than twice as many Union cavalrymen. "This cavalry, with their gallant leaders, was holding the enemy in check, which was a great achievement...,"[56] he wrote.

Averell ordered Oley's and Schoonmaker's commands to dismount and rush forward. Dupont's guns were also sent into action, and "...a sharp contest ensued."[8] Despite the increase in men and guns, terrain, trenches, and artillery were too much for Averell's Cavalry. It began to take casualties and fall back. Some Confederates left the breastworks and fought forward. It was no rout; the cavalry fell back in good order. It was plain to see that the cavalry had no chance to take the works without taking unacceptable casualties. Averell sent a note to Crook to bring in the infantry.

During this time, Duffié continued to push McCausland slowly back over the Forest Road. Early and Hill were swiftly riding toward the sound of fighting on the Pike. Also approaching the town from the north was Lt. Carter Berkeley with his two artillery pieces. Berkeley, a Staunton resident, was not familiar with the terrain in the Lynchburg area.

Only after Crook received Averell's courier did he let his true feelings show; "After waiting...I had to do all the work as it was, for I got no material assistance from anyone else."[73] Crook knew that there was "...a strong force in trenches between us and the city."[102] Crook was a good soldier: he would move them.

Crook had apparently seen Hunter's mistake in ordering the cavalry to attack a fortified position. He was ready when the messenger arrived. It appears that Crook neither requested nor received artillery support.

First Crook sent Second Brigade under Col. C. B. White to reinforce Averell's Cavalry. He didn't want a retreat turned into a rout.

He then sent Col. J.M. Campbell and the Third Brigade to flush the Rebels out of a section of woods on the Confederates' right.

The time was probably past 4:30 p.m. It appears that Early and Hill arrived on the scene at this time. Early rapidly surveyed the situation and concluded that Imboden could not hold the line very long against an infantry assault. Early was unsure as to the progress on his outer-defense line. If Hunter could move forward and attack the new line in force before it was ready, Hunter might achieve a victory. The more time Hunter spent going to a Quaker Church, the better chance Early felt that he would have. Early and Hill turned their horses about and galloped toward the new defense line.

As Crook's Second Brigade fell in behind Averell's retreating cavalry, the cavalrymen were more than willing to give up their position. They didn't want to be caught between their infantry and the Rebel trenches. The cavalry drew off to the Confederate left.

The Second Brigade moved forward "double-quick."[105] It was the Rebs, who were falling back. Those few of Imboden's men who had left the breastworks fell back to their positions. The Twelfth and the Ninety-First Ohio were apparently in the lead of the Second Brigade when it came "...under a heavy fire of grape, across some open fields...."[104] Then both regiments took considerable casualties including Colonel Turley of the Ninety-First with a fracture of his right thigh. The "double-quick" was slowed to a snail's pace. The infantry was having no more success against Imboden than the cavalry had had. Near the meeting house, Rebel Maj. Stephen P. Halsey was struck in the belt buckle. The bullet was nearly spent. The buckle broke half in two, but Halsey was not hurt. The guns sent to support Averell were now used to support Crook's men. The battery was not able to silence the Confederate artillery on the hill. A stalemate developed in the center.

Third Brigade on Imboden's right was continuing forward, but the cavalry McCausland had left (now commanded by Jackson) was making the movement a slow one.

With the center halted, Imboden was keeping a weary eye on both flanks. The advance on his right was threatening to cut off the Pike as an escape route. The cavalry massing on his left might round that flank also.

It appears that Berkeley's Battery rolled across the James River Bridge and into town during this time. The sound of battle four miles away could be heard

*Re-creation: Imboden's
men at Quaker meeting
house.*

in the city. Because many new units were in the city, because command changes had been made, and because all of the new commanders were at the front, Berkeley was unsure how he was to proceed. Inner-defense unit commanders knew that they were to stay in place but little more. A frustrated Berkeley decided on his own volition to move his guns toward battle. No one would take charge or give answers. The battle sound was straight ahead. Berkeley assumed that the shortest distance between two points was a straight line. The straight line went straight up Ninth Street to the top of a hill. They would go straight up the hill and into battle. With little rest for men or horses, they started forward.

During this time, Early had galloped to his troops working on the line. He told them to drop the shovels and get their guns and move as quickly forward as possible. Troops under Ramseur were at the redoubt. Some of these men had served in "Stonewall's Foot Cavalry." They moved forward at a run as "everything hinged on speed."[103]

Back at the church, Imboden knew that Early's men were supposed to be on their way, but they were not in sight. One of his guns, probably a 20-pounder, became "disabled."[101] Imboden was trying to hold the line until Early arrived. He could not have known that the advance of Early was only minutes away. He did know that the Union had pushed back the portion of his cavalry under Jackson. The road to the rear was cut. Jackson was continuing to fall back along the road, but it would allow him to move his cavalry safely toward town. Now he saw Averell's Cavalry make the expected move upon his left. If Averell advanced farther, the escape route up Fishing Creek would be taken. Imboden had held as long as possible. There was no Early to reinforce him. He had gambled that Early would come in time. There was no time to organize a retreat or to remove the artillery or spike it. His men had to run, and run now, for their lives.

Imboden had bought the defense of Lynchburg every second that he could, but it was reported: "Imboden's men were finished."[103] "Imboden's men stampeded."[113] "Momentary panic seized Imboden's fazzled men and they started to break for the rear."[103] The cavalrymen jumped on their horses which were tied behind the church out of harm's way. They galloped down the hill and raced along Fishing Creek toward the city. It seems that when they disappeared from the hill that the Union was unaware of the direction in which they traveled.

The Union soldiers did not know why the artillery and small arms fire decreased so rapidly. They just knew that it had decreased. The artillery was now unanswered from the hill. The cavalry and the infantry surged forward, and "...charged the Rebel position, driving the enemy in great confusion."[34] One soldier said "I noticed many of their horses were down and a few men...."[105] Averell's Cavalry ran upon the works; "...the West Virginia boys (were) clearing the Rebel barricades with a vault, and (were) using their clubbed muskets and bayonets in close quarters."[109] The Ninety-First Ohio was "gallantly capturing and bringing off the field a rifled gun...."[16] Crook took his just credit: "I defeated their troops, captured their artillery, and drove

their troops off the field."[73] General Hunter concurred: "Crook's Infantry...
made a brilliant advance upon the enemy, drove him from his works back...."[8]
Strother said, "...Crook's troops (were) driving the enemy in confusion."[11] The
Yankees had captured four pieces of artillery and many prisoners. As the
Union advance swept over the hill, only the one gun with the Ninety-First was
taken along. The other guns and ammunition were left on the field "by
mistake."[8]

The chiefs who had looked worried were beaming. They assumed that
they were facing "the bee," McCausland, who had stung them so many times
since Meadow Bluff. They had dealt him a critical blow, killing, wounding,
and capturing many of his men and artillery pieces. Was this the final desperate
act of the only soldiers between them and Lynchburg? It would appear so.

As soon as Jackson's men became aware that Imboden was high-tailing it,
they knew that their smaller force must do the same. They leaped onto their
horses and galloped down the Pike. "Here, and at this moment, the rout of our
grey-back friends became suddenly complete..,"[109] wrote one Union soldier.
The Union soldiers saw the Southern cavalry running down the road and
assumed that was the end of the whole force, unaware that Imboden's men
had moved down the hill and were now galloping toward town along Fishing
Creek.

Jackson's Cavalry had only moved a few hundred yards when a bugle
sounded. It was blown by a local boy Junius Tinsley, who had marched off to
war under Stonewall Jackson. He was blowing the horn to let the cavalry know
that the infantry was on its way. Most of the intended audience was galloping
down Fishing Creek.

When Jackson's men saw the few breathless men running toward the
Union advance, they knew what was likely to occur. There were too few of
them, and there was no time to form a line. The Union advance would eat
them up. An infantryman saw the cavalry coming and concluded, "Jackson's
Cavalry also ran...."[113] The cavalry knew that its infantry was only "...seven or
eight hundred yards from the Yankee infantry."[36]

Jackson's men halted and formed a skirmish line. They must slow the
Union advance until more infantry came forward. The Union advance was at
Jackson's front before the infantry came from the rear. The few Union soldiers
at the head of their advance saw the cavalry halt and form a line; they began
slinging lead at the new Rebel line. Jackson's men returned their fire.

As the men in the infantry arrived, they realized what the cavalry had done
for them: "They cheered all the time, especially loudly when they neared our
cavalry line and could hear the whistle of the bullets,"[36] said one cavalryman.

The Union soldiers pursuing the retreating cavalry did not realize that
infantry troops were moving toward them. One Yankee wondered how
"...they were keeping up a rapid fire with diminished numbers."[105]

As more and more Union and Confederate soldiers arrived, Jackson knew
that his work was done. According to one soldier the infantry "...took the
places of our dismounted cavalry, which withdrew and remounted."[36] It
started across country toward McCausland. The Northern attackers did not

see them ride off.

Early was very near the head of his troops. One soldier wrote: "During the war I saw General Early under fire on several occasions, and I do not hesitate to say that I have never known a man who seemed to be so utterly destitute of fear and so entirely insensible to danger."[114] Another soldier described Early: "General Early is about six feet high, and but for a stoop of the shoulder, caused by rheumatism, would be of fine figure. He is about fifty years of age, apparently well preserved, and a person who would be singled out in a crowd. A large white felt hat, ornamented by a dark feather, and an immense white, full cloth overcoat, extending to the heels, give him a striking and unique appearance. His face is remarkable and none could be more expressive of pertinacity and resolution. The will to do — the soul to dare, are unmistakably stamped on every lineament and expressed in every feature. The massive head, the broad, high forehead, the dark, piercing eye, the well cut nose, the compressed lips and thick set jaws are characters in which nature has written self-reliance and inflexible determination."[104]

Another writer recalled that Old Jube wore a "...broad, white slouch hat with its black feather!"[112]

Early arrived in time to see the cavalry withdraw. He galloped up to the defense line, "...stood up in his stirrups and, shaking his fist at the enemy, he bellowed out at them: 'No Buttermilk Rangers after you now, you damned Blue-Butts!'"[112] Others nearby recall Early cursing and damning the Yankees in similar terms.

Early was anxious to show those "damn Yankees" that they were now facing a crack unit of mean Confederate veterans. As soon as he had enough men on the line, he ordered an attack on the Union advance. His men "...in a frenzied counterattack...by regiments of the old Stonewall Brigade"[6] pushed the Yanks back. Perhaps Bugler Tinsley met his fate here. One soldier recalled, "Poor Tinsley! His last bugle call, like the bagpipes at Lucknow...but on that field he found, in a soldier's duty and with a soldier's glory, a soldier's death."[56]

The Union forces fell back and re-formed. They did not suspect that the troops they were now facing were infantry, not cavalry. The last time they fought the cavalry, the Southern horsemen were fighting dismounted. The artillerymen came forward. "They continued to fire over our line — helping us to drive the Rebs...,"[105] recorded one Union soldier.

Early had no artillery to provide counterfire. He directed his troops to fall back towards the protection of the new defense line. Early said, "The Yankees outnumbered our men and were constantly trying to flank, but every effort was repulsed."[36]

At the inner-defense line, soldiers watched "...the shells...exploding in the air while the Federals were fighting and pursuing Imboden from the beginning of the engagement...."[30] A lady recalled that she "...went on College Hill and watched the fighting...it was very exciting to watch the cannon-fire from both sides and the explosion of shells on the opposite side. It was fascinating beyond all description. I could see our troops moving and taking new positions, and could see the Yankee batteries doing the same thing, (she may have been observing McCausland and Duffié on the Forest Road) and then the fearful reality of the scene was forced upon me by a line of ambulances which was kept busy bringing the wounded men into town."[115]

Jackson's Cavalry traveled across country toward its old commander McCausland. The last report that Jackson had on the Union's advance was hours old. In the early morning, it was reported that the Union cavalry was advancing upon the Forest Depot; Jackson had set his course for that area.

Duffié had pushed through the Forest Depot and was attacking McCausland near the railroad bridge over Ivy Creek closer to Lynchburg. Duffié had his wagon train at a safe spot in the rear of the column at Forest Depot.

When Jackson arrived and surveyed the scene, he saw the wagons. Captain Moore with the Fourteenth Virginia decided the train was "...guarded by a brigade of infantry."[36] The need for supplies for this part of McCausland's command was great, and the prize below was tempting. Jackson recognized that it was neither a full brigade nor an infantry; otherwise he might not have attacked. The safe wagon was suddenly and "vigorously attacked"[36] by yelling, mounted Rebels. The startled defenders started running along the Forest Road toward Duffié. Few of the Confederates continued the pursuit. Greed and empty bellies caused most men to stop and "...see what was in these wagons...."[36]

The lack of pursuit allowed the Yankees to re-form and get reinforcements. Soon, "...those who were in front were driven back upon those behind them, confusion ensued, and we had to abandon all we had already taken except a few prisoners and a small number of wagons and horses,"[36] recorded a soldier.

Re-creation: Cavalry action near Forest Depot between Duffié's and Jackson's men.

When Jackson lost control of his men, he lost a valuable prize, a wagon train; he also lost eight to ten men,[36] killed, wounded, or captured. All the killed or the wounded, except Captain Smith of the Seventeenth Virginia, were left in enemy hands. Smith was taken to the nearest house away from the fighting. The last time his comrades in arms saw him, a resident was "...carrying water from a near-by well, bathing his face, when he was practically dead."[36]

Back in Lynchburg, Carter Berkeley was learning that in this city the shortest distance between two points may not be a straight line. His tired horses and men started up Ninth Street toward the old courthouse on the top of the hill. The straight up-grade was too much. He swung down a block to his left and started up an equally steep Eighth Street. Since the horses could pull no farther, he put "...several men at each wheel."[56] The guns and their powder wagons crept forward. Sweating men and horses moved the guns about one third of the way. "...There is a limit to human and equine endurance...;"[36] that limit had been reached. Guns, horses, and men could go no farther. About this time, the troops of Imboden's command were coming into town. They had apparently followed Fishing Creek to the Campbell Courthouse Road and then cut back into town. As they passed the foot of the hill, they saw Berkeley's plight. The men had been routed at the church; they knew every gun might be needed to stop Hunter. Without hesitation, they "...jumped from their horses, reinforced the steaming party, and soon had the guns to the top of the hill...."[56]

Once at the top of the hill, neither man nor beast was rested. Both rushed toward the battlefield on the Pike. As Berkeley galloped forward, Early was retreating. The Union Infantry advanced under a curtain of artillery fire. The exploding artillery shells had set part of the woods on fire. One soldier said it was "...now burning fiercely with a mighty crackling and roar, only pierced by the terror-stricken screams of the mangled men who lay beneath the flaming canopy of leaves and branches...."[59] Some Union soldiers stopped to help these men and others who were wounded. Most of the Union soldiers kept up the advance.

Apparently Berkeley's two guns had arrived at the redoubt only shortly before Early's retreat moved into the new defense line. Berkeley's guns were the only ones on line. Berkeley, a fighter, knew Hunter's massive artillery was moving toward him. He didn't want to leave the field after the defeat at Piedmont. As Imboden refused to consider supporting his artillery, he had to leave the battle. Without orders, he was preparing to fight.

The Yankees had been steadily pushing Early's Infantry back for almost two miles. Both sides had suffered a few casualties, but there were no signs of panic in the ranks. The sun was sinking low when Early's men moved back to the works. There along the line was the rest of Ramseur's and Gordon's Brigades.

Averell's Cavalry was the first Union unit to discover that the South was no longer running. "The enemy, driven to his field-works, received reinforcements, and confidently advanced to charge my line,"[8] recorded Averell. It was the Union who was retreating. When Union commanders realized that the Rebs had turned, they ordered the infantry and the artillery forward. Averell admitted that it was hard holding his position while he was waiting for infantry support. When the infantry and the artillery did arrive, they began to push the Rebs back to their earthworks — "...the boldness of the enemy was severely punished...."[8]

As the Union line began to approach the works, it came in range of Berkeley's guns in the redoubt. It was "...load, ram, fire! Load, ram, fire!"[103] As at the church, it was the Twelfth and Ninety-First Ohio that advanced in the center. They came under Berkeley's guns — "...the Rebel gunners evidently being skillful hands in the management of their pieces."[16]

Hunter came forward to get a closer look. Berkeley's guns sent ordnance flying close to the staff. Hunter withdrew apparently without seeing the defense work.

The Twelfth and Ninety-First Ohio were taking considerable casualties, but they were unable to advance. It appears that they too withdrew somewhat to lessen the effect of Berkeley's guns.

Dupont brought his batteries forward to a close range. Soon they were pouring "...shell, grape and canister..."[16] into the Rebel line.

Early did not know why this one Confederate battery was on line, but he was glad Berkeley was there. He knew Berkeley would need help to maintain the new line. He sent word back to the inner-defense line to send Lurty's and Floyd King's Batteries forward. He was familiar with these units. One account also states that only two guns of the Botetourt Artillery were requested.

As darkness approached, artillery fire increased. A Southern writer said that when the Yankees realized that they were not going to be able simply to walk into Lynchburg, they "...began a sullen artillery duel...."[103] Strother said that the cannonade was conducted with "great fury."[11] A common soldier echoed that it was a "furious fire."[16] Non-replaceable Union powder and shell were being flung at the Rebels. Few soldiers were aware of the extensive earthworks to their front. One soldier who did see them was not impressed, calling them "...thin field works."[105] Every soldier knew that the cannonade was only a prelude to a general assault. At darkness, the cannon fire ceased with no order to attack. The Yankees had pushed the Rebels all day; there was a grand cannonade: "...to the surprise of the troops...while the attack had been gloriously successful...it was halted in the enthusiasm of victory."[59] Lynchburg was only a stone's throw away. Many Federal soldiers felt that with one more push it would be theirs. Most men wanted to fight on. Some of their officers, including Colonel Powell, went to see Hunter with "...strenuous objections..."[7] that he had called a halt to further action. It was too dark to continue Hunter declared; his order would stand. The officer of the Ninety-First Ohio returned and told his men that Hunter would allow no further attack that day. "The curses that greeted this order were long and deep and loud...."[7] But the apex of opportunity was abandoned when the musketry of the evening sank into a random shot...."[59]

During the afternoon, Duffié had slowly pushed McCausland back. Because of the dense woods and the narrow road, Duffié was uncertain of the size or the composition of the force at his front. Near dark, Duffié halted his command near Clays Mill about five miles out of Lynchburg. Clays Mill was on the Blackwater Creek near the Virginia-Tennessee Railroad. When Duffié stopped his pursuit, McCausland continued to fall back across Blackwater Creek nearer Lynchburg, looking for a good defensive position. At that point, both the Forest Road and the Virginia-Tennessee cross the stream. The road bridge was burned, and McCausland assumed a position on the high ground overlooking the stream. By dark, fighting had ceased on the Forest Road also.

The attacks stopped near dark. Southerners said that they had "...arrested the progress of the Federals...."[58] Northern sources said they had "...utterly beaten and demoralized..."[109] the Rebels and "...had shut the enemy within..."[17] Lynchburg.

Duffié posted pickets. McCausland dug in. Both sides feared that they would be attacked during the night.

A bright moon was starting to shine as Hunter's men began to dig in from the Quaker Church forward to the outer-defense line of the city. The advance of the Union line was "...within speaking distance of the Rebel line."[83] Both sides could hear the sounds of shovel, hammer and axe as men threw up breastworks. Sharp-shooters of both sides kept keen eyes for any "...incautious man of either party (who) exposed himself too openly."[16] Early's men near Richmond had had more experience at trench warfare than most troops in the Valley. Southern "...sharp-shooters, many of whom, (were) armed with long-range rifles, and concealed in the tree tops, do severe execution,"[83] noted one soldier.

The artist, Strother, who had drawn many scenes in the Valley and who knew the people, was usually the one who selected the house to be used as quarters for the Union high command for the night. This night it was Hunter who chose the quarters. Hunter had Crook, Averell, and their staffs follow him as he turned north off the Lynchburg-Salem Pike onto a country lane. The First New York (Lincoln) Cavalry escorted them. Hunter knew where he was going, and he knew something of the terrain between his army and the city.

The group approached a "...beautiful residence...."[109] Hunter explained that the owner, Maj. George Christian Hutter, (U.S. Army retired) was an old acquaintance of his. Hutter was an elderly man, but once he and Hunter had served together long ago before the war. A soldier was led to believe that Hunter was "...in some degree of cousinship..."[109] with Hutter. Hunter was related to many of the people that he had burned out on his raid.

Any friendship that had once existed had been erased by time and the war. Hutter unwillingly opened his home "Sandusky." The cavalrymen surrounded the house and then entered. To make sure that it was safe, all family members were made prisoners. After the area and the house were secure, Hunter entered and had the former United States Major and Army Paymaster Hutter and his family released. It is assumed that Hunter attempted to open a cordial dialogue with the man just made prisoner in his home. There is no indication that Hutter either accepted or spurned Hunter's cordial overtures.

Hunter informed Hutter that his house was to be used as headquarters for the army commanders that night. The first order of business was for Hutter to

"Sandusky" — Lynchburg.

provide food for the men who had invited themselves to stay for the night.

The Signal Corps established a post on one of the chimneys of the house to keep the generals in communication with the army. Other soldiers continued the practice of looting. Hutter "had one only daughter, the divine..."[109] Ada Hutter, age eighteen, and she saw the Yankees looting. She was glad that a Southern soldier had stolen her brother Risques' horse "Rebel" earlier in the day so that no Yankee would sit upon "Rebel". The Yankees entered her room and stole her clothing and valuables.

When the food was served, it appears that Hunter allowed Hutter and his daughter to be seated. Hunter "...talked freely with Major Hutter, having known him as an army officer before the war."[106] Thornton Hinkle, the correspondent with the *Cincinnati Gazette*, might have also been present.

It was a jovial and happy time for the unwelcome guests. The army had moved approximately seventeen miles that day. Hunter's men thought that they had finally given that pesky bee, McCausland, a thorough mauling, capturing his artillery. They had no idea that they were facing Early. They were sure that the only forces between themselves and Lynchburg were those under Breckinridge. They had thoroughly beaten those forces at Piedmont; they thought that they could do it again the next day. The officers "...boasted that they would eat supper in the city Saturday night."[106] One officer said "Hutter observed that such a job would be difficult. Lynchburg citizens would resist...."[78] Hunter boasted that "...he could take Lynchburg easily and that the people had better not make any resistance."[106] Hutter said that even if Hunter took the city the Confederates would move to "...Amherst Heights and shell Hunter in the city."[78] "Good!" retorted Hunter. They "...would merely help him destroy the city."[78]

The young and pretty Miss Hutter confronted and condemned the aged Hunter for the wanton destruction of the Virginia Military Institute. In a high-handed manner, Hunter said, "You need not make a fuss about that, for I intend to burn the University of Virginia also."

Hunter and most of his staff would probably agree with a Northerner who wrote: "Thus far Hunter's campaign had been not only vigorous, but brilliantly successful."[17]

The conversation turned from battle and war to a more personal level. A New York soldier was close enough to hear the conversation which he labeled as "...ludicrously, though painfully amusing, to hear...."[109] The General and Strother inquired from Hutter as to the "...health of 'Cousin Kitty,' 'Aunt Sallie,' 'Cousin Joe,' or 'Uncle Bob'...(while all the time Union soldiers were) cleaning out smokehouses and granaries by wholesale...(leaving) the Rebel side (of the family) without a week's food in the house, without a single slave to do their bidding, and with horses, cattle, sheep, bacon, pigs, poultry, and so forth, things only to be recalled in ecstatic dreams."[109]

Strother noticed that the supper was good. Everyone noticed the beautiful Ada.

Averell learned that Ada's horse had been stolen. He probably believed that one of his cavalrymen had ridden off on the animal. He offered to replace the animal. This act of kindness changed Ada's opinion of all damn Yankees. All but one of them was still low life vermin, but Averell the man, not the Yankee, was a gentleman. Her true Southern heart beat faster for this dashing, handsome gentleman, even if he was dressed in the hated blue. Ada declined the offer, and there is no evidence that Averell attempted any flirtation with this sweet Southern belle, but he probably did.

Averell probably flirted with Ada, but the New York soldier could not take his eyes off her. He was smitten. He recalled "...her pure silvery voice...cheek blanching...clear olive pink...proud wooers must have come from far and near to court the sunshine of her smile...."[109] There was no room to attempt an advance upon this fairest Southern maiden in a room filled with generals. The soldier had to admire and hope from afar.

Strother had estimated that the Union had lost "...forty men killed and wounded";[11] it was estimated that Southern losses were much higher and that the artillery and seventy men[58] had been captured. Because none of the Union generals even suspected that they may be facing a different enemy than they had previously defeated, no prisoners were interrogated. Casualty reports began to trickle in. The Thirty-Sixth Ohio Infantry had three killed and seven wounded. The Twelfth Ohio reported seven killed and nine wounded. The Ninety-First Ohio lost its commander, Col. John A. Turley, who was severely wounded. It had a total of one officer and eight men killed and three officers and nineteen men wounded. The Eleventh West Virginia Infantry reported three wounded and two missing.[8] Company D, One Hundred and Twenty-

Third Ohio Infantry lost three killed and six wounded.[53] Crook was upset that Lt. Cyrus Roberts of his staff had been seriously wounded. Dupont was upset when one of his batteries reported "...empty ammunition chests...(and) no grain or feed for the horses...."[8] Not all was rosy for the Union Army. Col. Daniel Johnson of the Fourteenth West Virginia sent in no casualty figures for the day, but he wanted to be on the official record about one man under his command. He said the men of the Fourteenth had "...displayed great courage and heroism...with the single exception of First Lt. William H. Gillespie... (who) exhibited great cowardice, by dodging behind trees, stumps, etc....fell entirely behind...did not rejoin...until...the firing had ceased."[8]

The newspaperman, Hinkle, had been listening to these stories of victory, but these last fragmented reports caused him to ponder. Was Strother's estimate much too low? Had this day's victory caused much more than high command believed? He excused himself and followed a newspaperman's nose to try and find the truth.

Because Duffié was separated from the main army, Hunter received no casualty report from him.

Near dark at the outer-defense line, the action decreased. Col. Floyd King, a Southern gentleman and battery commander, rode to the houses near his guns to inform the people to move their families and their valuables to the cellars and to stay there until the danger had passed. Most people took his advice.

Near dark, the Botetourt Artillery received orders to move from Church Street. Because other artillery units had been moved from the inner-defenses to the outer-defenses, the Botetourt was assigned to the line on College Hill. Finally the guns could be unlimbered and positioned, and the horses could be unharnessed so that both man and beast could rest.

When it became clear to Early that Hunter was through fighting for the day, he returned to Lynchburg. The ailing Breckinridge was in a hotel there, but Early decided to headquarter at his brother William H. Early's house near the Washington Hotel.

Despite the sharp words that had passed between him and Rodes, Early knew that Rodes was a good soldier and would move his command and Terry's Brigade to North Garden Depot by this evening if at all possible. The slow empty trains had been sent over the rickety track toward Rodes in the afternoon. The big *if* was the railroad. If all went well, Rodes should start arriving some time near dawn in the morning. Would that be in time? Would Hunter launch a massive dawn attack, breach his lines, and move upon troops of questionable value in the inner-defense line? Time was all Early needed, and he would be more than willing to take Hunter on in combat. Early devised a trick to buy time. If he could make Hunter believe that Lynchburg had received massive reinforcements during the night, Hunter would not attack at dawn. He would be compelled to wait for light and reconnaissance parties to report before attacking. There was a switch engine with some cars on the Southside Railroad. These were ordered to move out from Lynchburg and then return to the city, blowing the whistle often. A band played loudly and soldiers shouted and cheered for the return of the empty trains. Early wanted Hunter to believe reinforcements were arriving in town. The train, the band, and the soldiers repeated their play many times throughout the night. A tired Early hoped that Hunter would believe his scheme as he retired for a few hours. The big question was would the Yankee Army hear and believe?

The signal station at Sandusky was busy. The first recorded time, 10:00 p.m., came from the One Hundred-Sixteenth Ohio Infantry which reported "...we heard the whistle of a locomotive and the rolling of a train."[14] Soon many regiments were telling headquarters, "We could hear the locomotive whistles as the trains came. We could hear the music of the bands, the rattle of the drums, the shouts of the troops and the populace. All night Lynchburg was in a fever of preparation. The next morning was lurid with forebodings."[59] The good soldier, Crook was also taken in. "...We could hear trains...bringing in reinforcements."[73] Hunter was not convinced, but he knew the high cost his army must pay if he was wrong. There would be no dawn attack until Rebel position and strength was ascertained. Early had won.

Some Confederate troops not at the city were fooled also. They believed that they were being reinforced.

Many Union troops remained unconcerned about reinforcements. They were sure that they would push into Lynchburg tomorrow. Some of the men who used to call Hunter "Black Dave" had now decided he was okay after all. Some affectionately called him "Uncle Dave."

Strother was not bothered by the train noises. He records that he went to bed and "slept profoundly."[11]

At Forest, Miss Lottie Hutter, the daughter of Maj. Edward Sextus Hutter, would spend the night on the roof of her home. She believed that the Yankee who threatened to burn the house in the morning, would attempt to carry out his threat that night, but the Yank did not return that night.

It is uncertain what time that night General Nicholls summoned the tax collector, Major Saunders, to his office. Apparently Saunders' comment that Hunter might not attack Lynchburg but march against undefended Danville, had been bothering Nicholls. Saunders' account of the incident, written long after the war, shows some errors in time and command structure, but it is apparent that the Confederate commanders believed a march south by Hunter was a possibility. Imboden detached "...fifty picked men"[91] and placed them under Saunders. The command then moved south of Lynchburg to watch the bridges over the Otter and Staunton Rivers. If Hunter were to move in that direction, bridges would be burned and the high command at Lynchburg notified.

The Union Army had left Buchanan relatively intact, but new fires burned that night. Most residents believed that Negroes had set the fires. It was rumored that Northern troops had told the blacks to continue to burn even after they left. It is not known how many houses and buildings were burned. Because no one was caught in the act, the townspeople did not know if the arsonist was white or black.

An important business, Obenshain's Tavern, was burned. It was "...truly

Obenshain's Tavern — Buchanan.

distressing to see the poor little children (Obenshain's) running about the
streets crying just as they had been dragged from their beds." The writer
continued, "There is a feeling of dread and uneasiness throughout the whole
community...whose house may go next."[92]

The time was approaching midnight. Early's army had been in town for
approximately eleven hours. The lines were only a few yards apart, and still an
event had not occurred. Why it had not occurred is not known. From the first
of the campaign, the Jessie Scouts had been providing good to excellent
service to the Union Army. Now that the army neared its goal, the Jessie Scouts
were failing miserably. Many other towns in the Valley that had less confusion
and fewer troops than Lynchburg were easily penetrated by these blue-bellies
with gray-backs. Lynchburg should have been penetrated and Hunter
informed of Confederate strength. Hunter had a major intelligence failure
within sight of his ultimate goal. It appears that Averell had failed to direct the
Jessie Scouts properly.

Newspaperman, Hinkle, made his way to the field hospital to get a better
idea of what the day's advance had cost the Union Army. When he entered the
compound, he noted, "...a great many of our brave boys have been killed or
wounded."[102] He went to see the head physician. When he entered the doctor's
quarters, he was shocked. Even the doctor could no longer cope with the
blood and the pain. Hinkle said, "I put Medical Director to bed *Drunk*."[102]
Hinkle then tried to help some of the drunken doctor's patients. Hinkle said

that he passed "...from group to group of the dead and dying. One little group, all the victims of only one shell, are mere boys, some of them fearfully mangled. It all appeals to my sympathies most powerfully...I shall never be able to forget the pitiful moans and cries of the poor anguished victims, nor can I describe the scene."[102] This is war.

All along the line there was movement. Neither army was familiar with the terrain. Commanders sought advantages for their units. The moon provided some light as leaders looked for the advantage of high ground or the protection of a ravine. One Ohio soldier, tired and disgusted, said, "...Our regiment had been moved from one point to another several times."[14]

Rebel commanders were doing the same. A voice called out in the dark, "What brigade is that?" The leader replied, "Gordon's Brigade of Early's Division. Who do you'uns belong to?" Perspiration broke out as the Ohio Yankee shouted back, "The same."[60] The nervous Yank quietly withdrew his men. There was no engagement, nor was Hunter's headquarters informed that it was Early's men at their front.

It was near midnight when both armies discovered that the other side was dismantling a rail fence between them. The rails were being carried back to reinforce breastworks on both sides. The Confederates decided that it was their fence and that the Yanks would have to fight for the next rail, and "A lively fire started...."[105] A major with the Eighteenth Connecticut was almost made prisoner. The Yanks decided that if the rails meant that much to the Southern boys, they could just have them. The Yanks withdrew and the firing stopped except for an occasional shot.

Twice within minutes at different points along the line, the individual Federal soldiers had backed down when the Confederates appeared. A change was occurring.

Only Strother and a few of the Union high command with a false sense of complacency slept well. Other Union officers heard the music and worried. Many soldiers spent the night marching and building defense works. The Union soldier seemed to suffer more: "The regiment did not get much rest during the night, *fearing an attack*."[41] Many Confederates rested in the inner and outer-defense lines. Many Southerners cheered for empty trains while the band sent musical barrages toward the enemy.

Saturday, June 18

On Saturday, June 18, the sounds of trains and men digging continued throughout the night hours. Periodically the sound of horse and rider could be heard. There was trouble communicating between the main army and Duffié at Clays Mill. As the crow flies, there was relatively little distance that separated the two army groups, but there were no roads on the Union side of the line that even faintly followed a direct path. Hours would be lost if Duffié used the roads to send a messenger to Hunter. The messenger would have to ride back toward Liberty several miles and take a road to New London and then proceed several more miles toward Lynchburg and Hunter.

Instead of losing time, Duffié was losing messengers. As riders attempted to go cross-country in the moonlight, they got lost and confused by the hills and the streams. Duffié records that he had sent several couriers to Hunter with reports and requests for orders but had not received a reply.

At Sandusky, Averell was complaining because he had heard nothing from Duffié. Averell, who had sent scouts looking for Duffié, complained that Duffié "...had lost himself on the extreme left."[8]

The sound of all those trains had finally prodded Averell into action. Scouts, presumably including Jessie Scouts, were sent out to obtain information.

Averell ordered Powell to circle Lynchburg to the south and attempt to cut the Southside Railroad. Powell was aware that many Union messengers were riding around lost in the darkness; since he was determined that it would not happen to his cavalry unit, he recruited a local for a guide. He might have used the point of a gun to instill a spirit of voluntarism in the Southern citizen.

After a brief rest, General Early arose at 2:00 a.m. He wondered if Hunter had fallen for his empty train trick and if the full trains from North Garden Depot would arrive in time.

Shortly after he arose, Early might have been informed that Breckinridge was feeling much better and believed that he could assume limited duty. Early ordered Breckinridge to move his troops from the inner-defenses to the right of the Lynchburg-Salem Pike on the outer-defensive ring. Vaughn had been relegated to operations with his brigade only. The brigade was moved from the inner-defenses to a hill overlooking Ivy Creek and the railroad bridge. There the men of the brigade began erecting an earth fortification, later known as Fort McCausland.

When Union troops and officers heard Breckinridge's troops marching forward in the darkness, they assumed that these were the reinforcements that were coming in on the trains they had been hearing.

Early rode along the line and inspected it. He made some readjustments in its course. This readjustment necessitated more vigorous digging and activity. Apparently Early did not request any additional artillery be sent forward. Perhaps he was waiting for his personal artillery which should arrive some time past daylight. He knew and trusted these units.

The occasional sharpshooters' round still pierced the night.

These night sounds increased the anxiety in Union camps. There was a fear that the Confederates would launch an all-out night attack. Both the infantry and the artillery were ordered to be ready to receive an attack. A Union soldier said, "At about 3 a.m. we were quietly roused, and stood to our arms, in anticipation of being attacked."[83] Worried officers sent messengers to their generals at Sandusky.

The drowsy generals received some reports. Both Crook and Sullivan were convinced that the Southern Army had been reinforced. Hunter was of the belief that no reinforcements could have been sent from Lee because Grant was pressing him hard at Richmond. The generals moved toward their troops.

The commotion in the Hutter house woke the sleeping family. The smitten soldier who had watched the beautiful Ada at the dinner table the night before was awakened in time to see her enter the drawing room. She went to the window and opened the blind and looked toward the east for any sign that the dawn would come again. While staring into the darkness, she said, "Oh, how I pray for peace." Then turning and staring directly into the soldier's face she addressed him with her silvery voice, "Do not misunderstand me, however; do not think I crave, or would accept, that peace you talk about — the peace of subjugation; for I am Southern in every fibre...."[109] It was the soldier's big chance. He saw that her "...eyes kindled brighter, her cheek took a deeper flush, and her musical voice swept upward..."[109] but the soldier's mouth would not work. It was stuck tighter than a clam with lockjaw.

His silence did not make her mute. She continued, "This dress I wear — I have carded, and spun, and cut out, and put together with my own hands. Oh, we have given up everything for the cause, save the barest necessaries of life; and I cannot believe that God would allow a people to suffer so much as we have done, if not intending to reward us with final victory."[109] If she had only said the word, the soldier would probably have conceded the war and would have willingly become her prisoner. Words and feelings were there, but the mouth just wouldn't work. Within a few minutes, the two would part never to see each other again. He knew something of her patriotism, but she would never know of his romantic feeling for her.

The first fingers of early dawn light were reaching upward from the eastern horizon when Captain Duncan roused his 200 men of the Fourteenth Pennsylvania Cavalry. They had been detached at Liberty and sent to see if Breckinridge was at Balcony Falls, but Breckinridge was not there. There is no report that the Fourteenth even attempted to destroy the locks on the James River as it passed Big Island, heading toward Lynchburg. It is assumed that the cavalrymen were riding over the Lexington Pike toward Lynchburg. There could have been some gray-back, Jessie Scouts among the blue-clad cavalrymen. The Pike was guarded by a handful of Home Guard men near Lynchburg.

Locks on James River canal near Big Island.

Back in the pre-dawn darkness near Sandusky, Averell probably informed
Hunter that Duffié was "lost." There is little doubt that Averell missed an
opportunity to take a verbal jab at Duffié's competency. Since Hunter wanted
all of his strength to be used against the city, he directed Averell to send most of
the First New York Cavalry to Duffié. It was intended that the First New York
would prod Duffié into making a vigorous attack. The First New York might
have also secured a local guide.

It was a cool morning, but as the sun broke through, it was bright and clear
with a promise of a hot day. The lines were only a few hundred yards apart,
and each studied the other's fortifications. One soldier reported: "About
sunrise, the Rebels opened the ball...."[83] The Confederates had seized the
initiative during the night, and with daylight, they continued pressing the issue.
Sharpshooters' fire increased as the sun rose. The long-range rifle perhaps with
telescopic sight, in the hand of a Southern marksman was taking a telling effect
on the Union infantry.

Even with the sharpshooter fire Hunter at times exposed himself. He
recalled, "...I reconnoitered the lines, hoping to find a weak interval through
which I might push with my infantry, passing between the main redoubts
which appeared too strong for a direct assault."[8] Despite what his generals
were saying, Hunter remained convinced that the troops he saw were the same
ones he had defeated at Piedmont.

While Hunter was reconnoitering on the Lynchburg-Salem Pike, Duffié
had started advancing slowly toward the city on the Forest Road. It was
Duffié's hope that he would receive orders from Hunter. Because McCausland
had withdrawn across Ivy Creek, Duffié encountered only an occasional
incoming round from one of McCausland's skirmishers.

As Duffié moved toward the city, the Botetourt Artillery was moving out
of the city. Early had recognized the weak defense on the city's north and had
sent the artillery to reinforce McCausland.

The Confederates had started the action with sniping at dawn. At
approximately 7:00 a.m. Southern "...guns on the Salem Pike opened a slow
fire, probing Federal positions, but could stir up little reaction."[103] Dupont
realized that he had no ammunition to spare.

Hunter wished a better look at the redoubt on the Pike. The staff foolishly
rode forward to open ground. Confederate gunners saw the party of riders
(perhaps forty in number) but probably didn't know their identity. The group
offered a perfect target, and apparently all the guns within range opened on
the staff. Rebel gunners slung hot lead. One Union soldier recalled, "...The
projectiles whistled just over our heads...."[47] Hunter knew that the time for
musing was past, and all of the riders made for the woods. Apparently
Southern gunners attempted to follow their prey with shell across the terrain.

Union gunners recognized that their leader and his staff were under fire.
Most Union guns replied to the Southern fire. Captain Glassie with the First
Kentucky Battery recalled that his guns did not fire at first because he was
caught during one of the many continuing troop locations. He rushed the guns
to a new location and soon was able to join in the cannonade.

Once the staff was safely in the woods, Dupont had time to contemplate those Rebel guns. "The marksmanship of this Confederate battery was so far superior to anything we had encountered..."[47] he wrote later. The train whistles, the more aggressive Rebs, and now these guns: Dupont was now convinced that he was facing a different enemy.

He approached Hunter and said, "General, this is the work of some new artillery. The people with whom we have been dealing could never have made such good practice." The short-tempered Hunter dismissed this latest suggestion of new troops by replying, "...This is nonsense and...the only hostile guns at Lynchburg were those whom we had met at Piedmont and previously throughout the campaign."[97] Hunter's reply did not change Dupont's theory, but the gruff tone of his voice let Dupont know quickly that Hunter wanted no more discussion on the subject.

Not only was there increased cannon fire, but more rifles smoked along the line. It seems that the long-range rifles were besting their Union counterparts.

Early's men had studied under General Lee. They had graduated at Cold Harbor. They were more accustomed to heavy cannonades and trench warfare than their foe across the line. Hunter's counterfire did little damage to the Confederates in comparison with Union losses. For example, the chaplain with the Eighteenth Connecticut wrote that the men were relaxing and enjoying an after breakfast smoke when the cannonade suddenly started. Two-timed fused shells exploded in rapid succession. When smoke and dust cleared, the Color Bearer, Serg. C.A. Tourtelott (Co H) and Private E.R. Wood (Co B) lay severely bleeding. Wood's leg was "shattered."[41] Bursting shells were accented with screams of anguish. Soon the Regimental Commander with the Eighteenth, Colonel Ely, joined the casualty list with a throat wound from flying shell. Hunter and the regiment had lost a good and trusted leader.

Dupont, who was near the Confederate line, could see that his artillery was not doing much damage. He knew that the powder supply was not high and that there would be no replenishment unless they took Lynchburg. With Hunter's blessing, Dupont left the staff to go and move the guns off line to save powder. This withdrawal of the artillery caused Hunter's other generals also to leave to shift troops back.

One Union infantryman noted, "The Rebels did some of the best artillery firing we ever saw, and our battery had scarcely opened fire before it was obliged to retire to shelter."[14]

It took Dupont twenty to thirty minutes to complete his backward movement. Since the Union cannons had been removed, Southern gunners slowed their firing rate. Somewhat of a lull developed. Only occasional cannon or rifle fire came from the Southern line and then only when Northern soldiers exposed themselves.

One soldier with the Fifth West Virginia had gotten fed up with all the maneuvering in the dark. He said, "...It appeared that the general didn't know what to do."[21] The soldiers were tired and frustrated, and they almost universally believed that the Rebels had been reinforced. All had confidence, however, that they could defeat the Rebs one more time and take their goal only a couple of miles away.

Not all men can be soldiers. Not all men in soldiers uniforms can tolerate death, blood, and noise. Colonel Johnson of the Fourteenth West Virginia Infantry had complained about the cowardice of Lieutenant Gillespie. Neither the lecture nor the night of relative quiet had settled Gillespie's nerves. At the first sound of cannons "...he again abandoned his regiment, (and) went to the rear...,"[8] said Colonel Johnson. Colonel Johnson "dismissed"[8] Gillespie from the service.

On the far right, Duffié had been advancing very slowly. At 9:00 a.m.,[8] the advance struck McCausland's pickets on the north side of Blackwater Creek. Although it was only minor resistance, Duffié's advance stopped and called for artillery support. Soon the artillery was brought on line, and shelling of the pickets south of Blackwater Creek began.

As the Union commenced the cannonade, the four Confederate guns from the Botetourt Artillery were facing toward the battle sounds. They arrived and took position on the Halsey farm near Ivy Creek.

With the increase in artillery pressure, Duffie's advance pushed forward. One Union soldier noted that the "Confederate skirmishers drew back slowly, contesting each inch of ground...."[103]

Duffie wanted to launch a vigorous attack, but the terrain prevented it. The road was narrow, the landscape was broken, and the foliage was thick. Duffie dismounted most of his men and sent them forward. Because of the thick undergrowth, Federals could not operate as a unit. They moved forward in small groups and as individuals. Because of the foliage, they were uncertain where their own troops were and only "...occasionally a puff of smoke would pinpoint a man lurking behind a tree...."[103] They knew that the Rebels were there, "but no line of battle showed itself....McCausland's men had refined delaying tactics to an art...."[103] Despite their difficulty, overwhelming Union numbers forced McCausland's men in a "brisk encounter"[8] to start falling back.

McCausland's pickets had done the job, and they began to fall back across Blackwater Creek and took position with McCausland's main body on the hills above the creek. Here Vaughn's Infantry supported them. Duffié states that it was the South that partially destroyed their own rail bridge as they retreated.

As the last of the pickets crossed the small stream, the advance of the Union cavalry began to emerge. By now the Botetourt Artillery was in position. It began to shell the Union formation. The definitive history of the unit states that all six guns of the battery were deployed, "...two 3-inch ordnance rifles were located just to the right of the road...near the Soap Stone Quarry...two 6-pounder Smooth Bores and the two 12-pounder Howitzers were located to the left of Forest Road."[77] Southern artillery "...did great execution."[101] A member of the artillery battery recalled we "...were just in time to drive the enemy back from the railroad and a railroad bridge over Ivy Creek they were trying to burn."[76] Apparently small groups of Union cavalry made several uncoordinated attempts to cross the stream, but each attempt was turned back by cannon fire and McCausland's small arm fire.

An incident occurred that shows the abundance of Confederate artillery and Early's apparent lack of knowledge that he had this much fire power available to him. One of the Botetourt guns burst while it was being fired. There was unused artillery simply sitting idly in the city. The battery commander told Lt. F.G. Obenchain and his crew to take the disabled gun to the city and "...get a new one."[76] It seems inconceivable that Early would allow any artillery to remain parked instead of having it on line.

Through the dense trees, Duffié could see the stream, the hills, and some of McCausland's breastworks. He could hear Southern artillery booming. Could that be entrenched infantry at his front? Duffié halted the advance and began to consider his next move. There were occasional shots exchanged, but hostilities were at a minimum.

McCausland sent word to Early about the Union advance, and added that the lines were now stable.

Back in the city, hospital staffs were ordered "...not to leave their posts...expected great numbers of wounded...."[78] The city rumor mill was still active. There was much talk, especially among the citizens and Home Guard, that Hunter "...had the aid of several notorious local traitors...."[56] Rumors stated that Hunter was not only receiving intelligence on the city's defenses but that locals were actually directing Union troop movement upon the city. These supposed traitors were roundly condemned. The local leading Powell's Cavalry as it moved toward the Southside Railroad, south of the city, was a hero, not a traitor. Since the dark early morning hours, the Yankee column had been wandering through the hills getting no closer to its objective. It took several hours of daylight riding before Powell realized that this guide was taking him on a trip to nowhere. The "...command was led in the wrong direction, it was thought intentionally, by the citizen guide, whose life paid the penalty of the act."[34] Powell attempted to determine his location and then moved toward the railroad. The adventurous engineer, Lieutenant Meigs, accompanied the cavalry outfit.

Back near the Salem Pike, one soldier noted: "Our national flag was made fast to the roof of a large barn, in plain view of the enemy. They tried to dislodge it. It afforded us some amusement as we watched them waste their ammunition."[18] Another Yank with the One Hundred Sixteenth Ohio was not amused: "Their sharp-shooters were...extremely accurate in their aim; they seemed to know the ground perfectly."[14]

It seems clear that the morale factor was swinging decidedly to the Confederates' favor. A Southerner said, "We had an abiding faith in the ability of 'Old Jube' ...to thrash Hunter most soundly."[116] On the Union side, low morale was leading to griping, especially about the lack of food. When an officer informed Hunter that the soldiers were complaining, Hunter said, "Tell them there is plenty of food — in Lynchburg."[109]

The train whistles of the night before had colored the judgement of most of Hunter's generals. They believed that massive reinforcements had been moved to their front. Crook's perceptions were typical of the other officers. When he looked through his field glasses, he saw "...the vast increase of troops...."[73]

Hunter was struggling with the same issue. How could it be? How could General Lee have sent a large force if Grant was still applying pressure at Richmond? Hunter had marched and fought from Winchester. Now the spires of the churches only two miles away in Lynchburg could be seen. Could he have come this far, lost so many men, and at the fringe of his goal, be turned back? Hunter was trying not to accept this new opinion of his generals. Everyone the night before had agreed that it would be easy to take Lynchburg, and he did not want that opinion changed.

Strother had been noting the Confederates' use of long-range rifles. He was close to Hunter when one of the bullets passed by. Strother stated, "The sound of these rifles suggested the presence of Richmond troops among the defenders."[11] Strother was still in the good graces of Hunter. Strother was the only member of the staff that had supported the burning order for the Virginia Military Institute. Hunter could not ignore Strother's opinion. Hunter decided "To settle the question...."[8] He sent orders for Sullivan and Crook to advance upon the works.

On the other side of the line, Early was probably lifting his eyes heavenward. "He could not be called a man who walked humbly with the Lord...."[123] The profane general was not praying. It was near 10:00 a.m. The sun was high in the sky. Where the hell was Rodes? Early had expected the second half of the Second Corps by now, but the trains to transport Rodes were only now pulling into North Garden Depot.

While orders were passed and preparations to attack were being made along the Salem Pike, Duffié was receiving two full squads of the First New York Cavalrymen from Averell. The orders to Duffié were as follows: "Do what must be done, but do it more vigorously...."[103] It was 10:30 a.m., and Duffié was determined to carry out orders. He placed one column on the Forest Road and flanked that column with a column to each side. A Southern observer wrote that he "distinctly saw a large body of cavalry, which he supposed to be about 4,000 drawn up in line of battle...."[101] Duffié also positioned his two artillery pieces to support the attack.

The Southern defenders had dug in and were waiting. The Botetourt Artillery was now back to full strength: Lieutenant Obenchain had returned with a new gun.

Blackwater Creek is narrow but deep. There was swamp land to the side of the Forest Road bridge. Because the banks leading toward the Confederate position were steep, Duffié would be forced to attack on a narrow front.

Apparently Southern cannons started to bark when the advance of Duffié's army came in range. The Union artillery replied in kind. McCausland believed that the Union was getting ready for a mass assault; he sent orders to the artillery to change their ordnance from long-range shot and shell to short-range lethal canister.

Southern guns fell silent as the Rebel artillerists switched ordnance. Duffié believed his artillery had "...silenced Confederate batteries. Encouraged he ordered the attack...."[103] The First New York attacked the Confederate right across the stream while two squadrons of the Twelfth Pennsylvania Cavalry charged the bridge in the center.

The morale of these Union troops was high. One Rebel said, "They charged upon our fortifications with great spirit yelling defiance and at the top of their voices."[101] Some troops taunted the Confederates by shouting, "Come out of your holes, you damn Rebels, we've got you now, come out of your holes."[101]

Fire did start coming out of the Confederate holes. Duffié was unaware of "...the enemy's infantry, which lay concealed beyond the bridge...."[8] One soldier noted that "When those infuriated wretches got within reach of our grape and canister our boys let fly a volley at them which did terrible execution."[101] The previously silent Rebel guns "...opened from all their works."[8] "Two other volleys were poured into them, when they broke and fled,"[101] reported another Rebel soldier.

Duffié saw the attack on the right and center break "...and the men fell back, badly chopped up."[103] Hoping to pull victory from defeat, he sent orders to advance to the Fifteenth New York on the left. The men of the Fifteenth were aware of what had just happened and started the advance. When Confederate gunners turned their attention on the new advance, the Yanks quickly retreated. They took virtually no casualties. There were many men lying dead and wounded on the left and near the bridge. Duffié's grand assault had lasted only a few minutes, but that was long enough to convince Duffié that he would not use the Forest Road to ride into Lynchburg.

McCausland sent a courier to Early to inform him of the preceding action and that of their present position.

It was "at 11:00 precisely...,"[101] and the smoke was clearing on the Forest Road when Hunter started his attack along the Salem Pike. Early was ready. The redoubt, the rifle pits, and the breastworks were mostly dug and manned. Berkeley's artillery was presumably still in the redoubt. Chapman's and Lowry's Batteries were also in or near the redoubt. Part of Bryan's guns were to the right of Chapman's and Lowry's. Lurty's Battery was on the left of Salem Pike near the redoubt. The first and the third sections of Bryan's Battery were held in reserve near the Spring Hill Cemetery on the far left.

Hunter advanced Sullivan toward the city along the right side of Salem Pike. Dupont's Artillery occupied the center, and Crook's army was on the left. Two squadrons of Averell's Cavalry were sent to the extreme left.

The high ground was narrow toward the tollgate with steep ravines to the left and right. It was heavily wooded on the left but largely open to the front and the center. The advance would be made along a narrow front.

Apparently Early had just finished filling his canteen at a well near the tollgate and had ridden back past the defensive line when the skirmishing began. The Federals opened "...a brisk fire..."[56] on the Confederate pickets who returned the fire, and artillery on each side roared. A Southern observer could clearly see the Confederate skirmish line approximately 100 yards in advance of the defensive line. However, within minutes the line was not visible. Smoke from rifles, cannons, and exploding shells combined with dust to hide the action. Along the line massive Union infantry advanced. The pickets knew that it was their job to prevent an attack from being launched and surprising the defenders at the main defense line. They were not expected to hold the line against a massive attack. The soldiers in the Southern picket line broke and ran for about fifty yards. Here they regrouped. A "gallant major"[117] helped re-form the men. With the Confederate artillery support, the line held for twenty minutes. The cannonading was described as "furious."[101]

Sullivan attempted to advance on the right over open ground. The fire from the skirmish line and defense works was too great. Once within Confederate gunners' range, Sullivan made virtually no progress.

Because of the woods, Crook could move closer.

The gallant major who had rallied his men was shot in the neck. He was taken to the rear. The increased Union pressure was too much, and the Rebel pickets broke. They used a ravine going toward Fishing Creek as they tried to escape. Not all of them made it.

The brisk action had lasted forty-five minutes.[8] The Union Army had cleared out the Confederate skirmishers, then they faced the main defensive works. The objective of the push was not to take the works but to gain information. There were but few Union soldiers killed or wounded. There were no accounts that any Confederates died, but some were wounded. The Union forces didn't want to kill the Confederates: they wanted to capture them. The Federals had succeeded in taking five prisoners.[96] Confederate artillery and sharpshooters kept the Northern Army pinned down, but the Southern prisoners were sent to the rear for interrogation.

Hunter was probably present when the prisoners were brought in. Soon it was learned that these were Early's men from Richmond. This was proof positive that Sheridan's Cavalry had been defeated and had turned back and that Lee had the upper hand on Grant and could send a large force to Lynchburg. Hunter also learned that "...the remaining divisions (of Early's army) were coming rapidly, by rail...It was now evident that the Army of West Virginia was in a critical position, two hundred and fifty miles from its base with ammunition nearly exhausted and commissariat entirely so...."[16]

Hunter could no longer deny the facts. He knew that he was in trouble. When the balance of Early's force arrived, he would face a superior army with a supply base. Hunter had no supply base.

It was Hunter's opinion and the opinions of most of his army that, "We must and would take Lynchburg at all hazards; rations we must have and we could only get them in Lynchburg. We could never retreat, that was impossible; if we were not all captured we should most certainly starve."[118]

Early sent orders to send the remainder of Bryan's Battery from the Cemetery to his position on the Pike. Other units may have also been moved forward to strengthen the line.

It was uncertain what thoughts were coursing through Gen. David Hunter's mind. Maybe the words of Crook spoken at the war conference in Staunton came echoing back: "Things change; things change." Maybe then Hunter realized that he had squandered one of the most valuable commodities of war

— time. The short marches, the frequent rest days, time wasted burning, especially at Lexington — these delays wasted valuable time. Perhaps he thought about Averell's plan to be at Lynchburg in five days. After agreeing to the plan, Hunter had only himself to blame for abandoning the timetable. It was now abundantly clear to him that the hand of time was now a closed fist to him and the whole Union Army. Hunter probably wondered if Early on the other side of the line realized that now time was his weapon.

While Hunter contemplated the situation and looked for options, Chief-of-Staff Strother rode to the front line to assess the situation.

At the front, a cannon spoke and a shell exploded occasionally. The air whistled with a periodic bullet from a sharpshooter's rifle, as "...General Early rode leisurely..."[117] forward to assess the situation. The Union artillery had destroyed an ambulance and killed a couple of horses but had done no real damage to troops or fortifications. Early saw either a weakness or an opportunity in the line. He sent men forward with picks and shovels to throw up rifle pits. Early anxiously scanned Hunter's line for an indication of the Federals' next move. Would the Union regroup for a mass attack on his line? Early wished to seize the offensive, but without Rodes he dared not. It would cost the Confederacy its life if Lynchburg fell: that far outweighed the benefit of beating Hunter. The risk was too great if he lost, to launch an offensive move upon Hunter. Early continued to watch, bringing men on line and waiting on Hunter and Rodes.

At 12:30 the booming of guns could be heard along the Forest Road near Ivy Creek. Duffié later claimed that he had launched another attack on the Confederate works. This claim was probably not true. Duffié knew that a cavalry attack upon entrenched troops, part of which were infantry, that were supported by superior artillery would simply lead to another repulse. Confederate observers were probably more accurate. One Confederate stated: "Finally they gave it up, placed a battery on the high grounds beyond the railroad, and spent the rest of the day shelling us. We replied in kind...."[76] Another Confederate said that he saw the Union cavalry "demonstration." When the cannonade started, "We were then entertained for about one hour by a pretty artillery duel."[91] Duffié knew that if the short-tempered Hunter heard all the racket from the cannons, he would think that the cavalry was fighting as hard as possible. Duffié would later also claim that McCausland attempted to seize the offensive and turn his flank. Probably it was not true. If Early would not allow himself to go on the offensive, would he dare allow the cavalry to attack in a sector where he had never personally inspected? Never! Duffié checked the paper attack on his flank by sending a force to oppose it. Duffié won an action, and never a shot was fired nor were any troops moved.

General Early, hearing the cannons boom, was deeply concerned. McCausland must hold until Rodes arrived. Early could not leave his line upon the Pike. Hunter had two infantry divisions that might attack at any time.

General Hunter also heard the cannons boom. The heat was oppressive and so was Strother's report from the front. Strother said that both officers and soldiers were hugging the ground for dear life. The Confederate sharpshooters were shooting at anything that moved. Men were hiding behind trees and beside logs, and lying in depressions. He told Hunter of a conference he had held with Colonel Thoburn and General Sullivan while "...lying on the ground on some boards."[11] Sullivan told Strother to inform Hunter that the enemy was "...very much strengthened and were pressing his hand. He was sustaining himself with difficulty...(but would) attack if ordered but he felt assured it would end in disaster."[11] Strother went on to quiz Sullivan. If Hunter did order an attack, where should it be made? Sullivan replied, "He had no choice...so convinced was he (Sullivan) that the enemy was strongly reinforced."[11] Hunter was "dissatisfied"[11] but issued no orders. Hunter knew that time and options were running out for him. While his boss agonized, Strother took a nap.

Finally Averell returned from his movement on the Confederate far left. Had Averell attacked, Hunter wanted to know. Averell replied in the negative for "...they had encountered a large body of Rebel cavalry in that quarter...."[56] Hunter was elated. Not that Averell had remained inactive but that a large section of Early's line was manned by a weak cavalry unit which had been pushed back and mauled repeatedly. (Imboden's Cavalry was not on the line, but it was at the inner-defenses). It was going to be Piedmont all over again! Just as at Piedmont, Hunter saw only defeat and retreat until the weak spot on the Confederate right was found. Now the weak spot was on the left, but the result could be the same.

Moments ago Hunter was awash in bad news and defeatism. Now with equal force, waves of optimism and hope filled his thoughts. It all came together clearly. Duffié's loud action on the Forest Road must be commanding Early's attention to focus on the right. Perhaps Early would shift men from the line to meet Duffié and weaken the center or left. Sullivan was on the Confederate right near Salem Pike. His report was that of a defeated man. The man Hunter needed, the good soldier Crook, was on the right. He was nearest the weak point in the line.

Time was critical. Hunter must strike before the balance of Second Corps arrived. He issued hasty orders.

Apparently both Averell and Dupont were near headquarters. Hunter told them of his plan to pull Crook off line and send him to attack the Southern cavalry. This plan would weaken the center. Dupont said, "...I had no hesitation in telling General Hunter that the artillery could repel a frontal assault upon our center...."[47] Dupont began making arrangements and shifting guns to hold the center if Early attacked.

Hunter told Averell to take position in the rear. The cavalry would be used when Crook turned the flank. No doubt a platoon was sent to Crook to lead his command to the Rebel line manned by cavalrymen.

Crook received his orders to move a brigade off line undetected and to go to the Confederate left and to look for the weak spot. Writing much later, Crook states that the movement was made "...with my division...(in the) morning...."[8] Other accounts place the time near 1:00 p.m. with one brigade or less. Crook states that he made "...a *reconnaissance* for the purpose of turning the enemy's left."[8] (Reconnaissance clearly indicates far fewer men than the whole division).

Crook sent a request to Dupont to send him artillery support once he moved off line. Dupont sent Carlin's Battery (six guns) to Crook, leaving Dupont twenty-six guns to defend the narrow front.

Hunter also sent orders to Sullivan and the infantry to demonstrate in order to hold the Rebels' attention so that Crook could move off line undetected.

While Hunter issued orders and troops deployed, Hunter's chief aide, his Chief-of-Staff, snoozed.

Soldiers grumbled about being deployed again and again. Captain Glassie with the First Kentucky Battery complained: "I am again changing my position; he (Dupont) ordered me to the extreme left of the line...supported by the Eighteenth Connecticut Infantry. I moved under cover of a hill...where my guns were well covered until I was ready to open."

It was approximately 1:00 p.m. General Early had been listening to Duffié's guns and watching with a weary eye the movements to his front. Rodes had not arrived; surely this was the big push that Early had been anticipating since dawn.

At the precise time, Glassie issued orders. He later reported, "...I ran my guns up by hand and opened directly on the enemy's flank, surprising and driving them from their guns."[8]

With Duffié's guns still sounding, Early heard the Union artillery at his front open and saw the infantry advance. "This is it," he thought. Southern guns joined the fray. When all the noise interrupted Strother's nap, he returned to duty. On the other side of the line, Early records, "...an attack was made on our line, to the right of the turnpike...."[119] A Southern defender said, "I had seen a great deal of fighting, but had never seen such bulldog tenacity."[36]

The Rebels thought that it was the main attack, but it was only a demonstration to allow Crook to pull off line. Early was happy that the attack "...was handsomely repulsed with considerable loss to the enemy."[119] A Union soldier back from the battle who did not know that it was only a demonstration came to the same conclusion as the Rebel general. He recalled, "Various charges that we made up the hills on which the earthworks stood were heavily repulsed...."[109] Neither the Rebel general nor the Yankee soldier saw "...Crook's men (as they) disappeared in the woods."[60]

Hunter's plan was working. The level of activity decreased along the Pike. Again orders were sent, and many units changed position.

The attack was brief but noisy. Early scanned the Union line and wondered was that it? Was Hunter beaten? Some artillery and infantry units were clearly seen falling back. Was Hunter "...a malignant and cowardly fanatic, who was better qualified to make war upon helpless women and children than upon armed soldiers?"[56] Had Hunter lost the stomach for a fight?

Some time on June 18, General Lee personally telegraphed General Early. The message might have been delivered during this time frame. Usually it was Lee who was one step ahead of Grant, but now it was Grant who was knocking at the door in Petersburg before Lee was aware that he was there. Grant almost took Petersburg before Lee could react. Lee sent the following telegram to

Early:

> Grant is in front of Petersburg. Will be opposed there. *Strike as quick as you can*, and, if circumstances authorize, carry out the original plan, or move upon Petersburg *without delay*.   R.E. Lee[8]

Early believed that Hunter's force was larger than his, but it had exhibited no fire in the last attack. Early sent orders that his unit was going hunting for Hunter.

Occasionally artillery still boomed, and balls whizzed through the air. A soldier in the open had a short life expectancy. When lines stopped moving either forward or backward soldiers began to dig into mother earth for protection. Some of Crook's troops on the left of the Pike started digging into loose ground. These were the best holes they had ever dug. Out of the ground they began to pull "...prized hams."[56] The Yankees didn't know how the hams had gotten there, but they were very grateful. The hams had not been planted for the Yankees but to keep them from feeding the Yankees. Part of the land they were fighting on belonged to C.H. Moorman. He had packed several wagons full of valuables, took the stock, and most of the slaves and had left the area before the Yanks arrived. He had left his wife, daughter, an old male slave, and several female slaves to guard the house. As he moved off his land, he discovered that one wagon was too heavy. To lighten the load, he buried the hams near his property line. The Yankees "...enjoyed a very fine lot of old Virginia hams, always valuable, but especially so under such circumstances."[56]

Early did a good job of rapidly and secretly massing his troops behind the earthworks. Hunter had no idea he was about to be attacked.

Some reports state that the Confederate attack started about twenty minutes after Crook drew off line, which would place the time between 1:30 and 2:00 p.m. One account stated the battle opened at approximately 2:00 p.m.; another, that it was over at 2:00 p.m.

A soldier with the Thirty-Fourth Massachusetts Infantry wrote, "Our scouts are coming in from the front, with the information that the Rebels are in line of battle!"[83] Either the reports were unconfirmed or were not passed on to Hunter. Hunter said the "...movement was so unexpected and rapid as almost to amount to a surprise...."[8] The same Massachusetts soldier records, "...our skirmishers are busy. Here they come! Closely followed by the Johnnies, who are charging, and yelling like made!"[83] Another soldier recalled that he was making coffee when they came upon us "...in one grand outburst so unexpected and deafening, that for a moment we were paralyzed."[105]

The Rebel yell sounded, and Southern cannons boomed along the line. "The roar of their artillery and the bursting of shells as they tore through the woods, breaking off limbs which fell among us in showers was deafening and somewhat appalling,"[83] wrote a Union soldier.

Glassie was proud that his Kentucky boys had surprised the Confederate artillery and had driven it back. It was the Rebels turn to act. Perhaps it was Bryan's Battery that was taking deadly aim. The Union gunners attempted to return the fire. Dupont, who saw the danger that the whole battery might be captured, sent word for it to move rapidly toward the center. Glassie indicates that some cannons were disabled before his orders arrived. He had to replace wheels damaged by Confederate fire before he could fly toward the center.

Hunter became aware that a full-scale attack was under way. Hunter believed that Early was aware that a brigade under Crook had been pulled off line. Hunter thought Early was attacking because he believed that Hunter's center was weak. Hunter and his staff dashed forward to assess the situation: "The Rebel yell of attack sounded along our whole front...The storm of yells and musketry rapidly approached...."[11] "Leaping over their defenses, the enemy's infantry, with terrific yells, assaulted the Union left and center, held respectively by Sullivan's Division and the artillery brigade, my twenty-six remaining pieces opening with a roar,"[47] said Dupont.

The Southerners, wanting revenge for Piedmont, the Virginia Military Institute, Governor Letcher, and a hundred other atrocities of Hunter, began to breach the center of the Union line. Dupont who had told Hunter that his guns could hold the center, then had reason to worry that the Rebels would make him into a liar.

Sullivan on the right was faring no better. "Brigadier General Jeremiah Sullivan's First Infantry Division broke under the initial shock, and some of his units fled toward the rear,"[103] recorded a soldier.

Dupont sent orders to outlying guns to concentrate at the center along the road. His guns fired both to the front and to the two sides. With Dupont's aid, Sullivan's Infantry began to recover from the sudden Rebel onslaught. A soldier under Sullivan said, "...Our batteries opened upon them, with terrible effect."[83] The Eighteenth Connecticut was moved forward to form a line of battle to receive the Rebel attack.

The center was lightly manned with regiments which had been under Crook. Crook by then was at least two miles away. Without their leader, the regiments began to disintegrate under Rebel pressure.

As Hunter rode forward, he saw "...groups of fugitives (beginning) to appear through the woods."[11] The center was giving way. Hunter believed that Early knew that Crook had moved off line; therefore, Crook's attack would be no surprise. Crook would serve no purpose detached so far away. He was needed in the center. A courier was sent to recall Crook.

Hunter sent orders, and part of Averell's dismounted cavalry moved toward the center, if not all.

Hunter considered the situation desperate because he "...was now actually engaged with a largely superior force...."[16] "The general and staff drew their swords and rushed in...,"[11] said a staff officer.

On the Confederate right, the One Hundred and Sixteenth Ohio Infantry was re-deploying. The Confederates attacked the infantrymen coming through the woods and hit them both from the flank and the front. The One Hundred and Sixteenth was falling back. Sullivan sent two regiments forward to stop the Southern attack. These two regiments were sharply repulsed and sent reeling back upon the One Hundred and Sixteenth in disorder. The One Hundred and Sixteenth opened ranks to allow the cut-up regiments to fall back through.

The Eighteenth Connecticut Infantrymen were having better luck stemming the Southern tide. Southern infantry was beyond effective range of its own guns, but within effective range of the Union's. The Confederates charged toward Snow's Maryland Battery, but the Eighteenth Connecticut turned them back twice.

The aggressive Southerners continued to press Sullivan, who continued to fall back in good order. His regiments were not crumbling under pressure.

The courier reached Crook, and the general and his brigade started back on the double-quick.

Hunter and his staff began to rally the broken regiments and faced them toward the Rebels. Some cavalry troops arrived on the double-quick. Dupont's guns worked the attackers over. Sullivan continued to fall back until he was in a rough line with Hunter. Here Hunter was determined to hold the line. A cavalryman said, "We were...truly exposed to a terrific cross fire from two batteries. Shot and shell tore threw (sic) our open ranks."[105] Sullivan's troops stopped retreating. Hunter rode the front. Men saw "...the lion-like bearing of the commander."[11]

A shell exploded near a soldier; he saw five or six of his comrades go down. "'Twas so near me, I felt the force of the explosion for an instant stunned me."[105]

Both sides poured volley after volley into the other and "...the storm of musketry shook the earth."[11] The Confederates pushed Sullivan from the crest of a hill on the right. Just as the Southerners advanced to the crest, the Thirty-Fourth Massachusetts Regiment, which had been lying in ambush, rose and gave "...them a volley, and, charging (drove) them back...."[83] Through smoke, fire, bullet, and shell, the Union line held.

Because Confederate artillerists were afraid that they would hit their own men, they could not fire at the Union formations directly in front of their troops. A Union defender noted that the shells, "...for the most part, pass high over our heads."[83]

The furious fighting had been raging for about half an hour when the Union commanders heard a cheer coming from their men. The line was stable. The Rebel attack had been halted. Hunter could breathe more easily; the center wasn't breached.

Early saw an opportunity to break through on the right. Two Union regiments had been mauled and sent scurrying from the field in that sector. They key was the battery of guns. If the guns could be taken or forced back, the line might collapse. The Union artillery was on a hill, giving it and the two regiments that defended it an advantage. Despite their advantage, the possible reward (breaking the Union line) was worth the risk. Early began to assemble his troops to attack that point.

What Early could not know was that Crook's Brigade was rapidly approaching the Union line. Crook had his brigade "...well in hand."[47]

Early renewed his attack on both the front and the right. The force of the renewed attack was too much for Sullivan to resist. Sullivan's Division "...was somewhat broken and retiring in some confusion, the enemy advancing against it,"[8] concluded one historian. Dupont ordered the First Kentucky from the center to the left. Dupont apparently felt that the line was breaking. Some gun carriages and horses were struck before the battery retreated.

Hunter realized that Crook's advance was nearing. He sent orders, and Crook sent "regiment after regiment"[11] toward the attack. Bryan's Southern guns opened on the advancing troops. Dupont's Batteries opened on Bryan in an attempt to silence the Confederates. On the line "...the fire was tremendous."[11] "There was a continuous crash of musketry, intonated plentifully with artillery."[59]

Soon Dupont had eight to ten guns trained on Bryan's four. "A violent artillery duel ensued...,"[30] remembered a soldier. One of Bryan's guns was malfunctioning, and it was withdrawn. Bryan kept hammering the infantry and the artillery with three guns. Despite the mismatch, Bryan got the better of his more numerous foe. Federal guns were for the most part firing too high "...the projectiles were passing ten feet over them."[30] Not a man, beast, or carriage of Bryan's was scratched, but the Federals could make no such claim. It is assumed that other Confederate units were also experiencing the same sort of action.

Hunter and his staff continued to send every man they could find toward the smoke and fire along the line. Was Crook in time? Would the line hold? A Union officer stated that "...presently great and continued cheering from the front told us the enemy had been routed...."[11]

Hunter rode toward the front. Crook and his troops pressed forward. Sullivan's and Crook's units and fragments of units meshed. The Confederate attack was halted. Sullivan, who was among Crook's troops, "...rode up and directed that if the enemy gave way to pursue him closely and charge his fortifications."[8] Sullivan might have been shouting the order to his One Hundred and Sixteenth Ohio Regiment, but the commander of Crook's Fifth West Virginia Infantry alongside heard the same order.

The South said that they "...retired to the intrenchment...."[30] The Federals said that the enemy had been "...driven back into his works."[11]

By this time, Southern gunners had forced the Union artillery to fall back. The One Hundred and Sixteenth and the Fifth forced the Rebels to retreat. They had their orders. Crook probably wondered why one of his regiments, which he kept well in hand, was attacking without orders. The two regiments were advancing without proper artillery or infantry support on their flanks. Other units or fragments of units saw the two regiments press forward and they too joined the attack.

The appearance of Crook's troops had proved too much for Early's men on the Confederate left. The lines were now breaking, and the cut-up units fell back rapidly toward the safety of the breastworks. The Fifty-Fourth Pennsylvania Infantry had joined the chase on the Confederate left. During the run, when a cavalryman's haversack strap broke, he asked a buddy to lend him his pocket knife to punch a hole in the sack and tie it. While he was on the ground working on the sack, his buddy and several others stood close by "...when a shell burst close in front, killing and wounding 'Big' Bill Wents and five others...I threw my haversack away and ran faster ahead to overtake my company,"[120] recalled the cavalryman.

To prevent a rout, Early formed a line "...in a deep ditch, concealed by thick weeds and underbrush..."[8] at the base of the hill. Southern fire caused the Yanks to slow down but not stop. The Federals rushed upon the ditch, and the Southern line fell back again. The Union had the advantage in numbers and in charging from high ground. Once the Confederates were forced from the ditch, the lines broke as Confederates raced up hill. Because of the hill to their front, Confederate gunners could not see to fire upon the advancing Yankees.

Spearheaded by the One Hundred and Sixteenth and the Fifth, it appears an advance took place along the whole Union line. The Rebels were falling back. It appears that neither Hunter nor his staff gave orders to advance. Only the two regiments in front had orders; the others followed.

Because of the ditch, the valleys, the contours, and the change in direction of some of the regiments, a few minutes halt was called in many regiments. Some of Crook's men simply needed a rest. They were winded, having double-quick marched over two miles and then with little rest thrown into battle. A unit of cavalrymen stopped a few minutes to drink from a small hot and murky stream. Others stopped, but the One Hundred and Sixteenth and the Fifth chased after the Rebels. This placed the two regiments out front with a gap on both sides and to the rear.

From the crest of the hill to the rifle pits and breastworks, there were approximately 800 feet of open ground. The Confederates fell back across the open ground and the One Hundred and Sixteenth and the Fifth were right on their heels. Because Confederate and Union formations were very close and in some cases intermeshed, Confederate artillerists withheld their fire. They saw the situation, but could not open fire on their own men.

Hunter and his staff moved forward with the troops. Hunter realized that some units were moving toward the works: "...waving his sword (Hunter) led them back to their original position."[7] Strother could see the soldiers of the One Hundred and Sixteenth in advance of the Fifth as they "followed"[11] the Confederates to the works.

Early's men jumped into rifle pits just outside of the breastworks. They attempted to stop the Union onrush, but the charge was too great to resist. The Federals "clambering over them...pushed on to their second line...."[14] As the One Hundred and Sixteenth slowed to clear the rifle pits, the Fifth came alongside or into the same area. Together the units swept upon the main breastworks.

While this action was occurring, soldiers had reached the crest of the hill and started over the 800 feet of open ground somewhat closer to Salem Pike. There were no Confederate troops immediately in front of them. Confederate gunners did not hesitate. Most artillery had switched to canister load for more effective short-range work. As the Union soldiers attempted to cross that short 800 feet, they "...were met with such a storm of grape and canister..."[8] that their line was shocked. The hail of lead and iron riddled any unit that even attempted to cross open ground. One soldier remembered the experience: "The line was formed. We then advanced prepared to charge the Rebel breastworks, distant less than 800 feet. We were met by such a terrific shower or rather a storm of musket fire, shot, and canister that our line wilted down. Every man dropped hugging the ground close as he could."[105] Another soldier recalled, "So severe was the firing...that hardly a tree escaped the enemy's shells, some being cut down and others had limbs cut off, while many bore marks."[18] The Fifth West Virginia Infantry lost almost thirty men in a few minutes, including Lt. D.J. Thomas.

Officers and men lying prone or protected by the hill could see that "...the One Hundred and Sixteenth Ohio even planted its colors on Early's breastworks."[17] They could see but offered no help to their cut-off comrades. A New York officer saw, "...one Ohio regiment getting over their works, and that part remaining therein — either from pride in their achievement, or because (they were) unable to fight their way out again."[109] The Color Guard led the attack, waving the flag, "...their dauntless courage inspired the whole regiment to charge over and up the enemy's second line."[14] Serg. Fred Humphrey was carrying the flag when he "...fell, terribly wounded...."[14] The flag did not hit the ground before a Federal corporal grabbed it, but he was also wounded. The captain of B Company, Edwin Keyes, was hit by a musket ball in the knee. Dupont's Batteries which had not repositioned yet could offer no effective artillery support.

The Fifty-Fourth Pennsylvania Infantry saw what had happened to other units that dared to cross the deadly 800 feet. The infantrymen made no attempt to cross but moved first down the hill and then to the Confederate right.

Any man with the One Hundred and Sixteenth or the Fifth could have told that New York officer, that pride had nothing to do with their position within the Confederate line at that moment. A soldier with the One Hundred and Sixteenth said, "...we fought hard against desperate odds, waiting for help, which we felt would surely come...."[14] A West Virginia boy wrote, "By some misunderstanding the Fifth and one other regiment made a fierce charge on the enemy's breastworks...."[21] The men suddenly realized that they were all alone and that no help was likely to come.

The Confederates realized the same thing: no help was available. Early ordered a battery sent about 100 feet inside the breastworks toward town. It then aimed directly at the breastworks the Yanks had just breached. The battery was probably brought from the cemetery where it had been held in reserve. With canister at 100 feet, it was an awesome force to use against the Yankees. At the same time, Southern soldiers (the Twelfth and Twenty-Third North Carolina Infantry) drove from both sides of the breach along the innerwall of the breastworks toward the breach. They used the breastworks to shield themselves from any Union fire across the open field and from any Union soldiers in the breached breastworks.

The three-pronged attack was too much pressure for the Yankees. The One Hundred and Sixteenth and the Fifth began backing from the main breastworks. Their blood mingled with that of the former Southern defenders.

Back across the open field, no help was coming. One unit admitted that it lay so prone that for awhile "We did not return the fire."[105] Soldiers lay prone in fear for their safety. One Yankee saw something out of the corner of his eye and exclaimed, "My God...the Color Bearer of the Thirty-Fourth Ohio (mounted infantry)...had stood up and held his colors in contemptuous defiance of the Rebs...It was a brave but foolish act...." A Rebel sharpshooter soon found his mark and the Color Bearer "...dropped on his knees, but still kept his flag flying."[105] The bearer fell dead, and the colors sank to the ground. Another soldier picked up the colors but knew better than to stand with them.

Farther along the line to the Confederate left, the Fifty-Fourth Pennsylvania soldiers came over the crest. Between the Confederate breastworks and them there were a house, stable, and ice house — all occupied by Johnnies. The Union commander yelled "Charge!" and, "simultaneously with the order, both the officers and men gallantly rushed forward with a shout...."[8] The Federals charged about 200 yards toward the structures, and the Confederates ran toward their breastworks. The Federals took the structures, but it was an empty victory. When they advanced toward the main objective, they were mowed down. The regiment had only 420 men when it entered battle that day. The unit lost a total of 55 killed, wounded, and missing. A loss rate of approximately 13%. "Here we received the hottest musketry fire of the day, and it was here that most of our comrades fell,"[8] recalled a soldier. The Fifty-Fourth fell back rapidly to the hillcrest. Two units at the breastworks would receive no aid from this sector.

Officers on the hillcrest could see that the men of the One Hundred and Sixteenth and the Fifth "...were very badly cut up,"[21] and could offer no support. The Confederates pushed them from the main works; the Yankees climbed into the same rifle pits that they had just taken from Southerners attempting to stop their onslaught.

Confederates crossed the breastworks above the desperate Yankees' left. The Rebels used trees in advance of the breastworks to shield their movements from the army across the open field. When the men of the One Hundred and Sixteenth and the Fifth saw the Southerners, they knew that they would be attacked from both sides; they were ordered by Capt. Edwin Keyes to withdraw. Keyes had been wounded in the left knee but he still led an orderly withdrawal. He then was hit again, this time in the left shoulder. Some of the men did not make it to safety. Some of the Ohio soldiers carried the wounded Captain Keyes with them.

A soldier with the One Hundred and Sixteenth Ohio said he knew that Captain Keys and Color Sergeant Fred. E. Humphrey were badly wounded. A total of 13 men were killed or wounded from the One Hundred and Sixteenth. A West Virginian saw 7 or 8 of his buddies lying dead, 13 wounded, and he didn't even count the ones taken prisoner.

Records indicate that the One Hundred and Sixteenth Ohio had 12 killed, 25 wounded, and 10 captured during the two days of fighting. Of the 25 wounded, 3 would die of their wounds.

Records indicate that the Fifth West Virginia only lost 2 killed, 13 wounded, and 8 captured from June 10 until the end of the campaign. Most of the losses occurred at the breach in the Rebel breastworks.

As the remainder of the two regiments withdrew from the field, Hunter knew that there was no reason to expose his army to additional fire at this time. He issued orders, and the advanced units fell back across the hill.

As the Yankees withdrew, wrote a Union cavalryman later, "The Rebs saw the movement, and we noticed many (of them) jump over the breastworks forming a heavy line of skirmishers...."[14] An infantryman recalled, "The Rebels were now shelling the woods with great fury, and being still within range of the grape and canister, also the rattle of small arms, the hurling and crashing of flying missiles, the explosion of shells, and the yells of the victorious enemy, combined to make one of the wildest battle scenes we ever witnessed."[14] It does not appear that General Early had issued orders, but the Confederate soldiers were anxious to continue the attack.

The Eighteenth Connecticut saw some Rebels trying "...to sneak through a ravine to get to our battery." The Eighteenth charged and the Confederates fell back. When the Eighteenth pursued, it was caught in "...a cross fire by our own men and the enemy."[18] When the Yankees on the line saw their colors with the Eighteenth, they stopped firing, and the Eighteenth raced back to the hill. The counterthrust was short-lived. The Federals fired from the crest of the hill at the few advancing Rebels. Within minutes, the Confederates returned to the breastworks, and the Union ringed the hillcrest 800 feet away.

After one and one half hours of fighting, "The Union losses were about two hundred, and the Confederates must have been severe,"[17] observed one witness. The lines were roughly where they were before the ordeal of fire.

In the One Hundred Sixteenth Ohio, word began to spread about the condition of the wounded Capt. Edwin Keyes. "...The officers and his men gathered about him to bid him farewell...,"[14] wrote a member of the regiment. But it was the comforters who received comfort. Keyes sang "Rally Round the Flag" to his comrades in arms. Somewhat later both Keyes and Humphrey were taken to the field hospital in the Hutter barn.

The generals and the men on both sides began to contemplate the meaning of the previous one and one half hours. A soldier with the Thirty-Fourth Massachusetts Infantry saw that 4 of his outfit lay dead and 45 were hurting. The lines were near the same spot as before the battle; was their sacrifice in vain? "No," stated the soldier. *We are not whipped!* In fact, we are holding our own, and a little more."[83] Another soldier said, "We put in a hard day and were only holding our position, nothing gained."[18]

The soldiers' general did not share the same view: "...The display of Rebel aggressiveness shook Hunter badly."[60] Union high command believed that Early had attacked because he knew that Crook had pulled a brigade off line. Dupont commented to the general that they were lucky. He said, "Had the Confederates waited until Crook's turning movement was further developed, they might have been able to crush Sullivan before Crook could have come to his assistance; but by attacking prematurely they threw away their chances of winning the battle."[47] Hunter "feared"[103] Early would attack again. "Our whole force was massed to receive the charge...,"[59] he wrote.

Hunter knew that he must remain on the defensive, but he could praise his men, saying that they acted "...with the greatest steadiness..."[8] "...and that the artillery was rapid and efficient."[47]

On the other side of the line, Early was not rejoicing either; "The enemy's forces showed no signs of weakness or timidity...."[56] "Old Jube" knew that he was lucky. If all the units of the Union Army had shown as much daring as the ones that breached his line and planted the hated Stars and Stripes upon his breastworks, he might now be conducting the defense of Lynchburg from the inner-defense line with young boys, old men, cripples, wounded, and the rabble of the Southern Army. The stockade was emptied of the prisoners caught for desertion, robbery, murder, and other crimes. They were on the inner-defense line. Hunter's repulse of the attack had "...made Early cautious."[103] Early decided to remain on the defensive and wait for Rodes to arrive. Early would not attack Hunter in haste again. Before he took the offensive, he would have his men in position and a definite order of attack.

The heat was oppressive. Dupont was taken from his horse because he had suffered a sunstroke. After being cooled with water, filled with fluids, and a brief rest, he resumed command. A soldier with the Fifth West Virginia Infantry estimates that sixty men were overcome by heat in his regiment alone.

It was probably between 3:00 and 4:00 p.m. when a train pulled into Lynchburg. It was not Rodes, for it came over the Southside line, carrying two generals and their staffs. Ransom and Elzey had come from Richmond under Lee's orders. Gen. Robert Ransom, Jr., became over all commander of the cavalry, which made Imboden his second. Ransom was a thirty-six-year-old major general from North Carolina.

When the shells started bursting shortly after noon, Thornton Hinkle, the journalist, knew that men were getting killed on the lines. He decided to look in a safer place for his story; he visited some field hospitals. He saw and talked with some of the men wounded in the early morning skirmishing. One man was Edward Wood of the Eighteenth Connecticut. Hinkle wrote, "Both of his legs have been cut off at the knees by one cannon ball."[102] He also comforted some men by combing their hair. After he left the field hospitals, he had a difficult time finding food for lunch.

A nurse with the hospital in Lynchburg said, "I have been constantly engaged with wounded soldiers. My work, however, is much reduced, as the men have been scattered about to the different hospitals...There are three wounded Yankees...I have talked with (one) a good deal and found him very intelligent and very sick of the war. He says he has been kindly treated...here and does not intend to fight any more. The Yankees are mixed up with our men and are treated exactly alike. They seem well contented."[115]

Back on the line on Salem Pike, the Confederate artillery was having a field day, firing at the Yankee infantry. As most of Dupont's guns were still off line, there was little counterfire. "Bryan's guns commenced shelling everything in sight,"[30] said a soldier. General Early had decided to go on the defensive. He sent orders to the artillery to slow the firing rate "...and save their ammunition for tomorrow...."[30] When the staff officer told a gun crew of Bryan's to cease firing, a gunner informed the officer that the gun was primed and the fuse cut. They were hoping to hit some Union cavalry about a mile away. "Okay," said the staff officer, "but listen at the effect on our men."[30] The gun spoke once more and, "...instantly a rattle of musketry passed along the line clear on out of hearing."[30] The staff officer continued, "Do you hear? Everytime you fire our men think *there they come!* and bang away at nothing."[30] Although occasional burst and shots were fired, the level of activity decreased.

At about 4:00 p.m., Early heard the trains rumble into town over the Orange and Alexandria. Rodes had arrived! Early believed that he could hold Hunter in check on the Pike, but he had doubts about the line on the Forest Road. He directed Rodes to that section. Despite the fact that his artillery had not arrived because it was sent over the road, Early could breathe more easily and start plans to smash Hunter at early light.

Across the line, Hunter and his staff observed: "About 4:00 p.m. the car whistles at Lynchburg indicated that the Rebels were being reinforced — drums were beating, and there was great cheering and rejoicing."[41] Southern prisoners taken that morning had told Hunter that the balance of Second Corps was expected at any time. It was here. With the steeple spires of Lynchburg in view and with the fate of the Confederacy only two short miles away, Hunter knew that he had failed. At Staunton, the fate of the Confederacy was in his hands. Because of his flaming hatred of slavery and the desire to punish slave-holding Virginia, men and animals had marched, sweated, burned, fought, looted, bled, and died for nothing. Instead of being a brave, victorious hero to the Norther nation, he would be a defeated, incompetent coward, sneaking away from a fight under the cover of darkness.

Some time in the afternoon a courier arrived from Duffié. Hunter could expect no miracle from that flank. Duffié informed Hunter that he was stuck. "I am awaiting some demonstration from the rest of the line (meaning Hunter on the Pike), as I cannot move forward alone...I am almost out of ammunition,"[8] he wrote.

Dupont summed up the facts from the Northern point of view very well. "With but little ammunition and less food, we now found ourselves in a hostile country several hundred miles from our base, from which we were entirely cut off, and confronted by a force of Confederate veteran troops under Early much greater than our own. Everyone recognized the extreme peril of the situation, and it was quite evident that in the event of our supplies of food or ammunition becoming exhausted, the larger part of our command could not hope to escape capture and that we would lose our trains and artillery."[47]

Hunter echoed, "My troops had scarcely enough ammunition left to sustain another well contested battle."[8] Hunter, fearful, wrote: "The morrow would find him (General Early) in a condition to assume the offensive...."[8] "In the situation, (Hunter) saw no recourse but to retreat."[47]

A non-military man said, "We can go no farther, so the General decides we must retreat."[102] Another writer said Hunter "...had simply lost heart."[7]

The decision was not accepted well by some officers. "Averell was excited and angry...(and) said he was not afraid of them,"[11] stated one soldier. The good soldier Crook received the news and remained, "...cool and matter of fact."[11]

Which way to run? At first glance, it would appear that Hunter should retrace his steps: first to Liberty, then over the mountain to Buchanan, and straight down the Valley. Hunter had not listened to Crook's advice, and he had ignored Grant's orders to move from Staunton to Rockfish Gap and destroy the railroad to Lynchburg. His failure to follow orders had eliminated his best escape route. Hunter knew that Early could move troops by rail and be in Staunton long before his Army of West Virginia would arrive.

Hunter's best hope lay in sneaking away, avoiding the Peaks of Otter, and going for Salem, and then to the mountains of West Virginia.

Hunter sent couriers toward Duffié and Powell to inform them of the retreat and order their return to the main army. Staff officers and couriers bustled about the general, making preparations to retreat. Some common soldiers saw the activity, and the rumor mill started. Some soldiers were sure that another attack was planned; other soldiers said they were about to retreat. "We thought we were going to Lynchburg that we had an awful large army and nothing could stand before it."[118] The rumors flew but "...neither our own soldiers nor the enemy knew anything until nightfall...."[109]

Saunders and his fifty picked-men were detailed to guard the bridge over the Otter and Staunton Rivers. Saunders could hear the sounds of battle. "...After hearing the cannonade at Lynchburg, I became satisfied there was no use guarding the roads longer." Saunders and his men rode back toward town. Apparently, it was not long before some of Powell's men arrived at the unguarded bridge and burned it. It is probable that a civilian rode to Lynchburg to tell of the Union force.

By near 5:00 p.m., Rodes had moved the advance of his infantry troops on line. It appears that McCausland's Cavalry moved somewhat to the rear, giving the infantry the line. Duffié reported that Rebs "...opened along his whole line with artillery and small arms, compelling my skirmishers to retire to the other bank of the river. From my position on the field I could see numerous reinforcements marching down the hill from the city...This led me to the belief that large bodies of reinforcements were arriving and being thrown into my front."[8] To keep up the good show for his boss, Hunter, Duffié had his cannons firing all afternoon; he was low on powder. With the increased pressure, Duffié wondered if he could hold the line against an all-out attack. Duffié sent a courier to Hunter to inform him of the new troops coming from the city.

A Lynchburg citizen also wondered if the Yankees could hold the line. She saw the increase in troop strength, "...but for some reason (Early) did not attack."[115]

Many of Duffié's command were caught by surprise by the increased fire. A three-man party had been sent to Ivy Creek with every empty canteen in the outfit. One man posted himself as a lookout while the other two rode down the hill to the stream. With the canteens finally filled, the two rode back toward the lookout on the hill. It was then that the Southern line came alive with renewed fire. The men could see their dismounted comrade waiting for them to return when a Confederate shell came crashing. Their comrade fell prone. The two raced to the scene to recover the body. As they approached the limp body, they were surprised when "...he jumped up unhurt." One of the mounted two yelled angrily, "What did you fall for, if you were not hurt?" "Why, I thought if they saw me fall they would think I was killed and they wouldn't shoot again,"[9] was the soldier's answer. The three rode back unharmed. The balance of Second Corps was serving notice that it had arrived. There was no concerted attack.

Back at Staunton, the telegraph was finally back in service. The townspeople then learned that Hunter was "banging on Lynchburg's door." Also in Staunton, the Federals had dumped some artillery shell in the creek. The town boys and some slaves were recovering the projectiles for the Confederacy when one apparently was dropped. An observer noted: "One exploded...while a Negro man was opening it, killing the man. The fragments (both man and shell) flew to a great distance."[43]

To cover his withdrawal, Hunter decided that he would try to deceive Early to gain time. The troopers "...were ordered to maintain a firm front and with skirmishers to press the enemy's line at all points."[8] It was near 4:00 p.m. when withdrawal movements started. There were about five hours of daylight left. Hunter knew that if Early discovered the retreat that he would start "...an attack which under the circumstances would probably have been fatal to us...."[8]

Most of Hunter's wagon train had been sent north over the Peaks of Otter on the morning of June 17. What train was with the army was kept well to the rear out of the fighting. Hunter divided his supply train. "A portion of his train was kept in full view of the enemy, but the greater part was quietly moved to the rear, and headed towards Liberty,"[41] stated an observer.

Just like the previous evening, the Hutter house served as a signal station to coordinate troop movements. Hunter soon moved his headquarter staff into the house.

The common soldier did not know that he was being sent to the lines to keep "...up a bold front,"[11] "...our men believing firmly that they were to enter Lynchburg as conquerors if it cost them a week's steady fighting."[109] The higher ranking officers knew they were to keep "...the enemy in their intrenchments, with occasional firing between sharpshooters and skirmishers until..."[8] dark. "Active demonstrations (were) being kept up by his (Hunter's) cavalry and artillery to mask his (Hunter's) infantry and wagon movements."[117]

Union soldiers not on the line, "...buried our dead, and gathered in our wounded."[83] Old Glory was taken from the barn where Confederates had used it as target practice.

Hunter sent orders that there were to be no fires made along the line. There would be no one left to keep them going, thus Early might become aware that the retreat was on.

Hunter ordered that under the cover of night, Averell's Cavalry would move forward and take the infantry's position and keep up a steady fire. Thus, the slower moving infantry could start the march, and the cavalry could ride later and join the army. The noise from the steady cavalry fire might help cover the noise of the infantry moving off line.

If Early discovered the movement and attacked, Hunter wanted his best division to repel the attack. Crook's Infantry would form the rear guard of the army.

Early on the other side of the line had no reason to suspect that Hunter's army was beaten. In fact, it was just the opposite. First there was the breach in lines and now the increase in activity on the line.

Now that Rodes was here, Early's subordinate generals began to petition Early to attack. An officer noted, "Aggressive, dauntless John Gordon echoed the theme: attack now."[103] Early's generals "...Breckinridge, Gordon, Ramseur, and Rodes all expected to attack."[103] "Early's troops expected to be ordered forward...everyone in Lynchburg expected that their deliverer would smite the vandal Hunter in righteous punishment."[103]

One biographer noted: "More than ever before, Jubal knew the loneliness of command...Early pondered the obvious question: when should he attack?"[103] His hasty attack of the early afternoon had almost ended in disaster, the enemy breaching his breastworks. There would be no attack that day. They would attack at first light and bag the Yankees "body and boots."[109] Early believed that time was now his ally. He knew that the Federal Army's stealing and looting were not just a form of punishment for the South. He knew that the Union Army needed to steal the food to keep it going. Early was aware that little pillaging had taken place in the last two days. The longer he waited to engage Hunter's army, the weaker that army would be. The next attack would be well planned. It was reported that "During the afternoon when Early was making his dispositions for a battle on the next day, Hunter was making his arrangements to steal away in the night."[30]

Not all officers and staff were with Hunter as he moved toward the Hutter house "Sandusky." It appears that Averell received a courier from Duffié. Duffié's message seemed to say that Confederate troops were not coming from town (Rodes's command) but going to town. Averell interpreted the message to mean that the Confederates were retreating in that section. Averell sent a messenger to inform Duffié to launch an all-out attack at once. Averell hoped that this retreat could still be stopped and that Lynchburg could be taken.

Major Hutter had uninvited guests for the second evening in a row. The two parties looked the same, but they were different people. Friday night's guests were arrogant, boastful, loudmouths. Saturday night's guests "...took their meal at the same board in perfect silence."[101] The soldiers had told Hutter not to expect them for supper this evening because they would be dining in Lynchburg, but now they came back, downcast.

It seems that the silence was broken briefly when Averell came dashing in with the good news: Rebs were retreating from Duffié's front. Apparently all the generals and staff members turned on Averell. They knew that Duffié's little cavalry and two pieces of artillery could not do what thousands of infantry and approximately forty guns had been unable to do. "I did not give the slightest credit to the news...,"[11] said Strother. Averell informed the general that he had sent word for Duffié to mount an all-out attack. Hunter could not believe "...the stupidity and conceit of that fellow, Averell..."[8] in ordering the attack. Hunter immediately called for a courier to race to Duffié and countermand Averell's order. The army was retreating, not attacking.

The beautiful Ada had been observing the contentious officers. She hated the Yankee blue, but her true Southern heart beat faster for the one general in blue. She watched as "General Averell retired to the back porch after supper very moody."[101] She had some romantic feelings for this Union soldier but none for his goals. She was glad that the soldiers were down, defeated and silent. She wrote, "Good...they are only drinking the bitter gall prepared for us."[121]

While Ada was watching Averell, Dupont was watching Hunter and said, "He remained dazed in the initial stages of the movement and relied heavily on Crook for advice. Indeed, Crook, ...probably made the actual decision to..."[47] retreat via Liberty, Salem, and the Kanawha.

While Hunter and his staff were melancholically eating supper, Major Hutter attempted to escape. He was trying to reach Southern lines to tell them of the retreat. One soldier said, "Major Hutter, having retired to a back chamber of his house, attempted to pass out of the building when he was informed that he was a prisoner."[16] He was an unwilling guest in his own house.

After dining, Hunter and his generals returned to the field to supervise the withdrawal. Apparently Averell lingered. He knew Hutter's farm and pantry had been cleaned out by his fellow Yanks. Averell asked Hutter if he had anything left to eat. Hutter said "No." Averell said, "Go out into the herd and take your ten cows and drive them into your field, and if you don't find yours, take ten of the best and add five for interest."[106] Hutter could not locate his ten, but he had fifteen belonging to someone else when the Union Army left.

It was about 6:30 p.m. when the courier from Hunter located Powell and his West Virginia boys about twenty miles from the main army. One report indicates that Powell made it all the way to Campbell Courthouse where a brief skirmish occurred in which two Rebs were killed and six captured.[16] No report was found to verify this fact. Powell was informed that the lines around Lynchburg had been strengthened and that Hunter had ordered a retreat. Powell's command had burned a bridge and started a flurry of rumors among the citizens. Chief Engineer Meigs was along for the ride and the fun. Powell started back toward the main army.

At 7:00 p.m. on the Forest Road, "...an officer of General Averell's staff came to me (Duffié and) ...directed me to make a general advance of my line...."[8] Duffié, contemplating this order, stated that if he had obeyed the order, "...my loss must have been very great, if not my whole command sacrificed...."[8]

Duffié had not been able to attack all afternoon. What was he to do? At the time he decided to "obey," he noted: "...A few moments afterward, an officer of Major General Hunter's staff came to me, stating that the whole army was falling back..."[8] and that his order of withdrawal would arrive within an hour. Duffié's command had been saved.

It was near sundown[122] when two Jessie Scouts made their way down the Lexington Turnpike heading toward Lynchburg. These Jessie Scouts were either part of Duffié's command or of the troops sent to look for Breckinridge at Balcony Falls. They stopped at Mrs. Narcissa Owen's home "Point of Honor" and asked for food. She believed that they were just another couple of hungry Rebels. When they learned that she was the wife of the president of the Virginia-Tennessee line (Robert Owen), they seemed to be interested in every word she said. The Jessie Scouts knew that her husband was in the position to know, and they asked her about troops in the city. The two pretended to be concerned that Hunter was about to capture them and Lynchburg. She ticked off the names of the generals and the size of the command of each to reassure the soldiers that Hunter wasn't just going to walk into the Hill City. With their blue-bellies full of food, and their heads full of knowledge, they thanked their hostess, an unwitting informer and left, going north.

Some time in the evening, Early started receiving reports of military activity south of the city. This was Powell's Cavalry. Early had no accurate information on the size, the consistency, or the intention of this force. He worried about an attack on "...Lynchburg on the south where it was vulnerable...."[119] Early thought that Hunter might bypass the city, cut the canal and the Southside Railroad, and move on Danville and Richmond. To obtain information and to slow any possible advance from the south, Early sent orders to Imboden's Cavalry at the inner-defenses. Soon Imboden and his command were moving south over the Campbell Courthouse Road looking for Yankees.

As the vale of darkness began to obscure the lines, Hunter's army went into full retreat. Cavalrymen dismounted and moved to the breastworks, and most of the infantry began pulling off line with orders to be as quiet as possible. Some infantrymen had to stay because the cavalry did not relieve them. The cavalrymen kept firing toward the Confederate lines to cover the noise. Troops assembled on the Salem Pike and started marching westward. Only then did many realize that they had been defeated. Some comments from several sources were recorded: "Why are we to retreat?...Oh, Lee has sent enough men from Richmond to eat us up...so it is best for us to get away before we are surrounded and captured."[120] "The march that night was dreary...."[14] "We are a sick, tired, discouraged lot of Yankee soldiers,"[18] said some Union soldiers.

The remainder of the wagon train which Hunter had placed for Rebel viewing left. Some of the lucky wounded got to ride in the ambulances. Hunter used approximately 90 ambulances to transport the wounded. Because of a communication mistake, "...about 150 wounded which Doctor Hayes had in a temporary hospital...(were) left because he had no notice of the move."[11]

Hunter wanted high command to believe that it was a "mistake," but it was no mistake. The make-shift hospital was only a few feet from his temporary headquarters. Hunter deliberately left his wounded in Hutter's barn because they would slow the army.

Orders were sent to the troops that there would be no fires allowed on the line. As each regiments's turn came to move off line, the orders were whispered and "...not a word spoken until we reached a road"[120] (the Salem Pike). Once to the road, the troops held their position until there was room for them to start a hurried march.

If the Confederates had discovered the retreat and attacked, it would be a disaster for the Federals. In order to prevent a disaster, Crook and his crack troops formed the rear guard.

Opposing troops were so close that the enemy's "...conversation could be distinctly heard."[41] As more and more regiments pulled off line, members of the remaining regiment realized that they were "...in a perilous situation."[41] Although it was dangerous, some troops had to maintain the front. Some soldiers became curious about what was really going on and "...defied orders and stood up to look around. They were hit by Rebs high up on trees, and hid by the thick June foliage; who were watching for just such a mark,"[105] recorded a Union soldier.

Not all went according to plan: in the darkness "We left Lieutenant Goodrich, with his company upon the picket line, entirely ignorant of the intended retreat,"[83] said another soldier.

Lieutenant Goodrich was not the only one staring into the darkness, uninformed. Since shortly after 7:00 p.m., Duffié had been waiting for orders to retreat. By 10:00 p.m. he decided that he had waited long enough and started to move back up Forest Road. Duffié sent a courier to Hunter to inform him of the movement, and began to retreat.

On the other side of Blackwater Creek, a Rebel reported that, "...about 10 o'clock there was a great commotion in the Yankee camp. We could tell this from the rumbling wagons and the peculiar jolting of artillery over rough roads. Headquarters was informed...."[36]

Early was still near the line on the Salem Pike. He was directing some troop movements himself. Despite the increased firing by the Yankees, he was determined to attack at dawn. Unlike his hasty attack of that afternoon, he was going to deliver Hunter's army a well-planned death blow. From what little information is available, Early's plan can be partially seen.

Early's plan called for massive movements of his troops. At 10:00 p.m. the corps received orders to move from the inner-defenses and occupy the most important part of the Salem Pike defense line. Early was turning the redoubt on the Pike over to the corps.

Placing weak troops in a critical spot shows that Early was no longer thinking defensively. It can be assumed that the other troops of the inner-defense line were sent to the outer-defense line. It appears that Early had decided to organize his army behind the line and charge his infantry forward at dawn. Most of the artillery was pulled off the line and organized. The artillery would go in motion with the infantry. According to the attack plan, the Confederates would not find themselves extended beyond their artillery support.

Apparently as Early was directing troop movements, he received the messenger from the Forest Road. What did this Union movement mean? Was the flank attack being recalled to the main army? Was Hunter retreating? Was it a diversion or a regrouping? Early returned the courier with orders for part of McCausland's Cavalry to proceed as directly as possible to Valley Pike Road near Buchanan. Early wanted to know if Hunter was retreating, and if he was, Early wanted Hunter slowed. McCausland was just the man to do it.

"...Not before midnight did it become clear to the Confederates that Hunter's forces were in motion. Even then it was thought he was merely changing lines."[86] Early had not changed his mind about a dawn infantry attack, but now his cavalry was separated from the main army. Imboden was on his way to Campbell Courthouse, and part of McCausland's Cavalry was on its way to Buchanan.

A cavalryman with McCausland remembered that it was about 11:00 p.m. when they were ordered "boots and saddles" and off to God knows where: "...in a short time we were plunging through forest, (and) across rivers and creeks...."[36]

Back at the Salem Pike, Early didn't want Hunter to discover his troop movements; the troops "...were warned not to speak...."[71]

On the Forest Road, Duffié decided to halt his column after a three-mile retreat. He wanted definite word from Hunter before he continued to withdraw.

Near midnight, the courier Duffié had sent to inform Hunter that he was falling back returned. The courier said that he could not locate either Hunter or any staff officer; the army was mostly withdrawn and heading west over the Salem Pike (Highway 460 roughly follows Salem Pike). This news was enough for Duffié who ordered his troops to move.

It was probably near midnight when Powell's Cavalry approached the old battle line. In the darkness, the cavalrymen had a close brush with some Rebel pickets. When he was challenged, Powell shouted back that "...they were reinforcements from Richmond looking for a place to camp."[59] The answer satisfied the picket, and Powell's command rode forward unharmed.

As a private with the Thirty-Fourth Massachusetts started the march, he knew that they had been defeated. In the gloom of defeat, he paid his adversary a compliment: "Rebel soldiers fight splendidly and there are no better soldiers to bear burdens...."[118] Unlike other outfits, the Thirty-Fourth left, "our dead and most of the wounded...."[118]

Hunter's defeated army was exhausted by marches, fighting, sleepness nights, and little food. One soldier said "Our men had but one cracker (hardtack) a piece in two days...,"[14] but they could be proud because they had done a great job of pulling off line undetected. "Not a single wagon or ambulance was captured...General Hunter...displayed fine generalship in conducting the fight at, and in his retreat from Lynchburg...."[41]

Strother summed it up well: "This withdrawal in the face of a superior force was well conducted and successful."[11] Another soldier said, "The Rebels had but little to boast of on their part. It was greatly to the discredit of their

commanders that the whole Yankee army was not captured."[41]
Just like the battle at Piedmont, counting the cost in wounded, dead, and missing is very difficult because figures vary widely. Following is an assortment of figures and sources.

A Prototype of a Confederate Hospital Center in Lynchburg, Virginia —
Peter Houck:
85 mortally wounded — Union.
"Buried only seventy-five Federals, the estimates of Federal deaths run as high as 250 — many probably being buried in fields around the city."
117 wounded Yanks in Hutter's barn. At the barn: "I noted a large and a small pile of limbs, the larger at least 4 feet high, indicating the surgeon had been busy...."

Lynchburg in the Civil War — George Morris and Susan Foutz
Union — 250 killed, wounded or captured.
Confederate dead were considerably fewer.
Union — 12 wounded left at Mrs. Lizzie Plank's house.

A Virginia Yankee in the Civil War — David Hunter Strother
Union 500 killed and wounded.

A History of the Lynchburg Campaign — Milton Humphreys
Union 250-300 killed and wounded.
No Confederate returns.

"The Lynchburg Virginian" June 21, 1864
Union losses 800-1,000 including "90 odd" in Hutter's barn plus other wounded in other homes.
Confederate — 6 killed, 95 wounded.

The Shenandoah Campaigns of 1862 and 1864 and the Appomattox Campaign of 1865 — The Military Historical Society of Massachusetts
Union: from 6/10 - 6/23: 103 killed, 564 wounded, 273 missing, total 940.
Confederate: no figure given.

Lynchburg and Its People — W. Asbury Christian
Union: 100 killed, approximately 500 wounded and missing.
Confederate: 6 killed, 95 wounded.

War of the Rebellion Official Records of the Union and Confederate Armies — War Department

No. 2.

Composition and losses of the Union Forces June 10–23.

[Compiled from nominal lists of casualties, returns, &c.]

Command.	Killed. Officers	Killed. Men	Wounded. Officers	Wounded. Men	Captured or missing. Officers	Captured or missing. Men	Aggregate.
FIRST INFANTRY DIVISION.							
Brig. Gen. JEREMIAH C. SULLIVAN.							
First Brigade.							
Col. GEORGE D. WELLS.							
34th Massachusetts, Capt. George W. Thompson.	......	b	1	41	.....	....	47
5th New York Heavy Artillery (Companies A, B, C, and D), Lieut. Col. Edward Murray.	......			4	.....	....	4
116th Ohio, Col. James Washburn	......	5	1	29	.....	....	35
123d Ohio, Col. William T. Wilson	......	3	......	14	.....	1	18
Total First Brigade	......	13	2	88	......	1	104

Composition and losses of the Union Forces June 10–23—Continued.

Command.	Killed. Officers	Killed. Men	Wounded. Officers	Wounded. Men	Captured or missing. Officers	Captured or missing. Men	Aggregate.
Second Brigade.							
Col. JOSEPH THOBURN.							
18th Connecticut, Col. William G. Ely	.....	....	1	8	......	....	9
1st West Virginia, Lieut. Col. Jacob Weddle	......	1	2	16	......	11	30
4th West Virginia, Col. James H. Dayton	......	....	......	1	......	....	1
12th West Virginia, Col. William B. Curtis	......	2	......	15	......	....	17
Total Second Brigade	......	3	3	40	......	11	57
Unassigned.							
2d Maryland, Eastern Shore, Col. Robert S. Rodgers.	......	1	......	5	......	10	16
2d Maryland, Potomac Home Brigade, Lieut. Col. G. Ellis Porter.	......	2	......	14	......	6	22
Total unassigned	......	3	......	19	......	16	38
Total First Infantry Division	.. ....	19	5	147	......	28	199
SECOND INFANTRY DIVISION.							
Brig. Gen. GEORGE CROOK.							
First Brigade.							
Col. RUTHERFORD B. HAYES.							
23d Ohio, Lieut. Col. James M. Comly	.....	....	......	3	......	6	9
36th Ohio, Col. Hiram F. Devol	.....	3	1	10	......	3	17
5th West Virginia, Col. Abia A. Tomlinson	1	8	1	26	.....	6	42
13th West Virginia, Col. William R. Brown	.....	....	.....	8	.....	1	9
Total First Brigade	1	11	2	47	. ....	16	77

Second Brigade.

Col. Carr B. White.

Command	Off. K	Men K	Off. W	Men W	Off. C	Men C	Aggregate
12th Ohio, Lieut. Col. Jonathan D. Hines	.....	7	...	11	......	1	19
91st Ohio, Col. John A. Turley; Lieut. Col. Benjamin F. Coates.	1	8	3	21	....	......	33
9th West Virginia, Col. Isaac H. Duval	.....	.....	.....	15	.....	3	18
14th West Virginia, Col. Daniel D. Johnson	......	1	......	11	.....	4	16
Total Second Brigade	1	16	3	58	......	8	86

Third Brigade.

Col. Jacob M. Campbell.

Command	Off. K	Men K	Off. W	Men W	Off. C	Men C	Aggregate
3d and 4th Pennsylvania Reserves (battalion), Capt. Abel T. Sweet.	......	......	......	......	......	..	....
54th Pennsylvania, Maj. Enoch D. Yutzy	......	11	1	36	......	14	62
11th West Virginia (six companies), Col. Daniel Frost.	1	5	......	20	......	6	32
15th West Virginia, Lieut. Col. Thomas Morris	......	6	......	54	......	21	81
Dismounted cavalry	......	6	......	23	.....	1	30
Total Third Brigade	1	28	1	133	..	42	205

Artillery.

Capt. James R. McMullin.

Command	Off. K	Men K	Off. W	Men W	Off. C	Men C	Aggregate
Kentucky Light, 1st Battery,* Capt. Daniel W. Glassie.	......	......	......	5	.	.....	5
Ohio Light, 1st Battery, Lieut. George P. Kirtland.	.....	1	.....	4	...	..	5
Total artillery	......	1	......	9	....	......	10
Total Second Infantry Division	3	56	6	247	......	66	378

*Detachment 3d and 4th Pennsylvania Reserves, attached.

Composition and losses of the Union Forces, June 10–23—Continued.

Commana.	Killed.		Wounded.		Captured or missing.		Aggregate.
	Officers.	Men.	Officers.	Men.	Officers.	Men.	
FIRST CAVALRY DIVISION.							
Brig. Gen. Alfred N. Duffié.							
First Brigade.							
Col. Robert F. Taylor.							
1st Maryland, Potomac Home Brigade	......	...	......	2	......	......	2
1st New York (Veteran)	......	1	......	5	......	1	7
15th New York	......	2	1	14	......	23	40
21st New York	......	3	2	3	......	5	13
Total First Brigade	......	6	3	24	......	29	62
Second Brigade.							
Col. John E. Wynkoop.							
1st New York (Lincoln)	......	......	......	2	......	1	3
20th Pennsylvania	......	1	......	8	....	66	75
22d Pennsylvania	......	1	......	2	....	2	5
Total Second Brigade	......	2	.....	12	......	69	83
Artillery.							
1st West Virginia Light, Battery B (section)	.....	1	......	1	......	......	2
Total First Cavalry Division	......	9	3	37	......	98	147

SECOND CAVALRY DIVISION.

Brig. Gen. WILLIAM W. AVERELL.

First Brigade.

Col. JAMES M. SCHOONMAKER.

	Killed Off.	Killed Men	Wounded Off.	Wounded Men	Capt. Off.	Capt. Men	Aggregate
8th Ohio		8	4	54	1	15	82
14th Pennsylvania				18		9	27
Total First Brigade		8	4	72	1	24	109

Second Brigade.

Col. JOHN H. OLEY.

34th Ohio (mounted infantry)		1		4			5
3d West Virginia*							
5th West Virginia				1		2	3
7th West Virginia		2		13		8	23
Total Second Brigade		3		18		10	31

Third Brigade.

Col. WILLIAM H. POWELL.

1st West Virginia	1	1		1			3
2d West Virginia		3		13			16
Total Third Brigade	1	4		14			19
Total Second Cavalry Division	1	15	4	104	1	34	159

ARTILLERY.

Capt. HENRY A. DU PONT.

Maryland Light, Battery B				1	1	24	26
New York Light, 30th Battery				2	1		3
5th United States, Battery B			1	2			3
1st West Virginia Light, Battery D				5	1	17	23
Total artillery			1	10	3	41	55

*Served with Second Infantry Division, and its losses are embraced with the dismounted cavalry.

106   OPERATIONS IN N. VA., W. VA., MD., AND PA.   [CHAP. XLIX.

Composition and losses of the Union Forces, June 10-23—Continued.

RECAPITULATION.

Command.	Killed.		Wounded.		Captured or missing.		Aggregate.
	Officers.	Men.	Officers.	Men.	Officers.	Men.	
First Infantry Division		19	5	147		28	109
Second Infantry Division	3	56	6	247		66	378
First Cavalry Division		9	3	37		98	117
Second Cavalry Division	1	15	4	104	1	34	159
Artillery			1	10	3	41	55
Grand total	4	99	19	545	4	267	*939

Record of the 116th Regiment Ohio Infantry Volunteers in the War of the Rebellion — Thomas F. Wildes
(The official records show 5 killed, 30 wounded, none captured. The detailed diary account seems to indicate that official records are in great error on this unit and therefore suspect for all units and the totals).
Union losses: 12 killed, 22 wounded, 10 prisoners.
Confederate losses: no figure.

Wildes details his account with the name of each man, for example, under killed:

Company A
Private James A. Boyd
Private Jefferson Gatten

Company B
Private Charles C. Davis

Company D
Private Moses F. Starr
Private Micajah Gowdy
Private Evander B. Hamilton

Company E
Private George H. Blair
Private George M. Coulter
Private Jacob Kernan

Company F
Private William Fisher

Company I
Private Gilbert VanHorn

Company K
Private George Lyons

(He also lists each man's name that was taken prisoner and each man wounded with a description of the wound: adding credibility to his figures).

Hunter's official record states that the 116 Ohio's losses were 25.7% fewer than which Wildes states.

Remains of viaduct from James River canal — Lynchburg.

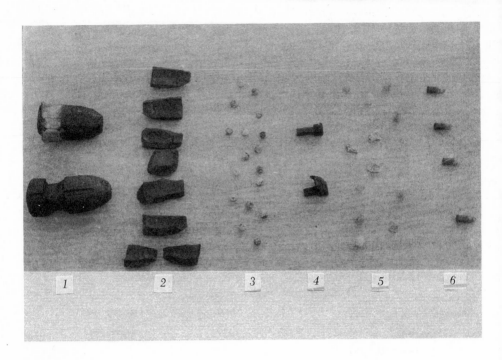

Recovered from the battlefields at Lynchburg.

1 - Hotchkiss shells

2 - Fragments of Hotchkiss shells

3 - Round balls

4 - Timed fuses

5 - Dropped and fired minie balls

6 - Dropped Spencer rifles bullets

(Courtesy: the Lloyd Jones collection)

Chapter XI

Sunday, June 19 — Monday, June 20

Hunter's army marched throughout the dark early morning hours of Sunday, June 19. The soldiers knew that they were a beaten army. Many worried that the Rebels would discover the retreat and attack them. "It was a fearful night,"[18] said one soldier.

The moon offered some light as the weary, depressed, and hungry army struggled over rough roads and forded streams. Some of the men had only two pieces of hardtack to eat in two days. The soldiers were hungry and exhausted. "...A great many (were) dropping down by the side of the road, would fall asleep on the road, and it would be almost impossible to arouse them,"[53] observed one soldier.

Some of the stolen cattle were slaughtered and cooked along the road. As they marched, some units were lucky enough to receive a half pound of beef for each man. Other units received nothing.

Hunter had down-played McCausland's efforts to slow his advance on Lynchburg. On the retreat, Hunter adopted the same tactics: "...trees were felled and blockades of fence-rails and stones were made to impede pursuit."[16]

The weary army trudged west for fourteen miles. About 3:00 a.m., the advance came to a dead halt at Big Otter River. Since the Union forces, who had bridged the stream on their advance to Lynchburg, had no plans of returning this way, they destroyed their own bridge. Now the army halted: the bridge must be rebuilt.

Hunter called for Chief Engineer Meigs to start the bridging. When Hunter was told that Meigs was out thrill-seeking with Powell's Cavalry, Hunter exploded. The whole army was in danger, and Meigs was gone again. Hunter replaced Meigs with Capt. Franklin Martindale of the First New York Cavalry.

Some officers accused Hunter of being in a daze on the retreat, but at the river he showed no signs of mental unfitness. Having disposed of that pest Meigs, Hunter decided to continue. He sent a courier back to Duffié, telling him to report immediately in person to headquarters when his cavalry joined the main army. Hunter also told Duffié that from now on he would receive his orders directly from headquarters and would answer directly to headquarters. Duffié was no longer under Averell's command. Hunter strongly disliked Averell on a personal basis. When Averell ordered Duffié to attack, Hunter decided that Averell should not command beyond his own cavalry.

Hunter decided to send Averell on a mission so secret that he would not

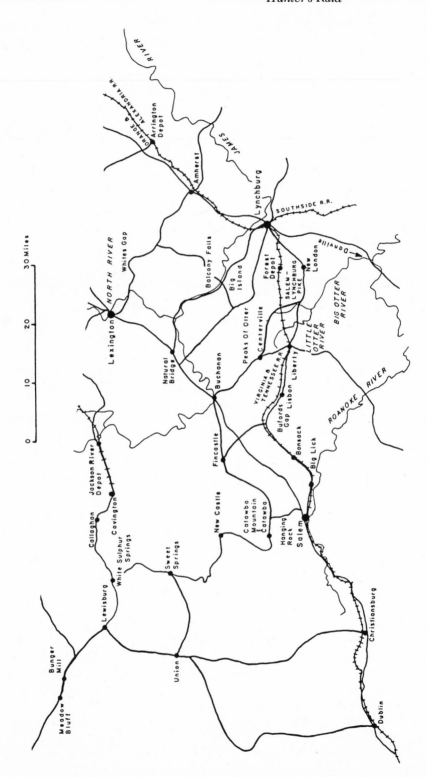

even trust a Union courier to deliver the marching orders. The message Averell received read: "Brig. Gen. W.W. Averell will report immediately in person at these headquarters for confidential instructions."[8]

Once the courier left, Hunter had his Chief-of-Staff prepare a written order for Averell when he arrived at headquarters.

Hunter also set the marching orders for the retreating army. "First, one strong regiment of cavalry: second, train; third, one good regiment of infantry (Sullivan's); fourth, four batteries of artillery; fifth, one division of infantry (Sullivan's); sixth, one battery of artillery; seventh, one division of infantry with four pieces of (Napoleon) artillery (Crook's), eighth, cavalry and horse artillery."[8]

It was still dark at the Big Otter when a courier was received from Powell's Cavalry. Hunter was glad that this cavalry detachment was back safely, but he was unhappy that the Southside Railroad still worked; Powell had "...retired without accomplishing anything."[11] Powell's Cavalry had reunited with Averell near New London. It is assumed that Meigs learned that he had been replaced when the courier returned to his unit at New London.

It was still dark when Averell galloped into Hunter's camp to receive his orders. "General: You are directed to move with your command...southward upon the Richmond and Danville Railroad...cutting the road...the release of the U.S. prisoners at Danville being one of the most important objectives...you will use every effort to accomplish this purpose."[8] "On receiving the paper he read it with a gesture of violent dissatisfaction,"[11] reported an observer.

It is unclear if Averell made his dissatisfaction known to Hunter or simply rode back to New London. Back with his command, Averell grumbled that Hunter was the cause of their retreat and misery. At Staunton, Averell had set forward a plan to march directly on Lynchburg. Hunter accepted the plan and then wrecked the whole time-table by staying in Lexington, burning when he should have been marching. There was much tension between the two generals.

Only the advance was halted at the river; the rest of the army kept moving. Horses that couldn't keep up the pace were shot. Men who couldn't keep up the pace were left along the road.

As Captain Martindale worked on the bridge, the army rested, ate, and slept. One man recalled that he was too exhausted to eat; "I lie down and fall asleep in a furrow of a ploughed field, thoroughly done up."[102] While others slept, some soldiers had their first cup of coffee in two days.

It is believed that it was still before dawn when Martindale completed the bridging and the army continued the retreat.

Back at Lynchburg, it was uncertain how much sleep General Early had gotten. He had been assembling his men to launch a dawn attack to crush Hunter. Early was aware of the Union troop movements on the Forest Road, but it wasn't until the early morning hours that pickets reported that the Union Army was no longer entrenched along the Salem Pike. Early sent pickets and scouts forward to attempt to locate Hunter and try to determine his intentions. Miss Moorman, who lived on the Forest Road, informed some soldiers near her house that the Yanks had retreated.

Early knew that he had stopped Hunter, but he did not feel that he had defeated him. Early had no idea that Hunter was low on ammunition. He believed that Hunter would continue the fight. Early was aware of the Union cavalry activity south of the city. Had Hunter realized that Lynchburg was poorly defended from that direction and made a night move to attack from the south? Had Hunter decided to sever the Southside Railroad, thus stranding Early in Lynchburg and then moving to Danville and then to Richmond?

Shortly before dawn, Early had his answers. Couriers came in to report that the Forest Road was open. Other scouts reported that Hunter's main army was headed due west over the Salem Pike, not south.

Early concluded that Hunter was withdrawing. Lynchburg was no longer the object of the attack. "Relieved of any chance of error, Early ordered a pursuit as quickly as the troops could get out of the ditches and into the roads."[103] When Early's men advanced past the Quaker Church, they found three pieces of artillery. They mistakenly believed that these were Union guns left in haste. They were Confederate guns abandoned by Imboden, which Hunter had mistakenly forgotten and left on the battlefield since the seventeenth.

The soldier whose feet were too sore to march at Charlottesville again reported to the regimental physican. The doctor examined the soldier's feet and told him to report to a Lynchburg hospital. The soldier's patriotism exceeded his pain. Ambulances are usually used to transport hurting men away from the battle. This time in reversal one was used to transport a foot-sore soldier back toward battle.

Early guessed that Hunter was retreating in the same direction as he had advanced. Early was determined to seal Hunter off and destroy him.

During the night, Early had ordered Jackson's Cavalry to cut across country to the Valley Pike Road. He then sent orders to Elzey with McCausland's Cavalry to move at once toward the base of the Peaks of Otter.

The cavalrymen were to lead the way with Breckinridge's Infantry (now under Ransom) to follow. They were to proceed to Centersville and to the Peaks of Otter Road. With any luck when Hunter started up the mountain, he would be caught by Elzey and Ransom in his front and Early in his rear.

Imboden had been sent over the Campbell Courthouse Road to locate the Yankees that had burned the bridge. Early sent a courier to him to rejoin the command moving over the Salem Pike. By early light, the Confederates advanced. Hunter's advance units were now fourteen miles and eight hours ahead of the Rebels, but other units were strung out for miles back toward Early.

It was near daylight when Jackson's Cavalry came out of the woods near Buchanan. Since there was no sign of the enemy, a courier was sent — probably over the Peaks to Early. The command rested and held position.

At the redoubt on the Salem Pike, a cadet recalled, "I must have slept soundly, for when I awoke it was broad daylight. The men were beginning to talk aloud, and several were exposing themselves freely. No enemy appeared in our front."[71] The corps was not called upon to chase Hunter.

Not too far away, a Union soldier with Duffié's command also woke up. He had fallen asleep before the retreat: he was alone and shocked when the sun rose. The soldier wandered near the Moorman house.

When he met Miss Moorman, he asked her what had happened to his comrades. She told him that "...they had been whipped and had retreated...and informed him that he was her prisoner. (The shocked Yankee)...at once surrendered to her."[56]

Near daylight, Duffié linked with the rear elements of Hunter's army near New London. The general was relieved that his whole command had been safely pulled off line and linked. A courier was sent to Duffié to move his cavalry to the advance and not stop until he had seized Bufords Gap (now Montvale). Once over the river, Hunter and his staff slept.

Word of Hunter's retreat began to spread throughout Lynchburg. The citizens knew that the general who "...knew no mercy, and was a stranger to the feelings of humanity..."[106] would not be coming to town.

Citizens began to drive their wagons to the battlefield and recover the wounded, mostly Yankees.

Valuables which had been hidden in anticipation of Hunter's visit, began to re-appear. Some were hidden so rapidly and under such mental strain that the owner could not recall where certain items were. Some valuables never re-appeared.

There was some outrage channeled against fellow citizens suspected of guiding Union units. One citizen demanded that the "...name should be known, that the execrations (sic) of generations to come might be poured out upon this vile traitor, who deserves to be ranked with Judas and his kind."[106]

Near the river, Dupont slept only about one hour. When he awoke, he found that Hunter had not issued a marching time for the day. He went to see the general about 6:30 a.m. The general was awake. Dupont asked Hunter for a marching time. "I think we ought to get away by nine o'clock or thereabouts,"[47] Hunter leisurely answered.

Dupont thought the general had lost his mind. He told Hunter "...it is necessary to realize that our men, knowing that they have but little ammunition and less food won't stand five minutes, so greatly are they demoralized by hunger and exhaustion. Our sole chance of safety lies in moving instantly."[47] Dupont was still not sure that Hunter had a good grasp on reality, but at least Hunter gave orders to march after 7:00 a.m.

Dupont and the army were running for their lives. The men were "tired, foot-sore, hungry, and about played out, but must keep pushing on or be taken prisoner."[18] In his report Hunter contends that the army moved "...at our leisure."[8]

Before one of the ambulances departed, a grave was dug for Lt. F.L. Torrence of the Twelfth Ohio. He had died since they left Lynchburg.

Back along the Salem Pike near New London, a Union soldier straggled. He was "...a young boy in his teens, sick, foot-sore, weary, desiring but one thing on earth, to get back home."[111] Most of the straggling Yankees' next home would be a Confederate prison. This boy was more fortunate. Dr. J.T.W. Read took pity on the boy and took him into his home. Read did not notify authorities.

It appears that Ramseur's Division of Early's command struck the rear of Averell's Cavalry near New London. The twenty-seven-year-old North Carolina general was still recovering from a wound received at Spotsylvania Courthouse as he led Early's troops. A few shots were fired on Henry C. Lowry's place one mile east of New London as both armies moved along the road.

A Federal trooper recalled: "We did not eat breakfast in peace. Our mounted men were driven back on us and we stood to arms. Coffee cup in one hand, carbine in the other — drinking our coffee, but keeping a watchful eye on the Rebs...skirmishing now."[75] The cavalrymen knew they were there to slow the Rebs, not fight them. The cavalry mounted and moved forward, closer to Crook and farther from the Confederates. Occasionally the cavalry would dismount and fire before the Rebs advanced. The cavalrymen knew that they were facing infantry, but their Northern generals, riding ahead, believed it was Rebel cavalry against their cavalry.

One fairy tale says that Hunter stopped at a house on the way to Lynchburg. The owners invited the general in and got him drunk. Because of this delay, Lynchburg was saved. On the retreat, it was Early's turn to be a character in a fairy tale. According to this tale, Early made the mistake of stopping at Doctor and Mrs. T.N. Kabler's place in New London. "...Mrs. Kabler regaled him with such delicious wine of her own vintage that he temporarily lost sight of his determination to capture the enemy and allowed them to get such a start that it was impossible for his men to overtake them...."[97]

It is known for certain that at 9:30 a.m., General Early sent General Lee a dispatch from New London. Early briefly informed Lee of the combat at Lynchburg. He then said, "The enemy is retreating in confusion, and if the cavalry does its duty we will destroy him."[8] Early should have added one more "and if;" (and if Hunter retreats the way he came). Hunter was not even considering that route.

"To say that the citizens of Lynchburg were wild with joy at their deliverance expresses but mildly — their gratitude was unbounded,"[10] said one citizen. The Sunday morning church bells rang clear and churches were filled. Many prayers and petitions had been sent heavenward since last Sunday's service. Many prayers of thanks and praise were offered by grateful people because the Almighty had answered their prayers. The citizens rejoiced but for only a little while. In silence, many contemplated "the ever growing list of those we knew who were being killed and wounded...Daily...comes word of misery and suffering, the ever arriving wounded who both drained our hearts and our small supply of food, clothing and comforts...the Yankees (who) ...could not destroy the spirit of Virginia, were starving it into impotence."[115]

It was evident that there would be no fighting that day at Lynchburg. There was no reason to continue holding the corps under arms. "The Corps of

Cadets was given a holiday"[91] by a rightfully proud Colonel Shipp. The Home Guard returned home, and many invalids returned to the hospital. The Southern prisoners returned to the stockade, but many were soon freed because of their service at Lynchburg. Some rejoined the army; many were dismissed from service.

Members of the corps joined the townspeople and toured the battlefield. They recalled that "about one hundred dead Yankees were strewn over the field, many of whom were nude and terribly torn by shells; others were shot through the head and heart, showing the accurate aim of our men. Some were fierce-looking, heavily bearded foreigners, while others were beardless boys."[106]

Another Lynchburg citizen said that he "...counted 83 Federal soldiers in a space of ... 6 or 8 acres."[91] He went on to say that in the area near Salem Turnpike, "...I think the number could be safely estimated by hundreds...."[91]

A Lynchburg newspaperman said: "...We counted some 40 odd dead Yankees who lay stiff and stark nude."[101] The newspaperman indicated the corpses had been stripped "...by their particular friends, gentlemen of African descent."[101] There was little doubt that slaves and free blacks had taken clothing, but many Southern boys wore Yankee shoes.

The corpse of a Yankee in a turnip field drew the attention of one young boy who said, "One arm was thrown over his head, and a turnip was still in his mouth...."[10] The long-distance Rebel rifles were devastating.

Another Yankee was found. His leg below the knee had been shattered by a Rebel bullet. He apparently bled to death behind the tollgate fence post. "That was the nearest approach to Lynchburg of any one of Hunter's army,"[117] reported an observer.

There were only a few Southern dead. One of Ramseur's North Carolina men was found near the Pike. His body was buried at Lynchburg, but a comrade took the soldier's new bandanna soaked with blood back home to his friend's mother. The body of another Confederate was found on the back steps of a house where he had bled to death. The body was taken to a nearby woods and buried.

As corpses of horses and men are a health hazard, they had to be buried rapidly. By far the largest number of graves were for Federals. "As these young men were laid away in unknown graves in the land they sought to despoil, many who stood near thought of the mother far away waiting for the returning boy who had gone down to the darkness of the tomb...(Hunter's men) were left to be buried by their foes, or else devoured by dogs or vultures,"[106] said one citizen.

Some of Hunter's regiments had buried their dead. Near the Quaker Church were headboards for five men of the Ninety-First Ohio Infantry: First Lt. George Straup, Co. K; Lewis Graham, Co. C. Across the road from the graves, "...a man was laid out in a blanket with a piece of white paper pinned on his breast, marked Robert J. Simpson, Co. I, First VA. Lt., Infantry."[12] Not far away another grave had a wooden name board, but because of haste, the corpse was only half buried. "...The legs of a Federal soldier were exposed."[117]

Near Dr. William Owen's spring about fifteen bodies of "badly muti-lated"[117] Federals were found. Confederate artillery had done its work; it was time for the grave digger to do his work.

Union "...wounded were left at different points amongst the families of the people they had robbed...."[101] Abraham Planks was in the ranks killing and wounding Federals. At his home in Lynchburg, his wife, Lizzy, was caring for twelve of the enemy.

The largest number of Federal wounded was in George Hutter's large brick barn which was used as Hunter's main field hospital. The wounded too serious to even consider transporting were left there with at least one Union doctor and his staff.

Strother estimated that 150 wounded were left. The Union doctor stated, "...there were 85 wounded men,"[117] and one Confederate. This mangled mass of humanity would defy description. A Confederate physician after a quick look at the horribly wounded said, "I believe...that not over five of their wounded would recover."[117] Another source said that at least four or five[16] died that day. When a nurse at a Lynchburg hospital heard of the wounded at the Hutter place, she exploded with anger: "Hunter's whole campaign seems to have been a farce. He was gallant where there was no enemy and a coward when they were in sight,"[101] she said. She was venomous that the coward Hunter would run and leave his brave wounded men.

Not only did the townspeople see wounded on the Hutter farm; they also saw fifteen cows. One by one, the neighbors began pointing out their cows in Mr. Hutter's field. Soon Hutter had no cows left.

Some of the cadets had asked permission to enter the Hutter barn hospital to view their wounded enemy. The doctor granted them permission. Carter H. Harrison was one of the cadets. As Carter passed one Federal, he saw C.H.H. monogrammed on the Yankee's sock. That was his initials, and a second glance told him these were the socks that his grandmother had knitted for him. Inspecting further "...I discovered that he had rigged himself entirely in my under clothing...,"[91] declared Carter.

Carter summoned a doctor. The Yankee claimed that he had bought the clothes in Lexington. The truth was that they had been stolen from one of the cadet trunks. Soon Carter was again wearing his own socks and underwear. Other cadets may have had similar experiences.

The wounded Union soldiers were removed to the Lynchburg hospitals. They were grateful for the attention they received and offered thanks and gifts of money and clothing to the staff. A doctor visited a Union soldier whose leg he had amputated. Even this man was grateful. He pointed to where his leg had been and said that he had the best stump in New England. The doctor observed that there were good feelings between the common soldiers of both sides. He concluded that the bitterness and the hatred must come from those who made the war, not those who fought it.

As the citizens inspected the area, they found "...a large number of guns, pistols and swords, both on the battlefield and on the route of retreat. Knapsacks, haversacks, canteens, etc, were also profusely strewn around...."[16]

Hunter's army left a path of destruction behind. One resident recalled: "Dressed chickens, a dead sheep, large portions of beef thrown away, all attest to the robberies perpetuated upon our people many of whom had been plundered of all their flocks and herds, whilst even their furniture has been wantonly destroyed."[101] Another resident reported the following: "The scenes of desolation...are positively appalling. The people were stripped of everything; fences were torn down, crops trampled up...hogs, sheep, cattle, poultry, were stolen...when not needed for food were wantonly slaughtered and left to rot on the ground."[16]

Now that Hunter's much disorganized army was retreating, old men and boys came out with squirrel guns and rifles and fired from concealed positions upon the fleeing columns. One of Hunter's staff said two Federals were "...treacherously shot in cold blood"[109] in New London. As some Federals moved past the Callaway Cemetery west of New London, locals rose and fired from behind the cemetery walls. Five Yanks fell dead and thirteen[97] were wounded before the locals ran for their lives.

Despite the force march and harassment by locals and Early, Union soldiers found time to steal food and valuables. Capt. W.M. Smith's house near New London was ransacked. A Federal infantryman complained that by the time the infantry had arrived the cavalry had already cleaned the place out.

Sometimes the Union didn't just steal, they left something. After looting one house the Federals left a mortally wounded friend with the now destitute lady of the house. She only had water to offer the dying man. "He was left by his own comrades to die, and was indebted to the poor woman whom they had robbed of all she had, for the small comfort that was afforded him in his dying hour."

As Early's Infantry forces pressed the rear of the column, the Union cavalry could not take the pressure. The cavalry at times split off to the flanks, thus forcing the infantry to fight rear guard actions with the Rebels. To share this burden on the rear guard infantry units, the commanders rotated the regiments that brought up the rear.

It had been very hot with no rain for some time. By mid-day, the temperature was sweltering, and the dust formed a pall over the Pike from Lynchburg to Liberty. At this hour, the advance of Hunter's army began to enter the town for a second time.

On the other side of the Petersburg line at Bermuda Hundred, Grant was getting anxious about Hunter's Army of West Virginia. Southern partisan and local forces had cut Hunter's communications back to Beverly. Because of these forces, Grant decided not to attempt to send supplies, including ammunition, to Hunter. Grant's orders to Hunter were specific: move on Lynchburg and then toward Richmond. If Hunter was forced to pull back, he was to return up the Valley. On June 19, Grant got a captured copy of "The Richmond Examiner" from the day before. It stated that Hunter was banging at the door of Lynchburg. Trying to prepare for contingences, Grant ordered Sheridan to ready his cavalry for yet another attempt to link with Hunter. Grant also ordered the cavalry to be readied at Beverly, (W) Virginia to help

Hunter.

As the last of the Union infantry moved over Big Otter River, it is probable that the bridge was burned, but there is no record to verify this action. It appears that three bridges had been destroyed since June 16.

With no bridge, Early's artillery was halted, but the infantry forded the river and continued the chase. At about 1:00 p.m., R.C. Saunders and his fifty "picked" men caught up with Early. These men were part of Imboden's Cavalry, which had been placed under Saunders to guard bridges south of Lynchburg. They had not done a good job.

Early was happy to see any cavalry units. Early ordered Saunders to "Go forward...charge those fellows and don't stop for a little shooting."[91]

Saunders rode forward about one mile before he saw the Yanks. The fifty charged but "...were driven back with what appeared to me very little shooting. Nobody was hurt."[91] Apparently Imboden had picked his fifty worst men. Saunders' command scattered.

It took Saunders a while to gather his men and re-form. He then started toward the Yanks again. As the column crossed a small stream, "A Yankee officer rode up on the hill some *four hundred yards* to our front and opened fire upon us with a repeating gun."[91] The picked fifty retreated from one Yankee at four hundred yards. Since Saunders could not stop the pack from running, he took on the single Yank. "At the crack of my gun I noticed the officer fall forward upon his horses neck and go off slowly...."[91]

As the wounded officer rode back, his men ran and Saunders "...joined the retreat."[91] As Saunders and the fifty ran, they met Gilmor's partisan battalion.

Gilmor's men were there to fight, and soon it was the Yankees who were running. Soon Saunders and Gilmor were back to the place where the Union officer was hit, and sure enough there was "...a Yankee soldier lying on his face in the broomstraw."[91] A Confederate began to kick the Yankee body. Much to Saunders' surprise, the Yank sat up "...and began to rub his eyes."[91] A disbelieving Saunders asked, "Are you hurt?" The Yankee soldier replied, "No...been asleep."[91]

If General Early had gotten a report on Saunders' role in the action, it would have "...reflected clearly Early's firm suspicion of his troopers..."[103] damn, buttermilk rangers.

It appears that outriders had moved faster than any of the armies approaching Liberty. The advance warning had allowed many to flee town and to hide their valuables again.

One report states that the advance Union scouts reached Liberty about 8:00 a.m.,[100] but the main columns did not enter town until past noon. A citizen said, "...They did worse than when they went through."[100] The Yanks stole horses to replace those shot along the road. There was little food for the Yankees to steal in town because they had stolen most of it on the advance.

Uncle Billy Haden, Micajah Davis' slave, started hiding valuables again. Edward Burks, who had stayed at Woodford and hidden on the advance, now left town on the Union's retreat.

Mr. Rosebrugh's slave was no Billy Haden. The slave had seen where the family valuables were hidden. When the Yankees arrived "...his Negro informed (them) where it was (hidden) and that is the way he (Rosebrugh) lost it...."[100] At another home, the slave returned armed and dressed in a Union uniform. The former slave was with a company of Federals.

Most of the citizens had left town, but the ladies who stayed "for the most part...were respected...except that the scoundrels cursed some of them...."[100] At least one slave who had run away with Hunter as he advanced toward Lynchburg changed his mind and returned home.

Some Masons had taken the jewels and other valuables from their Masonic Hall. As Union soldiers passed the Hall, they saw a sign reading "Bedford Sentinel." Rebel newspapers were fair game. When some of the girls of the town realized that the Hall was to be burned, they ran to the soldiers and pleaded that it not be burned. When the Yankees were told that the newspaper had not published since the war started, they decided not to burn the Hall. The lie of a Rebel girl saved the building.

Because Hunter knew that his army, like locusts, had eaten through Liberty once, he continued to move the army through town. Some of Hunter's officers forced their way into homes in Liberty and got both food and rest. One resident said, "The retreating army was completely demoralized, and its depredations laid waste in Bedford County some of its finest residences."[124] About three miles west of town, Mayor W.W. Leftwiche's home was looted and burned. The army caught some wagons leaving town with valuables. These were plundered and destroyed. Thomas Patton, John Cofer, Dr. D.P. Jones, Samuel Miller, and many others lost every horse the Yanks could lay hands on. J.W. Holt seventy-nine years old, lost both his horses and slaves to the Yanks.

At "Wheatley," Robert Mitchell's plantation two miles west of town, the family was getting ready to eat dinner when the uninvited guests arrived. One story indicates that Union soldiers gathered up the four corners of the tablecloth and exited the house with food, dishes, and all. Of course, most any farm animal encountered was soon a meal for the Yankees.

"Wheatley" — Liberty (Bedford).

The defeated and humiliated soldiers spread rumors throughout the population, but at least one citizen didn't believe them. "The Yankees said (that) they met all of General Lee's army at Lynchburg...They also said that Richmond had fallen, compelling Lee to fall back to Lynchburg...Ridiculous fools!"[100] was the citizens reply.

As the Federals retreated up the ridge from Little Otter River, they found a very narrow passage for the road. The road had been cut through a bank. On the right was a cliff, and on the left was a wall of logs to hold back the embankment. Retreating men "...had cut the throats of the teams of three or four wagons, chopped some of the wagon wheels off, and thus blockaded the road."[91] Saunders' command had to stop for some time as it cleared the road.

Many slaves took the opportunity to run. One Union soldier reported: "The ever faithful colored people were now flocking to our army by the hundreds. Many of them carried heavy loads of provisions, which they gladly divided with the soldiers, and told us where flour, meal, bacon, hogs, and other eatables were concealed."[14] The Yankee soldiers followed the escaped slaves back to the master's plantation and stole at will.

Hunter "...was called a good fighter but was regarded as careless of the wants of his men. It was a common saying among a certain class of his men that he thought more of the Negro than he did of a soldier, because Negroes rode in the wagons while wearied and wounded soldiers marched."[41]

When Saunders came upon a Negro man, his wife, and children, that were between Hunter's rear and the Rebels' advance, the Negro man hailed Saunders and said, "Ketch them Yankees and kill them."[91] Saunders knew that the man was lying through his pearly white teeth and knew where his real sympathies lay when he saw the bundles that the family were carrying. These slaves just couldn't keep up with the Northern Army.

Fleeing Negroes.

Soon Saunders spied three or four Yanks ready for a fight, waiting about four hundred yards away. Again, Saunders brought his fifty on the line. Some of the fifty had "long-range guns."[91] The less than gallant fifty left Saunders and trotted to the rear.

Soon Gilmor's Cavalry came and drove the three or four furious Yanks off. After the danger passed, the fifty non-heroes rejoined Saunders.

From Lynchburg to Liberty, the Confederates had passed the carcasses of over a hundred dead horses and mules. When the animals gave out, they were "cruelly shot."[16] The South had bagged about forty Union soldiers who had given out also.

By 3:00 p.m., most of the Union infantry had moved through Liberty and had gone into camp about three miles west of town. The tired and hungry army had moved over twenty-six miles from Lynchburg. Those that had food or had stolen food ate. Some soldiers shared with their comrades. Some of the soldiers had nothing, but to stop and rest was a joy in itself.

By 3:00 p.m., McCausland under Ransom was at, or approaching, the Peaks road leading north from Liberty toward the mountain. Elzey had moved with Breckinridge's Infantry over Big Otter and to Early's rear. Because the bridge was still out, no artillery was west of the Big Otter. Imboden was still en route toward Early, but his exact location was not determined. Saunders' and Gilmor's cavalry units were approaching Liberty. Early, with Ramseur's command in advance, was close behind the small cavalry units.

By 3:00 p.m., it appears that Hunter had heard rumors concerning the Confederate cavalry moving toward the road to the Peaks of Otter. Hunter believed that Early was sending his cavalry to hold Bufords Gap. "If (the enemy is) successful, we will probably have to surrender,"[102] concludes Hunter.

Duffié's Cavalry headed the army. It had had only two to three hours' rest, and the Gap was still sixteen miles away. Hunter sent Duffié orders "...to move forward immediately..."[8] and to take and hold the Gap, "...at all hazards."[11] As Duffié departed, he knew that he must achieve his goal or sacrifice the whole command in the effort. Duffié had two guns of the First Kentucky Battery with him.

By 3:00 p.m., Averell's Cavalry, the rear guard, had gone into camp in Liberty. Some of the cavalrymen had broken into houses for food and shelter.

Averell received a report that the enemy was approaching, and he sent a request to Crook to detach an infantry regiment to support his cavalry. All the reports that Crook had received indicated that it was Confederate cavalry that had been skirmishing with the Federal rear. Averell's superior cavalry should hold off any Southern advances. Besides, Crook was tired of his infantry doing the fighting for Averell's Cavalry. Request, denied!

It was shortly after 3:00 p.m. when the advance of Saunders' and Gilmor's Cavalries became aware of the exact location of Averell's Cavalry at the east edge of town. The Confederates dismounted and formed a line. As they advanced, Averell's men came on line also. Some men were located behind a stone wall for protection, some along the road, and some stayed in the houses.

"The balls were whistling lively around our heads and we were beginning to suffer,"[116] recalled one Reb cavalryman. Averell's superior numbers and firepower slowed the few Confederates.

A note of graveside humor then occurs. Private William Ashby was advancing next to his colonel, Charles O'Ferrall. Bullets were whistling about. The next step may be the last step, but Ashby's next step was in a hole. He almost fell, but as he recovered, he calmly turned to his colonel and asked if he "...didn't think Virginia was rather hasty in going into this thing (the war)."[116]

Gilmor soon concluded that Averell's forces were too much to attack and that he would fall back and wait for Early's Infantry.

Re-creation: Confederate Cavalry firing on Union Cavalry — Liberty (Bedford).

Averell saw the dismounted Confederate cavalrymen fall back. At 4:00 p.m., he saw the dismounted men moving forward again. He knew that there was an increased number of them. What he did not know was that these dismounted men were Early's Infantry under Ramseur.

Just south of town, Mrs. Burks heard the shooting. Her husband had left their house, Woodford, earlier. She had had one very distasteful encounter with the Yanks, and she didn't want a second one. Gathering her children, she fled Woodford. Because the children were small, she knew that she couldn't go far; she decided to seek refuge at a neighbor's farm house.

Most of the remaining citizens scurried to their cellars.

East of the town, Ramseur formed his infantry in battle array. By this time, General Early was on the scene. Early exposed himself to enemy fire as he directed his infantry into position. He was close enough to hear the Federal officers shouting orders to their men. Early, long ago, had lost his fear of death, but a member of his staff, John Goode, had not. Goode did not like being out there with the general because, "...bullets were flying thick and fast and buzzing about our ears."[114] If Early would take cover, so could I, thought Goode. He said, "General...You may be shot down at any moment."[114] General Early paused, saw the fear in Goode's eyes, and with a satirical smile replied, "Do you think so, Goode?"[114] Then he continued directing his troops in the same manner as before.

Early charged his Infantry forward against Averell's Cavalry. The Yanks didn't hold the stone fence long. Early's Infantry tore into the cavalry. "A severe skirmish ensued."[11] An officer reported, "...We could hear the rattle of a fight. Our lines were evidently being forced back."[11] The truth was that the initial attack had breached the cavalry line in several places. There were dead and wounded Federals in roads and yards. The first line of Averell's command was being chopped up. Troops ran on foot or on horse away from the advancing infantry. Some Federals in the houses found their paths of retreat cut off. Their only choice was surrender or die.

Re-creation: Early's Infantry advancing on Liberty (Bedford)

Averell himself went back to the center of town and attempted to form a skirmish line for his troopers to fall back through. He sent an urgent message to Hunter. Averell estimated the force to his front to be between 1,500 to 2,000[8] cavalrymen. Averell asked for infantry and artillery support.

When Hunter received the message, he began to form a line of battle to receive the Rebs. Hunter anchored the right of his line on a rise, part way up Wingfields Mountain. The trees had been cut from the Valley to that point. The rise gave a commanding view to the front and to the left. Hunter placed the artillery from the rise back across the Salem Pike and anchored the left side on a smaller hill but one with a commanding view. Four guns of the First Kentucky Battery were to hold the road. Because of the confusion of the retreat, the divisions, the brigades, the regiments, and the companies were disorganized. Any unit found anywhere was sent to some point along the line. The Eighteenth Connecticut was ordered "...to lie down behind a hill in ambush."[18] Crook's regiments were intermingled with Sullivan's. Despite the problems, a line was formed.

Back in town, Averell's second line only stood a brief time before Early's onslaught. Although the Union slowed the Confederate advance, it could not stop it.

Saunders was close to the advance of Early's line. He heard a woman's scream coming from one of the houses. The screams persisted even after the Federals were driven back. He entered the house and followed the screams to a locked second story bedroom. Thinking Yankees may be in the room, he cocked his pistol and forced the door open with his shoulder. Upon entering, he found no Federals, only a screaming woman and a pile of smoldering clothing.

After the smoldering clothes were extinguished and after the woman was somewhat calmed, she told him what had happened. "...Three or four Yankees had burst into the room, took...clothes, piled them in a heap and...(after) applying a match had gone out, locking her in."[91] She was screaming because the Yankees had meant to burn her alive.

When Saunders left the house, not surprisingly, he could not find his famous fifty. He wandered toward the shooting and attached himself as an aide on Colonel William E. Peters' staff of the Twenty-First Virginia Cavalry.

Not only was Averell losing men and ground; his ammunition was also running low. One cavalryman said, "...We had left but twelve rounds of cartridges per man...whenever a man fell, either killed or wounded, there would be a dozen squabbling over him in a moment for the precious contents of the cartridge-box...."[109]

Within two hours, Averell's men had no claim to the town of Liberty. "...We were again in Confederate lines...much to the relief of all,"[100] said one citizen. Averell's loss was 122 men[8] killed, wounded and captured. Schoonmaker's Brigade suffered the heaviest loss.

Averell raced from town because his cavalry had been routed. Early's Infantry was right behind as it raced out of town. The Yanks "...were closely pursued and hard pressed."[100] About two miles west of town, Averell's forces fell back through the Union line to safety. The Confederates in hot pursuit did not know that the line was there until the cannons roared and until the infantry rose and fired.

When Early heard the first cannon, he knew that he had struck the main Union line. Early knew that an army is a large animal with a will of its own. Armies cannot stop charging in an instant. Some units continued to move forward toward Hunter's deadly line. Now it was the South's turn to suffer. A man on the line remembered that the cavalry "...re-formed in our rear, came again to the front, advanced, we follow(ed) in support, then charged, driving the Rebs back in confusion."[75] A Union soldier on the line observed, "After a sharp fight they were routed...."[75] Early's men quickly re-formed ranks. Officers saw the battery on Wingfields Mountain anchoring Hunter's right. They attacked toward the gun. Union men who had chased the retreating Rebs, were now themselves chased back to their line. In a brief but bloody encounter, the South attempted to breach Hunter's right and take the guns. A witness said, "...The Eighth Ohio Volunteer Cavalry bore the brunt, losing over 70 men in a few minutes."[75] Southern casualty figures were not given; the line was not breached.

Early sent orders, the attack was halted, and the troops were pulled back. Early was not about to let his fine infantry be chopped up by Hunter's cannons. Early decided to wait for his artillery before attacking again.

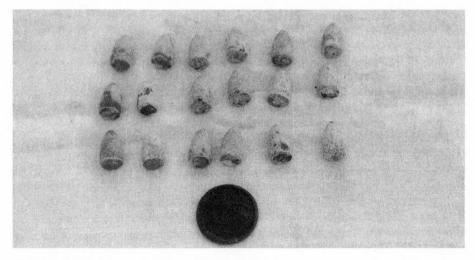

U.S. Cavalry .50 cal. Cosmopolitan rifle projectiles.

U.S. Rosette — (part of horse's harness)

All recovered at Liberty (Bedford)

Courtesy: Pat Trout collection.

Early, believing that Hunter would retreat north from Liberty over the Peaks of Otter, sent Ransom with the cavalry to intercept Hunter. When Early found Hunter's main army west of Liberty, he apparently concluded either that Hunter was aware of the Confederate presence north of town or that Hunter didn't want to retreat through Buchanan where the bridge was out. That was the probable reason that Hunter had continued west. A quick look at the map showed that Hunter's best route of escape was Bufords Gap and then north toward Fincastle. Early believed that Hunter would move that way tomorrow.

On the other side of the line, Hunter had not thought of attacking-only running. Because Early was upon him, Hunter decided that he could not afford to lose any troop strength. Averell was notified that his orders to attack Danville were "suspended."[8]

Rifle fire was exchanged between the two lines until dark. Union cannons were mostly silent to conserve powder. Hunter believed that Early would have his artillery up soon and might launch a night assault. Hunter issued orders to post a strong watch, and soldiers not on watch were to sleep on the lines with their guns ready.

Near dark, Mrs. Burks and her children made it to a "nearby farm house."[102] Mrs. Burks and her neighbor were not on good terms. Whether it was a personal dispute or whether the neighbor's sympathies were as pro-Northern as the Burks's were pro-Southern is not known. What is known is that "...she was refused entry."[102] Mrs. Burks and her children spent the night on the neighbor's porch. During the night a minie ball, presumably Northern, narrowly missed her head.

Hunter was convinced that if Early didn't attack during the night an attack would come at dawn. Hunter did not believe that he could repel an attack. The army must be gone by first light. Hunter issued orders for a night march to begin at midnight, but the wagon train started earlier. Trees were felled, and shouting kept up to cover the noise the wagons made.

Dupont states that it was actually he who got the army moving. By sunset, when Dupont had received no marching orders, he went to find Hunter. Because of the confusion of the retreat, it took him some time to locate the general. He found Hunter in a cottage on the Salem Pike. When he entered, Hunter was lying down. Hunter said that he was "feeling unwell,"[10] and that his adjutant "...is ill in an ambulance,"[10] and that he didn't know where any of his generals were. Once again Hunter is described by Dupont as being "dazed"[10] and not able to grasp the critical situation. With Hunter's approval, Dupont wrote the marching orders and personally delivered them to the various commands.

As the sunlight disappeared, Confederate artillery began to arrive in Liberty (another indication that the Union forces had burned their bridge at Big Otter). Shortly after dark, the advance of Imboden's Cavalry began to arrive.

Early knew that Hunter's troops were weary, but so were his. Early knew that Hunter's troops were hungry, but so were his. Early's men were in the line of battle at dawn; they had no extra food to carry and slow them down. They had force marched all day and overtaken Hunter despite his six-to-eight-hour lead. Early's supply wagons weren't even in Lynchburg when the army left. The only wagons were those of McCausland's and Breckinridge's. McCausland had his wagons north of Liberty. Only Breckinridge's were available to supply both army groups.

It appears that Early decided to wait for his supply train and artillery coming from Lynchburg. He believed that he would be supplied by dawn and have the artillery of the Second Corps. Early would attack at dawn.

A citizen of Bedford had witnessed the beaten Federals in town and could compare their fighting spirit to that of the Confederate troops there. There was no doubt in his mind that if the Yanks "...made a stand for a pitch battle, we would...(whip) them terribly."[100]

If the Confederate cavalry could get in front of Hunter and delay him, then Early's force might be able to crush the Federals. Early studied the map and quickly deduced that Hunter would cut north toward Fincastle. The road to Fincastle must be blocked. Early sent word to Ransom (McCausland's Cavalry) north of Liberty on the Peaks Road, to start over the Peaks at dawn. Imboden's Cavalry at Liberty would also start that way at dawn. At least, some of the artillery at Liberty was sent to Ransom and McCausland. The fast-moving cavalry should be able to outrun Hunter's Infantry.

Monday, June 20

Records do not indicate that Early was aware that Hunter's army started pulling off line at midnight. It is possible that Hunter was giving him the slip for a second night in a row. It is also possible that Early was aware of the move but chose to wait until dawn to pursue for several reasons. Perhaps Early wanted his army re-supplied and rested before pursuit and battle. Early knew that Hunter's weary men would not make many miles in the dark. Rest and light would allow Early to reclaim any advantage that Hunter might gain by a night march. Also Early remembered that his fast-moving infantry was able to overtake Hunter's forces after their night march from Lynchburg.

Whether Early was aware or not, Union units began to move off line near midnight.

Dupont was glad to see that Hunter was more alert after his rest. Hunter was in a better condition, but most of the troops were not. One officer noted, "The men were so weary they could sleep under any circumstances."[41] Units began to pull off line at midnight and moved to the Salem Pike. As space became available on the road, other units were roused and sent to the road. It would be near dawn before the last regiment was started toward Salem.

The exhausted men were in a very deep sleep and were very hard to arouse. Many soldiers who chose to move a little off from their outfit were not awakened as their comrades marched off. Even with "...the full moon shining gloriously,"[11] officers could not find all of their men. Many were left.

Some of the troops of the Fifth West Virginia couldn't march until they had buried a soldier from Pennsylvania. He had crawled from an ambulance and in the dark had died.

It was near 1:00 a.m. when the advance of Duffié under Col. John Wynkoop reached Bufords Gap. Much to Duffié's relief, the Gap was not occupied. He would not have to sacrifice his command to take it; he could rest his command there.

Duffié knew that the Gap was secure, but no one with the main army had that information, and rumors were rampant. One officer noted, "Some were in dread that we might fall into the hands of Rebel raiders."[11] A private said, "We were hurried on by the not cheering news that the Rebs were trying to get in our front...our situation would be desperate."[75]

Despite the worrisome rumors, "The men were so tired that they would go to sleep in the ranks. I went sound asleep quite a number of times, while walking...,"[14] stated one groggy private.

A mounted man said, "I sleep some in my saddle, some on the back step of an ambulance, and in the seat with the driver, some in the little ten minute halts."[102] The man was very hungry and was grateful when, "Lt. Herman Koenigsberger of the Twenty-Eighth Ohio gives me some scraps of cracker scooped out of his coat pocket."[102]

Some soldiers clung to the tail boards of the wagons, allowing the horses to pull them through the dark. A private said, "We limped along stubbing our toes in the dark, wishing for daylight."[75] Anything the soldiers had except guns, ammunition, and food, was thrown away.

It was still dark when the Union forces entered Lisbon (now Thaxton) Station. The depot was burned, and General Hunter himself assisted in pulling down the telegraph lines.

Dawn was just breaking when the advance of Hunter's army was entering Bufords Gap. When Hunter was informed that the Gap was secure, he sent orders to Duffié to continue his advance toward Salem. Duffié was to destroy railroad bridges and telegraph wires as he went. By taking out the telegraph, the Federal forces prevented the Confederates from communicating rapidly to the west concerning Hunter's advance. Taking out the railroad bridges would stop the Confederates from transporting any troops directly upon the main army body. Duffié was also to send scouts to Fincastle and Salem to get intelligence information.

By dawn, Early, aware that the Union Army was in full retreat, set his forces in motion. Moving west from Liberty, Gordon's Brigade was on the point, followed by Rodes, Ramseur, and Breckinridge. The artillery was distributed among the infantry units. Many sleeping Federals became Southern prisoners. Moving north from Liberty, Imboden moved his cavalry toward the Peaks. Before leaving Liberty, Early officially placed Breckinridge back in command of his old army. The hoped-for supply train had not appeared. The army started marching on an empty stomach.

Ransom with McCausland's Cavalry started north over the Peaks. Because it had not rained, scouts could easily see the wagon ruts and the horseshoe prints left in the dirt road, indicating a wagon train had moved over the mountain also going north. No doubt, citizens along the road also informed the officers of the train, an excellent target for the cavalry.

McCausland knew that "Mudwall" Jackson's Cavalry had been sent to block the road at Buchanan: perhaps it had intercepted the train.

Early assumed that Hunter would cut north toward Fincastle. The cavalry should be able to hold the road and delay Hunter. The infantry could then overtake him. "The aim of all strategy is to limit every opportunity to those desired by the strategist: Early wanted Hunter pinned to one road, encircled and cut to bits."[103]

As the cavalry wound over the mountain, an officer observed that a group of soldiers had stopped off of the road. A staff aide was sent to get the men moving so that the column would not be slowed. When he arrived, he saw men stripping bark from a tree. The aide "...asked what in the world they were about?"[91] The men replied that they were gathering rations and continued stripping until they had enough. When they had finished, they remounted and continued moving. As one man mounted, he gave the aide a strip of the bark. The aide sampled it and "...found it palatable and...nutritious."[91]

CONFEDERATE STRAGGLERS.

By David Hunter Strother.

Some time in the morning, scouts from Hunter's army saw the dust on the mountain and went to investigate. When they were near enough to confirm that it was the Confederate cavalry, they raced to Hunter with the news.

It was near 8:00 a.m. when some Union regiments were allowed to stop and make breakfast. Some regiments cooked freshly slaughtered cattle and sheep. One man had two or three flapjacks. One private recalled that we, "halted...for breakfast, though we had nothing to cook but coffee, black as soot, strong enough to float an iron wedge. We drank it."[75] Another soldier observed that when most men had little or nothing to eat, others always seemed to have an abundance. There was much stealing of food; one soldier took from another.

Members of the One Hundred Twenty-Third Ohio were taking their meager breakfast near the railroad at Lisbon when the general's orders arrived. The Company was sent to burn ties and destroy a water tank near the depot.

Some time in the morning, location unknown, a cavalry outfit stopped for breakfast. The rifles were placed in stands. Most of the soldiers were cooking their food, but a slave was cooking for the regimental colonel. A shot rang out, and cavalrymen rushed toward the sound. A cavalryman heard the shot and saw the commotion as soldiers dashed. From somewhere beyond the wall of soldiers, he heard "...a woman scream, a scream so full of agony, prolonged till it died in a low wail. Presently out from the crowd came a veteran in tears carrying a wee toddling child across his extended arms, the mother holding on to him, dragging herself along, sobbing and moaning."[75]

Apparently the mother and child had come sightseeing to the Federal camp. The child knocked over some rifles. One discharged, killing the child.

The cavalryman continued, "My God! ...an innocent child...the mother wringing her hands and wailing in the most pitiful agony. The whole making a picture so vivid that while memory lives in me I never can forget."[75]

Early was correct: rest and daylight soon made up for Hunter's five or six-hour head start. Moving since daylight, the advance of Early came upon the rear guard of Hunter near Lisbon about 8:00 a.m.

The Federals fell back rapidly but not before losing one dead and two wounded.[124] Breakfast was cut short for many regiments, and some had no breakfast at all. Both infantry and cavalry units formed a line of battle and waited for further Rebel advances. Other units were rushed forward on the retreat road toward Bufords Gap.

As the advance of Gordon's men came upon Hunter's skirmish line, they decided to wait for more forces before attacking.

During the time that the Confederates were waiting for more forces to move forward, the Federals withdrew. Before they withdrew, they removed twenty severely wounded men from their ambulance and left them on Dr. D.P. Jones's porch.

The soldiers knew that the Confederates were there: "The Rebs were closely escorting us, yet were cautious."[75] A cavalry private said, "...Early's men...were like blood-hounds on (our) tracks...."[116]

There were occasional shots fired between the advance of Early and the rear of Hunter as both armies moved toward Bufords Gap. An exhausted Union soldier complained, "We have not stopped long enough to learn the names of the places that we pass through...the rear guard reports that many of our boys are falling into the hands of the Rebels as they are worn out and cannot keep up...."[18]

By this time Duffié's Cavalry had left the Gap heading west toward Bonsack Station. The heat was not as bad that day, but the dust filled the air and choked men's throats. Duffié burned every railroad bridge between Bufords Gap and Bonsack Station.

Sullivan's Infantry was in advance of Crook's as the army moved toward the Gap. The infantrymen did their share of burning and looting as they moved. Many private homes near the tracks were plundered and torched. Fires were started on the tracks, and rails were bent. The infantrymen discovered some rolling stock, (railroad cars) which they pushed toward ravines where the bridge had been destroyed; "...the cars are run over into the deep ravines. They go down with a great crash."[18]

It appears that local citizens fired at the Federals because of the destruction they were visiting upon them. William Ferrel may have fired on the Yanks and was riding away, or he may have simply been running when he "...was shot through the head...."[124] Apparently Calohill Williamson had shot at the army. His horse was shot from under him, but he did escape. William Coleman lay in ambush, "A lieutenant riding up, Coleman took aim and shot him dead...."[124] Six or seven of the lieutenant's men fired at Coleman, but he escaped.

Not far from Petersburg, Grant had received more Confederate newspapers. They indicated that Hunter was retreating west. Grant concluded that since Sheridan could not reach Hunter he would allow Sheridan's Cavalry to be assigned to other duties.

Near Beverly, forces were still being collected so that they could be sent to Hunter's aid. The problem for the Union high commanders was to determine where Hunter was and the condition of his army. They knew that Early was after the retreating Hunter; it was believed that Hunter's whole army might be destroyed.

The wagon train had made it to Bufords Gap well before noon. The horses were unhitched but not unharnessed. The poor beasts were allowed to rest and graze. Many of their number that could no longer pull their load were shot.

About noon, the advance of Hunter's army was close to the Gap. As the men approached the Gap, they could see open farm land on both sides of the road. The mountain abruptly closed in, leaving only a hundred-yard-wide opening for the road to go through. The Buford family owned land and ran a tavern in the Gap itself.

There is little doubt that Duffié's men had cleaned out the stock of food and beverage well before the first infantry units arrived. The Bufords lost seventeen horses and forty-nine[132] cows in minutes.

The army had moved sixteen miles in twelve hours and needed rest. The Gap was a super defensive location. Hunter's staff members worked efficiently and deployed troops and guns as they arrived at the Gap. The open

Bufords Tavern — Bufords Gap (Montvale).

farm land gave an unobscured view of almost one half mile looking east from the Gap. Cannons were placed on the foothills entrance to the Gap. The Union defense line, approximately one quarter mile in length, was anchored to the mountains on both sides. Captain Town sent signal parties to establish stations on both mountains. Once the stations were in place, Confederate moves in the Valley could be easily seen and reported to the general's staff.

As the weary army began to fill the Gap, Strother noted, "Our cavalry looks very much used up and demoralized."[11] Most of the cavalrymen didn't unsaddle their horses; they just dismounted, lay down, and slept. An infantryman sarcastically said, "It was almost noon when we stopped for breakfast."[14] Another infantryman recalled, "Less than half rations are issued...."[83] Another infantry regiment saw some pigs. Since the men of the regiment were so tired that they couldn't run fast enough to catch them, they had to shoot their dinner.

At the Gap, Hunter received scouting reports. The scouts had sighted McCausland the night before and reported that they had seen "...a heavy force of cavalry...(moving) northward in the direction of the Peaks of Otter."[8] Hunter also heard "...a rumor that John Morgan is in front of us...."[11] (John Morgan was the vicious Commander of the Confederate Military Department of Southwest Virginia). Hunter, worried that he might have to face cavalry to his front, sent part of the First New York Cavalry to move to Bonsack with specific orders to guard the road coming from the north.

As Hunter moved west, he destroyed railroad depots and telegraph wires, but not before the operators reported his position as he moved. Jacob Bonsack, owner of the Woolen Mill in the community that bore his name, knew that the Yanks were approaching. Jacob also realized that it was very likely that his mill would be burned; he had much of the machinery moved to another building, maybe in Salem. When Duffié arrived, Jacob's mill went up in flames. Duffié also burned the depot and destroyed the telegraph lines.

Federals broke into George Gish's house. They stole food and scattered flour that they couldn't carry. The supply of meat was carried off except for one ham that was hidden behind a corner cupboard.

At one house, the residents put their flour in sacks and placed them under their feather ticks. They were not discovered. Another unnamed resident wasn't as lucky. He had acted on a rumor several weeks earlier and had sent his flour and cured meat to a relative for safe keeping. When the rumor proved untrue, he retrieved his food. When the rumor that Hunter was near reached him, he did not react. This rumor was correct, and the Yanks carried off, "...flour, wagon, horses, and all...."[125]

At Albert Reed's home, the Yanks stole turkeys and clothing. At Samuel Wood's, they stole six horses, many hams, and a slave named Charlie.

Many of the community's citizens felt their losses less acutely when they heard that David Plaine had been cleaned out. David had galled many of his neighbors because of his pro-Union sympathies. It was only right, thought the neighbors, that the Union should punish one of its own. The peace-loving Quaker preacher, John Moorman, told the Federals "...he was as good a Union man as any of them...."[132] His sacred calling and words of strong Union support, didn't even slow the hordes that ransacked his property.

Some of the citizens offered the looting Yanks stiff resistance. For example, when Mrs. George Riley saw a Federal enter her springhouse, she followed. The Yank was found bent over a jar of cream with his posterior high in the air. The homemaker gave it "...a kick and he went head first into the spring race."[125]

Mrs. Arbuckle saw her husband's finest boots come down the steps on Union feet. She grabbed an object and hit the Yank in the head, "...causing the blood to flow...."[125] As the dazed, now barefooted, Yankee recovered, he asked, "Old woman, how many sons have you in the army?"[125] The barren Mrs. Arbuckle lied, "I have twelve, and I wish to God I had twelve more."[125]

When comrades saw one of their own come from the house, bleeding and barefoot, they asked him what happened. The soldier told them. That was his second mistake in the last few minutes. Not only had he lost a bloody encounter with Mrs. Arbuckle, but his buddies would tease him unmercifully, saying that he had marched and fought furious Rebels only "...to be whipped by a woman."[125] The Yank had seen better days.

Within this general time frame, Ransom (with McCausland's Cavalry) had made it over the Peaks to Buchanan. There he joined with Jackson's Cavalry and learned that Jackson had sent no troops after Hunter's wagon train heading north past Fincastle.

On the way over the Peaks, the column had been halted by two pretty girls who told the officers of the outrages committed against them. "They implored us not to spare the Yankees when we caught them,"[91] recalled a Rebel officer.

Ransom had learned through couriers that Imboden's Cavalry was approaching. Several factors led Ransom to make a command error. The road leading from Bufords Gap to Fincastle must be blocked before Hunter arrived. Because of General Early's scathing condemnation of Imboden, Ransom believed his leadership was needed with that cavalry column. Ransom was anxious to direct troops toward Hunter's wagon train.

Ransom issued orders that McCausland was to proceed and block the road. McCausland's Cavalry had rested about an hour and a half. Ransom would wait and take personal command of Imboden's Cavalry and send troopers after the wagon train. Because McCausland was well in advance, Ransom would be forced to use couriers to attempt to keep abreast of the situation to the front. He might have to make command decisions based not on personal observation but on information relayed through scouts.

Back at the Gap, most of Hunter's men believed that they were to spend the night in rest, but the news the scouts brought forced Hunter to continue the retreat. Hunter was concerned that the Confederate cavalry seen moving north over the Peaks would intercept him. If that cavalry didn't intercept him, Morgan's might. Hunter didn't want his weary army to tangle with this fighter, who knew no mercy. At 3:00 p.m., couriers were sent to Duffié to push forward and occupy Salem. Hunter's wagon train was sent forward.

It appears that Hunter was with Sullivan's Infantry about two and one half miles west of Bufords Gap. Crook and Averell had the rear guard duty at the Gap. At 2:00 p.m., Hunter became aware that Southern forces were moving en masse toward the Gap. Despite the information, Hunter apparently decided to remain where he was and let George do it (George Crook).

Early had been pursuing since daylight. He was anxious to take the Union on in battle. Now was his chance!

Crook began to wake his men and move the troops on line. One soldier complained that they had barely had time to eat when they were ordered to fall in.

As Early's men approached, the Union line opened fire. Early rushed forward and surveyed the Federal position. At the crest of a hill, Early could see Union cannons on the foothills over cleared farm land about one mile away.

Early remembered what had occurred at Gettysburg; he sought other options besides a frontal attack across open fields.

Early formed his center with Ramseur's Brigade. The artillery was brought on line. Early directed Gordon to move his brigade to the left and try to find a way to outflank the line. Early gave the same orders to Rodes on the right. Elzey (Breckinridge's Cavalry) was held in reserve.

Gilmor's Independent Partisans were there. They saw the Union signal station on the right observing troop movements. They decided to blind

Hunter's "eye" on the mountain. Apparently the signal men were watching the main forces under Early and did not see this small band of cavalry circle far to the right.

Perhaps unaware of Gilmor's action, orders were sent to Opie's cavalry unit to attack Hunter's left on the mountain. The foliage was thick but Col. Sturgis Davis pointed to the area where he believed the Federals were. Opie dismounted his men and started up the mountain. The trees and underbrush were so thick that he couldn't see more than five feet ahead.

Within minutes of Rodes's and Gordon's departure, the signal station relayed their movements to Crook. Crook sent a courier to Hunter with the information. A message also arrived at headquarters from Averell. He said, "...We must prepare to fight immediately and this is the crisis of our fate, as this battle will save or ruin us."[11]

Instead of riding to the line for a personal assessment, Hunter sent word for Crook to report to his headquarters.

Apparently in Crook's absence, Rodes made contact with Crook's forces; "...heavy skirmishing broke out...."[103] Southern cannons opened to support Rodes on the right. Union cannons returned the fire. Despite the noise and the danger, some Union soldiers were so exhausted that they didn't even wake up.

During this time frame, Gilmor's Cavalry had reached the base of the mountain where the Union signal station sat. The cavalry dismounted and started scaling the mountain.

While Gilmor's men climbed the mountain west of the Gap, Opie's men were already on the mountain closer to the Gap. Opie was moving toward the spot where Col. Davis had said the enemy was posted. He was only about halfway there when shots rang out and one of his men fell, wounded. He was already in contact with the Yanks.

The brazen Opie decided to pretent to be a Union man. "Cease firing, you damned fools; you have killed one of your own men!"[20] he shouted. This tricked the Federals and they stopped firing.

Opie moved to the wounded man. He saw the wound and knew the trooper was badly hurt. He whispered to his fallen comrade that the group was going to fall back, and that to attempt to move him in his wounded condition would expose the whole unit to enemy fire. Opie then ordered his men to fall back. Opie told the wounded man he must be left, but he promised to come back for him as soon as he could. The wounded man said it made no difference because he was going to die anyway. He asked Opie for a sip of water. Since Opie had no water to give to the dying man, he bid him adieu, and followed his men down the mountain.

Crook and Hunter were in conference. Crook grumbled to himself that he had to run the whole army: "General Hunter had gotten so now that he would do nothing without first consulting me...."[73] Crook advised Hunter to move with Sullivan toward Salem and then toward the Kanawha Valley; he (Crook) would hold the Gap as long as possible or until dark and then follow. Hunter agreed. The Rebel cannonade cut the conference short, and Crook returned to the line.

Soon Hunter with Sullivan began to move toward Salem.

A Lynchburg newspaperman was still some miles away from Early's front when he sent the following dispatch back to his paper: "...From the fact that heavy cannonading was heard in that direction, it was supposed that he (Early) had overtaken them and the two forces were engaged in a fierce contest."[101]

Back on the line, the Union managed to capture a Confederate. The soldier was taken to Crook for interrogation. Soon Crook learned that this man was not from a dismounted cavalry unit but one of Rodes's men. The normally composed Crook said that it "...gave me much alarm."[73] Up to this point, Crook thought that he was dealing with some cavalry backed with artillery. Now he knew he was facing all of Early's army. The stoic Crook complained, "The lowest of everything fell on me and my division...I was in the advance all the time and now, in retreat, I was kept in the rear all the time, and had to do all the fighting."[73]

In this same general time frame, Opie was working his way down the mountain toward his unit. Opie heard a movement in the bushes ahead. Was it friend or foe? Opie called out, "Who are you?" "Who are you?"[20] was the reply. It sounded like a kids' game but these men were deadly serious. Opie yelled, "I was the first to make inquiry; who are you?"[20]

The voice in the bushes raised the ante, "If you don't say who you are, I will order my men to fire."[20]

Opie knew his life rested upon the right answer. To keep his country a secret he yelled, "My name is Opie."[20]

The voice in the bushes replied that his men had been sent to reinforce Opie. Opie then knew which team they were on. He joined the unit and discovered that most of the soldiers were age seventeen or under. He led the unit back up the mountain.

Crook probably didn't know it yet, but Gilmor's Cavalry had surprised and overrun the signal station on the mountain. Gilmor's men captured two Federals (the first losses recorded in the Signal Corps).

Now it was the Confederates turn to observe the enemy. It is possible that Gilmor's men could see smoke from the fires at Bonsack. They could surely see Sullivan's Infantry rapidly heading west. They sent this information to Early.

When Early received the news, "There was a momentary fear that the enemy would head for Wytheville or Saltville."[55] Since Hunter had not succeeded in capturing Lynchburg, he might be attempting to move directly against the South's only sources of salt and lead. The Confederacy might fall even though Lynchburg was saved.

Early believed that his cavalry should be at the junction of Valley Pike and the road to Fincastle. It was clear that Hunter would not be retreating in that direction. Early had sent no messengers to the cavalry because he was unsure where they would be needed. If the infantry broke the Union line, he wanted the cavalry to push through and reap havoc on the Federals. Because Early knew the Union was retreating, he wanted his cavalry to block that retreat. A courier was sent to Ransom. It was imperative that Ransom occupy Salem before the Yankees arrived. From Salem, the telegraph was to be used to call the Home Guard out. Home Guard units were to be activated from Salem to Lewisburg and from Salem to Christiansburg. There would be some forces to oppose Hunter whichever way he moved out of Salem. A courier was also sent to Fincastle to have that Home Guard unit move toward Salem. The cavalry continued over Valley Pike which roughly runs where Highway 11 is today. Other couriers spread the word to friends, neighbors, and to the workers at the Catawba Iron Works, northwest of Fincastle.

Although Early's cannons had been roaring on line they were doing little damage. If they were able to force a Union gun off line, the gun would simply be rolled behind the crest of a hill. In the event of a frontal assault by Early, the gun could be brought on line rapidly. Early ordered the cannons to reduce their rate of fire to conserve ammunition. Early would have to wait and see if Rodes or Gordon could find a pass through the mountains and flank the main line at the Gap.

Both flanking brigades found "the ground confusing...."[103] They were making no headway. Scouts were sent to find natives who could direct brigade movements. Valuable time was lost as the two brigades waited. The news the scouts brought in was not good: "...All the men, except the old ones, had gotten out of the way, and the latter, as well as the women and children, were in such a state of distress and alarm that no reliable information could be obtained from them."[114]

On the mountain, Opie knew where his enemy was. He led the unit of young men close to the spot where his man had been shot. Opie halted the unit. He then crawled forward to the wounded man. After briefly checking him, Opie crawled forward another two or three yards. As Opie peeped from the underbrush, he saw a Federal unit lying on the ground two marks deep. Opie quietly crawled back to the unit of young men. He informed the captain of the situation and moved the unit forward.

Near the spot where the wounded man lay, Opie shouted, "What command is that?"[30]

A voice replied that they were Ohio soldiers and requested that they not be fired upon. The captain of the young men shouted "Throw down your arms and surrender. We are Confederate soldiers."[30]

The roar of musketry was his reply. The bullets passed well over the Southern unit.

The Ohio soldiers decided not to stop and determine the strength of the Southerners in the bushes. They retreated. Opie and the unit opened fire on the fleeing Yanks. Opie fired his pistol at one Yank who dropped his gun as he ran. Opie recovered the rifle with a pistol ball in the stock.

The Confederates chased the Yankees a short distance. Here the Yanks established a line. Both sides slung lead, but few casualties were taken. Opie believed he was to be reinforced by infantry. With ammunition running low, he broke off contact with the Yankees. Some men in the unit picked up the mortally wounded Confederate and descended the mountain.

When Col. Davis became aware that Opie had retreated, he became angry and demanded, "Why in the hell didn't you hold your position...?"[30] The

Burnside carbine — captured by Capt. John N. Opie. Courtesy: Hiram Opie.

brazen Opie retorted, "Why in the hell didn't you charge on the main road with your regiment of infantry?"[30]

It was past 5:00 p.m. when McCausland received the messenger meant for Ransom. McCausland was still back toward Buchanan. McCausland sent a courier toward Ransom and Fincastle with Early's orders. Then McCausland started toward Salem.

As Rodes and Gordon could find no passage through the mountains, they issued orders that the army would have to struggle directly over the mountains. It was hard climbing and slow moving as the army inched upward. Because of trees, cliffs, and ravines, units could not stay in any formation. The generals worried that even if they did succeed in conquering the mountain, they could not re-form the brigade for an attack. The sun was sinking rapidly. Some soldiers did make it to the mountain tops by dark, but there was no way to re-form an attack. Early "...reluctantly called off the fighting after dark."[103]

Union signal men had observed the Confederates as they tried to find a passage around the Gap. When they saw the army starting up the mountain, they moved down to their army and reported the movements to Crook.

Early knew that Hunter was retreating. The troops in the Gap would be withdrawn during the night. Early was determined not to allow Hunter the entire night to march ahead. In the dark, Early sent orders that his army would start the pursuit, "...long before dawn."[103] General Rodes was to take the point, and the others would follow.

On the mountains, both Rodes and Gordon were having trouble finding their men and moving them back down the mountain to encamp.

By dark, Crook had started most of his infantry toward Bonsack. Crook knew the rear guard was facing infantry, not cavalry; this evening he did leave one of his infantry regiments (Colonel Hayes's Twenty-Third Ohio) and an artillery battery with some of Averell's Cavalry. Averell sent Jessie Scouts toward Fincastle and Liberty. Most of Averell's Cavalry had followed Sullivan's Infantry.

Citizens as far away as Salem attended prayer meetings to beseech their God to stop Hunter and to spare them. In one church, a member, Dr. Bittle, prayed and told fellow members that he was placing himself and his property in God's hands for protection. He wasn't going to hide one thing he said.

A member of the congregation returned home and told his wife not to hide anything. He said, "...Doctor Bittle prayed so eloquently that..."[127] he was sure Hunter would not be able to do them any harm.

As Crook pulled off line, he said that the enemy had "...attacked us with considerable vigor."[73] Hunter, who never witnessed any of the fighting, belittled both Early and Crook when he wrote, "The enemy...made some feeble demonstrations, but was easily repulsed."[8]

The citizens as far back as Liberty were aware of the day's battle. Rumors circulated. One rumor states that Early had overrun the Union and captured six cannons.[100] An angry population cried out for revenge: "We sincerely wish that he (Hunter) may be caught and hung by Early. Such a man deserves no better fate...."[101] Another citizen wanted to punish the whole army, not just Hunter. He said, "It is a pity we could not surround and kill, not capture or wound, every scoundrel...."[100]

Early had not captured Hunter's army, but he had bagged at least 250 prisoners[101] since he left Lynchburg. Some of Early's men were foot-sore. The rations in Breckinridge's supply train were long gone. Early had not been re-supplied since Lynchburg. Hunter's army had left no forage for Early's army. The Rebels were as exhausted and hungry as were the Yanks.

The Federals continued to retreat all night. The hungry Yankees entered "...A bad road filled and choked with wagons, artillery, pack horses and mules, and weary men hardly able to walk on, many apparently sleeping as they walk."[9] "The suffering of our men (wrote one private) is something fierce...Many are barefoot...."[18]

The infantry flanked the roads and the artillery and wagon train filled the center. Men picked honeysuckle and strawberries to eat and hastily rejoined the march. Sometimes soldiers had to trot to keep up with the wagons. More men and horses gave out as they moved.

The destruction of the railroad continued. Strother said, "Burning bridges and railroad stations lighted our way."[11]

Despite the misery, there was some humor in the ranks. A soldier who lost his knapsack at the battle of Lynchburg, picked one up on the road. Another Federal had discarded the weight of an empty bag. When other members of the unit saw their comrade retrieve the empty pack, they, "...laughed...seeing I had nothing in the shape of rations to carry,"[75] recalled the soldier.

An infantryman saw a wagon which was constantly blocking and slowing the column. Hunter saw the same thing: "Snatching the whip from the hand of the astounded wagoner, our commanding general soundly castigated the offender with the instrument with which the latter was wont to belabor his own beasts!"[10] said an observer.

With each mile, more and more men straggled. Some fell in the road and some, along the road. All were sound asleep by the time they hit mother earth.

TEAMSTERS.

By David Hunter Strother.

Straggling decreased troop strength and decreased the speed of the column. Some officers decided to stage a play to motivate the men.

A private saw a cavalryman ride up to his major and whisper a few words in the major's ear and then ride off. In a few minutes, the major shouted, "Halt! Silence. Listen."[75] The men froze. Shortly they "...heard a few shots mingled with the cry 'I surrender, I surrender.' We muttered curses."[75] The ruse worked, many Federals believed that their stragglers were being shot even when they had tried to surrender.

More slaves ran with the army. An infantryman said, "Some of them took their master's buggies and loaded them with young nigs and rode along quite stylish."[118]

Back at Bufords Gap, Crook pulled the last of his troops off line. (The fires were kindled before the rear guard pulled off). The fact that Early's Infantry had been sighted moving along the base of the mountain preyed upon Crook's mind: "My greatest fears were that Rodes's Division had either gotten in our front or had come in on one flank. In either case I felt certain of disaster."[73]

Crook elected to share the pangs of hunger with his men. "One ear of corn was all that I had,"[73] said Crook.

Crook remained at the rear of the column in case of Rebel attack. He wanted to try to prevent straggling. First, he told stragglers that they would be taken prisoner if they didn't move faster, but "...that fact had no terrors for the poor, worn-out wretches."[73] Then he tried shouting and haranguing his men, but they still continued to straggle and fall by the road.

There in the dark, Crook said, "I felt the whole responsibility on my shoulders. I had no confidence in those in front (Hunter, Duffié, Sullivan, and Averell). I was so worn out that it was only with the greatest exertions I could keep awake."[73]

Some time between 10:00 and 11:00 p.m., Crook's column came to a sudden halt. Crook went forward to investigate.

On the other side of Bufords Gap, the Confederates saw the Union's campfires burning lower and lower. At 11:00 p.m. it was discovered that Hunter was gone. Early had already decided for a march to begin in the early morning hours of June 21.

Gilmor's Cavalry was independent of Early's command. It appears that the small band of partisans started their pursuit before midnight. They went cross-country, following the north base of the mountains.

Crook's column was halted between the Gap and Bonsack because some Union artillerists had simply abandoned a cannon that got stuck in the mud at a stream crossing. The artillery unit followed Sullivan, but it was in front of Crook. Units approaching the gun saw that the road was blocked and took the chance to fall out and to fall asleep. Soldiers were so exhausted that they didn't even consider moving the obstacle. Finally, some officers rode forward and employed the men to move the gun. It was near midnight before the column again began to move. Because Sullivan moved and Crook didn't, it "...left a gap of some miles in our columns."[73]

Near midnight on Valley Pike Road, a group of slaves running from their masters heard the cavalry approach from the east. They hailed the horse soldiers out there in the dark, telling them that they were going to run north with them. Their greeting was answered by rifle fire. The runaway slaves ran for their lives. They had hailed the wrong army. This army was the advance of McCausland's Cavalry.

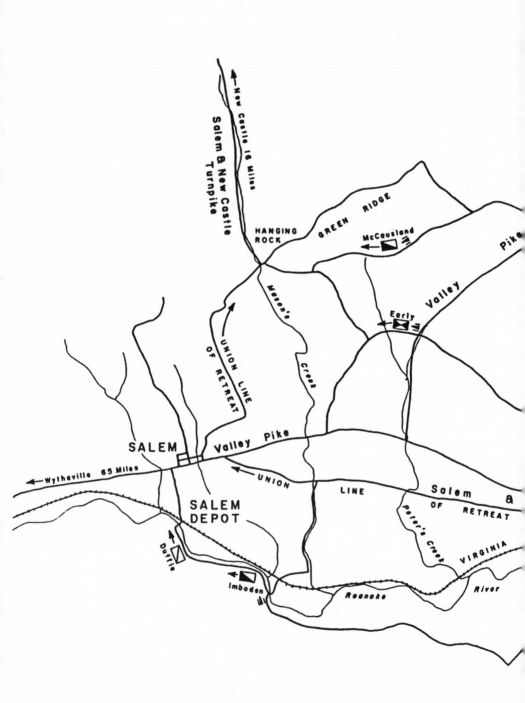

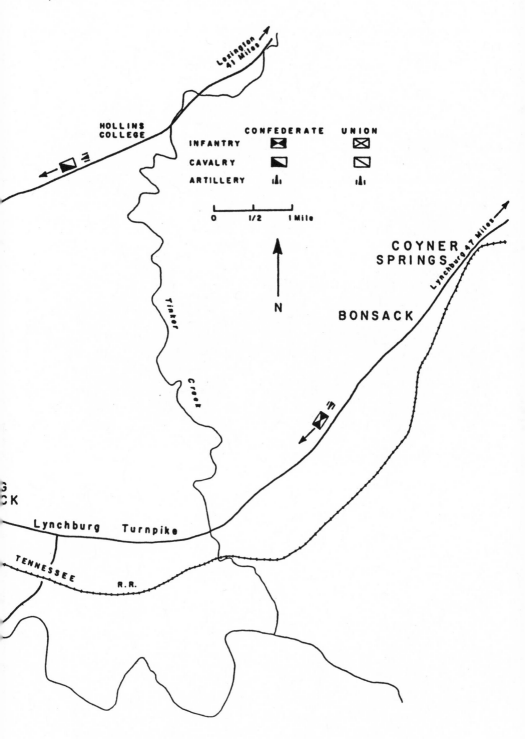

Re-creation: Confederate Scout.

Chapter XII

Tuesday, June 21 — Wednesday, June 22

As McCausland's forces rode toward Salem over Valley Pike Road on Tuesday, June 21, the dark early morning air was pierced by a whistling soldier. One of his companions near the head of the column praised the music, saying "I never heard such whistling, popular airs, operatic airs, hymns, chants, anything and everything."[91] Despite the music, McCausland knew that it was a desperate ride. All depended on his getting to Salem before the Union Army. If McCausland was successful, Hunter might be destroyed; if he was unsuccessful, the Confederacy might be destroyed.

Somewhat to the rear was Ransom with Imboden's Cavalry. Fast-riding couriers were sent to keep separate parts of the army informed. Ransom had received a courier from Early, stating that the infantry would be in motion well before daylight. Early believed that his cavalry could make it to Salem before Hunter. Early instructed the cavalry to hold the town if possible until the infantry arrived. In case the cavalry couldn't hold, axes were to be secured from Salem citizens. When and if the cavalry was driven from town, the axes were to be used to fell trees on the major roads leading both west and north out of town. If the cavalry could fell enough trees, the infantry could catch and defeat Hunter.

Averell had sent scouts over the Creeley Gap Road (now alternate Route 220) north from Bonsack. These scouts observed the Confederate cavalry heading toward Salem. They raced back toward Bonsack with the news. Averell sent word forward to Duffié's advanced cavalry column and told him to post heavily all roads leading toward the Salem Pike. The pickets were to be placed four miles distant from the Pike to prevent the Confederates from cutting the road.

While the Confederate infantry slept near Bufords Gap, Gilmor's Cavalry continued working west along the north base of the mountains. In the dark, the cavalry came to the Creeley Gap Road and encountered Averell's picket (part of Powell's West Virginia Cavalry). From the musket fire, Gilmor determined that there were fewer Yankees than Rebels; he pressed and attacked.

Powell's men sent a courier back to the main infantry column then moving over Salem Pike through Bonsack. Crook dispatched two companies of the Thirty-Sixth Ohio over the Creeley Gap Road.

A decision was made to ambush these Rebs. A member of the Thirty-Sixth recalled, "We were ordered to jump down over the retaining wall on the low side of the road and wait till our few mounted men passed then give the murderers (the soldier believed that the Rebel cavalry was shooting stragglers when they tried to surrender) a volley from ambush. Here was a trap, every man eager for revenge. On and past went our mounted rear guard, saw us, but spoke not. Soon the Rebel advance turned the bend. Now we held our breath, nervously handling our carbines. Here they come round the bend. Just when almost in the trap, one excited comrade yelled aloud 'Here they are!' The Rebs heard and turned and fled. We took a near cut through the bushes to head them off at the neck of the bend below, but only fired a volley at long-range, crippling them some and scaring them...."[75]

Gilmor knew that he had encountered more than an isolated foraging party. He pulled off the road and continued across country, still heading west and parallel to Salem Pike. It is not known how many miles the cavalry had ridden before it ventured toward the Pike. When the cavalry reached the Pike, it was surprised to find no Union soldiers. Gilmor quickly surmised that there was a gap in the fleeing Union column. A strong picket would not have been posted on the Creeley Gap Road if the whole Union Army had passed through Bonsack. Gilmor was correct. The gap had been caused by one Union cannon stuck in the mud.

The Union rumor mill began to report and distort the sighting and the action of the Confederate cavalry. It was believed that the Bee, McCausland, was back upon them. One soldier lamented, "It is galling to our brave soldiers to retire...before the men they had so often overcome and routed."[16]

Farther toward Big Lick (now Roanoke) outriders were spreading the news that Hunter would soon be upon them. Valuables began to disappear from sight. John Trout packed his wagons with slaves, and animals and headed toward Yellow Mountain. At Ferguson's tobacco factory, there were two barrels of brandy. The owner didn't want the Yankees there, much less drunken Yankees. He had the barrels rolled out of the factory and broken open. The slaves then tried to catch some of the liquid without success.

At a house near the factory, hams were placed in barrels and covered with ashes. Only one ham was left hanging for the Yankees to discover and steal.

One homemaker hid valuables in the chimney.

A boarder, Mrs. Mitchell in Big Lick, didn't hide a thing, "She boasted that she was not afraid of the Yankees (and) that she would tell them plainly what she thought of them...."[126]

Outriders were sent toward Salem and toward Botetourt Springs, which is on the campus of Virginia's first woman's college, Hollins College, located on Valley Pike. The college President, Dr. Charles Cocke, was well aware of what had occurred when Hunter visited Washington College and the Virginia Military Institute in Lexington. Mr. Cocke, "...had prepared a paper in which he had set forth the defenseless position of his college family...to be delivered to the first (Union) soldier who reached campus."[127]

Sometime near midnight, Duffie's Cavalry entered Big Lick. The railroad station, some track, and the telegraph wire were the first things destroyed. The soldiers then started filling their stomachs. Hogs were caught, slaughtered,

Hollins College — Botetourt Springs.

cooked, and eaten. Some cattle were taken with the cavalry as it left town.

The owner of the tobacco factory had his smokehouse broken into, and all the meat was removed. One domestic slave begged the soldiers to leave her something. Because she was black, they did.

In one barn, the slats of the corncrib were kicked in, allowing the corn to spill on the ground so that horses could eat, too.

Mrs. Mitchell's speech was brave; when a Federal came, calling to her, "...she went out to meet him and answered his questions very politely...."[126] The soldier took what he wanted. As he got ready to leave, the brave Mrs. Mitchell asked, "Won't you have something more? Won't you have some water?"[126] He thanked her and left.

One lady told a newspaperman, the damn Yankees "...stole my cow, flour, meal, meat, land...rifled our trunks, took all my gold and silver money, my silver plate...every kind of kitchen utensil, knives, and forks, cups and saucers...tore the clothes...stole my children's (unreadable)...tore down fences, grazed our oats, and destroyed nearly everything we had...the Negroes insulted the ladies...one buck nigger smacked a young girl's face...One officer...told my servant woman if she would go he would take her behind him. She told him she did not want to go, as she had a good master. (A male slave that was rented from another family but working in Big Lick) did go...our loss is not less than $15,000 at the lowest calculation...(Not only were her possessions gone but her spirit was also broken) I am for the first time in my life a beggar."[132]

One Union soldier bragged "...every bridge or culvert that was burnable was burned so that through the whole country for miles shone the light of these traces of our devastating march."[16]

General McCausland saw the light from the burning bridges. He came over Valley Pike by Hollins College. It is likely that outriders informed him of Hunter's presence. The Yanks had burned Big Lick and were moving toward

Salem. McCausland knew that the race was lost. It is likely that he halted the column and sent word back to Ransom.

Ransom believed that Hunter had three choices. He could stand and fight or he could move west and attempt to destroy the leadworks in Wythe County and the saltworks in Saltville or he could retreat north. The cavalry could do nothing about the first option; it could try to slow or stop a possible flight west or north. Ransom sent orders to McCausland to attempt to get in front of Hunter somewhere on the Salem-New Castle Road. Imboden's Cavalry would move cross-country to Salem Pike and attempt to circle Hunter's army and block Valley Pike heading west from Salem. Ransom was hoping that this might slow Hunter enough so that Early could strike him.

Ransom became ill; the lack of food and rest were probably the contributing factors. He stopped at a house on Valley Pike. He didn't formally release command, but he had no direct command of either McCausland's Cavalry or Imboden's Cavalry.

McCausland pushed forward along Valley Pike and then turned the column northward over what is today Cove Road. The column passed the Dunkard Church in the night. Once on Cove Road, McCausland could swing due west toward the Salem-New Castle Road as it passes through the gap in the mountain where Mason Creek flows. The gap is named Hanging Rock because of the large outcropping of rocks at the gap's south end. McCausland knew that Union forces were ahead of him, but he did not know their numbers or consistency. He believed that it would be risky to move his tired cavalry to the road where the Union infantry might be waiting. The time was between 3:00-4:00 a.m. when McCausland decided to camp the next couple of hours until dawn at Greenridge before proceeding to block the road.

Hanging Rock.

Apparently Imboden's Cavalry continued along the road that follows Peters Creek going toward the Roanoke River. At approximately 4:00 a.m., it stopped near the river. Horses grazed and rested. Men came out of their saddles and fell asleep on the ground.

Before Duffié left Big Lick, the Home Guard was forming at Salem. There were two units at the Salem area. One unit was composed of home folk and the other was composed of students at Roanoke College. The composure of the Home Guard and its leaders during this time frame were not determined. Not only did the Home Guard turn out to fight, but also outriders were sent over the roads heading both north and west from town to inform the populace that Hunter might soon be upon them.

It was still dark when Duffié, closely followed by Sullivan, left Big Lick. One report stated that Duffié was approaching Salem by as early as 2:00 a.m.[128]

Salem is an old town. It grew up on the Valley Pike long before the railroad came to this section of the state. The Salem depot of the Virginia-Tennessee Line was built more than a quarter of a mile from town. Duffié was probably at our near the depot at 2:00 a.m. As he moved toward the town proper, some Home Guard troops fired on his column. The gallant, fearless Duffié halted his command and called for reinforcements from Sullivan's Infantry. Shots were exchanged between the cavalry and the Home Guard, but no casualties were recorded on either side. Sullivan sent two companies of the Hundred Twenty-Third Ohio forward. Apparently the Home Guard heard the reinforcements arriving and fled. The Union Army occupied the town without further opposition.

Salem, like the other towns, soon felt the heat of the Union Army. The depot was burned, the telegraph wire destroyed, and plundering continued. One unit stole a sheep which was quickly butchered. Soldiers broke into homes and looted at will.

An officer near Hunter saw this scene repeated time and time again as ladies ran to Hunter begging for protection from his army. Hunter gave them all a pat answer, "Go away! Go away, or I will burn your house!"[14]

The army had moved over twenty-five miles. At Salem, Hunter received the courier from Bonsack, stating that the Rebel cavalry was sighted on Valley Pike heading west. This news bothered Hunter.

Hunter had the springless wagon carrying his favorite prisoner, Angus McDonald, parked close to his headquarters.

Back near Bufords Gap the first rays of the sun were starting to warm the air, and so was General Early's tongue. His command was supposed to move well before dawn; now the sun was moving, but his army was sitting. He surely sent a courier to Rodes, demanding an explanation and movement! One soldier noted even privates "...were impatiently discussing the cause of the delay."[30]

Rodes was befuddled. This was the first time that he had heard that he was to form the advance of the army and be gone while it was still night. One account said that the delay was due to "...a mistake of the messenger..."[119]

from Early to Rodes.

An artillerist at Bufords Gap later set forth three areas where Early had erred: (1.) the marching order from Early to Rodes was issued verbally, not written; (2.) only one courier was used to convey the order; and (3.) Early had chosen the wrong messenger. The artillerist who had served in the Valley knew the courier personally; therefore, it is likely that the courier was from the Valley also. The artillerist gave no name but said that the "...single messenger who turns out to be a blockhead and his blunder is allowed to delay the whole army...."[30]

The belated march began shortly after sunrise. Crook's rear was miles and hours in advance of Early's advance under Rodes. Of course, Ransom with the cavalry was ignorant of this fact and believed that the infantry had started a hot pursuit at an early hour.

Hungry and tired men with blistered feet raced. One army retreated for its life; another pursued with the hope for vengeance.

An incident occurred that some accounts indicate took place at Bonsack, but it was more likely to have occurred at Bufords Gap. General Early was already having a bad day, which had just started. His army was late moving; and as he passed Bufords Tavern, Mrs. Buford beckoned the general to tarry a little longer. He stopped. Apparently, Mrs. Buford had been able to hide some of the tavern's finer whisky from the thieving Yanks. She divided that meager stock with the general. She "...cordially supplied him with two saddle-bags of good old Southern whisky."[129] As Early was leaving, William Cook rode up to the general, dismounted, and handed him a message. Early gently laid the saddle-bags aside and read the note. Just then "...Cook's horse went berserk...."[129] Men moved from the horse's path, leaving saddle-bags to be smashed. The horse stamped the bags. The bottles broke. As the aroma rose in the air so did Early's temper. "...The General went nearly as berserk as the horse,"[129] and "...the old General cussed like a sailor,"[125] recorded some observers.

The advance of Crook was well past Bonsack, but it was not at Big Lick when the sun rose. Crook recalled, "While dragging our weary bodies along, nearly exhausted, unconscious of any danger, all of a sudden we received a volley...."[73] Gilmor's men gave some of Crook's men permanent rest. Union soldiers dashed for cover. Others lay in the road bed for cover, thus joining the wounded and the dead. Very soon they were returning Confederate fire. Other Federal units rushed forward. Gilmor's Partisan Rangers had done their work; they retreated, unscratched.

The dead were buried, the wounded were given transport, and Crook's column continued marching. It was Crook's men who had stopped because one cannon was left on the road, but Crook was angry that Sullivan had continued to march, creating the gap which allowed Crook's column to be attacked. Sullivan was probably unaware that Crook's column had halted.

When one of the troopers with Imboden (between Big Lick and Salem) awoke near dawn, he "...noticed the sleepers all along the line with horses walking in and out amongst them."[91] Soon the command moved across

Three grapeshot recovered near Gish Mill (between Bonsack and Big Lick [Roanoke]). Courtesy: *Lance M. Hale.*

Roanoke River and entered the Salem Road, which ran south of the stream along the railroad tracks. The command started west toward Salem. It could not know that it was in the gap between Crook's advance and Sullivan's rear.

The cavalry had only moved up the river a few hundred yards when the Yankees fired on it. Imboden had some of his men dismount, and he sent them forward as skirmishers. Soon the Union cavalry, rear guard, was being pushed toward Salem.

After retreating some distance, the two companies (one from the First West Virginia Cavalry and one from the Second West Virginia Cavalry) formed a skirmish line by lying at the edge of a wheatfield. Because the wheat was high, the advancing Confederates could not see how very few Yankees opposed them. The Union also brought a gun on line.

The Confederates halted, and they, too, brought a battery forward. When Saunders saw the battery commander "...a beardless young fellow with a Lieutenant stripe...(with the) voice of a boy not yet attained to manhood,"[91] he had little confidence. The guns were run up a steep hill to the left of the Union line. Saunders watched as the gun was aimed. He soon changed his mind about the lieutenant: "I had my glasses to my eyes. I never saw so destructive a shot. It struck one of the enemy's guns, dismounted it, and the shell exploded. It seemed to me that it had killed all the gun crew."[91] The next shot was aimed at the Union cavalry; it, too, found its mark. Saunders was impressed.

The Yankees were impressed, also. They sent a battery to the right of the Confederate battery. Soon "...shot fell among us fast and furious...A big ball came near scooping me out of the saddle,"[91] Saunders recalled. This was no place for an older man who wanted to become even older. Saunders informed the young lieutenant (whom he now admired) that he had other pressing duties farther back from the fighting. The fearless lieutenant replied, "I was thinking it was about time"[91] (that Saunders would be leaving).

The Union trooper rode to Hunter with the news. It was estimated that the Confederates were attacking with a force of 1,000 men.[83] The cavalry commander requested infantry and artillery support to stop the attack. The only good news that Hunter received was that Colonel Ely was sufficiently recovered again to command the Eighteenth Connecticut.

Hunter had heard the sounds of battle. The courier from the cavalry arrived with the request for support. One soldier said, "...the Rebels made a fierce attack on the rear, with both musketry and shells."[16] About this time "...the Rebels suddenly sent three shells right into camp."[102]

Hunter's weary brain was in turmoil. How could the Rebels attack his rear? The thought now occurred to him "...that Crook was cut-off."[11] Hunter had relied heavily on Crook during the retreat. One writer even described Crook as being "the brains of the army."[73] Hunter could neither rely on Crook for decision making nor on Crook's troops. It appears that Hunter made an incorrect assumption as to the fate of Crook's whole division. Hunter evidently believed that Early had cut-off Crook and trapped him. The last report placed the Rebel cavalry on Valley Pike. This report must be that of Early's attacking the rear.

Hunter was badly shaken. The newspaperman with Hunter's staff said that he was very near and watched Hunter "...while he rapidly issued his orders to meet this unexpected attack. He seems to be unduly excited, almost panic-stricken."[102]

In his panic, Hunter tried to save what he could of the army. He ordered Sullivan to send a brigade to the rear to slow the Rebels. He ordered Dupont to send a section of cannons to support the infantry.

Horses could move faster than men so Duffié's Cavalry was told to push straight to New Castle. The wagon train was to follow as rapidly as possible. The wagon train was said to have 147 wagons (probably including the 90 ambulances). Two wagons were reported filled with stolen silver.[101] The balance of the horse-drawn artillery was then sent. The excited general pushed and shoved soldiers, officers, and teamsters as he demanded that his orders were to be obeyed at once.

The Eighteenth Connecticut was part of the brigade Sullivan had ordered to the line at the rear. The Eighteenth had been stealing and cooking steadily, preparing for their best meal in days. There was hot, strong coffee with plenty of sugar, "a nice soup, well flavored," fresh mutton, and other delights. The meal was half cooked when they were ordered to move. One soldier proclaimed, "This was downright provoking."[41]

The infantry brigade moved about a half mile and formed a line with artillery support.

When Imboden saw the infantry and the artillery, he knew that he had advanced as far as possible. He could not know that he was sitting in the gap between Sullivan's rear and Crook's front. Imboden knew that Early was to advance his infantry past midnight. All Imboden could do was to harass and hold the Union rear and wait for the arrival of Early. It appears that Imboden detached some of his cavalrymen and sent them to aid McCausland. Because Imboden was engaged in a holding action, he didn't need all of his troops, but McCausland may need every man he could get to stop a union advance toward New Castle.

Imboden had become engaged south of Salem near dawn. Hunter had ordered that Duffié's Cavalry, the wagons, and the artillery should run toward New Castle. It was probably near 6:30 a.m. when Duffié left Salem. Because of the reports of Confederate cavalry heading over Valley Pike, Duffié had to be concerned that the road to New Castle would be blocked.

Duffié raced out of Salem closely followed by the train and the artillery. The cavalry went through the gap at Hanging Rock and followed the road along the base of the mountain, going west and then turning north. No picket was posted on the Green Ridge Road. As the cavalrymen started up Catawba Mountain, they found that the road was blocked by fallen trees.

Various sources indicate that the trees were cut by the Salem Home Guard, McCausland's men, or organized workers probably from the Catawba Iron Works almost twenty miles away on the Fincastle Road. Because of the location of the fallen trees, the first two groups appear to be eliminated. Why would Salem Home Guards go approximately four miles before they cut their first tree? If McCausland had had the trees cut, why weren't they felled at the intersection of the Green Ridge Road and the New Castle Road? The lack of cutting from that point strongly indicates that McCausland, like Early, failed to march on time. Had McCausland moved at daybreak, he would have been in the gap at Hanging Rock to oppose Duffié. Apparently, workers coming down the mountain saw Duffié's column coming up the mountain and started cutting trees.

It was approximately 7:30 when Duffié's Cavalry was halted by the trees. Most of the wagon train had passed Hanging Rock Gap and had spread along the road to the base of Catawba Mountain. The artillery came to a halt in the gap at Hanging Rock.

Duffié's men started clearing the road, but because of the number of trees, it was known that it would be some time before the column could proceed. A courier was sent back to Hunter at Salem. As the courier passed, he informed the wagoners and the artillerists that they would be going nowhere for awhile. The weary men knew that it was a good time for a rest. Some slept, and some started fires to cook the breakfast they had not gotten at Salem.

McCausland had stopped before dawn near Green Ridge, approximately one half mile from Hanging Rock Gap. Because of the mountains that surround the Gap, the noise of the wagon train was muffled; it was probably the smoke from the artillerists' campfires that drew McCausland's attention.

McCausland rode toward Hanging Rock Gap. When he reached the crest of the hill and peered down into Hanging Rock Gap, he was greeted by a cavalryman's fantasy come true. There, camped below, was the tailend of the Union supply train and several artillery batteries. They appeared to be completely unprotected by either the infantry or the cavalry.

Every fiber in McCausland's body wanted to attack! McCausland was a good leader, but he was also a good soldier. Ransom was in command. McCausland sent a courier back to the ailing Ransom, who was at a home on Valley Pike, asking for permission to attack. McCausland drew up his line on the hill and waited.

Ransom received the courier. Ransom believed that Early had started his march some time after midnight and that he should be approaching Salem very soon. Ransom did not know that Early had not left until dawn, nor did he know that Crook was separated from the main force and that Imboden had engaged at Salem. Ransom knew that if McCausland attacked, he probably could not hold the Union column long enough to allow Early to overtake Hunter. Ransom sent a courier back to tell McCausland to hold his position and to wait for Early.

Ransom sent one courier to inform Imboden at Salem and another courier across country toward Salem Pike. It was expected that the courier sent to the Pike would locate Early's Infantry approaching Salem.

While couriers raced, Duffié's men had succeeded in clearing the road at least partway up the mountain. A courier from Duffié moved down the road, informing teamsters and artillerists to start making preparations to move.

McCausland observed the Union making preparations to move, and he believed that his position had been discovered. McCausland sent another courier to Ransom. This time he "...begged to be allowed to attack...."[91]

Ransom received McCausland's courier, but he had not received any courier from Early. Ransom realized that it was ridiculous to try and command both Imboden's Cavalry and McCausland's Cavalry when he was with neither. He relieved himself from command and sent a courier to McCausland.

It was approximately 9:00 a.m. when the courier arrived at Hanging Rock Gap. Now McCausland learned that "General Ransom (had) turned the command over to me (McCausland)."

McCausland passed the order to attack. The Fourteenth, Sixteenth, Seventeenth, and Twenty-Second Virginia Cavalries were ready.

McCausland's men occupied the slightly wooded ridge line. Approximately 100 yards below them were the end of the wagon train and the artillery. The wagoners and the artillerists were not heavily armed; there were some pistols but very few rifles. Because of the steep slope, the Union artillery would be completely useless. The guns could not be elevated to fire on the Confederates. In short, the Yankees were like fish in a rain barrel.

Years later, Carter Berkeley would claim that his artillery outfit fired the first shot. The battery was on a hill at the south end of the Gap. The road from Salem runs almost one half mile due east before turning north through the Gap. The Federal column on the road offered a tempting target.

Berkeley recalled that he had waited and watched for two hours. When the Federal column started moving, Berkeley decided that he had waited too long: "I ran out a gun without orders and fired into the moving column."[30]

Whether it was Berkeley or McCausland that fired the first shot, the conflict was on. McCausland's men opened fire from the hillcrest.

The Yankees were caught by surprise. Many of the poorly armed Federals panicked. Some ran across Mason Creek to the mountain away from the Confederate line. Some streamed out of both ends of the Gap. Some took cover near the wagons. Others returned the Confederate fire. There was much firing from the hill, but relatively few Union soldiers were struck. The first shots from the Confederates weren't aimed at the men but at the horses in harness. McCausland wanted to make sure that the wagons and the artillery could not be taken from the Gap.

It seems that Carlin's Battery was near the north end of the Gap, followed by Snow's Battery. Apparently, all but one gun of Von Kleiser's had turned north into the Gap when the Rebels struck.

Union horses began to fall throughout the Gap. (At least thirty[41] were struck in the initial firing). The guns and the wagons could not move. Confederate fire from the hill easily overwhelmed the few poorly armed Federals. Within minutes, the Union had eight to ten men killed and forty to fifty wounded.[130]

McCausland's men reloaded and charged off the hill toward the stalled and battered column. They yelled to the penned-down Yankees to surrender. Approximately 100 Union[101] soldiers responded to the call. One of the prisoners was Captain Von Kleiser.

McCausland's men began to secure the Gap, but action was taking place at both ends. South of the Gap, Von Kleiser's one gun had unlimbered and started to return Berkeley's fire, but Berkeley's cannon found its mark, and the Union's gun barrel blew away from the caisson. One of the men running out of the north end of the Gap was Captain Carlin. He had the Signal Corps send a flag message forward to Duffié, who was now approaching the top of Catawba Mountain. Duffié, unaware of the situation that had developed, sent only one regiment back down the mountain to aid the horse-drawn vehicles.

McCausland first disarmed and herded the Union prisoners; then he sent troops to secure the ends of the Gap. Some of his hungry men had already started plundering the Union wagons, reducing his effective strength.

The north end of the Gap was secured easily and quickly because there were only wagoners in that direction. The south end of the Gap was posted, but the Union controlled the road heading east toward the Gap. McCausland made no attempt to attack the Union forces controlling the road. Berkeley's Battery forced the Federals approximately one half mile back down the road. It was McCausland's hope that he could simply hold his position until Early arrived. Hunter's Union Army had suffered a considerable loss. Again, figures vary widely, but it appears that McCausland had captured between twelve and fifteen wagons and fifteen pieces of artillery plus the one remaining gun of Von Kleiser's which Berkeley had destroyed. The artillery was the queen of the battlefield, and Hunter's army had lost approximately one half of its strength in just a few minutes.

McCausland knew that he could not hold the Gap against a determined Union attack. He began sending the captured soldiers up the hill toward the old Southern line. They would be placed under guard back from the hill toward Green Ridge.

The dead and the wounded horses that had prevented any Union attempt to move wagons and cannons slowed McCausland's efforts as he tried to move the vehicles out of the Gap. A soldier with the Fifth West Virginia Infantry said, "The roads were...narrow and poor, much unlike the excellent macadamized turnpikes we had been on."[21] A private with the Thirty-Fourth Massachusetts wrote, "It was impossible for one team to pass another."[118]

Dead and wounded horses were replaced, and one by one the wagons (some times carrying slightly wounded prisoners) were pulled off. The severely wounded were left where they lay. Apparently little or no medical attention was given to them.

One Southern soldier was delighted to find "...many wagons loaded with gunpowder, boots, shoes, and other equipment and plunder taken from houses along the line of march."[28] Some escaping slaves might have been caught.

Since shortly after dawn, Crook had been able to march unmolested by any Confederate troops. With daylight, the hungry soldiers left the Salem Pike to loot any nearby house.

The citizen who had been so moved by Dr. Bittle's prayer that he had placed his property in God's hands and not in hiding, soon wished for a second chance. One source said, "...The poor man had reason to regret the quality of his faith, for the invading soldiers made way with everything in sight."[127]

The soldiers entered Leroy Campbell's house and stole at will. Mr. Campbell noted that his "...slaves...were terrified. One half-grown girl attempted to crawl beneath a trundle bed and got her head caught between the side piece and the floor. There she lay, kicking furiously and screaming at the top of her lungs."[127]

The Federals pillaged the Wheeler farmhouse. They stole food and then headed to the barn to steal the horses. When a soldier mounted Miss Lelia Wheeler's favorite horse, she decided that the damn Yankee had gone too far. She raced from the house with a pistol in her hand. She aimed the weapon straight at the soldier and told him to dismount or die. The soldier replied, "Lady, I am not afraid of your pistol, but I do admire your bravery." Not only did he return her favorite riding horse, but he also had the other stolen horses returned.

At another house a Union soldier decided to get a cool drink of water before starting his plundering. The colored cook saw the soldier and called to him, "My gawd, man! You hain't dun drinked dat water, is you? We done been drapping dead cats and every old thing in dat well."[127] The sweet, cool taste of the water in his mouth, now became a churning, nauseous pain in his stomach. The soldier left without stealing a thing.

A female slave lamented, "They took old Charlie, and Pappy (Master Albert Reed) said he had expected to marry me off on old Charlie."[127]

One soldier searched a house but could find only one jug of black strap molasses. Because the molasses was so easy to find and food was more difficult, some soldiers became suspicious. The thieving Yankee recalled, "...our boys were afraid to taste it, (the molasses) fearing Governor Letcher's

A BUSHWHACKER.

By David Hunter Strother.

order had been...truly obeyed...to poison and bushwhack..."[75] any Yank. The soldier decided to drink the contents anyway, telling his buddies, I "...might as well die at once by poison as be starved and tortured to death by inches as we now were."[75] The molasses was not poisoned.

Because Crook's army was spread over such a long distance, it is difficult to locate any one unit and a particular moment in time. It is known that the advance of the column had passed Big Lick and was approaching Salem by the time the engagement started at 9:00 a.m. at Hanging Rock.

Because Early had failed to march at an early hour, the rear of Crook's column had not been attacked. The advance had been hit by the Partisan Rangers. Since Crook seemed more concerned about an attack from the front than he was about one from the rear, he moved to the front of the column. Crook was normally cool and composed, but the fatigue was showing. He was angry and grumbling because of the gap between his column and Sullivan's.

Imboden had been skirmishing with the Federals near Salem since shortly past dawn. Imboden was unaware that he was sitting in the gap between two Union armies. Crook moved his command off the Salem Pike and toward the battle sounds.

Apparently Union troops at Salem were aware of Crook's approach before Imboden. They brought more guns and troops on line. It was hoped that the Confederate cavalry would be caught and destroyed between the two armies.

Crook may have believed that the cavalry to his front was the unit responsible for the attack on his advance at dawn. He was eager for revenge.

Imboden quickly found himself in a difficult situation. There were overwhelming armies to his front and to his rear, and a river on his right flank. His only choice was to move to his left across country. Imboden was either very lucky or very skillful to have retreated without being crushed. He maintained such a good show that the Yanks on the Salem side of the line did not charge. None of his artillery was captured.

There are many possible reasons that General Early was not informed, or fully informed, of this action. Because he was pressed hard, Imboden might have sent a courier to Early, or the courier might have been captured. If the courier did make it to Early, Early might not have understood that there was a gap in the retreating Union column and that one column was several hours behind the other.

Imboden pulled safely off line. He then swung westwardly around Salem toward Valley Pike. He would attempt to slow Hunter if Hunter chose that road.

With Imboden out of his way, Crook entered Salem with an exhausted army. When the column quit moving, men lay by the side of the road and slept.

Hunter had panicked when Imboden struck his rear near dawn. When the rear guard had halted the Confederates, Hunter had calmed down. The noise of the engagement at Hanging Rock (two miles north) had caused him concern, but as the noise had decreased, he was less anxious.

Near 10:00 a.m., Hunter got the good news that Crook was coming into Salem. Hunter felt better. Crook had not been cut-off and destroyed. His best troopers were rejoining the army. The general upon whom he relied heavily was back.

Crook let Hunter know in no uncertain terms how angry he was that Sullivan had marched off and left him during the night. Had Early attacked, his division would have been subject to annihilation.

Hunter immediately flew into a rage and "Cursed General Sullivan for being a coward, etc., who tried to lie out of it...."[73]

It appears that Crook, Sullivan, and Averell, along with Strother, were with Hunter at approximately 10:30 a.m. when the first couriers arrived from Hanging Rock. The messengers said, "...Our artillery en route with the train had been attacked and was *all captured*."[11] Crook said, "They brought information that the enemy was occupying the Cross Roads."[73] A soldier probably echoed Hunter's thoughts when he said that the cavalry attack on the rear was made, "...to detain us long enough to enable another body of their troops to gain the Gap, on the road between Salem and New Castle, through which we must pass, if we pass at all."[83]

Two Confederate cavalry prisoners were brought to the generals for interrogation. They informed the generals that it was Imboden who had struck the Yankees' rear east of Salem and that it was McCausland who was in the Gap. The prisoners believed that Early had been re-supplied and was marching close behind the Union Army. The prisoners said, "Early's division is...20,000 strong and they have thirty days' rations and are determined to drive us out of Virginia."[11]

The army was cut in two factions, and the road was blocked. Strother summed it up well: "It seems as if we are getting into an ugly position, (the) artillery (is) gone and (the) cavalry (is) worthless."[11]

Hunter ordered Averell and Sullivan to move toward the Gap and attack. Crook's army was too spent to move. When Averell and Sullivan left, Crook and Hunter conferred. What should they do if the wagon train and the artillery were captured and if the Gap could not be taken? It was decided, Crook recalled, that "...if such was the case to strike south and follow the Virginia and Tennessee Railroad down to Knoxville."[73] (Knoxville at this point in the war was in firm Union control). While Crook rested, Hunter dashed toward the Gap.

McCausland had held the Gap for almost an hour. Twelve to fifteen wagons had been removed from the Gap. Some of the artillery and powder wagons had been pulled off. Most of the prisoners, including the wounded, had been removed. J.S. Moore with the Fourteenth Virginia, captured one Yank, who told Moore that he had nothing to eat but sassafras leaves and birch bark. Moore's warrior heart was broken. He gave the soldier some hardtack and a piece of raw meat. The Yankee gobbled them down. Moore surprised the Yankee by telling him that he was free to rejoin the Union Army and simply left the Yankee unguarded.

Re-creation: Confederate Cavalry forming skirmish line to protect Berkeley's cannons.

At the south end of the Gap, Berkeley's Battery had a high position overlooking the road heading toward the Gap. It appears that the battery had pushed Union troops back almost a half mile off the road.

Averell's Cavalry moved the two miles from Salem toward Hanging Rock. It was greeted by fire from Berkeley's Battery and forced off the road to the right and into the woods. Berkeley sent word to McCausland in the Gap about the approach of the cavalry. Berkeley, no doubt, requested troops to support his position.

McCausland probably sent men to Berkeley. He also spurred his men in the Valley to work harder. McCausland knew that he had only a limited time to get the captured artillery removed.

While the infantry was still en route, it appears that Averell's Cavalry made an attempt to move up the hill to the left of Berkeley's Battery. Averell's men, some armed with Spencer rifles, were turned back.

The troopers fell back from the base of the hill where they saw their major general. One cavalryman observed, "Hunter is angry."[9] The unit was quickly re-formed. Hunter let the troopers know that they *must* take the hill and force the battery back. "Move up! Move up, lively there,"[9] commanded Hunter, pointing at the hill. The cavalry started toward its target with renewed determination. Dupont brought a battery from Salem (Fifth U.S. Battery) and started shelling the Confederate position.

As the cavalry was approaching the hill, the infantry was approaching the bend of the road heading toward the Gap a half mile away. One soldier recalled that he was thinking about his fatigued, hungry body, and the hot sun boiling down, when "...General Hunter suddenly appeared in front looking blacker and more savage than ever."[41] The soldier watched Hunter dash about in a near panic issuing orders. In his tired state with the prospect of deadly battle near, the soldier decided that Hunter's actions were quite humorous. "...One could hardly restrain from laughing," he wrote, "to see the gruff old general fly about...."[41]

Averell's Cavalry reached the base of the hill. Schoonmaker's Brigade was closest to the Rebel position. It was either trailed or flanked on the right by Oley's Brigade. The hill was very steep. One cavalryman recalled, "The horses dig their toe corks into the hillside, climbing almost like cats...."[9]

There was no discounting of these cavalrymen's courage. Before the units reached the top, Schoonmaker's Brigade lost approximately thirty men.[11] Averell complimented his men, saying that they did their duty "...in a brilliant manner...."[8]

Berkeley saw the cavalrymen at the base of the hill, Federal cannons on the road, and the infantry approaching on the road. He sent word to McCausland in the Valley that there was no way to maintain his position and began pulling his battery off line. The Confederate cavalrymen protecting Berkeley's Battery also pulled off.

When McCausland received the message from Berkeley he knew that time was running out. McCausland had no knowledge of the gap between Crook and the balance of the army. McCausland assumed that he had struck the

Re-creation: Battery B; 5th U.S. Artillery under Dupont pounds Confederate position.

Re-creation: Union Cavalry under Averell prepare to attack the hill one more time.

Re-creation: Massed Union Infantry fire a volley into Confederate position.

middle of the retreating army, that there was infantry somewhere to the front, and that the infantry now arriving was the infantry that formed the rear guard. McCausland sent orders to pull any guns that could be moved out of the Gap. Any guns that could not be moved immediately were to be disabled. At the south end of the Gap, McCausland recalled, "I blew off an ammunition wagon...."[91] Other wagons were set afire.

Cavalrymen rarely used their swords in battle. At the Gap, they used them as axes as they chopped the wheels of powder wagons and cannons. Wounded horses were put out of their misery. Harnesses were slashed, and the other horses were led toward the north of the Gap. The guns were spiked, probably by driving the vent pick in the vent hole and then breaking it off.

Now that there was little or no fire coming from Berkeley's former hilltop position, Union troops raced over the one-half mile of open road toward the Gap. Dupont limbered up the battery and moved forward with the infantry.

Confederate resistance on the hill collapsed; the men started running back toward Green Ridge. McCausland was moving troops through the Gap toward the north.

It is possible that Dupont got at least one gun into service and fired on the fleeing Rebs. McCausland lost only two men killed in the Gap and an unknown number wounded. Most of his loss might have been a result of Dupont's guns. Because there were so few men left with McCausland, Union rumor mills said the column had been attacked by guerrillas.

Re-creation: Small band of Confederate Cavalry fire one last volley before leaving Hanging Rock Gap.

The total number of horses killed in the narrow valley might have numbered as high as ninety.[128] Mason Creek received the discharge from the wounded and dead horses, and "...the creek ran red with their blood that day."[129]

One infantryman said, "The fight was a lively one"[75] but short. McCausland's men fled while Union troops streamed into the Valley. A few of McCausland's men were captured, but McCausland had inflicted great loss with very little personal loss.

When a Union cavalryman saw the carnage in the Valley, only one word came to mind: "Disaster."[109] There was little time for the common soldiers to observe their surroundings. Many were ordered up the hill to catch McCausland who made no attempt to resist the increased Union pressure but fell back. He knew that he had done the best job that he could. Without infantry support, he could do no further damage.

The detachment Imboden had sent toward McCausland earlier in the morning began to arrive as McCausland retreated back toward Valley Pike. One of Imboden's men recalled seeing six cannons and approximately fifty Union prisoners.[91]

Saunders could not understand why the cavalrymen were pulling off the artillery. He expressed his astonishment to a sergeant: "...The Yankees surely could not have fought"[91] (well).

The sergeant snapped back: "Oh, yes, they did fight, and we have left some brave men down there."[91]

A major nearby heard Saunders' statement and jumped down from his horse and confronted Saunders. "I think you ought to withdraw that remark. See here,"[91] he said, showing Saunders his broken sword and empty revolver. (The sword was probably broken on a caisson wheel and the pistol emptied into wounded horses, but Saunders did not know that).

Saunders then said, "I desire to apologize most amply to you and your men."[91] The apology was accepted.

Apparently, McCausland sent Saunders to make sure that one of the Southern batteries retired with the column. When Saunders arrived at the battery, he found the men were asleep. They may have slept during the entire engagement at Hanging Rock.

Once the battery was on the road, Saunders rode toward the rear of McCausland's column to hurry any stragglers forward. He observed two small groups of mounted troops, leisurely coming together. When they united, there were six troopers in all. Saunders rode to them and heard their conversation.

One trooper asked his comrade, identified only as "Jim," "...What do you think we found on that fellow (motioning toward a Union prisoner) when we caught him?"[91]

Jim replied that he did not know, and his buddy continued, "Why, women's finger rings, earrings and other things."[91]

Jim became angry, "Damn him! He ought to be lost!"[91] (Shot).

Saunders probably interrupted the men and told them that they should move with the rest of the column and then rode off.

Within minutes, Saunders heard the report of a pistol. Later he saw that the six men did join the retreat, but there was no Union prisoner.

Chest used as money chest by Huffman family on Greenridge (engagement of Hanging Rock) — Family gold was wrapped in carpet rag balls. Yankees broke open chest and emptied contents but did not find gold wrapped in carpet rag ball. Courtesy: Lila Huffman.

More of Hunter's men moved into the Gap. One soldier said that he was "...astonished to find the ruins..."[16] of the batteries and wagons. Smoke filled the air from the burning wagons. The concussion of an exploding artillery shell (from the burning wagons) occasionally filled the valley. An infantryman saw the severely wounded. He recalled, "Some lay bleeding whilst others were lamenting for the poor horses and lost guns."[118] Physicians started to care for the injured.

Dupont and his men made an inspection of the guns and the harnesses. Dupont replaced the wheels and the harnesses of four of the guns. Because of damage, lack of horses, harnesses, and wheels, "...to my bitter regret..."[47] said Dupont, eight pieces were abandoned. Federals spiked any unspiked guns, rolled barrels toward the creek, and burned the carriages.

While some of the men cared for the wounded, others gathered prisoners, worked on the cannons, and stole food at the home of John Garst in the Gap. Mrs. Mattie Garst thought that it was bad enough that the Federals had stolen every bite of food in the house, but she grieved to her dying day that they had also burned her wedding clothes.

While working in the midst of the destruction, some soldiers began to wonder who was at fault. One Massachusetts private angrily stated, "Someone had evidently blundered!"[83] Another soldier said that this destruction was "...a desolate monument to somebody's inexperience and guilt."[16]

Averell never missed an opportunity to give Duffié a verbal jab. Averell said, "It was found...that General Duffié had neglected to observe any of the instructions he had received. Not a single precaution had been taken by him to prevent the attack...."[8]

Many other officers were also quick to point an accusatory finger at Duffié. In his official reply, Duffié said, "My orders were to clear out this Gap and take the train through. This I did."[8]

A private with the Twelfth Ohio Infantry knew where the blame lay. "This was wholly the fault of General Hunter, who had neglected to make a proper disposition of his guards...,"[31] he said.

In his early morning panic of issuing orders and physically pushing soldiers, Hunter had failed to provide protection for the wagons and the guns. He had seen only disaster and had rushed to try to save some of the army. His panic was in some measure the cause of the disaster.

Because his subordinates had addressed the question of who was at fault in their reports, Hunter could not avoid the issue in his official report. Hunter, true to his personality, said he didn't know who was at fault "...through some inadvertence the proper guard did not accompany the artillery."[8] He also stated that only "two batteries"[8] were lost. Federal figures clearly state that eight guns were abandoned and four guns were restored, and the Confederates carried off between three to six guns; a total of between fifteen to eighteen pieces.

The two batteries that Hunter had referred to were Carlin's and Snow's. Both batteries had six 3-inch guns; a total of twelve pieces. It is clearly stated that the captain of the artillery, Von Kleiser, was captured. It is highly unlikely

that he would have been captured if his unit had not been involved. By adding
Von Kleiser's four Napoleons to the twelve guns of Carlin and Snow, the
figures are more balanced.

During the action at Hanging Rock, Crook was at Salem. He needed food
and rest as much as did his men, but he would not allow himself any sleep. He
was struggling with an impossible problem: how to retreat over 300 miles to
Knoxville without food, train, artillery, and with a superior, well-supplied
enemy at the army's rear.

A courier was sent to Crook from the battlefield. Crook received with both
relief and anger the news that the Gap was open. He was grateful that the short
way north toward safety was open, but he was livid toward Averell: "General
Averell had a lot of bummers, who he called scouts and spies, who were
thoroughly unreliable and worthless."[73] Reports that the road was closed had
caused Crook to worry and lose much needed rest.

Back at the Gap, part of one of Averell's regiments, the Second West
Virginia, was ordered to remove and destroy the artillery ammunition even
from burning wagons. (At least one of the wagons contained ammunition
captured at the Battle of Piedmont from the Boys' battery, this accounts for the
recovery of projectiles of a much larger caliber than was fired by either Union
or Confederate cannons at Hanging Rock). About fifteen men from Companies C and H were dismounted and placed under Lt. J.W. Ricker's
supervision.

As Ricker approached one smoldering wagon, he remarked that removing
the contents would be dangerous. Major Carman who accompanied Ricker,
said that the ammunition "...must be destroyed at once."[34]

Against his better judgement, Ricker ordered that the contents were to be
removed and thrown into the creek. The oldest member of the party, Private
Thomas Warman, was told to enter the wagon and hand the packaged ammunition to others who would take it to the creek. Warman entered the wagon,
but other soldiers protested that it was too dangerous. Major Carman became
angry and yelled so loudly that even a member of the Garst family some ways
off could hear the major, who "With loud and angry oaths and calling them
cowards,...again ordered them to destroy the powder...."[129] Once the men
returned to work, the major left the area, probably to check on other working
parties.

"In a few minutes a fearful explosion occurred on the ground, and a few
seconds later the powder in the wagon exploded with fearful effect, killing and
wounding over half the guard,"[34] a private wrote.

A member of the Garst family later reported that six men were killed and
ten wounded.[16] A private on the scene sadly recorded the names of five of his
comrades who were killed. The only death in Company C was that of Marion
McMillin. Marion was the youngest of William McMillin's six sons, all Jackson
County Ohio natives. Marion had five brothers in Company H, Second West
Virginia Cavalry. When he was old enough, Marion (still referred to as "baby"
by his brothers) joined the Second West Virginia and was assigned to
Company C. At least two of his brothers rushed to the scene, and "...it was with

almost broken hearts that two of his brothers, Emerson and Murray, looked upon the dead body of their idolized Marion,"[34] said one witness.

From Company H, Privates Benjamin Prim, William Garvin, and Issac More were killed. The private with the Second West Virginia said that he would sorely miss Corp. Scott Gard, also killed along Mason Creek. The soldier described him as "...one of the finest athletes in the regiment...the wit of the regiment (also a prankster)...a gleam of sunshine...(who) lightened the burdens of others...Alas! the cruel hand of fate was...to include him in the needless sacrifice of five lives."[34]

Many of the wounded had the clothes blown off their bodies (partially or wholly).

Lieutenant Ricker was sitting on his horse near the wagon when the explosion occurred. His hat was blown off, and his saber scabbard was shattered. Some comrades observed that within minutes some of his hair turned white. His mount was also frightened. Later in the day "His faithful horse dropped dead...."[34] The incident was so traumatic that Lieutenant Ricker suffered from mental distress for the remainder of his life.

Miraculously, Private Warman was not killed. He was blown out of the wagon and sailed through the air over the remains of the lead horse. He "...was picked up in an insensible condition."[34]

The casualties were the result of "...folly and stupidity..."[16] said one report. Another account stated that it was called an accident, but it was "...official stupidity, as was, indeed, the loss of the artillery."[59] The number of casualties that McCausland had inflicted had just increased.

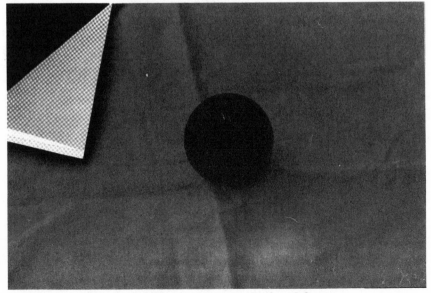

Cannon projectile from engagement of Hanging Rock — Salem.
Courtesy: Roanoke City Library.

Projectile from Hanging Rock. Courtesy of Roanoke County
Sesquicentennial Committee.

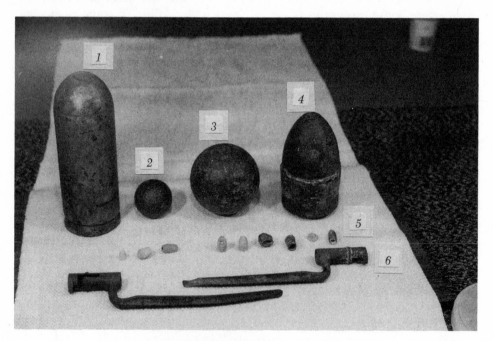

From Hanging Rick (Greenridge)- Salem
1- 20- pound Parrott
2- canister from 24-pound
3- 24- pound solid shot
4- 14- pound Hotchkiss
5- Minie balls
6-Broken and refiled bayonets
courtesy: Harry Huffman collection.

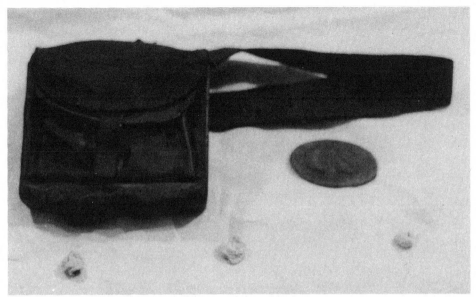

From Hanging Rock engagement — Salem
Cartridge box (probably taken from dead Yankee)
Confederate belt buckle
Three shot rifle balls
Courtesy: Allan and Keith Wingfield collection.

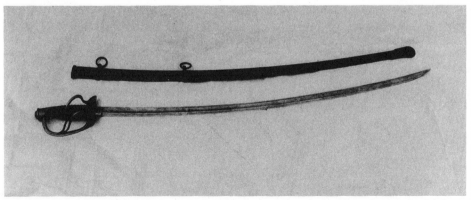

Sword of Pvt. McClanahan Ingles, Co. E, 25th Va. Cavalry used at Hanging Rock — Salem.
Courtesy: John Jeffries collection.

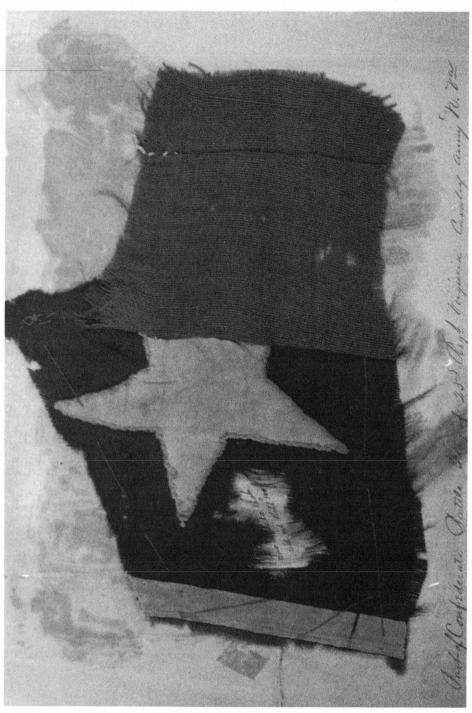

Small piece of the battle flag of the 23rd Regiment Virginia Cavalry. Courtesy: Major Marshall Vass Hale, USAF-Ret)

It is uncertain as to the date or the location, (but it occurred somewhere near White Sulphur Springs) and only one account includes a reference to the attack on Hunter's supply train that left from Liberty, moving north. The accounts of the Southern prisoners with the train make no reference to the affair. It was probably conducted on a small scale during a very brief period. Evidently that part of Imboden's command sent after the train did attack, "...but due to the cowardice and persistent disobedience of a colonel commanding one of (the) regiments,"[28] it was a failure. Any wagons that the Confederates seized were quickly retaken by the 100-day volunteers, and the train continued north without further harassment.

Mid-day was approaching. Hunter's army had retaken Hanging Rock Gap. Hunter realized that because of the action, there were holes in the retreating column. Orders were sent to Duffie to halt his forward motion and to picket any road entering the Salem-Newcastle Pike. Word was sent back to Crook to move from Salem to the Gap as soon as he felt the command could march.

Since shortly past sunrise Early had been pushing his hungry foot-sore army in an attempt to overtake the Union Army. John Worsham with Company F, Twenty-First Virginia Infantry — Gordon's Division — recalled that the men "...were padding along the dusty road as thirsty and hunger-ridden as mortal men could be..."[103] when they spied some ladies. As they approached, they saw two huge washtubs. "The young ladies gave us an invitation to come forward and partake of some ice water and Brandy Julep... the tubs were repeatedly emptied and filled."[103] Grateful soldiers had a drink, wished their hostesses well, and continued the march.

It was probably near mid-day when Early received the dispatch from Ransom. The courier told Early that McCausland was at Hanging Rock, waiting for the infantry before attacking. Early passed through Big Lick and force marched across country toward Hanging Rock. By the time he left the Salem Pike, the engagement at Hanging Rock was over, and McCausland was beginning to retreat.

No record has been found to indicate the exact time and place where Early's advancing infantry met McCausland's retreating cavalry. Early indicates that it was near Hanging Rock.

McCausland reported to Early, who had had a bad day. The general said, "The best news to come...that day...was that Hunter had turned off from his route toward Southwest Virginia...."[103] The lead mines and the saltworks were no longer threatened; the Confederacy would not fall by Hunter's hand. A quick glance at the map showed Early two things: (1.) there was no way to send the cavalry and get to the front of Hunter's army to slow it so that Early's Infantry could catch Hunter; (2.) it also showed that Hunter had no easy way out of the Valley which ran to Lewisburg, (W) Virginia. Hunter could not easily re-enter the Shenandoah Valley. Later Early wrote, "I was glad to see Hunter take the route to Lewisburg, as I knew he could not stop short of the Kanawha River, and he was...disposed of for some time. Had he moved to Southwestern Virginia he would have done us incalculable mischief...I should...have been compelled to follow him."[119]

If Early did not know before, he soon found out that Ransom had relieved himself of command.

After receiving the good news that Hunter was going north, Early wanted to know the details of the engagement. Early later wrote, "...on arriving there (meeting with McCausland) it was ascertained that the enemy's *rear guard* had passed through the gorge. McCausland had struck his column at *this point* and captured ten pieces of artillery, some wagons, and a number of prisoners...."[119] Both generals assumed that the infantry brought forth against McCausland was the rear guard of Hunter's army.

McCausland said, "Had an attack been made when we first reached their *rear,* Hunter would have either lost his entire train or been compelled to fight Early a pitch battle."[91] The Lynchburg newspaper later echoed McCausland, saying that Early had lost "...the golden opportunity of the war."[101]

Neither Early nor McCausland realized, even as they spoke, that a golden opportunity was still theirs. Only then was Crook's Division preparing to leave Salem. If Early had known of Crook's plans, Crook would most probably have been overwhelmed.

Early knew nothing of Crook's Division at Salem, but he did know of General Lee's instructions quickly to dispose of Hunter and march on Washington. The chances were remote that he could inflict any greater damage on Hunter. He would start operations toward the Yankee capital.

Before he could move far, his army needed food and rest. Early had fought at Lynchburg and had marched sixty miles in three days with no food. His supply trains still had not arrived from Lynchburg. Early wrote later, "I had seen our soldiers endure a great deal, but there was a limit to the endurance even of Confederate soldiers."[119] Early was not interested in further pursuit. The army camped for the night.

McCausland asked for permission to continue following Hunter. Early gave permission for a limited pursuit. As Early would need the cavalry when he moved north, McCausland could pursue for only a single day.

At Hanging Rock, Hunter received a dispatch from Duffié. He reported that the road going toward New Castle was clear. Some of the organized workers who had felled trees were running toward that town. Duffié said that he *would* destroy a facility, probably the Catawba Iron Furnace. (Note: Duffié referred to the facility as a "factory" that he believed was located on the top of Catawba Mountain. No record has been discovered of any business other than a tollgate, located on the mountain. It can be only conjecture that a local citizen might have identified the organized workers who felled the trees as being from the "Catawba Works." Duffié may have deducted that the "Works" was a factory on Catawba Mountain. The Catawba Iron Works was located approximately ten miles east of the north base of Catawba Mountain toward Fincastle. There is no record that these works were destroyed, and Duffié makes no mention in his official report of destroying any facility on Catawba Mountain).

Workers were proud that iron from the Catawba Mountain Furnace had been used to armor plate the Virginia, later referred to as the Merrimac. The furnace was a massive work that could produce up to forty tons of iron a week. It also provided living quarters for the workers.

Duffié informed Hunter that the road was steep and rough. Duffié suggested that worthless wagons be discarded so that the horses could pull essential wagons and artillery up the mountain.

Because Averell had been critical of Duffié's failure to picket the Creeley Gap Road, which runs north from Bonsack, Duffié sent a dispatch directly to Averell. He let Averell know that he had posted "...all roads three or four miles."[8] Duffié also said that his advance was skirmishing on the New Castle Road. Some of the iron workers possibly had been reinforced by locals from New Castle, who had fired on the Federal Cavalry.

Duffié's one regiment finally arrived at Hanging Rock, but the engagement had been over for some time. The regiment was used to guard the train going back up the mountain.

When Hunter received word that Crook was preparing to march, the Federals in the Gap started forward. Averell's Cavalry was in the advance to guard the road. (Duffié's Cavalry was almost in New Castle), and Sullivan's men were in the advance in the rear, and some units marched with the horse-drawn pieces. Hunter did not want to repeat Hanging Rock.

Crook assumed that Early would be following closely north from Salem; between Salem and Hanging Rock, he placed troops to ambush Early. Early was not following, and the ambushers later rejoined the army.

Prompted by Duffié's report and the sight of Catawba Mountain, General Hunter decided to abandon as many of the wagons as possible. He sent word to Crook to abandon his wagons also, but Crook kept all serviceable transportation and destroyed very few wagons.

Because fellow Yankees in advance had stolen all the food, Crook's men could gather very few supplies.

As the advance of the Union Army began the ascent of Catawba Mountain, it discarded much baggage. Saddles from dead horses and empty wagons were burned. One cavalryman was proud to note, "None of the men threw away their arms."[109]

The three-mile ascent was a rigorous climb for rested and fed man and beast; for this army, it was an almost impossible ordeal. "The road was very crooked and the ascent steep,"[118] complained one soldier. There had been no rain for some time. Every step taken only increased the dust in the air. There were very few springs for the soldiers to drink from.

"Stragglers everywhere," noted one soldier; "many had thrown away their arms."[75] Until this mountain, the stronger soldiers had helped the weaker, but now even the strong barely had the energy to keep placing one foot in front of the next. A private with the Eighteenth Connecticut remembered that it was every man for himself. "It is either push ahead or be left and made a prisoner,"[18] he said. Some couldn't continue. "They had left the road and lain down hidden as they supposed by the dense undergrowth, unable to walk a foot farther, will-power gone, reckless of consequences."[75]

Even some of the cavalrymen were exhausted. One man wrote, "I find I cannot stand it any longer. I simply cannot ride horseback any farther."[102] This man was luckier than most. Soon he was riding in a buggy pulled by two mules. The buggy might have been one that run-away slaves had stolen from their master. The slaves might have been forced to walk. One soldier characterized the march as one of "unspeakable suffering."[75] Another infantryman added that many men "...fell by the roadside, and are supposed to have died for want of attention."[31]

Some men could not make it to the top of the mountain. "The mules and (the) horses began to fall..."[21] stated one West Virginia soldier. A cavalryman seems to over estimate when he said horses were "...dying now by many hundreds daily."[109] One infantryman said that he counted 101 dead horses and mules[75] on Catawba Mountain.

Most of the men, animals, and wagons did make it over the mountain. One soldier reflected the condition of the whole army when he said upon making it to the top, "I was nearly played out."[118]

Some of Sullivan's men had started up the mountain by noon. Some of Crook's column did not reach the base of the mountain until 4:00 p.m.

No exact time was available, but it was before dark that McCausland started his cavalry after Hunter.

After resting the infantry, Early sent his army to Botetourt Springs (Hollins College) to camp. As his army marched toward Botetourt Springs, Early decided to visit the battlefield at Hanging Rock. It is very likely that the mapmaker for the army, Jed Hotchkiss, accompanied Early.

One of the general's companions said that as they approached the area that "...there appeared to be a rapid cannonade ahead, and a dense smoke arose among the hills."[30] The cannonade was caused by burning wagons and exploding artillery shells.

A cavalry aide who had been with Imboden earlier in the day told Early, "General, there would have been a different story to tell if you had come up with your army as your dispatch of last night said you would do by 6 a.m."[91] The profane general unleashed a verbal tirade against that courier whom he had sent to notify Rodes that he was to start the march at an early hour.

The two Confederates and all the Union dead, including the ones killed by the wagon explosion, were still unburied. An aide wrote, "The number of dead that lay in the narrow space showed that the struggle had been a desperate one."[91]

General Early could see and hear the exploding ammunition, but he continued forward. An aide cautioned the general, but "...he made no remark but rode on...."[91] Early and his staff were about thirty to forty feet away from a smoldering wagon when three or four shells exploded in rapid succession. None of the staff was hurt, but Early's horse bolted. An aide noted, "His horse plunged violently and came very near unseating him. I was so mad at the needless exposure...that I would not have cared much if it had thrown him — not very much if the fall had broken his neck."[16] McCausland almost increased his casualty figures.

As the sun set, Early's Infantry went into camp at Botetourt Springs. Some troops did not reach the Springs and camped along Valley Pike.

McCausland had started up Catawba Mountain and went into camp near its foot.

Crook's Division went into camp ("which meant a few steps off the road, and lay down"[75]) on the top of Catawba Mountain.

Hunter was with Sullivan's Division, and they camped at the foot of Catawba Mountain on the north side. They had moved approximately twenty-seven miles that day.

Averell's Cavalry pushed to within seven miles of New Castle before making camp.

Most of both the Union and Confederate armies would rest for the first night since they had left Lynchburg.

Only Duffié moved during the night. Hunter had ordered him to push through New Castle and secure the road at the junction of the Fincastle and Sweet Springs Roads about five miles north of Fincastle. No doubt, Duffié's men terrorized citizens and stole food and horses as they advanced through New Castle.

Wednesday, June 22

Duffié had pushed his command to the junction of the Fincastle and Sweet Springs Roads by dawn on Wednesday, June 22. The troopers secured the crossroads. Duffié also learned from the citizens that there were no Confederate troops in the area. Duffié sent a courier back to Hunter to keep him posted on conditions ahead of the infantry.

At 4:00 a.m., some of Sullivan's Infantry started marching. Hunter was very worried that Early would catch his army today. The air was filled with rumors which led Strother to record, "Our position will be a gloomy one if the reports we hear are confirmed."[11]

Hunter directed the Signal Corps to establish a post on the top of Catawba Mountain. If Early's forces were observed coming up the mountain, the infantry was to be alerted by signal rockets.

Signal station by David Hunter Strother.

Meanwhile near Petersburg, Grant was becoming increasingly worried over the fate of the Army of West Virginia. He had received no direct communication from Hunter since before the attack on Lynchburg. Grant received word that John Hunt Morgan was withdrawing his "terrible men" from Kentucky and was coming into Southwest Virginia. Grant believed that it was possible that Morgan might attack Hunter from the west.

On June 22, Union high command issued a clarification in a matter not directly related to Hunter's movements but related to the disposition of contraband with all Union armies. The revision stated that henceforth, "...all slaves who are *brought* to the recruiting rendezvous and found physically disqualified for military service, and *who do not desire to return to their masters*, but seek military protection, shall not be rejected, but enlisted and muster into U.S. service, with a view to transfer to the quartermaster's department."[8] To fill draft quotas, slaves were taken by force from their masters. Those physically qualified for service were not given the option of leaving service to return to their masters.

It was near dawn when Crook began moving his force off the summit of Catawba Mountain and headed north. Since Crook believed that the Confederates would pursue, he set up an ambush.

McCausland was in close pursuit. As McCausland's forces reached the top of the mountain, they saw a very few of the rear guard. When the Confederates gave chase, the Union ran, but this was all part of Crook's plan to lure the Confederates into a death trap.

The Signal Corps had not been told of Crook's ambush plan and was caught by surprise by the rapidly advancing Rebels. The officer said that the signal station "...was driven in by the enemy...."[8] A local rumor states that Confederates captured some signal rockets.

The Union continued to run, and the cavalry continued to pursue. Union soldiers ran down the road and passed their comrades concealed along the road. The Confederate cavalry followed until the head of the column was close to the north end of the ambush position. A Union soldier said, "...When the Johnnies had got well into the mouth of the trap set for them, our boys rose up, (and) fired...."[83]

The advance of McCausland's column was taken by surprise. Waves of smoke and fire rolled at it from Union rifles concealed in the underbrush. The mountain echoed with the reports of musketry, screams, shouts, cursing of men, and the anguished neighing of wounded horses. Within minutes, the Confederates that could were in full retreat up the mountain. Approximately eighty of the attackers were now Union prisoners; for eighteen Confederate soldiers[83] the war was over. (These figures were recorded by a man with Sullivan's Division well in advance. The figures come from hearsay and not from direct personal observation, therefore: it is likely the figures were exaggerated).

As McCausland reviewed the action, he quickly realized that he had lost much and that the Union had lost little. The cost of attacking the Union infantry was too high. McCausland would launch no further attacks. Crook concurred with his enemy's (McCausland's) decision and stated that "...he sensibly called off the chase...."[60]

At Botetourt Springs, the Confederate Army was waking up after the first sound sleep in many nights. The men were too tired the night before to appreciate their surroundings. That morning they realized that they were camped where the wealthy gentry's whims had been catered to before the war. The place where those of station and wealth had come to "take in the waters" was now their temporary camp. Dirty men with no money and holes in their clothes and some without shoes, frolicked in the playground of the rich.

Some time in the morning, Imboden's Cavalry came from Salem and joined in the fun.

The wagon train and the Second Corps' artillery arrived during the day. Hungry and tired men ate and rested.

There were almost no shoes in the supply train, but some men did get a new issue of underwear. Some of the Thirty-Sixth Virginia Infantry received outerwear also. One writer recalled that men "...walked around camp in their new shirts as proud as peacocks."[51]

The commander of the troops could not enjoy the fun and the relaxation. General Early had delayed his report to General Lee as long as possible. On June 19, Early had informed Lee that "if the cavalry does its duty we will destroy him." Hunter was gone.

Early knew that today's dispatch would disappoint his boss, but he made no excuses or offered any justifications. The facts would speak clearly of the situation. Having given Lee a very brief recap of the action at Hanging Rock, Early told him, "The enemy moved so rapidly that I could not attack him before he got into the mountains...."[8]

Early's brief report was enough for General Lee, who, of course, knew of Hunter's plundering, looting, and burning. It was Lee's sad task to write the President of the Confederacy, Jefferson Davis: "Although his (Hunter's) expedition has been partially interrupted, I fear he has not been much punished, except by the demoralization of his troops and the loss of some artillery."[8]

Citizens near Hanging Rock were having no joy on this morning. The armies were gone, but their carnage remained. The wounded soldiers were taken to homes and churches (including the Dunkard Church) and cared for. The two Southerners killed were buried on a farm near the Gap. The Union dead were buried in a mass grave. The sun would be sinking low in the west before the last of the horses were buried.

McCausland had decided not to attack the rear of Hunter's column, but the Rebel Army was not through with the Yankees yet. The Confederates had been the victims of Jessie Scouts on many occasions, but the Southern boys knew that two could play that game.

The uniform of some dead or captured Federal hid the identity of a Southern soldier. The disguised Reb rode near the head of Crook's column. When the column reached the base of the mountain at the Village of Catawba, the blue-clad Reb led the column off the main road, probably toward

Fincastle. A Union soldier wrote about those who dressed to deceive, saying, "They are sometimes very bold and risk their lives on one bold stroke."[118]

It was some time before the Union commanders realized that they were going in the wrong direction. It is probable that the disguised Rebel paid for his act with his life, but no record is available to verify his death.

To prevent another gap from developing, Crook sent Hunter word of the wrong movement. Hunter had to halt Sullivan's and Averell's columns until Crook could retrace his steps. Most of the Union regiments rested until near noon.

While the army was not moving, soldiers took the opportunity to loot houses along the road. One soldier noted, "The people among the mountains were nearly as hungry as the soldiers."[21] Another said, "The log houses of the mountain regions...looked anything but comfortable...the women were coarse, sallow, and altogether unlovely-gawky specimens of ill-dressed humanity, having ropy hair, and were barefooted or standing in clouted brogans, and exhibiting great clawing hands...."[41]

Mountain family by David Hunter Strother.

James Abott had his chickens stolen, garden plundered, wagon and horses taken and house looted, and as the invaders left, they burned his barn and corncrib.

Because residents had been hiding food and valuables in their feather ticks, the beds were among the first place the Union soldiers looked. At one home in Craig County, the soldiers forced their way into a bedroom. There in the bed lay a woman whose extended stomach was clearly evident as it pushed the blanket up. The soldiers, learning that the lady was in labor, withdrew without disturbing the mother-to-be. It was a false pregnancy. The woman's issue turned out to be a ham.

One soldier returned to his unit with all he could find to steal: one sack of green tea.

At another house, soldiers broke in and demanded that flour be given to them. The lady of the house said that other Yankees had already been there and had taken all of her flour. The soldiers searched anyway and found three sacks of flour covered by ashes in the fireplace.

The Federals were pleased that they were encountering citizens who seemed to be pro-Union. One such family "...offered us all they had. We did not accept anything for they were very poor,"[118] noted one soldier. The Unionists were quick to sic the army on their pro-Southern neighbors who had oppressed them. A Federal cavalryman said, "There was a house nearby whose owner was said to have cut down trees to block the way. He needed to be taught a lesson."[118] After looting the homeowner's house and barn, soldiers then went after his beehives. An officer recalled that the men were "...devouring great chunks of honey with brutal greediness. The honey as they ate it was streaming down their clothes and clotting in their beards. The vengeful bees swarmed around their faces, biting and stinging. They scraped them off with their hands when they got too thick for comfort and went on eating like a herd of grizzly bears."[11]

Not all of the honey was consumed in chunks. Some of the stolen flour was used to make small cakes, known as "toe jam," and they were covered by honey.

All of the pro-Southerners' meat was stolen, and even five and ten gallon cans of lard were taken. The infantrymen dipped their canteen cups into the cans and ate pure lard.

Being a Unionist did not guarantee safety. One such resident approached the chief-of-staff. He gave the signs and code words that the secret Union Leaguers used. Strother knew that the secret signs meant that the resident had been actively supporting the Union Army with any intelligence he could gather, but Strother paid no heed to his request for protection. The pro-Union man's house was looted.

Some women of the area asked to see the old flag once more. When the Stars and Stripes was unfurled, the soldiers gave three cheers for the flag and three cheers for the women.

By noon, the whole Union Army was on the move toward New Castle. One soldier noted that it would have been an easy march except that the men were hungry and tired and had blistered feet. Every time the men forded a stream, they would pause to soak their feet.

When the infantry did pause, the wagons would continue without protection. Teamsters worried that they might be caught in another "Hanging Rock" situation. At one stream, the infantry heard firing from the wagon train ahead. Hearts raced, and soldiers rushed forward. One breathless soldier said, "We found it was only a ruse to hurry us up for we were the rear guard. The train had not been fired upon at all."[118] The teamsters had fooled them once but no more. "From now on we took our own time arriving...,"[118] said one infantryman.

The day's march did not lead up any mountain, but the hunger and the exhaustion of some of the men and animals was too great, and they couldn't proceed. Also the roads were "...very dusty, the dust completely blinding and nearly choking us at times,"[118] said a soldier. More wagons were burned because there were not enough horses or mules to pull them. One soldier lamented the deaths of so many animals that had pulled until they could pull no more and were rewarded for their efforts by bullets in their heads: "War is a cruel thing. I wish it was over,"[18] he said.

One soldier noted that the officers suffered as much as their men. Men were so hungry that they would "...pick up kernels of corn left by the horses."[60] Like their Confederate counterparts, some men cut bark from trees and chewed it. Some soldiers cut hunks of meat from the carcasses of dead horses and mules and ate it raw. A few stolen onions were considered a great prize. Hardtack crackers sold for a dollar a piece. The price of flour for only one meal was six dollars if anyone could be found with crackers and flour who was willing to sell.

One officer noted, "...many of my best men dropped out of ranks, completely exhausted by hunger and fatigue...."[8]

Union officers almost universally complimented their men. One officer's statement was typical of most: "The endurance of the men is wonderful, and the spirit of devotion to their cause, which enabled them to bear all the hardships they have seen, is worthy of favorable comment."[8]

Fun-seeking Lieutenant Meigs left the cavalry and attached himself to the Eighteenth Connecticut. He tried to convince the unit to go to the rear and attack the Confederate cavalry. The men's spirit was willing but the flesh was weak. They didn't want to march or fight if they didn't have to. Meigs would have to seek adventure somewhere else that day.

Because the deceiving Rebel had led Crook astray, the Union Army was late getting started on its march to New Castle. Duffié's Cavalry had gone through the town and was posted on roads about five miles in advance. It was evening when Averell's Cavalry began entering the town. One soldier estimated the population as being near 200 citizens.[21] After the twelve-mile march, an infantryman was less than impressed when he first saw the town. It "...was a poor, barren looking place, containing only a few dingy houses, and a poverty stricken people,"[41] he said. The artist, Strother, noted, "It is an airy and picturesque locality but the village is forlorn and insignificant."[11]

Fatigued soldiers with a constant fear of bushwhackers sometimes make mistakes. A movement startled a cavalryman and "...a small boy is accidentally shot."[102]

Averell's men began looting and destroying. Some horsemen rode their mounts into the courthouse. They burned some records, including deed book A, "...marriage records, and threw ink on other records."[3]

One man started chopping the newel post, apparently trying to turn it to kindling. Rumors stated that Averell ordered the courthouse burned, but the order was not carried out. Some Federals quartered their horses in the building overnight.

The town was small and poor; the army was large and hungry. There was little food to be stolen, and most of the Union Army went to bed hungry. Soldiers stole what they could. A man with Company C, Eighteenth Connecticut brought in one bag of flour. Another soldier wrote, "If anyone found anything for man or beast to eat that night, he was more fortunate than the writer."[41] When what little the citizens had was gone soldiers stole from one another. Some soldiers were even brazen enough to break into General Sullivan's private stores and steal coffee. It was past 10:30 p.m. when the last of Crook's rear guard stumbled into camp near town. By this time, there was nothing left to steal.

As Hunter entered the town with Sullivan's Infantry, he received an alarming communique from one of Duffié's cavalrymen: "...a force of twenty thousand men had passed near Fincastle, via Covington, to intercept us."[11]

Had Early quit pursuing and started to intercept wondered Hunter? A staff officer wrote, "The enemy's silence all day may also be accepted as an evil omen."[11] Hunter panicked again. The army must not rest but push on through the night he told his staff.

A staff officer said that the tired army should not be forced to move on the basis of rumor and that cavalry scouts should be sent to confirm the report.

General Crook then spoke up. If the road was blocked, Crook proposed, "...to move southward to the line of the Virginia and Tennessee Railroad by a narrow and rough road, blockading the road in the rear as we go. Striking this line we would move westward into Tennessee, destroying as we move, including the Wythe Lead Mines and Smythe County Salt Works, using up John Morgan in our route."[11]

Once again, Hunter deferred the command decision to Crook. If Crook said that it was okay to stay at New Castle, then the army would camp at New Castle.

There is no evidence that Generals Sullivan and Averell were even at the conference, so dependent was Hunter on Crook's advice. One officer said, "I found Averell as usual sparking some girls, one of them a buxom, dimpled beauty."[11]

The general's staff forced its way into the house "...of a poor woman on the outskirts of town...."[11] They would sleep in her soft beds.

As the generals and their staffs ate a fine meal and prepared to climb into soft beds, their hungry men also bedded down. One cavalryman complained that they camped "...on a poor, brier-covered farm."[9] An infantryman grumbled that he "...tried to find a place to sleep where one's body would not be cut with sharp stones."[41] Another soldier echoed that it was "...the rockiest place you ever saw."[14] But, he continued, because of exhaustion, he slept perfectly.

Members of another regiment arrived after dark. They took no note of their surroundings but began "...dropping down where they stood...almost instantly falling asleep,"[53] recalled one soldier.

McCausland watched the sunset as the Yankees went into camp. The one day Early had allowed him to pursue was ended. The mass of the Confederate cavalry began to move back toward Salem. Hunter's raid into the valleys of Virginia was over. McCausland left a small scouting party to escort Black Dave (Hunter) and his demoralized army north.

Beyer's rendering of White Sulphur Springs from his 1857 Album of Virginia.

White Sulphur Springs by David Hunter Strother.

Postlogue

The exhausted Federals continued withdrawing from Virginia valleys. Non-essentials like plunder and empty knapsacks had been thrown away many days ago. Some men had thrown rifles and their accouterments away also. One Union officer was surprised to see some infantrymen carrying "...a Wooden-Bedded Billiard table...."[109] When Captain Town of the Signal Corps was told of the billiard table being carried north on the soldiers' shoulders, he exclaimed, "Hang me, if I don't expect to see my rascals carrying a privy along with them, plank by plank, in hopes of setting it up for general delectation when they reach Meadow Bluffs!"[109]

More horses and mules were shot as the Union column marched. A legend said that it took the residents a week to bury the approximately 250-300[14] abused and destroyed animals. Approximately 50 wagons were burned because there were no animals left to pull them.

Federal troops began to arrive at the White Sulphur Springs Hotel in the late evening of June 23, but most of the troops did not get to look at their surroundings until the next day. When the sun rose, soldiers were astonished. What follows are but a few of the comments made by different soldiers. "A glorious place the White Sulphur."[104] One officer who had visited the place before the war now found it, "...desolate and forlorn...."[11] Gone were the wealth, the laughter, the gambling, and most of the slaves. The hotel had been converted into a Confederate Hospital. The hotel was described as "mammoth,"[11] "...three stories high, about four hundred feet long, with an L of about one hundred and fifty feet."[83] "The main hotel could accommodate over 1,000 guests."[109] The hotels were made of "...red brick and white stucco...with terraces and rows of tributary Italian and Swiss villas farmed out to separate families...."[109] The water of the Springs was clear and cold, but the sulfur content made it smell "...as if a thousand baskets of the rottenest eggs or worst decayed mackerel ever known lay festering at its bottom."[109] One soldier said, "I could not bring myself to quench my thirst...."[11]

Upon entering the hotel, a soldier marveled at a dining room measuring 300 by 50 feet, "...resplendent with mirrors...(and) furniture which is of the richest quality...."[109]

As there was no food to steal, the soldiers occupied themselves in the mineral springs baths. One soldier reported: "There are two large baths, one for ladies and one for gentlemen, with dressing rooms for each."[14] There was a skylight about 20 feet square. "The water can be graduated from 3 feet deep to 6, at the pleasure of the bathers,"[14] he said.

One soldier got enough nerve to drink the water. It had "...a sickish, sulphurish, metallicish, nastyish taste...."[14]

Hunter looked at the beauty and the elegance of the hotel and said, "Burn it!" Hunter said he had heard rumors about the attack made on the wagon train sent back from Liberty. According to the rumor, both a Mrs. Lewis and the hotel operator were involved in supplying the Confederates with information. Hunter ordered that Mrs. Lewis's home and the hotel be burned.

Mrs. Lewis soon called on Hunter to try and dissuade him from burning her house. Chief-of-staff Strother sided with the lady. Hunter countermanded the order.

When young Dupont heard that Hunter was going to burn the hotel and surrounding properties, he believed it violated "...the specific instructions of the United States Government,"[47] but he knew that Hunter had disregarded orders many times. Dupont decided to use subterfuge. He said, "General, I hear that you intend to burn the buildings here when we leave."[8]

"Yes, I intend to burn them all down,"[8] retorted Hunter.

Dupont told Hunter that it would be a mistake to do so. Dupont argued that the Union would soon be operating in the area and would need the hotel. Hunter then decided that he would be striking against the South by refusing to burn the Southern property. Young Dupont could smile as he left the old general — his mission accomplished.

The Union Army continued to Meadow Bluff, Crook's and Averell's former supply base, but there were no supplies. Because of Confederate Partisan Ranger activity, the supplies had either been moved north or destroyed. The weary and disappointed army turned toward Charleston, (W) Va. Near Gauley Bridge, the first supplies arrived. In the scramble to get food, men began fist fights throughout the army.

The army camped at Gauley Bridge. It had been almost one month since the army had started the march, which had covered almost 500 miles and had cost Hunter almost 1,000 men. Hunter's command was sore-footed, broken-spirited, bone-weary, and starved.

Lynchburg was the object of Hunter's raid. By this time, the Home Guard was released from duty, and most of the convalescents were back in the hospitals. Union prisoners were being sent to more permanent housing. Many Confederate prisoners held in the stockade previous to the battle were being released. Some rejoined the army; others were released from service.

The cadets returned to their burned-out school (V.M.I.). The president of Washington College allowed the corps temporarily to be housed at his school. After the war, citizen Robert E. Lee accepted the presidency of the college. Somewhat later, the name was changed. Today Washington and Lee University is recognized as a leader in the academic field.

As the news that Hunter was running north began to filter back to Lynchburg, the newspaper gleefully boasted: "...We predict that this is the last Yankee trip to Lynchburg."[16] There was a feeling of goodwill, brotherhood, and safety in Lynchburg. Many people and groups of people felt that they could claim some measure of credit for the salvation of the city. The common soldiers, wounded soldiers from the hospitals, nurses, doctors, Home Guard, railroad employees, homemakers, members of the corps, scouts, artillerists, and even "...Northern men who, having made their homes here, (and had) cast their lot with us to defend the cause upheld by the South,"[10] could claim a major role. One family at New London often bragged that they saved Lynchburg by getting Hunter drunk and delaying his arrival. Imboden believed that his holding action at the Quaker Church made all the difference. General Early wanted to claim the title, "Savior of Lynchburg."

The government of the city of Lynchburg passed the following resolution on June 24, 1864:

"Resolved: That the thanks of the City are due, and are hereby tendered to Lieutenant General Jubal A. Early and Major General J. C. Breckinridge, and the officers and soldiers under their command, for their timely and efficient services in driving the enemy from our borders.

And to Brigadier General F. T. Nichols, commander of the post, for his untiring and successful efforts to meet, with the local forces, the advancing foe.

And to Major General D. H. Hill, and Brigadier General H. T. Hays, for their co-operation in organizing the local forces, and constructing the lines of defence.

And to Lieutenant Colonels Richard E. Burks and E. J. Hoge, though themselves on crutches, who generously volunteered and were placed in command of the convalescents.

And the cadets of the Virginia Military Institute, a noble band of youthful heroes, for their promptness in the hour of danger.

And to Brigadier General McCausland, and the officers and soldiers under his command, for their gallantry in opposing for ten days the march of a greatly superior force, thereby retarding the advance of the enemy on our city until a proper force could be organized for its defence.

And to Major Generals Wade Hampton and Fitzhugh Lee, and the officers and soldiers under their command, for the defeat of Sheridan, thereby preventing a junction of the enemy forces at this place.

Resolved that the authorities and the citizens gratefully acknowledge our obligations to the defenders of Lynchburg; they will ever find seats around each fireside, and plates at every board, and old and young will greet them at the threshold, and bid them welcome, thrice welcome to our homes and hearths.

A copy teste. James O. Williams, *Clerk.*"[106]

The city government was a political body eager to have the goodwill of all and the ill will of none. Members didn't wish to elevate one man or group above another, but the common citizen did.

The newspapers informed the people of McCausland's efforts to slow Hunter at each turn, creek, and town. The citizens had also heard of the punishment McCausland had inflicted on Hunter at Hanging Rock.

By June 27, a formal committee of "...tribute to McCausland"[101] had been organized and had collected over $1,000. The fund quickly rose to $3,000. A beautiful sword and a pair of silver spurs were purchased for the peoples' choice. Citizen pressure forced the City Council formally to present McCausland with the tokens of admiration from the populace on July 7, thus formally recognizing McCausland as the "Savior of Lynchburg." The formal presentation was to take place on September 10, but McCausland wasn't there because he was involved in another action in the Valley.

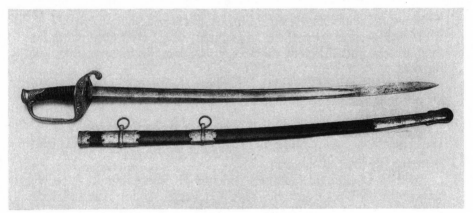

Gen. John McCausland's sword (Lynchburg Museum System).

There has been much debate as to who stopped Hunter and where the critical action took place. People of the time and historians since have selected a person or group and pointed to a particular action and proclaimed their choice as the savior of Lynchburg.

The name of one man has never been put in nomination for that honor. It is possible that this man would probably not wish to have his name entered. Even to this day in Lynchburg, the name is preceded or followed by coarse and derisive adjectives. It appears to this writer that Gen. David Hunter was the "Savior of Lynchburg." He allowed his personal hatred of slavery to supercede his military mission. The time "Black Dave" wasted warming his vengeful heart with punitive fires allowed the South time to reinforce the city. The Confederacy would survive for almost one more year. The responsibility for the pain, the wounds, the deaths, and the destruction that would occur could be placed directly on Hunter.

Mrs. McDonald had a bad premonition when her husband, Angus, and young son, Harry, left Lexington as the Union Army approached. Harry escaped from the wagon train. He left his youth in Union captivity and spent the balance of the war fighting for a Southern man's rights.

Angus's rheumatism would hardly allow him to walk; he could not run away. He was imprisoned at one of the worst camps possible (Elmira Prison) for those suffering from his type of ailment. Insufficient food, few blankets, poor medical care, and the icy winds off the Great Lakes caused Elmira, New York, to be the final resting place of too many Southerners.

McDonald survived imprisonment and returned to the capital of his beloved Confederacy. He died there at the home of his son, never reaching Lexington or never seeing his wife again.

Views of slavery contrast sharply between Northern and Southern writers. This is due in part to two major reasons: what did the writer see and what did the writer want to see? Northerners mostly saw run-away slaves that had little love for their masters and a desire for freedom. The escaped slaves told stories, sometimes exaggerated, of the horrors of slavery, reinforcing some Northern writers' prejudice that slavery was "evil."

Southern writers mostly saw the faithful, devoted, and beloved slave. Runaways were most often field hands that might not have had a personal relationship with their masters. Southern writers saw slaves protecting their master's property and caring for their master's family. No matter which of the popular rationales the master adopted to justify the institution of slavery, most Southerners viewed slavery as "good."

The sociology of slavery cannot be simply summed up as "evil" or "good." It was as complex as the various individuals, institutions, ideologies, economics, and political pressures involved.

Before the war, many Southerners had a deep worry, although not often spoken, that the slaves would revolt. The war came and most of the white men left their plantations to serve. There is no record of a slave rebellion occurring during the war. Southerners could argue that if slavery was evil, then slaves would revolt at the first opportunity; because there was no general revolt, Southerners could say that slaves were, on the whole, satisfied with their roles in life.

It appears that Hunter had learned nothing from his failure to capture Lynchburg. It appears that his attitudes had not changed. After the army had rested but before he left command, Hunter paid a visit to his cousin Andrew Hunter's house near Charlestown. The two cousins had similar ages but clashed on political views and personalities. Andrew was a Southerner; Hunter was a Northerner. Andrew was described as "...a man without an enemy."[116] Hunter could almost be described as "a man without a friend."

Hunter arrested his Southern cousin without charge, refused Andrew's request that the contents of the house be removed before the house was burned, and then camped on the farm for several days, allowing men and beasts to despoil the whole place.

Hunter visited nearby Sheperdstown and burned the fine home of Alexander Boteler. As with his cousin Andrew, Hunter allowed nothing except the occupants to be removed from the house. Hunter was, indeed, the black sheep of the family, for Mrs. Boteler was also Hunter's cousin.

Hunter also had the home of Edward I. Lee burned. The outrage and the anger of Mrs. Lee in her letter to General Hunter are evident.

Shepherdstown, VA., July 20th, 1864.

General Hunter —

Yesterday, your underling, Captain Martindale, of the First New York Cavalry, executed your infamous order and burned my house. You have the satisfaction ere this of receiving from him the information that your orders were fulfilled to the letter; the dwelling and every outbuilding, seven in number, with their contents, being burned. I, therefore, a helpless woman whom you have cruelly wronged, address you, a Major General of the United States Army, and demand why this was done? What was my offense? My husband was absent — an exile. He never had been a politician or in any way engaged in the struggle now going on, his age preventing. This fact your chief-of-staff, David Strother, could have told you. The house was built by my father, a Revolutionary soldier, who served the whole seven years for your independence. There was I born; there the sacred dead repose. It was my house, and my home, and there has your niece (Miss Griffith), who has tarried among us all this horrid war up to the present moment, met with all kindness and hospitality at my hands. Was it for this that you turned me, my young daughter and little son out upon the world without a shelter? Or was it because my husband is the grandson of the Revolutionary patriot and "rebel," Richard Henry Lee, and the near kinsman of the noblest of Christian warriors, the greatest of generals, Robert E. Lee? Heaven's blessing be upon his head forever! You and your government have failed to conquer, subdue or match him; and, disappointed, rage and malice find vent on the helpless and inoffensive.

Hyena-like, you have torn my heart to pieces! for all hallowed memories clustered around that homestead; and, demon-like, you have done it without even the pretext of revenge, for I never saw or harmed you. Your office is not to lead, like a brave man and soldier, your men to fight in the ranks of war, but your work has been to separate yourself from all danger, and with your incendiary band steal unaware upon helpless women and children, to insult and destroy. Two fair homes did you yesterday ruthlessly lay in ashes, giving not a moment's warning to the startled inmates of your wicked purpose; turning mothers and children out of doors, your very name execrated by your own men for the cruel work you gave them to do.

In the case of Colonel A. R. Boteler, both father and mother were far away. Any heart but that of Captain Martindale (and yours) would have been touched by that little circle, comprising a widowed daughter just risen from her bed of illness, her three little fatherless babes — the oldest not five years old — and her heroic sister. I repeat, any *man* would have been touched at that sight. But, Captain Martindale! one might as well hope to find mercy and feeling in the heart of a wolf bent on his prey of young lambs, as to search for such qualities in his bosom. You have chosen well your agent for such deeds, and doubtless will promote him!

A colonel of the Federal army has stated that you deprived forty of your officers of their commands because they refused to carry out your malignant mischief. All honor to their names for this, at least! They are *men* — they have human hearts and blush for such a commander!

I ask who, that does not wish infamy and disgrace attached to him forever, would serve under you! *Your* name will stand on history's page as the Hunter of weak women and innocent children; the Hunter to destroy defenseless villages and refined and beautiful homes — to torture afresh the agonized hearts of the widows; the Hunter of Africa's poor sons and daughters, to lure them on to ruin and death of soul and body; the Hunter with the relentless heart of a wild beast, the face of a fiend, and the form of a man. Oh, Earth, behold the monster! Can I say, "God forgive you?" No prayer can be offered for you! Were it possible for human lips to raise your name heavenward, angels would thrust the foul thing back again, and demons claim their own. The curses of thousands, the scorn of the manly and upright, and the hatred of the true and honorable, will follow you and yours through all time, and brand your name *infamy! infamy!*

Again, I demand why have you burned my house? Answer as you must answer before the Searcher of all hearts; why have you added this cruel, wicked deed to your many crimes?

HENRIETTA E. LEE

Not only did the deaths and the destructions of Hunter's raid generate letters and accounts of the horror, but they also generated works of literature.

This incident has been so beautifully and fully told in verse by the wife of General F. H. Smith that this story would be incomplete without its reproduction:

"He lived the life of an upright man,
 And the people loved him well;
Many a wayfarer came to his door,
 His sorrow or need to tell,
A pitying heart and an open hand,
 Gave succor ready and free;
For kind and true to his fellow-man
 And a Christian was David Creigh.

"But o'er his threshold a shadow passed,
 With the step of a ruffian foe;
While in silent words and brutal threats
 A purpose of darkness show;
And a daughter's wild, imploring cry
 Called the father to her side —

His hand was nerved by the burning wrong,
  And there the offender died.

"The glory of autumn had gone from earth,
  The winter had passed away,
And the glad spring-time was merging fast,
  Into summer's ardent ray,
When a good man from his home was torn —
  Days of toilsome travel to see —
And far from his loved a crown was worn,
  And the martyr was David Creigh.

"The tramp of your men is at our door,
  On an evil errand come;
But for love of them whose garb you wear,
  I invite you to my home."
So spoke the southron! the Chaplain thus:
  "Though sick and weary I be,
I can't break bread 'neath a southern roof,
  Since the murder of David Creigh!

"Here where he lived, let the end by told,
  Of a told of bitter wrong;
Here let our famishing thousands learn,
  To whom vengeance doth belong.
Short grace was given the dying man;
  E're led to the fatal tree,
And share the grace to our starving hosts,
  Since the murder of David Creigh!"

Our hosts were stayed in their onward cry,
  Exulting in power and pride,
By an unseen hand — defeat and unrest,
  Our banners march beside;
And a heavier burden no heart hath borne,
  Than the one that came to me,
With the dying words and the latest sigh
  Of the martyr David Creigh.

The beast of the desert shields its young,
  With an instinct fierce and wild,
And lives there a man with the heart of a man,
  Who would not defend his child?
So woe to those who call evil good —
  That woe shall not come to me —
War hath no record of fouler deed,
  Than the murder of David Creigh.

The Bicentennial Pageant "Echo of Liberty" of Bedford County, 1954, devoted a scene to Hunter's sweep through the county.

A play by Edwin Warehime, "The Waves of War," reminds the descendants of those who fought of Hunter's visit to Lynchburg.

The engagement at Hanging Rock has been the cause of no fewer than three poems.

THREE PRESIDENTS AT HANGING ROCK

On the outskirts of Salem, Virginia,
In the Civil War's '64,
History was being made:
Three future Presidents were in the roar.

Hayes, Garfield, McKinley —
General Averell retreated for no gains,
Land trap held by Rebel's McCausland;
Cannons shot up troops and wagon trains.

Hayes, Garfield, McKinley
Fought the good fight at Hanging Rock.
Wonder it is they survived
So history could tell and talk.

Captain McKinley lived through Hanging Rock's holocaust;
As President McKinley he signed into laws
Panama Canal and the Great White Fleet.
Our luck was better than it ever was.

Never in battle's fitful fight
Had three men destined to be
President of these United States
All survived to set their enemies free.

It is fitting that these three soldiers
With military and political ties
Knew Hanging Rock's fight and freedom —
That on this Rock history lies.

Lee's Command by Albert J. Russo, MD

HANGING ROCK

A grim black mountain stands beside the tombstones of the brave,
You look at Hanging Rock and think of everything they gave;
The loyalty they offered, and the lives they could not save,
That grim black mountain looks just like a grave at Hanging Rock.

The wind that blows on Hanging Rock, a hundred years has sighed

And to the lost and lonely souls all respite has denied,
But echoes still a sweetheart's voice who stood alone and cried,
"I knew him as a baby, but he died at Hanging Rock."

So many men lie dead now, for their country, for their state,
What makes a man leave everything and turn to such a fate?
What makes him leave his children, leave his home, and leave his mate?
They left their love behind, and took their hate to Hanging Rock.

They heard the call of bugles and they came, by day, by night,
And each man knew his cause was good and prayed to God for might.
But how could either one be wrong, or either one be right
When brother turned on brother at Hanging Rock.

And somewhere in the muster were three strong and fearless men;
McKinley, Hayes, and Garfield faced the battle fire again.
But one day peace would come, and though they didn't know it then,
They'd lead their country as they'd led their men at Hanging Rock.

A war's a time for killing, and there's no time to repent
Till men are lying dead, and all the shot and powder spent.
But God knew what would happen, and before all time He sent
A grim black mountain there, a monument at Hanging Rock.

Patsy Bickerstaff Curley

Yonder clift of rock so steep and high,
Thrills many a passer as he goes by,
And with all its beauty so sublime,
The soul cries out to climb! TO CLIMB!
But the rugged rocks beckon him away
And point to the path of an ancient day,
Which leads to the top where he can see
How McCausland's men could fire so free.

This Marker across the chasm deep and wide,
Shows where gallant soldiers fought and died,
The Boys in Gray from that very spot
Fired on the Boys in Blue an unfriendly shot,
For hours cannons roared, shot and shells were flying,
The villages were terrified, brave men were dying,
This battle was fought on June 21st, 1864,
A Confederate victory of the Civil War.

Author Unknown

As Hunter's starved troops withdrew north, both the soldiers and the generals knew that they had failed. The capital of the Confederacy, Richmond, still stood, apparently as indomitable as ever. Soldiers from the highest to the lowest ranks knew that it was going to be difficult to explain how such a mighty army could fail to take such a weakly defended position as Lynchburg after such a glorious victory as Piedmont.

Many Northern soldiers, newspapermen, and writers decided to find victory in retreat. By ignoring the fact that Hunter had failed in his main mission to stop the flow of salt and lead and cause Richmond to fall, authors could find victory. One newspaper told Northern readers, "The result of the campaign...had been eminently satisfactory; and everything that had been ordered or expected had been thoroughly accomplished, with but comparatively little loss."[16]

A Northern writer echoed, "...extremely successful, inflicting great injury upon the enemy."[17] Other pro-Northern reports gave lengthy accounts of railroad and track equipment destroyed, of casualties inflicted, of ordnance destroyed, of supplies plundered, of factories laid waste, and of weapons captured. No Northern accounts claimed victory for destroying beautiful Southern homes, hanging civilians, looting, ransacking Washington College, or burning the Virginia Military Institute.

Even General Averell ignored the fact that the army had failed in its major objective. He stated that the campaign's "...greatness as a military achievement will be recognized by history."[11]

A cavalryman under Averell suffered no self delusion. He knew that he was bone-weary, starving, and running because the army had lost. He knew that accusatory fingers would be pointed. He wrote, "Who was to blame? Certainly not the rank and file."[34]

In retreat, the Union soldiers had been tried by indescribable hardships. The majority of the Federals had shown stamina, courage, and valor.

Most of the Union officers praised their men. Duffié's words are eloquent: "I am pleased to testify to the gallantry, efficiency and fortitude of the troops...In every action the greatest bravery has been manifested...everyone did his duty...."[8]

Who was to blame? Almost every finger pointed toward David Hunter, but there are always some who disagree. One officer in Hunter's army wrote, "Hunter's only fault was that his tender and noble heart did not allow him to execute one-tenth part of the severity of his orders...."[109]

Hunter's adjutant, Lt. Col. Charles Halpine, jumped to the general's defense, declaring that when God made Hunter, "He took the world's finest clay and broke the die after the cast was perfect."[5] Halpine called his superior, "...the purest, gentlest, bravest, and most honest gentleman...free from any vice...incapable of any baseness...absolutely pure."[5] Even Lincoln referred to Hunter as "...so good and true an officer, man and friend."[5]

The few who spoke eloquently of Hunter and his success were drowned out by the vindictive shouts of the many. Many writers branded Hunter as incompetent and demanded his immediate removal. One Northern writer who wished to avoid harsh recriminations against any member of the United States Army, simply stated, "...that had the generalship that guided the movement been equal to the spirit and courage of the troops, Lynchburg would have fallen into our hands."[59]

After Sigel had been driven from the Valley, Grant was quick to reprimand and remove him from command. Grant did not treat Hunter in the same manner. Perhaps Grant was so relieved to receive the news that the Army of West Virginia had not been annihilated in the valleys of Virginia that he took no action against Hunter.

Despite Grant's lack of speed, Hunter could see the handwriting on the wall. The letters spelled the end to his command. True to his character, Hunter accepted no personal responsibility for the defeat. Hunter stated that he had been "...selected as the scapegoat to cover up the blunders of others...."[5] Hunter later placed blame by writing, "...I dashed toward Lynchburg, and should certainly have taken it, if it had not been for the stupidity and conceit of that fellow Averell...."[8]

After a private meeting with Grant in August, Hunter was convinced that there was no way to hold command of the Army of West Virginia any longer. To spare Grant from the pressure of relieving him, to spare President Lincoln the pain of approving Grant's request, and to spare the army and the United States any feelings of division, Hunter asked to be relieved of command. Maj. Gen. David Hunter no longer commanded an army.

Averell stated that the campaign's "...greatness as a military achievement will be recognized by history." In the South, and particularly in the valleys that witnessed Hunter's achievements, history recognizes the terrorism of the campaign, not the military achievements.

Words from one Southern writer's pen state: "War is not a gentle occupation, and its customs are harsh...But putting non-combatants to death, insults to women and children, the wanton destruction of household goods and clothes, the application of the torch to dwellings, factories and mills, or the destruction of public buildings, works of art and science, is a style of warfare long since relegated to the savage. The disgrace of reviving the barbaric strife in modern times was reserved for Hunter."[56]

General Imboden spoke of Hunter's atrocities: "The United States Government could not stand it, his army could not stand it, as many of his prominent officers yet living tell how keenly they felt the stigma such acts —beyond their control — brought on them."[23]

The memory of Gen. David Hunter runs deep in the valleys of Virginia. Even today his name brings forth curses and oaths muttered with the most intense anger from the darkest side of the human spirit of the descendants of those who fought Hunter or felt the wrath of his hatred for his parent's native state. A Southern gentleman said of Hunter: "...It would be a greater charity than can be shown him to speak not at all. The mildest terms that can be applied to him are renegade and coward."[131]

It appears that Hunter had learned nothing or altered any of his attitudes because of the campaign. He accepted no blame for the failure. He continued to burn Southerners' homes while he was in command of the army.

It is to be remembered that most of Hunter's military career had seen him as a major. Only after riding Lincoln's train did he start wearing a major general's uniform. Some months after leaving the Army of West Virginia, Hunter wrote Grant: "...I beg that you will give me a command of some kind...give me a division, a brigade, or a regiment."[8] Hunter had not been able to cope with the command of an army. He constantly called on Crook to make decisions when the going was rough. In his communication to Grant, Hunter seems to admit that he was only a major in a major general's uniform.

One writer indicates that Hunter might not have been upset because he was considered "...the war's highest ranking pyromaniac. It was fitting, for Hunter had long considered himself an agent of death and demolition, a tool of retribution to be wielded against the enemies of his nation, no matter how horrid such retribution might appear."[5]

> "...The memory of General David Hunter will live and be handed down through the generations to come — it may be, in the long future, only by legend and tradition — in connection with deeds that illustrate how far the passions, fanaticism, and hate engendered by civil war can drag a man down...."

General J.D. Imboden

"Lest We Forget"

David Creigh's grave — Lewisburg, (W) Va.

Caldwell House — Hunter threatened to burn house while passing through Lewisburg, (W) Va.

Gen. Jubal A. Early's grave marker, Spring Hill Cemetery — Lynchburg. (Early lies at the far end of where the Confederate left was anchored during the engagement of Lynchburg).

State Route 116

Gen. W. E. Jones's grave — Glade Spring Presbyterian Church — Glade Spring, Va.

1932 monument at Hanging Rock.

1964 monument at Hanging Rock.

Ceremony at V.M.I. to honor cadets that fell during the war.

Re-dedication of Pest House Hospital — Old City Cemetery — Lynchburg — Summer 1988. Note: Some of the over-2,000 grave markers of Confederate soldiers can be seen in foreground.

Home of the Reverent James Morrison

    This home near Brownsburg is where David Creigh spent his final hours on earth.

Covered Spring at Harrisonburg

Courtesy: James O. Gunter & H. Clark Lee

Home of Dr. J. T. W. Read

This home at New London was visited by General Hunter.

Courtesy: H. Clark Lee & James O. Gunter

"The Piano That Saved Lynchburg"

The Read family and their descendants believe that the music from this piano so charmed General Hunter that he temporarily forgot about the urgency to attack Lynchburg. While the music and drink flowed, Southern forces were able to prepare the defense of the city. Thus, this piano saved Lynchburg and the entire Confederacy!

General Early's French made field glasses, liquor flask, boot pistol, Boker knife-for cutting tobacco plug, and field sword, he called his "fighting sword." All were used in the war.

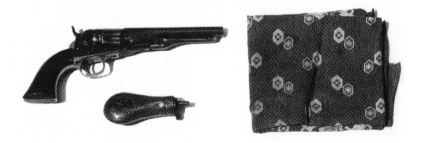

The pistol, power flask, and bandanna with maple leaf imprint were acquired by him when he was in self-imposed exile in Canada. Photos courtesy: Tad Darnall.

Text Notes

[1]*Elements of Military Art and Science* — by Henry Wager Halleck

[2]Dixie Gun Works, Inc. — Armament Listing

[3]*New River Valley Historical News Letter* — "Hunter's Retreat" — by James Looney

[4]*Sketches of War, the Lynchburg Campaign* — by Edward S. Wilson (xref59)

[5]*Civil War Times Illustrated* — "A Profile of Maj. Gen. David Hunter" — by Edward G. Longacre

[6]*Conquest of a Valley* — by Marshell Brice

[7]*Time-Life Books* — "The Shenandoah in Flames" — by Thomas A. Lewis

[8]*War of the Rebellion: Official Records of the Union and Confederate Armies* — Ed. War Department

[9]*First New York (Lincoln) Cavalry* — by William H. Beach, A.M.

[10]*Lynchburg and its Neighbors* — by Rosa F. Yancy (xref64)

[11]*A Virginia Yankee in the Civil War* — by David Hunter Strother

[12]*Presidential Anecdotes* — by Paul Boller, Jr.

[13]*Hayes of the 23rd — the Civil War Volunteer Officer* — by T. Harry Williams (xref60)

[14]*Record of the One Hundred and Sixteenth Ohio Volunteer Infantry in the War of the Rebellion* — by Thomas F. Wildes

[15]*The Civil War* — by Shelby Foote

[16]*The Rebellion Record: A Diary of American Events:* — Ed. Frank Moore

[17]*The Shenandoah Valley in 1864* — by George E. Pond

[18]*The Civil War Diary 1862-1865 of Charles H. Lynch, Eighteenth Connecticut Volunteers* —by Charles Lynch

[19]*The Confederate Veteran* — "Scouting Hunter's Raid to Lynchburg" — by James Z. McChesney

[20]*A Rebel Cavalryman* — by John N. Opie

[21]*Ironton Register* (Dec. 22-March 23, 1865) "Adventures, Struggles, Trials and Service of the Fifth Regiment Volunteer Infantry"

[22]*Diary and Letters of Rutherford B. Hayes* — Ed. Charles R. Williams

[23]*The Annals of the War* — "Fire, Sword, and the Halter" — by Gen. J.D. Imboden

[24]*Generals in Gray* — by Ezra Warner

[25]*A Diary with Reminiscences of the War and Refugee Life in the Shenandoah Valley 1860-1865* — by Mrs. Cornelia McDonald

[26]Tombstone of Eliza M. (Dunn) Jones

[27]Hand written letter — Virginia Military Institute Archives (xref75)

[28]*Wildcat Cavalry: A Synoptic History of the Seventeenth Virginia Cavalry Regiment of the Jenkins — McCausland Brigade in the War Between the States* — by John H. Dawson

[29]*Southern Historical Papers* — "Richmond Times Dispatch" (July 8, 1900) "General Hunter's Raid"

[30]*A History of the Lynchburg Campaign* — by Milton Humphrey

[31]*12th Ohio Volunteer Infantry* — by J.E.D. Ward

[32]*Greenbrier Pioneers and their Homes* — by Ruth Woods Dayton

[33]*Harrisonburg, Va. Diary of a Citizen* — by E.R. Grymesheneberger

[34]*History of the 2nd Regiment West Virginia Cavalry During the War of the Rebellion* — by J.J. Sutton, Washington and Lee University Archives

[35]*Journal of John Milton Hoge — Confederate Soldier* — Ed. Mary Bruce

[36]*Southern Historical Society Papers* — "General Hunter's Raid" — Ed. R.A. Brock

[37]*The Campaign of 1864 in the Valley of Virginia and the Expedition to Lynchburg* — by H.A. Dupont (xref47)

[38]Composite: *A History of the Lynchburg Campaign* — by Milton Humphrey
Conquest of a Valley — by Marshell Brice
The Annals of the War — "Fire, Sword, and the Halter" — by Gen. J.D. Imboden

[39]Composite: *Conquest of a Valley* — by Marshell Brice
The Annals of the War — "Fire, Sword, and the Halter" by Gen. J.D. Imboden

[40]*Sandusky Register Steam Press 1874* — "The Military History of the 123rd Regiment Ohio Volunteer Infantry" — Ed. C.M. Keyes (xref53)

[41]*A History of the 18th Regiment Connecticut Volunteers in the War for the Union* — by Chaplain William C. Walker

[42]*The War in Southwest Virginia 1861-65* — by Gary C. Walker

[43]*Annals of Augusta County, Va.* — by Joseph A. Waddell

[44]*"Untitled Article"* — *by Milton Shaver*

[45]*History of Augusta County, Va.* — by J. Lewis Pexton

[46]Composite: *The Campaign of 1864 in the Valley of Virginia and the Expedition to Lynchburg* — by H.A. Dupont
History of Augusta County, Va. — J. Lewis Pexton
Conquest of a Valley — by Marshell Brice
The War in Southwest Virginia 1861-65 — by Gary C. Walker
A History of the Lynchburg Campaign — by Milton Humphrey

[47]*The Campaign of 1864 in the Valley of Virginia and the Expedition to Lynchburg* — by H.A. Dupont (xref37)

[48]*Southern Historical Society Papers* — from "Richmond Times Dispatch" June 4, 1899

[49]"Untitled Article" by Mrs. David Beard

[50]*Civil War Times Illustrated* — "The Battle of Piedmont" — by William J. Kimball

[51]*36th Virginia Infantry* — by J.L. Scott

[52]*"Southwest Virginia Enterprise"* Feb. 20, 1914

[53]*Sandusky Register Steam Press 1874* — The Military History of the 123rd Regiment Ohio Infantry" — Ed. C.M. Keyes (xref40)

[54]*Southern Historical Collection* at University of North Carolina — "Letter of Major Archilles James Tynes, C.S.A."

[55]*Breckinridge* — *Statesman, Soldier, Symbol* — by William C. Davis

[56]*Southern Historical Society Papers* — "The Campaign and Battle of Lynchburg" — by Capt. Charles M. Blackford

[57]*Speech by Dr. Alexander McCausland*

[58]*The Military History of the Virginia Military Institute* — by Jenning C. Wise

[59]*Sketches of War* — *the Lynchburg Campaign* — by Edward S. Wilson (xref4)

[60]*Hayes of the 23rd* — *the Civil War Volunteer Officer* — by T. Harry Williams (xref13)

[61]*Southern Historical Society Papers* "General Hunter's Raid"

[62]*The Story of a Cannoneer under Stonewall Jackson* — by Ed Moore

[63]*Southern Historical Society Papers* "The Fourteenth Virginia Cavalry" — by J. Scott Moore

[64]*Lynchburg and its Neighbors* — by Rosa F. Yancey (xref10)

[65]*The Governors of Virginia 1860-1978* — Ed. Edward Younger and James Tice Moore

[66]Virginia Military Institute Archives "Correspondence of Superintendent Francis Smith"

[67]*Lynchburg in the Civil War* — by George Morris and Susan Foutz (xref78)

[68]*The Diary of Henry Boswell Jones of Brownsburg (1842-1871)* — Ed. Charles W. Turner

[69]*The Confederate Veteran* — "The Shelling of Lexington, Va." reprint in "Rockbridge County News"

[70]"The Action at Lexington, June 11, 1864" Prof. P.J. Thompson Virginia Military Institute

[71]*An End of An Era* — by John S. Wise

[72]*A History of Rockbridge Co. Va.* — by Oren F. Morton, B.L.T.

[73]*Gen. George Crook* — *His Autobiography* — Ed. Martin F. Schmitt

[74]*Lexington in old Virginia* — by Henry Boley

[75]William Watson Collection Washington and Lee University (xref120)

[76]*The Confederate Veteran* "Who Saved Lynchburg from Hunter's Raid" — by A.H. Plecker
[77]*The Botetourt Artillery* — by Jerald H. Markham
[78]*Lynchburg in the Civil War* — by George Morris and Susan Foutz (xref67)
[79]*Civil War Journal of Stonewall Jackson's Topographer* — Ed. Archie McDonald
[80]*A War Diary with Reminiscences* — by Henry D. Beall
[81]*The Philadelphia Weekly Times* April 9, 1892 — "The Capture of Buchanan" — by Gilberta S. Whittle
[82]*A Valley A Song* — by Julia Davis
[83]*Life with the 34th Massachusetts Infantry in the War of the Rebellion* — by William S. Lincoln
[84]*Personal Recollections of the Civil War* — by Mary Terry
[85]*History of the Shenandoah Valley* — by William Couper
[86]*Historic and Heroic Lynchburg* — by Don P. Halsey (xref131)
[87]*Iron Maker to the Confederacy* — by Joseph Anderson
[88]*The Shenandoah Campaigns of 1862 and 1864 and the Appomattox Campaign 1865* — the Military Historical Society of Massachusetts
[89]*Battles and Leaders of the Civil War* — "The Way to Appomattox" — Ed. Robert Johnson and Clarence Buel
[90]*The Civil War Almanac* — Ed. John Bowman
[91]University of Virginia — Daniel Papers Collection
[92]*Buchanan, Va.: Gateway to the Southwest* — by Harry Fulwiler, Jr.
[93]*Journal of the Roanoke Historical Society* — "Some Phase of the Civil War in the Roanoke Area" — by Goodridge Wilson
[94]*A History of the Southern Confederacy* — by Clement Eaton
[95]*Lee's Maverick General* — *Daniel Harvey Hill* — by Hal Bridges
[96]"Bedford Soldiers in the Civil War" — by Melvin Scott
[97]*The History of Bedford County, Va.* — by Lula Parker
[98]*Big Dan* — by Frank Cunningham
[99]Bedford City/County Museum — Historical Home Description File
[100]Bedford City/County Museum — Historical Letters File
[101]"The Lynchburg Virginian" Newspaper June 21, 1864
[102]Bedford City/County Museum — Historical Newspaper File
[103]*Jubal's Raid* — War Library & Museum of the Military Order of the Loyal Legions of the United States
[104]*Old Jube* — by Millard Hushong
[105]Hand written letter — Virginia Military Institute Archives (xref27)
[106]*Lynchburg and its People* — by W. Asburg Christian
[107]*John O. Casler's* — *Four Years in the Stonewall Brigade* — Ed. James I. Robertson, Jr.
[108]*Gen. James "Pete" Longstreet* — *Lee's "Old War Horse" Scapegoat for Gettysburg* — by Wilbur Thomas
[109]*Baked Meats of the Funeral* — by Private Miles O'Rielly
[110]*New River Valley Historical Newsletter* Vol. 1 No. 1
[111]*New London Today and Yesterday* — by Daisy L. Reed
[112]*The Vanishing Virginian* — by Rebecca Williams
[113]"Diary of Captain W.W. Old" ADC — Library of Congress
[114]*Recollections of a Lifetime* — by John Goode
[115]*Letters from Lee's Army* — Mrs. Susan Blackford
[116]*Forty Years of Active Service* — by Col. Charles O'Ferrall
[117]Jones Memorial Library — Historical Letter File
[118]*The Atlanta Monthly* — "The Great Skedaddle" — by William Stark
[119]*A Memoir of the last year of the War for Independence* — by Lt. Gen. Jubal A. Early
[120]William Watson Collection — Washington and Lee University (xref75)
[121]*The Journal of Ada Lawrence Hutter* — by Ada Hutter
[122]*The History of Lynchburg 1786-1946* — by Philip Scruggs
[123]*American Bar Association Journal* — "Jubal Anderson Early — Lawyer and Soldier of the Confederacy" — by George Farnum

438

[124]*A History of Bedford County* — Ed. Peter Viemeister

[125]*Community at the Cross Roads: A Study of the Village of Bonsack of the Roanoke Valley* —by Deedie Kagey

[126]*Journal of the Roanoke Historical Society* — "Big Lick Home Front: 1861-65" — by Mary Terry

[127]*Roanoke — Story of County and City* — Roanoke School Board

[128]Roanoke City Library — Virginia Room — Newspaper File

[129]*The Battle of Hanging Rock and its Centennial Commemoration* — Salem Library

[130]*The Confederate Veteran* — "Battle of Hanging Rock" — by Mary. Coates

[131]*Historical and Heroic Lynchburg* — by Don P. Halsey (xref86)

[132]"The Sentinel" Newspaper June 30, 1864

Index

(C) = Confederate   (U) = Union

M

Magazine Hill - 72

Mahoney, Richard (U) - 119

Maris, Serg. Matthew W. (U) - 121

Marquis (Boys') Battery [Capt. J. C. Marquis] (C) -64, 66, 83, 85, 89, 92, 94-5, 105-6, 113, 127, 282, 287, 289, 398

Martin, Corp. Robert (U) - 122

Martin, Capt. Walter K. (C) - 96, 103

Martindale, Capt. Franklin G. (U) - 214, 341, 343, 420

Martinsburg (W) Va. - 24, 110, 156, 159, 163, 214, 240

Maryland Battalion Cavalry (C) - 78

Mason Creek - 380, 387, 395, 397, 399

Mason, George (U) - 76

McAtlee, Mark W. (U) - 123

McBride, William (U) - 122

McCammon, Robert (U) - 120

McCann, Capt. Thomas K. (U) - 273

McCausland, Gen. John (C) - numerous

McChesney, Adam - 140

McChesney, James E. (C) - 138-40, 158, 161-2, 165, 177

McClanahan's Battery Maryland Artillery [Capt. John H. McClanahan] (C) - 25, 65, 79, 83, 85, 100, 107, 282, 286

McCoy, Stephen C. (U) - 120

McCulloch, Moses (U) - 119

McCulloch, Samuel (U) - 123

McCutcheon, J. R. (C) - 138, 140

McDonald, Col. Angus (C) - 164, 184, 192, 209, 213-6, 224, 234, 236, 240-1, 243-4, 246, 253, 261, 271-2, 381, 418-9

McDonald, Mrs. Cornelia - 176, 201, 234, 243-4, 418

McDonald, Harry (C) - 164, 184, 192, 209, 215-6, 224, 234, 236, 241, 243, 246, 253, 261, 272, 418

McFarland, Alexander (U) - 120

McGee, Wesley (U) - 122

McKinley, Lt. William (U) - 43, 175, 186

McMillin, Emerson (U) - 399

McMillin, Marion (U) - 398-9

McMillin, Murray (U) - 399

McMillin, William - 398

McMullin, Capt. James R. (U) - 337

McNeil, John H. (C) - 17, 58, 63, 67-8

McNeil's Partisan Rangers [Capt. John H. McNeil] -68, 72, 83, 96, 107

McReynolds, Col. Andrew T. (U) - 107, 156

Meadow Bluff (W) Va. - 17-8, 24-5, 27, 32, 38-40, 43, 45, 48, 50-1, 54-6, 152, 273, 277, 294, 415-6

Metz, William (U) - 120

Meechum's River Depot - 71, 129, 136-7

Meeks, Newton (U) - 119

Meigs, Lt. John R. (U) - 36, 40, 44, 67, 82, 199, 209, 232, 247, 276, 331, 341, 343, 412

Mechanicsville - 242

Mercer, Joshua (U) - 120

Meredith, Jonathan (C) - 124

Meredith, John W. (C) - 113

Methodist Church [New Hope] - 111

Middle [Fork Shenandoah] River - 74, 85, 87, 89, 105, 107, 110

Middle River Church of the Brethren - 110

Middle Brook - 132, 138, 140, 149

Middleton, Col. Gabrich (U) - 77, 81

Midway - 55, 163-5, 169, 191, 193

Miller, Lt. A. (U) - 160

Miller, Madison G. (U) - 121

Miller, Corp. Richard B. (U) - 120

Miller, Samuel - 276, 351

Miracle, Garrison (U) - 119

Mitchell, James (C) - 125

Mitchell, Robert - 351

Moffit, Eldridge (U) - 121

Montgomery, John J. (U) - 120

Montvale — See Bufords Gap

Moor, Col. Augustus (U) - 39, 40, 81, 87, 89, 90, 96, 146, 156

Moore, Edward A. (C) - 147, 262

Moore, J. S. (C) - 391

Moore, Rev. John - 365

Moore, Serg. W. W. (C) - 125

Moorman, C. H. - 318

More, Pvt. Issac (U) - 399

Morgan, Gen. John H. (C) - 8, 9, 10, 31, 73, 148, 151, 364, 366, 408, 413

Morris, Col. Thomas (U) - 337

Morrison, Rev. James - 163-4

Morrison, Joseph (U) - 122

Mosby, Gen. John S. (C) - 17, 48, 109

Mott, John W. (U) - 122

Mount Crawford - 53, 59, 60, 62-8, 70, 85

Mount Joy - 223, 237, 242

Mount Meridan - 75-6, 78-9, 87

Mount Sidney - 70, 71

Mount Torry Furnace - 235

Mountain Tenny Iron Furnace - 158

Mowder, Henry (U) - 121

Mowry, George - 131

Mowry's Hill - 69-71, 78-80, 106, 113, 129, 131

Mt. Jackson - 39, 44-5, 48-9

Muary River - See North River

Muhleman, Lt. Edward (U) - 113

Mulligan, William (U) - 146

Murray, Col. Edward (U) - 81, 336

Myerley, G. F. (C) - 125

N

Nadenboushe, Col. John (C) - 134

Narrow Passage Creek - 44

Natural Bridge - 73, 181, 219, 224, 232

Nelson County - 181, 184, 193, 216

Neptune, Fred F. (U) - 119

Newcastle - 384, 385, 390, 404, 405, 407, 411-413

New Glasgow Station - 182, 183

New Hope - 75, 86, 107, 108, 110

New London - 263-65, 267, 269, 273, 276-77, 280, 289, 343, 345-46, 349, 417

New Market - 8, 18, 21, 25, 27, 36, 40, 43-46, 48-9, 51, 53-55, 58, 60, 62, 83, 87, 90, 113, 132, 199

New Providence Church - 161

New River Bridge - 7, 9, 11, 17, 25, 48, 50, 83, 86, 151, 258

Newtown - 28, 30, 37, 40, 48, 51, 53, 55, 58, 60, 63

Nicholls, Gen. Francis T. (C) - 189, 190, 217, 228, 231, 243, 252, 253, 274, 276, 285, 303, 417

Niter Miners Corps - 50, 64, 66, 79, 80, 81, 83, 107, 124

Y Z